Goldmine

THE Beatles Digest

Compiled by the editors of Goldmine magazine

Published by

700 East State St., Iola, WI 54990-0001
715-445-2214
www.krause.com

Please, call or write us for our free catalog of antiques and collectibles publications.
To place an order or receive our free catalog, call 800-258-0929. For editorial comment and further information,
use our regular business telephone at (715) 445-2214

Library of Congress Catalog Number: 00-104627
ISBN: 0-87341-948-0

Printed in the United States of America

Table of contents

Introduction *by Greg Loescher* 4
Britain before The Beatles *by Bruce Eder* 7
The Hamburg days *by Gillian G. Gaar* 18
Collecting Hamburg-era Beatles stuff *by Gillian G. Gaar* 37
Interview with Jurgen Vollmer *by Ken Sharp* 39
Parlophone Records *by Bruce Eder* 46
Andrew Loog Oldham *by Dave Thompson* 49
Songs The Beatles gave away *by Robin Platts* 56
Who was the real Fifth Beatle? *by Allen J. Wiener* 62
The Mersey-Motown sound *by Bill Harry* 68
Interview with photographer Harry Benson *by Terry Ott* 72
Interview with producer Walter Shenson *by Gillian G. Gaar* 75
1967: A year in the life *by Gillian G. Gaar* 81
The making of *Yellow Submarine* *by Dr. Bob Hieronimus* 87
***Yellow Submarine* sails again** *by Mark Wallgren* 95
Interview with director Michael Lindsay-Hogg *by Bill DeYoung* 98
The evolution of "Get Back" *by Doug Sulpy* 101
The Beatles in person and on the air *by Charles Reinhart* 103
Beatles instrumentals *by Charles Reinhart* 110
The Beatles' Grammys *by J.G. Schuberk* 115
The lawsuit to break up The Beatles *by J.G. Schuberk* 121
John Lennon and Yoko Ono appear on *The Mike Douglas Show* *by Gillian G. Gaar* 124
John Brower says Albert Goldman's book is all wrong *by William Ruhlmann* 131
Late-80s Beatles solo records *by Allen J. Wiener* 134
Interview with George Martin *by Bill DeYoung* 136
Collecting non-Beatles Apple Records *by Tim Neely* 142
The solo Beatles' '70s chart invasion *by Casey Piotrowski* 144
Interview with Wings' Denny Laine *by Bruce Eder* 148
Harry Nilsson and John Lennon's *Pussy Cats* *by Dave Thompson* 155
Klaatu *by Mark Hershberger, Jaimie Vernon and Dave Bradley* 162
The Rutles *by Dave Thompson* 168
Niche Beatles collecting *by Chuck Miller* 176
The (Ex-) Beatles in 1974 *by Gillian G. Gaar* 178
Dark Horse Records *by Charles Reinhart* 186
John Lennon (1940-1980) *by Rick Whitesell* 191
John Lennon remembered *by* Goldmine *readers* 193
The Beatles' butchered cassettes *by Mark Wallgren* 195
Beatles 45 sleeves of the '90s *by Charles Szabla* 203
Yoko Ono's controversial career *by Gillian G. Gaar* 205
Yoko Ono speaks about her Rykodisc reissues *by Gillian G. Gaar* 210
Interview with Ringo Starr *by Robyn Flans* 223
Beatles guest appearances *by Belmo and Thomas Ramon* 236
Conversation with Ringo Starr *by Allen J. Wiener* 246
The making of the TV and video *Anthology* *by Gillian G. Gaar* 253
George Martin retires, releases *In My Life* *by Ken Sharp* 261
Chart domination of The Beatles after the breakup *by Casey Piotrowski* 272
Linda McCartney's obituary *by Dave Thompson* 274
Interviews with Ringo Starr and Mark Hudson *by Ken Sharp* 276
Beatles price guide *by Tim Neely* 282
Apple Records numerical listing *by Tim Neely* 302
Beatles resources *by Cathy Bernardy* 312

Meet *The Beatles Digest*...

OK, so it's all beat up! But this copy of *Meet The Beatles* is the first record album that I ever owned. My father bought it for me for my birthday at the time of its release in 1964. While it left my personal possession for many years, I eventually got it back, a bit banged up from the journey, but it's in my collection nonetheless. Today a near mint copy (mine is the mono version) would sell for $200. But with the condition my copy is in, it isn't worth much more than a greenback dollar to anyone but me (priceless is my price tag)!

At least I still have it, which is a better fate than what happened to my first Beatles 45, "Thank You Girl" b/w "Do You Want To Know A Secret." It would have been worth up to $65 in near mint today, although even when I had it, it was in rough shape. This 45, along with all the others I owned, ended up at my brother-in-law's family's household, and the 45s are long gone. You know the old story, "My mom threw out all my old records/baseball cards/comics, etc." That's why we have Mother's Day. They may think all the flowers, candy and other gifts are given to honor them, but it is really sort of a forgiveness day for all the things they threw out that could have made us rich today! ("Mom, I still love you, even though you threw out all my cool stuff.")

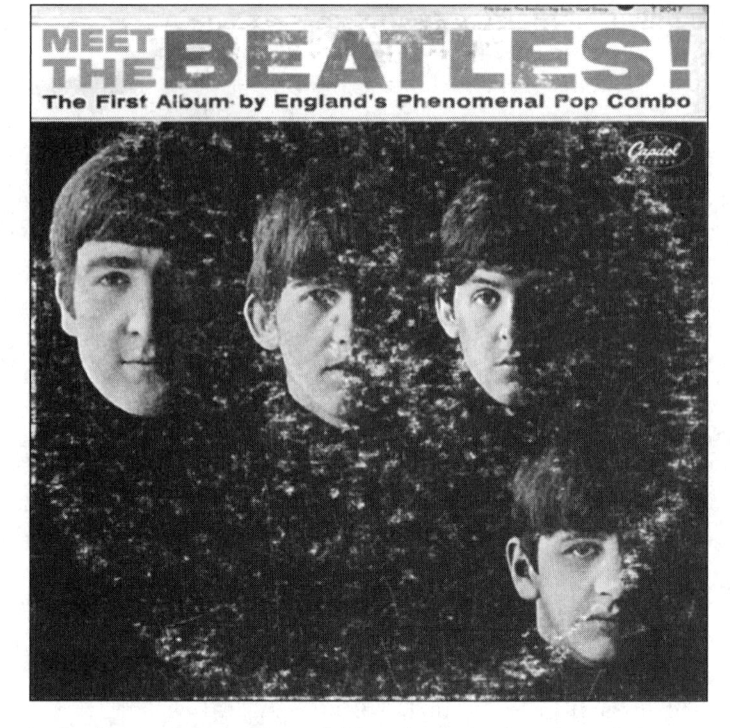

But I do have all of these memories of playing Beatles records as a kid, looking over the records and jackets with a fine-tooth comb. What young person is going to have a memory of their first Napster download? Big deal! It's about as exciting as remembering the first thing you photocopied.

One of the defining moments of The Beatles' American invasion was their appearance on *The Ed Sullivan Show* in 1964. For those of us around at that time, where we were when that show aired is as memorable as where we were when President John F. Kennedy or Martin Luther King was shot. I was at the home of some of my parents' friends when it aired. All of the adults in attendance thought The Beatles were pretty outrageous, but I knew something special was going on. Sure enough, it was Beatlemania from then on!

The hype for *A Hard Day's Night* was nonstop. I was as anxious as any Beatles fan to hear the new songs and see the movie. The hometown movie house that showed it was infamous for its owner coming out during a movie to tell kids to knock off the noise, and his appearance during the airing of *A Hard Day's Night* was no exception. The movie hadn't even started and the girls were screamin' their heads off. The owner warned the audience that he would stop the movie if things got out of hand. No one listened. As the movie rolled, the screaming intensified with every close-up shot of a Beatle. Eventually, the theater owner came back out and told everyone he was going to turn the sound off if there wasn't silence during the movie. The girls kept screaming. It didn't matter that the sound was turned off — you couldn't hear anything anyway! I was a bit perturbed at the time.

But the revamped *Hard Day's Night* is coming back to the silver screen this fall. So even though I have seen the video since the original showing of the movie, now I should be able to both see the movie and hear the soundtrack at the same time on the big screen (unless the same Beatles fans show up that "ruined" the first screening!).

These are just a few Beatles moments in my life. There have been many. The Fab Four's influence has permeated several generations as well as just about every musician. Their music will easily be listened to for decades to come. In fact, The Beatles are to pop and rock music what Mozart and Beethoven are to classical. The Beatles had chart success (as noted in several articles in *Beatles Digest*) well after their breakup. The *Anthology* series and *Live At The BBC* put them back in the #1 slot in the '90s, and for good reason.

Earlier in 2000, "In My Life" was dubbed the greatest pop song ever by a group of 20 famous songwriters including The Beach Boys' Brian Wilson, Jerry Lieber, Hal David (Burt Bacharach's songwriting partner), Elton John, and Paul McCartney. That song also happens to be my favorite Beatles song, off of my favorite Beatles album, *Rubber Soul*.

Another measure of The Beatles' continued popularity is Beatlefest, which has been around for more than 25 years. The first one I went to was in Chicago in 1986. It freaked me out. There were hundreds, no, thousands of teenaged girls screaming during Beatles videos. Many of the fans were wearing vests covered with Beatles pins. At that time, some of these young fans weren't even born when The Beatles broke up. Thirteen years later, at Beatlefest 1999 in Chicago, the same thing occurred, only this time, the young fans were almost young enough to be the daughters of the young fans from 1986! Wild.

So what is this *Beatles Digest* you purchased? It's the third in *Goldmine's* annual reprint series of articles that were published in the magazine. Over the years, we've had lots of requests for article reprints, but coming up with a viable format to collect the articles was the dilemma. The solution led to 1998's *Classic Rock Digest*, which covers classic rockers from the '60s and '70s and includes a bonus CD, and 1999's *Roots Of Rock Digest*, which focuses on the early years of rock 'n' roll right on up to the British Invasion.

When coming up with ideas for our 2000 *Digest*, we thought that focusing on a single artist would be the way to go. The Beatles made sense as the topic for the first *Digest* we published on a single group. *Goldmine*'s best-selling issues of the past decade or so have always been Beatles issues, and they have usually been the largest in page count as well. There really is no group out there that compares to The Beatles in terms of collectibility (although Elvis Presley and Kiss fans might disagree!). If you have any suggestions for topics for future *Digests*, please drop us a line (*Goldmine*, Editorial Dept., 700 E. State Street, Iola, WI 54990, or e-mail us at mr.postman@krause.com).

Putting this *Digest* together is a team effort. Two on the team who did the bulk of the work are *Goldmine* associate editor Cathy Bernardy, who tackled this project like a Blue Meanie (on top of doing her regular *Goldmine* duties), and Stacy Bloch, from Krause Publications' book department's production team, who was getting designed pages back to Cathy faster than she could keep up (which is a good thing). Cathy spent a lot of time tracking down photos to use in the *Digest* and also used her exceptional organizational skills to keep track of the stories — a feat in itself — as they flowed to various desks around the building.

Also to be thanked is Tim Neely, our *Goldmine* price guide expert, for providing us with the Beatles price guide used in this *Digest*. Tim's work the past four years has been devoted to developing *Goldmine's* record database, which as of this writing has close to a quarter of a million entries. As a result, he has published a number of price guides including Goldmine *British Invasion Record Price Guide*, cowritten with *Goldmine* writer Dave Thompson. (For more information on our *Goldmine* book lineup, check out our web site at www.goldminemag.com or call 1-800-258-0929 and ask for a current catalog of products.) Tim also brought in from his collection a number of the records and sleeves depicted in the *Digest*.

All of the *Goldmine* writers who have contributed Beatles articles over the years are to be thanked as well. Without their enthusiasm and desire to write about The Beatles, this special Beatles edition of *Goldmine*'s *Digest* series would not have been published.

Of course, the biggest thanks goes to The Beatles themselves. Their incredible legacy will be hard to repeat, much less top, for a long time to come. Besides being just way cool, which can be said about a lot of bands, John, Paul, George, and Ringo created some of the world's best pop music, which only a handful of artists can achieve. The songwriting team of Lennon/McCartney is one of the most successful and best of the 20th century.

And it wasn't just a few really good songs either. It's hard to find a clunker in The Beatles' repertoire! In fact, each "period" of The Beatles' recording history would have been a huge contribution to music. Combined, it's monumental. Hardly a day goes by without hearing a Beatles song or someone covering one (even on Muzak!).

The breakup of The Beatles in 1970 sent shockwaves through Beatleland. I remember that when I heard the news, it was hard to take it seriously. It just seemed so out of place, so unbelieveable and inconceivable. Beatles 4-ever, so we thought. Looking back now, it's easier to see why things happened the way they did. Who among us could have handled the pressure of being the most popular, successful act in the world? Trying to constantly come up with new material amid the explosive dynamics of fame, success, money and interpersonal relationships had to be exhausting.

Of course, the breakup didn't stop the Fab Four from creating more great music. As outlined in several chapters of this book, each Beatle had a solo career with high and low points.

Lennon's solo outings were inconsistent in my estimation. Some of his individual songs from this period were among his best ever, such as "Imagine," "Woman," "Instant Karma (We All Shine On)" and "(Just Like) Starting Over." But a lot of his solo material was erratic in quality, partially due to Yoko Ono's musical influences. His final album, the #1 *Double Fantasy*, showed strong glimpses of a revived Lennon ready to tackle the world. All of us wonder what great music he would have produced had he not been assassinated in 1980. It ranks as one of the saddest moments in rock history.

On the other hand, McCartney's solo output was a lot more consistent, chart-topping and more poppy. With his band Wings and as a solo artist, he has so far produced 10 #1 hits, more than 20 Top 20 hits and seven #1 albums. While not a big fan of his solo work in general, I think his 1997 *Flaming Pie* album is outstanding and his best effort to date.

Ringo Starr also had strong chart action imediately following the breakup: seven straight Top 10 hits, including two consecutive #1s. His happy-go-lucky tunes and retained Beatles attitude was latched onto by a new generation of Beatles fans during the mid-70s pop explosion. His chart output has slacked off tremendously since the mid-70s, despite the successful All-Starr Band tours of the '90s.

Which brings us to George Harrison. I am going out on a limb here (OK, throw still-sealed "butcher" cover albums only, please!): I think of all The Beatles, Harrison's solo output is the best and most consistent. His #1 *All Things Must Pass*, the first triple album in rock history, is chock-full of goodies, as is his other #1 album, *Living In The Material World. Concert For Bangla Desh* was a 1972 Grammy winner and Album Of The Year. 1987's *Cloud Nine* is fab, as is Harrison's work with rock supergroup Traveling Wilburys (Bob Dylan, Tom Petty, Jeff Lynne, Roy Orbison — could it have gotten much better?!).

Of course, these are just my short takes on the Fab Four. I know you have yours (thanks for all the butcher covers!). Beatles fans can spend hours (and often do) analyzing and philosophizing about The Beatles' songs and history. It's a pastime that's fun and will never go out of style. We hope that you'll have hours of fun with Beatles Digest as well.

Beatles 4-ever.
— *Greg Loescher*
Editor
Goldmine magazine
Oct. 1, 2000

Photo credits

John Lennon and Yoko Ono photo copyright 1971 Sherry Barnett: page 209
Fanzine courtesy of *Beatlefan*: page 312
Magazine courtesy of *Beatlology*: page 312
Photos copyright Cathy Bernardy/*Goldmine* magazine: page 28, 93, 94, 316
Photo of *Yellow Submarine* memorabila copyright Cathy Bernardy/*Goldmine* magazine; display of materials by Jeff Augsburger at Chicago Beatlefest, 2000: page 92
Photos copyright 1999 Gillian G. Gaar: John Lennon statue, 41; Cavern Club, 51, 53, 55; Pete Best, 67; Blue Meanie, 88; cab, 89; banner and stamp presentation, 91; Abbey Road Studios, 243, 265; George Martin, 267; The Remnants and Liverpool Institute, 317
Books photos courtesy of Genesis Publications: pages 32, 33, 43
Photos courtesy of Glenn A. Baker Archives, Australia: Billy Fury, 14; Billy J. Kramer And The Dakotas, 61; The Beatles with Jimmy Nichol, 63; Dave Clark Five, 69; The Beatles, 122; Wings, 150; Harry Nilsson, 157; The Rutles, 170, 174; John Lennon, 192; Ringo Starr, 249; The Beatles, 254; Linda McCartney, 275
Fanzine courtesy of *Good Day Sunshine*: page 313
Butcher cover courtesy of Good Rockin' Tonight: page 177
Posters courtesy of the Pete Howard collection (www.postercentral.com): page 29, 54, 65, 226
Poster photo courtesy of Pete Howard: 8, 40, 64
Photo of The Beatles in Hamburg, copyright 1960 Astrid Kirchherr/K&K/Star File: page 19
Photo of Ringo Starr copyright Bob Klein: page 278
Yellow Submarine memorabilia set-up shot copyright Krause Publications: page 96
Photo of John Lennon and Yoko Ono on *The Mike Douglas Show* copyright Michael Lehsnov: pages 125, 127
Yellow Submarine video courtesy of MGM Home Entertainment, Inc.: page 96
Photo of The Beatles with George Martin courtesy of Michael Ochs Archives: page 264
Motown Museum photo courtesy of Motown Historical Museum, Inc.: page 71
All sheet music courtesy of Orpheus, Toronto: pages 22, 30, 52, 57, 59, 60, 70, 73, 82, 90, 104, 117, 138, 145, 149, 152, 180, 188, 189, 206, 232, 247, 248, 266
Promo photos courtesy of Orpheus, Toronto: pages 106, 228
Photos courtesy of Pictorial Press, U.K.: Andrew Loog Oldham with The Rolling Stones, 53; Brian Epstein, 66; George Martin, 137; Yoko Ono, 217
Photos of Klaatu copyright 1981 Bob Reid: pages 163, 165
Photo of boxed set courtesy of Rhino Records: page 129
Rock Hall photo courtesy of The Rock And Roll Hall Of Fame: page 317
Photos of *Hard Day's Night* and *Help!* filming courtesy of Walter Shenson: pages 77, 78
Cover photo courtesy of Star File
Pussy Cats album courtesy of Dave Thompson: page 161
Beatles cassettes courtesy of Mark Wallgren: pages 197-199, 201-202
Photos copyright Chris Walter/Photofeatures: The Beatles, 50, 83, 107; John and Julian Lennon and Eric Clapton, 99; John Lennon and Yoko Ono, 132; George Harrison, 187; Plastic Ono Band on *Top Of The Pops*, 214; Ringo Starr, 225
Cartoon copyright Marty Winters: page 159

Britain before The Beatles

Guys named Cliff, Tommy, Adam, and Billy...

by Bruce Eder

Who started English rock 'n' roll?

That's a lot like asking who started American rock 'n' roll, except tougher to answer, partly because the story of early British rock 'n' roll has its beginning, as does all rock music, in America. It was not only American records that first whetted the appetites of listeners on the other side of the Atlantic, but also America's cultural influence going back to World War II that made possible the whole phenomenon of British rock.

In the beginning, in America, when the record business fully took root in the period immediately ahead of World War II, there were established the urban musical genres of jazz and early rhythm 'n' blues, which were interrelated through popular music; there were the rural genres of hillbilly music and the blues, and there was folk music, which, as it became organized through the process of recording, developed along different political and sociological lines and crossed over with the blues in terms of definitions and audience.

Then came World War II, and the historical figure who is as much a nonmusical mover in the birth of rock 'n' roll as any man who ever lived: Adolph Hitler. The fight against Hitler involved the greatest temporary mass migration of American males ever witnessed, with millions of them going over to Europe to fight. The dislocation in their lives and those of their families back home and the desire to make up for lost time when they got back, stirred America's cultural melting pot in a way that no phenomenon before ever had. Individuals and families were uprooted, long-established social structures were broken down, and in many cases the men doing the fighting got to know, hear and see more of their world than they ever would have by staying at home.

The results of this stirring of the pot included the birth of the suburbs, the restabilization of the big cities for the first time since before The Great Depression — and among numerous other social changes — the creation of large numbers of musically adventurous performers *and* an even more restless mass of younger listeners.

Not content with the established musical forms, the former began stretching the envelope in the 1940s, exploring not only more varied and daring styles but experimenting with the newer sounds available on electric instruments. Meanwhile, listeners coming of age in the early and mid-1950s found themselves on a social and cultural track very different from that of their parents.

This article originally appeared in Goldmine *issue #310, June 12, 1992.*

The mothers and fathers of the early '50s had lived through The Great Depression and World War II. They'd been through the wringer and were only too happy to settle down to the relatively complacent '50s. The typical pop music of the era, a well-crafted but bland extension of both the best and worst of Tin Pan Alley, suited them just fine.

But it didn't suit their children, for whom the war was but a vague early memory and The Depression not even that. Rather, their kids' cultural and musical lives were shaped by the social ripples radiating outward from the war — a stable, growing economy, more money in circulation than there had ever been before and more free time than any generation of children had ever known.

The house with the two-car garage and Patti Page singing on the radio were fine for parents, but the 14- or 15-year-olds growing up in this environment, relatively free of want and lots of time and hormonal-based energy on their hands, were bored stiff. And the earliest serious, hard rhythm 'n' blues-cum-rock 'n' roll, represented by classics such as "Gee" by The Crows, "Rocket 88" by Jackie Brenston, and "Shake Rattle And Roll" by Joe Turner, among many others, was one answer to that boredom.

(Note: This boredom and restlessness and the factors behind them also caused rock 'n' roll to be linked by its critics to juvenile delinquency. Rock's defenders often attributed that link-up to prejudice on the part of the critics, but the real picture is more complicated. The 15 years between the end of World War II and the country's redefining of itself in 1960-61 saw an entire generation of children raised in war-disrupted households — with fathers in the Army and mothers working days or nights in the defense industry — reach their teen years. Of necessity, they'd been raised differently than any other group of children in modern times, and that made them stand out; they were more daring, more independent, and more open to new ideas and ways of thinking than the previous generation of teenagers — and possibly, in some cases, more antisocial.

In actual fact, they probably weren't more troubled than earlier teenagers, but they were spotlighted against a relatively placid time in the lives of most adults. With no economic or military upheavals as a distraction, the teens, their tastes and their problems stood out more sharply. And between the children conceived as The Depression was ending and those conceived immediately after the end of the war in 1945, there were more teenagers around in the years 1953 through 1960 than the country had ever seen before.)

Teenaged life in Britain wasn't much different, only more constricted. Where Americans possessed a set of shared middle-class aspirations to cling to, which became even more real immediately after the war, the British still lived under a class system and under rationing nearly a decade after the last shot was fired. Their ruined cities could be repaired, their cathedrals rebuilt and the status quo maintained, at least for the older population. But among the younger ones, the seeds for a social upheaval had been sown.

From 1939 until 1945, virtually every able-bodied Englishman had served in uniform, and most of them, owing to the Empire's commitments in Burma and the Middle East, had served abroad. (This led to one of the great complaints of British soldiers overseas, who not only had to contend with the enemy but with worries about what the women they'd left behind might be tempted to do with any of the many hundreds of thousands of American soldiers — "oversexed, overpaid, and over here!" was the common lament — stationed in England.)

Rock around the isles

Many of the children raised during this period knew a degree of freedom and independence that would've been unheard of at any other time in history. After the war, the normal order was restored, at least on the surface — the country's relatively rigid class system was intact and adults fell back into it, albeit not always easily.

The first visible cracks in the British social contract began appearing in the '50s, with the emergence of gangs of so-called "Teddy Boys." Loutish youths, most widely seen in the South London area, they were more thugs than rebels. The "Teds" fell outside of any accepted manner of behavior and department, with their Edwardian dress and, by the standard of the day, unkempt hair — very much in a James Dean mold. They seemed always in the mood for a fight and made an enormous noise considering their relatively small numbers.

They might never have been more than a noise but for the fact that parents of lower- and lower-middle class teenagers often found their children looking up to the Teds, at least from a distance. By the middle of the decade, even firmly middle-class teenagers showed an affinity for their approach to authority, which was pretty much to ignore it — or, barring that, shove it off the sidewalk or kick it in the groin.

And one of the most celebrated manifestations of the Teddy Boys' influence was a passion — often expressed violently — for American rock 'n' roll. When Sam Katzman's pioneering exploitation movie *Rock Around The Clock*, featuring Bill Haley And His Comets, opened in Britain during the summer of 1956, authorities were caught by surprise by the audience reaction. Actually, Haley and his band had first hit the British charts in 1954 and 1955 with "Shake, Rattle And Roll" and "Rock Around The Clock," both on the British Brunswick label, with the former doing considerably better, reaching the #4 spot. "Rock Around The Clock," as it had in America, faded and then returned in 1955 for an extended stay at the top of the charts with the release of the movie *The Blackboard Jungle*.

But the movie *Rock Around The Clock* caused young audiences in England to express their enthusiasm, first by dancing

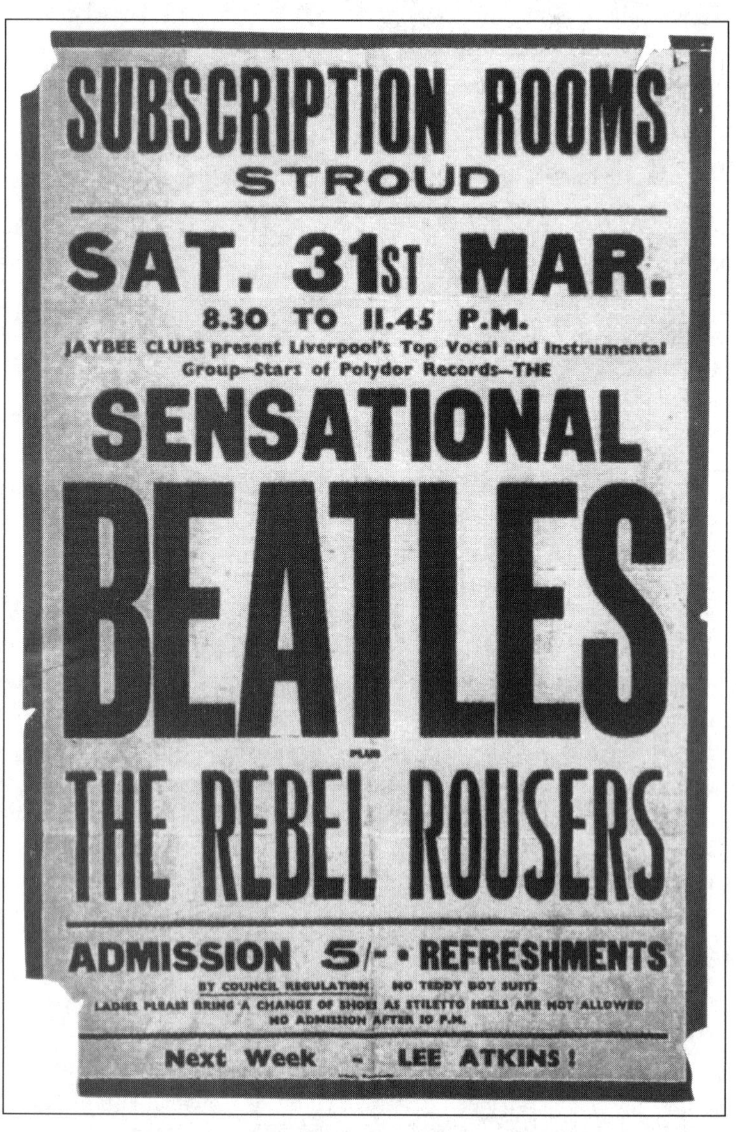

A 1962 Beatles concert poster warning kids not to wear "Teddy Boy Suits" or stiletto heels.

in the aisles (which was frowned upon but not serious) and later by tearing up the seats in the theaters in which it was running. The Rank Organisation, which had booked the film in its theater circuit, canceled the Sunday night showings of it in the South London area, Sunday being a favorite night for the Teds to prowl the streets.

Equally important to the development of home-grown British rock was a small but dedicated group of jazz musicians whose tastes and styles had been shaped by the wartime American "invasion." There had been jazz of a kind played in England almost as long as jazz had been established in America. Like many transplants from America, however, most of what was played was watered down in the process.

Meanwhile, in Manchester, 20 youths were arrested at a single showing of the movie, and reports of street disorders — many growing out of the aftermath of teenagers being evicted from theaters after refusing to stop dancing — spread throughout England, especially in the north. By the beginning of September, with *Rock Around The Clock* going into general release, the movie was banned from Brighton, Blackbum, Preston, Birmingham, South Shields, Wigon, Bootle and Gateshead, and police reinforcements were called out for the premiere showings in Edinburgh, Scotland.

The behavior that resulted in these bannings was new to England, and it led to calls for the ban of rock 'n' roll in England, much as it had in America. Even Queen Elizabeth II took notice of the situation, and a request was forthcoming from Buckingham Palace for a copy of *Rock Around The Clock*, intended for a private screening for H.R.M. (What Fred F. Sears, the director best remembered for *Earth Vs. The Flying Saucers*, and Sam Katzman, the producer, must've thought of this was anyone's guess.) Meanwhile, on the musical front, no less a musical figure than Sir Malcolm Sargent, conductor of the Royal Liverpool Philharmonic Orchestra — leading music institution in Liverpool — compared rock 'n' roll to "an exhibition of primitive tom-tom thumping."

Equally important to the development of home-grown British rock was a small but dedicated group of jazz musicians whose tastes and styles had been shaped by the wartime American "invasion." There had been jazz of a kind played in England almost as long as jazz had been established in America. Like many transplants from America, however, most of what was played was watered down in the process.

There were some brilliant artists, most notably Stephane Grappelli and Django Reinhardt, who had worked in Britain before the war, and a few homegrown figures that made international reputations for themselves: Marian McPartland, the pianist and composer, who came from a long musical heritage and began establishing herself immediately after World War II and who has enjoyed a long career in America and throughout the world, and pianist George Shearing, who also emerged in the middle and late 1940s and remains a giant in the jazz field. But mostly, jazz in England, like most other elements of culture, popular or otherwise, was hopelessly tradition-bound and almost as formalistic as classical music.

During and after World War II, the dominant form of jazz was known as "trad" and was based on American Dixieland jazz. It was popular enough but was placed firmly on a road to nowhere, locked into its own traditions and formalism. A small cadre of players began entering the jazz scene in England after World War II, however, who saw and heard things differently. Among them were guitarist Alexis Korner and guitarist-cum–harmonica player Cyril Davies, two budding American blues enthusiasts who felt even more passionately about the guitar and harmonica music that came out of the Mississippi Delta by way of Chicago than most bandleaders did about Dixieland jazz. And a guitarist named Anthony "Lonnie" Donegan.

Korner, of Austrian, Greek and Turkish descent, had been born in Paris in 1928 and got to England just as the French were surrendering to the Germans. He spent his teenage years in London and put a good deal of time into listening to American blues records brought over by the GIs stationed there. He hooked up with jazz band leader Chris Barber during the late '40s and by 1953 was playing blues as part of Barber's band. At around the same time, the Barber group added a new form of music to its set, a rhythmic, jangling sound called "skiffle."

Skiffle was a rudimentary form of American blues, transliterated by the British on the simplest possible instruments, mostly acoustic guitars, washtub bass and washboard percussion — ironically, not that different from the instrumentation that many a transplanted player from the Mississippi Delta might have used on first arriving in Chicago. Skiffle lacked the sophistication of jazz, but it had a lively beat, it was freer form than most of the jazz played in England and it had a raw, honest energy.

Korner quickly found an ally in Davies, a panel-beater by day whose love for American blues was the equal of Korner's. In 1954 the pair had started their own duo and a year later opened the London Blues And Barrelhouse Club upstairs at The Round House Pub in London. They began building an audience for serious R&B and attracted visiting Americans including Muddy Waters, Otis Spann, John Lee Hooker, Memphis Slim, and Sonny Terry And Brownie McGhee, as well as a growing cult of British enthusiasts.

All of this was underground activity, however, for neither the recording industry nor the British music press — which was every bit as tradition-bound as the majority of the musicians that it covered — were prepared to acknowledge the importance of American blues. Donegan, however, saw that there was something special in the way that younger audiences reacted to his sets with the Barber band.

A self-taught musician, Anthony Donegan was born in Glasgow, Scotland, in 1931 and spent his youth immersed in American folk music. He bought his first guitar at 17 and played his first show with a jazz ensemble in 1948, a year before being drafted. He got out of the army in 1951 and resumed his career, and it was after appearing on a bill at the Royal Festival Hall with his idol, Lonnie Johnson, that Donegan changed his first name to Lonnie. He joined Barber's band on banjo soon after, and it was as part of the Barber Band's *New Orleans Joys* album in 1954 that he first cut "Rock Island Line," with Barber on bass and Beryl Bryden on washboard.

Late in 1955, Donegan self-produced and self-financed a version of "Rock Island Line." The record, released by Decca, surprised the music world by climbing to #8 on the British charts during a 13-week run and then re-entering the charts twice, in April for an additional three weeks, rising to #16, and in May for 17 more weeks, during which it hit the #2 spot.

"Rock Island Line" made Donegan an overnight sensation, and suddenly the featured player in the Barber Band's skiffle set was a star. The single, released by London Records in America, enjoyed a 17-week chart run in the United States that peaked at #8. Donegan found himself in the enviable position of entertaining offers from American record companies and concert promoters and demands from an eager British public for more of his music. But even more important than his commercial success was the effect that Donegan had on British youngsters.

American rock 'n' roll had begun showing up on the British charts the year before, and while "Rock Island Line" wasn't quite American rock 'n' roll or about to challenge Chuck Berry's "Maybellene" or Elvis Presley's "Heartbreak Hotel" for sheer ballsiness, it did have a beat. It was sung in a bluesy manner — and it was played by someone British.

Sales of guitars in England skyrocketed, fed by the resulting skiffle boom, in a manner that was unequaled until the chart breakthrough by The Beatles seven years later. By 1957 it seemed as though half the youth in England — including John Lennon, Paul McCartney, and George Harrison — were strumming acoustic guitars and scratching out beats on old washboards on street corners throughout the Sceptered Isle.

Additionally, although skiffle never caught on in America, Donegan got to tour America, something almost unheard of for a young British musician on his first break into stardom. He and his band, which featured Denny Wright on guitar, Mickey Asliman on bass, and Nick Nicholls on drums, came to the United States in February 1957 in an exchange that permitted Haley And His Comets to play England.

Other skiffle acts followed in Donegan's wake, most notably the Chas McDevitt Skiffle Group, who hit with "Freight Train" in 1957, and The Vipers, a band discovered by George Martin, with "Don't You Rock Me, Daddy-O" and "Cumberland Gap." Although none of these acts made it to the end of the decade as serious chart contenders, Donegan endured, placing 25 singles — the second largest number of chart singles by a British recording artist after Cliff Richard — including "Jack O' Diamonds" and "Grand Coulee Dam," into the British Top 20 between 1956 and 1962.

He also recorded several albums, of which the best and most representative are *The Lonnie Donegan Showcase*, made up mostly of the songs that he and his band knew best, and its more elaborate follow-up, *Lonnie*, both released on Pye.

Meanwhile, the British music business, alerted to the drawing power of American rock 'n' roll and the riotous reception given to *Rock Around The Clock*, splintered into various factions in deciding what to do about it. Most of the trad-jazz outfits, such as Barber's band, ignored it, preferring to think of rock 'n' roll as something beneath them, while a few, such as bandleader Humphrey Lyttleton, expressed outright hostility toward the music and its audience.

There were a few jazzmen, however, who were bored stiff by the whole trad scene and who saw in rock 'n' roll a chance to break out of the pack and energize their playing and their audiences. During the summer of 1956, there came the announcement of the formation of several rock 'n' roll bands out of converted jazz outfits, most notably from drummer Tony Crombie and singer Art Baxter.

Crombie, a self-taught musician who toured with Lena Horne and Carmen McRae, had formed his first jazz group in 1954. In 1956, he rechristened it The Rockets and, as Tony Crombie And The Rockets, led Britian's first homegrown rock 'n' roll band. The group was signed to EMT and managed to chart one single, "Teach You To Rock"/"Short'nin' Bread," into the lower reaches of the British charts during October 1956.

Baxter, a former singer with Ronnie Scott's band, followed suit that fall by forming the Rockin' Sinners and landed a recording deal with Philips Records. Throughout 1956, there were other attempts to cash in on the rock 'n' roll "craze" by bandleaders Ken MacIntosh and Victor Sylvester, drummer Eric Delaney, trombonist and bandleader Don Lang (whose band became a fixture as the house band of *The Six-Five Special*, one of the earliest British television shows to feature rock 'n' roll) and an outfit called The Kirchins, among many others. It should be pointed out, in fairness, however, that not only the British jazz acts jumped on this bandwagon — Lionel Hampton also added a rock 'n' roll set to his stage act and could be seen in one Alan Freed jukebox movie sandwiched somewhere in between Chuck Berry and Little Richard.

Sales of guitars in England skyrocketed, fed by the resulting skiffle boom, in a manner that was unequaled until the chart breakthrough by The Beatles seven years later. By 1957 it seemed as though half the youth in England — including John Lennon, Paul McCartney, and George Harrison — were strumming acoustic guitars and scratching out beats on old washboards on street corners throughout the Sceptered Isle.

The record companies themselves were at a loss. Decca/London, which had most of the distribution for American rock in Britain thanks to its contracts with Chess, Imperial and Liberty Records, among other U.S. labels, benefitted tremendously from the popularity of figures such as Berry, Fats Domino, Bo Diddley, Eddie Cochran and others. But they and every other label in England were looking for homegrown talent that they could push on the public.

England wanted rock stars of its own — not just bands that could play dance music with an occasional vocal by some soloist, but a charismatic personality, with a voice that could sell records. The answer seemed to come during 1956, in the form of Tommy Steele (real name Tommy Hicks), a merchant seaman who had sung aboard ship and played a little guitar. Steele frequented the 2 I's, a coffee bar (or, more properly, an espresso bar), so named for the Irani brothers who founded it at 59 Old Compton Street in Soho, where Steele occasionally sang and played guitar.

Ironically enough, there had been word around the record industry about the young singers frequenting the 2 I's and other coffee bars like it, and producers had started to look over the talent in the area. In his book *All You Need Is Ears*, Martin, then the newly installed head of EMI's tiny Parlophone label, confessed to having been at the 2 I's and having seen Steele perform and to have passed on him. Instead, Martin signed up the group backing him, a skiffle group called The Vipers, only to see Steele snapped up by Decca Records the next day.

Steele was signed to a three-year Decca contract at the end of 1956 and was immediately booked for national television appearances and a concert tour. Within weeks, his first single, "Rock With The Caveman," was released and reached #13 on the British charts. It was a good beginning, and his success seemed assured when, less than three months later, his cover version of "Singin' The Blues" chased Guy Mitchell's version up the charts, halted one spot behind it at the #2 position for a week, and then replaced it in the top spot the following week.

Four of Steele's next five singles were major hits, sailing into the British Top 20, and "Butterfingers," written by Lionel Bart, stayed on the English charts more than four months during 1957. His next single, "Shiralee," taken from the film of the same title, reached the Top 10 and was followed by a double-sided hit of "Water Water" and "Handful Of Songs" at #15, and, after a lapse with "Hey You," he jumped to #3 with "Nairobi."

Steele was everything a British record company executive in 1957 could have wanted. He was young and talented (he occasionally even wrote songs), with an ingratiating Cockney personality and was interested in a long-term career. Unfortunately, this also meant that he was not exactly the kind of "rebel" personality that most young listeners looked for in a rock star. His songs rocked, sort of. Listening to them today, they seem a little pallid, but they have a beat, the electric guitars are there (albeit not played too interestingly or daringly) and, as the list of names shows, they certainly emphasized "rock" in their titles.

But Steele wasn't threatening in the manner of Presley, hadn't the sly, knowing, sexual side of a Berry or Bo Diddley, and next to Holly's records, his songs sounded like someone going through the motions of playing rock 'n' roll. Additionally, it soon became clear that Steele had bigger career goals than rock 'n' roll. As early as 1958, even as he honed his talents and grew in confidence, he was aiming at a broader audience with a pop music sound, and he was starting to appear as an *actor* in his films, rather than as a singer who acted.

Steele's first album, *The Tommy Steele Stage Show*, was a 10-inch long-player featuring Steele's backing band, The Steelmen, in what was purported to be a live recording of his act. As with most Decca "live" recordings until The Rolling Stones' EP *Got Live If You Want It*, the circumstances are somewhat dubious, as is the rocking nature of the proceedings. "Rock With The Cavemen" is included, but none of it is really much more than a fairly anemic variation on American rock 'n' roll.

Steele's second album, *The Tommy Steele Story*, was the soundtrack to the movie of the same title, shot less than six months after the release of his first single. It isn't a bad album, consisting of most of Steele's hits up to that time, but for Steele the rocker, the album and the movie were the beginning of the end. In 1958, his only album was the soundtrack to *The Duke Wore Jeans*, and he wouldn't get another long-player out until 1960 with *Get Happy With Tommy Steele*, a collection of soft pop, folkish and romantic ballads from his singles and EPs of the prior year.

Steele was a success, however. Despite being banned by the South African government, he was an all-around wholesome entertainer who quickly outgrew his rock sound and graduated to television, motion pictures and the stage. Not that he didn't occasionally return to something with a beat — as late as 1959, Steele cut a credible cover version of Freddy Cannon's "Tallahassee Lassie."

If the goal of British rock 'n' rollers was to emulate Elvis Presley the singer, it was the goal of their managers and record companies for their stars to emulate Elvis Presley the personality. Steele's career became the established pattern for the 1950s: young singer (and sometimes guitarist) comes along with a good song and is idolized by the young audiences and works his way into the hearts of their mums and dads with a few well-placed smiles and a ballad or two thrown onto their records and into their television appearances. He tours the country once or twice as a rocker and then softens his sound and image, moves into pop music and cabaret with perhaps a movie or two, and is never of interest again to anyone under the age of 30 — all in two years.

The most publicized of the singers who followed immediately in Steele's wake were a fairly nondescript group, whose abilities and recordings anticipated the teen idols of late 1950s/early 1960s American music. They were an amazingly malleable lot, mostly under the management of Steele's original comanager Larry Parnes and christened with stage names such as Vince Eager, Johnny Gentle, Duffy Power, and Dickie Pride. None of them mattered much to rock music, partly because the music didn't matter much to them — they were pre-packed as product and might just as well have been pop singers (which is how most of them started, in any case) as rock singers.

Part of the problem that the British branch of rock 'n' roll faced was that the industry was run in exactly the opposite manner from its American counterpart. In America, a singer would presumably have had to have made a record before appearances could be booked on television or movie contracts signed. In England, the reverse was true. Rock stardom, such as it was, flowed from television appearances, concert bookings and film contracts, with records a mere "tool" used in securing the larger career.

The recorded repertory generally consisted of a cover of a recent American hit, perhaps followed up with a similar cover, backed by an "original" by some British songwriter, with a novelty tune somewhere in the release schedule as well. But the repertory hardly mattered, because most of the studio musicians working in England during the late '50s had little innate understanding about rock records or what made them work. Without a blues or rhythm 'n' blues tradition to work from, there was no British equivalent to Memphis, Nashville or Chicago, with large contingents of experienced players to draw from.

The one exception, in terms of relative talent, to emerge in Steele's wake was Terry Dene (real name Terry Williams) — the Dene don who showed up at the 2 I's and impressed its co-owner, Paul Lincoln, who signed Dene up as a client. Lincoln wisely saw that Dene had a style that was reminiscent of Steele. What he couldn't see were the signs of personal instability that later became evident.

Dene was signed up to appear on Jack Good's teenage variety show, *The Six-Five Special*, and a record contract followed. His first single, "A White Sport Coat," placed respectably in the British Top 20, but his next two records faltered. A series of untoward incidents followed, including bouts of public drunkenness and a well-publicized "breakdown." And Dene's being drafted into the British army fairly well ended his career. He re-emerged as a Christian evangelist after a failed comeback attempt.

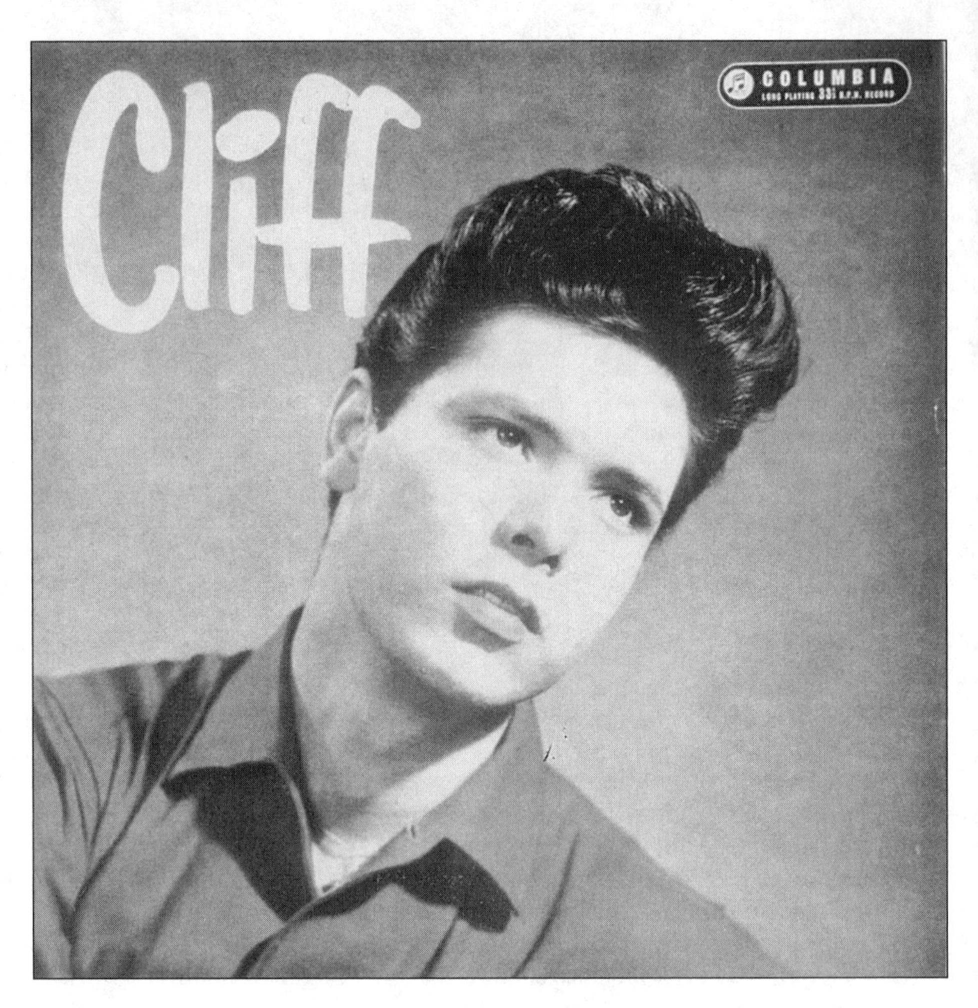

Dene's career was one of the first in England to be closely tied to the fate of *The Six-Five Special*. The series itself was the creation of promoter Jack Good, who was later responsible for *Oh Boy!* and *Shindig*. The show was a loose-knit assembly of music acts, covering light jazz, pop, folk, skiffle, and a smattering of rock 'n' roll, most of it provided by the John Barry Seven and the occasional guest such as Donegan, and it was a success as far as it went.

The program's decline coincided with the attempt to sell its stars as stage attractions, on the first all-British rock package tour, billed as "The Six-Five Special." Sources differ as to the success of this tour — pop historians claim it was a rousing success, but the music trade papers of the era are filled with stories of attendance dropping precipitously as the dates wore on. It is possible and, in fact probable, that the public was willing to accept the free and convenient entertainment offered by the *Six-Five* musicians on their television sets, but being asked to shell out money to see them was overplaying the value of what they had to offer. In any event, by 1958, *The Six-Five Special* was on the ropes, both as a live attraction and a television show and was revamped completely by mid-year in an effort to save it.

Oh Boy!

Out of the near-primordial era of 1956-57, little of lasting value in British rock other than Steele's records and those by Donegan had emerged. The seeds were planted for greater things during this period, however, and this soon became apparent in 1958. Jack Good was lured away from the BBC by ITV, Britain's independent television network and came up with the first television show devoted entirely to rock 'n' roll, *Oh Boy!*

Ask anyone growing up in England during the late 1950s about *Oh Boy!* and you'll likely get a glowing smile of remembrance. *Oh Boy!* was the first television show that a lot of British teens can recall looking forward to each week. Indeed, it set the stage for such successor programs as *Ready! Steady! Go!* in England and *Shindig* in America. And with its freer format, it was able to draw on a new wave of talent that had evolved in the period from 1957 through 1958.

The best of these, by far, was a young Indian-born Briton named Harry Webb, rechristened Cliff Richard and backed by a quartet called The Drifters, who were hastily renamed The Shadows to avoid any confusion with the American rhythm 'n' blues quartet. Richard, a Presley enthusiast from the word go, had started out with the Dick Teague Skiffle Group, invited in with the help of drummer Terry Smart, whom he knew from school, and learned the guitar after joining.

Richard and Smart eventually split off to form their own band, initially with guitarist Norman Mitham, and eventually hooked up with an R.A.F. enlisted man named Ian Samwell, who came in on lead guitar. By the time of their second booking at the 2 I's, Webb and The Drifters had become Cliff Richard And The Drifters (the original name considered for the band was The Planets).

EMI/Columbia producer Norrie Paramor got hold of a demo record, and the rest, as is said too often, is history. A recording session was eventually set up for the spring of 1958, at which two songs, "Schoolboy Crush" — a piece of fluffy romantic rock — and a hot-rocking Ian Samwell original titled "Move It" (written, so the story goes, while the band was traveling on a bus) were recorded, with Ernie Shear sitting in on lead guitar and Frank Clarke playing bass.

Cliff Richard And The Drifters' first single, released in the summer of 1958, was more than a hit record, however. It was a shot heard 'round the world — or, at least, all around the British isles. For one thing, Good, newly installed as the leading music promoter in England thanks to *Oh Boy!*, had the good sense to flip the single over, insisting that "Move It" was the song that should be plugged. The rest of the country seemed to agree, and "Move It" was the song that propelled Richard and his band to the #2 spot on the charts and earned them a spot on *Oh Boy!*

Although it isn't well known in America, where it has never had an official release in more than 34 years, there aren't many rock songs as good as "Move It." From the steely, metallic guitar opening through the cascading lyric stream strung out as an homage to rock 'n' roll to the rippling solo (subsequently imitated, adopted and claimed for ownership by The Shadows' eventual lead guitarist, Hank B. Marvin), to the slow fade with Richard in the most quaking and shaking Elvis-like frenzy of his career, it does just what its title promises. It moves, and it doesn't stop.

But even more amazing than its beat and its sound was the fact that "Move It" had been written by an Englishman and recorded as an original by a British act — and even though sessionmen were involved on two key instruments (a fact not generally known at that time or cared about by most listeners), it was recorded in an out-and-out hard-rocking manner, exactly the way the band would play it on its own.

Among the hundreds of thousands of teenagers watching *Oh Boy!* on the night of Sept. 13, 1958, when Richard And The Drifters made their debut, were John Lennon and Paul McCartney. Both of the teenagers were enthralled by "Move It" and had vowed to watch at their respective homes to see how the song's opening guitar part was played and to try to figure out how to play it. The story goes that McCartney figured it out first and rode over to Lennon's house on his bicycle to show him.

Richard's career was made by the combination of his EMI/Columbia singles and his appearances on *Oh Boy!* He and The Drifters, whose membership would soon coalesce around the "permanent" membership assembled for their first major tour — Hank B. Marvin on lead guitar, Bruce Welch on rhythm guitar, Samwell on bass, later replaced voluntarily by Jet Harris, and Terry Smart on drums, subsequently replaced by Tony Meehan — recorded a live debut album on two dates in early February 1959, at EMI's Studio No. 1, simply titled *Cliff*.

If "Move It" was the breakthrough record in British rock 'n' roll, *Cliff* was no less vital as an album. Most important, it was truly a live album, with no serious audience embellishments and minimal doctoring (as far as one can tell) of its performances. And the performances themselves were fast, hot and sure, perhaps more restrained than one would've gotten from an American band of the period, but not flaccid in the least. The covers of American standards such as "That'll Be The Day" and "Whole Lotta Shakin' Goin' On" were more than respectable (in addition to "That'll Be The Day," the group covered "Donna," and it should be remembered that these two live dates took place barely a week after the deaths of Buddy Holly and Ritchie Valens).

All in all, Cliff Richard And The Drifters — who renamed themselves The Shadows after the release of the first album — were the first top-flight British rock 'n' roll band to get a serious hearing from the public and major exposure on television. The effect of their arrival on the rock scene in Britain was tantamount to blasting a hole in a dam. Suddenly, the island was flooded with serious electric bands and singers who were not ashamed in the least of expressing themselves physically on stage, in the manner of a Presley, or a Richard (although Richard later reined in his stage moves after a series of near-riots at his early shows). And for the first time, there were record company executives, envious of Norrie Paramor's success, willing to hear them and record them that way.

Actually, many of these acts had been around for a long time. The John Barry Seven (originally The John Barry Five) had started out as a light-jazz ensemble in the mid-1950s and made a name for themselves on *The Six-Five Special*. Barry's own training as an arranger, supposedly acquired initially through a Stan Kenton correspondence course, had kept him busy as music director of several television shows, including *Oh Boy!*

Barry, in turn, was responsible for rescuing a forgotten failed alumnus of *The Six-Five Special*, Adam Faith (real name Terence Nelhams), from oblivion. Faith had first recorded a pair of failed singles for EMI in 1957 following two appearances on the fading show and a stint in a skiffle group called The Worried Men. He'd returned to work in the editing department of Rank Films when Barry remembered him and recommended the singer to the producers of the television series *Drumbeat*. Faith tested well and became a key character in the series, which ran from 1959 through 1960.

By 1959, Faith was back in the recording studio with Barry as his arranger and Barry's band backing him up, and the result was a #1 single on Parlophone titled "What Do You Want." "Poor Me," released only three months later, also topped the charts, and April 1960 saw him back at #2 with "Someone Else's Baby." By the time *Drumbeat* was off the air, Faith had a devoted following and was one of EMI's top recording artists. In the early 1960s, he put together a backing band called The Roulettes, featuring Russ Ballard on guitar, who subsequently split off on his own to make an outstanding series of recordings during the early part of the British Invasion.

There were, of course, numerous others at work in England during this period that never got the kind of press or television exposure of the Johnny Gentles and Vince Eagers of the world. One of Martin's early discoveries was Neville Taylor, a former R.A.F. radar technician who became a singer in the early '50s and was signed by Martin to the Parlophone label. Although Taylor never saw any chart action, he and his band The Cutters became a fixture on the *Oh Boy!* program.

Janice Peters also recorded for EMI but never got as far as a regular spot on television. Listening to her singles "A Girl Likes" and "This Little Girl's Gone Rockin'," it's easy to understand why — her frantic, raunchy and uninhibited approach to rock 'n' roll, in a manner that anticipated Lene Lovich, made Peters as formidable as Brenda Lee, Wanda Jackson and almost any other American female rocker of the era.

Similarly, transplanted American jazz singer Bertice Reading, who did manage some appearances on *Oh Boy!*, busied herself cutting genuine American-style R&B such as "Rock, Baby, Rock," for EMI. It didn't sell many copies, but the results endeared Reading to perceptive fans at the time and earned her a small spot in British rock posterity.

And finally, on the outer fringes of the early British beat, there was David Sutch, who billed himself as "Screaming Lord Sutch." Decked out in clothes that looked like hand-me-downs from a medieval rummage sale and fronting one of the hardest playing bands in Britain, Sutch carved a special niche for himself in the hearts of British youth. More recently, he has been making periodic runs for a seat in the House Of Commons, with a similar lack of restraint.

Richard and Faith divided up the top of the British charts between them during the post-1959 period. Although they were superior to virtually any British rock singers who had come before them, they repeated a well-established pattern — both softened their sound after an initial burst of success with loud rock 'n' roll. Faith, in particular, was never a powerful singer in the Presley vein, and his conversion to balladry made sense.

In Richard's case, however, the loss to music was greater. He was a stylist clearly influenced by Presley but hardly a clone. Richard's baritone was strong, his sound genuinely exciting, and his repertory, augmented by an occasional contribution from Samwell ("Dynamite," in particular, was truly fierce, if a little mechanical) was the best England had ever seen. "Livin' Lovin' Doll" was as worthy a piece of work as ever made the British charts, but it only got as high as #20 in early 1959 after a sixweek run, and its follow-up, "Mean Streak," only made it to #10.

The change in Richard's music came with "Living Doll," a much gentler number released during the summer of 1959 that shot directly to the #1 spot, a feat matched by its follow-up, "Travelin' Light." These were both acoustic guitar-driven numbers, sung in a style reminiscent of Ricky Nelson rather than Presley. Richard himself was evidently more comfortable with this sound, and it came to characterize the rest of his career. The Shadows remained Richard's backing band, at least officially, on every single through "A Girl Like You," released in the spring of 1961, after which they worked on roughly every other single, up through 1966's "In The Country."

If Richard and Faith held the top of the charts with their softer, more romantic approach, there were some rivals on the scene who tried — and to some extent succeeded — with a harder, sharper-edged sound. Marty Wilde (real name Reginald Smith) was actually a *Six-Five Special* retread, having appeared on the old show after being discovered in a London coffee bar by impresario Larry Parnes in 1956. He was signed to the Philips label in 1957.

Wilde's first three singles — one of which was a cover of "Honeycomb" — made no chart impact whatsoever, but his fourth, "Endless Sleep," a moody and brooding number, rose to #4 during the summer of 1958. Wilde went hitless again until the following spring, when his cover of Valens' "Donna" got to #3. He followed it up with a version of "A Teenager In Love" that reached #2 and "Sea Of Love," which made it to #3. These songs all allowed Wilde to explore the dark, brooding side of his voice and persona, which strongly resembled that of Gene Vincent. He was genuinely a menacing and romantic figure, with a keen musical sense as well. Wilde's support band, The Wildcats, were also Eddie Cochran and Vincent's backup band during their appearances on the BBC, although he later dropped them in favor of The John Barry Seven.

Unfortunately, Wilde was too intense a figure to see much more chart success. After "Bad Boy," an eerily Vincent-like number that reached #7 on the British charts and rose to an unprecedented #45 in America (resulting in a somewhat disappointing tour of the United States), he failed to get anywhere near the top spot again, apart from his #9-placing cover of Bobby Vee's "Rubber Ball" in early 1961. Wilde's chart run ended late in 1962 with "Ever Since You Said Goodbye," at #31.

Fortunately, Wilde had acquitted himself well before the public — unlike many other rock singers who turned to occasional movie roles, he understood his limitations and

Billy Fury

stuck to supporting parts in films such as *Jet Storm* and *What A Crazy World*, in which he got good notices from critics and the public alike.

What's more, his sense of matters musical was undiminished, even during the period after 1962 when he broadened his sound into more of a pop vein for the cabaret circuit — Wilde's lead guitarist during this period was Justin Hayward, future key member of The Moody Blues, who credits Wilde with teaching him a great deal about music.

It was in 1960, however, that they recorded the song that they would always be remembered for, "Shakin' All Over." Released on EMI, the single rose to the #3 spot and became an inspiration for budding R&B players such as Pete Townshend and Roger Daltrey, with its raw, grinding beat, crisp and raunchy guitar sound, and soulful vocal performance by Kidd.

But better than Wilde and even Richard, was another Parnes discovery who represented the apotheosis of pre-Beatles British rock: Billy Fury.

Strangely enough, Fury hailed from Liverpool, where he'd grown up (real name Ronald Wycherly) in a neighborhood not far from Ringo Starr. He was a tugboat worker at the time he first approached Larry Parnes in 1958, to try to sell him a few songs. Instead, Parnes realized that Fury himself had potential as a singer and signed him, with the usual change of name. A Decca recording contract followed in short order and Fury broke into the charts with his own song, "Maybe Tomorrow," which rose to #18 in a pair of appearances during the winter of 1959. Another original written by the singer himself (who often used the pseudonym "Wilburforce"), "Colette," rose to #9 during the spring of 1960.

Fury's four subsequent singles were far more modest in their success, but in the meantime, he did something that no British rock 'n' roller had ever done before — he recorded a great rockabilly album, in the form of his debut long-player, *The Sound Of Fury*.

Driven by Fury's dark, strong voice — truly a Presley-styled voice, without any of the pronounced mannerisms that Richard displayed — and Joe Brown's dexterous and loud lead guitar, *The Sound Of Fury* reached #18 on the British charts. This was only a modest showing, especially compared to the #4 spot achieved by Richard's debut album, but its importance lay not so much in how many people heard *The Sound Of Fury*, as in who heard it: Keith Richards, for one, has extolled the record's virtues for years in interviews, and it has long been a favorite record among his generation of rock stars.

Fury's career after 1961, however, quickly took on a shape reminiscent of those of Richard, Faith, and Wilde, as he shifted over to softer, more pop-oriented material, such as the orchestrated "Halfway To Paradise," which rose to #3 on the charts. He saw major success with this material right up until the summer of 1963, when the emerging Liverpool sound overwhelmed all of the older competition. Although Fury continued to chart singles up through early 1966 with "I'll Never Quite Get Over You," he would only reach the Top 10 twice more in eight more tries.

Ironically, his overall sound hadn't changed that much. He was not able to switch gears from Presley to Nelson's style in the way that Richard had, and his 1962 feature film *Play It Cool* includes some great, hard-rocking vocals in a nicely raw and basic electric band setting. If Fury was the most talented of the British rockers, however, then Johnny Kidd And The Pirates were the best of the integrated singer/band ensembles. Formed in 1958 by Kidd (real name Frederick Heath), they had an early success with their first single, "Please Don't Touch." It was in 1960, however, that they recorded the song that they would always be remembered for, "Shakin' All Over." Released on EMI, the single rose to the #3 spot and became an inspiration for budding R&B players such as Pete Townshend and Roger Daltrey, with its raw, grinding beat, crisp and raunchy guitar sound, and soulful vocal performance by Kidd.

The Pirates themselves were a somewhat fluid group, a trio with a rotating membership. Two original members, Alan Caddy (lead guitar) and Clem Cattini (drums), left Kidd in 1961 to form the core of The Tornadoes and were duly replaced by ex-members of The Redcaps, the backing band for Cuddly Dudley (a regular on *Oh Boy!*) This second lineup became the most famous and enduring version of The Pirates, with Mick Green (a genuine legend, and a deserving one) on lead guitar, Johnny Spencer on bass, and Frank Allen on drums.

They went on to become one of the greatest live rock attractions in British rock history, a loud, hard-rocking outfit whose sound served as the model for the eventual configuration of The Who, The Small Faces and other bands. Also legendary was Kidd's stage act, played out in full pirate regalia with eye-patch and prop sword, which was among the most unrestrained in British history up to that time.

Unfortunately, the public seldom got to hear The Pirates' best music on record during their original period together. EMI producer Walter J. Ridley, who had released the bone-crunching "Shakin' All Over," tended to favor pop ballads and standards in his subsequent choice of material, that were ill-suited to Kidd's raunchy vocal capabilities or the band's grinding, powerful sound. More than 20 years after the group's last hit, however, and Kidd's death in a car crash, See For Miles Records unearthed a brace of unreleased songs and odd B-sides that showed the group off to its greatest advantage, doing serious rhythm 'n' blues.

Meanwhile, Alexis Kerner and Cyril Davies, who had parted company from Chris Barber at around the same time as Donegan, had been toiling in obscurity between 1956 and 1962, playing the blues and developing a sound. Their work finally came together in a brief flash of recogition and success in 1962 with the Decca Records release of *R&B From The Marquee*, the vinyl testament to their residency at the famed London club as leaders of the group Blues Incorporated. The album, which featured saxophonist Dick Heckstall-Smith, Keith Scott on piano, and Long John Baldry as guest vocalist, became the first British blues album to make the English charts.

Kerner and Davies would never again know such unchallenged mastery in the still-embryonic field of British blues, however, only a year later, Blues Incorporated alumni The Rolling Stones would capture the market and the definition of British blues on Decca. In less time than that, however, the original Blues Incorporated would cease to exist, due to a dispute between Kerner and Davies over the addition of horns to the band.

Davies left the group during 1963 and recruited the former members of Screaming Lord Sutch's band (including Nicky Hopkins on piano and Carlo Little on drums) into a new group, The All-Stars. Cyril Davies And The All-Stars got a recording contract with Pye Records during 1963 but only managed to record a handful of sides before Davies' sudden death from leukemia during January 1964.

The rest of the rest

British rock prior to 1963 was focused largely on featured singers, such as Richard, Fury, Faith and Wilde. Bands and instrumental soloists mattered a lot less to the public and press, even when they were associated with these performers.

The major exception was The Shadows, who quickly emerged as England's leading instrumental group behind Bruce Welch and Hank Marvin's steely guitar sound and their crisp if somewhat mechanical recordings. The quartet, whose rhythm section after the departure of Jet Harris and Tony Meehan was a floating one, had a clean, elegant sound that suited the British producers of the era, quite unlike The Ventures (with whom they were frequently compared) in America. "Apache" was their initial hit, a #1 single during the summer of 1960, that was followed by the less successful but still popular "Man Of Mystery," "F.B.I.," "Frightened City" and a return to the top spot with " Kon-Tiki."

"Wonderful Land," "Dance On" and "Foot Tapper" would also top the charts, with "Atlantis" reaching the #2 spot during the summer of 1963, before their fortunes faded with the arrival of the Liverpool sound.

The group's success heralded a whole generation of instrumental outfits, among them The John Barry Seven (who actually predated The Shadows but didn't start doing full-length albums under Barry's direction until 1960); The Tornadoes, under producer Joe Meek, whose "Telstar" hit #1 during the summer of 1962 in England and America (a first for a British rock band); and The Outlaws, whose lineup featured a teenaged Ritchie Blackmore on lead guitar.

Although they never had any major success of their own, with the singles "Swing Low" and "Ambush" making #46 and #43 on the charts respectively, The Outlaws also served as the backing band to singer Mike Berry — all were produced by Joe Meek and played on "Tribute To Buddy Holly," a #24 hit in the fall of 1961. Berry and The Outlaws followed this with an even bigger chart success, "Don't You Think It's Time" (#6 in early 1963).

The beauty of British rock 'n' roll before The Beatles was that it didn't die on the vine. Even the unsuccessful acts served as guideposts, primers and even a farm system of sorts for what the music would become when it emerged, fully formed and fully grown, in 1963 and 1964.

Even one of the more regrettable teen idols, Cuddley Dudley (real name Dudley Haslop), served this purpose — his backing band, The Redcaps, included future members of The Pirates, as did the early instrumental group Les Hobeaux. Blackmore found an early home in The Outlaws, and Jimmy Page would play lead guitar on his first hit single, as a session man for Jet Harris And Tony Meehan on "Diamonds," their 1962 post-Shadows hit single.

Even these acts ended up contributing directly to the Liverpool sound and its successors in an odd way. Mick Green of The Pirates, who started out as a member of The Redcaps, went on to play lead guitar in The Dakotas, backing Billy J. Kramer. And Nicky Simper, one of the latter-day bassists with The Pirates, was subsequently recruited by ex-Searcher Chris Curtis into his proposed group, Roundabout. The band and the name didn't make it, but after a six-month wait they were back together — Simper, Blackmore and Jon Lord among them — as the original Deep Purple.

In the end, the best of the most famous early British acts survived. Faith, Joe Brown, Fury (who died of heart failure early in 1984, after years of health problems), Donegan and Wilde kept their musical careers alive in one form or another into the 1980s. Richard remains a pop star with a major international following and occasionally even reunites with The Shadows — who are still a going concern, at least part time, more than 30 years later — for a one-off concert. And even those old jazzmen Tony Crombie and Chris Barber were still working as of the '80s, although neither features skiffle or rock 'n' roll in his act any longer.

Early British Rock — A Select Discography

Lonnie Donegan

Singles (U.K.)

Label/#		Title (A-side)	Year
Decca	F10647	Rock Island Line	1955
Pye	N 15036	Lost John/Stewball	1956
	NJE 1017	Skiffle Session (*EP*)	1956
	N 15071	Bring A Little Water Sylvie	1956
	N 15080	Don't You Rock Me Daddy-O	1956
	N 15087	Cumberland Gap	1957
	N 15093	Gamblin' Man	1957
	N 15108	My Dixie Darling	1957
	N 15116	Jack O' Diamonds	1957
	N 15129	Grand Coolie Dam	1958
	N 15148	Sally Don't You Grieve	1958
	N 15158	Lonesome Traveller	1958
	N 15165	Lonnie's Skiffle Party	1958
	N 15172	Tom Dooley	1958
	N 15181	Does Your Chewing Gum Lose Its Flavor	1959
	N 15198	Fort Worth Jail	1959
	N 15206	Battle Of New Orleans	1959
	N 15223	Sal's Got A Sugar Lip	1959
	N 15237	San Miguel	1959
	N 15256	My Old Man's A Dustman	1960

Albums (U.K.)

Label	#	Title	Year
Pye	NPT 19012	Lonnie Donegan Showcase	1956
	GGL 0135	Golden Age Of Donegan	1962
	GGL 0170	Golden Age Of Donegan Vol. 2	1963

Adam Faith

Singles (U.K.)

Label	#	Title	Year
Parlophone	R 4591	What Do You Want	1959
	R 4623	Poor Me	1960
	R 4643	Someone Else's Baby	1960
	R 4665	When Johnny Comes Marching Home	1960
	R 4689	How About That	1960
	R 4708	Lonely Pup	1960
	R 4735	This Is It/Who Am I	1961
	R 4766	Easy Going Me	1961
	R 4807	Don't You Know It	1961
	R 4837	The Time Has Come	1961
	R 4864	Lonesome	1962
	R 4896	As You Like It	1962
	R 4930	Don't That Beat All	1962
	R 4964	Baby Take A Bow	1962
	R 4990	What Now	1963
	R 5039	Walkin' Tall	1963
	R 5061	The First Time	1963
	R 5091	We Are In Love	1963

Albums (U.K.)

Label	#	Title	Year
Parlophone	PMC 1128	Adam	1960
Columbia (EMI)	33SX 1125	Best Girl (*soundtrack*)	1961
Parlophone	PMC 1162	Adam Faith	1962
	PMC 1249	Faith Alive	1965
Warwick	WW 5113	20 Golden Greats	1981
See For Miles	CM 121	Not Just A Memory	?

Albums (U.S.)

Label	#	Title	Year
Amy	8005-M	Adam Faith	?

Billy Fury

Singles (U.K.)

Label	#	Title	Year
Decca	F11102	Maybe Tomorrow	1959
	F11128	Margo	1959
	F11158	Angle Face	1959
	F11189	The Last Kiss	1959
	F11200	Colette	1960
	F11237	That's Love	1960
	F11267	Wondrous Place	1960
	F11311	A Thousand Stars	1960
	F11334	Don't Worry	1961
	F11349	Halfway To Paradise	1961
	F11384	Jealousy	1961
	F11409	I'd Never Find Another You	1961
	F11437	Letter Full Of Tears	1962
	F11458	Last Night Was Made For Love	1962
	F11485	Once Upon A Dream	1962
	F11508	Because Of Love	1962
	F11582	Like I've Never Been Gone	1963
	F11655	When Will You Say I Love You	1963
	F11701	In Summer	1963
	F11744	Somebody's Else's Girl	1963
	F11792	Do You Really Love Me Too	1964
	F11888	I Will	1964
	F11939	It's Only Make Believe	1964
	F12048	I'm Lost Without You	1965
	F12178	In Thoughts Of You	1965

Albums (U.K.)

Label	#	Title	Year
Decca	LF 1329	The Sound Of Fury	1960
Ace Of Clubs	ACL 1083	Halfway To Paradise	1961
Decca	LK 4533	Billy	1963
	LK 4548	We Want Billy	1963
	TAB 37	Hit Parade	1983
Polydor	POLD 5069	The One And Only	1983
See For Miles	See 32	Billy Fury	198?
Decca	820-627	The Sound Of Fury +	1988

Cliff Richard

Singles (U.K.)

Label	#	Title	Year
Columbia (EMI)	DB 4178	Move It	1958
	DB 4203	High Class Baby	1958
	DB 4249	Livin' Lovin' Doll	1959
	DB 4290	Mean Streak	1959
	DB 4306	Living Doll	1959
	DB 4351	Travellin' Light	1959
	DB 4351	Dynamite	1959
	SEG 7971	Expresso Bongo (*EP*)	1959
	DB 4398	Voice In the Wilderness	1960
	DB 4431	Fall In Love With You	1960
	DB 4479	Please Don't Tease	1960
	DB 4506	Nine Times Out Of Ten	1960
	DB 4547	I Love You	1960
	DB 4593	Theme For A Dream	1961
	DC 756	Gee Whiz It's You	1961
	DB 4667	A Girl Like You	1961
	DB 4716	When The Girl In Your Arms Is The Girl In Your Heart	1961
	DB 4761	The Young Ones	1961
	DB 4828	Do You Wanna Dance	1962
	DB 4886	It'll Be Me	1962
	DB 4950	Bachelor Boy	1962
	DB 4977	Summer Holiday	1963
	DB 7034	Lucky Lips	1963
	DB 7089	It's All In The Game	1963
	DB 7150	Don't Talk To Him	1963
	DB 7272	Constantly	1964
	DB 7305	On The Beach	1964
	DB 7372	The Twelfth Of Never	1964
	DB 7420	I Could Easily Fall	1964
	DB 7496	The Minute You're Gone	1965
	DB 7596	On My Word	1965
	DB 7745	Wind Me Up	1965
	DB 7866	Blue Turns To Grey	1966

Albums (U.K.)

Label	#	Title	Year
Columbia (EMI)	33SX 1147	Cliff	1959
	33SX 1192	Cliff Sings	1959
	33SX 1261	Me And My Shadows	1960
	33SX 1320	Listen To Cliff	1961
	33SX 1368	21 Today	1961
	33SX 1384	The Young Ones	1961
	33SX 1431	32 Minutes And 17 Seconds	1962
	33SX 1472	Summer Holiday	1963
	33SX 1512	Cliff's Hit Album	1963
	33SX 1541	When In Spain	1963
	33SX 1628	Wonderful Life	1964
	33SX 1709	Cliff Richard	1965
	33SX 1737	More Hits By Cliff	1965
	33SX 1769	Love Is Forever	1965
	SX 6039	Kinda Latin	1966

Rock 'n' roll dreams

The Beatles in Hamburg

Conversations with Tony Sheridan, Astrid Kirchherr, and Pauline Sutcliffe

by Gillian G. Gaar

On Dec. 27, 1960, The Beatles appeared at the Litherland Town Hall Ballroom in Liverpool in a performance widely regarded as being a turning point in their career. The band, in one form or another, had been playing in the Liverpool area for over three years, and in May 1960 had gone on its first tour (albeit a mere seven days in Scotland, backing singer Johnny Gentle).

The Beatles had not previously been considered one of the city's top beat groups. Yet the band that stood on the Town Hall stage was far removed from the previously named Silver Beatles (or "Beetles"); as they stomped through a powerhouse set of rock 'n' roll classics, the audience surged to the front of the stage, screaming and later besieged the group for autographs. What had happened to change the group can be summed up in a single word: Hamburg.

Had it not been for the "Hamburg Experience," The Beatles might well have carried on playing the same Liverpool circuit for a few more years until their energy and ambition had faded, eventually splitting up and leaving the world none the wiser about their existence. But three months of playing in Hamburg, Germany, to an audience of gangsters, hoodlums, sailors on shore leave, prostitutes, strippers, "slumming" nightclubbers and art students had changed the group irrevocably from hobbyists into professionals.

Before arriving in Hamburg, the group had played no more than 60 or so shows; in Hamburg, it was expected to play for four and a half hours every week night and six hours on the weekends. It was a back-breaking schedule that forced a group to sink or swim. By the end of 1961, it was clear which path The Beatles had taken. They were one of Liverpool's top draws, had returned for another successful season in Hamburg, made their first professional recordings and had acquired a manager in Brian Epstein.

But strangely, for being such an important period in their lives, the Beatles' Hamburg years have yet to be examined in depth. There are books that focus on just about every other aspect of their career (the early Liverpool years, Beatlemania-era tours, the Apple years), but the story of their Hamburg sojourns has been largely relegated to one or two chapters in Beatles biographies.

So although the general public undoubtedly knows that The Beatles came from Liverpool, most would be unaware of how their trips to Hamburg helped forge them into the group that would later take the world by storm.

This article originally appeared in Goldmine *issue #374, Nov. 25, 1994.*

That situation changed dramatically in 1994, primarily due to the release of the film *BackBeat*. Though the film was not as great a success in the U.S. as it was overseas (particularly in Britain), a number of music and entertainment magazines ran stories about the film, often illustrated with Astrid Kirchherr's historic photos of the early Beatles. For the first time in many years, Kirchherr granted several interviews, both to promote the film and the publication of *Liverpool Days*, a collection of photos by herself and Max Scheler.

Pauline Sutcliffe, the sister of Stuart Sutcliffe, the original "Fifth Beatle," also gave numerous interviews and put in appearances at different Beatles conventions to promote exhibits of Stuart's artwork and the publication of her own book, also titled *BackBeat* (subtitled *Stuart Sutcliffe: The Lost Beatle*), and cowritten with Alan Clayson. As a result, more people have begun to realize that the story of The Beatles' early years lies as much in Hamburg as it does in Liverpool.

The group appeared in Hamburg on five separate occasions before finding success in Britain. The story of how a Liverpool group came to play in the seedy bars of Hamburg's notorious red light district known as the Reeperbahn involves a number of curious twists and turns, coincidences and the hand of fate, a story that was largely overlooked in *BackBeat*.

It began in 1960, when Allan Williams, a small-time entrepreneur and friend of The Beatles, discovered that the steel

One of Astrid Kirchherr's famous Beatles shots, including Pete Best and Stuart Sutcliffe.

drum band he'd engaged at one of his clubs, The Jacaranda, had departed for Hamburg. The group then contacted Williams, inviting him over to survey the club scene and promote his other groups. Williams duly took up the challenge and arrived in Hamburg with a reel-to-reel tape containing recordings of different Liverpool bands. During his stay, Williams did make contact with one club owner, Bruno Koschmider, but found that the tape he'd made had been damaged during his journey and was unplayable.

Discouraged, Williams returned to Liverpool. But unknown to him, Koschmider's curiosity had been roused by his visit, and Koschmider set out to England to obtain some rock 'n' roll groups himself. Not surprisingly, he went to London, not Liverpool, where he first discovered Tony Sheridan and brought him over with a newly assembled group, The Jets. The group proved to be highly successful with German audiences, and when it moved on to another club, Koschmider returned to England in search of other groups.

Meanwhile, back in Liverpool, Williams was having new problems. Working with promoter Larry Parnes, Williams had secured summer work for another of his groups, Derry And The Seniors. In anticipation of this work, the band members had quit their day jobs and were irate when Parnes summarily canceled their booking. To smooth the situation over, Williams drove the group to London, took them to the 2 I's coffee bar and talked the manager into letting the band perform that night, By chance, he encountered Koschmider at the 2 I's and was at last able to introduce him to rock 'n' roll, Liverpool style. After watching Derry And The Seniors play, Koschmider agreed to hire them, and the group arrived in Hamburg on July 24.

The Seniors were also successful, and Koschmider soon contacted Williams about sending over other Liverpool groups. Williams first considered Rory Storm And The Hurricanes, and Cass And The Cassanovas, but both groups were presently engaged elsewhere. Gerry And The Pacemakers were then approached but turned the offer down. Finally, Williams asked The Silver Beatles, whose lineup then consisted of John Lennon, Paul McCartney, and George Harrison — all on guitar — and Stuart Sutcliffe on bass.

The group found a drummer in Pete Best, a member of another band, The Blackjacks, who were playing their final gigs before the other members returned to college. Best eagerly accepted the offer, the group dropped the "Silver" from its name and hit the stage at Hamburg's Indra Club, formerly a strip club, on Aug.17, 1960.

After the Indra was closed in October, The Beatles moved on to The Kaiserkeller, where Derry And The Seniors were playing. When The Seniors' contract was up, Rory Storm And The Hurricanes arrived. Shortly after The Hurricanes' arrival, Williams arranged for Lennon, McCartney, and Harrison to make an amateur record with two members of the group, singer/bassist Walter Eymond and drummer Ringo Starr; it was the first time The Beatles played with their future drummer.

But the group's first trip to Hamburg would end ignominiously, due to the ever-present rivalries between club owners. The Beatles had become friendly with Tony Sheridan And The Jets and were sitting in with the group at the Top Ten; this enraged Koschmider, and he canceled their contract. The group was not initially dismayed, as plans were quickly laid for them to move to the Top Ten officially, but Koschmider was still intent on retaliation. First, the German authorities were alerted to the fact that Harrison was only 17, hence a minor and not allowed to play in German nightclubs; he was duly deported. Next, McCartney and Best were deported on trumped-up arson charges.

Without their group, Lennon and Sutcliffe were at loose ends; Lennon eventually followed the other three members back to Britain, while Sutcliffe remained in Hamburg with Kirchherr, now his fiancée, not returning to Liverpool until February 1961.

But once their deportation mishaps had been cleared up — and Harrison turned 18 — the group returned to Hamburg on four more occasions; April to June 1961, when they played at the Top Ten (after which Sutcliffe left the group); April to May 1962, when they played at the Star Club; and, with their new drummer Ringo Starr, Nov. 1-14 and Dec. 18-31, 1962, again at the Star Club. Their second and third trips to Hamburg saw the group recording as backup musicians with Tony Sheridan, and their final show of 1962 was also taped on primitive equipment. They then returned to Liverpool; within two months, the group would have its first #1 when "Please Please Me" topped the charts. Like their time in Liverpool, their Hamburg period was now behind them.

Those interested in studying The Beatles' Hamburg years have a number of sources they can turn to. Hunter Davies was the first to examine The Beatles' Hamburg period in depth in his authorized biography of the group, simply titled *The Beatles*, which, for the first time, gave readers a clear sense of the impact the Hamburg period had in the band's development. Other biographers who gave further insight into this period include Philip Norman, in *Shout!*, Ray Coleman, in *Lennon*, and Mark Lewisohn in both *The Beatles Live!* and *The Complete Beatles Chronicles*. Jurgen Vollmer's *Rock 'n' Roll Times* and Gareth Pawlowski's *How They Became The Beatles* are pictorial records of the early Beatles, and two other close associates of the group tell their side of the story in *The Man Who Gave The Beatles Away*, by Liverpool promoter Allan Williams, and *Beatle! The Pete Best Story* by Pete Best.

Best's book is due to be reissued by Plexus this month, perhaps in response to the interest generated by *BackBeat*, but he is no longer interested in giving interviews. "It's all been in print and done before, so I don't really go in for that side of things now," he explained. "I think what I've had to say has already been said before."

Nonetheless, Best does appear at Beatles conventions, meets with fans on other occasions and even plays with his group, The Pete Best Band, "as need demands or if we want to do it or if we get asked to do it. It depends, you know."

There are also recordings available from the Hamburg years. The eight songs The Beatles recorded with Tony Sheridan, first released in 1961, have been repackaged innumerable times since the early '60s. On six of the numbers, where The Beatles only served as backing musicians, it's difficult to assess their skill as musicians, though their recognizable whoops of delight (especially from McCartney) are a testament to their energy, and their backing harmonies on "Why" are the clear forerunner of their later work on such songs as "This Boy." Their own numbers offer a clearer look at their developing talents: "Cry For A Shadow" is a lighthearted parody of The Shadows' instrumental style, and Lennon's ragged vocal on "Ain't She Sweet" displays the punishing workout the group's vocal cords were put through on a nightly basis.

The band's New Year's Eve performance in 1962, first released on the double-album *Live! At The Star Club In Hamburg, Germany, 1962*, gives a better indication of what the group sounded like on stage. Though the band rushes through their set at a breakneck pace (a clear indication of their desire to hurry through the engagement in order to rush back to England in order to promote their next single), the range of material, from "Falling In Love Again" to "Twist And Shout," is fascinating and a last look at the band's vast catalog of cover songs.

Like the material recorded with Sheridan, the 30 tracks from the Star Club performance have been repackaged many times since their first appearance in 1977 (after The Beatles tried unsuccessfully to prevent their release). There was initially some confusion about the origin of the tapes used to make the record; the liner notes claimed they'd been recorded by Ted Taylor, of Kingsize Taylor And The Dominoes on a night when Starr just "happened to be 'sitting in' for Pete Best."

In fact, since the recording date was Dec. 31, 1962, Starr had been a member of the group for more than four months. And according to Bill Harry's *The Ultimate Beatles Encyclopedia*, it was Adrian Barber, formerly a member of Cass And The Cassanovas and The Big Three, who made the original recording when he was stage manager at the Star Club, on the PA/recording system he'd designed for the club himself.

There are also speculations that amateur recordings of a Beatles rehearsal previously believed to have been done in the spring of 1960 in Liverpool were actually done in Hamburg that fall. Even at this early date, whether spring or fall, the harmonies on "The One After 909" are strong and confident and not far from how they would sound when the composers would finally release the song a decade later. The most complete sessions are available on the bootleg LPs *The Quarrymen Rehearse With Stu Sutcliff* [sic] *Spring 1960*; *The Quarrymen At Home* (also on CD), and *Liverpool May 1960*, and the CD *The Quarry Men: 58 To 62*.

In addition to *BackBeat*, an earlier film also looks at The Beatles' Hamburg years. The 1979 made-for-TV feature *The Birth Of The Beatles* is one of the few films actually about The Beatles (i.e., not "inspired" by them, à la *Sgt. Pepper's Lonely Hearts Club Band* or *I Wanna Hold Your Hand*) and was filmed in London, Liverpool and Hamburg. Considering the medium for which it was intended, this is a decent effort to tell The Beatles' story, though the usual "artistic license" is freely taken, despite Best's billing as "Technical Advisor."

Stephen Mackenna, as a thoughtful and sometimes angry Lennon, is the only character who makes much of an impression; Rod Culbertson's Paul is ambitious and eager to please, but the rest of the group is relegated to occasional one-liners. The music was provided by Beatles soundalike band Rain.

BackBeat ostensibly presents a more "realistic" look at The Beatles' time in Hamburg, which means there's far more rough language and nudity, though the same artistic liberties are freely taken with the story. "As long as one is keeping true to the inherent truth of the situation, then I think it's legitimate to use creative license," director Iain Softely explained, adding, "Just the fact that something is fact isn't enough to give one the sense that it's the truth or that it gives a true picture. You don't know how much people's memories are filtered by time having passed."

Lennon (played by Ian Hart) is again the dominant character, with Sutcliffe (Stephen Dorff) and Kirchherr (Sheryl Lee) coming in a close second; McCartney (Gary Bakewell) is clearly a secondary character, and the other Beatles are again relegated to the occasional one-liner, more understandably in this case, as *BackBeat* is really the story of Lennon, Sutcliffe, and Kirchherr. The music was provided by a grunge supergroup featuring Greg Dulli, David Pirner, Mike Mills, Don Fleming, Thurston Moore, and Dave Grohl and was produced by Don Was, who also wrote the instrumental music for the film (the rock and instrumental numbers appear on separate soundtracks). *BackBeat* is now out on video.

The best audio/visual documentation of the Hamburg years may well be The Beatles' own forthcoming *Anthology* video series, when The Beatles themselves will share their memories of the period. But the stories about the other people who were participants in the Hamburg scene often concentrate solely on their relationship to The Beatles, overlooking the rest of their lives.

Now, Sheridan, Kirchherr and Pauline Sutcliffe discuss the role and the influence The Beatles had in their lives-and vice versa.

Tony Sheridan

Despite a career that's spanned almost 40 years, Sheridan will forever be remembered as the man who first recorded professionally with The Beatles. "It's a bit strange being attached to this legend," he admitted. "It's been a bit of a bind sometimes, 'cause everybody wants to know the usual stuff, how it was. And the question they always ask in the States is, 'Well, Tony, what about the millions you didn't make? Don'tcha miss the millions you never made?' This is a typical American thing to ask, isn't it? And if you told them, 'Well, I'm not in it for millions, I'm in it 'cause I like doing it, 'cause I'm obsessed with what I'm doing,' it's very difficult for Americans to swallow that. But it's the truth."

Sheridan was born Anthony Esmond Sheridan McGinnity in Norwich, England, in 1940. Though he played classical violin as a child, he was equally intrigued by the new sounds that arrived in England along with the influx of American soldiers during World War II. "I was five years old at the end of the war, and there were a lot of American influences in our part of England," Sheridan said. "The music was blaring out from all over the place. So I grew up with these sounds, but I never got to hear them at home. They weren't even allowed! Then I heard electric guitar. I forget who it was, probably something like skiffle, Lonnie Donegan or something. And that told me straight away, this is what I'm going to do, nothing else. I wanted to be a painter as well, which I still am sometimes, but music got the better of me.

"First I got an acoustic guitar," he continued, "and it was difficult enough to get hold of that. But I got an acoustic in my hometown, an old beat-up one, and I was very happy with that. But when I went down to London later on, in the late '50s, I heard Buddy Holly and all these sounds, and I wanted to do something like that. So I got myself an electric guitar."

After playing with local groups, the lure of a future in show business led to Sheridan's arrival in the British capital. "It was a time of revolution," Sheridan remembered, "and rock 'n' roll music was definitely the side of the revolution that people like myself and kids of our age saw and felt and wanted to do. We weren't interested in any sociological issues or anything else. We just wanted to get hold of a guitar and do this music. It was more than just music for us. It was breaking out of our past completely, breaking away from our roots, if you like, and opting for something which was strange to us. 'Cause it wasn't our music. We were copying, you see? We got hold of this stuff and put our own feelings into it a bit. Then The Beatles came, and everything changed a bit, but in the beginning we were just looking for something to grab hold of, to get us out of the rut."

Sheridan soon found work playing with such homegrown talents as Marty Wilde and Vince Taylor And The Playboys and also formed his own group with bassist Brian Locking and drummer Brian Bennett, who would later join The Shadows. Sheridan just missed out on the opportunity to be a Shadow himself; the band's manager, John Foster, stopped by the 2 I's one day to ask Sheridan to join the band but ran into guitarist Hank Marvin instead and offered him the job.

The story illustrates how a small, tightly knit music scene was beginning to grow in England. "The London scene in the late '50s was concentrated around Soho, the West End of London, the so-called red light district, where the coffee bars were," explained Sheridan. "You could hardly hear a word of English there sometimes. It was skiffle music initially. This was before Elvis really got off the ground. Bill Haley was going too, but for us he was a bit too exotic. We were more into earthy sounds, blues more than anything else."

Television producer Jack Good provided a focal point for the burgeoning musical movement with the creation of one of Britain's first rock series, *Oh Boy!*, which featured Sheridan as a regular performer. "It was quite active, that whole scene," he said. "I'd been playing with all sorts of bands. The scene was such that it was fairly close-knit and you knew everybody. For instance, the band that went with Cliff Richard later on, The Drifters — they later changed their name to The Shadows — we used to back all sorts of people together as a trio, on TV and on stage. We'd got onto television very quickly, 18, 19 years old and on national television every week. In fact, I was the first guy to be allowed to play electric guitar live on British television. It's a dubious honor, but it's true!"

Sheridan also performed as a backing musician for touring American performers, including the legendary Gene Vincent/Eddie Cochran tour in the spring of 1960. "I was one of the first to get involved with actually playing with these people, which was also something anybody would've given their right arm to do in those days," Sheridan said. Unfortunately, this particular tour would end in tragedy, when the two rock 'n' roll stars, along with Cochran's girlfriend, songwriter

WHY

Words and Music by BILL CROMPTON and TONY SHERIDAN

RECORDED

BY

THE BEATLES

with

TONY SHERIDAN

ON

POLYDOR

52 275B

22 Denmark Street, London, W.C.2.

2/6

Sole Selling Agents:-
PETER MAURICE MUSIC CO. LTD.
21 Denmark Street, London, W.C.2.

Sharon Sheeley, were involved in a car accident that claimed Cochran's life following a show at the Bristol Empire.

Sheridan said he was nearly involved in the crash as well. "They all wanted to go back to London, because Bristol was dead after 10 o'clock at night." he remembered. "They wanted to go back and have some fun and hired a car. But there was no room in it for me, so I had to stay behind." (Most other rock histories state that Cochran, Sheeley, and Vincent were actually headed for London Airport and a return flight to America.)

But despite his growing acclaim as a musician, Sheridan never came into his own as a performer in England. "I wanted to record, of course. Everybody wants to record," he said. "I was playing on other people's records, playing with singers like Vince Taylor and Vince Eager. I nearly got my own recording contract in Britain, but somebody else got it instead. I don't know why. Probably because they were not as mad as I was. I had a reputation for being a bit wild, you see. And the British record company in question was looking for somebody more... a cleaner-image person. So they took somebody else."

Sheridan's career was further hampered by his admitted penchant for independence, which caused television producers and music industry promoters to regard him as being too temperamental and unreliable to deal with.

Soon after the Vincent/Cochran tour, Sheridan was approached about appearing in Germany. "In England, there weren't enough opportunities to play," he explained. "There weren't clubs, for instance, in the sense that we know them today. There was just the coffee bar scene in Soho. It was just shillings we were playing for. Enough to get a hot meal and some cigarettes and live wherever we could.

"Now in Germany, a chap who had a club in the red light district of Hamburg [Bruno Koschmider] had tried out a couple of German singers and had a lot of success, but they were pretty bad, because you can't sing rock 'n' roll in German, and they didn't have the feel or anything. So he wanted to put what he thought was authentic [rock 'n' roll] in. So he sent somebody to London to have a look and brought us over, among other people.

"It was June in 1960," Sheridan continued. "I didn't have any particular group, so I got a group together to come over to Hamburg, sort of a makeshift group, and we went over and did the gig with great success. I guess we were, for a German audience, authentic. We didn't look at ourselves as being that authentic, but in Germany they certainly accepted us straight away, and that just exploded overnight. And this really got the Hamburg thing off the ground, because the moment some British artists were there, the whole scene started blossoming and clubs were opening on every corner, almost. There were about 200 British groups in Hamburg at the height of all this, in the early '60s."

The first Hamburg stop for the new band, which called itself The Jets (and included Del Ward, Ricky Richards, Pete Wharton, Colin Milander, and Iain Hines), was The Kaiserkeller. "It was a cellar, like it sounds, a big, dirty, stinky place, and we had to 'rough it,'" said Sheridan. "Which we didn't mind doing, because it was part of the image. A lot of us were putting on this James Dean image and a bit of Elvis as well; that was half the job. The other half was the music. But at least half of it was looking the part. And we fooled a lot of people!

"We were earning fairly good money and playing every night; we loved it. I mean, eight hours a night sounds like a lot of work, and it is a lot of work, and it was a lot of work in those days, 'cause we didn't really look after ourselves and we didn't eat properly. We didn't sleep enough, we were doing too much beer and all sorts of funny things, doing speed now and again. But of course, that was all part of that scene, and out of that a lot of things happened.

"I moved on to the Top Ten, a few months after the Kaiserkeller," Sheridan continued. "And that being on the main street of this area, it took all the business away from the other club. That caused a lot of animosity.

"There were some ugly things bubbling under, gangster stuff. The bosses who controlled half the area weren't too happy about what was going on in the other half. The musicians were sort of oblivious of this, thankfully. But now and again we could sense what was going on. People would try to get us to play somewhere else for a little more money and this sort of thing, bribe us. But basically we felt good in the Top Ten club and it just escalated again. It was like a second explosion, if you like. And that's when, late 1960, everything was really in gear, records and everything. We had everything we wanted."

Once other British musicians began arriving in the city, they naturally sought each other out, for companionship as well as music-making. "It was a very tight little society of two streets, practically," said Sheridan. "We lived in two streets and we knew everybody. Part of the charm of the whole situation was coming together after the show and playing just for ourselves in little clubs and bars and all sorts of places. We always had instruments with us wherever we went. It was a good way to get free beers! We never had any money, 'cause we used to spend it too quickly. We were just enjoying the adoration of that time in Hamburg."

Though a variety of groups, including Gerry And The Pacemakers, The Swinging Blue Jeans, and Freddie Starr, would eventually play the Hamburg circuit, Sheridan admitted he had a special interest in The Beatles. "If you're an obsessed musician, you have an eye for other obsessed musicians," he explained. "Those sort of people naturally attract your attention. And what happened in Hamburg was that people like us thought we were something special, but it wasn't in a big-headed way. We were just different. We sensed our difference.

"We came together not just to string our guitar around our necks and get on the stage, we were into much more than that. We were into the lyrics and the melodies and the phrasing and the licks and solos and harmonies and all sorts of things. And we were interested in things like photography and art as well, 'cause we'd all done a bit of this at one point or another in our lives. So there was a clique of us, and I think we excluded a lot of other musicians. We didn't want to exclude anybody, but we did think that we were perhaps a bit more promising than most of them.

"And the impression I got from the rest of The Beatles was that they were more promising. They had more charm, personality, all these things which I felt that perhaps we had ourselves. I think as a mirror, they gave us a good feeling seeing them doing their thing. I think perhaps we gave them something like that as well."

The Decca version of "My Bonnie" came out in the U.S. in 1962 and is today worth $10,000 in near mint condition.

Though Sheridan has his own specific memories about each individual Beatle, he added, "I can't tell you a lot more than you already know. I think most people have got a pretty good image of what John Lennon was and what he was on about and what he was trying to do. In a nutshell, that was what he was in those days too. And Paul McCartney was basically Paul McCartney, except of course a 20-year-old version, which had slight differences. But the differences were mainly things that had to do with the music. Like he was playing piano on stage, a bit of guitar, a bit of bass, and messing about a bit more. And we were all fumbling, we were all very naive. We were practically kids. It wouldn't be wrong to say we were kids, especially George, of course."

As a budding guitarist and junior member of The Beatles, Harrison especially looked up to Sheridan, who was more than happy to spend time teaching him how to become a more proficient guitar player, which earned Sheridan the nickname of "The Teacher."

"George was very keen," said Sheridan, "very keen on learning anything he could. And there was practically nobody else that he could look up to, to get that sort of crash-course training. I was slightly older, and so I knew a bit more, and I was into weird chords and things. George was not looked upon by the others as being especially good, although they liked his image, and they liked the way he stayed in the background a bit. Of course, he wanted to be more in the forefront, but he could only do it by improving his knowledge and gaining a little more of whatever it was that was needed, which he did."

When The Beatles returned to Hamburg on their second trip in April 1961, Sheridan's fortunes as a recording artist were looking up, as he'd finally secured a contract with Polydor in Germany as a solo artist. When the time came to make a record, he arranged to have The Beatles, who were already backing him at the Top Ten, accompany him in the studio.

"I got a contract, and I asked The Beatles to come in and do it with me 'cause that was the group I was playing with at the time," Sheridan said. "So we just went from the stage into the studio, did the same thing a couple of times, in glorious mono, and we did it. That was it. The LP was done in about three hours or something. That was the way we used to do it in those days, which had a lot to be said for it. Even in the late '60s we were still making an LP in an afternoon.

"And it's quite possible when you know what you're doing before you go in. But today it takes half a day to get the drum sound and all this rubbish. In those days it was nothing like that. There was no real messing about. You got a crate of beer and a tube of pills to keep you awake, and that was more or less the same with most of the groups."

Details of exactly when Sheridan's sessions with The Beatles took place, as well as information regarding the specific songs recorded, varies greatly. Lewisohn's *The Complete Beatles Chronicle* lists June 22 and 23 as the dates of the first session, with the musicians assembling in the auditorium of a children's school to record two traditional numbers, "My Bonnie" and "When The Saints Go Marching In" (called "The Saints" on record), Hank Snow's "Nobody's Child," Jimmy Reed's "Take Out Some Insurance On Me, Baby" (a.k.a. "If You Love Me Baby"), and a Sheridan original, "Why (Can't You Love Me Again)."

The Beatles were also allowed to record two numbers without Sheridan, the standard "Ain't She Sweet," with Lennon delivering a raucous vocal, and an instrumental parody of The Shadows' style, "Cry For A Shadow," a rare Lennon/Harrison composition (Sutcliffe did not play on the recordings, though he attended the sessions as an observer). The sessions were produced by Bert Kaempfert, who'd recently had a #1 hit in the U.S. with "Wonderland By Night." Sheridan And The Beatles recorded together again the following year, during The Beatles' third trip to Hamburg in

April 1962, when they recorded "Sweet Georgia Brown," and possibly "Skinny Minny" and "Swanee River."

The song selections are curious, given the musicians' interest in rock 'n' roll, but Sheridan explains the choice of material was determined by what Polydor and Kaempfert perceived as being commercial. "The main thing was to sell records from the point of view of the record company and the producer," he said. "Kaempfert had a very commercial outlook on things, and the choice of songs was basically a product of a discussion, a heated discussion sometimes, about what to do and what not to do. 'My Bonnie' was a compromise, 'cause nobody really wanted to do that for the first record. But we did it, and we did it as best we could. But it was more tongue-in-cheek than anything else. In fact, I copied the version, more or less — well, not copied, but I got the idea and did it in a rock 'n' roll style like Gene Vincent's. He used to do it that way too. And it turned out quite well and it sold quite well straight away.

"I don't think Kaempfert really cared whether or not I sang 'My Bonnie' or John or Paul or anybody else," Sheridan continued. "I don't think he cared that much about who actually sang the song, but he did care about who was in town to make the next couple of LPs. And 'cause I was the one who was hanging around doing fairly well, he didn't really have a choice. I was the only one who had that amount of popularity at that time. But the next record, he said, the next single, you've got to do a ballad in German, which I did, which was entirely wrong. I shouldn't have done that. So he was really just out to make some money quickly from us."

Though he was the first producer to work with The Beatles, Kaempfert missed out on seeing their potential. "Kaempfert had the right sniffer, but he wasn't able to actually see deep enough into it to see what The Beatles could have done," said Sheridan. "I think his main thing was to get this atmosphere that he saw happening in front of his eyes. He would sit there and he used to boggle at what was going on. And he got this down on record and I think that was all he wanted to do; he gave The Beatles away to Brian Epstein. He had no idea at that time what could have happened with them. And not many others did in England. It's one of those things that I'll personally never understand. 'Cause Epstein went 'round all the companies in Britain, all the big ones, and they all turned The Beatles down, with one exception.

"And that was practically the same in Hamburg," he continued. "Nobody appreciated their talent. Everybody saw that they were funny people and they messed around on stage a lot, and this was basically what they were famous for in Hamburg. Not their music so much. They weren't so good, you see. None of us were. But we had a certain way of putting it over and getting through the spirit of the times, which was very important for the kids. It was the feel of rock 'n' roll which got them dancing, not so much the power of the sound. We didn't have any loud instruments. We were quiet in those days; if you heard it today you'd think it was ballads. But the energy was the thing."

"My Bonnie"/"The Saints" was first released on Polydor in Germany in June 1961, credited to Tony Sheridan And The 'Beat Brothers,' a name chosen over "Beatles" as it sounded too much like "peedles," German slang for penis. The single reportedly sold more than 100,000 copies in Germany (though, typically, Sheridan would receive little in the way of royalties) and originally featured a slow introduction in German on copies labeled "rock" and English on copies labeled "twist." The German intro appeared only on the original single; the English intro occasionally, though not always, appeared on subsequent reissues of the song (including Polydor's *The Early Tapes Of The Beatles* CD). It was this German single that brought The Beatles to the attention of Epstein, then a record shop manager in Liverpool, and by the end of the year he would persuade the group to let him be their manager.

In 1962, "My Bonnie"/"The Saints" was also released as a single in the U.K. (again on Polydor, credited to Sheridan And The Beatles, the first release to use their name) and the U.S. (on Decca, again calling The Beatles The Beat Brothers). The two songs also appeared on Sheridan's album *My Bonnie*, released in Germany in June 1961, and the original version of "Sweet Georgia Brown" appeared on Sheridan's *Ya-Ya* EP, released in Germany in 1962. But the other songs from the Sheridan/Beatles sessions remained unreleased until The Beatles found international success in 1963 and '64; the songs then appeared on innumerable singles and albums released in both the U.S. and U.K. to indifferent success (though "Ain't She Sweet" did make the U.S. Top 20 and the U.K. Top 30).

The camaraderie between the musicians was such that The Beatles, said Sheridan, even extended an offer to Sheridan to join them. "There was mention of it," Sheridan said. "'You want to come back and play in Liverpool with us? You want to come back and play in England?' Of course, at that time they were not big. It wasn't a question of saying, 'Would you like to join The Beatles, we're big!' That, of course, never happened! But had I wanted to go back, it would have been no problem at all. But for me there was no point. I didn't look back toward Britain, as many of them did. In Hamburg, we were making a pretty large impression on a lot of people. And I didn't really want to move. I felt good doing what I was doing. But on the other hand, I was one of the very few who was recording and who had a name and who was earning money, etc. I had practically everything I had not had in London, so I had no reason to drop it and go back and try and start anew. So I said, 'No, no, I've got everything I need here.'

"Later, of course, there was no question of my joining," he continued. "Everything was pretty much settled as soon as Epstein got the band straightened out and got them dressed up, taught them some manners. And secretly, people like myself, we were quite happy that we were being really 'authentic!' We frowned upon the pop world. For us it was either authentic or it was unauthentic."

Sheridan admitted he was not a fan of The Beatles' early records. "I'll tell you," he said, "bearing in mind my impression of what they had to offer, what they could do, the possibilities and the potential, the first records they made — 'Please Please Me' and 'Love Me Do' and all that stuff — I thought, 'Ah, they've sold their soul. They've forgotten the reason they wanted to play. Ambition got the better of them.' I really don't know what went on in their heads to actually let themselves be molded by Brian Epstein in the way he did. Obviously, they had a lot of trust and respect for him, but they actually let Brian change the whole thing, from top to bottom: the music, the manners, the whole lot. And I personally felt that they'd sold out by doing this.

"And I still feel, if, say, John and Paul had the chance again, they might've done something in a much more rhythm 'n' blues vein," Sheridan continued. "This was the music they were getting into in those days. It wasn't this bubblegum stuff that they came out with, which was basically just pop, wasn't it? I mean, they were into the guts of the music and suddenly, here we are, "Please Please Me" — this is for 15-year-old girls or younger. I think they sold out, at the beginning. Perhaps they did it consciously, thinking, 'Well, as soon as we make it we're going to do what we want,' which they obviously did. But I don't think they reckoned with George Martin having that creative influence on them. He did have a wonderful, from a musical point of view, influence on them, and I think that did them a lot of good. Had they not had him, I think they might have just turned into a rhythm 'n' blues band, doing their own stuff, maybe, but certainly not with that amount of musical expansion that went on.

"Later on, of course, they came out with some wonderful stuff, and I was very happy to hear what they were doing," Sheridan added. "One of the nicest things for me was to hear a particular chord or harmony that I'd taught George. To hear these suddenly coming through one of The Beatles' tracks from the late '60s was quite gratifying 'cause I knew where he got certain things. But that's the way it happened, you know; everybody learned from everybody else."

As the British beat group scene began to take off in England and British groups began finding success at home, the music scene in Hamburg naturally began to decline. "'Round about '64, '65, the impetus went out of it somehow," Sheridan said. "The energy got used up very quickly and the air went out of it because too many people started to try to make too much money out of the whole thing. I think it burned itself out somewhere along the line — the creativity side of it did. There wasn't this little colony anymore. A new thing was going on, and this was back in Britain itself. And in Hamburg, nothing much happened, as far as British music was concerned."

Many British musicians now returned to England, but Sheridan, true to his independent nature, stayed in Hamburg, "I didn't really want to go back," he explained. "I was still acting out my rebel thing and being known for that and having a good time, basically. I was a wild guy. I wasn't doing things that people were telling me to do, and I was doing everything I wanted to, doing it my way. Really, I wanted to go to the States, you see, But I never made it to the States until much later, in '78."

As the accompanying discography shows, Sheridan continued making records for Polydor in Germany, recording a mix of rock 'n' roll classics and original numbers. After The Beatles' success, Sheridan also re-recorded the vocals to "Sweet Georgia Brown," with new lyrics that made reference to them, but this was marked the only time he tried to capitalize on his association with the group. In the late '60s, Sheridan went over to Vietnam, where, if he hadn't yet made it to America, playing for U.S. soldiers seemed to be the next best thing.

"I got to know the Americans very well over there," he said, "and their way of life even, 'cause the whole thing was mini-States. That's the way it's done when the Army's somewhere. They bring everything in, all the mod cons [modern conveniences] and comforts and things.

"For me, the dream was America," he continued, "but I never was able to make that jump in the '60s before I went to Vietnam. When I went there, I was confronted with this very different situation, with guys who knew exactly what I was singing about. Just coming out of Hamburg, of course, half the audience had no idea what you were singing about, 'cause they just didn't understand it. But in Vietnam everybody did. And this was a great experience, playing for an authentic audience, if you like, for the first time. That's what it amounted to for me."

Sheridan's time in Vietnam led to rumors that he'd been killed, and an obituary was even published in a British music paper. In fact, Sheridan was alive and well and had returned to Germany, where he continued to record for Metronome Records and various other labels. When a new Star Club was opened in Hamburg, Sheridan was chosen to head the bill, cheered on by Starr and Harrison, who were in the opening-night audience.

In 1978, he finally traveled to America and recorded the album *World's Apart* with Elvis Presley's TCB Band. The album was produced by Klaus Voormann, an old friend from the Hamburg days, and released in Europe. Since then, Sheridan has also released the albums *Novus*, *Ich Lieb Dich So* (a collection of German songs released by Bear Family), *Dawn Colours* and *Here & Now*. He also continues to perform regularly in local clubs in Germany.

"Nothing has really changed," he said. "In order to understand exactly what I mean, you'd have to understand that I'm one of these persons who's never tried to 'make it.' Success is something I'm not after and never have been after, so I'm doing what I always have been doing, music and writing. Just for myself, basically, writing songs and making the occasional record as the chance comes along, without really going to beg for it, as most people have to do. I'm doing live gigs, solo acoustic gigs, and of course the rock 'n' roll stuff and rhythm 'n' blues stuff with a band."

Sheridan also remains in touch with the members of his one-time backing group, though he said, "None of us have ever tried to keep up any sort of contact. Quite honestly, being over here and them in the rest of the world somewhere, it's a big gap and it only bridges itself when one of them comes over here. But I've seen all of them. I saw John before he left the way he did. I saw him on a plane, I think, going to Australia or something. Paul I've seen a few times in the last few years, but it just sort of happens. He'll phone and say, 'What is old Tony Sheridan doing?' He actually phoned me up once when I was at a club. I was playing on the stage and the boss said, 'There was this creep on the phone, he said he was Paul McCartney, so I put the phone down on him.' I said, 'What? It could have been!' And he phoned up again and it was him. So little things like that, they do happen now and again."

His connection with The Beatles also means he's frequently approached to appear at conventions, which he does "just for the adventure, the laugh. It's a bit of a joke, really. So much time has gone by, I can't associate really intimately with my own past even, let alone anybody else's. So if I have to say something, I try to be as honest and as forthright as I can about this subject, but at the same time I try to get over that I'm a different person, I'm not the same person. 'Cause they want to hear it like nothing's happened. They'd love to see you appear without the gray hair and without the beard, with your leather jacket on. They'd like to see you like that. But I can't do that, not being that person anymore.

"In fact, I don't know who Tony Sheridan was, quite honestly. But if I say that, then they look at you very strangely and think 'This guy's some sort of nutter.' Especially in America, you've got to be careful what you say, and just try and play the game without losing face and without losing your own integrity. So it's a bit of a juggling match, this convention thing. But it's not unpleasant.

"Looking back, in retrospect, it's so far gone now," Sheridan continued. "It's over 30 years ago, and so much has happened to me personally, especially in the last 15-20 years, it's a very small component of my life now. And it becomes smaller and smaller as I go on. I look back now through the wrong end of a telescope, and it's little. And other people see it as something big, which I can't grab at all.

"But I can only say what I feel about it, and how I saw it, and how it was at that time as far as I remember. But it doesn't mean a thing to me at all. I'm not in the slightest bit sentimental or nostalgic about it. So it's a bit strange when people come up with this theme again and again and again. These are people who are nostalgic about something they've never even experienced themselves. So it's very strange for me to not be that enthused about the subject in the way they would like, perhaps, to have it presented.

"It's the same for McCartney too," Sheridan added. "I was with him in Paris about six months ago. I went to see him, 'cause I went to see Screamin' Jay Hawkins, who lives in Paris. And Hawkins knows him too. I think McCartney helped him a couple of times when it was necessary. And we went to see Paul, and I experienced how Paul really got uptight about some of the stupid questions that the Parisian journalists were throwing at him. The same old crap. And he got visibly upset, and after 20 minutes, instead of staying there 30 minutes or whatever, he got up and just left, just like that, visibly perturbed. So he's not into that either.

"If you ask him if he's sentimental he'll probably say yes. In fact, I know he would. He'd probably say the past is the only thing we've got. But at the same time he can get too much of people harping on this stuff. And it's been blown up out of all proportion as well. It wasn't that important, the past. A lot of people would like to see Paul go back to doing 'Fool On The Hill' and 'Lady Madonna,' that sort of stuff. Which he could no doubt do. It's a lot of pressure, I think, for somebody like Paul knowing that the whole world wants him to get together with the rest of them and perhaps Julian Lennon too, or whatever. He can never drop The Beatles, and I think he suffers a bit from that."

Unsurprisingly, Sheridan's own eyes are fixed clearly on the future, and his dream is America. "It'd be nice to do something constructive in America next time, like record with some really juicy musicians," he said. "I'd love to do that. That would be, for me, a similar experience to, say, The Beatles getting together again from the point of view of the fans. I would get as excited as a fan would at being able to do this with American musicians, which I've practically never done. I've never had an American group, you see. I've played with American musicians sometimes, but not very often. But being part of a group, I'd like to try that. For me that would be latching onto where my rock 'n' roll days left off.

"I had an offer to go over to Japan and do my waxworks act with a Japanese-looking Beatles band," he continued. "Which I would find very difficult to do. So I said, 'If we go do something in Japan, I just want to be myself and play with some good musicians: a little jazz, a little blues, a little something in there, a little creativity going on.' Which was the same thing we did in Hamburg in those days — look at it like that.

"Whatever happened in Hamburg in '60, '61, '62, let's do it somewhere else, not necessarily the same thing but with the same components. That means you get together with some good people and you have a good time and you're creative. So what I would like to do is the same thing as I did in those days, except transplanted into now. Basically be creative and have a lot of fun doing it with right people, in the right time, the right place. Who knows? And if it happens I'll be very happy."

Astrid Kirchherr

Kirchherr is best known for her striking photos of The Beatles taken during their first stay in Hamburg, which were later reproduced around the world. Ironically, though, people would probably be more familiar with the photographs than they would with the photographer's name. In a sense, it could be said that The Beatles' success overshadowed Kirchherr's budding career as a photographer in much the same way their success also overshadowed Sheridan's career as a musician.

But unlike Sheridan, who continues to perform, the constant focus on her association with The Beatles caused Kirchherr to stop taking photographs altogether. Nonetheless, her haunting portraits of the young Beatles provide a poignant documentation of their Hamburg years.

Kirchherr was born in Hamburg in 1938, the daughter of a Ford Motor Company executive. She grew up in the suburb of Altona, and after leaving school in 1953, she decided to develop her interest in painting and drawing by enrolling at Hamburg's Meister Schule in 1957 to study art.

"I originally wanted to become a fashion designer," she said. "But when I was in my second term we had a new professor, Reinhart Wolf, the photographer. And I immediately felt that was the thing to do. I stopped everything and just did photography, because he was such a great teacher. We became very good friends, and he taught me an awful lot. Mr. Wolf's whole personality and the pictures he had done himself really turned me on to photography. Sometimes you just need a little peek into something which will then influence your whole life, and that's what Mr. Wolf did by encouraging me and showing me all his pictures."

By the time Kirchherr left the Meister Schule, Wolf offered her a job as his assistant. "He had by then built a big studio," she said. "We used to do advertising stuff, because that makes the most money. Some of it was quite interesting, but most of it was pretty boring. My main interest was in people, portrait photography. That's what I always wanted to be, a portrait photographer. But as you know, to live on portrait photography is very hard."

As a result, Kirchherr was only able to work on her portrait photography in her spare time, but Wolf allowed her to use his studio and darkroom. She eventually took pictures for album covers, but found the experience unsatisfying: "They told me what to do, so there's not much artistic feeling about that," she said. "And I did one cover for Tony Sheridan, but

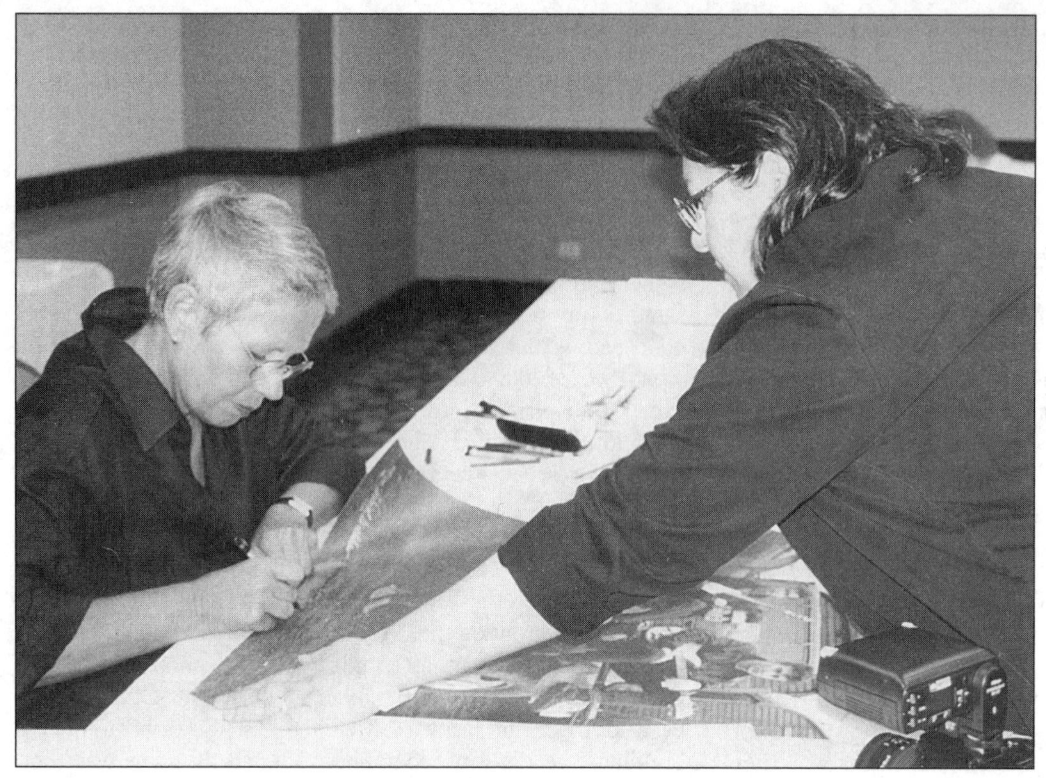

Astrid Kirchherr autographs one of her photographs for a fan, Florence Gerage Eskin, at Chicago Beatlefest in 1999.

that was later. And some other ones I can't remember. I think it was mostly for classical music. But my main interests were people and portrait photography, all the time."

By this time, Kirchherr's circle of friends included artist/deigner Klaus Voormann, who had met Kirchherr at the Meister Schule and was now her boyfriend (he would later design the cover of The Beatles' album *Revolver* and play on their solo albums), and Jurgen Vollmer, another photographer. Though the three friends regularly spent time together, visits to Hamburg's nightclubs were not yet part of their schedule.

"There weren't any clubs, really," Kirchherr said. "For amusement, we listened to Johnny Mathis and Frank Sinatra and The Platters. But most of all I liked classical music and jazz, before I ever came across rock 'n' roll. And the first time I heard rock 'n' roll was by Elvis and Bill Haley. I liked it, but I didn't particularly like the look of Elvis and I of course, didn't like the look of Bill Haley! So the music was fine, it was all right, but I never got over-excited with it."

But Kirchherr's feelings about rock 'n' roll would change quite suddenly in October 1960, due to a quarrel she had with Voormann. After wandering the streets of Hamburg, Voormann found himself in the Reeperbahn, where the electrifying sound of raw rock 'n' roll drew him into The Kaiserkeller, where Rory Storm And The Hurricanes were working through their set. Following The Hurricanes, The Beatles took the stage, and their act overwhelmed Voormann even further. Shortly after, he convinced Kirchherr and Vollmer to accompany him to the club, where they were equally won over by the groups, particularly The Beatles.

"I'd never, ever experienced anybody like that before," remembered Kirchherr, who was captivated not only by the band's sound, but also their presence. "It was everything," she said. "It was a mixture of their great gift and talent and their wonderful looks and their charm and their individuality, which really impressed me. And most of all, their personality."

Kirchherr's next move was obvious: she had to take their photographs. "They had such great faces," she said. "And when I asked them to do pictures of them, they were so sweet and they did everything I wanted them to do. They were wonderful models. I enjoyed taking pictures of them."

About a week after first seeing the group, Kirchherr took them to Der Dom, a local park where a fun fair was being held. The band posed with their instruments, the most famous picture being a rare shot of all five members together, looking tough yet somehow vulnerable.

"That's the way I saw them, at the time," Kirchherr explained, "being dressed like Teddy Boys and acting like Teddy Boys, but they were still so individual, each one of them. That's what I wanted to show, in my pictures; that they were not just little Teddy Boys, that there's something more behind it all. Behind their faces and behind their eyes, each one of them. So that is what interested me, by taking their pictures. And I've got an awful lot of pictures. If you take a picture of a person, you do at least three or four rolls, but sometimes there's only one picture good on it. So the rest you never show anybody. They're kept in a hiding place. So I really don't know how many pictures I've got."

Kirchherr, Voormann, Vollmer and their friends soon became regulars at The Kaiserkeller, the first intellectual following The Beatles had ever had. At first, the cultured art students mixed uneasily with The Kaiserkeller's usual rough clientele, but as more of the "Exis" (as Lennon referred to the students, taken from "existentialist") arrived, the two disparate groups developed a tolerance for one another due to their mutual love for The Beatles.

Though they were fans of the group. no one suspected they were observing history in the making. "None of us ever thought The Beatles would be changing the world, as far as music is concerned," admitted Kirchherr. "We used to make jokes about it. George used to say, 'Oh, you just wait when

A 1960 poster.

we are as big as The Shadows!' And John would say, 'Oh, no, no, no, no, not The Shadows, we want to be as big as Elvis!' But we just joked about it. Nobody was serious. And I didn't expect them to be changing the world. Not at all. I knew they would go somewhere, each one of them individually, because they were highly talented and highly intelligent and individualists. But I never ever expected this great fame at all."

In addition to taking photographs, Kirchherr and her friends influenced the group in other ways, imbuing the band members with an artistic sensibility not common to a rough-and-tumble rock 'n' roll group. Shortly after meeting them, Kirchherr became romantically involved with Sutcliffe, and she soon introduced him to her own distinctive ideas in clothes design: smart leather suits and jackets without lapels (a few years later, Vollmer would try to persuade Lennon and McCartney to wear bell-bottomed trousers, but they refused, afraid of looking too "queer").

Kirchherr also styled Sutcliffe's hair in the "pilzen kopf" "mushroom head" cut worn by other bohemian young men. Though the laughter of the others prompted Sutcliffe to quickly comb his hair back into the usual ducktail, he eventually adopted the new look on a permanent basis. Harrison was the next member of the group to approach Kirchherr about having his hair styled in what would be known as the "Beatle cut" in a few years' time.

But most importantly, Sutcliffe's romance with Kirchherr marked the beginning of the end of his tenure with the group. The two became engaged in late 1960, and during The Beatles' second season in Hamburg in 1961, Sutcliffe elected to remain in the city with Kirchherr, enrolling at Hamburg's State School Of Art. But Sutcliffe and Kirchherr remained a part of The Beatles' inner circle, attending their shows regularly, with Sutcliffe occasionally sitting in for a laugh.

In 1962 The Beatles would return to Hamburg three more times to play at the Star Club, by which time Sutcliffe would be dead from a brain hemorrhage. Within another year, The Beatles, with their new drummer Ringo Starr, would be the rising stars in the British hit parade and on the verge of conquering the world. They returned to Hamburg one final time on June 26, 1966, at the end of a tour of Germany.

By that time, Kirchherr's pictures of the group had appeared in newspapers across the globe and on album covers such as *Best Of The Beatles*, a 1966 release featuring songs by Best. Her dramatic style of photographing the group in half-shadow also inspired the cover photograph of the *With The Beatles/Meet The Beatles* albums. It was the height of Beatlemania, but Kirchherr received no money or recognition for her photographs.

"The thing is, when I did the pictures, nobody knew them," she explained. "So each one of them got a big pile of pictures for their mums and dads and aunties and everybody. And when journalists started to become interested in The Beatles, they used to ask for pictures, so they gave them the pictures I did. But because I did the pictures for them personally, I didn't stamp them [with a photographer's credit]. So nobody knew who had done them. And my pictures went all round the world and I never got a penny for it."

Neither did she receive recognition for her pictures of other English groups. "I did a lot of pictures," she said. "The Undertakers, Cliff Bennett, Rory Storm, King Size Taylor, and Gibson Kemp [whom Kirchherr would later marry]. You name them and I took their pictures! But it was the same thing again. We became friends, and I liked some of their faces, and I said, 'Come on, I'll take some pictures of you.' I never got paid for it, but that's my fault. I'm not blaming anybody. When you do things like that, you don't think about it. Especially The Beatles pictures. They are my closest friends and they enjoyed the pictures so much and loved them so very much I just gave them to them.

"But my other pictures are hardly shown," she continued. "Everyone is just interested in my Beatles pictures. Some of them were shown when I had an exhibition in Japan [in March 1994] and they didn't only want my Beatles pictures, they wanted the ones I chose. So that was quite an interesting exhibibition because it didn't only show Beatles pictures."

[A number of Kirchherr's non-Beatles pictures can be seen in a profile of the photographer that ran in the May 16, 1994

VOCO - INSTRUMENTAL

MY BONNIE

05513

GIL MUSIC CORP.

2.95

issue of *People*, which features a photograph of Kirchherr standing in front of a wall filled with her photos.]

And despite her impressive portfolio, Kirchherr also found it difficult to develop a career as a photographer. "In those days, it was a man's world, really," she said. "And there weren't many women who were photographers." But in 1964, her association with The Beatles did lead to an assignment for *Stern* magazine.

"The Beatles were at their highest point of fame, and no journalist could get near them," Kirchherr explained. "So a friend of mine, Max Scheler, who was working for *Stern* magazine, asked me if I could help him by introducing him to The Beatles. And so said, 'Well, I'll ask them.'

"And so I gave George and John a call and told them the situation," she continued. "And they said, 'Well, it's all right if you come over, and you can take pictures, but only if they pay you for it. If they don't pay you anything, forget it.' So that's what I told Max, and he cleared all that with *Stern* and that is how we were invited to be with them on the train when they did *A Hard Day's Night* and went to their homes. George and Ringo used to share a flat then, in London, and I stayed there. And so after the London thing, we went to Liverpool and took pictures there as well, of all the unknown groups in Liverpool."

With Beatlemania then in full swing, it was easy for Kirchherr to get a sense of how things had changed for the group in the previous four years. "They had an awful lot of stress going on," she said. "It wasn't anything like in the good old Hamburg days. And everybody was screaming and they couldn't walk in the road anymore. But our relationship hadn't changed. To me, we were friends and that's it, if they are The Beatles or not." Kirchherr would soon become caught up in the madness surrounding The Beatles herself, though to a slightly lesser degree.

Thirty years later, Kirchherr's and Scheler's photographs of The Beatles and their hometown would appear in Genesis Publications' limited-edition book *Liverpool Days*. Kirchherr's friendship with the group is clearly evident in the shots of her in Harrison's parents' house going through his birthday presents, and in Harrison's and Starr's London flat, Starr teaching her a new dance. And there are also evocative shots of children playing games in the streets of Liverpool.

But the situation may not have been as comfortable as it appeared. In a new introduction in the 1985 edition of *The Beatles*, Hunter Davies makes a reference to an assignment Kirchherr received from a "famous German magazine," quoting her as saying, "John said I should agree. I might as well make some money out of it for a change. This other photographer took some nasty pictures of them, when he shouldn't have done. They used all his."

Kirchherr was now working as a freelance assistant and stylist. "I liked styling," she said, "because that is something creative and you can get your own ideas across and it's much more creative than just being an assistant. If, for example, the photographer has got to do a still life, the photographer tells the stylist what ideas he's got, and the stylist has got to get it together. That means the location, what things he would like to have in the still life. Styling I always liked very much."

But though Kirchherr was also trying to get people interested in her own work, it was only her Beatles connection that interested the media. "When The Beatles were still going 'round on tour, there were people phoning me every day," she recalled, "wanting an interview and wanting to meet me and doing this and that and everything. I didn't like that at all. They do misinterpret you all the time. All they wanted to know is how this hairstyle came to be, which is nothing. It's so stupid! But that's all they wanted.

"I told Hunter and I told Ray [Coleman], and they did the right story, that I only cut Stuart's and George's hair," Kirchherr continued. "I never cut John's and Paul's hair, because Jurgen Vollmer did that. But all the press in the whole world, they say Astrid, the one who invented the Beatles haircut. And that's stupid. They wrote that I was a hairdresser and mad things! I just got fed up with it, so I'd rather say nothing.

"And they still wrote about me: that I was homeless and really weird things. Albert Goldman [in *The Lives Of John Lennon*] wrote that I was a witch and I had a circle of people 'round me. Can you imagine it. This man has never spoken to me! And that is why I couldn't be bothered talking to people about it. I wanted to start going on and doing my thing, portrait photography, but nobody was interested in my other photography except of The Beatles. So I was completely fed up and gave it up."

One of Kirchherr's last published photographs was a shot of Harrison taken for the inner sleeve of his solo debut album, *Wonderwall Music*. Today, Kirchherr says she has no regrets about leaving the field.

"Not at all," she said. "I did my bit, and I was quite happy doing it while I was doing it. But that's it. I'm not all that into it anymore. My main interest is in living in peace and paying my rent and paying everything else I've got to pay. I can't be bothered sitting down worrying how can I pay my rent next month because I haven't got a picture to do. So I'd rather keep it like it is. And whenever there is an opportunity I take it, if not, that's it.

"But I'm not bitter about it at all," she continued. "Not at all. Because I do stand on the ground with my two feet and I'm not somewhere high up in an artistic sky, dreaming of being a big photographer but knowing I can't afford a studio. I don't want to live on photography now and struggle and go 'round and show my pictures because the standard is so absolutely high that you can't compete with it. And I haven't got the money to buy myself a big studio and have thousands of cameras and flashes and everything. So it's not worthwhile."

In the intervening years, Kirchherr has been a restaurant manager, and, in the mid-80s, she worked as the manager of Boermoos, a hotel Voorman then owned on the Baltic. She now works part-time at More Music, a music publishing house in Hamburg. "It's nothing much," she said. "I go there whenever they need me, so I've got a lot of spare time. This past spring I wasn't working there at all, because I had to do all this film stuff. So there's nothing exciting about that job. What's exciting now for me is getting all my pictures together and developing them and discussing about exhibitions and things like that. That's what I'm mainly doing now. This last spring I was just going from here to everywhere. I went to Japan for 14 days, to open the exhibition there, and to open the film and do interviews and it was nonstop from March up to June. So I was very, very busy."

As the years passed, though Kirchherr had left photography behind, her past nonetheless managed to catch up with her.

Voormann introduced her to a friend of his, Ulf Kruger, who one day asked Kirchherr about the proceeds from her photos. "He just asked me, 'You must be quite well off with all your money from your Beatles pictures,'" she remembered. "And I said, 'You're joking!' And he said, 'Well, we've got to do something about that. Would you like me to get your things together for you?' And so I very happily said, 'Yes, please,' and that's what he did. And ever since he has been working with my pictures. He's organizing exhibitions and posters and everything. And so things are happening. Not only happening, but I get paid for it. And that's a change."

As a result of having finally secured management, Kirchherr's photos are being exhibited more frequently; in 1994, exhibits have been held in London, Japan, New York and Washington, D.C. Kruger also looks after Voormann's and Vollmer's work (Vollmer published his own book of Hamburg photos, *Rock 'n' Roll Times*, in 1982, a year later in the U.S.). One upcoming project involving all three artists is another book for Genesis Publications, *Hamburg Days*, which will feature photos by all three and illustrations by Voormann.

"But Klaus is still doing the drawings," said Kirchherr, "and he's a perfectionist like you've never seen anybody before in your life. So it's taking him a long time to do all these drawings, and I don't know when the book will be coming out."

Kirchherr's involvement in the *BackBeat* film also brought her, and Sutcliffe, greater recognition for the roles they played in The Beatles' development. Kirchherr agreed to be a participant in the film's creation because of director Iain Softley's assurances that the film would focus on Sutcliffe, not The Beatles.

"I met Iain 10 years ago," she recalled. "He phoned me and asked if he could come to see me in Hamburg, because he was interested in doing a movie about Stuart. And he was the first one who asked me about Stuart only. So I thought, well, I want to know what he's got to say, and I said, 'Yeah, OK, come over and see me.' And he did and we got on very well together. And all through these 10 years, he never disappointed me, that he didn't want to sneak in doing a Beatles movie and was just telling me it's about Stuart."

Once the film was released, Kitchherr found herself in a new situation: giving interviews. After her initial experiences with the press in the '60s, Kirchherr had stopped doing interviews, with, she said, two exceptions: Hunter Davies and Ray Coleman (though her quotes in Philip Norman's *Shout!* do appear to be direct quotes). But in the wake of *BackBeat*, she has found it to be a more welcome experience.

"It has changed now," she said. "Because of the movie, they are more interested in 'What was Stuart like?' and 'Tell me about Stuart.' Journalists ask me about him because they want to get to know him. And of course they ask me about John and George and Paul, but that's all right, and I see that as pretty natural and normal, because they were Stuart's best friends. Before, it was just so ridiculous I didn't like to talk about it."

"And the wonderful thing is that, through the movie, people recognize Stuart," she said. "They know his name now. And that is what I like. And that is what I wanted, so that people know him, and don't say, 'Oh, well, a fifth Beatle, who was that? Was that Pete Best?' And that is why I helped doing the movie. Because I wanted his name to be realized. And I wanted his wonderful art to be shown to the public. And you know what it's like when you want to put an exhibition into an art gallery of somebody nobody knows? You don't get one foot in. But now, because of the movie, Stuart's sister is getting offers from well-known art galleries to show his pictures. And that is why it was all worthwhile."

Pauline Sutcliffe

In the 1980s, following her mother's death, Pauline Sutcliffe, Stuart Sutcliffe's younger sister, inherited the task of looking after her brother's artwork. Since Stuart's tragic death at the age of 21 in 1962, his work had been seen in various exhibitions, but he was still chiefly known for his status as a former Beatle, not for his achievements as an artist.

"There's not really been sufficient media coverage of the complexity of his work," Pauline Sutcliffe, who now works as a therapist, told *Goldmine* in 1990. "There hasn't been enough interest in doing that. So people don't realize just what a large body of very good work that he's left. Whenever there's a request for an illustration of his work, newspapers and publishers usually want a representational piece, one that photographs well and works well in black and white. They work on the notion that you have to have a representational piece, which is a bit condescending or patronizing, isn't it? As if abstract art is so inaccessible nobody would be interested."

***Hamburg Days*, by Genesis Publications, came out in 2000.**

Pauline has seen that situation change considerably in the past few years. Prior to 1990, her brother's work rarely appeared in more than one exhibit a year. Pauline set about changing that by setting up a company that cosponsored a series of one-man shows, held at Sotheby's in London, Glasgow's Barbizon Gallery and the Bluecoat Gallery in Liverpool in 1990, before the exhibit toured Cologne in Germany.

This endeavor helped to generate more interest in Stuart's artwork, and this past year has been especially busy; exhibitions have held in London, Liverpool, Japan and Toronto (at BeatleRama), and the release of *BackBeat* and publication of the book of the same name have given Pauline the chance to talk more about the less-publicized aspects of her brother's life.

Stuart Fergusson Victor Sutcliffe was born in Edinburgh, Scotland, in 1940. After the birth of a daughter, Joyce, the

Genesis Publications' *Stuart: The Life And Art Of Stuart Sutcliffe*, comes with a reproduction of Sutcliffe's art school sketchbook.

Sutcliffes moved to the Merseyside area where Pauline was born in 1944. Stuart exhibited an interest in artistic pursuits at an early age, though as Pauline said, "When artistic activities are part of the familiar backdrop to family life, one doesn't think of it as anything unusual. And given that many of one's friends were from interesting families, mine didn't stand out in any way. We were not exceptional or particularly different."

Though he sang in the church choir, visual art, not music, proved to be his forte, and in 1956 he enrolled at the Liverpool College Of Art.

Back in Liverpool earlier this year to oversee an exhibition of Stuart's work at his old art school, Pauline was able to look at her brother's original registration form. "We were just gasping on realizing that he was 16 years and three months of age when he started at the art school," she said. "That's a very, very young person, no matter how mature they might be for their age."

A year later, in 1957, Lennon entered Liverpool College Of Art and was introduced to Sutcliffe by Bill Harry, another Art College student who would later start the city's first rock paper, *Mersey Beat*. Sutcliffe and Lennon became close friends and shared a flat together, and Lennon eventually extended an offer to Sutcliffe to join his group, then known as The Quarry Men.

Sutcliffe agreed and joined in early 1960, spurred on by having sold one of his paintings in the biennial John Moores Exhibition held at Liverpool's Walker Art Gallery for £65, a prize he used to purchase a bass. He also gave the group a new name in "Beatals," a play on Buddy Holly's Crickets. The name was further amended to the Silver Beats, Silver Beetles and Silver Beatles, before the Silver was finally dropped when the group went to Hamburg that August.

But despite Stuart's longtime interest in the arts, Pauline found his interest in being a rock musician surprising. "That was most unusual," she said. "I didn't know anybody who had a brother who was in a pop group. Especially a brother who was at art school, who was also in a pop group. I hardly knew what pop groups were, and neither did most of us. Trad jazz was the middle-class cultural pursuit of young people, rather than rock 'n' roll. One could just almost marginalize it, 'Oh, well, art student' — it was almost like a fad, do you know what I mean?"

Nonetheless, Pauline was happy to go along and hear her brother's group play, "long before they ever hit The Cavern," she said, "and when they had hardly formed as a group, at least of the people who we're talking about — George, Paul, John, and Stuart. It was long before Pete. You know all that stuff about the Fifth Beatle — well, Stuart was the fourth. But somebody pointed out to me he can't ever be the fourth, because the four Beatles are John, Paul, George, and Ringo. So even though Stuart predated Pete and Ringo, he can't ever be considered a fourth Beatle.

"I saw them in some grimy dump when they were hardly formed," she continued. "They didn't have much in the way of instruments, but for me were an utter delight and brought forth the reportage back home that they could actually play a whole tune. So low were my expectations, because I wasn't aware that he could play anything, you see. I used to go to quite a lot of the gigs, until Stuart went to Hamburg. When he was back from Hamburg, I'd still go see them, but with him usually. I was 'Stuart's Little Sister' and wasn't there to enjoy the social milieu, just simply to be there because my brother was there. They still mostly did covers in those days; I remember Paul McCartney singing 'Bésame Mucho,' which was regarded as some sort of sloppy aberration on his part, but of course we girls loved it. But I liked the real old rock 'n' roll stuff."

Pauline was able to see the group in a more casual setting when they visited Stuart at home, though she added, "We've also got to remember the difference in age, and I was four years younger than Stuart, and when you're teenagers, that's a lot of difference. John in particular seemed intimidating. George never did. I always thought he was just sweet and cute. And I liked Paul, but I thought he was too distant, whereas John had a different, other quality to him that was more frightening, really. He was such a radical even then. He didn't pay lip service to social convention. Even though he might be in your home, he certainly wouldn't conform in any way to the manners of that time, which I was both shocked by but also secretly admired."

With one tour under their belts by summer — the week-long stint in Scotland backing Johnny Gentle — The Silver Beetles were now offered their first international gig in Hamburg. The band had convinced each of their families it was a not-to-be-missed opportunity, but Pauline recalled her mother still had apprehensions about the trip.

"Hamburg to me was like going to the moon," she said. "We hardly traveled to Manchester airport in those days, and I had never been abroad. So even conceptually I couldn't think where Hamburg was. I could look it up in an atlas, but it seemed to be some sort of exotic world that I didn't know anything about. Yet on the other hand I was aware of the distress it was causing to my mother, because she foresaw that it would play havoc with his professional aspirations."

Stuart's mother wasn't the only one concerned about the impact a trip to Hamburg would have on his studies. By 1960, Stuart was considered one of the Art College's premier students, and his instructors regarded the trip as an unnecessary interruption of his studies. But in the end, the College agreed to let him resume his course work when he returned from Hamburg, and, perhaps to assuage his family's worries, Stuart kept up a regular correspondence about his activities.

"He was a very prolific letter writer," Pauline said. "But, of course, I discovered over the years he was not an accurate reporter of what exactly was going on. From the family homey perspective that he used to report — 'Tonight we had dinner with so-and-so, and Nielsa [Astrid's mother] came along,' or, 'I'm going for my morning paper and I'm taking the dog for a walk as well' — it was almost home from home, except we didn't have a dog!

"It was as if he was trying to replicate a home away from home," she continued. "A proper disciplined family structure and a work regime and regular meals and so on. That was mostly after he'd left the group, I have to say. But although there was a lot of intimacy in his letters, they certainly weren't over-revealing, as to just exactly the conditions they were living in and working in and just how utterly punishing it all was. And how decadent it all was. That was certainly a revelation."

But Stuart's initial period of time in Hamburg not only played havoc with his college studies, it also affected his ability to be an artist, and his creation of visual art lapsed. "Some disillusion did set in for a little while," said Pauline. "And some of that was to do with his disenchantment with his final post-graduate year that he expressed a real wish to do here in Liverpool, though I think as we got older we realized he was doing that as much to please his mother as for any real desire on his part. But of course once he got fired again, in no time he was doing both [art and music]. And of course that was often attributed to some of the symptoms that he was starting to develop. He was burning the candle at both ends, really."

After Stuart returned to Liverpool in February 1961, he applied for the Art College's teacher training course and was surprised when the college reneged on their past assurances to readmit him and turned him down. Back in Hamburg in March, Stuart realized that his pull toward art was greater than his pull toward music, and he quit the group and enrolled in art college once again. His "candle burning" now began in earnest, perhaps hastened by the blinding headaches that increasingly troubled him. Whatever the inspiration, Stuart's works were now burning with an intensity missing in his earlier creations.

"[Art critic/author] John Willett describes it as an explosion," Pauline said, "in terms of his range and the depth and the texture and subtlety of his coloring and so on. Which must've had something to do with the international flavor of art school in Hamburg, especially studying with someone who was as well known as Eduardo Paolozzi was [Stuart's instructor in Hamburg]. Plus his own development anyway, which was always fairly rapid.

"So what we see is a young artistic life. We're talking about a span of five or six years, which is regarded as very tiny

Selected Tony Sheridan Discography

by Gillian Garr

Label	Record #	Title	Year
U.S. Singles/EPs			
Decca	31382	My Bonnie/The Saints	1962
MGM	K 13227	Why/Cry For A Shadow	1964
Atco	6302	Sweet Georgia Brown/Take Out Some Insurance On Me, Baby	1964
Atco	6308	Ain't She Sweet/Nobody's Child	1964
U.S. LPs/CDs			
MGM	SE 4215	The Beatles With Tony Sheridan And Their Guests	1964
Atco	SD 33-169	Ain't She Sweet	1964
Polydor	24-4504	The Beatles — Circa 1960 — In The Beginning	1970
Polydor	823 701-2	The Early Tapes Of The Beatles (*CD*)	1987
German Singles/EPs			
Polydor	NH 24 673	My Bonnie/The Saint	1961
Polydor	NH 24 821	Ich Lieb Dich So/Der Kiss Me Song	1962
Polydor	NH 24 849	You Are My Sunshine/Swanee River	1962
Polydor	NH 24 948	Madison Kid/Let's Dance	1962
Polydor	EPH 21 485M	Ya-Ya (*EP*)	1962
Polydor	NH 52 025	Ruby Baby/What'd I Say	1963
Polydor	NH 52 099	Veedeboom Slop Slop/Let's Slop	1963
Polydor	NH 52 315	Jambalaya/Will You Still Love Me Tomorrow	1964
Polydor	NH 52 324	Skinny Minny/Sweet Georgia Brown	1964
Polydor	EPH 21 610M	My Bonnie (*EP*)	1964
Polydor	NH 52 906	Sweet Georgia Brown/Nobody's Child	1965
Polydor	NH 52 936	Do-Re-Mi/My Babe	1965
Polydor Int.	NH 52 944	Shake It Some More/La Bamba	1965
Polydor Int.	421-009	Vive L'Amour/Hey! Ba-Ba-Re-Bop	1965
Polydor	?	Just You And Me/The Creep	1966
Polydor	NH 52 733	Wolgalied/Alles Aus Liebe Zu Dir	1966
Polydor	NH 52 834	Ich Will Bei Dir Bleiben/Ich Lass Dich Nie Mehr Wieder Gih'n	1967
Polydor	?	Jailhouse Rock/Skinny Minny	1968
Polydor	?	Die Grossen Vier (*EP*)	1968
Festival	?	I've Been Loving You Baby/I've Had My Yesterdays	1969
Metronome	M 25 529	Ich Glaub An Dich/Monday Morning (*as "Carole And Tony"*)	1972
Metronome	?	I Was All Alone/Come Inside (*as "Carole And Tony"*)	1973
Metronome	M 25 551	Whole Lotta Shakin' Goin' On/Skinny Minny Reprise	1974
German LPs/CDs			
Polydor	ST 237 112	My Bonnie	1962
Polydor	ST 237 629	Just A Little Bit Of Tony Sheridan (*also released on CD: Polydor 831 998-2D2*)	1964
Polydor	?	The Best Of Tony Sheridan	1964
Polydor	?	Meet The Beat (*also released on CD with extra tracks*)	1965
Polydor	2459247	What'd I Say	1968
Metronome	MLP 15 489	Tony Sheridan Rocks On	1974
TS	76001	On My Mind	1976
Antagon	ALP 3217	Worlds Apart	1978
MSP	MSP 250 185	Novus (*also released on CD*)	1984
Bear Family	BFX 15249	Ich Lieb Dich So	1986
CGD	20 605	Dawn Colours	1987
World Wide	201089	Here & Now! Music (*also released on CD*)	1990
Miscellaneous			
?	?	Right Behind You, Baby/I Like Love (*note: as backing musician for Vince Taylor And The Playboys*)	1959

indeed. And yet the quality and the depth of experience in his work and the quantity is quite breathtaking. But of course there certainly is a marked transformation in that last 18 months, where they say about artists, 'They've found their voice.' And that's clear; I can take one of his Hamburg works out anywhere; the work from that period is so consistent and clearly his. His style is there, whereas prior to that he was experimental and derivative."

Unfortunately, Stuart's artistic renaissance was to be short-lived. Doctors in neither Hamburg nor Liverpool could pinpoint the cause of his headaches, and Stuart died little more than a year after his return to Hamburg, on April 10, 1962. The official cause of death was "Cerebral paralysis due to bleeding into the right ventricle of the brain." It was later learned that Sutcliffe's brain was expanding, and that if he'd survived he might not only have been blind, but also paralyzed. As Kirchherr put it simply in *Shout!*, "He would have preferred to die."

Following Stuart's death, his mother took on the task of storing and promoting his artwork, a legacy that Pauline is now in charge of. "I think that the ratio of what I have and what was produced is that I've probably got about 90 percent of it," she said. "My mother had kept all his early work from Liverpool art school. My brother had entrusted it to her care. And the late work, the Hamburg work, was delivered back from Germany by Astrid and her family. So the work that's out is mostly work that's been purchased or acquired when my brother was an art student. When students trade they trade pictures of one another."

Pauline's work with her brother's artwork is two-fold. First, she ensures that it is stored and looked after properly. "The practical and technical aspects," she said, "like making sure cellotape doesn't touch it, which some of it has in the past, 'cause it rots. Making sure that they're not exposed to damp. And if there's exhibitions, it's very time-consuming because people come to select. I used to have a security store arrangement, so I'd have to arrange to get work out. Or people might want a transparency for a book or a magazine, and they might need half a day to select something, and sometimes they select something that there isn't a transparency for, and they've either got to send photographers or it goes on and on and on.

"So it's time consuming," she continued. "It's expensive, but it's wonderful to have the experience I had today, when I walked into his old art school, and I've never been in there before, ever, into this wonderful exhibition hall with fabulous roof light and see my late brother's work in his art school and think about how proud he might feel about that. So the rewards are tremendous. I'm sure he'd be very pleased to have a one-man show in his old art school."

One welcome development in the wake of the renewed interest in Stuart's work due to *BackBeat* is that Pauline is now more often on the receiving end of exhibition requests, rather than having to promote her brother's work to disinterested parties. "Mostly we've exhibited in non-commercial galleries," she said. "The works have usually been in public spaces like the Bluecoat and like his art school now. They're usually done with dedicated gallery directors who are publicly funded and their galleries are too. So we're always having to think about costs, 'cause it's very expensive to move art from A to B. So that's an investment I made in getting his work shown.

"But now, of course, it is more likely that I will be approached to show his work, like in Japan, for example. It's in Canada at the moment. It's going to be opened there in October. And that's all been funded either through sponsorship or other organizations."

Pauline has also been involved in two book projects about her brother. One is a limited-edition book set for publication by Genesis that Pauline originally worked on with Mike Evans. "I'd been asked for years by various other potential collaborators to do a book, and I really didn't feel I wanted to do it," she said.

"I didn't know these people, which was a good reason to begin with! Also, they had in mind less of a creative vision than I was personally interested in. Whereas I used to know Mike Evans when I was in my late teens in Liverpool. He'd contacted me to borrow a dozen pictures to go on tour in Japan and in Germany and then in Liverpool at the Walker Art Gallery, in an exhibition that illustrated the book that he'd written, *The Art Of The Beatles*. I liked Mike's book very much. And we re-met in London when he was having his book published, and I said yes to doing a book with him.

"And so we did the usual stuff," she continued. "We presented it to a number of publishers who were not interested. I think they thought, 'Yawn, yawn, here comes another Beatle book.'"

Sutcliffe and Evans finally secured a publisher in Genesis, whose well-made, limited-edition books fit in with Sutcliffe's wish for a "definitive catalog" of her brother's work "It will have lots of letters and writings and photographs as well as being lavishly illustrated," she said. "The main focus is on the artist without denying a very important part of his life."

But despite the interest on Genesis' part the book has still taken a number of years to complete. "I think in the early days, Brian [Roylance, of Genesis Publications] didn't think that Stuart was known enough and that it would sell enough," explained Pauline. "And then other priorities take over, like George and Eric in Japan [George Harrison's *Live In Japan*, 1991], and now he's put Astrid's book out, and he's got one with Bob Gruen, and Yoko's doing the text for that [*Sometime In New York City*]. Now whether that'll be out before Stuart or after Stuart I don't know. The rumor is it's going to be out in the spring!"

Contacted this past August, Genesis says its next book will be Gruen and Ono's *Sometime In New York City*, with the Stuart Sutcliffe book planned for publication "some time next year").

In the interim, Pauline was approached by Alan Clayson to cowrite a book on her brother as a tie-in with the *BackBeat* film. "Alan was already known to the publishers," she explained. "The film company had been approached by him, and they persuaded me that I should do it with them. So I didn't know Alan at all. We were put together in that arrangement. It worked surprisingly well, given the limited amount of time that we had to get it out in."

Clayson had previously written books on two of The Beatles, *The Quiet One: A Life Of George Harrison* and *Ringo Starr: Straight Man Or Joker?* The Clayson/Sutcliffe book, *BackBeat: Stuart Sutcliffe: The Lost Beatle* (published in the U.K. only, by Pan), is the first biography of Sutcliffe, and, in refreshing comparison to most other Beatles-related books, does offer new information both about Stuart and the early years of The Beatles, even though Pauline did not always find the collaborative process an easy one.

"Alan already had a number of books published," she explained "He had his own style and way of doing things. And sometimes it was difficult, but we met all our deadlines and we got it done. I expect he thinks he made a lot of compromises and I for sure feel I made millions [of compromises] in lots of areas. I didn't think Alan's research was anything [like] deep enough. But he having much more familiarity with publishing and writing, I'd have to prove it, if I differed on a perspective or a perception. I might have to write six pages of things in order to disabuse him of a fixed idea he might have about something.

"Also, the publishers wanted me to use a lot more of my professional insights and background as a psychotherapist. And it was awfully difficult to interweave a very different voice and different styles of writing about things. So it's a small miracle in a way, that book, because we come from extremely different perspectives, life and people."

The fact that the book was so tied up with the film was another sticking point. "There were some things that I didn't cause too much of a storm about," Pauline admitted, "knowing that at some point in the future there's going to be this glorious limited-edition art book where the emphasis will be very much on the artwork. But I did have some thoughts about the cover. The original cover was going to be a wonderful portrait of Stuart in a fabulous blue wash that they managed to superimpose onto one of Astrid's photographs. And clearly we didn't have a great deal of influence when it came to the cover because of the tie-in with the film. So I personally don't like the cover.

"And see, with hindsight, the cover has got very little to do with the movie," she continued. "And books of films have a certain market, and pop biographies have a certain market, but they're not necessarily the same market. And so the life of the movie book is much shorter. So commercially, I don't think it's going to turn out to be a good idea, in that, if you like, the book on Stuart dies with the film, the film's life."

Not only does the cover use the characters from the film, with a photo of the real Sutcliffe consigned to the back page, a color insert features five pages of movie stills as opposed to three pages of Stuart's artwork.

Nonetheless, Pauline does have kind words for the movie. "I suspect that it's going to become a cult film," she said. "I think we might have a *Rocky Horror* here! You'd be amazed at the number of people who've said, 'I didn't manage to get to see the film and I can't wait for the video!' The movie was very well received in Britain as a piece of film, irrespective of its subject matter. The view was that Softley, for a first directorial job, had done remarkably well. And I think it's a good film. I don't think it's a good film about my brother, but I think it's an extremely good film."

As a result of the film's success, Pauline has taken advantage of the renewed interest in her brother and, like Kirchherr, has let herself be more available for interviews and convention appearances. "I come to conventions now either because I'm signing books or we're going to be staging an exhibition," she explained. "So I come to talk about Stuart as a painter as much as those early years with the group. And I was delighted at the level of interest in him in Chicago [at Beatlefest], really delighted. There were 7,000 people at it."

Pauline's next convention appearance will be at the Los Angeles Beatlefest, held Nov. 26-27, where there will also possibly be an exhibition of Stuart's work. Her return to Liverpool this past August was not only to open an exhibit of her brother's work at the Art College, but also to announce the founding of a scholarship in Stuart's name. The scholarship was the creation of Liverpool resident Colin Fallows and the PR company of Shirley and Melody McLean.

"The coming together of those forces has been quite remarkable," said Sutcliffe. "Colin has been absolutely fantastic. And the McLeans, quite independently of their professional lives, have had the same idea as Colin, even though they're from Scotland and he's from Liverpool."

And so, 32 years after his death, it appears that the perspective on Stuart Sutcliffe may finally be changing. Known for so long as the one-time Beatle who was also a painter, *BackBeat*'s focus on the relationships between Sutcliffe, Lennon, and Kirchherr helps keeps Sutcliffe's role in the group in perspective, while allowing his accomplishments as a visual artist to take precedence.

"I absolutely hope you're right," said Sutcliffe. "It did occur to me that that could be the wonderful paradox that *BackBeat* may have brought about. Because, as you know, the *BackBeat* film was Astrid's film. It's not inspired by me in any way. I get a credit, but that's for the use of the art.

"And I actually said to her, 'cause we met up in Japan in March, 'Why did you do it now, 30-something years later?'" she continued. "And she said, 'Because I felt he wasn't given his place, and he was ignored.' And so I related to her a similar story, how it was just impossible to shake the other half, the Beatle who painted. And that I had a funny feeling that now that *BackBeat* was acknowledging him as a Beatle — that's foreground, isn't it, really, even though he's a painter — that we may well have this wonderful paradox, that he will actually now emerge as a painter who Beatled!"

Collecting Hamburg-era Beatles stuff

by Gillian G. Gaar

This article originally appeared in* Goldmine *issue #374, Nov. 25, 1994.

Though on the surface there might not seem to be many items to collect in conjunction with The Beatles' Hamburg years, a closer look shows that there is actually a wide range of Hamburg-related collectibles.

Most obviously, of course, are the recordings The Beatles made there, and collecting every permutation of the Beatles/Tony Sheridan sessions or the 1962 New Year's Eve show would take considerable effort. The first songs released from the sessions with Tony Sheridan were "My Bonnie"/"The Saints," released in Germany in June 1961, on Polydor. This record was credited to Tony Sheridan And The Beat Brothers and featured a slow introduction in either German (on copies marked "rock") or English (on copies marked "twist").

The German intro only appeared on this original single. But two fan club recordings did resurrect it from the vaults. In 1978, a single of "My Bonnie"/"Cry For A Shadow" was issued (on Polydor) in a limited-edition run of 500 in conjunction with a Beatles convention being held in Kohn, West Germany. And in 1992, a seven-inch EP issued in Sweden (also on Polydor) was issued with the intros in both languages (though, strangely, the intros were not followed by the rest of the song) and the original "Sweet Georgia Brown." Ringo Starr's "Just A Dream," Cream's "Badge," and Roger Daltrey's "Giddy" appeared on the B-side.

The next songs to surface from the sessions were "Why" and "Cry For A Shadow," which appeared on the German Polydor EP *My Bonnie*, which also included "The Saints" and the title track. The EP was released in September 1961. The following year, the German EP *Ya-Ya* was released in October 1962, with "Sweet Georgia Brown" (the other tracks did not involve any of The Beatles). Aside from the 1992 Swedish EP, this marked the only appearance of the original take of "Sweet Georgia Brown."

"My Bonnie"/"The Saints" was first released in the U.K. in January 1962, on Polydor, credited to Tony Sheridan and The Beatles. The first U.S. release of the single followed in April 1962, on Decca; the single was credited to Tony Sheridan And Beat Brothers. The single was reissued in the wake of The Beatles' success on MGM in January 1964. MGM also released "Why?"/"Cry For A Shadow" in March 1964, and the album *The Beatles With Tony Sheridan And Their Guests*, released in February. This LP had all songs on the MGM singles, along with numbers by the other Beat Brothers and The Titans.

Atco released the other four songs from the Sheridan sessions: "Sweet Georgia Brown" (with new lyrics) b/w "Take Out Some Insurance On Me, Baby" in June 1964 and "Ain't She Sweet"/"Nobody's Child" in July. An album, also titled *Ain't She Sweet*, was released in October. In 1970, Polydor released *In The Beginning* (circa 1960), the first time all eight songs had been released on one record. The Polydor CD, *The Early Tapes Of The Beatles*, released in 1987, also contains all eight songs.

The songs from The Beatles' New Year's Eve show on Dec. 31, 1962, were first released in the U.S. on Lingasong in June 1977, packaged in a double album titled *Live! At The Star Club In Hamburg, Germany 1962*. There were substantial differences between the U.S. set and the U.K. set (released in May 1977), with the U.S. version containing the songs "I'm Gonna Sit Right Down And Cry (Over You)," "Where Have You Been All My Life," "Till There Was You" and "Sheila," none of which were on the U.K. version.

Instead, The U.K. set contained "I Saw Her Standing There," "Twist And Shout," Reminiscing" and "Ask Me Why," which were not on the U.S. set. After countless reissues of the material, Audiofidelity Enterprises did collectors a favor and issued *Historic Sessions* in the U.K. in 1981, which contained all 30 tracks. This still remains the easiest way to get all 30 tracks. Or, if you prefer a CD, pick up the U.K. issue of Baktabak's *1962 Live Recordings*, released in 1988.

As far as actual Hamburg collectibles, Iain Hines, a member of The Jets, revealed in an article that the Top Ten club made cigarette lighters bearing the club's logo as a promotional item, as well as embroidered bowling jackets. The Star Club also issued bags with its logo. Sound World, in Germany, sells reproductions of club contracts, along with limited-edition, autographed art prints of Astrid Kirchherr's and Jurgen Vollmer's work, books and other items. They can be contacted at Sound World Publishing House, P.O. Box 2709, D-21317, Luneburg, Germany, U.S. address: Christel Detsch, 3218 4th Ave., Kearney, NE 68847.

Washington, D.C.'s Govinda Gallery is another place selling Kirchherr's photographs, and Genesis's limited-edition books (such as *Liverpool Days* and *Hamburg Days*) are also available from them: Govinda Gallery, 1227 34th St. N.W., Washington, D.C. 20007; (202) 333-1189 and fax (202) 625-0440. You can also order books directly from Genesis at 2 Jenner Road, Guildford, Surrey, England GU1 3PL. Call: + 44 (0) 1483 540970 or fax: +44 (0) 1483 304709, e-mail: info@genesis-publications.com, order online at www.genesis-publications.com, or call toll free: 1-800-775-1111.

Other books that depict or discuss the Hamburg period include *How They Became The Beatles* by Gareth Pawlowski (Dutton); *Beatle! The Pete Best Story*, by Pete Best and Patrick Doncaster (Plexus, U.K. only); *The Man Who Gave The Beatles Away* by Allan Williams and William Marshall (Elm Tree Books, U.K. only); *Rock 'n' Roll Times* by Jurgen Vollmer (Overlook). The April and May 1994 issues of *Mojo* also feature extensive write-ups on the Hamburg scene. Back issues can be ordered (for £7.25) from *Mojo* Back Issues, Tower Pub., Services, Ltd., Tower House, Soverign Park, Lathkill St., Market Harborough Liecs, England, LE16 9EF.

There are also a number of items released in conjunction with *BackBeat*. Along with the standard one-sheets and press kits, a special promotional boxed set was released in the U.K. consisting of a video (an "electronic press kit"), copies of the soundtrack on CD and cassette, and three booklets "Stuart Sutcliffe: The Lost Beatle, "The *BackBeat* Band" and "The Making Of *BackBeat*." Other promotional items included a white T-shirt with artwork from the poster, a black mock-turtleneck T-shirt with the *BackBeat* logo and drum sticks also marked with *BackBeat* logo.

Two soundtracks were released from the film, both on Virgin. The first features rock 'n' roll classics played by a grunge supergroup. The second contains instrumental music by Don Was (who produced both soundtracks). The cover also features many reproductions of Stuart Sutcliffe's artwork. In the U.K. "Money" and "Rock 'n' Roll Music" were released as singles, and "Please Mr. Postman" was released as a promo CD single. *BackBeat* is now available on video.

As a tie-in with the film, Polydor issued a seven-inch EP containing "My Bonnie," "The Saints," "Ain't She Sweet" and "Cry For A Shadow." In Japan, Polydor released "My Bonnie'/"Ain't She Sweet" on a three-inch CD.

Trivia

by Marc A. Catone

1. What were the original titles for "Yesterday," "I've Just Seen A Face," "It's Only Love," "Eleanor Rigby," "For No One," "And Your Bird Can Sing," "Tomorrow Never Knows," "With A Little Help From My Friends," "Everybody's Got Something To Hide Except For Me And My Monkey," "Don't Pass Me By," and "Sun King"?
2. How did John Lennon record the fast version of "Revolution"?
3. What were "The Magic Circle" and "A Doll's House"?
4. What date is generally acknowledged as the official breakup of The Beatles?
5. After The Beatles split up, John Lennon, George Harrison, and Ringo Starr briefly considered performing with the addition of Kaus Voormann on bass. What was the proposed name of this new group?
6. Who were Bonnie Jo Mason and Rainbo, and what do they have in common?

Answers

1. "Scrambled Eggs," "Auntie Gin's Theme," "That's A Nice Hat-Cap," "Daisy Hawkins," "Why Did It Die," "You Don't Get Me," "The Void," "Badfinger Boogie," "Come On-Come In," "Some Kind Of Friendly," and "Los Paranois."
2. While lying on his back on the studio floor, playing the guitar and singing the words.
3. The working titles for *Rubber Soul* and *The Beatles* (*The White Album*) respectively.
4. April 10, 1970, when McCartney announced he had left.
5. The Ladders.
6. The former became known as Cher, the latter as Sissy Spacek. Both did novelty songs about The Beatles. Cher did "Ringo, I Love You" in 1964, produced by Phil Spector. Spacek, in response to John's nudity on the "Two Virgins" album did "John, You Went Too Far This Time" in 1968.

Jurgen Vollmer

The great photographer remembers when rock 'n' roll was still dangerous and The Beatles were just a bar band

by Ken Sharp

According to a letter written by John Lennon, "Jurgen Vollmer was the first photographer to capture the beauty and the spirit of The Beatles, (tho I say it myself)! We tried very hard to find someone with his touch after we returned from Hamburg, Germany... nobody could. He loved rockers... and rock and roll... the photographs speak for themselves."

Lofty praise indeed, but one look at Vollmer's stunning collection of photographs of The Beatles in Hamburg will make you an instant convert.

Vollmer's terrific new book, *From Hamburg To Hollywood*, a lavish limited edition tome (Genesis Publications) capturing the photographer's most striking work has just been published.

Along with his friends, Astrid Kirchherr and Klaus Voormann, Vollmer was one of the fortunate ones to have witnessed The Beatles' formative years on the club circuit in Hamburg, Germany. Vollmer was inspired to take up photography while working as an assistant for renowned German photographer Reinhardt Wolf. Little did he know that some of his earliest forays into photography would be of such profound historical significance.

Transfixed by The Beatles' exciting and powerful brand of rock 'n' roll and the whole "rocker" subculture, Vollmer became a regular to such Beatles haunts as The Kaiserkeller and The Top Ten club. Afraid to shoot photographs of The Beatles during their marathon nightly performances — the hostile "rocker" crowd preyed on outsiders — Vollmer arranged an afternoon photo shoot at The Top Ten club. His groundbreaking images culled from that session remain among the most affecting of the early Beatles. That very same day, Vollmer took the legendary portrait of John Lennon, wearing his trademark leather jacket, standing defiantly outside a doorway, a photograph that graces the cover of his 1975 album, *Rock 'N' Roll*.

Vollmer is also vitally important to The Beatles saga as the creator of the "Beatles" haircut, as he recalls in the accompanying interview.

In recent years, Vollmer's exemplary work photographing the likes of Madonna, John Cougar Mellencamp, and Arnold Schwarzenegger has solidified his reputation as one of the world's most gifted photographers. Much of Vollmer's essential work — Beatles and otherwise — is lovingly chronicled in his latest project, *From Hamburg To Hollywood*.

This article originally appeared in* Goldmine *issue #451, Nov. 7, 1997.

Goldmine: *What inspired you to become a photographer?*

Jurgen Vollmer: Actually I was at Hamburg Art School and wasn't interested in photography. I went to become a graphic designer. I studied painting and drawing. I never took pictures myself. I never had a camera. In that school there was a professor named Reinhardt Wolf, and he became a very successful photographer in Germany. One of his pupils was Astrid Kirchherr. I didn't know her. Another pupil at that art school was Klaus Voormann, and they were a couple. Astrid asked me if I could model for her. She wanted to take pictures of me. I did that a few times. Through her I met Reinhardt Wolf, her professor. He became very busy then as a photographer, and he gave up being a professor at the school and just became a brilliant photographer. So he needed an extra assistant. Astrid was already assisting him, so he asked me. I had enough of the art school. It wasn't the kind of surrounding I liked. I took a chance and became his assistant without ever having taken a picture. This was in 1960. Then I got into it.

Do you feel to become a great photographer that you're born with an innate eye for composition, an innate gift?

Yes, you either have it or you don't. There are certain things you cannot learn. If you don't have that eye, it doesn't matter how long you go to photography school, you won't get it. Really good artists, they have it right away. They're born with it. If you don't have the eye, forget it.

Did you sense that you 'had it'?

It's very difficult to say. Of course everybody who is creative thinks, 'Oh, I'm the greatest.' That goes with the profession. We're all a little bit suffering from illusions of grandeur. I didn't think about it that time. See, I followed my natural desire. I wanted to take certain photos. I didn't think about if I could make money from it. It was from a natural desire of wanting to photograph something.

Bring us back to that fateful night when you, Astrid and Klaus first went to see The Beatles.

That happened in the fall of 1960. People like me were artsy types, we were called "Exis" after the French existentialists. I brushed my hair forward for many years already. That was already a revolutionary act at that time. It seems so strange for young people to imagine that. Even employees in a bank will brush their hair forward now. At that time Germany was a very bourgeois country. They had all this kind of irregular haircuts. You never saw anyone with long hair. This was many many years before the hippie period. If your hair was even a little bit longer than most, people in the street would say things. And the same was with the clothes you wore. I loved Paris. I'd been to Paris a few times even before I went to art school. Whenever I had a little bit of money I went to Paris. There I felt a freedom of spirit. People were more tolerant. There was this whole area, the Left Bank, where a lot of like-minded people more or less looked like me. Bohemian. I felt totally at home there. Klaus was a little bit of the same and Astrid was a little bit different, but nevertheless we were all outsiders in Hamburg. We were old-time jazz, Dixieland jazz fans. We went to jazz festivals.

That's where we were all the time before we got into rock 'n' roll. Klaus, by coincidence, worked in the port area called The Grosse Freheit where The Kaiserkeller club was. He'd never been inside. He had heard from the street this great rock 'n' roll sound and he dared to venture inside. In those places only very dangerous, rock and tough rockers went. The rockers were our worst enemies. Some of my art school friends had been beaten up by rockers. So Klaus went in and saw The Beatles on stage and thought they were great. Of course they were totally unknown at that time. He stayed a very short time. The next day he came to the studio where Astrid and I worked and said, 'You have to come see this band!' We, of course, were a little hesitant, but we went anyway. There are certain moments you remember all your life. That was one of them. When I went in there I was so fascinated by the whole thing. There were these dangerous-looking guys in the audience. I was incredibly afraid but fascinated by them. Not quite by The Beatles yet, the whole atmosphere, by the rockers, the audience. The Beatles were all the way in the back on the stage. I couldn't see them at first. We went though this mass of rockers and went close to the stage, which felt somewhat safer. There were five guys in The Beatles at the time, John, Paul, and George. Pete Best was the drummer, and Stuart Sutcliffe was playing bass. The Beatles played one hour, and then the other band came on and played for an hour. They were Rory Storm & The Hurricanes, and Ringo Starr was on drums. But we only had eyes for The Beatles. I was particularly fascinated by John Lennon. He projected the image of a young Marlon Brando in *The Wild Ones*. Totally menacing-looking. I didn't dare go close to him, which is funny because what we found out later, not only we but the entire world, was that he was actually a softie. It was just an act, this rough and tough rocker look. They played only American rock 'n' roll, covers. Hearing the rock 'n' roll not on the radio in your little safe haven in an apartment, now in these surroundings with all these rockers, it was just mind-blowing.

It was one of the all-time greatest moments in my life. It was so fascinating. I was so fascinated by The Beatles and the rockers that I immediately decided that I had to photograph them. I

A 1962 poster ushering The Beatles off to their two-month stint in Hamburg, Germany.

couldn't photograph The Beatles or the rockers at night in that club because you had to keep a very, very low profile. Of course we got very, very menacing looks. We were strangers there. We were outsiders. The Beatles recognized us up front. We applauded after they finished a song. Nobody applauded there. The rockers weren't there to see The Beatles. It was a place to pick up a girl or pick a fight. It was a social place. Of course from then on, they had a several-month engagement and we came every night. We saw them every day for two or three months. I must have seen them at least 60 times then. So we were applauding, and The Beatles looked at us strange. Stuart fell in love immediately with Astrid. He was intrigued by us. He talked right away to us, the first hour when Rory Storm was playing, he came to our table and talked to us. Astrid didn't speak English but Klaus and I did. At that time Klaus and Astrid were still a couple. They were on the verge of breaking up, but they were still together. I noticed immediately that Stuart had the hots for her. He asked me all kinds of questions about Astrid. Stuart was actually the closest to us. He wasn't really a rock 'n' roller. He was an artist, that's why he immediately came to us. Stuart didn't try to project this rough and tough rocker look. He didn't care about that. His heart wasn't in the music. Often I saw Paul and George look at Stuart, for he had played a wrong note. I am not a musician. I am a visual person. But I don't really hear if chords are wrong unless somebody plays particularly bad. I saw the looks Paul and George gave him. John never looked at Stuart with a look like that. They were good friends. Then after meeting Stuart, it didn't take long before they all came to our table except for Pete Best, who took a little while longer.

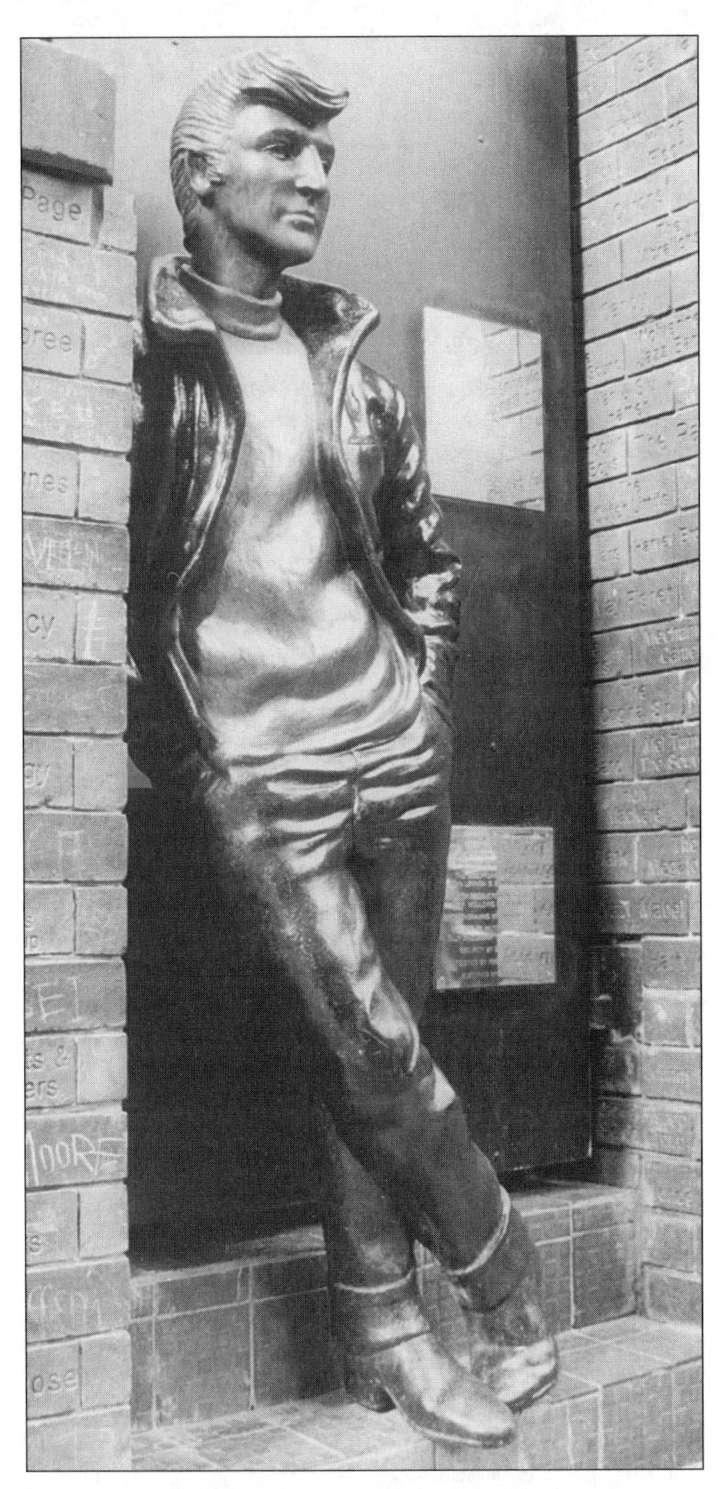

A Liverpool John Lennon statue, based on the famous photograph by Jurgen Vollmer.

Share your impressions of each member, starting with John. You felt uncomfortable with John.

He'd make some nasty reflections, so I felt ill at ease. He had an edge. You felt, "Oh my God, if I say something wrong now, he will make a nasty reflection." But he was great. He kept his distance. He also seemed very arrogant, but it was just an act. I figured it out once I got to know them. They had to play in front of an audience, so he couldn't be natural, the rocker image with the pompadour hairstyle and the duck tail, etc. And also this sort of Marlon Brando, cool guy. Paul was a little different. He was actually very friendly. He was always smiling, smiling at the girls. He was always very nice, a gentleman par excellence. George struck me as very shy. He was a cute little guy [laughs], the baby of the band. To me he was harmless. You weren't fearful of him.

How about Pete Best?

I thought that as a photographer that Pete was the best-looking. He was a great looking guy with beautiful hair and very quiet, also harmless. I never got to know him well. We didn't hang out with him that much.

Could you sense a division between Pete and the rest of the band?

To tell you the truth, I didn't notice it. But George in particular was often with Pete. They were often together. I didn't feel any animosity towards Pete. They were always very harmonious among themselves. But I thought he didn't quite fit. George was shy but George was with it. He was not as aloof like Pete was. Pete was always in the background, a little dreamy, like this whole thing didn't really concern him.

What were The Beatles' shows like back then?

They played one hour and then they had an hour rest. And then that hour Rory Storm played and this went on the whole night long. They played a long time. It was very, very tiring. The only way to survive it was to take these pills, preludins. They got it from the owner of the club [Manfred Weissleder]. They couldn't survive playing this hard, playing real heavy rock 'n' roll without any kind of substance.

George has said that The Beatles were never better than in Hamburg.

I can't imagine that they could be any better than they were in Hamburg, any more energetic, any more giving it all. I think it was due to the atmosphere, due to the rockers. Just as I was drawn in by the rockers' atmosphere. But this was authentic, rock 'n' roll, the raw sex appeal of it. You felt the guys were after the girls, the girls were after the guys. There wasn't any of this bourgeois bullshit. There were a lot of fights. There wasn't an evening where I wasn't afraid. People were throwing chairs at each other. When they were already on the ground they'd kick each other with these pointed shoes. But the funny thing is The Beatles got so used to it that they just continued to play. There was in all this violence a sexual atmosphere that is the core of rock 'n' roll. I remember George always sang "Roll Over Beethoven."

You saw The Beatles at three different Hamburg clubs. Tell us about them.

Nothing tops The Kaiserkeller. The Kaiserkeller was great. It was a real rock 'n' roll cave. There were absolutely no artistic types there except for us. It wasn't tiny, but it wasn't that big either. It was an old building and it looked like a cave. It was all done up like a boat, it had a maritime theme, these little booths were done like little boats. It's funny, I remember being so afraid to go to the toilet. You always came very early, not only so you didn't have to go through the rockers then, but to go to the toilet I was afraid. Beer was thrown in my bag without any provocation. Now The Top Ten club was on the Reeperbahn. The Kaiserkeller was on a side street in the Grosse Freheit. The Top Ten was a little bit better, still predominately rock 'n' rollers, but by that time, it was the next spring in '61 when The Beatles came back to Hamburg. The Beatles wore black leather jackets, had an Elvis haircut, a pompadour and the ducktail. They arrived in Hamburg in April '61. To some extent mainly to my influence in the artistic community in Hamburg, I knew a lot of people at that time. I always tried to bring people to see The Beatles. Some would never go back, but some would bring other friends. It had a little bit more of a mixed audience which absolutely did not exist in The Kaiserkeller. I read a lot of nonsense about this time. Don't believe it, The Kaiserkeller was full of rough, tough rockers and Astrid, Klaus and me. There was nobody else. In the fall of '61 I immigrated to Paris. The Star Club opened while I was in Paris.

Tell me about when John Lennon and Paul McCartney visited you in Paris in the early '60s before they became successful.

Like I said before, I had been to Paris quite often. I was obsessed with Paris. I couldn't take the bourgeois society, and I was drawn to that city. I had talked to The Beatles about it, and John was particularly interested in Paris. I was living in Paris for about a month in a hotel. I got a job working for the famous American photographer William Klein. He was more of my kind of photographer. The photos he did were more my kind of style. John and Paul had no money. The Beatles had to work hard for the little money they made. They didn't even have the money to take the train, so they hitch-hiked from Liverpool to Paris. They came to my hotel and I couldn't get them a room at my hotel because it was full. They stuck out in my quarter, The Latin Quarter, among the students and the Exis. I had talked to them about always buying my clothes in a flea market in Paris. So they wanted the same kind. So I took them to the stands at the flea market. They bought similar clothes to what I wore. I typically wore black turtleneck sweaters, which very few people wore at that time,

John Lennon's *Rock 'N'Roll* album.

and corduroy jackets. I remember John bought a green corduroy jacket at the flea market. I can't remember exactly what Paul bought. I was one of the first to have kind of bell bottom pants. I wore pants that had a touch of being wider. I remember Paul was very intrigued by that. He said they couldn't buy those pants. People back in Liverpool might think they're queer.

Wasn't that the trip where you gave John and Paul their first "Beatles" haircut?

Yes, I had already had my hair combed forward, a long time before I even went to art school. A lot of nonsense has been written and said about the haircut. I combed it forward as a revolutionary act against those bourgeois horrors in Hamburg. There was all very bourgeois haircuts. I went to the barber and they always cut it too short. So I cut my own hair, but I never cut anybody else's hair. So when John and Paul came to Paris I also gave them the haircut. In Hamburg they laughed about the haircut and said how strange I looked with it. I didn't convince them to do it. It was their idea, their desire to have their hair like mine. I liked this rather crazy haircut. I took them up to my hotel room and cut it. First Paul and then John. They left Paris and they never brushed their hair back again. In an interview with George in the mid-60s he was asked by the interviewer how The Beatles haircut came about. He said I only brushed my hair forward after John and Paul came back from Paris. That's the story of the haircut. Don't let anyone tell you any different. Paul said the same thing in '88: "The Beatle haircut was effectively a Jurgen haircut."

Share the concierge story.

I wanted to introduce John and Paul to my girlfriend at that time, a really Bohemian girl with long black hair, great figure, mysterious look. At the same time I wanted to impress her knowing such great musicians. So I made an appointment at this cafe and I was already there with John and Paul. So when she came she was so put off by them. She didn't want to sit down, she was so shocked by their look, for it was the rocker look. She said how dare I introduce her to those rockers. We were shouting at each other in French, and John and Paul were just sitting there looking at us, smiling and had a great time making fun of us while we were carrying on. Then she rushed away. So that gives you an idea of what kind of impression they made in Paris back by the way they looked. So when they first came to Paris, I tried to get them a room. My hotel was booked. But the whole area was all full. I told them for tonight I have two mattresses and for them to put them on the floor and sleep. But I said we had to wait until the concierge had gone to bed. It's not allowed to take somebody up to your room at night — during the day, but not at night. So we sneaked it and suddenly the light is switched on and the concierge, this fat French woman, comes out and started to scream at us. In the afternoon I had asked her if my friends could stay at my place for just one night and she said, "No, no, no!" She was screaming at us, "Out, out, out!" We had to pass by her to leave, and John turned at the exit and said, "I didn't like the service here anyway Madame!" And then he said to Paul, "Shall we try the Ritz?" [laughs] Then when I cut their hair, there was hair on the floor, and I just kicked it under the bed. The next day the concierge, when she saw the hair on the floor, she started to screaming again at me. It was kind of funny. I think John and Paul stayed in Montmarte where there are a lot of prostitutes. We went there and I got them a small room.

Genesis Publications' *From Hamburg To Hollywood*, featuring the work of Jurgen Vollmer.

Tell us about your classic photos of The Beatles taken at The Top Ten club.

It was impossible to take photographs during the show. Even though there was a mixed audience and it wasn't quite as dangerous as The Kaiserkeller, it was still too dangerous to have run around with a camera. The rockers wouldn't have tolerated it. So The Beatles were actually sleeping above the dance floor. I had taken pictures of George already outside. He had visited me. Those portraits you see of George I had done at the lake then. You have to understand, that was my first year that I had gotten into photography. I hadn't any experience. I didn't even own my own camera. I had to borrow one. I am a live photographer. I hate those kind of sterile photographs. It was very fashionable back then. I wanted to get something more out of it. I wanted to get into the interior of the people. I wanted to say something essential about the people so they all don't look like corpses. I wanted lively expressions.

So you shot those photos of The Beatles during the day?

Yes, I arranged that they come down in the afternoon when the club was closed. So I remember it was the middle of the afternoon and John hadn't put on his leather jacket and I said that I wanted that image. He grumbled something, half asleep, and went up and got his leather jacket. Then he came out and he looked perfect again. I didn't have a flash at that time. This was 1961, and flash was not a thing everybody had. So I had directed all the lights in the club towards the stage and had put The Beatles closer together so that they are standing all in the light, closer together than they'd normally play in the evening. So then they played just for me. And I was just running around and taking my pictures. At one point I stood on this table and almost fell down and they all laughed. I took 10 rolls of The Beatles. I took the photos without any purpose. I just wanted to do it, for what, I didn't know. I just wanted to do it. Before they saw those photos, I think it was the same day, we went out. I always had this certain backyard in the poor district in mind. I liked those mysterious backyards, they exude mystery. I had that in mind. I saw John standing there, the real rock 'n' roll image. You had to go through a house in order to get to the backyard. That was the alley of the backyard. It still exists by the way. I put John there and told him not to move, to just stay like this. The other three Beatles, Paul, George, and Stuart — Pete Best didn't come with us. As you can see from the contact sheet here, they had to walk by John 12 times. To me, their pointed shoes were very amusing. I'd never seen anything like this. So I wanted them in focus and their body out of focus. I just wanted John to be recognizable with the brick and everything. But you can't foresee how the bodies will be in composition perfectly, just John. I had to do it over and over again and of course they complained. I did it 12 times. Several are OK, but the one I liked, John when he was in New York in '75 had contacted me when he was putting together his *Rock 'N' Roll* album. He wanted to use that image for the cover.

Had John seen some of the alternate shots of the photo that would later adorn the Rock 'N' Roll *album?*

No. Back then, I would always give them enlargements. When I gave John the enlargement of this at the photos from The Top Ten he said, "Thank God you made me wear my leather jacket." He didn't realize that I would actually take good photos. They didn't realize that one could actually take great photos.

So when you gave The Beatles the photos from The Top Ten club, were they blown away?

No, see that wasn't their style. They weren't blown away by anything. They were playing it cool. Just like nobody would applaud at The Kaiserkeller, this is part of it. You are cool, you don't show your emotions by applauding. It just was not done, not from rockers. But they liked them. But John did say, "Good thing you made me wear my leather jacket." I wanted him to wear it because it was very important.

Take us back to what one would witness walking down the Reeperbahn.

It's quite different today than what it was like back then. Now it's really catering for those awful tourists, those bourgeois assholes that go there. I live in Hamburg, but I never got back to that area. But back then it had some sort of authenticity at that time in the '50s and early '60s. It was a real working-class area, everything was very authentic. That was the rockers' neighborhoods. There were no chic restaurants, just disgusting little kiosks. When I compare it to today, there's all kinds of restaurants. Nothing was chic, it was rough.

There was a red-light district. At that time there were no prostitutes in the street, there was only that closed street where they were sitting in the window. But today there are many more prostitutes standing in the streets. They didn't allow that sort of thing at that time. There might have been bars where the prostitutes used to hang out, but they weren't really out on the streets.

Pete Best said a lot of criminals used to come to see The Beatles perform.

Yeah, there were criminals, of course. It was all part of it. There were no bourgeois people in that part of Hamburg. It was their neighborhood. Certainly the reason that The Beatles projected that rough and tough image, if they had shown their softie side, that wouldn't be a very practical thing to do in front of their rocker audience. They had to project and act like they were one of them, just for safety reasons.

You and Astrid both shot photos of The Beatles back in Hamburg. Was there any competition between you?

No, not really. Astrid and I were never really that friendly. We weren't enemies, but we were different. Astrid never wanted to meet anybody. But I was very curious about everything. If there was some interesting person in Hamburg, I wanted to meet them. But Astrid just wanted to be alone with Stu.

How would you characterize Stu and Astrid's relationship?

I had left for Paris then, but I was always a little bit suspicious. It was a couple who were in love. If Stuart had lived on, I have my doubts whether he would have stayed with Astrid. She had many friends in her life, and they all apparently had left her. She never stayed with one for a longer period of time, so I suppose that would have happened to Stuart too.

Did you see the film BackBeat*?*

Yeah I saw it. It was totally unauthentic and totally boring. I had kind of looked forward to it to bring back a little bit of the memory, but it was ridiculous. Astrid was nothing at all like she was shown in the movie. I wasn't even mentioned at all. I guess out of the jealousy reason, I don't know what it was. The movie rings false. I was very disappointed by the movie, particularly it came across so boring and it was anything else but boring, that period. There was some sort of energy, excitement, mystery. It was a different world. Nothing came across in that movie. I was totally disappointed.

John also visited you in Paris in 1966.

Yeah. But before I talk about that I wanted to mention that when The Beatles were playing The Star Club in 1962, I came back to Hamburg and tied it together to when they were playing there. The Star Club was more established. It didn't have that authentic rock 'n' roll feeling. It was gone by that time. The Star Club was definitely the most harmless place of the three. Also when The Beatles came to Paris in 1964 and played the Olympia, George called me.

I had now slowly became aware that my rocker friends had become such big stars. I saw them on the cover of magazines and publications. It was a little strange feeling. So when they came to Paris I was of course very intimidated that suddenly it's the famous Beatles. I was supposed to go to their hotel, The Georges Cinq, and then go to the concert. I didn't have the courage to go to the hotel. In their eyes I wasn't a photographer, I was a friend. We'd hang out all the time. Besides The Kaiserkeller and The Top Ten, we spent some private time together during the day. They just wanted me to come over to go with them from the hotel to the Olympia and watch the concert. But I was too shy to go to the hotel. So George said, "Why don't you go to the stage door and we'll let you in there?" So I went to The Olympia, and it was a madhouse. There were hundreds of girls, screaming. I could barely get to the stage door because I had to go through the masses of people. And there of course were security guards waiting there. I said, "I have an appointment with The Beatles." [laughs] I couldn't even get past them. George didn't realize that you just can't go in there. I couldn't go to the show. The next day George asked me why I didn't come. I explained it. He said there's no reason to be shy, we're all together and then we'll go there. I said all right. So I hung up the phone and I just couldn't do it. It sounds crazy, but I was very shy at that time. I mean it's unbelievable that suddenly those guys I was hanging out with in Hamburg looked up to me. They wanted to be like me, they wanted my haircut, they wanted my clothes. We also talked about books I was reading then with John. Suddenly they were the stars. I felt like a little cockroach. And I'm supposed to go like a cockroach and meet these superstars!

So I called back the hotel and I didn't want to be connected with George... I said to them, "Could you please leave a message with Mr. Harrison. I'm called on an assignment and I have to leave Paris right away so I can't go there." I swear to you that is the truth and it was the last of it.

So then in '66 John called me one day and he was in Paris for two days. He was on his way to Spain for shooting the movie *How I Won The War*. He spent two days in Paris and was registered under a fake name. He was with Neil Aspinall. So John said to come over to the hotel and I should ask for whatever name he was using. I drank a couple of glasses of red wine [laughs]. I couldn't drink alcohol. If I drink two glasses of wine I'm half drunk. So I go there and there's John Lennon, and suddenly I see him and he's a famous guy. So I was so confused and of course I was half drunk and I couldn't walk straight. So John made fun of me. He walked like me, like a drunk. We had a good time.

So after a little while you forget that this is the famous John Lennon. It's John from Hamburg. Then he seemed to be the same guy. One of the first things he wanted to do was go back to the flea market. He discussed it with Neil Aspinall and asked, "Can we risk it?"

He had cut his hair short for the movie. It wasn't as long. So he disguised himself and he put big glasses on. We went and I realized for the first time in my life how horrible it must be to be a famous person, for he was absolutely paranoid. He was always afraid if somebody recognized him.

At one point we were in this flea market at this small cafe. Then he noticed that a group of people across the street had recognized him. They were watching him. So we managed to get out of there quickly. Then it was very crowded at the flea market. I can't remember whether he bought something or not. We tried to get a cab, but we couldn't get a cab.

Then I said, "Why don't we take the bus?' And John said, "What, a bus?" And it was so absurd that John Lennon would take a bus. Not that he is snobbish but to go with normal people who might recognize him, he was completely paranoid. But I made him go on the bus. There was a platform on the bus that we were standing on. So at least as we got further into Paris, so that he could try again to get a cab there.

The flea market was in the suburbs, Porte de Clingancourt. Nobody recognized John on the bus. They really didn't expect John Lennon riding a bus [laughs]. But then we got out and took a cab. We were together for two days. His son was very small and he wanted to buy some clothes for him. I took him to stores there. It was just like the old days.

When did you reconnect with John?

It was in 1975 when he had split from Yoko. I moved to New York in '69. In '75 he had contacted me through his then-girlfriend May Pang who had run into me somewhere. She had me meet up with John. Then also Klaus had phoned me up. He was in New York playing with John for the *Rock 'N' Roll* album. So I got together with Klaus and we visited Yoko Ono, who of course was separated from John.

Then the next day I was supposed to meet John. He had given me an appointment at the studio where they were recording. So I came to the studio, and I was very excited. I waited for him and he came out and took me in his arms. Then he put his arm around my shoulder and guided me into the studio and said, "I want you all to meet one of my oldest friends."

He was very very nice to me. He knew that I was a little bit sensitive, so he wanted to put me at ease. And I think also, as we all know, that John had made a great transition to a saintly kind of human being. Before he was more the rocker. But he was definitely now totally human. He invited me to do the layout for the *Rock 'N' Roll* album, which I did. So I came back to the studio, and he said, "It's beautiful Jurgen. It's beautiful." He liked it very much. In the '70s in New York I was mainly a designer. And then somebody had done a bootleg of the record called *Roots*. So they had to rush the real thing out because they didn't have the time to make this foldout thing which was my design. All they did was use my photo on the cover. They put something on the back that was just a rush job. That's how John explained it to me.

They cropped the front cover in a way so the pointed shoes aren't in it. But still it's great. After that I had met John again. I had done an extensive report on rock 'n' roll fans, it was for my first book, *Rock 'N' Roll Times*. I showed John the layout and asked him if he could write something. Then he wrote an introduction. I was supposed to see John again at one point when Klaus was in New York, but I got cold feet and I canceled that appointment. I'm such an idiot. Today I wouldn't be like that.

You met up with Paul on his 1989 world tour.

Yes. I went back to Hamburg and it happens that Paul was on tour and in Hamburg. He called Astrid and he invited both of us to his concert. I got over being shy, but I was still a little bit excited. We spent at least an hour with him in the green room. He was great. He was so nice I couldn't believe it. Paul hadn't seen me since '62 and this was now '89. Of course I recognized Paul McCartney, but how would he know that it was me? [laughs]

But he said, "Of course I recognize you." The publishers of my new book asked Paul if he would write something and he did. Paul also called me in Hamburg. Unfortunately I wasn't there, but he left a message on a answering machine. I had written a stage play about the Hamburg Beatles period. It also has music and I needed his authorization to use some Beatles songs, and he sent a fax immediately to my agent giving him the authorization. On the answering machine he said, "It's Paul McCartney and I'm just wanting to wish you the best of luck with your stage play. Hope you're well."

To order your copy of *From Hamburg To Hollywood* by Jurgen Vollmer or for a free color prospectus please contact:

Genesis Publications
2 Jenner Road
Guildford, Surrey, England GU1 3PL
Tel + 44 (0) 1483 540970 or Fax: +44 (0) 1483 304709
e-mail: info@genesis-publications.com
Order online at www.genesis-publications.com
or call toll free: 1-800-775-1111

The price is $267, including shipping. Interest-free installment plans are available.

Parlophone Records: The starting point for The Beatles' invasion

Laughed at by EMI execs, in 1962 the subsidiary took on a life of its own

by Bruce Eder

In June 1962, Parlophone Records was one of the smaller record labels in the EMI organization — not much more than a poor relation to its more prominent and respected rivals, Columbia (the U.K. label, not the American company of that name) and His Master's Voice (HMV). By July, the company had auditioned and signed The Beatles, who would make Parlophone the most visible and successful of all the EMI labels and reshape the various units of the company around the world.

The relationship of The Beatles to Capitol Records in the United States is well-known to most serious fans and collectors. Capitol was the label by which most of their tens of millions of American fans discovered the group, and entire books have been written — most recently *Songs, Pictures And Stories Of The Fabulous Beatles Records On Vee-Jay* by Bruce Spizer — about the effect that Capitol had on The Beatles' fate in America and that The Beatles had upon Capitol. The history and fate of Parlophone is part of their story that relatively few Americans know.

This article originally appeared in Goldmine *issue #523, Aug. 11, 2000.*

Parlophone Records' origins go back to the German-based Carl Lindstrom company, through which the company was founded. The Parlophone logo, often mistaken for the pound sterling symbol, was actually an old-style German "L" for Lindstrom. In 1927, The Columbia Graphophone Company purchased Parlophone from Lindstrom. In the process, it also acquired the services of the label's manager, Oscar Preuss (1889-1958). By June 1931, The Columbia Graphophone Company had merged with its largest rival, The Gramophone Company, to form Electric And Musical Industries Ltd., better known as EMI. Parlophone became part of a huge conglomerate that included not only Columbia but also the powerful HMV label and two budget labels, Regal Records and Zonophone Records (later merged into Regal Zonophone).

The 1930s were not a prosperous decade for the new company. Various units of EMI were consolidated, and parts of the smaller labels' rosters were shifted elsewhere. Parlophone finished the 1930s weaker than it had started them, with its strongest and most popular artists — most notably Victor Silvester (1900-1978), the leader of the most popular ballroom dance band in England — shifted to Columbia or HMV.

Preuss did his best to keep Parlophone alive for more than a quarter of a century, largely running the label and many aspects of its day-to-day operations with help from only one secretary. In 1950, he interviewed a young job applicant, a Royal Air Force veteran, oboist and graduate of The Guildhall School Of Music named George Martin.

Martin, born in 1926, was engaged as his assistant. He wasn't much more than a glorified gofer at first, but soon he was managing recording sessions.

His musical training made Martin a natural to supervise classical recordings — among Martin's earliest credited sessions was the recording of Ralph Vaughan Williams' "Song Of Thanksgiving," a large-scale choral work written to commemorate the end of World War II (reissued on CD by EMI in the early 1990s), and a series of recordings by the German conductor Dr. Karl Haas and the London Baroque Ensemble, performing the music of Haydn, Bach, Mozart, and Handel.

Parlophone's big artists in those days, however, were its pop musicians, including Humphrey Lyttelton And His Band. Squeezed by his rival EMI labels, Preuss had kept Parlophone alive by cornering certain music at the margins — most notably the Scottish market for dance music. If there was one locale where Parlophone did rate alongside Columbia and HMV, it was Scotland. The company's Scottish roster included band leader Jimmy Shand, vocalist Roberto Inglez (a.k.a Bob Ingles), pianist Annie Shand, and accordionists Mickey Ainsworth and Jimmy Blue.

It was through Martin that Parlophone opened up another new niche market — comedy. It all began with Peter Ustinov, a fellow member of the London Baroque Society with Martin, who used to entertain his friends with his comical takes on classical music. That led to the recording of a single, "Mock Mozart" b/w "Phoney Folk Lore," the recording of which, involving Ustinov taking on upward of a half-dozen voices, was the *Sgt. Pepper*–scale project of its day. Its success opened Parlophone to an array of new artists, including Spike Milligan, Bernard Cribbins, and — the closest thing to a superstar that Parlophone had — Peter Sellers. They all became recording stars because of Parlophone's struggle to stay afloat in competition with Columbia and HMV.

In 1955, with the retirement of Preuss, Martin became the head of Parlophone Records. Within a year, new forms of music — skiffle and rock 'n' roll — were making themselves felt. Parlophone was just hungry enough and just low enough on the EMI totem pole to bother with these new phenomena, which were beneath the notice of Columbia and HMV.

In the fall of 1956, Martin visited the 2 I's coffee bar in London, where all of this activity seemed to be focused, and saw The Vipers Skiffle Group, led by guitarist Wally Whyton. He signed them soon after, and The Vipers became one of the top skiffle bands in England, even releasing music in America as The Original Soho Skiffle Group.

The Vipers scored a Top 10 U.K. hit with a Whyton song, "Don't You Rock Me Daddy-O," and were successful for the label. Martin later admitted that working with The Vipers was excellent experience for producing a band whose members couldn't read music, preparing him for a key future signing.

Parlophone kept slogging along, selling lots of records by Sellers and company but not getting too much respect. EMI's management did assign one new artist, a popular young singer/actor named Adam Faith, to Parlophone, which gave the label some pop-rock credibility. Though Martin and company likely didn't know it, in the guise of Faith's backing band, The Roulettes, Parlophone had one of the better rock 'n' roll groups in England.

But Parlophone was still a poor relation, thought of — like its most popular releases, the comedy records — as a joke.

He didn't know it at the time, but Martin was in a position to change that in April 1962 when he had a meeting with the neophyte talent manager from Liverpool named Brian Epstein, representing The Beatles. Martin didn't like the music that he heard on their demo, but in later years he admitted to being intrigued by the fact that two or more of the members were singing — which was unusual in in those days — and by their roughness, which seemed to hint at untapped potential. An audition at EMI's Abbey Road Studio No. 2, run by Martin's assistant Ron Richards, who was more adept at dealing with rock 'n' roll, was scheduled for June 6, and a tape was made. In July 1962, the group was signed to the label. Martin's colleagues at Columbia and HMV were so accustomed to Parlophone's specialization in comedy, that they suspected these "Beatles," whoever they purported to be, might really be Sellers.

They thought differently a little more than six months later. By then, the group's second single, "Please Please Me," had been released and was dominating the charts, the radio, and the consciousness of Britain's youth like no record ever cut by an English band. Over the next year, the group racked up sales so high — with LPs and EPs that outsold most rivals' singles — that the U.K. record charts had to be reconfigured to accomodate them.

Change swept over Parlophone as well with the subsequent signings of Billy J. Kramer & The Dakotas, The Hollies, The Paramounts, and Cilla Black, among others. Parlophone ended up as EMI's top rock 'n' roll label and its most profitable operation of the 1960s. (Of course, in America, we scarcely heard the name Parlophone or, for that matter, George Martin. EMI's American outlet, Capitol Records, affixed its name — and the

The 1967 Great Britain *Magical Mystery Tour* EPs, with pop out centers.

name of its producer, usually Dave Dexter Jr. — to Beatles releases, it barely touched Black's output and passed on The Hollies and Kramer, who ended up on Imperial).

The irony was that Martin wasn't part of the boom years he had jump-started. After 35 years of being the laughing stock of the EMI organization, Parlophone — through The Beatles (and, to a lesser degree, The Hollies) — had been transformed into the biggest cash cow in the history of the corporation, and the man who'd brought it about was no longer there.

Treated poorly for years in terms of salary and respect, Martin left EMI to form A.I.R., an independent recording studio, in 1965 — his sole stipulation to the company on exiting is that he would continue to produce The Beatles.

Parlophone signed some good artists, such as Rainbow Folly and Locomotive in the mid-to-late 1960s, though none of them were as promising as one of Martin's A.I.R. discoveries, The Action. For a time, it looked as though Parlophone might become EMI's psychedelic and progressive rock imprint.

By the end of the 1960s, however, a new problem had come up, due precisely to The Beatles' success. From the spring of 1963 onward, the quartet had so thoroughly dominated the Parlophone release schedule with their sales, chart placements and the attenion that they received that other Parlophone artists were eclipsed. Parlophone may not have been Apple, but it might as well have been, insofar as it was identified with The Beatles in England. Indeed, Harvest Records was created as a haven for all of the non-Beatles progressive and psychedelic acts on Parlophone and the rest of EMI.

In the 1970s, EMI was reorganized and most of its individual labels, other than Harvest and the HMV classical label, disappeared. By that time, Parlophone was best remembered by serious Beatles fans, including tens of thousands of Americans who had sought out the group's original U.K. discs. The name reappeared in the 1980s as a logo and on the original Beatles CDs from EMI, although the Apple name and logo was affixed to the vault-raiding Beatles' BBC collections and the *Anthology* series.

A recent Parlophone 45 for Gene Vincent's "Blue Jean Bop" by Paul McCartney, which features an old-time label and sleeve.

Trivia
by Marc A. Catone

1. All of The Beatles eventually married, but three of them divorced wtheir first wives and later remarried. Name the order in which they married, then divorced and then remarried.
2. What was the date and location of the last paid concert performance by The Beatles? What was the date and location of the last public performance by The Beatles?
3. Which member of The Beatles appears on two songs recorded and written by Donovan and what did he contribute to each song? Which Beatles song does Donovan appear on and what did he add to it?
4. Name the seven original Beatles compositions, all recorded by the band, which contain a reference to the drinking of alcoholic beverages, the contemplation of the same or the name of a particular alcoholic drink. Hint: alcohol only!
5. In 1967, George Harrison and wife, Patti, visited Golden Gate Park in San Francisco. What song did George briefly perform to the hippies hanging out in the park?
6. How many takes were required when The Beatles recorded "Twist and Shout"?
7. When did the first recording of The Beatles occur? What was the lineup of The Beatles? What songs did they record? What singer did they back up on the recording? Where did this recording session take place? Who arranged the recording session?

Answers

1. John, Ringo, George, and Paul. John, Ringo, and George. John, George, and Ringo.
2. Aug. 29, 1966, Candlestick Park, San Francisco, Calif., was the last time an audience paid to see The Beatles. Jan. 30, 1969, atop The Apple Building, London, England, The Beatles played for passersby during the lunch hour as part of the filming of the movie, *Let It Be*.
3. Paul McCartney appeared on Donovan's "Mellow Yellow" and "Atlantis" doing background vocals on the former and vocals and tambourine on the latter. Donovan did bird whisltles on "Blackbird."
4. "I Don't Want To Spoil The Party," "Norwegian Wood," "When I'm Sixty-Four," "Rocky Raccoon," "I'm So Tired," "I Me Mine" and "Her Majesty."
5. "Baby, You're A Rich Man."
6. One. And it's a great one.
7. The first professional recording of The Beatles occurred in the fall of 1960. The Beatles consisted of John Lennon, Paul McCartney, George Harrison, Stuart Sutcliffe, and Ringo Starr (who was not a regular member but was sitting in for The Beatles' drummer, Peter Best). They backed Lu Walters, bass player from Rory Storm And The Hurricanes (the group Ringo was then drumming for) on the songs "Fever," "Summertime," and "September Song." The session took place at a tiny studio, called Akustik Studios, located behind the main railroad station in Hamburg, Germany. The recording session was arranged by Alan Williams, The Beatles' booking agent at the time. There were four copies made. Starr and Williams have lost theirs. Storm had one, but he is deceased. Walters had a copy, but no one has ever heard from him again.

The Beatles meet the Loog

by Dave Thompson

This article originally appeared in Goldmine *issue #451, Nov. 7, 1997.*

Although history remembers him best as the mastermind who dragged a scruffy suburban blues band out of obscurity and into immortality, Andrew Loog Oldham was carving swaths through the British pop overground for a full three years before he discovered The Rolling Stones. Just 18 years old, a career in PR had already seen the former public schoolboy representing the likes of former Shadows Jet Harris and Tony Meehan, Sam Cooke, Kenny Lynch, and the dancer Peppi. As 1962 rolled to an end, his office at 93-97 Regent Street, in the heart of London's west end, was also handling Mark Wynter, one of the teen sensations of the age.

Independent PR men were a distinct rarity at the time, as Oldham recalls: "There was someone over at Decca, Tony Calder, who I'd run into a couple of times, someone else who was getting a fiver a week for looking after Cherry Roland, and there was Tony Barrow, also at Decca but moonlighting for a new band called The Beatles. What we all had in common was a sense of priority. We were all independents, even Calder and Barrow, which meant that we rarely had any direct contact with the actual record labels."

That was probably for the better. Record companies at that time still regarded their protégés as "five-minute wonders" — here today, gone tomorrow, and a handful of tenacious one-offs aside, they were not far from being wrong. Indeed, the idea that an artist might survive more than a year or two at the top of the pops was about as reasonable as the idea that an artist would employ an outside publicist, and Oldham recalls, "There was one woman working in the Pye press office, who 'hated' me because of what I was doing with Mark Wynter." Wynter, of course, was a Pye Records artist.

"People like her, though, didn't interest or bother me in the slightest. They were simply time-servers. For me, working with someone like Jet Harris was a dream come true, because it's what I'd wanted all my life or thereabouts. I've always believed that it's only if you want something really badly that you get it, and it infuriated me to see that other people had it that didn't even want it that much in the first place."

In January 1963, Wynter released his latest single, "Go Away Little Girl," a follow-up to the smash hit "Venus In Blue Jeans." It was already shaping up to be as massive when Oldham and Wynter traveled up to the ABC Television studios on Aston Road North, in Birmingham, to film his spot on the following weekend's *Thank Your Lucky Stars. Thank Your Lucky Stars* was one of just two pop-oriented programs on British television at the time (the other was the BBC's *Juke Box Jury*), and one of those rare shows that truly captured a moment in time, before most people were aware that the moment had even happened. Week after week, the hottest Top 20 acts were blasted into a transfixed nation's dining rooms; week after week, the stage sets within which those acts would perform seemed more garish and extravagant than before.

As Wynter and Oldham walked in, they were confronted by four monstrous metal hearts that the props men themselves were staring at in disbelief. What the hell were they all about? Wynter ran through a quick rehearsal, "did his bit," says Oldham, "as confidently and gracefully as ever," and then it was time for the filming to start. Everyone settled back to watch everyone else, and at the foot of the bill, they all watched as the metal heart boys came on, four kids with tightly buttoned gray suits, fringes that flopped to their eyelids, a left-handed bassist and a fab new waxing called "Please Please Me." It always baffled people how The Beatles landed such a prestigious television performance so early on in their career. *Thank Your Lucky Stars* was not a talent contest. You had to be established, with at least one big smash under your belt, before they'd even consider letting a band perform. Yet here were The Beatles, their first single a lowly Top 30 minihit, their second single scarcely out of the traps, being blasted across the country. "There had to be some funny business going on," Oldham mused as he watched. He just wondered what it was.

It was Brian Epstein, The Beatles' slight, dapper manager, who finally put him out of his misery. A week or so before, Epstein had been invited down to London to meet Dick James, one of the mere handful music publishers who actually showed an interest in the pre-Merseybanged Beatles.

After 10 minutes in the great man's presence, though, Epstein was feeling distinctly underwhelmed.

"His office was tiny, a little mess annexed to a bigger mess, in the middle of Denmark Street, which was always a mess. So Brian asked him, 'Mr. James,' — at that time, Brian called most people Mister someone — 'Mr. James, if I let you publish 'Please Please Me,' what can you do for me?'

"And Mr. James picked up the telephone and called Peter Jones (the show's producer), played him the record, swapped a few pleasantries, then told Brian The Beatles were on the show. Then he asked, 'Now can I publish the damned song?'"

Oldham remembers the band's performance. Metal hearts or not, "The Beatles were good. Better than 'Love Me Do,' better than Tony Barrow had told me. I asked Brian if there was anything I could do to help them along. And though he didn't say 'Funny you should ask that,' by the look in his eye, I knew he thought it."

Oldham was hot right then. Wynter, Harris-Meehan, Kenny Lynch, the word was out on the teenaged daredevil who turned everything he touched into megaselling gold, and Epstein had heard it. Slowly, politely, he outlined his current "predicament."

Barrow was still nominally handling The Beatles' publicity, mailing out press releases and photos to the papers. But that wasn't enough any more. Epstein needed someone who could supply the personal touch, make phone calls, take people to dinner and most of all, travel outside of London to meet the provincial press, all the things that Oldham had been doing for Wynter without even thinking about it.

The early 1960s were the age of the great syndicated newspaper columnists, the journalists who seemed to have gathered in a vast herd on the outskirts of London, filing their entertainment tales with 25, 26 different newspapers, all over the country.

The strange thing was, Oldham realized, nobody else seemed to have figured out that if you telephoned one writer, you could suddenly have your client's name splashed all over 26 different papers! So he started calling, introducing himself and the artist he was working with, "and the writers loved it. Nobody ever telephoned them; they worked from press releases and record company hand-outs, and it was actually a very lonely profession, to the point where I almost felt guilty, calling in and chatting them up, then extracting payment for my time with another plug!"

Barrows' activities at Decca precluded anything as adventurous as this, anything, in fact, beyond some part-time pushing. And Epstein needed someone full time. "By the time I left the studio," Oldham continues, "I'd got a new job, as a publicist for NEMS Enterprises, and a retainer of 15 pounds a month."

The Beatles made it on talent and their absolute uniqueness. But as Oldham confirms, there was also a lot of luck involved there as well. The history books claim, and the British nation's chilblains agree, that the winter of 1962-63 was one of the worst on — or off — the record, a season when everything froze, from the English Channel to the hastily commissioned snowplows that you would find gaunt and ghostly, locked in the banks beside roads they'd been trying to clear. Concerts were canceled, cinemas closed, sports slid to a standstill.

Beyond The Cavern

Oldham recalls, "A lot of people, me included at the time — thought people went mad for The Beatles that weekend because they recognized a special talent. No, they went mad because The Beatles were on television, and that weekend it was so cold there was nothing to do but stay in and watch television."

"Please Please Me" entered the British chart at #16, within a month it was sitting at #2 and it was time to put the boys on the road.

As the temperature continued to drop and their record sales soared through the roof, The Beatles' first journey into the world beyond the caverns where they were born and bred involved trundling round the tundra in a bus with Helen Shapiro. The rest of the tour, which included another of Oldham's clients, singer Kenny Lynch, made its own way about in whichever fashion it could.

The Beatles were placed at the foot of the bill, a four-song set that they would debut in front of a packed Bradford Gaumont on Feb. 2, 1963.

"It was the first time I'd seen them live," says Oldham, "and it probably wasn't the most ideal circumstances. But still they electrified me," beating out the winter chill

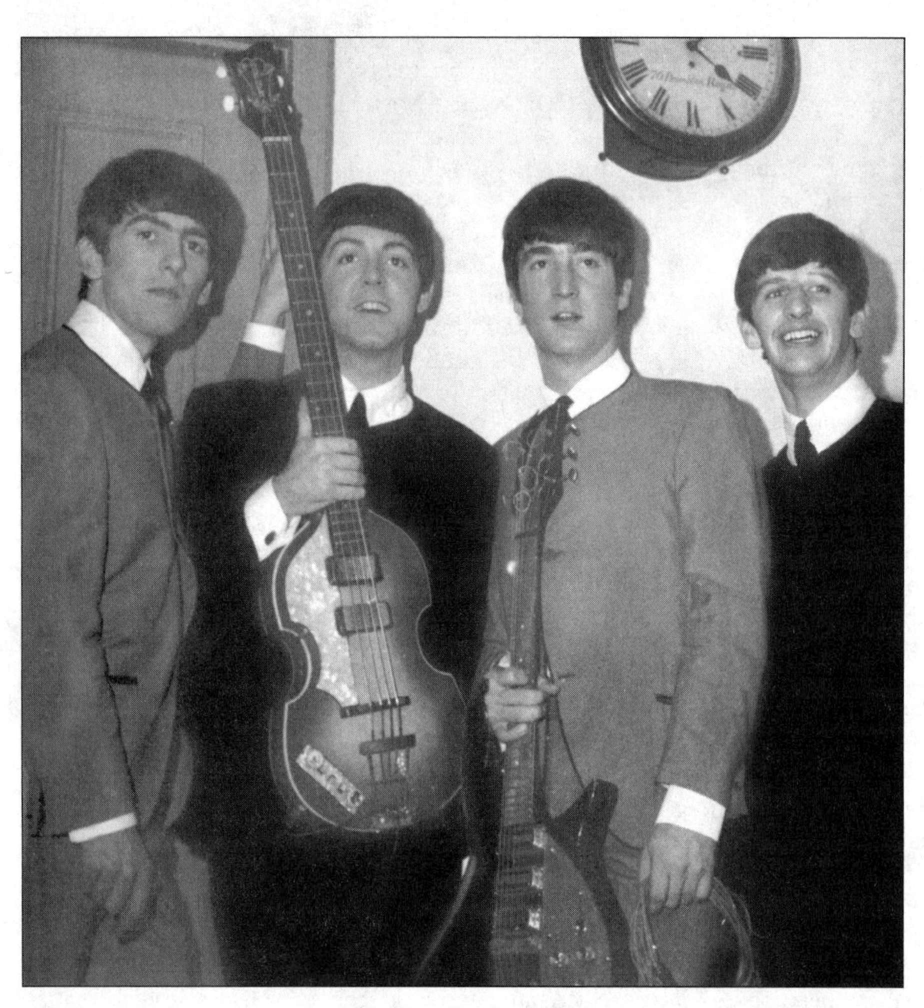

The Beatles in 1963.

with an opening "Chains," slamming straight into "Keep Your Hands Off My Baby," exploding with "A Taste Of Honey" and suddenly closing, "Please Please Me."

"It was their confidence that struck me the hardest. Of course they were old troupers. Brian had already sent me a thick file of cuttings documenting the band's Hamburg apprenticeship and Liverpool looning. But at a time when even the hardest-bitten pro still pulled out the pleasers whenever they played, it astonished me that only one of The Beatles' four songs was actually familiar to their audience. I was already beginning to see where Brian got his quiet confidence from."

The Beatles were back in Liverpool next, for two prearranged shows at their home ground, The Cavern; they rejoined the tour on Feb. 5 in nearby Doncaster, then everyone poured down the country for the next night's show in Bedford.

The tour was going well, with The Beatles drawing at least as strong a reaction as the acts who were billed above them. That, of course, was nothing out of the ordinary, as they had a hot single, and each night's crowd was fresh. Bedford, though, was different, almost from the moment the buses arrived at the venue.

"The audience by the stage door was larger, louder, and far more female than we had seen before," Oldham recalls. "At the stage door, we sat in the car for a few moments, waiting for the doorman to force the crowd back enough for us to pass through. That had never happened before.

"Inside, if anything, the tension was even greater. The Beatles had been pushed up the bill, and the audience was restless throughout the opening acts — Danny Williams, Kenny Lynch, The Honeys, The Kestrels, The Red Price Band. Then, as we reached the end of the final interval before The Beatles took the stage, an almost unearthly calm descended on the place.

"It wasn't silent. People still talked, moved around, shouted to friends on the balcony. But it was muted, as though everybody was waiting for something but hadn't quite figured what that something might be."

Then the house lights dimmed, the curtains swam open, and Oldham will never forget the question that slammed unbidden into his brain: What is going on out there?

It's starting...

Screaming. The entire audience was screaming. "It sounded like pigs were being slaughtered. I was standing at the side of the stage, next to Brian, and the effect was like being hit with a steamroller, a roar of noise, a wall of noise, which drowned our voices, drowned the band, swamped everything in its own keening mass. And it didn't relent.

"Then I looked at Brian. And suddenly I knew. He was standing there smiling, his chin resting in one hand, and at first I was reminded of a businessman on the tube, reading Andy Capp in the paper on the way home to his supper. Then I sensed, rather than heard, the words that his lips were gently mouthing.

"'It's starting,' he said. 'Just like I said it would. It's starting.'

"I blinked. My eyes were watering, from the sound, I thought, until I felt the lump that shook in my throat. My God, what was happening? To me, to the theater, to the world? I thought I'd seen it all, the Little Richard berserk audiences, slashing seats and spitting teeth; the Mark Wynter screamies, flinging arms and wetting seats; the Billy Fury scholars, black leather and sneers, all Elvis out of Surbiton; I'd seen all these things, and I'd been impressed.

"But they were nothing compared to this. Nothing. The Beatles were the first group who ever compounded all of these elements, who grasped exactly what show business is meant to be about.

"There was an aura of emotion, a naked emotion so pure that even though it's right in front of you, you couldn't believe it was really happening. And while it didn't happen every night, once you'd experienced it, that was enough. That was it for anybody else who was on the tour. The Beatles had taken over, and nothing would ever be quite the same again."

The site of the new Cavern Club in Liverpool.

Concerts were canceling all over the country, as the ice got into heating systems and the janitors' bladders froze full of whisky. But The Beatles' tour rattled on, fueled by the momentum of the Liverpudlians' sudden fame. In between dates, they recorded their first album, all 14 tracks in the space of a day. They squeezed in some TV and went back to the 'pool, and every time Oldham saw them again, they looked bigger and brighter than ever.

"Christ, The Beatles were keen. One day on the road, Paul walked shyly up to Helen Shapiro and told her he and John

PLEASE PLEASE ME

Recorded by **The Beatles** on PARLOPHONE

DICK JAMES MUSIC LIMITED 132 CHARING CROSS ROAD. LONDON. W.C.2

Sole Selling Agents

CAMPBELL CONNELLY & CO. LTD. 10 DENMARK STREET, LONDON, W.C.2

2/6

Andrew Loog Oldham (left) with Charlie Watts and Keith Richards of The Rolling Stones.

had written a song for her, 'Misery.' She turned it down, so they gave it to Kenny [Lynch] instead."

The Shapiro tour finally inched to an icy halt on March 3. Six days later, The Beatles would be off again, third on the bill behind Chris Montez and Tommy Roe, visiting Americans with monster hits up their sleeves. But "Please Please Me" was #2 by now, battling for the top slot with Frank Ifield's "Wayward Wind," and that was a little harsh on the Americans, who of course had come over expecting that they would be the stars of the show. Twice a day, early house and late, the journalists descended upon the theaters like a plague, and all you could hear was "Beatles Beatles Beatles." The tour was precisely one concert old when The Beatles were pushed to the top of the bill.

The tour opened on the eastern edge of London, at the East Ham Granada, then wound its way through the end of the month, with little more than hysteria for history to record. Oldham shrugs, "Every show remains clear in the mind's eye, but individual nights blur into one, all of them except Bedford, where we returned on March 12.

"John had been building up to a heavy cold for a few days now, but even before we checked into our hotel, it was painfully obvious that he wouldn't be leaving it again in a hurry."

Paul most accessible

The band locked themselves away to try and weigh their options. Cancellation, of course, was out of the question. For a start, it would probably turn into a riot, but more than that, it was against their natures to pull out like that. The set, six songs, was taken apart, then reassembled around Lennon's absence, and that night, Redford was treated to a show that would remain unique in the annals of Beatledom history for another 33 years — a three-man Fab Four, the first ever show by the Threetles.

The phenomenon continued, unabated, unstoppable, and Oldham was drawn into the maelstrom like everyone else. But he admits, "The Beatles themselves were never so interesting to me as Brian. In fact, I rarely ever used to think about the acts themselves; so far as musicians were concerned, I would simply work out who was the most accessible member of the band, then take everything else to the boss.

"At this stage, it was Paul who struck me as the easiest to talk with, but even he deferred to Brian. There really was something about the man, something intangible and in truth, overlooked by all but the most dispassionate histories, but which made him the center of attention even when he wasn't in the room. More than that, though, he was only the second British manager I had met who measured up to the Americans, people like Jim Lee (who handled Chris Montez). Nobody I'd seen outside Mark Wynter's manager, Ray MacKender, seemed so in control of what they were doing. When you sat down with Brian, you were looking at a man who had a vision that nobody was going to get in the way of, the kind of vision that gives you the power that makes sure people listen to you — 'I want this done, I want that done,' and it would be done.

A vintage Cavern Club sign.

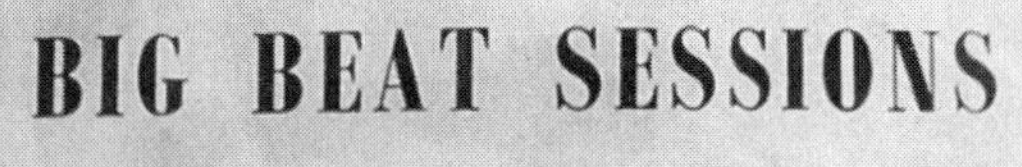

Who do you suppose won this battle of the bands?

"And I could see him — it's not so much what they say, but what they don't say that counts, and the attention he would get from all the people running around on *Thank Your Lucky Stars* that other people weren't getting. Brian would just stand there and watch 'my boys,' and even the technicians, grouchy buggers that they can be, would pay solemn attention to him, probably without even knowing why he had that presence.

"I sensed that right away it was a matter of knowing that what is sexual to you is sexual to other people, because if you don't love yourself, how can you expect other people to love you? That was a very great part of his vision."

Epstein's own sexuality, however, remained his own business. Although Oldham acknowledges that "one could pick up hints," he is also adamant that "It was not until a lot later that the more intimate details of his life came out. Certainly there was nothing going on between Brian and the band, not even with John with whom, of course, we have since been informed, Brian was hopelessly in love."

This, of course, is one of those tantalizing little legends that continues to swirl around The Beatles. Oldham, however, is unequivocal in his dismissal of it. "You could argue that Brian wouldn't have dared make a move on Lennon — in fact, a lot of people have, but that wasn't it. Simply, Brian didn't play favorites. The vision that he sustained and disseminated was the sheer totality of The Beatles, and beyond that, of the entire Mersey beat boom. Plus, he was very well-behaved. I never saw any other side of him. He was simply a very astute, very inspired, young man living out his dream.

"All the other people I met did what they did for the salary. Even I, condemning the drones who drudged through the day, would not, could not, have maintained my enthusiasm without a check every week. Brian could, and Brian did, because Brian was in it for a lot of other things. A lot of them I didn't understand at first, but still they made a kind of instinctive sense. His aura was more than simply powerful. It was obsessive."

Oldham was granted more than one glimpse of Epstein's instinct, of course, but one does stick in his mind.

The Beatles rarely came down to London, not unless they had an engagement there, so Brian, too, remained at home when he could, summoning the people he needed up there to be with him. "One day it was my turn, and after we'd swapped the usual pleasantries, he introduced me to the four scruffy looking gentlemen I'd seen sitting outside his office, telling me all the while that their record was a surefire #1.

"I just looked at them, glowering in their polyester coats with mock leather trimmings, and I thought, 'This lot?' Then Brian played 'How Do You Do it,' and it suddenly made sense. Gerry And The Pacemakers made sense." Effortlessly, it seemed, Epstein turned them 'round and cleaned them up, and suddenly he wasn't selling a group, he was selling a sound and an ideal. Mersey beat was born.

"How Do You Do It" went to #1 in April 1963. Three weeks later, it was knocked off the top by The Beatles' "From Me To You," which in turn was toppled by The Pacemakers' "I Like It." "It never ceased to amaze me," Oldham admits. "I could see what it was about The Beatles, but to see him be right about Gerry And The Pacemakers and then Billy J. Kramer — to me, Billy just looked like a lump, whose ineffectiveness was only compounded by the obvious affection Brian had for him. Even George Martin, when he first heard Kramer sing, told Brian he'd made a mistake, but Brian ignored him. 'My Billy,' he said quietly, 'will be a star,' and of course, 'my Billy' was."

Backed by a Manchester band, The Dakotas, Kramer's version of The Beatles' "Do You Want to Know A Secret?" went to #2, "Bad To Me" made #1, "I'll Keep You Satisfied" #4, and behind him, straining to kick their way out of the NEM-pire, a smorgasbord of scousers awaited their bite of the cherry. Epstein was untouchable.

Merseybeat exploded, and suddenly every city in the country had its own sound, jostling for attention. In Newcastle, The Animals and The Influence were howling the blues and screaming the odds at anybody who cared (or dared) to enter the Club A-Go-Go. In Birmingham, Mike Sheridan's Nightriders, in Southampton, The Soul Agents. New groups were popping up daily. Anybody who knew three other people who could play their instruments (or who looked like they could, it didn't really matter) was throwing together a band.

With only the most rudimentary knowledge of musicianship, anyone could bash out a few Chuck Berry numbers, and who knew when the fat cat from Decca or Pye might be lurking in the audience, just bursting to hand over a license to print money. And even if he didn't come, you'd still have fun, getting pissed, getting laid, and it certainly beat staying at home watching *The Adventures Of Twizzle* on the television.

Outside of Liverpool, the healthiest scene was in Manchester. Thirty-five miles from Liverpool, Manchester had developed its own self-contained network of ballrooms and clubs and a similarly cutthroat sense of ambition.

The self-styled kingpins of the Manchester scene were Kennedy Street Enterprises. Oldham knew the company vaguely; Tony Calder was working much the same beat for Kennedy Street as he was for NEMS, while Kennedy Street was also booking tours for various visiting Americans. It was inevitable that the two companies would come together eventually.

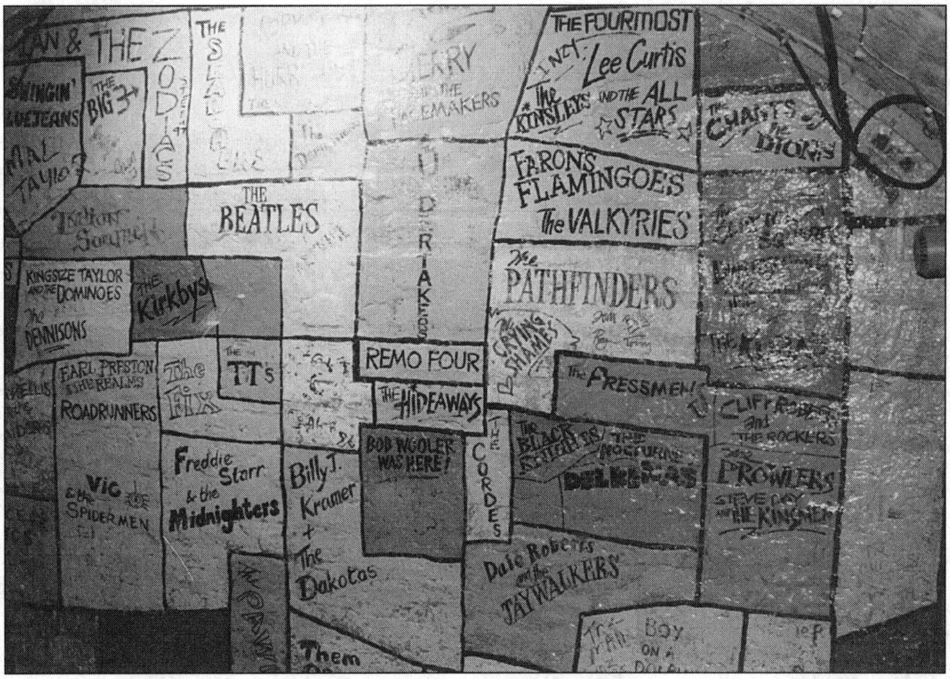

Inside rear wall of The Cavern Club.

"Thank you, goodbye."

The first joint scheme was a tour coupling The Beatles with Duane Eddy. Eddy canceled. The next time, it was Ben E. King, The Four Seasons, and The Beatles. That fell through as well. Finally, it was announced that Roy Orbison was coming over to tour with the Fabs, but he would not be the headliner. Very craftily, the advertising was arranged so that Orbison's name appeared in big, bill-topping letters. But it was The Beatles who closed the show every night, and if anyone wants to seriously consider portents and omens, Orbison's latest British single spelled out the fate awaiting anyone who wasn't suddenly mop-topped and suited. It was called "Falling."

Business and ambition collided. Oldham had already sewn up the Liverpool scene; now he dreamed of taking Manchester as well. Bands such as The Hollies and The Mindbenders were already out of the traps and cruising toward the heavens. Oldham remembers, "I immediately began working on my link with Tony Calder. I wanted Manchester." And he believes he would have got it as well, "if London hadn't begun beckoning once more."

One Sunday evening in April 1963, acting on a tip from journalist Peter Jones, Oldham made his way down to south-west London's Station Hotel. There he saw The Rolling Stones. There, he says, he saw the future.

"I was not a particular fan of R&B per se. It depended who was doing it, and could I smell a hit. I loved Johnny Otis' 'Willie And The Hand Jive.' It went to #2. But Willie Dixon was another story. And The Rollin' Stones were another again, the same story I'd heard four months before, when I stood at the back of the Bedford Granada while Brian Epstein mused and his lips moved slowly, 'It's starting.' And above the keening of the crowd, you knew that it was."

Suddenly, it seemed, life was no longer second-hand, bathing in Bedford in someone else's glow. He was in the eye of the storm. "I'd stopped thinking," he reflects. "Now I was feeling."

Oldham's first instinct, of course, was to contact Epstein. "After two days on the underground, three square meals a day and the calling of clients before they called me, I felt ready for a dry run. I phoned and asked Brian if I could meet him for half an hour outside his office. We ended up having drinks at his house that Thursday evening."

The Beatles' "Please Please Me" had pleased-pleased everyone, and now the team were readying "From Me To You." Brian's next group would be The Pacemakers, his next secret was Billy J. Kramer. Oldham told him about seeing the Stones, how great he thought they could be ("not were," he emphasizes), his position of being only a press agent and the need for management help and an agency, "But I didn't give a great performance," he shrugs, "because that really wasn't possible. How can you tell someone you've found something to change the world, when they're already changing it themselves?

"Brian had his agenda and the manners to give me the time of day. But on that day, the only time he heard me was when I said, 'Thank you, goodbye.' Brian had his own reality, and as I traced my footsteps home, I knew that I had mine.

"I remembered back to Bedford, and about the lump in my throat. Especially the lump in my throat, and with that, a knowledge which I'd even kept from myself until now. At that moment, as The Beatles came out and the screaming went up, I knew that as sure as eggs is eggs, like Elvis and Pat Boone, when The Beatles really made it, the public would demand an opposite attraction."

Oldham had seen how Epstein worked, how he had made The Beatles universally acceptable, universally appealing. A kid could say he liked The Beatles, and his parents could turn 'round and say that they like them too. But there was another kid who wouldn't want to share his heroes with his mum and dad. He wouldn't like them if his parents did, he wouldn't want to like them if his parents did. The kids already had The Beatles. Now they needed something that wasn't The Beatles.

It's for you

The songs The Beatles gave away

by Robin Platts

"John and I were a songwriting team and what songwriting teams did in those days was wrote for everyone — unless you couldn't come up with something or wanted to keep a song for yourself and it was a bit too good to give away." — Paul McCartney

Today, it may be difficult for us to imagine that The Beatles ever wrote a song that *anyone* might consider a throwaway, even The Beatles. How could any song penned by a Beatle not be a winner?

Yet, in their early days, when they were writing prolifically, The Beatles, John Lennon and Paul McCartney in particular, did give songs to other artists, songs they had no interest in recording — or at least releasing — themselves. This article takes a look at some of those songs and their fate, which ones rose to the top of the charts and which remained in obscurity despite having been written by a team that seemed to turn everything it touched into gold.

This article originally appeared in Goldmine issue #399, Nov. 10, 1995.

1. "I'll Be On My Way" (Lennon/McCartney)
Recorded by Billy J. Kramer with The Dakotas, March 21, 1963
Produced by George Martin

Billy J. Kramer was singing with a group called The Coasters when Brian Epstein "discovered" him and hooked him up with The Dakotas: Mike Maxfield (lead guitar), Robin MacDonald (rhythm guitar), Ray Jones (bass) and Tony Mansfield (drums). Epstein helped the group get a contract with Parlophone, where it was produced by George Martin. The group's first release, "Do You Want To Know A Secret?"/"I'll Be On My Way," would be the first of four Beatle-penned hits for the group (#2 in the British charts). The A-side had already been cut by the Fab Four (on their *Please Please Me* album) but the flip was given exclusively to Kramer and The Dakotas. The Beatles' own recording of "I'll Be On My Way," cut on April 4, 1963, for the BBC radio program *Side By Side*, was released 21 years later on the *Live At The BBC* album.

Between 1963 and 1965, Lennon and McCartney gave Kramer seven songs, more than they gave to any other artist. Part of the reason for this was undoubtedly the influence of Epstein, who was managing Kramer and The Dakotas.

"I'd done a lot of gigs with them," Kramer recalled, "and then Brian started managing me and he was managing them, so obviously it must have had some influence on them to do it. I was very fortunate that I was there and I did a lot of shows with these guys."

Kramer actually turned down several Lennon/McCartney songs that were offered to him. Some of these were recorded by other artists, but one in particular stands out in his memory.

"I was doing a summer season in a town called Blackpool," he recalled. "They were doing one of their last TV shows there, and I asked Paul for a song. And he sat in the theater and played 'Yesterday' and I said, 'No, I want a rock 'n' roll song.' And I turned it down."

2. "Bad To Me" (Lennon/McCartney)
Recorded by Billy J. Kramer with The Dakotas, June 27, 1963
Produced by George Martin

On June 27, 1963, Billy J. Kramer And The Dakotas recorded their second Parlophone single, "Bad To Me"/"I Call Your Name." Once again, both sides were Lennon/McCartney songs, but this time neither had been released by The Beatles themselves. The A-side appears to have been written with Kramer in mind.

"John and I would get together, 'Oh, we gotta write one for Billy J. OK, Birds in the sky will be...' and we just knocked them out," McCartney would later recall. "In our minds there was a very vague formula and we could do it quite easily."

As with most of their Lennon/McCartney recordings, Kramer and The Dakotas learned "Bad To Me" on the day of the recording session.

"I learned 'Do You Want To Know A Secret?' from a demo tape," Kramer recalled, "and the other songs, like 'Bad To Me,' they only played them on the actual day of the session." Kramer remembers Lennon playing "Bad To Me" to him on the piano, "And then he played 'I Want To Hold Your Hand.' I said to him, 'Can I have that one?' and he said, 'No, we're keeping that one for ourselves.'

"Bad To Me" proved to be even more successful than "Do You Want To Know A Secret?," reaching the #1 spot in Britain (it would subsequently reach #9 in the U.S.). In an August 1963 edition of *Mersey Beat*, McCartney said of the record, "His phrasing has a wistful feeling about it, and the sequences where he self-duets with his own voice have come out ideally."

A Lennon demo of "Bad To Me" (recorded in 1963) has appeared on various bootlegs, while The Beatles subsequently released their own version of "I Call Your Name" on the 1964 EP *Long Tall Sally*.

3. "Tip Of My Tongue" (Lennon/McCartney)
Recorded by Tommy Quickly, 1963
Produced by Les Reed

Like Kramer, Tommy Quickly was managed by Brian Epstein and it is likely that Epstein encouraged Lennon and McCartney to give him material. Quickly was given two Lennon/McCartney numbers to record, the first being McCartney's "Tip Of My Tongue." The single didn't chart and, despite a great deal of promotion by Epstein, Quickly only reached the charts once: His U.K. single "Wild Side Of Life" peaked at #33 in October 1964.

In June 1964, Lennon gave Quickly another song, "No Reply." Quickly learned the song from Lennon's demo and cut his own version. Though initially scheduled for an August release, the single was canceled, apparently due to Quickly's unsatisfactory vocal performance.

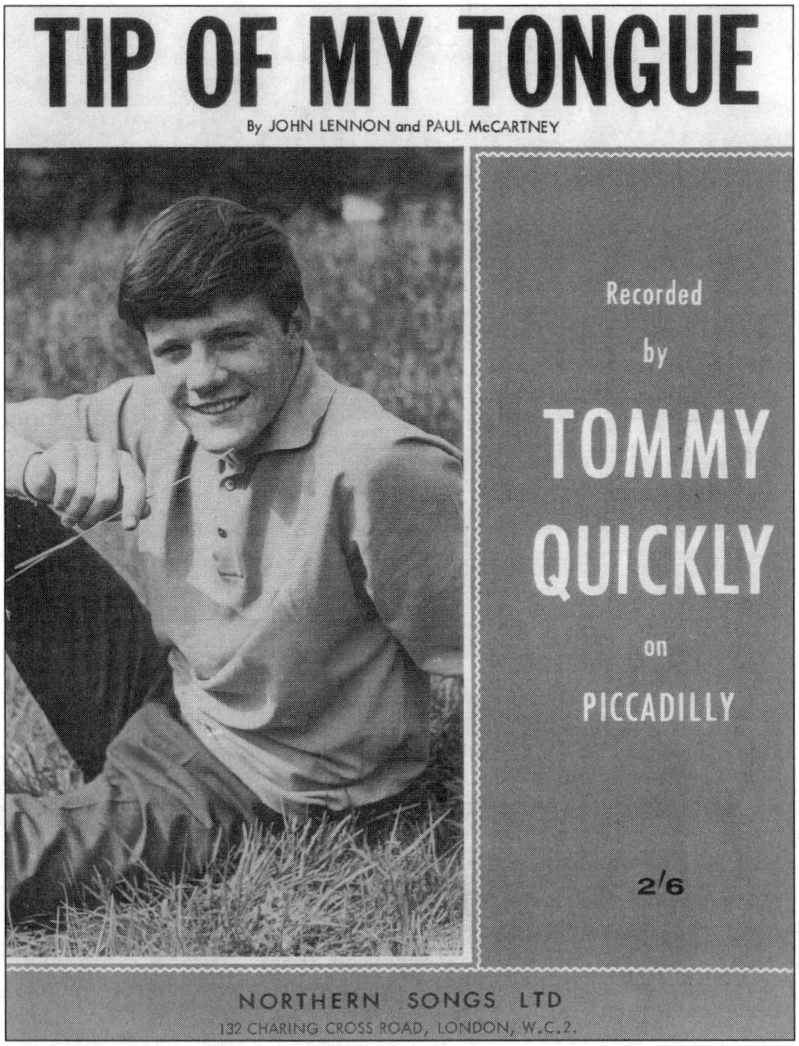

TIP OF MY TONGUE
By JOHN LENNON and PAUL McCARTNEY
Recorded by TOMMY QUICKLY on PICCADILLY
2/6
NORTHERN SONGS LTD
132 CHARING CROSS ROAD, LONDON, W.C.2.

The Fabs' own version of "No Reply" showed up on *The Beatles For Sale* LP, but the tape containing their November 1962 attempt at recording "Tip Of My Tongue" apparently no longer exists.

4. "Hello Little Girl" (Lennon/McCartney)
Recorded by The Fourmost, 1963
Produced by George Martin

Before signing with Epstein in 1963, they were known as The Four Jays, then The Four Mosts. As he had done with Billy J. Kramer And The Dakotas, Epstein got the group a Parlophone contract and a Lennon/McCartney number to record for their first single. The rechristened Fourmost — Brian O'Hara (lead guitar), Mike Millward (rhythm guitar), Dave Lovelady (drums), and Billy Hatton (bass) — cut an early Beatles song called "Hello Little Girl," which took them to #9 on the British charts. The Fabs had played this number for many years and recorded it as part of their Decca Records audition on Jan. 1, 1962.

"Hello Little Girl" was also recorded, though not released, by Gerry And The Pacemakers. Whether the song had been given to them first is unclear, but the recording probably dates from circa 1963.

5. "Love Of The Loved" (Lennon/McCartney)
Recorded by Cilla Black, 1963
Produced by George Martin

"Love Of The Loved" was also included on The Beatles' Decca audition tape. Their friend Cilla Black had already performed it on stage with them, so it was a natural choice for her first single.

Martin later recalled, "Brian [Epstein] brought me a girl singer named Priscilla White. All her friends called her Cilla, and Brian, for some reason best known to himself, didn't like the idea of Cilla White, so he'd gone to the other end of the spectrum and called her Cilla Black.

Cilla had been singing 'Love Of The Loved' at The Cavern, and we decided to record that, with a special arrangement I had written for trumpets." Cilla Black: "My very first single was 'Love Of The Loved,' which Paul actually wrote — he used to sing that one in The Cavern, way before they were famous. I think it was one of the earliest songs he wrote, with a few bits and pieces from John thrown in. We were all just kids in Liverpool together and I used to sing 'round the clubs. And my girlfriends, depending on what Beatle they fancied, used to say, 'Oh, please, George, let Cilla sing with you.' And, just to shut my girlfriends up, they'd allow me to sing with them.

"When Brian Epstein came on the scene and was managing The Beatles, it was actually John Lennon who told Brian about me. And I did my audition with The Beatles in Birkenhead. But Brian was not very impressed. It wasn't until a while later that he saw me singing with a modern jazz band, in a club called the Blue Angel in Liverpool. I didn't know Brian was in the audience, and I just got up and sang. They just asked me to fill in. I think their lead singer wanted to go off and have a smoke. So I did, and Brian just flipped. I owe that to John Lennon, because John told

Brian about me originally. But then Brian saw me [at the Blue Angel] when I wasn't nervous. I was singing in my own key, which I wasn't when I did my audition with The Beatles."

Black's version of "Love Of The Loved reached #35 in Britain.

6. "I'll Keep You Satisfied" (Lennon/McCartney)
Recorded by Billy J. Kramer with The Dakotas, Oct. 14, 1963
Produced by George Martin

Billy J. Kramer And The Dakotas' third Lennon/McCartney single was recorded Oct. 14, 1963 and gave them another hit, #4 in Britain and eventually #30 in the U.S. Lennon, who was at the session to teach them the song, suggested they also try another song of his, "I'm In Love."

Kramer: "I think 'I'm In Love' would have made a great A-side, but I just couldn't get it together on that day. I was doing a session and then they suggested I do that song. And we learned it there and then. And we just forgot all about it. We never completed it, I think maybe because The Fourmost brought it out some time later and had a hit with it."

Kramer's version of "I'm In Love" eventually surfaced on EMI's 1991 *Best Of Billy J. Kramer And The Dakotas* CD. Lennon's voice is audible among the studio chatter that precedes the track.

Note: A John Lennon demo of "I'm In Love" has appeared on several bootlegs.

This recording was probably made circa 1979-80, when Lennon did home demos of a number of his old songs.

7. "I'm In Love" (Lennon/McCartney)
Recorded by The Fourmost, 1963
Produced by George Martin

After Billy J. Kramer's version of "I'm In Love" was abandoned, the song was passed on to The Fourmost and gave them a #17 hit in Britain. (Though The Fourmost are remembered for their association with the Fab Four, their biggest hit was actually a non-Beatles number called "A Little Loving," which reached #6 in the British charts.)

Note: In 1969, Paul McCartney worked with The Fourmost again, producing and playing piano on the group's U.K. single "Rosetta."

8. "A World Without Love" (Lennon/McCartney)
Recorded by Peter And Gordon, 1964
Produced by Norman Newell

Peter And Gordon's "World Without Love" was the first non-Beatle U.S. #1 of the British Invasion. Like several of the songs given to other artists, it was a very early Lennon/McCartney composition.

"A lot of [our] early stuff is not very good," McCartney told *Mersey Beat* in 1964, "but every now and then we remember one of the good ones we wrote in the early days. And a lot of the numbers have been used — 'Love Me Do,' 'World Without Love,' 'Love Of The Loved' and a number of others."

"World Without Love" was eventually heard by Peter Asher, brother of McCartney's then-girlfriend Jane.

Peter Asher: "I'd heard it in passing. It didn't have a bridge. It wasn't until EMI had signed us up and wanted to make a record that I went back to Paul and said, 'Would you write a bridge for that song and may we do it on our first album?' and he said yes. Then I had to nag him a couple more times to actually write the bridge, and then he did."

9. "One And One Is Two" (Lennon/McCartney)
Recorded by The Strangers with Mike Shannon, 1964 (no production credit)

This song, originally offered to Billy J. Kramer And The Dakotas, is most likely an early Lennon/McCartney composition. By 1964, Lennon's and McCartney's songwriting skills had evolved to the point where they would probably not have written lyrics like: "One and one is two/What am I to do/Now that I'm in love with you."

Just prior to sending Kramer a demo of the song, Lennon apparently said, "Billy J.'s career is finished when he gets this song!" Kramer apparently felt the same way and the song was passed on to The Strangers with Mike Shannon. That version was released in May 1964 but did not reach the charts.

Note: A low-fi McCartney demo of this song has appeared on several bootlegs.

10. "Nobody I Know" (Lennon/McCartney)
Recorded by Peter And Gordon, 1964
Produced by Norman Newell

The second of four Lennon/McCartney songs given to Peter And Gordon. The huge success of "World Without Love" probably encouraged McCartney to write more for the duo. Another factor was his proximity to Peter Asher.

"We lived in the same house," recalled Asher. "He lived in my parents' house for a couple of years. We had rooms next to each other on the top floor, so he'd usually play [a song] to me when he'd written it."

"Nobody I Know" reached #10 in the British charts and made it to #12 in the U.S.A.

11. "Like Dreamers Do" (Lennon/McCartney)
Recorded by The Applejacks, 1964
Produced by Mike Smith

This early Lennon/McCartney composition was recorded by The Beatles as part of their Decca Records audition, but by the end of 1962 they had stopped performing it. When "Like Dreamers Do" was eventually released, it *was* on Decca but performed by The Applejacks, a Birmingham group consisting of singer Al Jackson, guitarists Phil Cash and Martin Baggott, organist Don Gould, bassist Megan Davies and drummer Gary Freeman. Released in June 1964, The Applejacks' version was a Top 20 hit in Britain.

12. "From A Window" (Lennon/McCartney).
Recorded by Billy J. Kramer with The Dakotas, Aug. 22, 1964
Produced by George Martin

Billy J. Kramer And The Dakotas had broken their string of Lennon/McCartney-penned hits with their fourth single, "Little Children."

"At that time they came along with two songs," Billy remembered, "One was called 'One And One Is Two,' the other I can't remember. I turned them down, and that caused a bit of bad vibes between Brian and I, because he thought I'd insulted them, because they were so successful by this time."

Kramer and The Dakotas returned to the Fabs' songbook for "From A Window," the last Beatles composition to be given to them.

Kramer: "It was Brian's idea to record 'From A Window.' I think Paul wanted to give it to Peter And Gordon and, when you think about it, it would have fit them."

The Lennon-McCartney/Martin/Epstein formula proved successful once again and "From A Window" reached #10 in Britain and #23 in America.

13. "It's For You" (Lennon/McCartney)
Recorded by Cilla Black, July 1964
Produced by George Martin

Cilla Black's second Lennon/McCartney–penned single fared considerably better than "Love Of The Loved," reaching #7 in the U.K. charts. McCartney would later recall, "That was something I'd written. You sometimes would pull one out of the drawer and say, 'Maybe this one would be good for you.'"

It has been reported that McCartney played piano on "It's For You." Black doesn't recall him playing on the track but remembers him being at the session.

"He was fascinated, because it was a Big Band, The Johnny Spence Orchestra. There were about 48 pieces in the band. We were in Number One Studio in Abbey Road, and it was just so exciting with all these musicians being there. Paul came along very, very excited, because [the song] was given an incredibly different feel, a jazz feel. When I got the demo of Paul doing it, it was just guitar — there was no arrangement whatsoever. I think it was Johnny Spence who did [the arrangement], but I'm sure George [Martin] had a very big hand in the arrangement."

McCartney's demo version of "It's For You" was cut at Abbey Road on June 3, 1964, the same day that George Harrison and Lennon cut demos of "You'll Know What To Do" and "No Reply," respectively.

Note: In the early '70s Harrison wrote a song for Black, titled "I'll Still Love You," which she did not release. The song was subsequently recorded by Ringo, for his *Rotogravure* album.

14. "I Don't Want To See You Again" (Lennon/McCartney)
Recorded by Peter And Gordon, 1964
Produced by Norman Newell

McCartney's third song for Peter And Gordon and the least successful of the duo's Beatles-penned releases. The single reached #16 in America but failed to chart in Britain.

15. "That Means A Lot" (Lennon/McCartney)
Recorded by P.J. Proby, April 7, 1965
Produced by Ron Richards
Arranged and conducted by George Martin

The Beatles made several attempts at recording "That Means A Lot" during the *Help*! sessions in early 1965. "The song is a ballad which Paul and I wrote for the film," John Lennon said at the time, "but we found we just couldn't sing it. In fact, we made a hash of it, so we thought we'd better give it to someone who could do it well."

That someone was P.J. Proby, an American singer who moved to Britain in the early '60s and enjoyed chart success there. Proby, who once toured under the name "Jet Powers," was notorious for his onstage trouser-splitting antics, which caused him to be banned from some venues. His dramatic version of "That Means A Lot" reached #30 in Britain but, like most of Proby's other singles, did not chart on this side of the Atlantic.

Note: P.J. Proby's most significant contribution to rock 'n' roll was probably his late '60s LP *Three Week Hero*. The musicians assembled to back Proby on the album were Jimmy Page, John Bonham, John Paul Jones, and Robert Plant, who subsequently formed a band and enjoyed some success in the '70s.

16. "Woman" (McCartney, as Bernard Webb and as A. Smith)
Recorded by Peter And Gordon, 1966
Produced by Norman Newell

By the mid-60s, there were those who claimed that any record bearing a Beatle's name would be a hit, regardless of its merits. To prove a point, Paul McCartney used the pseudonym "Bernard Webb" on Peter And Gordon's new single. [In the U.S., the song was credited to "A. Smith."] His scheme was discovered, but not before the record became a hit on its own merits (#28 in the U.K., #14 in the U.S.).

"Woman" is unquestionably one of the strongest compositions any of The Beatles ever gave away and could have held its own on, say, *Revolver*, had the Fabs chosen to record it.

17. "Catcall" (Lennon/McCartney)
Recorded by The Chris Barber Band, July 20, 1967
(no production credit)

"Catcall" was written by Lennon and McCartney in the late '50s, at which time it was titled "Catswalk." A recording of The Beatles rehearsing the number at The Cavern has surfaced and appeared on several bootlegs.

His desire to work in musical genres outside of rock/pop saw McCartney give the instrumental to Chris Barber's Jazz Band. By 1967, Barber's band had been a fixture on the British scene for many years, including a mid-50s stint with skiffle pioneer Lonnie Donegan, himself a big influence on The Beatles.

McCartney and Jane Asher attended the session for "Catcall" and theirs are among the voices heard imploring the band to "Play slower!"

18. "Step Inside Love" (Lennon/McCartney)
Recorded by Cilla Black, February 1968
Produced by George Martin, arranged by Mike Vickers

"Step Inside Love" was written by McCartney for Black to use as the theme for her TV series, *Cilla*.

Black recalled, "The BBC kept sending me all these very big 'There's No Business Like Show Business' kind of songs, which wasn't me at all. And I got a phone call out of the blue [from Paul] and he said, 'I know what they're all doing at the BBC. They're sending you all these songs, Billy Cotton Band show-type songs, and that's not you. You're the kind of person that should invite yourself into their houses, start off quiet and build up,' and he was totally right.

"And only half the song was finished when I did the show. I only did the opening part [at the beginning of the show], then the end bit to close it. There was no middle bit. And it caused such a storm. Everybody said, 'You really ought to put this out as a single.' And he quickly had to finish it. Apparently, he finished the middle in the bathroom, as the story goes [laughs].

"That record got me in really big trouble in South Africa. They said it had kind of prostitute connotations and it was banned."

STEP INSIDE LOVE
Words and Music by JOHN LENNON and PAUL McCARTNEY
Recorded by CILLA BLACK on Parlophone
NORTHERN SONGS LIMITED
60p

The February 1968 debut of *Cilla* featured Ringo Starr as a guest. The popularity of the TV show helped "Step Inside Love" reach #8 in the British charts.

19. "Thingumybob" (Lennon/McCartney)
Recorded by The Black Dyke Mills Band, June 30, 1968
Produced by Paul McCartney

"Thingumybob" was written by McCartney as the theme for a London weekend television sitcom. His use of a brass band for the recording again reflects his interest in pursuing different musical genres.

Peter Asher (who, by this time, was head of A&R at Apple Records) recalled that McCartney "always loved brass band music. It's a big thing in England. [All the mills and factories] in the north of England would traditionally each have amateur brass bands, assembled from the workers, and there would be a big competition. We'd been asked to do [the TV theme] and Paul said, 'I want to do this with a brass band.' So we found out who the competition winners were at that time and it was The Black Dyke Mills Band. So we went up north and did it there with them. We all drove up together."

At the time, McCartney apparently expressed interest in producing an album for The Black Dyke Mills Band, but "Thingumybob" failed to chart and the single remained a one-off effort for Apple. (McCartney did eventually work with the band again, on his 1979 *Back To The Egg* LP.)

"Thingumybob" was one of Apple's first single releases and was included, along with "Hey Jude," "Those Were The Days" and "Sour Milk Sea," in a rare promotional boxed set called *Our First Four*. The package was a 10-inch by 12-inch box, which included the four singles along with photos and biographies of each artist.

20. "Sour Milk Sea" (Harrison)
Recorded by Jackie Lomax, June 1968
Produced by George Harrison

"Sour Milk Sea" was written by George Harrison during The Beatles' early 1968 stay in Rishikesh, India. In his book *I Me Mine*, Harrison wrote that the song was "about meditation. I used 'Sour Milk Sea' as the idea of — if you're in the shit, don't go around moaning about it: Do something about it."

The Beatles recorded "Sour Milk Sea" during their May 1968 demo sessions for *The White Album*, suggesting that it was at first considered for inclusion on that LP. In any event, the song was recorded by Apple artist Jackie Lomax, formerly the vocalist with a Liverpool band called The Undertakers. The group had reached #49 in the British charts in 1964 with "Just A Little Bit," and after they split up, Epstein began managing Lomax's career. He cut singles with the Lomax Alliance ("Try As You May," 1967) and as a solo artist ("Genuine Imitation Life," 1968), before Harrison brought him to Apple.

Lomax's recording of "Sour Milk Sea" featured rhythm guitar work by himself and Harrison, lead guitar by Eric Clapton, drums by Starr and piano by Nicky Hopkins. Harrison put a fair amount of effort into Lomax's career at that time, producing his excellent *Is This What You Want* LP (on which "Sour Milk Sea" was included) and the subsequent 45 "How The Web Was Woven." McCartney also took a shot at producing Lomax (the "Thumbin' A Ride" single) but, despite a great deal of talent and Beatles assistance, his career never really took off.

In the early '70s, Lomax cut albums for Warner Brothers and Capitol, in addition to stints with Badger and Heavy Jelly.

21. "Goodbye" (Lennon/McCartney)
Recorded by Mary Hopkin, March 1969
Produced by Paul McCartney

Following the success of her debut single "Those Were The Days," Mary Hopkin asked McCartney, "Look, how about another single?"

McCartney promptly delivered "Goodbye," which he claimed to have written in just 10 minutes. He recorded an acoustic demo of the song, a lovely recording that would not sound out of place on *The White Album*, then produced and played guitar on Hopkin's version. The result was a very appealing single that reached #2 in the British charts and #13 in America.

22. "Come And Get It" (McCartney)
Recorded by Badfinger, September 1969
Produced by Paul McCartney

"Come And Get It" was written by McCartney for the movie *The Magic Christian*, which starred Starr and Peter Sellers. McCartney had originally been slated to do all the songs for the soundtrack himself but, when it became clear that he wouldn't have the time, he passed the project on to an Apple act called The Iveys. Paul produced their recording of "Come And Get It," which was basically a carbon copy of his own demo version.

In Mark Lewisohn's *Complete Recording Sessions* book, McCartney recalls telling the band, "Just copy this down to the letter. It's perhaps a little bit undignified for you, a little bit lacking in integrity to have to copy someone's work that rigidly, but this is the hit sound."

It was indeed the hit sound, a Top 10 hit on both sides of the Atlantic and the first of several big sellers for the newly rechristened Badfinger.

24. "Penina" (McCartney)
Recorded by Carlos Mendes, 1969

In a 1994 issue of the McCartney fan club magazine *Club Sandwich*, he was asked about his song "Penina" and if he was ever likely to record it himself. He replied, "I went to Portugal on holiday and returned to the hotel one night slightly the worse for a few drinks. There was a band playing and I ended up on the drums. The hotel was called Penina. I made up a song with that name, someone made inquiries about it, and I gave it to them. And, no, I shouldn't think I'd ever record it myself!"

"Penina" was recorded by Portuguese singer Carlos Mendes in 1969 and then by the Dutch group Jolla Herre in 1970. Presumably these artists learned the song from a McCartney demo but, if such a recording exists, it has not yet made the rounds on bootlegs. The Beatles were recorded playing a short, unfinished version of "Penina" during the January 1969 rehearsals for what would become *Let It Be*.

Billy J. Kramer And The Dakotas appeared in *Go Go Mania*.

Who was the real Fifth Beatle?

by Allen J. Wiener

In the earliest days of Beatlemania, a peculiar phenomenon followed the group. This was the notion that someone other than the four musicians must have been responsible for their success, since anyone with eyes could tell that these four affable simps couldn't have done it alone. Conventional wisdom, after all, held that The Beatles hadn't a lick of talent anyway and were entirely the product of some imaginative marketing strategist.

The credit was usually given to Beatles manager Brian Epstein or their record producer, George Martin, or big-name showmen who "gave them their start," such as Ed Sullivan. Thus, the idea persisted that there must be a "Fifth Beatle" lying somewhere behind the scenes. John Lennon particularly hated these suggestions and, referring to the Epsteins, Martins and Sullivans of Beatledom, angrily asserted that "They didn't make us; we made them!"

Once Beatlemania became the public madness it was, still others were eager to bestow upon themselves an equal share of the group's celebrity, dubbing themselves the "Fifth Beatle." So great was the avalanche of adulation and money that flowed down upon The Beatles that it must have been difficult to resist the temptation to somehow share in both.

The "additional Beatles" fall into several categories. First, there really were several musicians who played with The Beatles, some of whom appeared on Beatles records. Second were the "powers behind the throne," a few people behind the scenes who made significant contributions to the business and recording spheres of The Beatles' career. Most notable among these are Epstein and Martin. Finally, there were a number of sycophantic DJs who were able to get close enough, often enough, to ingratiate themselves to The Beatles and to convey to their listeners a feeling of involvement with the group.

The musicians in this collection probably have the most legitimate claim to the title "Fifth Beatle," since they actually did perform professionally with the group. The early members of Lennon's fledgling group, The Quarrymen, can be discounted. There is no evidence showing any contribution to Beatles success on the part of Colin Hanton, John "Duff" Lowe, Nigel Whalley, Pete Shotten or any number of others who were part of this group.

Even after Paul McCartney and George Harrison joined Lennon, The Beatles' lineup was far from final. Both Stu Sutcliffe and Pete Best were card-carrying, working members of the early Beatles during the harsh days in Liverpool and Hamburg. Sutcliffe, their original bass player, left the group while in Germany to devote himself to painting. His tragic early death was the first.

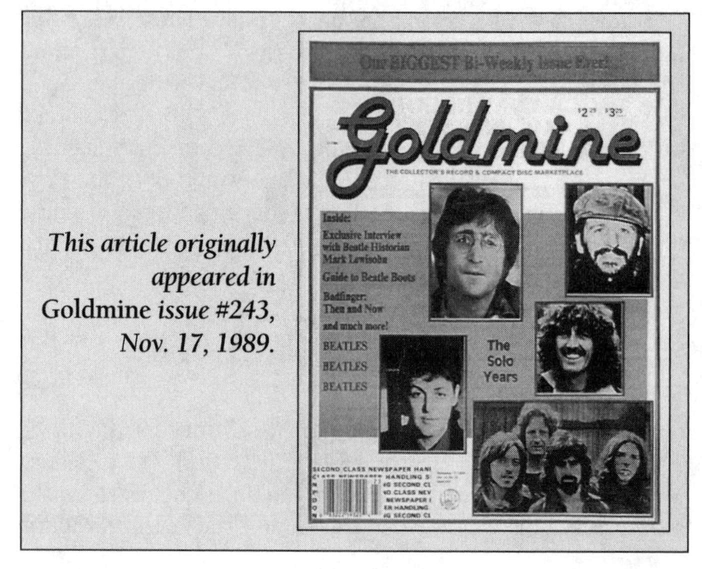

This article originally appeared in Goldmine *issue #243, Nov. 17, 1989.*

While tradition holds that Sutcliffe couldn't play bass any better than Yoko Ono can sing, recent revisionist history suggests that he was a competent, if unexceptional musician. Some of his playing can be heard on the bootleg albums *The Quarrymen At Home* and *Liverpool May 1960*, both of which have longer and more varied titles. These "Quarrymen" rehearsals are more probably Beatles rehearsals taped during the early Hamburg days.

The Best case has been rerun countless times, frequently by Best himself. Best was hardly the first drummer hired on by The Beatles, and his fame stems largely from the fact that he was their next to last. Best is better known for being replaced by Ringo Starr than he is for his drumming. He can be heard performing with the group on the same bootlegs featuring Sutcliffe, and he was The Beatles' drummer during the Decca audition on New Year's Day 1962, released on many legitimate and bootleg records.

Earlier than that, Best drummed as a Beatle when the group backed Tony Sheridan on several songs produced in June 1961 by Bert Kaempfert in a Hamburg studio. Best can also be heard with The Beatles on bootlegs of a few early BBC appearances. Finally, Best made a few records of his own with a group after leaving The Beatles.

Notable among these is an album, released one Christmas during the era of Beatlemania, called *Best Of The Beatles*. The title was clearly designed to catch the unwary eye of holiday shoppers filled with a tad too much Christmas cheer. There is nothing in any of Best's records to indicate that Martin was in any way misguided in recommending that The Beatles find themselves another drummer.

Regardless of their relative musical talents, both Sutcliffe and Best merit inclusion as fifth Beatles by virtue of their respective tenures with the group during its most difficult days.

An even smaller footnote in Beatles history belongs to Tommy Moore, the drummer who preceded Best. Moore had left a perfectly good job driving a forklift at the Garston bottle works to drum for The Beatles, who were then managed by Allan Williams and known as The Silver Beetles. By mid-1960, after only a few months with the future Fabs, Moore, who was older than the other members of the group, gave in to his girlfriend's badgering and quit The Silver Beetles to return to the security of the forklift.

Johnny Hutchinson enjoys the rare, if obscure distinction of having twice sat in with the Fabs. On May 10, 1960, still calling themselves The Silver Beetles, the group auditioned for Larry Parnes, a promoter who was booking supporting acts for Billy Fury. The tryout would actually net the Liverpudlians the dubious reward of backing Johnny Gentle, another of Parnes' singers, on a tour of Scotland. When the time arrived for The Silver Beetles to audition, Moore had yet to arrive. Hutchinson, then the drummer with Cass And The Cassanovas, sat in for Moore. He is immortalized in one of several photographs taken at this audition in which he looks totally bored, staring off into space as Lennon, McCartney, and Harrison seem to be pulling out all the stops while Sutcliffe lurks sideways in the background. Hutchinson relinquished the drum kit to Moore when he appeared about halfway through the 10-minute audition.

More than two years later, Hutchinson again served as The Beatles' drummer during one of the most awkward moments in their history. The event occurred on Aug. 16, 1962, only one day after Best's swan song with The Beatles at The Cavern Club and just hours after The Beatles officially dumped him but before Starr was able to join the group. Hutchinson, then with The Big Three, filled in as drummer at the Riverpark Ballroom, and on the following night at both the Majestic Ballroom Birkenhead and the Tower Ballroom in New Brighton. By the next evening, Ringo made his debut as a Beatle and Hutchinson returned to obscurity.

Neither is Rory Storm, leader of Starr's former group, The Hurricanes, omitted from the footnotes of Beatledom. Aside from appearing with his group on the same bill as The Beatles many times, Storm is said to have filled in for Lennon on Feb. 1, 1962, when The Beatles played the Thistle Cafe, West Kirby. One-time promoter Sam Leach claims that laryngitis prevented Lennon from appearing, but that he (Leach) was

Jimmy Nichol filled in for Ringo in Australia.

A 1962 poster touting The Beatles and their drummer's then-band Rory Storm And The "All Star" Hurricanes. Wonder where Ringo got his current band name...?

able to persuade Storm to fill in. Harrison, among others, says that he cannot recall this incident, and there is some doubt that Storm ever made this appearance as a Fifth Beatle. Since he gave up his valuable drummer to The Beatles, perhaps Storm ought to receive the benefit of the doubt.

During their famous Star Club performance of New Year's Eve, 1962, in Hamburg, The Beatles enjoyed the company of yet another guest member. On that occasion, immortalized on countless record releases, German bouncer Horst Fascher, a friend of The Beatles, did lead vocal on "Be-Bop-A-Lula" and "Hallelujah I Love Her So." Since this performance has enjoyed such wide dissemination on such a large number of releases, Fascher enjoys rather unique status among the legions of fifth Beatles.

One of the most notable substitute Beatles was Jimmy Nicol, yet another drummer, who filled in for Ringo at the start of group's 1964 world tour. Nicol performed with the Fabs from June 4 through the Adelaide, Australia shows at Centennial Hall on June 13. Some of these shows have appeared on bootlegs, and Nicol is heard on a few Beatles interview records. Decked out in a collarless suit and sporting a hastily engineered Beatles haircut, Jimmy Nicol was, for the briefest of moments, a genuine Fifth Beatle.

There are, of course, others who have been immortalized on Beatles records. Perhaps the most noteworthy of these is Andy White, once again an additional drummer. White was called into The Beatles' second recording session on Sept. 11, 1962, during which the second version of "Love Me Do" was cut, along with the single's B-side, "P.S. I Love You." The first version of "Love Me Do" had been recorded a week earlier with Starr on drums, but producer George Martin, among others, was not satisfied with Starr's work.

Contrary to popular myth, Martin was not even present at the Sept. 11 session: It was Ron Richards who produced that session and who brought White in, assigning Starr to a tambourine for the second version of "Love Me Do" and maracas on "P.S. I Love You," with White on percussion. Oddly, it was Ringo's version of "Love Me Do" that was released as the A-side of The Beatles' first single anyway, while White's version appeared on the *Please Please Me* album. Subsequent releases of the single replaced the A-side with White's version. When EMI released a 20th anniversary reissue of the single, the White version was mistakenly placed on the record. This prompted the release of a 12-inch single that included both versions as well as "P.S. I Love You."

Eric Clapton's work on "While My Guitar Gently Weeps" is well known, as is Billy Preston's on *Let It Be*. Preston enjoys the rare distinction of having his name appear along with that of The Beatles on the "Get Back" single. Then there were the two Apple scruffs, Gayleen Pease and Lizzie Bravo, who were hauled off the front steps at Abbey Road and into the studio to add backing vocals to Lennon's "Across The Universe." Vocal "support" was also lent by Beatles wives on tracks such as "Birthday" and "The Continuing Story Of Bungalow Bill." Yoko Ono, by virtue of the fact that she was present throughout the *Let It Be* sessions, and her influence on Lennon, should be included in our list.

Perhaps the least-known guest musician to serve The Beatles would be an excellent subject for a trivia question, for he is none other than Starr himself. It happened in Hamburg when Best was still drumming for The Beatles and Starr was doing the same for Rory Storm And The Hurricanes. On Oct. 15, 1960, while Best was apparently frying bigger fish, the other three Beatles joined Starr and Walter Eymond, also of the Hurricanes, in a small Hamburg recording studio. Eymond used the stage name Lou Walters and was nicknamed "Wally," thus giving him as many names as the girl in "Rocky Raccoon."

In the Hamburg studio, the group recorded George Gershwin's "Summertime," with Eymond on lead vocal. Several copies of the Hamburg record were cut, but only one is known to have survived. But for the presence of Eymond, this was the first gathering of the final four Beatles. After Lennon, McCartney, and Harrison had left, Starr remained while Eymond recorded "Fever" and "September Song." Starr later sat in with The Beatles several more times as a substitute for Best, usually at The Cavern Club. On those occasions, as at the Hamburg Studio, Starr was but another in a long line of "Fifth Beatles."

Another class of Fifth Beatles comprises individuals who were seen as either the brains or the "real talent" behind the group. This school of journalistic diarrhea held that The Beatles' success could only have been the product of some shrewd genius lurking behind the scenes. The most prominent among these was Beatles manager Epstein. A current biography of Epstein takes the title *The Man Who Made The Beatles*, lending support to the theory that the group itself was not responsible for its success.

Epstein deserves some credit for The Beatles hitting the big time. His marketing ideas, such as dressing the group in conservative yet mod suits and crowning them with unique haircuts, certainly caught the public eye. Epstein also intervened to curb the group's rowdy stage practices, including swearing, fighting, eating and food-tossing. He did his best to keep Lennon's loose verbal cannon from going off in public, and until the undeserved abuse Lennon took in 1966 for his "Bigger Than Jesus" crack, Epstein succeeded admirably.

Epstein also negotiated The Beatles' record deal with EMI, something that in retrospect seems to have been remarkably difficult to do. He got them onto *The Ed Sullivan Show* in the United States, garnering for The Beatles perhaps the single biggest promotional payoff in electronic media history. Moreover, "Eppy" really did have The Beatles' best interests at heart and wanted them to be successful for their own sake as well as for any profit he might realize from it.

There seems to be general agreement that much of Epstein's value to the group evaporated when The Beatles ceased touring. Once the group confined itself exclusively to the studio, there was little for Epstein to do. Even in those areas where he might have contributed, The Beatles had taken over much decision-making. In spite of this, Epstein's untimely death seems to have left a leadership void that was never filled. McCartney's attempts to do so seem only to have speeded the group's end. Maybe Epstein really was a Fifth Beatle, at least for a time. There can be no denying that he was a key player in the group's success.

Neither has Sullivan himself gone unnoticed by seekers of a Beatles secret weapon. So great was the impact of those first TV appearances, that Sullivan has sometimes been credited with responsibility for The Beatles' "overnight" success in the United States, and he has thus been viewed as something of a Fifth Beatle himself. This view enjoyed some prevalence in those early days of 1964 when the public was largely unaware of how long The Beatles had been around or of how popular they had become in Europe.

Indeed, the group's reputation preceded them to these shores and, well before the lights went up on Sullivan's stage, the mobs had gathered at New York's Kennedy Airport and Plaza Hotel. "Beatlemania" in America clearly preceded the *Sullivan* show, it did not stem from it, notwithstanding the publicity value of that appearance. The live broadcast that Sunday night in February symbolized and crystallized what was in fact already happening throughout much of the world.

Like Epstein, Beatles producer Martin has often been given a considerable amount of credit for the group's achievements. While his role has sometimes been exaggerated, Martin did play an important part in The Beatles' story and contributed artistically to their recording work. This was especially true in the early years when Martin was pretty much in control of things in the studio. He suggested arrangements and directed recording and mixing sessions. In the early years, it was Martin who decided which takes were scrapped and which were keepers. And it was Martin who did most of the mixing for Beatles releases in those days. Beyond that, Martin often played on Beatles records, noticeably providing a number of piano parts. In this regard, he enjoys special status in Beatles history.

However, as Mark Lewisohn illustrates in *The Beatles: Recording Sessions*, Martin's role diminished over time as The Beatles became more knowledgeable about recording techniques and began making their own decisions in the studio. This extended into post-recording work, including ideas for the use of sound effects and mixing techniques. Martin's role never disappeared by any means, and he continued to play an important part in recording sessions right up to the group's demise. Afterward, he frequently worked with McCartney.

Martin's contribution to The Beatles' success is as great as that of any other supporting player in the group's story, and he has a convincing claim to the title "Fifth Beatle." In addition to his hands-on-participation in nearly all of the

A 1961 poster.

Brian Epstein in 1964.

Kaufman can be seen with The Beatles in the documentary film *What's Happening? The Beatles In The U.S.A.*, which was shot during the early 1964 visit. In one scene, George Harrison is heard requesting that Kaufman play James Ray's "Got My Mind Set On You," which Harrison would record himself some 23 years later for *Cloud Nine*.

Kaufman's affiliation with the Fabs was not a brief one either. He was later welcomed on the *A Hard Day's Night* film set, where he again interviewed The Beatles. Several of Kaufman's interviews were released on a limited edition record, *Murray The K And The Beatles: As It Happened*, and have subsequently appeared on several other records, including *Timeless II*. On June 1, 1969, Kaufman was one of several visitors to the Queen Elizabeth Hotel in Montreal whose voices were part of the chorus on Lennon's recording of "Give Peace A Chance." Kaufman was parodied in the 1978 TV film *The Rutles*, played by Bill Murray, who naturally took on the name Bill Murray The K!

Kaufman was a popular and knowledgeable DJ, and he may have been friendly with The Beatles for a while. But, he was hardly a contributor to The Beatles' work, any more than any other DJ who sustained audience following by playing Beatles records and by pandering to the obvious public taste for Beatles product. But, in that giddy February in 1964, "The K" fit the Beatlemania scene perfectly. In that sense, he shares a small part of The Beatles' spotlight in one image of that magic moment.

The sycophantic DJ is better personified by Ed Rudy than by Murray "The K." It's not clear whether Rudy was actually a DJ at all.

group's recordings, he was the only record company official who was willing to give The Beatles a chance by offering them a recording contract. Given the benefit of hindsight, that is a fairly remarkable fact and a superb testimonial to the capabilities and judgment of British record company executives at that time.

A final group of would-be Fifth Beatles was peopled by any number of radio DJs who did their best to latch onto The Beatles once they reached American shores. Literally jockeying for position, each tried to achieve a closeness to The Beatles that would give them an advantage in radio coverage of the group's activities.

One of these, New York DJ Murray "The K" Kaufman, may well have coined the phrase "Fifth Beatle." He certainly used it in reference to himself often enough. He also went a long way in justifying the moniker. Murray "The K" was made welcome within The Beatles' inner circle and enjoyed unlimited access to the group. He was thus able to transmit live and taped first-hand interviews with the group to his radio audience during a period when most DJs would have traded their own blood to be in Kaufman's place.

The first issue of his initial interview/documentary album, *The American Tour With Ed Rudy*, referred to him as a radio reporter for the *Radio Pulsebeat News* independent audio news network. Rudy released at least four different Beatles documentary albums, one of them a promo issued only to radio stations.

The American Tour With Ed Rudy was recorded entirely during The Beatles' first U.S. visit. While side one is made up of clips from various press conferences and interviews bracketed around repeated barrages of blabber from Rudy, side two offers a unique telephone interview with Harrison conducted by Rudy. Excerpts from this interview have appeared on the legitimately released LP *The Beatles Talk Down Under (And All Over) Volume 2* and on the bootleg album *The Beatles Conquer America*, where it is falsely listed as a telephone interview with DJ Charlie Murdock of Miami radio station WQAM. The Murdock recording is simply an "open-end" interview using clips from Rudy's Harrison interview, with Murdock dubbing in questions. In fact, it may be this open-end interview that was

Pete Best, signing autographs in Liverpool during Beatles week in 1999. It was The Casbah's 40th anniversary.

released on Rudy's promo LP *Beatlemania Tour Coverage*.

Rudy also released *Great American Tour: 1965 Live Beatlemania Concert*, which includes a 1964 Beatles concert overdubbed by a group called The Liverpool Lads, and 1965's *Talk Album: Ed Rudy With New U.S. Tour*, consisting of clips from several press conferences and interviews from the summer 1964 U.S. tour with Rudy dubbing in the questions himself. Except for the Harrison phone interview, Rudy offers little except a big mouth that repeatedly refers to itself as yet another Fifth Beatle. In fact, Rudy is more interested in promoting himself than in providing press coverage of the Fabs. He isn't very successful there either. He introduces McCartney as Lennon and asks Harrison if The Beatles call Lennon "Johnny or Jack." Not very impressive for a fifth Beatle.

In any event, British DJs had preceded their American counterparts as close affiliates of The Beatles with more legitimate claims to a share of the group's status. Most notable among these was Brian Matthew of BBC Radio, who hosted many weekly shows with The Beatles and enjoyed a great rapport with them. Some of his banter with the group can be heard on several bootlegs containing BBC appearances. Bob Wooler, Cavern Club emcee/compere, also did a great deal to promote The Beatles. Neither ever thought of calling himself a Fifth Beatle.

No doubt readers will want to add more names to this list of fifth wheels. Names such as Dick James, Klaus Voormann, and Astrid Kirchherr spring to mind. Perhaps someone ought to start a contest to see who can name the most Fifth Beatles. Or, maybe a Beatles convention should be organized hosting as many of these people as can be located. Any additions to the names presented here are, of course, welcome, but the whole idea of a Fifth Beatle is really a little silly. Like all great artists, The Beatles were clearly the recipients of valuable help from a number of people. But they also deserve primary credit for their success, which was largely achieved through years of hard work and perseverance, not that the formula has paid off for every talented group or artist who has used it. A little luck and good timing help too, and The Beatles had their share of both.

In the end, there were only four Beatles, and each of them offered enough of an individual contribution to make the group something special and unique. Together, those four were truly one of a kind.

The Mersey-Motown sound

How Liverpool fell for Detroit

by Bill Harry

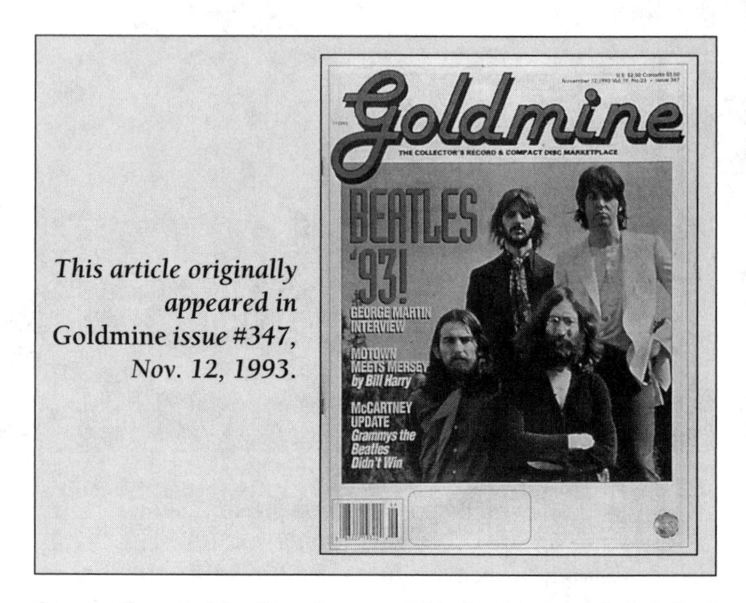

***This article originally appeared in** Goldmine issue #347, Nov. 12, 1993.*

I recently visited Detroit and during the trip Martha Reeves escorted me on a personal tour around Hitsville USA, Motown's own museum. One of the photographs displayed was of The Dave Clark Five together with The Supremes, and it was captioned "Liverpool Meets Detroit."

Later, when we went out to lunch, I was able to tell Martha that Dave Clark was not a Liverpool artist, although the ties between Liverpool and Detroit were stronger than anyone realized, and I was able to relate the rarely told tale of the Mersey-Motown sound.

Most people assume that the major influence in the birth of the Liverpool sound were American rock 'n' roll acts such as Buddy Holly, Carl Perkins, Elvis Presley, Jerry Lewis, Gene Vincent, and Little Richard. To a great extent, they are right, although the first major influence on the members of the group who were to become The Beatles was a British artist, Lonnie Donegan. The rock 'n' roll numbers began to appear in the repertoires of the Mersey hands from 1957, but a new influence was to creep in during 1962.

The Motown record label was created by Berry Gordy Jr. in 1961. Prior to that, he used the name Tamla Records. The name Tamla Motown was used on the European releases which, by 1962, were being distributed in Britain on the small label Oriole. The company was surprised to discover that its largest sales were in the Merseyside area. It began taking half-page advertisements in *Mersey Beat*, the newspaper I founded, and I began writing about the Motown artists each issue.

Oriole sent me the records to review, and I'd also take them to local venues to play. I remember receiving "Fingertips" by Little Stevie Wonder and taking it down to The Cavern to play. Ringo Starr came up to me and told me it was the best record he'd heard and asked if he could have my copy. I gave it to him and also arranged for Oriole to send him a complete set of their Motown releases.

Around that time, the Mersey groups began to perform what we called the Mersey-Motown sound. The Motown numbers stressed vocals, and the Liverpool groups adapted the numbers to their own style: beat group versions. The most popular example was by Faron's Flamingos, who took "Do You Love Me," a song by the vocal group The Contours, and rearranged it in the Liverpool rock 'n' roll style. Other Liverpool artists began to record their Mersey-Motown numbers, such as Ian And The Zodiacs, with their rearranged version of The Marvelettes' "Beechwood 4-5789" and Beryl Marsden with The Supremes' "When The Lovelight Starts Shining."

I actually traveled down to London for the recording session with Faron's Flamingos. Faron was lead singer and played bass guitar, Paddy Chambers and Nicky Crouch played lead and rhythm, and Trevor Morais played drums. John Schroeder produced for Oriole in a small studio off New Bond Street.

To create a party atmosphere, some crates of ale were brought in and friends and fans danced in the studio during the recording. The group's version of the number was a sensation, and we were all convinced they would have a major hit with it. Imagine the surprise of everyone when, after saying that Faron's "Do You Love Me" was a sure-fire hit, the company issued it as the B-side to a number called "See If She Cares." Everyone was despondent at the time, as we believed the number would have made Faron's Flamingos one of the top groups of the beat era.

Faron himself was to recall, "I remember after playing St. Helens one night I gave the words to Brian Poole in exchange for a large whiskey." Brian Poole And The Tremeloes then went shooting up the charts with the number, as did another London band, The Dave Clark Five. What was particularly frustrating to Faron was that the original Contours version was purely a vocal harmony number. Both The Tremeloes and The Dave Clark Five used Faron's own version of the number. Brian Poole hit the #1 position in the charts with it and it gave The Dave Clark Five their first chart hit.

So the Mersey-Motown sound, developed in Liverpool, brought fame to two of the groups in the rival South! With their next single The Dave Clark Five attracted headlines — "Tottenham Sound Has Crushed The Beatles" — and the London-based media in Britain promoted them as rivals to the Mersey sound. Yet in America the publicity drive was completely opposite. Rather than being pushed as London's answer to Liverpool, the group was promoted as if it was a Mersey beat band. Since "Glad All Over" had replaced "I Want To Hold Your Hand" at the top of the British charts, in America it was believed that The Dave Clark Five were the next big group from Liverpool. Epic Records exploited this belief by advertising them in *Billboard* as having "the Mersey sound with the Liverpool beat," which is why the Motown Museum displays their "Liverpool Meets Detroit" photograph.

Incidentally, Trevor Morais, drummer with Faron's Flamingos, was one of the leading Merseyside drummers. Listen to his performance on "Do You Love Me" and then listen to the Dave Clark version. Faron's Flamingos also produced exciting Mersey-Motown versions of numbers such as "Shake Sherry" and "Mickey's Monkey," but when they recorded "Do You Love Me," it was the first time that a Motown number had been covered by a British act on record, albeit in a completely different form from the original.

"Do You Love Me" was such an obvious hit that Faron and many Merseyside fans were dumbfounded when it was relegated to the flip side and a number that was catchy but rather dull was issued as the A-side. Faron wrongly assumed that the decision came because a number of young Londoners were taken from the street and asked which side they preferred. He thought they might have opted for "See If She Cares." They didn't.

The feeling that "Do You Love Me" was the most powerful side was agreed upon unanimously by everyone who listened to the numbers.

I happened to be present at a playback with John Schroeder, some Oriole executives and Don Agnes of Leeds Music, publisher of "See If She Cares." They all agreed that "Do You Love Me" was a blistering number and an obvious hit, but Oriole was a small label with not much money and needed a professional record plugger on the disc. Don said that he would plug the record on the radio, but only on condition that the Leeds Music number was the A-side. It was as simple as that.

In my office at *Mersey Beat* I had several Motown albums displayed on the wall. The Chants were frequent visitors and borrowed my LPs. When I eventually did get them back they were literally threadbare! The Chants and the black groups from the Liverpool 8 district were the nearest equivalent to the actual Motown groups that Liverpool had.

Excuse me if I digress for a moment to fill in the details of the black Mersey groups, all from the Liverpool 8 district, Liverpool's "Harlem."

Stanley House in Upper Parliament Street was a community center for both blacks and whites, an attempt to create racial harmony in a sea of prejudice.

John Ankrah formed The Shades, who began to rehearse and perform at Stanley House. They developed their vocal sound and changed their name to The Chants. Apart from Joe, they comprised Edmond Ankrah, Nat Smeda, Alan Harding, Eddie Amoo, and reserve singer Peter Ching.

They made their Cavern debut in November 1962. Being a vocal outfit, they needed instrumental backing, and this was

The Dave Clark Five.

MONEY

(That's What I Want)

Words and Music

by BERRY GORDY, JR. and JANIE BRADFORD

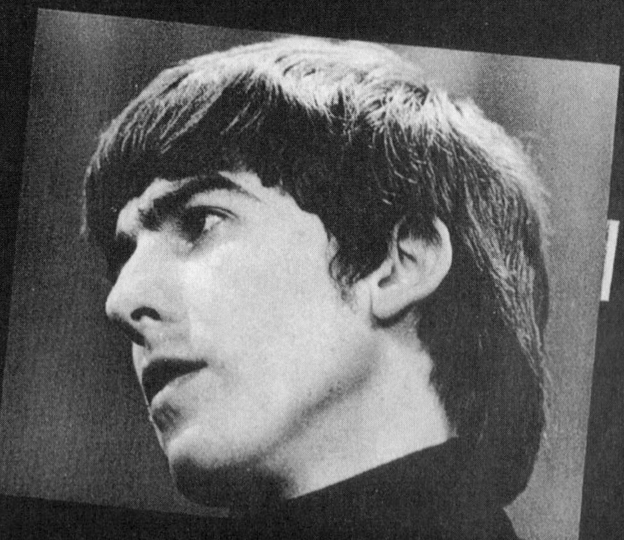

Price

75¢

JOBETE MUSIC CO., INC.

CPI Sole Selling Agents:
Cimino Publications Incorporated
479 Maple Avenue • Westbury, L. I., N. Y.

provided for them on an early Cavern appearance by The Beatles. Brian Epstein wasn't too happy about his prestigious local band backing a group of unknowns, but John Lennon insisted and the gig went ahead. The Chants were an immediate success and were able to engage their own instrumental backing band, The Harlems. Originally it was a trio comprising Dave Preston on drums, Vince Ishmael, lead, and Rob Eccles, bass.

Epstein became their manager for a short time, but it didn't work out and they signed with an impresario from Manchester, Ted Ross. They recorded for Pye Records and their second single, in January 1964, was "I Could Write A Book." When the historic all-Beatles panel of the TV show *Juke Box Jury* was filmed from the stage of the Empire Theatre, Liverpool, on Dec. 7, 1963, the first record to be played was The Chants' "I Could Write A Book." The Beatles voted it a hit, although it never became one. Several other releases followed, but chart success eluded them.

There were other black vocal groups springing up in the Upper Parliament Street area immediately following the local success of The Chants. These included The Sobells, who comprised Gilbert Benjamin, Edward Ankrah, Kenny Dans, and Bernie Winton; The Conquests, a four-man harmony group, and The Contrasts, a female vocal group.

When Bob Dylan appeared in Liverpool, he asked me to take him 'round the town at night to meet some Liverpool poets. I took him to the Blue Angel club, run by Allan Williams, which was the late-night hangout for the Mersey bands. They only served beer and spirits, so Dylan wanted to return to his hotel, the Adelphi, where he had boxes of Beaujolais. We were joined by The Scaffold and The Poppies and spent the entire night chatting in his room. The Scaffold were a trio comprising Mike McGear (Paul McCartney's brother), Roger McGough, and John Gorman. The Poppies were a black female trio. Dylan was impressed with them and arranged for the girls to go to London, where he acted as their recording manager and made a record with them, although to my knowledge it was never released.

In 1963 the Motown distribution in Britain changed to EMI's Stateside label and the Motown artists soon began to have their first British hits, particularly since The Beatles had started to mention the Motown acts in interviews.

1963 was also the year when The Beatles made their own Mersey-Motown recordings, with no less than three Motown numbers on their British *With The Beatles* album: "Please Mr. Postman," "You Really Got A Hold On Me" and "Money (That's What I Want)."

"Money" was also a number that had been part of the repertoire of numerous Liverpool bands. When The Undertakers came to make their second record, they chose "Money" as their A-side. As in the case of Faron's Flamingos, the record company put the obvious hit on the B-side and made "What About Us" the A-side. This also proved fortunate for another Southern group, Bern Elliott And The Fenman, who then had a Top 20 hit with the number, although they said that they had first heard it in Hamburg when The Searchers performed it at The Star Club, and they rushed back to Britain to record it.

Kingsize Taylor And The Dominoes, arguably one of the very best of the Liverpool bands, spent most of their career in Germany, where they recorded "Money" for Polydor. When Tony Jackson left The Searchers he formed The Vibrations and his first two singles for Pye in 1964 were Mary Wells hits, "Bye Bye Baby" and "You Beat Me To The Punch." The Fourmost had a modest chart hit on Parlophone with The Four Tops' "Baby I Need Your Loving," and The Trends performed two Motown numbers on their Pye single release in 1964, The Temptations' "The Way You Do The Things You Do" and Marvin Gaye's "You're A Wonderful One."

The Beatles continued to be enthusiastic about Motown artists and invited Mary Wells to be their guest during a British tour in 1964. I talked to Wells backstage at the Apollo, Ardwick concert and she told me, "I'd just love to record a number by John and Paul and I think I'll ask them about it." In fact, I discussed it with Lennon myself later that night and he told me, "We've got a number which we think will really be suitable for her." Nothing transpired, but The Beatles did request that she appear on their *Around The Beatles* television special and she recorded an album, *Love Songs To The Beatles*, singing 12 Lennon and McCartney compositions.

Epstein also became a fan of Motown artists and brought The Four Tops over to Britain to tour. When they appeared at the Saville Theatre in London, Paul McCartney designed a special backdrop for their show. Paul was later to forge a close association with other Motown artists, recording "Ebony And Ivory" with Stevie Wonder and "This Girl Is Mine," "Say, Say, Say" and "The Man" with Michael Jackson. Ironically, it was Jackson who eventually acquired control of the Lennon and McCartney song catalog.

The Motown Historical Museum, Detroit, Mich.

Photographer Harry Benson, on his famous Beatles shots

by Terry Ott

Photographer Harry Benson, now 69, had the good fortune in 1964 to be assigned (against his will) to a rising young pop group known as The Beatles. Working for the Exportriate Canadian Lord Beverbrook at *The Daily Express* in London, Benson was with the group as they exploded on to the world stage.

He framed some of the most memorable and unpretentious photographs ever taken of the Fabs. Benson's shots never looked strained and, despite manager Brian Epstein's almost total control over the group's early media exposure, Benson managed to manipulate The Beatles to his camera's listing.

From the Paris hotel room where a pillow fight "erupted" at Benson's urging to a Miami Beach gym with another cultural hero-to-be by the name of Cassius Clay (later known as Muhammad Ali), Benson captured the essence of the lads. His candid recollections of the meeting with Clay (revealed for the first time in the following interview) demonstrate Benson's knack for situational spontaneity, as well as his guts.

From 1964-66, Benson accompanied The Beatles on world tours and personal appearances. Unlike other so-called "Fifth Beatle" journalists, he never became part of the entourage. Looking back, Benson believes this is what gave him the advantage over photographers who followed the group as fans.

As his black-and-white photos reveal (Benson never shot the group in color because in his opinion 1960s color stock was "shit"), John, Paul, George, and Ringo never looked anything but fab through Benson's lens.

Deservedly, 35 years later Benson's Beatles shutter work is being celebrated in a new book, *The Beatles Now And Then* (Universe/Rizzoli) and in a tour of art galleries and museums throughout the United States. He remains a working photojournalist with assignments worldwide.

This article originally appeared in Goldmine issue #503, Nov. 5, 1999.

Goldmine: *How did you hook up with The Beatles in January 1964?*

Harry Benson: It was weird. I was going to Africa for the London *Daily Express* to do a story in Kenya one year after the independence. And then I got a call that night saying the editor wants me to go with The Beatles who were going on their first trip to France. I thought, "Oh Christ, I don't want to go with a rock group." You know, I'm a serious journalist. Anyway, I talked them out of it, or so I thought. About five minutes later, the phone rang again and they said, "You're going with The Beatles."

What were your first impressions of the Fabs?

As people they were very nice. And the first time I heard them play, I knew I was on the right job. The music was sensational. They had a gig in a suburb outside of Paris. I always remember Paul McCartney saying to the fans, "Come on, give us a cheer, we need confidence." Because at this point the fans hadn't started screaming yet.

Who was the most photogenic Beatle?

Paul was the cutest, but I would say the most photogenic was John Lennon. When he was young, you know he had a very refined nose and if you look at it, very fine features. But you couldn't get anything done without Paul. You could take a picture of three Beatles, but Paul had to be one of them.

What was your most memorable experience with The Beatles?

The most memorable for me was when we went down to Miami [after *The Ed Sullivan Show*] with Cassius Clay. I had this idea of taking The Beatles to meet Clay because he was a big-mouth, always doing funny things. So I went to see The Beatles and they said no. Lennon said they wanted to see Sonny Liston [who was fighting Clay for the heavyweight title on Feb. 25] because Clay was gonna get beaten by Liston. I went to see Liston, who didn't even look at me but told me he didn't want to see "those bums." So I went back to The Beatles, who still thought they were going to see Sonny Lis-

As Recorded by THE BEATLES on Capitol Records

I WANT TO HOLD YOUR HAND

Words and Music by JOHN LENNON and PAUL McCARTNEY

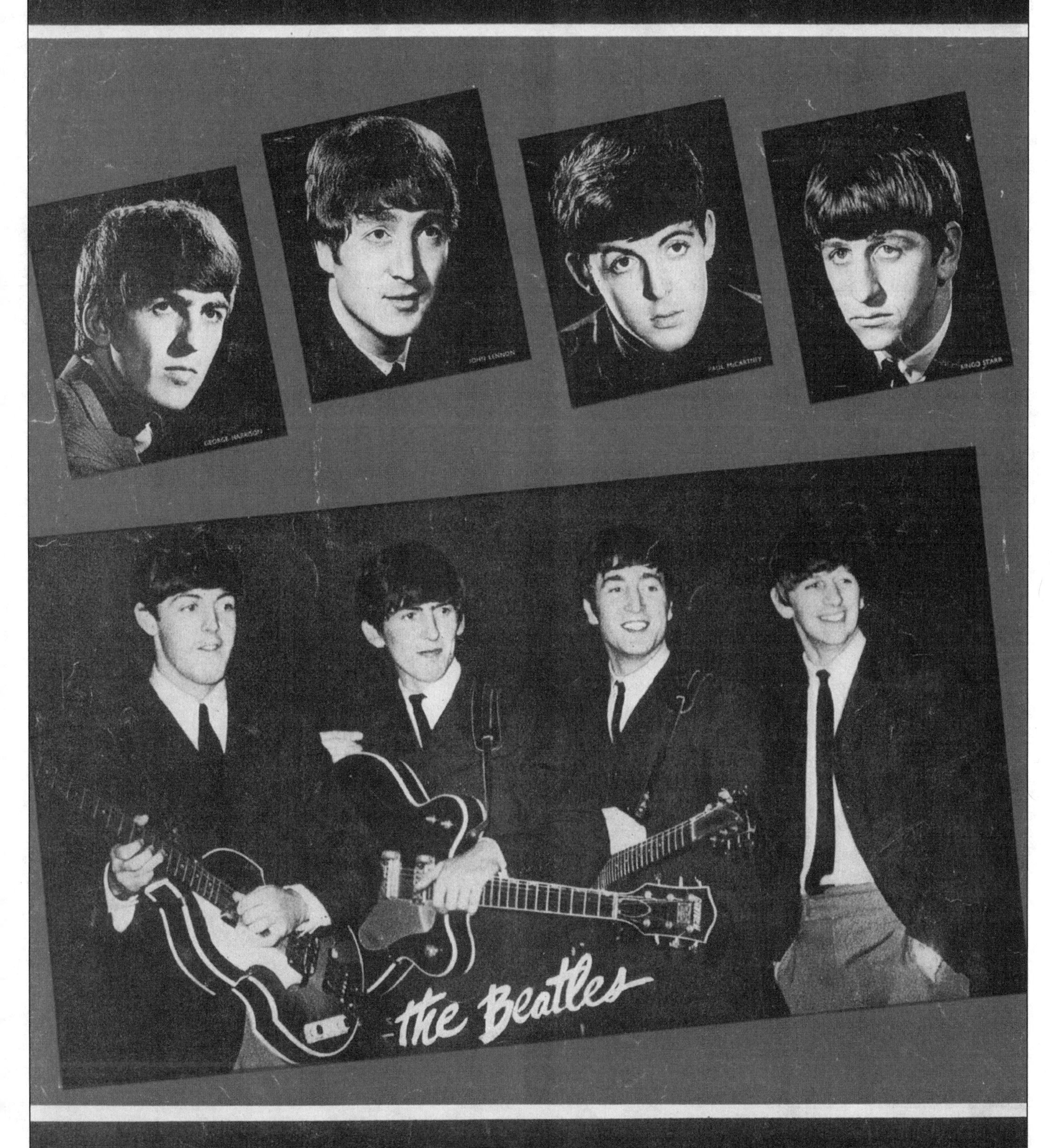

DUCHESS MUSIC CORPORATION .60 in U.S.A.

ton, but I took them to see Clay, who made them do all kinds of things. He had them all manipulated. Do this. Do that. Who's the greatest? Who's the best-looking? He had them lying on the ring floor. Afterwards, Lennon said to me, "You made us look like fools." Because you know, The Beatles were so cool, nobody made them look silly. They were the coolest ones. But Clay was way ahead of them in intellect. Don't believe the nonsense [reported several times after the photos appeared] that Clay had no idea who The Beatles were. He knew all about them. Afterwards, The Beatles wouldn't speak to me for a month.

How did the famous "pillow fight" shots take place?

We were sitting around late at night in the hotel room in Paris, and Brian Epstein comes in with a cable to say "I Want To Hold Your Hand" is #1 in the United States. I suggested, "How about a pillow fight?" And Lennon said, "No, that's stupid, it's childish. We don't want to be made to look like adolescents." Paul agreed with that and the other two just kind of nodded. I remember this as me being put in my place. But as Paul was sitting there drinking a whisky — they were always drinking — John comes up behind him and bangs him right across the back of the head [with a pillow] and that was it.

Through the years The Beatles' first American concert at Carnegie Hall has taken on almost mythical significance. What was your recollection?

It was too sedate. Too precious. I remember thinking it wasn't raucous enough. The audience was too high-brow. It was no big deal, you know.

You have said it was fun in the early days before world weariness set in.

Well, they started to go off to India, and that's where I left them. I could have gone, but I didn't want to. When I came to America with them I didn't come just to be a rock photographer. So I was then doing things on civil rights and being what I really wanted to be, which was a photojournalist. I'm not knocking it because The Beatles were very important in my whole career. I don't think I would have come to America without The Beatles and got out of the British sort of newspaper status quo kind of thing.

Why did you get along with The Beatles so well?

I got along with them because I wasn't hanging around them every minute. A lot of photographers and writers became kind of groupies with them, and then The Beatles got rude with them.

What are your feelings on the acclaim your photos from 35 years ago are receiving today?

Well, when I set out, when I started to do them, it wasn't to do a book. It wasn't to do museums. It wasn't to do galleries. It was to stay on the payroll at the end of the week. It was to have a fuckin' job. That was my whole thing. But professionally, it does make me feel I had my wits about me and I did it well. Looking back over my career, there are things I didn't do well, things I missed. But The Beatles I did well. The pictures hold up because they are not forced like a lot of the pictures were of The Beatles at the time.

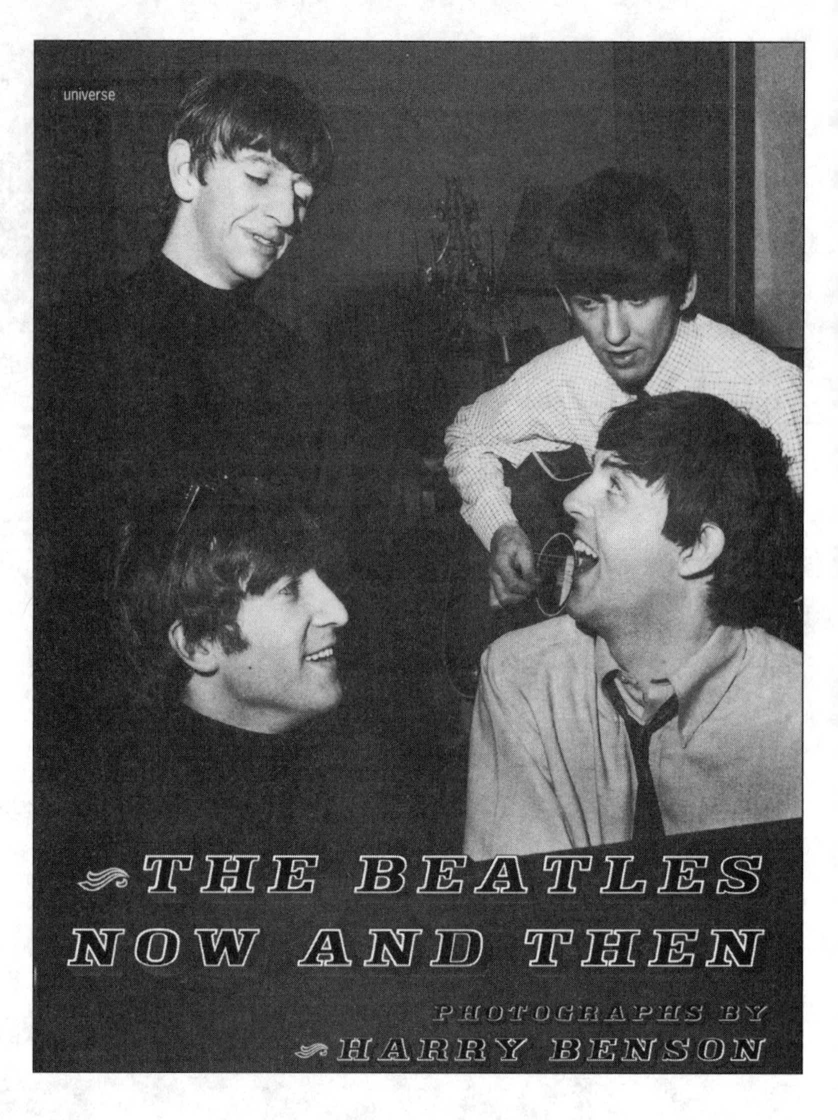

What are some of your memories from the 1964 American Beatles shows?

My favorite was *The Ed Sullivan Show*, but that was not really a concert. I remember places like Memphis where the police never knew what the hell hit them. They thought they could handle all the kids. The Beatles would be laughing up a storm about it afterwards. They had warned the police of what could happen, but they just said they could handle everything. And they couldn't. The kids were all over the place. And Lennon used to make jokes about spastic fans. He used to mimic them, and McCartney would tell him to cut it out. He didn't like it. I also remember the February Washington concert. [The Beatles had refused to fly to D.C. due to the "fookin' blizzard" and took a wild train ride instead.] It was a freezing cold night and afterwards we were invited to the British ambassador's residence, and the staff behaved awful. They called The Beatles "yobs [British slang for lower class] from Liverpool." It was rude, and the ambassador later apologized. But the concert itself was pretty good. Pretty refined compared to what was to come.

Acting naturally

The producer of *A Hard Day's Night* and *Help!* remembers bringing The Beatles to the big screen

by Gillian G. Gaar

Though The Beatles' '60s film career is generally thought to revolve around "the big four" — *A Hard Day's Night*, *Help!*, *Yellow Submarine* and *Let It Be* (with an occasional detour for *Magical Mystery Tour*) — a complete listing of their various film ventures encompasses a much wider range of movies. Think of *Pop Gear*, *What's Happening: The Beatles In The USA*, *The Family Way*, *How I Won The War*, *Wonderwall*, *Candy* and *The Magic Christian*, add in TV specials such as *The Mersey Sound*, *Around The Beatles*, *The Beatles At Shea Stadium*, *The Music Of Lennon And McCartney*, *All My Loving* and *The Rolling Stones Rock And Roll Circus*. Don't forget John Lennon's films made in collaboration with Yoko Ono, and you've got a filmography that covers virtually everything from documentary to live performance to feature films to avant-garde experimentation.

This article originally appeared in* Goldmine *issue #477, Nov. 6, 1998.

But it's still the big four that draw the most attention and receive the widest distribution. This is particularly true of *A Hard Day's Night*, released in 1964 at the crest of Beatlemania, and on the verge of a theatrical reissue next year, its 35th anniversary. Walter Shenson, who produced the film and today holds on to the film's residual rights, isn't surprised by the interest *A Hard Day's Night* has received — and hopes that interest will find new life in the future.

"It's the first Beatles picture, and it was everybody's introduction to The Beatles," he says. "You saw who they were and how they acted.

"It's hard for me to believe that it's 35 years since we've made *A Hard Day's Night*," he continues, "and 34 years since *Help!*" (released in 1965). At the time, it was hoped that Shenson would help The Beatles build a film career to rival Elvis Presley's. Instead, he only oversaw two movies before The Beatles lost interest in making feature films. Nonetheless, what began as a scheme by United Artists to commission a quickie picture in order to lay claim to a Beatles soundtrack album, resulted in two movies that are key in the history of rock film. The story of their creation, and their continued success in the decades since The Beatles' breakup, is one that Shenson has been constantly pressed to revisit.

Shenson began his career as a publicist, working for Paramount and Columbia in Hollywood, before moving to England in the 1950s. It was there he produced his first film, *The Mouse That Roared* (1959). Shenson met director Richard Lester — like himself, another American expatriate — when he hired Lester to direct the film's sequel, *Mouse On The Moon* (1963). Thus the key players were in position when United Artists approached Shenson the same year to ask if he'd be interested in producing a film starring this new British phenomenon, The Beatles.

"I said, 'You mean those kids with the long hair? What do you want to do that for?'" Shenson recalls. "And they said, 'Well, we would get the soundtrack album, and that's worth financing a low-budget film.' So the purpose of the film was for United Artists Records to have the distribution rights to the soundtrack album. The film was a bonus. I don't think anyone thought it would serve any other purpose than to have a soundtrack album. But the picture turned out awful good. And it eventually became more important than the soundtrack album."

In 1963, no one, even The Beatles themselves, realized the monumental impact they were going to have on the rest of the decade. The price the surprisingly low fee manager Brian Epstein asked for the group — a £20,000 advance and seven

A scene from *A Hard Day's Night*.

and a half percent of the film's net profits — was perhaps indicative of this (the fee was later raised to £25,000 and 20 percent of the profits). Likewise, would-be screenwriters were anxious to shove The Beatles into the usual pop film scenario, without consideration of their exceptional talents.

"You cannot believe what kind of scripts were submitted once it was announced we were going to make a picture," says Shenson. "Everybody was writing such corny stuff. Just silly! Most of these people didn't even know The Beatles." Shenson's first step toward investing some quality in the venture was to bring Lester aboard. "He was closer to The Beatles' age than I, so I figured they'd get along well," he explains. "And they did indeed, because he was very gifted, gifted in the right way as a director. He was willing to take chances and captured The Beatles as they were, rather than trying to turn them into actors. I wouldn't want to put any of The Beatles into a picture where they're not playing themselves, because they're not actors! I think that's why the films are so good, because the camera captured the real Beatles."

Finally, Shenson and Lester decided to commission a script themselves. "So many writers, screenwriters, journalists and people in London were submitting these terrible, terrible ideas," Shenson says. "They were insulting. That's when we decided we'd better start from scratch and do what we want. Then Dick and I came across Alun Owen, a screenwriter from Liverpool, and we thought, 'He'd be perfect, because he could write in their idiom.' Which he did. Once you got to know The Beatles, you knew they were very independent and had very good judgment about what they could do well. And so we tailored the script just for them.

"That's where Dick Lester and I did the right thing," Shenson continues. "Getting Alun Owen and deciding to make the film in black and white and to have that hand-held camera style. And although it was not original, not many people had been using it for feature films, just documentaries and things like that. And it appeared to us that The Beatles were black and white. And somehow or other black and white films have a documentary quality. They look more real than fiction. And it just worked beautifully. The style that Dick Lester put into the film couldn't have been better. And even though there was a script, the brilliance of the screenplay made it appear like there was no script."

Shenson and Lester's desire to produce a quality film despite their budgetary limitations broke with tradition as far as rock/pop films were concerned. With few exceptions (the tongue-in-cheek *The Girl Can't Help It* and Presley's *Jailhouse Rock* and *King Creole*), such films routinely sacrificed intelligent storylines and other "inessential" production values in their rush to get to the next musical number. Not that United Artists appreciated the attention being put into *A Hard Day's Night* at the time.

"United Artists would look at the rushes and say, 'We don't understand what they're saying,'" says Shenson. "And there's some Beatles colloquialisms that we let through because it was very much them. I didn't want to censor them in any way and I said to Dick, 'Just let it go. If the audience doesn't understand they'll get the drift.' It was part of them. I think that was the charm of the film."

Neither did UA appreciate the innovative camera work, which, during the songs in particular, clearly points the way to now-common video techniques. "When Paul sings 'And I Love Her,' we rigged up the set so that the camera would follow him around in a close-up, very tight," Shenson remembers. "And after I sent the picture off to New York, some executive called me. And he was a little bit hesitant. He said, 'You know, there's one shot where Paul McCartney's singing a song where the arc light goes right into the lens.' And I said, 'Yeah, it took us a half a day to get that.' And he didn't know what the hell I was talking about!

"We hung a camera operator from the ceiling on a bosun's chair, like a baby's crib hanging from a rope," Shenson continues. "And the assistant cameraman just pushed the guy with the camera around Paul. I mean, we didn't have expensive equipment to use. And I remember when I saw the rushes, right after they were developed, I went over to Dick Lester and I gave him a hug. I said, 'Gee, that's beautiful.' And he said, 'Yeah, I'm glad you like it.' And people ask was I aware of the fact that the light went into the lens! Yeah, I know! They just hadn't seen that stuff before. It was different.

"I think United Artists was just happy to get it out right away before The Beatles faded away. They kept calling me and saying, 'Do you think they'll still be popular when the picture comes out?' And I said, 'You're going to have it in a month! Don't worry!' And then they called and said, 'Oh, the picture's great. Do you think they're going to last?' And I said, 'I don't know if they're going to last or not. Just put the picture out! Don't worry if they're going to last! Because they're popular now and that's what you put the money into.' To be honest with you, I just hoped that people would come to see the movie to make it pay its backers back. Little did I know they got their money back the first hour! It was a very successful picture."

It was expected that *A Hard Day's Night* would be a success with Beatles fans; as Shenson says, "I think all the kids wanted to do was see The Beatles." But this fictionalized day-in-the-life of the Fab Four, where the biggest dilemma was whether the band would get to the TV studio on time for the big show, also won over adult critics.

"The thing that's most interesting about the picture, that I think has a lot to do with its continued success, is that nobody expected this kind of film," Shenson explains. "Everybody had heard of The Beatles. Seventy million Americans saw them on *The Ed Sullivan Show* before the picture came out. And there was a lot of Beatlemania. But I don't think anybody else expected as intelligent and artistic a picture as *A Hard Day's Night*. And that's one of the reasons it got such good reviews. It was a good film, but the raves came because it was unexpected. All a lot of people could think of was, 'Oh, they're the boys that go, "Yeah, Yeah, Yeah."' And that was it. And then when they saw the film, and they saw their personalities, The Beatles were not what they expected. They were witty, they were fun. You got that cuteness coming through, the decency."

All of which boded well for *Help!*, released the following year. Additional money was secured to make the film, which Shenson and Lester were determined to make as different from *A Hard Day's Night* as possible. "We didn't want to do that again," Shenson says. "So in *Help!* we had beautiful color and bigger locations, went to the Austrian Alps and to the Bahamas and all through England. It was a totally different kind of movie. And it's something Dick Lester liked very much. And if you look at that picture again, some of the camera work and the rendering of the songs is absolutely beautiful. I mean, the photography while they're singing against different backgrounds, you never see anything like that today. It's just beautiful."

Yet *Help!* failed to scale the critical heights *A Hard Day's Night* had. What had been seen as innovative and spontaneous in the first film was deemed calculated and forced in the second. The plot, concerning a mystical ring stuck on Ringo's finger, was admittedly light, and thus the songs were not worked in as naturally as in *A Hard Day's Night*. But as Shenson points out, the backgrounds for such song sequences as

Producer Walter Shenson chatting with John Lennon on the set of *A Hard Day's Night*.

"Ticket To Ride" and "Another Girl" make *Help!* arguably the first feature-length music video (fittingly, MTV would later honor Lester as the "founding father" of music video).

The Beatles' arrangement with UA called for three films, so following *Help!* Shenson looked for another property for the group. "We had a couple of other things that we tried to get together," Shenson says. "But I don't think The Beatles wanted to do any more. Maybe if we'd got a great script. But it was very difficult. We had readers and we had stuff being submitted. They didn't want to do another day in the life of The Beatles, and they didn't want to do anything like *Help!* The only thing I suggested, which is kind of funny because later Dick did this without them, was 'You ought to play 'The Three Musketeers.'" But they didn't. It's probably just as well that they didn't!"

The British playwright Joe Orton left an illuminating account in his diary of how potential screenwriters dealt with being tapped by The Beatles' entourage for a script. Orton, whose plays *Entertaining Mr. Sloane* and *Loot* were theatrical successes in London, was contacted by Shenson in January 1967 to rework a script titled *Shades Of A Personality*, which Shenson felt was "dull." "Somebody introduced me to Joe Orton because they knew I was looking for a writer," Shenson says. "And I met with him. And he said he'd like to take some time off to try something. And I said, 'Fine.'"

Shenson and The Beatles during the filming of *Help!*

Orton finished the script, now titled *Up Against It*, in February and sent it off to Shenson in March. Unfortunately, Orton's anarchic farce was not what Shenson had in mind for the Fabs.

"I read the script, and it was just terrible," Shenson says. "The Beatles were very interested in him because he was so hot at the time. But when I said, 'You want to read it?' they said, 'No, no, no, if you say it's no good, forget about it.' They didn't even read it, though I think Paul might have read it later. I know I was justified in turning it down. I didn't want to be responsible for the boys to do that kind of a script. It was pretty far out. I told Brian Epstein to read it, and if he wanted to do it, go ahead, just don't include me. But they all agreed not to."

The inability to find a suitable script temporarily ended Shenson's association with The Beatles. "It would've been nice to make a third picture," Shenson says, "but it became this big challenge. So I got on to other things."

Shenson eventually returned to America and rarely saw The Beatles again.

"I ran into Ringo once," he recalls. "And I sent something to John to see if he'd be interested in doing it when he was living in New York. And he wrote me a note back saying, 'Thanks, but no thanks.' It was very cute. What I do cherish is that he autographed a book of his poetry to me, something like 'To good old Walter from good old John.' And I received an invitation to attend the memorial service for Paul's wife in New York, which I couldn't go to. So I must be thought of OK! I was very glad to receive it, knowing that he put me on the list."

On returning to the U.S., Shenson briefly worked at a studio again. "I had an office at MGM, and they asked me to try and develop some things," he says. "But I went crazy, because I forgot that in Hollywood, pitches are made by committees! And my ideas never jumped at them, and I decided I'd better go off and do them on my own. I don't think I would be able to work at a studio. I'm just too old and I know too much. And I think a lot of the studios are guessing; they really don't know what they're doing. And the big thing these days is how many big stars can you get into a film, and they get very expensive. And I don't like that responsibility."

As Shenson continued to find success with critically acclaimed films such as *Rueben Rueben* and *Echo Park*, his previous association with The Beatles began to fade in the public mind. "I'm pretty low-key," he says. "A lot of people about don't know that. Like I'm trying to put together a small comedy now, and some of the people we're interviewing weren't born then, and they see I have a one sheet [for *A Hard Day's Night*] in my outer office and they come in and say, 'Oh, I didn't know you produced The Beatles' films!'"

But in 1979 he became caught in dealing with The Beatles again due to a clause in his contract with UA in which the rights to both *A Hard Day's Night* and *Help!* reverted to him after 15 years. "It was unusual, but United Artists did that," Shenson explains. "United Artists in those days was not a studio, they just put up the money and distributed films for independent producers. And it was in the contract with these low-budget pictures that the producer automatically got the rights back after 15 years. And when 15 years were up, I received a letter from United Artists, asking me what to do with the negative and all the prints and all that. I said, 'Keep 'em. Why don't you just keep distributing the picture?' And their attitude was, 'Oh no, they're all finished by now. Just take the stuff.' So they literally forced me to do it!"

Shenson did consider selling the rights to The Beatles. "They talked about it at one time," he says. "They have an accountant here. But he was a little smug and I just walked out of the room. But I deal with their manager all the time, Neil Aspinall. We call each other frequently. He's a good man. He's very dedicated, and they can trust him. So I own the rights, but they share in the profits. And believe it or not, I have to send them checks! It's kind of silly, but I do it."

Shenson's first project was arranging a theatrical reissue of *A Hard Day's Night* in 1982, though he concedes, "It didn't do very well. Maybe the timing was wrong."

The film was released on video the following year, with *Help!* released on video in 1987. Both films are currently available from MPI home video, who reissued both in 1995 with bonus footage. MPI also carries related Beatles videos such as *Magical Mystery Tour*, *The Beatles: The First U.S. Visit*, *You Can't Do That: The Making Of A Hard Day's Night*, *Ringo Starr And His All-Starr Band Live From Montreux* and the just-released *Ringo Starr And His Fourth All-Starr Band.* In 1992, *A Hard Day's Night* became the first feature-length film released in CD-ROM format, and *A Hard Day's Night* and *Help!* have also been released in laser disc and DVD formats by MPI, of which Shenson says, "My own feeling is that a lot of that stuff is just eyewash."

Nonetheless, Shenson invested in some "eyewash" himself when he arranged for both films to be restored in the mid-90s. "*A Hard Day's Night* is absolutely gorgeous now," he says. "The blacks are black and the whites are white. It's very sharp. *Help!* is also beautiful. Because of the color, you have to be careful. That can start to fade away. But we made a new negative and what they call an inter-positive, so we can make prints of it. They're both in first class condition. And they're in a vault here. I've been honored, because they have a vault at the Academy Of Motion Picture Arts And Sciences where they keep classic films, and they asked if they could hold them for us. Which meant one, I didn't have to pay for the storage, and two, they brag about the fact that they're sitting on the negatives of those two pictures. I think they're on the shelf next to *The Godfather*."

Shenson is also on call to speak about his work with The Beatles, appearing at Los Angeles-area colleges to screen *A Hard Day's Night* and talk to the class afterward.

"The first question I always ask is, 'How many of you had seen it before?'" he says of one such appearance. "And out of about 100, would you believe maybe six hands went up of college age kids that had seen *A Hard Day's Night*. And then they kept me there for an hour and a half, asking me all kinds of questions. I said, 'Do you feel the film is dated?' And they

> **"We think this will go out and do better business than some brand-new pictures!"**
>
> ***— Walter Shenson on the re-release of* A Hard Day's Night *to the theaters***

said, 'Oh, no.' One cute girl said, 'My skirts are just as short as they were in your picture.' And some boy said, 'And my hair is about as long as The Beatles' hair.' And the bottom line was no, it's not dated, it's just British."

Shenson also noticed a lack of awareness about the film when the restored version of *A Hard Day's Night* was screened at the Academy Of Motion Picture Arts And Sciences.

"A lot of older people came to see the film," he says. "And a lot of them are my friends. And they called me at home or caught me in the lobby and confessed that they hadn't seen the picture before. All of my friends in Hollywood, writers and directors and big people in the industry, they lied to me! They said they saw the picture and they hadn't! 'Why didn't you see it?' 'Well, we didn't want to go. There was a bunch of screaming kids in the audience.' I could understand. It didn't bother me, it's just that they said, 'My God, what a good movie!' And so I said, 'Fine, you should've seen it then.'"

The theatrical reissue of *A Hard Day's Night* will be of the print screened at the Academy, with a new soundtrack in direct mono, and the music in two-track stereo. "We have brought it up to date, technically," he says. "We think there's a big audience of younger people who know The Beatles, have been brought up with Beatles music and have not seen the film. I was very careful not to saturate television with *A Hard Day's Night* and *Help!*. AMC and PBS [stations that screened both films in the last three years], that's not a big audience. So there's a whole new audience of young people who have never seen the films. And we're not disregarding the older people who might want to go for nostalgic reasons. So I think we have a pretty good potential audience for the film, don't you?"

Shenson's reason for giving the new print a theatrical, rather than a straight-to-video, reissue is economic. "You make more money!" he says. "We think this will go out and do better business than some brand-new pictures!" The reissue will also include new behind-the-scenes footage after the film's final credits and possibly the inclusion of the song "You Can't Do That," cut from the film's concert sequence (and included in full on the video *You Can't Do That: The Making Of A Hard Day's Night*). A theatrical reissue of *Help!* may follow, along with a video release of both upgraded films.

Scene from *A Hard Day's Night*.

Shenson also hopes the *Hard Day's Night* reissue will tap into the interest generated by *The Beatles Anthology*. "When The Beatles came out with their *Anthology*, there was a huge surge of interest, and that was reflected in big videocassette sales," he says. "And there were only clips from *A Hard Day's Night* and *Help!* in the *Anthology*, very little. The video cassettes sold like hell, and this interest created a new audience. There are an awful lot of very young people that were not around or were babies during the period that The Beatles were really high. And now there's another generation. I talk to people who have little girls nine or 10 years old that are Beatles fans. And that's because their parents were. So there's always been an ongoing audience, even a growing audience. And it's just going on and on and on."

And as to what has made these two Beatles films live on with audiences is something Shenson admits he's not totally certain of.

"I think the fact that the films were witty and entertaining, apart from featuring The Beatles," he says. "The films were intelligent. They're not silly. They look like they were made by filmmakers who know what they're doing. Plus the fact that The Beatles' charm and their personalities really jump out at the audience. They have that magic that movie stars need."

A magic that has made both films classics of their era.

A year in the life: The Beatles in 1967

by Gillian G. Gaar

Though it seemed that something of historic significance happened to The Beatles every year of the 1960s, 1967 was, in many ways, the high watermark of their career. In hindsight, it was the last time The Beatles were seen as a group, presenting a united front to the world. Yet the year began with a sense of apprehension on the part of some fans, due to The Beatles' announcement that they planned to give up touring. This was a bold step at a time when groups regularly issued two or even three albums in a year, accompanied by tours and other personal appearances. The band's recorded output had dropped over the past year as well, with only one new single and album being released in Britain ("Yellow Submarine"/"Eleanor Rigby" having been taken from *Revolver*).

So it was both ironic, and a portent of things to come, that the first Beatles-related release of the year was not a record by the group but a solo album — Paul McCartney's soundtrack album for the British film *The Family Way* (a single from the album had been released only in the U.K. in December 1966, the same month the film had its world premiere). The record didn't chart, but it did mark the first time a member of the group had worked on a solo musical project (a year later, George Harrison's first solo album would also be a soundtrack: *Wonderwall Music*).

But as the album didn't prove to be a big seller (and the film wasn't released in the U.S. until June 1967), no one viewed *The Family Way* as a sign that The Beatles might be interested in taking on more outside projects. Indeed, in January, the group signed a new nine-year contract with EMI Records, and in April, they formed a business partnership, Beatles & Co., which would keep the group together legally for 10 years. Their contract with their manager, Brian Epstein, was due to expire in October, but it seemed likely it would be renewed, if under different terms.

Of more importance to The Beatles when the year began was the demand for a new single. The group had been working on three tracks since November '66, "Strawberry Fields Forever," "When I'm Sixty-Four," and "Penny Lane." January was spent completing "Penny Lane" and it was decided to couple this track with "Strawberry Fields" for the new single.

On Jan. 30 and 31 and Feb. 5 and 7, the group filmed promo films for each song. Much has been made over The Beatles' "pioneering" in the realm of what would eventually be called music videos. In fact, The Beatles were simply building on an existing format. Promo films with performers singing (or miming) their hit songs had been around since the 1940s. When rock emerged in the '50s, directors began looking for more interesting settings for their artists, though most films were still performance-oriented. Director Richard Lester had taken The Beatles to the next level in the "Can't Buy Me Love" and "Ticket To Ride" sequences in *A Hard Day's Night* and *Help!*, respectively, which featured no lip-

This article originally appeared in Goldmine issue #451, Nov. 7, 1997.

syncing from the group, something readily picked up and imitated on the TV series *The Monkees*.

When the films were screened on shows such as *American Bandstand*, the aspect fans were asked to comment on was The Beatles' physical appearance. Their long hair had provoked much comment in '63 and '64, and now the group's new moustaches came in for scrutiny. There were further ripples of surprise when the single (released Feb. 13 in the U.S., Feb. 17 in the U.K.) failed to reach #1 in Britain, resulting in the inevitable "Are The Beatles slipping?" articles (while in the U.S., "Penny Lane" reached #1, "Strawberry Fields" #8).

But there were those who better appreciated the incredible developments The Beatles were making in their music. Author Hunter Davies recalled being "amazed" by "Strawberry Fields" when Epstein first played it for him ("It was such a leap forward"). Davies, a journalist with the London *Sunday Times*, had long had an interest in The Beatles and had finally suggested the need for an authorized biography to McCartney in '66. McCartney agreed and helped Davies draft a letter to Epstein in December. By the end of January, Epstein had agreed. Davies could hardly have imagined the tumultuous events that would take place throughout the rest of the year that he would now be well-placed to observe first-hand.

Another writer given a sneak preview of The Beatles' first single of 1967 was the playwright Joe Orton. Orton's plays such as *Entertaining Mr. Sloane* and *Loot* had gained notoriety for his irreverent presentation of such taboo topics as death, religion and sexuality. The Beatles had been searching for a script for their third film for more than a year by 1967. A day after winning the *Evening Standard* award for *Loot* (the U.K. equivalent of the Tony), Orton was contacted by The Beatles' film producer Walter Shenson to look at and rework a script the group was considering.

Recorded by THE BEATLES on Capitol Records
SGT. PEPPER'S LONELY HEARTS CLUB BAND
Words & Music by JOHN LENNON and PAUL McCARTNEY
SGT PEPPERS
LONELY HEARTS
CLUB BAND
KEYS
05027
Maclen Music Inc.

The script, *Shades Of A Personality*, by Owen Holder, had The Beatles playing different aspects of one man's persona. Orton was attracted to the possible sexual ambiguities of the story; "Already have the idea that the end should be a church with four bridegrooms and one bride," he wrote in his diary.

He also decided to draw on two previously unpublished novels of his, *The Silver Bucket* and *The Vision Of Gombold Provost* (published postumously as *Head To Toe*). Of the latter book, he noted in his diary, "Miraculously, towards the middle of the novel four young men appear. Might have been designed with The Beatles in mind."

This statement was bizarrely misquoted in Roy Carr's *Beatles At The Movies* as "With its political assassination, guerrilla warfare and transvestism — it might have been designed with The Beatles in mind!" But Carr was right about the script's outrageousness, which contained all of the aforementioned elements. Orton regularly met with Shenson and had dinner with McCartney at Epstein's home where he heard the new Beatles single (Orton favored "Penny Lane"). He submitted his script, *Up Against It*, at the beginning of March. It was returned on April 4 with no comment. Orton's private assessment was "Fuck them," though in public he put on a more concillatory face, saying to the *Evening Standard*, "I must admit I always thought that the combination of The Beatles, whom I admire very much, and myself, was too good to be true."

In *Beatles At The Movies*, McCartney says the group wasn't interested in Orton's script because... "it was gay. We weren't gay." Actually, none of the characters The Beatles would've played were gay; all had female love interests (though they do end up marrying one woman). After The Beatles' rejection of the script, Orton rewrote it, eliminating one of the four male leads ("It's a much better script without the weight of the stars hanging on it," he wrote), and it's this version that was later published by Methuen. The script was later adapted by Todd Rundgren as a Broadway musical; most recently, *Up Against It* was broadcast as a radio play on the BBC in September '97.

But locating a suitable script was a side project for the group, who were in the midst of working on what would be their most acclaimed album to date: *Sgt. Pepper's Lonely Hearts Club Band*. After completing work on "Penny Lane," the next track the group worked on was "A Day In The Life" (a Feb. 10 recording session, devoted to recording the song's orchestral build-up, would be filmed), and gradually the idea of presenting themselves not as The Beatles but an alter-ego group developed. Buoyed by their enthusiasm and free to indulge in experimentation, work on *Sgt. Pepper* continued until April 21,

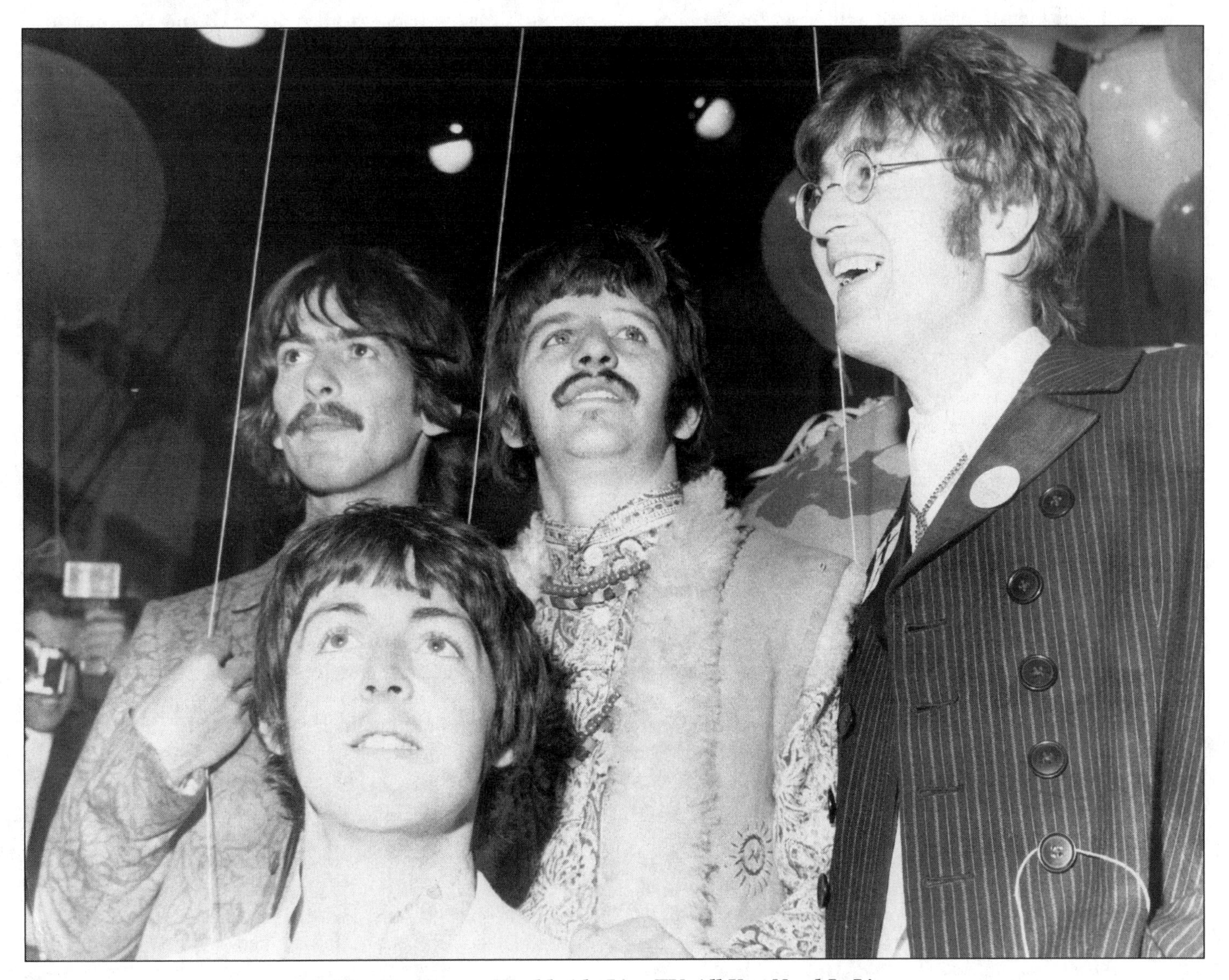

The Beatles on *Worldwide Live TV, All You Need Is Live*.

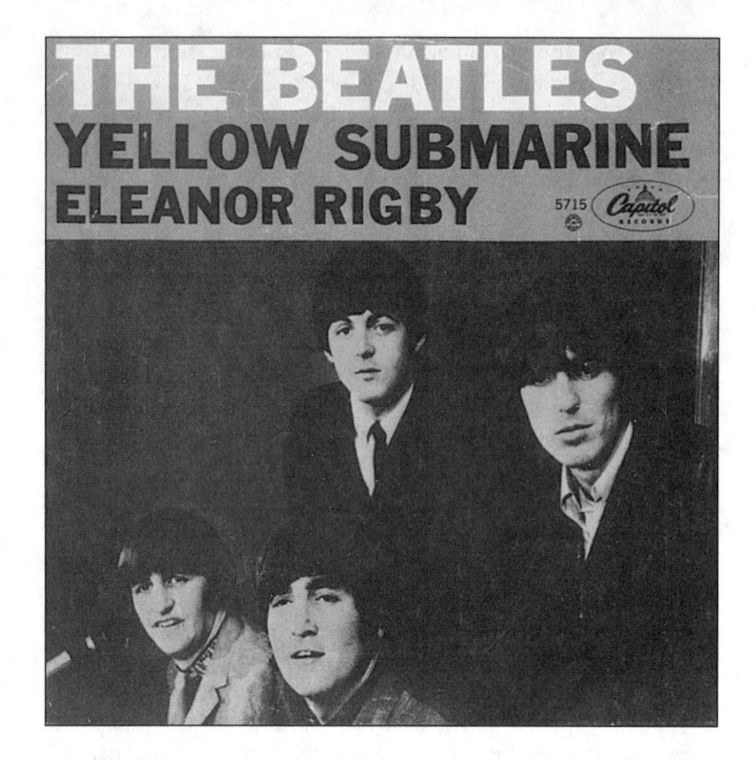

when The Beatles put the final touches on recording appropriately weird noises for the album's run-out groove.

The Beatles had spent longer on *Sgt. Pepper* than on any other album; as Mark Lewisohn noted in *The Complete Beatles Chronicle*, the 700 hours they spent on *Sgt. Pepper* was 318 times greater than the time they'd spent on their first album, *Please Please Me*. The recording sessions also marked the first time the group had used another studio besides EMI's, recording "Fixing A Hole" at Regent Sound Studio. Hunter Davies, present at recording and songwriting sessions during this period, duly documented his observations in his biography.

There were also elaborate preparations for *Sgt. Pepper's* cover. Peter Blake, working with The Beatles, had designed the striking front cover shot, which features the group decked out in satin uniforms, in front of a collection of favorite famous faces. EMI had worried that people would object to their appearance on an album cover and insisted that The Beatles contact as many living people as possible to secure their permission; they also insisted that Ghandi be removed. The cover photo was photographed by Michael Cooper on March 30. The rest of the album's presentation was equally elaborate; the gatefold sleeve had, for the first time, the album's lyrics on the back cover. There was also a sheet of cut-out "surprises," such as a cardboard moustache.

The Beatles hardly paused for breath when *Sgt. Pepper* was completed. Even as the album was being mixed in April, The Beatles began working on Harrison's "Only A Northern Song," which they'd first worked on in February. They then commenced work on *Magical Mystery Tour*, based on a idea McCartney had on a recent visit to America, having been inspired by the travels of author Ken (*One Flew Over The Cuckoo's Nest*) Kesey's gang of friends, the self-described "Merry Pranksters' (and immortalized in Thomas Wolfe's *The Electric Kool-Aid Acid Test*).

Magical Mystery Tour would provide the basis for The Beatles' next film, though before shooting had started yet another film project was announced. In order to finally resolve their three-picture deal with United Artists, it was agreed that The Beatles' third movie would be an animated feature, produced by the team that had been working on a Beatles animated TV series airing in the U.S. If The Beatles themselves were initially unenthusiastic, at least the film, eventually titled *Yellow Submarine* and released in 1968, wouldn't require their participation beyond contributing a few songs to the soundtrack (the group eventually filmed a brief sequence tacked on to the end of the movie).

The Beatles recorded the *Yellow Submarine* songs in a number of different studios, including Olympic Sound and De Lane Lea. Other sessions of the time produced endless jams and experimental tracks such as "You Know My Name (Look Up The Number)." Of greater importance was the impending release of *Sgt. Pepper*. On May 19, Epstein hosted a listening party for the press at his London home; photographer Linda Eastman, who had previously met McCartney May 15 at a Georgie Fame gig at the Bag O'Nails night club, was among those in attendance. The album was previewed in the U.K. the following day on BBC radio. Though scheduled for release in the U.K. on June 1, *Sgt. Pepper* was rush released on May 26; U.S. release followed on June 2.

The album generated instant acclaim, and it's hardly an exaggeration to say that *Sgt. Pepper* pushed rock to a new level; indeed, it can easily be regarded as the coming of age of rock. Quite simply, The Beatles took rock where no one else had dared.

"It was like throwing down a hat in the center of a ring," said John Sebastian of Lovin' Spoonful. "It was a tremendous challenge."

No one else had taken such a desperate variety of styles — Indian ragas, music hall, ballad — and blended them so deftly.

"Certainly the most brilliant of The Beatles records," wrote Joe Orion. "They get better all the time."

One artist who seemed to think so was Jimi Hendrix, who performed his own version of the title track when he appeared at London's Saville Theatre (owned by Epstein) on June 4, with McCartney and Harrison in attendance. The album was successful commercially as well, entering the U.K. charts at #1 where it remained for 22 weeks. In the U.S., *Sgt. Pepper* reached #1 in its second week, where it stayed for 15 weeks. In both countries, the album remained in the Top 10 until the following year.

The release of *Sgt. Pepper* was but one event in a memorable month. There was controversy about a *Life* magazine story in which McCartney said he'd taken LSD; he attempted to defend himself in a television interview on June 19 but was nonetheless roundly condemned around the world by moralists who believed Beatles fans would follow their example and become drug users themselves (the following month, The Beatles and Epstein would sign a petition published in the *London Times* promoting the legalization of marijuana).

Fortunately, the media's attention was soon deflected by a more notable occasion: The Beatles' appearance on the first-ever global satellite program, *Our World*. The Beatles would perform their archetypal Summer Of Love anthem, "All You Need Is Love," on the show, broadcast on June 25 from Abbey Road Studios' Studio One, and the remainder of June was spent on rehearsals. For the broadcast itself, The Beatles dressed in colorful attire and invited a number of friends, including Mick Jagger and Marianne Faithfull, Hunter Davies, and McCartney's brother Mike McGear. The group played to a backing track, with the vocals, lead guitar, bass, drums, and orchestra recorded live. Figures for estimated audience ranged from 150 to 400 million. Whatever the total, it was certainly the largest audience of The Beatles' career.

Immediately after the broadcast, John Lennon re-recorded his vocal, and the song, coupled with "Baby You're A Rich Man" (recorded in May) was released as a single on July 7 in the U.K., July 14 in the U.S. After the worldwide exposure via *Our World*, the single had little trouble reaching #1 in both countries.

The Beatles then took a well-deserved break during July, not returning to the studio until Aug. 22 to work on songs for *Magical Mystery Tour* (again recording at a new studio, Chappell Recording). A week and a half earlier, on Aug. 9, Joe Orton had been found dead in his flat, having been murdered by his longtime lover Kenneth Halliwell (an unsuccessful writer and artist), who then committed suicide. After reworking *Up Against It*, Orton had been in negotiation with producer Oscar Lewenstein and had scheduled a meeting with Lewenstein and Richard Lester on Aug. 9; the chauffeur sent to collect Orton, failing to get an answer, contacted the police. "A Day In The Life" was played at Orton's funeral. Orton's story was later told in the film *Prick Up Your Ears*, though his encounters with The Beatles as presented in the film are fictionalized.

Little did The Beatles realize that a new era in their own career was about to begin amid equally tragic circumstances. On Thursday, Aug. 24, Lennon, McCartney, and Harrison attended a lecture by the Maharishi Mahesh Yogi held at the Park Lane Hilton Hotel. Impressed by what they heard of the Maharishi's teachings of meditation and spiritual enlightenment, all The Beatles left the following day for a weekend seminar the Maharishi was holding in Bangor, North Wales. Brian Epstein was invited but declined to go, having arranged a weekend in the country with friends.

***MMT* album.**

***MMT* EP.**

However, when most of Epstein's guests failed to turn up, he returned to London Friday night, leaving Beatles aides Peter Brown and Geoffrey Ellis at his country home in Sussex. He spoke to his friends on the phone on Saturday, saying he would return to Sussex that evening. But when he failed to return or call or emerge from his room, Epstein's housekeepers became worried and a doctor was summoned, Epstein was found dead. The official ruling was "death by misadventure" (due to an overdose of prescribed medication), but, typically, conspiracy theories hinting at murder have continued to surface over the years, despite the lack of evidence.

The Beatles immediately returned to London from Bangor, though out of respect for Epstein's family, none of them attended the funeral on Aug. 29 (they did attend a memorial service held in October). A question of pressing concern was who they would choose to handle their affairs. The Beatles ultimately chose to manage themselves, a decision that would eventually degenerate into chaos. Epstein's business decisions have been criticized over the years because he did not secure as much money as possible for The Beatles; yet as subsequent events were to show, those advisors who did come on board with more concern for profits than The Beatles' well-being hastened the group's demise.

Certainly Epstein's organizational skills were sorely missed on the filming of *Magical Mystery Tour*. The group, along with a busload of friends and a film crew, set out for week's improvisational filming on Sept. 11. Working without a proper script was one thing; showing up unannounced in a small town expecting hotel bookings for nearly 50 people was another. Neither did The Beatles think of booking a studio for interior shooting. The bulk of the filming was completed in September, though shooting continued until Nov. 3, with footage for the "Blue Jay Way" sequence shot at Ringo Starr's house. The editing, which they'd expected to complete in one week, took 11 weeks. "If Brian had been alive," said Peter Brown in *The Love You Make: An Insider's Story Of The Beatles*, "it never would have happened the way it did."

With recording of the *Magical Mystery Tour* songs completed, The Beatles' final project for the year was shooting promo films for their next scheduled single, "Hello Goodbye" at the Saville Theatre (the single, b/w "I Am The Walrus," was released Nov. 24 in the U.K., Nov. 27 in the U.S.). Two of the promos were straightforward performance films, the group dressed in their *Sgt. Pepper* outfits for one and psychedelic "street" clothes in another. A third clip was made of outtakes. McCartney was cited as the director of the clips, though in a recent issue of *Beatlefan*, Tony Bramwell, another Beatles aide, said he was primarily responsible for directing the clips. Later, to circumvent a "miming ban" the Musicians' Union had passed, another clip was edited for British TV, containing no performance footage.

While waiting for *Magical Mystery Tour* to be screened on TV, The Beatles kept busy with a variety of projects. Lennon's friendship with the Japanese artist Yoko Ono (whom he had met in November 1966) was furthered by his financing of her show, *Yoko Plus Me*, which opened Oct. 11 at London's Lisson Gallery, though Lennon's sponsorship remained anonymous. On Oct. 18, *How I Won The War*, the Richard Lester-directed film that was Lennon's only solo film outing, had its world premiere in London, with all The Beatles in attendance. Lennon had been attracted to the film's antiwar slant, but the story proved too abstract and self-consciously "arty" for most people; others felt it was disrespectful to the nation's military. This did not stop United Artists from releasing a single from the film, credited to "Musketeer Gripweed [Lennon's character] And The Third Troop," which featured a very brief spoken-word contribution from Lennon.

In December, Starr flew to Rome to begin shooting his solo film outing in the film *Candy*. With McCartney on vacation, Lennon and Harrison were the only Beatles on hand when a party for area secretaries of the Official Beatles Fan Club was held Dec. 17 at London's Hanover Grand Film And Art Theatre. Attendees were treated to an advance screening of *Magical Mystery Tour* and *The Beatles At Shea Stadium*. The Beatles held a similar party for their friends on Dec. 21 at the Royal Lancaster Hotel, encouraging everyone to attend in costume.

Magical Mystery Tour was finally screened for the public on BBC 1 on Dec. 26. The reaction was fast and furious, with critics writing off the film as "rubbish." The free-form nature of the film, essentially a series of musical set pieces linked by a vague storyline (The Beatles and friends on a surreal trip through the countryside), was not exactly the mainstream fare a holiday audience expected, and the film was further hampered in that it was screened in black and white (color sets not being as common in Britain at the time, though *MMT* would be screened in color on BBC 2 on Jan. 5, 1968). McCartney quickly put in an appearance on *The David Frost Show* to answer the critics.

The film may well have done better had it been simply a collection of the musical numbers, which furthered the experimentation of the "Penny Lane" and "Strawberry Fields" promo films. Certainly the music was warmly received. In the U.K., the *MMT* songs had been released as a double EP set and reached #2 in the singles charts ("Hello Goodbye" was at #1), while in the U.S., an album fashioned out of the *MMT* songs and the group's other 1967 singles also reached #1 (as did "Hello Goodbye"). Earlier in the year, there had been plans to make a similar collection of promo films based on

Magical Mystery Tour was finally screened for the public on BBC 1 on Dec. 26. The reaction was fast and furious, with critics writing off the film as "rubbish." The free-form nature of the film, essentially a series of musical set pieces linked by a vague storyline (The Beatles and friends on a surreal trip through the countryside), was not exactly the mainstream fare a holiday audience expected.

the *Sgt. Pepper* songs (which is why one of the "Day In The Life" sessions had been filmed). Had the group opted for this plan with *MMT*, people might have focused on the imaginative ways "I Am The Walrus," "The Fool On The Hill," "Blue Jay Way," and "Your Mother Should Know" were visualized instead of remembering the film for the critical bashing The Beatles received.

Aside from Epstein's death and the critical failure of the *MMT* film, 1967 had been another remarkably successful year for The Beatles. And they were already laying plans for the new year, which would see the group attempt to take full control of their business, via their newly established company Apple Corp. Apple Publishing Ltd. had been founded in September. A London boutique, simply called "Apple," had opened on Dec. 7, following a preview party Dec. 5 that Lennon and Harrison had attended. On Dec. 11, Apple Music signed their first group, Grapefruit. The Beatles hoped that by handling the group's business themselves, they would be free from interference by the "men in suits" that characterized big business to them. The outcome would be quite different, but at the end of 1967, the future looked rosy indeed.

Life in the *Yellow Submarine*

The making of The Beatles' animinated movie

by Dr. Bob Hieronimus

In the almost 30 years since The Beatles broke up, everything the four of them ever touched or contributed to has been written about, analyzed and reanalyzed, interpreted, lauded and criticized. So why is so little still known about what is arguably one of their most vibrant (certainly most colorful) creations, the animated feature film, *Yellow Submarine*? Released in 1968 (July U.K., November U.S.), *Yellow Submarine* created a style for a generation of animators and artists and advertisers — remember the 7-Up green submarine ads? Even the "All Around The World" video by one of 1998's hottest bands, Oasis, seems to emulate much of the style and characteristics of this influential film.

The history of *Yellow Submarine* has fallen into a Sea Of Holes like the one depicted in the film, perhaps in part because The Beatles themselves had almost nothing to do with the actual creation of this project and in fact were ready to renounce it entirely until they saw the finished product. After the massively hysterical premiere of the film at the London Pavilion that clogged up all of Piccadilly Circus on July 17, 1968, John, Paul, George, and Ringo have continued to speak fondly of *Yellow Submarine* and indeed have watched and rewatched their copies of the video over the years just like the rest of us around the world lucky enough to have purchased it while it was briefly available on the market.

Obviously, to say The Beatles had almost nothing to do with the creation of *Yellow Submarine* is ridiculous in one respect, because their songs were the inspiration for the very foundation of the plot, and they do star in the film, although in animated form with voice actors portraying their voices. But just after the release of the *Sgt. Pepper's Lonely Hearts Club Band* in what was to become known as the Summer Of Love, 1967, The Beatles were busy balancing at the pinnacle of their careers. During the short time span in which *Yellow Submarine* miraculously fell into place, the following monumental events occurred: the design and production of their own *Magical Mystery Tour* film and album through the fall of 1967, manager Brian Epstein dying in August 1967, John meeting Yoko, Apple Corps' formation, leaving for India to study with the Mararishi in February of 1968, and in May beginning to record *The White Album*.

Yellow Submarine has not been available on video in the American market for several years. The film has been subjected to several ownership disputes over the years and recently ended up back at Apple under a sub-corporation known as Subafilms. Although it is rumored that Apple is working on remastering the negative of *Yellow Submarine* for a limited theatrical and video release in 1999, nothing has been officially announced as of this writing.

This article originally appeared in Goldmine issue #477, Nov. 6, 1998.

"There was a tremendous complication with the music," said John Coates, the Director of TVC (TV Cartoons), the London animation house that produced *Yellow Submarine*. "Because some of it was Lennon and McCartney or it was Northern Songs, some of it was, oh, that other publishing company, and they could never get together and sort that out. And it wasn't until Michael Jackson bought up the entire music that it became a video. You know, for years and years people were asking what happened to the video of *Yellow Submarine*, and it wasn't able to be released because they couldn't clear the music rights. And I think that's got a lot to do with its going from one place to another. I do know that here in England the BBC had it and it's been aired three times on the BBC and got amazing audiences every time. And our Channel 4 has acquired the rights here and are about to put it out again."

John Coates was credited as Production Supervisor on the film but says what he actually did would better be described as Line Producer in today's terminology. He managed the 200 artists and was the hands-on boss, while Al Brodax, who is credited as Producer, should actually be titled Executive Producer, since he was the big boss. Writer Erich Segal remembers him fondly as 'Big Al."

"Known as such, because he wasn't big," said Segal.

If Apple re-releases *Yellow Submarine* in spring 1999 as hoped, people may be fortunate enough to watch it on the big screen again.

The first thing American audiences will notice when watching *Yellow Submarine* for the first time in years is that it contains a full three minutes they have never seen before. This is known as the "Hey Bulldog" sequence, a really catchy, rollicking song that is one of the least-known Beatles tunes since it came out only on the soundtrack album for this film. Strangely enough, the "Hey Bulldog" sequence got the axe even though it was one of only four new songs The Beatles wrote especially for the film.

It was hard enough squeezing those four contractually obligated songs ("It's All Too Much," "All Together Now," "Only A Northern Song" being the other three) out of them. At that time The Beatles were still suspicious of the producers. When first presented with the idea for a full-length feature produced by the same company who had produced the ABC-TV Beatles cartoon series, The Beatles balked and refused to be represented by something they were afraid would make them look like "the bloody Flintstones" as John Lennon called it.

It was not until they saw the designs of an up and coming Czechoslovakian designer working in Germany for an avant-guard magazine called *Twen*, did they begin to feel more comfortable about the project. Lennon was particularly impressed with Heinz Edelmann, who remembers lunching with The Beatles during the production. Edelmann recalls they ate at a peculiar, supposedly hip, SoHo restaurant where he and Lennon mostly talked about the works of Aldous Huxley. Paul McCartney seemed to bond with one of the animation directors, Jack Stokes, who was also hired to design the titles for their *Magical Mystery Tour*. The tale of Stokes and Edelmann lunching with The Beatles is retold in *Beatlefan* issue #112.

It has been years since most people have taken the trip to Pepperland, so a refresher course is in order. As the tranquil narrator's voice rolls in over psychedelically colored clouds that open into the rainbow filled utopia of Pepperland…

"Once upon a time… or maybe twice… there was a place called Pepperland." The film begins on a peaceful day in this happy kingdom, when a concert by Sergeant Pepper's Lonely Hearts Club Band is savagely interrupted by an Antimusic missile attack launched by their arch enemies, the Blue Meanies. The Chief Blue Meanie and his assistant Max, send out their 99 numbered henchmen, the dreadful flying glove, Apple Bonkers and an assortment of villains, most of which are obvious caricatures of society's various ills, all drawn with humor and acerbic wit by Edelmann's graceful hand. There are the Butterfly Stompers, the Hidden Persuaders with guns in their shoes, the Snapping Turtle Turks with their mouths in their bellies and the Count Down Clown with his nose cone nose. Determined to rule the world by stomping out music, happiness and love ("A world without

Who Were The Blue Meanies?

by Dr. Bob Hieronimus

The Blue Meanies were all entirely the creation of Heinz Edelmann, although John Lennon for some reason later in his life declared that Al Brodax had stolen some of these monsters from original Lennon ideas. Edelmann recalls that he originally intended the Meanies to be red as an obvious Cold War reference, but that either his assistant misunderstood his instructions or ran out of red paint, and when he came in the next day the Meanies were blue instead of red! The memories of Millicent McMillan, Edelmann's assistant, however, are somewhat different. She recalls Edelmann's original intention being to make the Meanies purple, but that she suggested they would look better as Blue Meanies, and he agreed. There are even more theories about who the Blue Meanies were supposed to represent. Some say the KGB, the police, the Nazis, but most of the co-creators considered them a blanket reference to the establishment status quo.

"I have the dubious distinction of having coined the phrase 'Blue Meanies,'" Erich Segal says. "See Blue Meanies in your dictionary… Blue Meanies meaning policeman. Remember the Chicago Riots? They were called the Blue Meanies? I coined that phrase." Notice some of the Blue Meanies are wearing Mickey Mouse ears, which background artist Alison DeVere says was done as a direct jibe at Walt Disney. Brodax also claims to have encouraged the anti-Disney atmosphere during the production, saying he put signs up in the studio something like "Disney: Do The Opposite!"

Brodax also added that if you look carefully at the profile of his King Features assistant, Abe Goodman, you will find that it matches the Chief Blue Meanie. Charlie Jenkins agrees, saying that even Brodax was used as a model for the Blue Meanies. Jenkins remembers that when the Blue Meanie characters were first introduced by Edelmann, "Brodax got cold feet, because he realized what Heinz was doing. Heinz didn't like those [people] from King Features at all. He abhorred them. They were quite mean, always trying to cut things down, pare it down. He didn't like them, so he invented Blue Meanies around King Features people. It was a personal and political comment by Heinz about the producers."

Apple/Paul McCartney PR man Geoff Baker and The Chief Blue Meanie greet arrivals at the *Yellow Submarine* premiere, Philharmonic Hall in Liverpool during Beatles week in 1999.

music is a Blue world!"), the Blue Meanies turn Pepperland into a police state populated by grey lifeless statues.

Old Fred is the conductor of the Band and he flees the attack and reaches the Lord Mayor, who puts him into the *Yellow Submarine* for a last-minute escape in search of help. The sub surfaces in Liverpool and begins to follow a depressed Ringo, radarlike, as he wanders aimlessly about the streets of Liverpool in boredom ("Liverpool can be a lonely place on a Saturday night. And this is only Thursday morning!") Ringo notices he's being followed and runs up a large hill to a strange house called "The Pier." For this scene, Special Sequences designer Charlie Jenkins used a photograph of a real building in Liverpool, which he says sits on top of Penny Lane. Old Fred follows Ringo into the house, explains about the Meanie attack, and enlists Ringo's aid. They proceed to round up the others. John materializes out of a great literary creation, Frankenstein; George appears out of haze of transcendental meditation; Paul emerges from a concert playing classical music.

The Beatles board the *Yellow Submarine* and head for Pepperland. They are detoured through the Seas of Time, Science, Monsters, Nowhere, Phrenology, Green and Holes. They undergo time warps, chase Lucy through her "Sky With Diamonds," climb clocks, become ancient and infantile, are molecularized, actually "disappear up their own existences" and almost drown in an avalanche of apples, among other adventures.

A *Yellow Submarine*–themed cab in Liverpool.

Ringo takes a liking to the superintellectual Boob, a poetic personification of the "Nowhere Man," and takes him along on the trip. In the Sea Of Holes the Boob is captured by a Blue Meanie. A pepper-powered sneeze propels The Beatles through the Sea Of Holes where they finally find the Sea Of Green, which is the entrance to Pepperland. After unbonking the Lord Mayor, he remarks how much The Beatles resemble the original Sergeant Pepper Band. Disguised as an Apple Bonker, The Beatles infiltrate the musical instrument compound, and when armed with their guitars and instruments, The Beatles go to battle using their "All You Need Is Love" philosophy to win their antagonists over to the side of peace. They do not use any violence. Instead they transform their enemies into friends.

The film closes with a brief appearance by the live Beatles who warn us that newer and bluer meanies have been seen within the vicinity of this theater. There's only one way to go out! And that's singing!!! All together now…

Although most Americans will mistakenly guess that it was Peter Max who designed what later became known as "*Yellow Submarine* Art," the real genius behind this look is Czechoslovakian-born artist Edelmann. For the past 30 years Edelmann has been a professor at the Stuttgart Academy Of Fine Art while continuing to work in advertising, poster design for films, book design and illustration, magazine illustration and earning his acclaim as "one of the best designers in Europe," (in the words of Milton Glaser, founder of Push Pin Studios, New York). Edelmann's reluctance to talk about *Yellow Submarine* is another reason the real story about how this film came to be is not well known. *Yellow Submarine*

Real People And Places Seen In *Yellow Submarine*

by Dr. Bob Hieronimus

Watch the "Eleanor Rigby" sequence in *Yellow Submarine* carefully and you will see real photographs and "animated film" of many of the co-creators of this movie who are discussed in this article. The man trying to escape from the phone booth is the owner of the artists' favorite pub, The Dog And Duck. The fellow playing with the Jack Russell dog is the publican. The fellow in the motorcycle helmet with a tear running down his goggles is their handicapped messenger boy, Brian Endel. On the roof tops you'll see duplicates of two umbrella holding gentlemen: Director George Dunning and Art Director Heinz Edelmann. All the football (soccer) players, both teams, were made up of photographs of Tony Cuthbert, one of the film's animators. The woman who could be posing as Eleanor Rigby, who is carrying a fish bowl when the *Yellow Submarine* passes over and is reflected in it, is background artist Alison DeVere. The two ladies eating Fuller's Chocolates in the window are bookkeeper Ellen Hall and her friend, Phyllis Davis. Al Brodax, pipe in mouth, is seen in one of the alleys of Liverpool, and Abe Goodman, the film's production coordinator can been seen in profile on another street. Animation Director Bob Balser appears on a multistoried building looking as if he's about to leap. According to Brodax, Old Fred was modeled after a waiter at "Wheelers," another favorite drinking haunt of the *Yellow Submarine* crew. Charlie Jenkins, however, the Special Effects Designer who designed this scene, disagreed, saying that Jack Stokes was the model for Old Fred. Stokes was the Animation Director for the Pepperland scenes.

In the Sea Of Time a man in a derby hat holding a pocket watch is Sottish animator Ian Cowan, a watercolorist who worked closely with Edelmann and did much of the film's background work.

only a northern song

by george harrison

APPLE FILMS present a KING FEATURES production

The Beatles
Yellow Submarine

Nothing is Real
Starring
SGT. PEPPERS LONELY HEARTS CLUB BAND
From an original story by LEE MINOFF Based upon a song by JOHN LENNON and PAUL McCARTNEY
Screenplay by
LEE MINOFF and AL BRODAX JACK MENDELSOHN and ERICH SEGAL
Design HEINZ EDELMANN Produced by AL BRODAX Directed by GEORGE DUNNING
An Animated Live-Action Extravaganza
COLOUR BY DELUXE

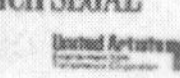

has felt like an albatross, he says. Edelmann is internationally renowned for his poster illustrations and typography and has had several one-man shows in Europe, the U.S. and Japan. He grew so annoyed at consistently being asked if held ever got to meet The Beatles while working on *Submarine*, that his daughter, Valentin, now an accomplished designer in her own right, remembers it was a forbidden topic in their house. He has granted this author numerous exclusive interviews on the subject over the past five years but wrote in a recent letter after explaining a lengthy answer, "Let anyone who mentions *Yellow Submarine* in my hearing after this be flattened into a carpet by a bolt of lightning and eaten by moths!"

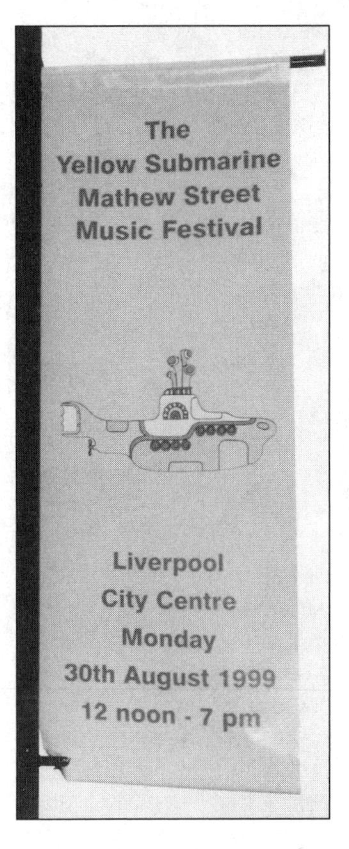

Beatles week in Liverpool in 1999 was abuzz about *Yellow Submarine*'s rerelease.

Without knowing what happened behind the scenes, it may be hard to imagine that the creation of something that exuded so much peace and love and flower power is remembered by its designer with such distaste. Edelmann was originally hired for a two-month job to create the designs for *Yellow Submarine* and then planned to return to his job in Germany. But because of lack of direction, the floundering for a script that went through dozens of rewrites and rebirths and other complications, Edelmann ended up staying in London for the entire year. He felt enormous pressure as he was called upon to design almost nonstop for the entire production ordeal of 11 months. He took on a schedule of sleeping for only four hours every other day and as a result, his health took a terrible beating. He also suffered a bout of food poisoning and almost lost his eyesight from the strain. It took two years to recover his health from the project, understandably leaving it as a painful memory.

With no one trumpeting around the claim that he was the designer responsible for *Yellow Submarine* Art, American pop artist Max received the mantle by default. Many assume it was Max's work, and he is often referred to in print or when being introduced on television as the one who did *Yellow Submarine*. Max says he does not usually take the time to correct people because he believes he inspired the look of the film anyway, so it was his gift to the world in a sense. According to Max, Al Brodax, the film's producer, originally tried to hire him to design the film, but they couldn't agree on terms. It is Max's opinion that Brodax specifically sought out Edelmann as a designer with a style similar to his own because he knew that The Beatles had already expressed their admiration for the Peter Max look. Brodax denies that this encounter ever happened, even though Max claims to have a contract to back up the story. Brodax says he's mixing it up with another contract for an *Alice In Wonderland* feature that they did discuss doing together, but never did they discuss doing *Yellow Submarine*. Brodax has even threatened to sue Max if he doesn't stop allowing himself to be identified as the man responsible for *Yellow Submarine*.

"I never claimed any ownership to the *Yellow Submarine*," Max says. "...[It's just that] I probably styled the direction in which it went."

The truth is undisputable, however, the designs in *Yellow Submarine* all came completely out of the head of Edelmann, who says he was only vaguely aware of Max's work at the time and did not consider it of any great importance.

The Lord Mayor of Liverpool and Deborah Willhite of the U.S. Postal Service unveil the *Yellow Submarine* stamp at Liverpool's town hall.

While Edelmann did work on the film but does not like being associated with it, and Max did not work on the film but enjoys being credited for it, more than 200 other artists who really did work on the film remember the frantic-paced 11 months as a strange but precious jewel in their lives. As animation director Bob Balser said, "It was a fantastic experience. It's something that could never happen again. You could never gather the kind of people we had together."

The artists hailed from all over the world: Belgium, Czechoslovakia, Holland, Canada, U.S., Australia, France, Japan, England and Scotland. Many of those who filled in colors and traced and painted were students at local art schools whom John Coates arranged to have bussed in for the overnight shift. And they did it all for less than $1 million.

The man who spearheaded the idea to do an animated feature film starring The Beatles and their songs was Brodax, who had headed the motion picture/television department at King Features for years before. Brodax was also responsible for the ABC Beatles cartoon feature, which The Beatles loathed so much they insisted on a contractual agreement that the series could never be shown in the U.K.

Brodax explained that The Beatles "had a three picture deal, and... I had done The Beatles television series, the cartoon series which was highly successful (receiving a 45-50 ratings share), and during that whole period it was my ambition to do a full-length feature. All the time running like a fugue throughout this was the presence of Brian Epstein, who was a very difficult person. But he did make the promise that if the cartoons were successful, I'd have a short feature. Grabbing at this straw, I understood that The Beatles wanted more than anything else to go to India to get their lives straightened out with this guru. I'd had problems, at least three to four years with contact with them. At this time, I suggested that they could go to India, with my blessings and have a feature produced while they were in residence in India, and all they had to do was sign a piece of paper. I'd do the work, thereby fulfilling their contract of the three-picture deal with United Artists. So they latched on to this, and that's truly how the *Submarine* happened."

Unfortunately, by the time the approvals were given to go ahead on an animated feature there were but 11 months to complete it because of a prescheduled opening at the London Pavilion the following July 17, 1968. This was seen by many to be an impossible task since similar animated productions normally require at least two years and twice *Submarine*'s minimal budget. It is still not clear if *Yellow Submarine* was accepted by United Artists as the third film. According to Peter Brown and Steven Gaines, *Submarine* was rejected (perhaps because of the minimal input by The Beatles), and thus the need for the fourth film, *Let It Be*, to finally complete their UA contract.

"It was part of a deal [Epstein] did with United Artists," says Beatles producer Sir George Martin. "And when Brian committed [The Beatles] to the picture, he said that they would provide new songs. They said, 'Well, we're not going to write any decent songs. We'll give them all the rejects we didn't really want."

It wasn't until one of their infrequent visits to the TVC Studios to observe the production that they became enthusiastic and volunteered to do the voices and do some new songs. Unfortunately, it was too late. (The voice of John was John Clive, the voice of Paul was Geoffrey Hughes, the voice of George was Peter Batten and the voice of Ringo was Paul Angelus.)

Brodax and King Features originated the idea to produce the film and are credited as the producers, but TV Cartoons of London is where the film was actually created. The TVC animation studios in London were originally set up in the summer of 1957 to produce TV commercials, and in 1966 they had already won several awards when contracted to produce The Beatles cartoon series for King Features that ran on ABC until 1968. Many of the same artists who worked on *Submarine* still work with TVC today, and several of them have been there since the cartoon series. Since *Submarine*

Who Was The Boob?

by Dr. Bob Hieronimus

There is a great deal of speculation about the Boob and who he is supposed to be parodying. The Boob is one of the two names kept from Lee Minoff's original screenplay, but Minoff had the name attached to a chartreuse shaggy seal! Minoff says, "The Nowhere Man was based on the director of my play, Jonathan Miller, who... was a great intellectualizer... and really helped to ruin it when it finally got to Broadway... Miller could do everything. He was a writer, a doctor, a director, blah, blah, blah. But I felt he was ultimately full of shit."

Other researchers have assumed that screenwriter Erich Segal was the inspiration for the Boob, since he was a professor of classics at Yale at the time. Segal says no, but adds: "People think that The Boob was based on a professor at Yale, a friend of mine, called Jeremy Adams because he's called Jeremy Boob, but I don't remember if that's true or not. Jeremy Adams thinks so, and since he was flattered, I told him it was true. But I don't know... The Boob [was] sort of me, too, I mean, you know, I wrote those words at that particular segment. I wrote every word of it."

A display of *Yellow Submarine* memorabilia at Chicago Beatlefest in 2000.

A Blue Meanie bathroom set, believe it or not! A cup, soap dish and toothbrush holder.

many of their productions have won Emmys, Oscar nominations and other international awards. They have recently completed their final productions: *Oi! Get Off Our Train* and *The Bear*, both due for release at Christmas 1998.

After The Beatles' disappointment with the TV series, Director George Dunning was determined to turn out a quality piece for the longevity that a feature film has. Most of the creators involved credit Dunning as the one who kept the *Yellow Submarine* from slipping into the easier, sloppier product it could have become when facing the insane time crunch and the lunacy of artists painting madly before there was a solid idea what the story was going to be.

Many *Yellow Submarine* fans believed this film had been carefully planned and written, but a little research dispels that myth. Much of the dialogue and witticisms we hear in *Yellow Submarine* are the work of Erich Segal, who followed up *Yellow Submarine* with the blockbuster *Love Story* and is currently a Fellow at Wolfson College, Oxford. Segal claims that he was number 40 in a long line of revolving writers who were tried and replaced in a desperate attempt to find something The Beatles and the production team would approve of. Treatments or contributions by Joseph Heller and Tom Stoppard are rumored to have existed at one time. Brodax disputes this number, saying the total number of writers was closer to four or perhaps six — but not 40!

Because there never was a complete script from beginning to end, much of the essential "plot" was devised by designer Edelmann and the other artists. Edelmann remembers the stress of facing the unmovable deadline without a clear script/story/idea to animate.

"I think everybody was unhappy. There were about five or six completely different versions floating around, one centering about the problems of Old Fred and Mrs. Old Fred and was a sort of middle class suburban romance at that point.... There were two characters remaining from the previous script. One was a character called The Boob and the other one was Old Fred. I did Pepperland and the Meanies and... the plot which is nothing terrifically original, the rough plot, and I did all the characters.... And then I think everybody contributed to that. Then when we were about 15 minutes into the production Erich Segal came on to write bits of the dialogue. And then later on, [parts of] this was rewritten by Roger McGough."

Animation Director Bob Balser confirmed how the storyline evolved over the 11 months. "Unfortunately, there was never a storyline. They had an idea to do a film about a trip in a *Yellow Submarine*, certainly because of The Beatles' *Yellow Submarine* song. And when I got there, there was really no concrete story. And this is, I think this is probably one of the most interesting aspects of it, it's this film was created as we went along."

Balser remembers starting his artists working on animating the songs while waiting for a script.

Again Brodax's memories conflict with the others. "Well, we had a script. A lot of people deny that, but we had a fairly loosely written script, a beginning, middle and an end, that Erich and I had from the onset and once we started production. We did have to stitch it together, but the chaos that people speak of at times was really engineered chaos because it's what gave us our edge. They really didn't know where they were going all the time, except I knew, and Erich knew, and Stokes and Balser knew."

A *Yellow Submarine* cookie jar.

Brodax found Segal when he was a young assistant professor of the classics at Yale University. Segal remembers a frenzied three weeks when he was flown to London and stayed in the Londonderry Hotel where he wrote practically nonstop, around the clock, only being allowed one hour off every 24 to go for a jog around Hyde Park.

***Yellow Submarine* model kits.**

"I had three weeks, and I got this thing on course. Because 24 hours a day and... three weeks on that film was like 12 weeks on any other film. As I said, they were divided into groups of four. They were working four times as fast, with four subdirectors.... I wrote the thing in four parts at once. Because Balser had divided the artists up into teams of four. So unlike live actors, [for example] Tom Cruise can only be in one room at one time. If you're drawing them, you could have four guys drawing four Ringos, and Ringo could be in four different adventures at once. So I ended up writing the middle, the end, the beginning in no particular order. Messengers just kept coming back and forth to my room to get material. Very early in the morning, I was allowed to see dailies, which are the rough sketches. They used to do pencil sketches of the story... with my dialogue across, to see how it went. And I never left my room except to see these penciled drawings and to speak to 'Big Al' Brodax."

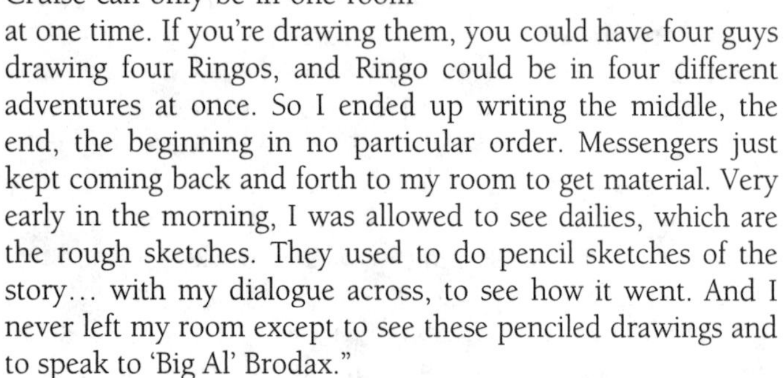

The writing credits on the film are split up between four people, with Brodax, Jack Mendelsohn and Lee Minoff being the other three. But there is a fifth person given no credit at all, who is remembered fondly by most of the co-creators as having contributed an important Liverpudlian flavor and hometown jokes. His name is Roger McGough, and he was a friend and an early influence on Lennon. He was recently awarded the MBE and is described by Edelmann as an "English poet and pop singer who is still around and still has got some reputation." McGough's contributions can be heard in the Sea Of Monsters and in the opening sequence of Ringo in Liverpool, among others, but his name does not appear anywhere in the credits.

McGough's original contract precluded his receiving a film credit, but he accepted his fate with grace. "From my point of view," he said, "I had no quarrel, really, because it had been made clear from the beginning there was no credit. You go into it with that in mind — that's it. Maybe later on when you realize you've done a lot of work, it would have been nice."

Depending on who you talk to, the production budget ran dry about three months before completion, and many of the crew members resorted to guerrilla-style tactics to remove from the clutches of King Features several portions of the work for protection until the budgetary conflicts and control over the studio was regained. It was a David and Goliath scenario that resulted in this quaint little film about a big rock 'n' roll band being preserved in animation for future generations. It was created by a studio that had never done more than five to 10 minute features, without a script, underbudgeted, in a mere 11 months and without the assistance of those whom the film was about. Looked at as a whole, *Yellow Submarine* symbolizes what the '60s were all about: the establishment's power vs. the artists' love.

Dr. Bob Hieronimus is completing his long-delayed history book on the turbulent journey of the Yellow Submarine, *which should see publication by the summer of 1999. His previous research interpreting the Great Seal Of The United States can be found at the White House, in the Congressional Record, and in the files of the late Egyptian president, Anwar El-Sadat.*

Yellow Submarine sails again!

by Mark Wallgren

Whoever said that history cannot repeat itself obviously never encountered The Beatles! In September 1999, the world witnessed the resurfacing of The Beatles' animated motion picture classic, *Yellow Submarine*, which was reissued on home video by MGM Home Entertainment, accompanied by a brand new *Yellow Submarine Songtrack* album from Capitol Records, with all of these featuring specially remastered and remixed versions of more than a dozen Beatles songs.

Originally premiered in London in July 1968, *Yellow Submarine* has charted a most remarkable course over the past three decades. Critically applauded for its unique and inspired pop art animation, it achieved considerable financial success upon worldwide general release in late 1968 and early 1969, as did its companion soundtrack album. It popped up again in 1970 on a double bill supporting The Beatles' documentary *Let It Be*. During the '70s, the film would occasionally be shown on television (John Lennon would later tell the story of how his son Sean first learned of The Beatles after viewing the movie on TV one afternoon). However, it would not be until the late '80s that MGM could issue *Yellow Submarine* on home video, although it soon went out of print, owing in part to the various legal squabbles surrounding The Beatles and Apple during that period.

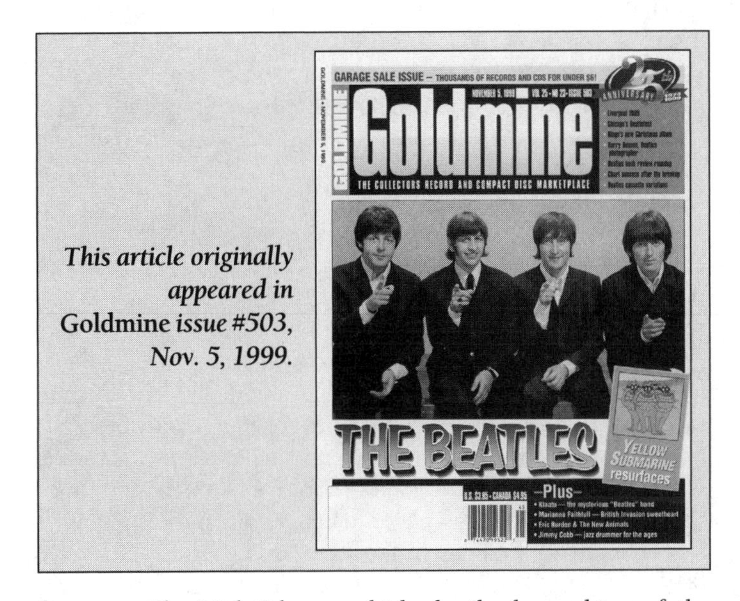

This article originally appeared in* Goldmine *issue #503, Nov. 5, 1999.

New home video

Now, more than a decade after it was last made available on the home video market, MGM Home Entertainment has re-released *Yellow Submarine* with a digitally renovated picture and remixed 5.1 Dolby Surround Sound soundtrack. MGM's Special Edition DVD is the definitive home video version of this remarkable film, offering a true state-of-the-art audio and visual experience. Presented in its original wide-screen format, the DVD presents a unique six-channel mix of the soundtrack that engulfs the home viewer as never before.

"Really to me, the biggest improvement we made in the movie is the sound," said Bruce Markoe, MGM vice president of feature post production, "the fact that we were able to remaster all of their songs in six-track digital format from scratch from the original session masters, and as well we enhanced the sound effects in the movie too. Hearing it in the six-track format is a huge improvement over what their songs sounded like before. So really the only way to hear that is in the theater in DTS digital sound or on DVD if you have a Dolby digital home theater system that can reproduce it, and even in a very modest home theater setting the sound is incredible. For most people who hear it, there's kind of a big 'Wow' factor."

In addition, the special edition DVD contains a considerable number of value-added elements for both fans and collectors including: the original theatrical trailer; the behind-the-scenes featurette *The Mod Odyssey*, which details the making of the movie; a special feature-length audio commentary track presenting John Coates, one of the film's animators, and Heinz Edelmann, the film's designer; video and audio interviews with selected cast and crew; original pencil drawings; three original storyboard sequences including two from footage that was not featured in the final film ("Battle Of The Monsters" and "Pepperland"); a special music-only track highlighting The Beatles' songs sans dialogue or added sound effects; more than two dozen behind-the-scenes still photos of The Beatles; and an eight-page full-color booklet filled with background information on the film.

The new *Yellow Submarine* VHS home video presents the fully restored film in the standard television (pan-and-scan) format, although it does not include any of the value-added elements. Even so, the VHS edition offers a greatly improved soundtrack.

According to Markoe, "The VHS actually has what we call a four-track stereo (mix). For most people, if you play it back through your television it's just two-channel, left and right stereo. But if you have a Dolby Pro Logic receiver, then you can decode the VHS cassette and you'll get four channels, left, center, right and a mono surround channel, so it is certainly an enhancement even over the *Songtrack*."

MGM has also done a remarkable job restoring the movie's fabulous colors. Hailed as one of the most innovative and landmark animated features at the time of its release, much of the film's rich and vibrant colors had drastically faded in nearly 30 years of storage.

"We had a lot of problems. The lab had to work really hard to get it, but they eventually got it to where I think it turned out real well," added Markoe.

"Hey Bulldog" sequence restored

American fans (and worldwide home video collectors) will be especially thrilled to view, at long last, the infamous "Hey Bulldog" scene, familiar to British audiences but deleted from the U.S. version of the movie. Contrary to some reports indicating that this "extra" song simply made the film drag, that is hardly the case. In fact, the inclusion of the "Hey Bulldog" scene not only provides audiences with an additional full-length Beatles song (easily the strongest of the four "new" numbers), but it also helps to push forward the storyline and brings a much-needed musical jolt late in the film.

The inclusion of "Hey Bulldog" is no simple cut-and-paste insert. Its genesis actually begins with the preceding scene wherein Sgt. Pepper's Band is seen performing inside of a giant bubble. Ringo then removes the hole from his pocket and places it on the side of the bubble, allowing the smoke to escape. This is where the British and American versions differ quite drastically.

In the newly released MGM home video, which features the original British version of the film, the smoke is seen completely emptying from inside the bubble, accompanied by 20 seconds of the instrumental opening of "Baby You're A Rich Man," which is heard faintly in the background (the song is faded before the first words are sung). With the smoke completely emptied from the bubble, Sgt. Pepper's Band descends down the steps of the bandstand and exchanges greetings and various dialogue with the four Beatles (for 30 seconds). Ringo then attempts to sound "charge" on the bugle, but his rendition is absolutely horrendous. Paul delivers his next line, "Beatles to battle... charge!" rather lethargically (Ringo is the only Beatle seen standing behind Paul during this line). The two sets of Beatles scatter, with the "real" Beatles diving for cover behind a large set of bushes, which are immediately attacked and destroyed by the Blue Meanies, forcing the Beatles to seek cover inside a nearby player piano (wherein their four alter egos have already sought refuge). At this point, the song "Hey Bulldog" commences. At the completion of the song, Sgt. Pepper's Band is seen running away, followed by three of The Beatles, before panning directly across the hillside to a shot of Ringo running straight toward the screen and then cutting to Ringo pushing his head through a bush to discover Jeremy the Boob being held prisoner by the Blue Meanies. Jeremy is not heard until after Ringo speaks to him first. From this point forward, both versions of the film feature the same concluding scenes.

Lunch boxes, model kits and pins were just the tip of the *Yellow Submarine* marketing iceberg.

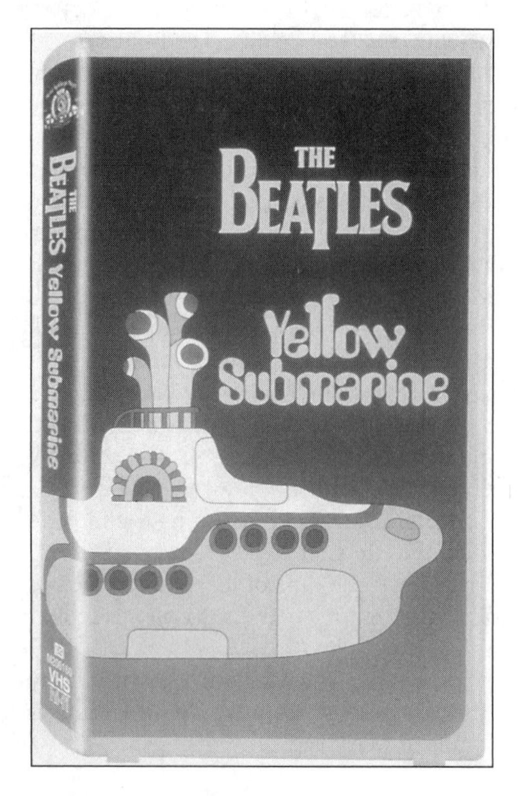

***Yellow Submarine* was re-released in 1999 with the "Hey Bulldog" song included.**

In the original American film (i.e. 1988 MGM home video version), as the smoke bellows out through the hole in the bubble, Sgt. Pepper's Band is seen performing inside, while the four Beatles stand at the base of the bandstand, dancing and singing along with the first verse of "Baby You're A Rich Man." As they do, the smoke continues to pour out (it never finishes escaping).

The song is abruptly cut after the first verse. Ringo is shown playing a perfect-note bugle-charge, the action pans to Paul (with John and George visible directly behind him), and he yells out in an excited voice, "Beatles to battle." Thereupon ensues approximately 30 seconds of additional battle footage, as the Blue Meanies are repeatedly foiled in their latest attacks (e.g. flowers repeatedly shoot out of their guns and various weapons, giant versions of the word "yes" pop up), during which loud and wildly anarchic saxophone and percussion music plays throughout. This new battle is eventually segued to the shot of Ringo running toward the screen (during which the audience hears Jeremy reciting additional lines) and subsequently pushing his head through the bushes to find Jeremy being held prisoner. This alternate sequence of events was in fact written and animated especially for the U.S. version of the movie back in 1968, once the decision was made to drop "Hey Bulldog."

Markoe personally supervised the new reconstruction and added, "To me, the 'Bulldog' sequence and the scene before it, continuity-wise, make much more sense to the story than the American version. If you're just trying to follow the story of *they rescue the guys* in the American version, all of the sudden they disappear. Now, they interact, they come down, talk to each other, and then the 'Bulldog' scene itself is the two sets of Beatles confusing the dog, and then they all run off. You never quite have a resolution as to what happened to the other guys, but it makes a little more sense to me. I think it worked out."

Altogether, the British version (i.e. new home video release) contains about four and a half minutes of footage (including the song "Hey Bulldog") otherwise not previously available (ironic to note, even the original '80s home video released in Britain presented the American version of the movie!). Conversely, the American version (i.e. original home video issues) contains approximately one minute and 10 seconds of footage that is not seen in the British version (and is no longer available on home video). Since the newly released widescreen DVD already contains substantial bonus material and is unlikely to be altered, it would appear that the only likelihood of this now-deleted U.S. scene resurfacing in the future may rest solely with the outside possibility that it could be included as a future bonus item should MGM decide at some point to issue the widescreen version of the movie on VHS. In the meantime, anyone considering trading away their original '80s MGM home video of *Yellow Submarine* may wish to hold onto it after all.

A *Yellow Submarine* enamel pin.

From soundtrack to *Songtrack*

Whereas the original 1969 *Yellow Submarine* soundtrack album presented a scant six Beatles songs alongside the instrumental score performed by the George Martin Orchestra, Capitol Records' brand-new *Yellow Submarine Songtrack* contains 15 newly remastered and remixed Beatles songs as featured in the movie. As wonderful as the visuals are, the new soundtrack is equally, if not even more, impressive. Remarkably, Markoe was able to convince Apple chief Neil Aspinall to allow the songs to be remixed (by Abbey Road engineer Peter Cobbin, assisted by Paul Hicks and Mirek Stiles) to take advantage of today's state-of-the-art audio technology, with the strict understanding that if any of The Beatles were dissatisfied with the results, they would never be used.

Listeners will immediately notice a new clarity and separation in the music. Among the songs benefiting the most from this treatment are the new mixes of the songs earmarked for the film. "Hey Bulldog" is much cleaner and features a much stronger Lennon lead vocal than the original version. "Only A Northern Song," previously released in a horribly compressed, fake-stereo, albeit mono version, is perhaps the most improved number of the lot.

The one disappointment with the *Yellow Submarine Songtrack* is that many fans were hoping it would contain the original, full-length version of "It's All Too Much" (8:16), which has never been officially released. Although the version of the song at the end of the film is only (2:30) in length, it contains an otherwise unavailable verse not found on the officially released albeit longer album version (6:23). The fact that both the edited film version and the regular album version have both been remixed would seem to strongly indicate that the entire full-length recording had to have been remixed.

Markoe said, "I knew there was a longer version of the song. I think we mixed the long version of the song. [Cobbin] did at Abbey Road when we did the 5.1 [mix]. I thought that they might release that on the *Songtrack* album." Given that the full-length version of "It's All Too Much" was not included on the *Yellow Submarine Songtrack*, could this be taken as a sign that Apple may be holding it back for a possible *Anthology 4*?

Until then, it's been reported that newer and bluer Meanies have been spotted in your vicinity, and the only known remedy for fans is to take a trip on the new and definitely improved *Yellow Submarine* (and *Yellow Submarine Songtrack*). A journey perhaps best described by George Harrison, "It's all in the mind, y'know."

A *Yellow Submarine* trading ard set from an English tobacco company.

Michael Lindsay-Hogg — father of the music video

by Bill DeYoung

If any one person could claim to be the father of the music video, it's Michael Lindsay-Hogg. The award-winning film director (*The Object Of Beauty*, *Guy*) cut his teeth doing rock 'n' roll television in England and directed some of the earliest clips by The Beatles ("Paperback Writer"), The Rolling Stones ("Jumpin' Jack Flash"), and The Who ("Happy Jack").

Lindsay-Hogg was at the helm of two of the '60s most legendary full-length productions: The Rolling Stones' *Rock And Roll Circus* and The Beatles' *Let It Be*. He went on to make videos with Elton John, Wings, Neil Young, Paul Simon and others.

The American-born filmmaker recently turned up as the director of *Two Of Us*, the VH-1 film that "reunited" John Lennon and Paul McCartney.

The veteran director knew he would get criticized by Beatles fans by taking on the VH-1 project. He did, after all, have a name to look after.

"Over the years Beatles projects had come my way, dramatic ones, and I didn't want to do them because I thought they were gonna be coming from the wrong place," he said. "But when I read it, I was really surprised to find I liked it. It seemed to me that [writer Mark Stansfield] had got the characters right and the idea of the dialogue right. Underneath, the movie is about friendship, which could happen to any people, not two famous people."

Born in New York City in 1940, Lindsay-Hogg moved to Ireland with his father following his parents' divorce. He went into television production, he said, because Irish TV was in its infancy in the early '60s and they needed, and would hire, anyone they could get.

In 1965 he was offered a job at *Ready, Steady Go*, a British music program that featured acts performing live, rather than miming their records. All the bands, he said, loved appearing on *RSG* for this very reason. The Stones were regulars on the weekly show, and they began a working relationship with Lindsay-Hogg that would last through the 1980s.

It was The Beatles, however, who with "Paperback Writer" broke the mold of live TV appearances to promote their latest single. "That was very daunting. It's hard to imagine if you're not from that generation how extraordinarily famous they were, and how powerful they were in the world.

"Doing it live was such a hassle for them because the audiences were so out of control," he said. "And they were powerful enough to say to the TV stations, 'Take it or leave it.'"

Lindsay-Hogg shot the Fabs miming their song, and "Rain," its B-side, in a country garden. "When we did 'Paperback Writer,' I'd wanted to have a kind of story video, like Paul playing a writer or something in his little garret," Lindsay-Hogg recalled. "But Brian Epstein didn't want that. He said story videos had no future and that the audience wanted to see them play."

This article originally appeared in Goldmine issue #513, March 24, 2000.

A year later, "Peter Brown called me. He said, 'The boys have a new album coming, and they want to talk to you about doing a kind of concept video. Can you meet them next week?' And I said, 'Sure, sure.'" The new album, of course, was *Sgt. Pepper*.

"Then he called me the day before the meeting and said they'd had a change of plan. What happened was, Paul had met some guy in a nightclub and the guy said he had a great idea about how they should be filmed, and it sounded good to Paul. They did 'Day In The Life,' but he shot it on infrared film, and all the images flickered. It was a disaster."

In September 1968, The Beatles' camp rang him up again.

"The idea of 'Hey Jude' was dictated by that four-minute chorus at the end," he recalled. "So I thought we needed something to shoot other than them singing 'Hey Jude.' I had this idea, and Paul and I talked it over, about getting an audience in. And that the audience shouldn't be just the usual kids. There should be a kind of cross-section of life — housewives, postmen, kids, mums and dads, everything like that.

"So we got that audience in, and that worked very well because it wasn't only the kind of teenybopper audience. And that was really the genesis of what became *Let It Be*, because we did, say, seven or eight takes of 'Hey Jude.' Between takes,

John Lennon and son Julian with Eric Clapton at The Rolling Stones' *Rock And Roll Circus*.

while we were getting the cameras ready again and seeing what had gone wrong in the previous take, The Beatles had nothing to do except stand there. And then they started to jam for the audience. They'd play old Motown songs and they'd horse around and stuff, and they enjoyed it. It was the first time they'd performed to any kind of audience since they stopped touring in '66."

Lindsay-Hogg was also at the helm for the famous clip of The Beatles rocking through "Revolution." "I remember John saying that day that the most important thing was to have a big close-up of him — not for ego reasons — on the lyric about Chairman Mao, because he thought that was the most important line in the song."

Lindsay-Hogg adored The Beatles. "They were very different from The Rolling Stones. The Stones were more accessible — like if you'd give Mick [Jagger] and Keith [Richards] an idea, you'd bat the idea around together. Whereas with The Beatles, if you gave them an idea or a concept, it was kind of like throwing a piece of meat into the bear pit. They'd paw it over and chuck it around between themselves, and they'd exclude you. They'd do it in a four-way tangle. And then they'd come back to you after a while with their opinion."

Doing Beatles work was fun but intense. "Your adrenalin was not asleep when you were working with them, because they had their own opinions and they were who they were. They were the greatest band and the greatest songwriters of, if not the last 100 years, the last 50 years."

The Stones were back next with an idea for Christmas of '68. *Beggar's Banquet* was their new album.

"After 'Jumpin' Jack Flash,' Mick and Keith wanted to do something else, although they didn't know what it was going to be. They had this idea to do a television special.

"They weren't going to look for financing from anybody else. So the Stones produced it, and because of that you could pretty much get anything you wanted, in terms of musicians. So I came up with this idea of a circus. And Mick and I talked about what kind of circus it would be. We thought it shouldn't be a kind of glamorous, Ringling Brothers, it should be like a small, little European traveling circus, which is a bit shoddy.

"We were going to introduce a new band, or a band which hadn't been around very long — and that was the Jethro Tull spot. There was another band we'd thought of, but it was a kind of heavy guitar band, and Mick didn't like that so much. We chose Jethro Tull, and we turned down Led Zeppelin. They'd sent in some demos."

Lennon made his first non-Beatles musical appearance on the *Rock And Roll Circus*.

"In the so-called supergroup spot, Mick had wanted Stevie Winwood," Lindsay-Hogg explained. "But about a week before shooting, Stevie got a cold or something and couldn't do it. So Mick thought, 'Christ, what do we do?' He thought the one who would be most open and available to getting a call on Monday, to shoot Thursday, was John Lennon. He called John, and John said sure.

"John had already been playing with Eric Clapton a little, and so then Keith said, 'Gee, I want to play with John and Eric.' That band came together in like 48 hours.

"And we didn't know that Yoko was going to sing. There was this black bag on the stage, and the poor violinist, he thought, 'Wow, this is my spot. I'm going to be playing rock 'n' roll violin with Lennon and Clapton!' And then this woman gets out of a bag — if you look at it again, you see this look of real consternation on his face, thinking, 'What happened here?'"

Although it was filmed in 1968, *Rock And Roll Circus* was not released or even publicly screened until the mid-90s. Here's why: "The Who had recorded at three in the afternoon, and they were very good," said Lindsay-Hogg. "The Stones had been there since noon because they were the hosts. As the day turned into evening and into night, other bands would come on. John did his spot about 11, finished that, and the Stones' setup didn't really begin until one in the morning. The Stones didn't start their set until 2 a.m. — they'd been there since noon. I think if a group of nuns had been sitting around for 14 hours, they'd have been in a pretty weird mood, too.

"We didn't get to 'Sympathy For The Devil' until six in the morning. And we thought, 'We're so tired, let's come back tomorrow.' But it was going to cost too much money 'cause the Stones were paying for it. So Mick said, 'If you can get the cameras right, and if the engineers can get the balance right, I will do it one more time. And then we're all going to go to sleep.'

"They were very different from The Rolling Stones. The Stones were more accessible — like if you'd give Mick and Keith and idea, you'd bat the idea around together. Whereas with The Beatles, if you gave them an idea or a concept, it was kind of like throwing a piece of meat into a bear pit. They'd paw it over and chuck it around between themselves."

— Michael Lindsay-Hogg, director

"Then we put the rough cut together. And in those days, they were all very close friends, but they were also rivals. And I think when Mick and Keith saw it, they thought, 'Hmm... The Who are really good.' And it was the last time Brian [Jones] played with them and he wasn't in good health... and one thing led to another, and then a year had gone by. It lost its momentum, and in those days if a rock 'n' roll show lost its momentum, it got put away."

Not long after, the Stones moved to France to escape Britain's suffocating tax laws. When their London office was shut down, pianist/road manager Ian Stewart took the cans of *Rock And Roll Circus* film. "He didn't tell anyone, because it wasn't important anymore," said Lindsay-Hogg. "But he thought it was worth saving them."

(Every so often, during a video shoot, Jagger, Richards or one of the other Stones would ask Lindsay-Hogg, 'Whatever happened to the *Circus*?')

After Stewart died in 1985, his widow went into their barn to take stock of what was there. "And there against the wall with a bale of hay on top of it and a rake and some gumboots are all these cans of film with the tape peeling off, OCK N OLL IRCUS."

After the *Circus* shoot, in January '69, The Beatles and Lindsay-Hogg's film crew gathered at Twickenham Studios, where the *James Bond* movies were filmed. It had been the director's idea to get the group into a large space where the equipment was — big mistake.

"Originally, *Let It Be* was supposed to be a short documentary that would support a TV special. But they're sitting there in a cold studio and nobody was getting on. They didn't know what they wanted to do. McCartney wanted to do a TV special, John said OK, George didn't... so we'd talk about it. One of them would say, 'Let's do it at The Cavern,' and I'd say, 'Well, you're bigger than The Cavern now. You're for the world.'

"Then the ideas got really fanciful, because The Beatles, they could do it. They were going to hire a boat and rehearse and bring the audience with us. The documentary would be about the rehearsal and you'd do the show."

But George Harrison got fed up with everything and quit The Beatles. Two of his conditions for returning were a) no more talk of a TV show, and b) let's get out of this place and go to the Apple studio like real musicians.

And so the bad vibes continued across town. "It was two, three weeks, two cameras, eight hours a day," said Lindsay-Hogg. "They'd come in between 11 and 1 and we'd grind it out and grind it out. You'd do 'Long And Winding Road' 30 times."

The Beatles came to ignore the film crew. "Originally, even though they'd hired us, they were sort of irked by the presence of the crew and the cameras," Lindsay-Hogg said. "But after a while that settled down, and I think we became no more annoying than wasps on a summer afternoon."

According to Lindsay-Hogg, it was his idea to film The Beatles performing on the Apple Records roof. "I didn't want *Let It Be* to get put in the closet because the momentum was gone. So the only way I knew to fix it was to have some sort of climax."

To his delight, the idea came out of "the bear pit" more or less intact. "Paul and I and Mal Evans went up on the roof and looked around and shouted to see what the echoes were like and jumped up and down on the floorboards to see if it would take the weight of the amps. And Paul said, 'Let's try and make it work.' Because Paul, to his credit, was always the one who was pushing ahead. Paul always goes forward, which is a very admirable thing.

"We got planks in to shore up the roof for the equipment, where we were going to do it on Thursday, but the weather was bad. So we decided we'd do it at 12:30 on Friday. And they were still arguing at 12:20 if they were going to do it. I thought, 'My God, it's awful, it's typical of this whole project.'

"Paul wanted to do it and George didn't, which was the usual breakdown of the personalities. And then John, who was the leader of the democracy, if he chose to be, said, 'Oh, fuck it, come on, let's do it.' And so we all walked up the little staircase and kind of into history, you know?"

The evolution of "Get Back"

by Doug Sulpy

January 1969 has to stand out as the most heavily documented period in Beatles history. Not only were 17 hours of multitrack tape recorded at Apple Studios between Jan. 22-31, but an additional 60-85 hours of mono recordings were preserved on film, thanks to the project that eventually came to be known as *Let It Be*.

The subject of The Beatles' *Get Back* sessions deserves (and will get) a book of its own. In this article, though, we'll zero in on one song, "Get Back," focusing attention on its genesis and development.

Paul McCartney came into the session of Jan. 9 with "Get Back" half-written. Interestingly enough, the idea for the tune very likely came from George Harrison, by way of his 1968 composition titled "Sour Milk Sea." This had been released the previous September by Apple artist Jackie Lomax. At the end of that recording Lomax can be heard singing a variation of the song's lyric, almost as the record fades: "Get back! Get back! Get back! ... I want you to get back now, you don't belong here..." This is, of course, is very similar to McCartney's "Get back to where you once belonged" hook. A simple coincidence?

For years, the story has been that "Get Back" started off as a political statement about racism. McCartney has stated as much, as has Beatles scholar Mark Lewisohn, but it's not true. "Get Back" began its musical life very much the same as it ended, except that the words were unfinished and the tempo was faster. True, the rehearsals did at one point contain topically oriented lyrics (hence McCartney's hazy recollection) but, as we'll see, this was more along the lines of an improvisational dead-end rather than a serious attempt to write lyrics for the song.

The earliest rehearsals show that "Get Back" began as an up-tempo hard-rock number, with very unfinished lyrics. Certain familiar phrases are there: "California grass... loner," "I left my home in Arizona" (note the usage of first person here), but many of the lyrics are unfinished and "Jo-Jo" and "Loretta" haven't been conceived yet.

Since he has no real lyrics at this point, McCartney improvises various place names to go along with "Arizona." This leads him to "Puerto Ricans," and, finally, to "Pakistanis," two similarly oppressed ethnic groups in the United States and England. From "Pakistanis" McCartney begins to improvise lyrics about discrimination. For inspiration, he would have needed to look no further than the morning's headlines, which were occupied with stories about Prime Minister Wilson's public comments on this subject. These were in response to statements made by British Member of Parliament Enoch Powell to the effect that too many non-white citizens of the greater British Empire were living on visas in England and competing for limited job opportunities. "All the folks around don't dig no Pakistanis,

This article originally appeared in **Goldmine** *issue #295, Nov. 15, 1991.*

takin' other people's jobs," sings McCartney. It must, however, be stressed that these are sarcastic comments based upon Mr. Powell's unacceptable attitudes and obviously do not reflect McCartney's own views.

Although the political references were ultimately dropped, McCartney did keep one improvised line from these rehearsals, about the song's as-yet-unnamed heroine, who "thought she was a woman, but she was another man." Again, this was very much a topical reference, "drag artists" being extremely popular (and socially acceptable) in Britian at the time. As The Beatles rehearse the song, 'Jo-Jo' makes his first appearance — name obviously made up on the spot, despite any stories you may have heard about any real-life individuals claiming to "be" Jo-Jo.

Our heroine develops a name, too. At first it's Teresa, and then "Sweet Loretta Martin." Unlike in the finished version of the song, her verse comes before Jo-Jo's, leading off the song. Later rehearsals would see "Martin" changed to "Modem," perhaps to avoid linking the character to George Martin, The Beatles' producer. The lyrics still have reference to things like "Pakistanis living in a council flat," but the racism aspect very quickly loses favor against the Jo-Jo/Loretta story and is soon dropped from the lyric entirely.

Oddly enough, the tempo of the song has picked up considerably by this time. This wasn't unusual for the group, and up-tempo renditions exist of a number of songs from this period, most notably "Two Of Us." It also seems to please John Lennon to perform the song at this tempo, perhaps because the *Get Back* sessions were lacking in newly composed "fast" numbers. The song also contains a few bars of drum solo from Ringo Starr, only the second recorded instance available (the other, of course, being the famous drum break on the *Abbey Road* track "The End"). If it had been kept in the song, the solo in "Get Back" would have been his first. This "fast" version is commonly attainable on the bootleg *Sweet Apple Trax* (or *Songs From The Past Vol. 3* on compact disc) and is in some ways as satisfying a performance as the legitimate release.

The Beatles returned to the song several days later. Although the political lyrics were now abandoned, the hard-rock feel of the song was still intact. With assistant Mal Evans transcribing the words, Lennon and McCartney attempt to polish off the lyrics of the song. Lennon suggests the name "Jo-Jo Jackson" for the song's hero, building upon "Jo-Jo" or "Jody-Jo," the name McCartney had used earlier. Lennon, refreshing his own memory of the lyrics, bounces the line "But he knew he couldn't last" off of McCartney, to which McCartney responds: "No. That's not good," effectively (and perhaps unknowingly) vetoing his own work! The song at this point sounds halfway between the jamming of the earlier "political" improvisation and the finished song as we know it.

The next time The Beatles returned to the song was at Apple Studios the following week. By this time it was essentially finished and the group began the familiar and occasionally tedious process of refining the song to a state of note-by-note perfection. The earliest Apple rehearsals show The Beatles perfecting the guitar solo and Lennon/McCartney harmonies. Interestingly enough, the group came into Apple on Jan. 23 and evidently recorded only this song. This single-song rehearsal is unique among all the January sessions, and there's no indication at this point why that Thursday session appears to have been abbreviated.

Although the Apple sessions are not as interesting or as lively as the Twickenham performances from earlier in the month, they're not without their share of humor, charm and occasional improvisation. At one point McCartney sings the entire song in German with the exception of the last verse, which is sung in pidgin-French! Another fascinating take is more than six minutes long. This performance was played on WABC radio in New York many years ago, where it was claimed to have been an unedited tape of the single — wrong, but an interesting explanation.

There's also a jazzy organ improvisation on "Get Back," entirely instrumental. On the 24th, a unique, basically instrumental version was attempted using slide guitar. This last performance is also of interest because the "official" log of these sessions (found in Mark Lewisohn's book *The Beatles Recording Sessions*) does not list "Get Back" as having been recorded this day. It's possible, of course, that the rehearsals might have been preserved by the film crew and not by EMI. Then again, EMI recorded McCartney's less-than-memorable performance of his song "Teddy Boy" from the same day, so it obviously was being too choosy as to what it laid down on tape. Until further information appears, this will have to remain on the list of *Get Back* session mysteries.

The story of "Get Back" winds to a close with the recording of the official release. A definite error does occur in *The Beatles Recording Sessions* when Lewisohn claims that a Jan. 27 recording of "Get Back" was used for the *Let It Be* album, while a Jan. 28 recording was used for the single release. In fact, both versions are the same (Jan. 28) recording. The single is simply longer than the album version due to the inclusion of the coda. The single version, in fact, once ran even longer. The tail end of that performance may be found as a "tag" to both the *Let It Be* film and commonly bootlegged *Get Back* LP. Comparing the beginning of the tag to the very end of the fade on the mono single mix of "Get Back," one will find the two join up quite nicely.

The final performances of "Get Back" were on the Apple rooftop on Jan. 30, where it was performed three times. The last Beatles performance of "Get Back," with McCartney improvising lyrics about the British police, can be heard in the film *Let It Be*.

As intimated earlier, the song "Get Back" is just one of hundreds of Beatles performances captured on tape during the January 1969 rehearsals. A collaborator and I have been working for years on a book about the *Get Back* sessions. If you feel you may be of assistance, please communicate with us at Schuberk, P.O. Box 751, New Monmouth, NJ 07748.

The Beatles

In person and on the air

by Charles Reinhart

In December 1963, The Beatles' name was not known to many Americans. However, by the middle of January of the next year, the radio was filled with Beatle music. The group was an "overnight" success in the U.S. But, like so many other groups who appeared to have rocketed to stardom, The Beatles had put in many long, hard years of work to get themselves into a position where they could gain success overnight. Even in their native England, it had taken them many years to get the recognition they enjoyed before storming our shores.

The Beatles built their reputation in four main ways: tightening up their musical sound and building a large repertoire of songs; constant touring during their formative years; many radio appearances; and after they had built a following, TV appearances to give the fans who couldn't see them live a chance to get a look at their heroes.

The story of The Beatles has been told many times and most of the group's history is known even to the casual fan. This history will concentrate on those four areas that made The Beatles what they are: superstars of the first magnitude.

This article originally appeared in Goldmine issue #132, Aug. 16, 1985.

Tightening their sound & building repertoire

Even before they became The Beatles, the group, then known as The Quarrymen, began to build a following by playing various locations around the Liverpool area. The Quarrymen played spots such as the St. Peters Church Hall, The Conservative Club, Wilson Hall, Finch Lane Bus Depot, Lathom Hall, St. George Hall, Grafton Ballroom, Blair Hall, Aintree Institute, the Blue Angel Club, and the Jackaranda Club. (The latter two clubs were owned by Allan Williams, who was to become the first manager of The Silver Beatles.)

In late August 1959, The Quarrymen became the regular band at Mona Best's Casbah Club. The Casbah was owned by the mother of Pete Best, who would later become The Beatles' drummer. At this point, The Quarrymen consisted of John, Paul, George, and Ken Wood on drums.

When Wood left, Best sat in with the group but didn't become their regular drummer at this point. Beginning in late 1959, the group underwent several name changes. They performed as The Moondogs, Long John And The Silver Beatles, The Silver Beatles, and finally, they settled simply on The Beatles.

In April 1960, Williams got The Silver Beatles an audition with British rock 'n' roll promoter Larry Parnes. Johnny Hutch sat in with the group on the drums. Parnes was not too impressed with the group's new bass player, Stuart Sutcliffe, a friend of Lennon's from art school. Parnes offered them a job backing singer Johnny Gentle on a tour of Scotland. They took the job, but adopted new names: Johnny Silver (Lennon), Paul Ramon (McCartney), Carl Harrison (George), and Stu de Steel (Sutcliffe). The group had to enlist the help of drummer Tommy Moore for the tour.

Williams managed to get The Beatles booked into the Indra Club in Hamburg, Germany, for August through October of 1960. Before they left Liverpool, McCartney asked Best to join them as their steady drummer. When the Indra Club closed, The Beatles moved to The Kaiserkeller. They stayed there for seven weeks, playing seven hours a night, alternating with Rory Storm And The Hurricanes, featuring Ringo Starr on drums.

In December The Beatles made an unscheduled, one-night appearance at the Top Ten Club. This infuriated Kaiserkeller owner Bruno Koschmeider, who had not given them permission to do so, and he reported to authorities that Harrison was underage. Harrison was promptly deported. After a fire in their room, McCartney and Best were also deported. Sutcliffe decided to remain in Hamburg with his girlfriend, Astrid Kirchherr. Lennon, alone in a foreign country, also made his way back to Liverpool.

The trouble they had in Germany in 1960 didn't deter The Beatles, and they returned to Hamburg in April 1961 for a two-month engagement at the Top Ten Club. In May, The Beatles were asked to back singer Tony Sheridan on his recording session for Polydor Records. Bert Kaempfert produced the sessions. Lennon sang lead on "Ain't She Sweet" and The Beatles also recorded the instrumental "Cry For A Shadow."

The tracks recorded at this session have been released many times over the intervening years. One of the tracks, "My Bonnie" was released as a single. On Oct. 28 of that year, a

LOVE ME DO

WRITTEN AND COMPOSED BY McCARTNEY AND LENNON

RECORDED BY **THE BEATLES** ON PAR R. 4949

ARDMORE AND BEECHWOOD LTD.
363. OXFORD STREET LONDON W.1.
Sole Selling Agents:
CAMPBELL, CONNELLY & CO. LTD.
10 DENMARK STREET, LONDON, W.C.2

2/6

lad named Raymond Jones walked into the NEMS record store in Liverpool and asked the man behind the counter for a copy of this single. The store didn't stock the record, but copies were ordered and the man, Brian Epstein, decided to find out more about The Beatles.

The Beatles returned once more to Hamburg in April 1962 to play the Star Club. While they were there, their new manager, Epstein, took tapes they had made for a Decca Records audition on New Year's Day to various record companies trying to get The Beatles a recording contract. When the group returned to Liverpool in early June, he had good news for them: They had an audition with George Martin of EMT on June 6. They were signed to the Parlophone label and recorded their first single, "Love Me Do"/"P.S. I Love You" on Sept. 11.

The Beatles returned to the Star Club for a short stay on Nov. 1, remaining there until the 13th. They returned again for their final engagement from Dec. 18-31. During this stint, fellow Liverpudlian Ted "Kinpize" Taylor recorded one of their shows. Nearly 15 years later in 1977, this recording was released as an album titled *Live At The Star Club In Hamburg, Germany, 1962* (Lingasong LS-27001).

In between visits to Germany, The Beatles played many venues in the Liverpool area. Among the clubs played were: Grosvenor Ballroom, Litherland Town Hall (where the first signs of Beatlemania were said to have started), Tower Ballroom, Jazzclub, Women's Institute, Majestic Ballroom, Grafton Ballroom, River Park Ballroom, Queen's Hall, and Winter Gardens. Of course, they also played the famous Cavern Club. The Beatles made their first appearance there on March 21, to be called The Swingin' Blue Jeans). They played The Cavern 294 times, with the last performance coming on Aug. 3, 1963. During that time, The Beatles went from being struggling artists with no recording contract to a group with a # 1 hit to their credit.

Not many of The Beatles' fans in Liverpool would argue that those long hours of hard work in Hamburg paid off in a much tighter group sound. The Beatles returned from Germany sounding different and better than many of the bands who had remained in England. The constant club dates in and around Liverpool gave The Beatles a ready market for their records once they had a recording contract.

Touring in formative years

The Beatles' first British tour came in early 1963, after they had two U.K. hits. They were not top-billed, however. That honor went to Helen Shapiro. Others on the bill were Dave Allen, The Honeys, The Kestrels, Kenny Lynch (who later recorded the Lennon/McCartney song "Misery"), The Red Price Band, and Danny Williams. The tour began Feb. 2 in Bradford and ended in Hanley on March 3, after visiting 16 towns.

After less than a week off, The Beatles embarked on a second tour on March 9. This time the headliners were Tommy Roe and Chris Montez. Also on the tour were Debbie Lie, Tony Marsh, The Viscounts, and The Terry Young Six. After 21 stops, the tour ended on March 31.

By mid-May, the group was back out on the road, this time headlining their own tour with Roy Orbison, Gerry And The Pacemakers, Ian Crawford, Louise Cordet, Erkey Grant, David Macbeth, Tony Marsh, and The Terry Young Six. This tour ran from May 18 through June 9 and covered 21 cities, making it their largest tour to date.

From Sept. 4-8, The Beatles did a short tour of five cities in mid-England. Mike Berry traveled with them.

Their first tour outside of England came from Oct. 24-29. During that time they played five Swedish cities and recorded a TV show, *Drop In*, which was broadcast Nov. 3, after they had returned home. Several of the Swedish shows featured local acts.

No sooner had they returned from Sweden than The Beatles set off on the fifth British tour of the year. Again the headliners, they were supported by The Brook Brothers, Peter Jay And The Jaywalkers, The Kestrels, and Vernons Girls. They played 36 dates from Nov. 1-Dec. 13, including the Royal Command Performance Variety Show (Nov. 4) and a charity show at the Grosvenor Hotel in London on Dec. 2. The day after the tour ended, The Beatles did a special show at Wimbleton Palais for the Southern England Fan Club Convention.

During the ensuing week, the group went into practice for their first Christmas Show. The show featured The Beatles as singers and also acting in skits. Their guests were The Barron Knights, Cilla Black, The Fourmost, Rolf Harris, Billy J. Kramer And The Dakotas (The Dakotas also had a solo set), and Tommy Quickly. Two previews of the show were held: Dec. 21 at the Gaumont in Bradford and Dec. 22 at the Liverpool Empire. On Dec. 24, the show opened at the Finsbury Park Astoria. The show then played every day (except Christmas and Sundays) through Jan. 11.

The Beatles had established themselves in England during 1963 and as a result the touring load dropped in 1964. There were only three official tours — of the world, the U.S.A., and England. The year started with the group in France for appearances at the Olympia in Paris. They were on the bill with Trini Lopez and Sylvia Vartan. They played three shows a day from Jan. 16 through Feb. 4. For the first time in quite a while, the shows were met with a less than enthusiastic response from the audience. The Beatles were hardly disappointed though; when they returned to England they learned that "I Want To Hold Your Hand" was #1 in the U.S.A.

The Beatles were soon in America themselves for appearances on *The Ed Sullivan Show* and two concerts. The first concert was held at the Washington Coliseum on Feb. 11. The show was filmed and later shown on TV. Years later several videos, including "Love Me Do" and "I Want To Hold Your Hand," feature clips from this concert. The next day, The Beatles played New York's Carnegie Hall.

On June 4, 1964, The Beatles set off on their first world tour with a show in Copenhagen. However, Starr was in the hospital and was replaced on drums by Jimmy Nicol. The group played dates in Denmark, Hong Kong, Australia and New Zealand. Ringo returned in time for the June 15 show in Melbourne, Australia and finished out the tour, which ended June 29 in Brisbane.

The stage was now set for The Beatles' very first American tour. It opened in San Francisco at the Cow Palace on Aug. 19. The supporting acts were: The Bill Black Combo, The Exciters, The Righteous Brothers, and Jackie DeShannon. The Aug. 23 show at the Hollywood Bowl in Los Angeles was recorded by Capitol Records but remained unreleased (except for bootlegs) until 1977 when a few of the tracks were finally released. Twenty-five concert dates later, the tour ended with a charity show at the Paramount Theatre in New York City.

Americans soon found there was money to be made from a Beatles tour. Charles O. Finley, owner of the Kansas City A's baseball team, even paid The Beatles $150,000 to play Kansas City on Sept. 17, which was to have been a rest day for the group.

Less than a month after returning to England, The Beatles set off on their final tour of the year. The British tour began Oct. 9 in Bradford and ended 26 stops later on Nov. 10 in Bristol. Touring with them were: Bob Bain, Michael Haslam, Tommy Quickly, The Remo Four, The Rustics, Sounds Incorporated, and Mary Wells.

As they had done the year before, The Beatles once again did a series of Christmas shows for the British fans. Opening night was Dec. 24 at the Hammersmith Odeon, London. There were then two shows a day, except Christmas Day and Sundays, through Jan. 16, 1965.

The Beatles were now an established group on a worldwide level, and as a result they toured less often and their tour dates diminished. In 1965, they made only three tours with the longest lasting only 12 dates. The first tour of the year was a European tour, which started in Paris on June 6. This time, The Beatles toured alone with no supporting acts. They played eight dates in France, Italy, and Spain, with the tour ending July 3 in Barcelona.

The Beatles' second American tour traveled to only 10 cities, remaining in two of those (New York and Los Angeles) for two days each. The tour ran from Aug. 15-31. The Shea Stadium concert in New York on the 15th was filmed and later shown on TV. The Beatles filled the 56,000 seats of Shea on two successive nights setting an attendance record that stood for many years. Like the year before, their concert at the Hollywood Bowl was taped and several tracks later turned up on the 1977 album, *The Beatles At The Hollywood Bowl*. Opening for The Beatles were The King Curtis Band, Brenda Holloway, and Sound Incorporated.

The final tour of the year was a nine-day blitz of England running from Dec. 3-12. Steve Aldo, The Koobas, Beryl Marsden, The Moody Blues, and The Paramounts were the supporting acts. This was all the British fans got for Christmas, 1965; there was no Christmas show like there had been the past two years.

On May 1, 1966, The Beatles played at the Empire Pool, Wembley, as part of the *New Musical Express* Poll Winners' Concert. Although the British didn't know it at the time, this was to be the last public concert The Beatles would ever do in England (not counting the Apple rooftop concert of 1969). There would be no U.K. tour that year. In fact The Beatles did

A scene from *A Hard Day's Night*.

only two tours: a short trip through Germany and the Far East, and the usual August tour of the U.S.

Touring with Cliff Bennett And The Rebel Rousers and Peter And Gordon, The Beatles played three dates (June 24-26) in Germany, then set off for Tokyo. They played the Budokan Hall there on June 30, July 1-2, doing two shows each day before nearly 11,000 fans each show. These shows were taped and shown on Japanese TV and have recently become available on videotape. The final stop of the tour was Manilla, The Philippines, on July 4. The estimated audience for that show was 100,000. The Beatles barely escaped Manilla with their lives when they inadvertently snubbed the President's wife and failed to attend her charity show.

On Aug. 12, The Beatles began their final U.S. tour with a show at the International Amphitheater in Chicago. The Cyrkle (who owed the spelling of their name to Lennon) and The Ronettes traveled with The Beatles on this tour. In all, The Beatles did shows in 14 cities (two in New York), with the last coming on Aug. 29, at the Cow Palace in San Francisco. This was to be the last concert ever by The Beatles. The show was taped but has never been released by Capitol; it has been issued on several bootlegs.

In four years, The Beatles had made seven tours of the U.K., three of America, two world tours, and one tour of Europe. In addition, they had staged two Christmas shows and done one long stint in Paris. Plus, when they weren't touring, they were playing various clubs and ballrooms around England. If a fan really wanted to see the group, he or she had every opportunity to do so. During that four-year span, The Beatles were probably the most visible group in the world. Constant touring sells records, and The Beatles sold millions during this time period.

Numerous radio appearances

Between touring and playing club dates, The Beatles also managed to perform on 53 BBC radio programs between 1962 and 1965, giving the non–concert going public a chance to hear them.

Their first radio show was broadcast March 8, 1962. The show, *Teenager's Turn*, aired from 5-5:30 p.m. with Ray Peters as host. The Beatles — Lennon, McCartney, Harrison, and Best — did three songs for the show: "Dream Baby," "Memphis" and "Please Mr. Postman." No Lennon/McCartney songs were performed on this first show.

At this point in time, The Beatles did not have a recording contract; they were booked for the show because of the talent they showed at an audition session, not because of any hit records they had. The Beatles appeared on just three more

The Beatles appearing on *Top Of The Pops*.

BBC radio shows in 1962. They were on *Here We Go* (the new name for *Teenager's Turn*) on June 15 and again on Oct. 26. On the first of these shows, they did one Lennon/McCartney song, "Ask Me Why," and two other songs: "Bésame Mucho" and "A Picture Of You."

By the Oct. 26 show, they had signed a recording contract with Parlophone and had recorded their first single: "Love Me Do"/"P.S. I Love You." They did both these songs on the show, as well as "A Taste Of Honey." Their final BBC appearance for the year came on Dec. 4, when they were on *The Talent Spot*. Once again they did "Love Me Do" and "P.S. I Love You," adding "Twist And Shout" for the show.

During 1963, The Beatles made 40 appearances on various BBC radio shows. Seven of those appearances were on the very prestigious *Saturday Club* program, with Brian Matthew as host. *Saturday Club* was, at the time, the only outlet for pop music on the BBC. It aired every Saturday morning from 10 until noon and its audience numbered in the millions. When The Beatles appeared on this show nearly every Briton interested in pop music heard them perform. Their first appearance on the show was on Jan. 26, 1963. They also appeared on March 16, May 25, June 29, Aug. 24, Oct. 5, and Dec. 21.

By the middle of 1964, The Beatles' popularity had grown to such gigantic proportions that the BBC offered them their own radio series, *Pop Go The Beatles*. At first, just four shows were ordered. The Beatles recorded an adaptation of "Pop Goes The Weasel" as the shows' theme song. The shows aired on Tuesday from 5-5:30 p.m. The first show aired June 4, with the others coming on June 11, 18, and 25. The BBC then ordered another 11 shows. The first of these was broadcast on July 16, with the remaining shows broadcast weekly through Sept. 24.

The presenter for the shows was Rodney Burke (Lee Peters handled the first four shows), and each week's show featured a guest artist. The guests included The Bachelors, The Searchers, Swingin' Blue Jeans, The Hollies, and Brian Poole And The Tremeloes, all of whom were relatively famous, and unknowns such as The Lorne Gibson Trio, The Countrymen, Russ Sainty, and The Marauders.

The Beatles in *Help!*

With all their other commitments, The Beatles didn't wish to continue with a weekly radio series but did agree to do an occasional special. These specials were titled *From Us To You* and featured The Beatles doing a reworked version of their "From Me To You" as the shows' theme. The first of these specials aired on Boxing Day (Dec. 26), 1963. The presenter was Rolf Harris, who you may remember for his hit, "Tie Me Kangaroo Down Sport."

The Beatles also appeared on nearly 20 other BBC radio shows during 1963. They made one appearance on *The Beat Show* (July 4). They were on *Easy Beat* with Brian Matthew four times (April 7, June 23, July 21, and Oct. 20). Their final two appearances on *Here We Go* were on Jan. 25 and March 12. On Nov. 3, they were on *The Ken Dodd Show* doing just one song, "She Loves You." They also made one stop on the show *On The Scene*, that coming on March 28.

On Feb. 20, they did their first live broadcast on *Parade Of The Pops*. They did three *Side By Side* shows on April 22, May 13 and June 24. They performed this show's theme with the resident band, The Karl Denver Trio. On June 3 they were on a show called *Steppin' Out*.

On April 18, the BBC broadcast a live show from the Royal Albert Hall featuring The Beatles and Del Shannon. The show was called *Swingin' Sounds '63*. During this show, Shannon heard The Beatles do "From Me To You" and asked them if he could record it for U.S. release. They agreed and he hit the charts with it in July (Big Top 3152). They also made one guest appearance on *The Talent Spot* on Jan. 29. On Nov. 4, The Beatles made an appearance at the Royal Variety Performance. The show was taped and broadcast on BBC radio Nov. 10.

In 1964, as the touring done by the group increased, their appearances on BBC radio shows decreased. They did only eight shows during the entire year. Three of those shows were *From Us To You* specials. The first of these came on March 30, Easter Monday. On May 18, they did another for Whitson Bank Holiday Monday. The final show was for August Bank Holiday Monday on Aug. 3. They also did three more Saturday Club shows: Feb. 15, April 4 and Dec. 26.

On July 16, 1964, the BBC premiered a new show, *Top Gear*, to play more progressive music. The show aired weekly on Thursday nights from 10 until midnight. Brian Matthew, an old friend of The Beatles by now, was the show's host. The Beatles were the show's first guests. They also appeared a second time on Nov. 26.

The Beatles made their final appearance on a BBC radio show on Monday, June 7, 1965. This was another Bank Holiday Monday Special, but this one was titled *The Beatles Invite You To Take A Ticket To Ride*. Denny Piercy was the host for the program. Just before noon on that Monday, "Ticket To Ride," the last song The Beatles would record especially for a BBC show, was aired.

The Beatles recorded 36 songs for the BBC that they never released as records. Many of these songs had been performed during their Cavern and Hamburg dates, but Americans never had the chance to hear many of these songs until the 1982 radio show, *The Beatles At The BEEB*. These songs form a very important part of The Beatles' history, showing us the artists whom The Beatles themselves liked. EMI has not seen fit to officially release any of these tracks, but many have found their way onto bootlegs.

The unreleased BBC material includes the following: "Beautiful Dreamer," "Bésame Mucho," "Carol," "Clarabella," "Crying, Waiting, Hoping," "Don't Ever Change," "Dream Baby," "Glad All Over," "The Hippy Hippy Shake," "The Honeymoon Song," "I Forgot To Remember To Forget," "I Got A Woman," "I Got To Find My Baby," "I Just Don't Understand," "I'll Be On My Way," "I'm Gonna Sit Right Down And Cry (Over You)," "I'm Talking About You," "Johnny B. Goode," "Keep Your Hands Off My Baby," "Lend Me Your Comb," "Lonesome Tears In My Eyes," "Lucille," "Memphis," "Nothin' Shakin' (But The Leaves On The Trees)," "Ooh! My Soul," "A Picture Of You," "A Shot Of Rhythm And Blues," "So How Come (No One Loves Me)," "Soldier Of Love," "Some Other Guy," "Sure To Fall (In Love With You)," "Sweet Little Sixteen," "That's All Right Mama," "To Know Her Is To Love Her," "Too Much Monkey Business" and "Youngblood."

TV appearances

The final way in which The Beatles made themselves visible to the fans during their formative years was by appearing on TV. In the years between 1959 and 1965, they appeared on no less than 35 U.K. TV shows, not counting appearances made by just one or two members of the group.

Their very first TV show was done in the summer of 1959. John, Paul, and George, appearing as Johnny And The Moondogs, appeared on a show in the Manchester area titled *Discoveries*. It was a talent show, and The Moondogs lost. As The Beatles, their first TV show was also broadcast from Manchester. This *Granada TV* show aired Nov. 7, 1962. By this time, the regular lineup for the group had been established and they had recorded and released their first single.

Their first national broadcast was on ABC's *Thank Your Lucky Stars* on Jan. 11, 1963. During the year, they made three more appearances on that show; June 29, Oct. 26 and Dec. 22, the latter being a special Christmas edition of the show.

Also during 1963, The Beatles appeared on the following shows: April 16, the BBC's *6:25 Show*; May 17, the BBC's *Pops And Lennie*; Aug. 19, Granada TV's *Scene At 6:30*; Sept. 7, ABC TV's *Big Night Out*; Oct. 9, the BBC's *The Mersey Beat*, a renamed version of the *Thank Your Lucky Stars* show aired June 29; Oct. 13, the BBC's *Sunday Night At The London Palladium*, which was viewed by 15 million.

Finally, their *Royal Command Performance* show of Nov. 4 was taped and broadcast Nov. 10. On June 29, 1963, Lennon made an appearance on *Juke Box Jury*, a record rating show. The Beatles were on the same show on Dec. 11, 1963.

In 1964, the group made 14 appear ances on British TV, as well as seven U.S. TV shows, mostly being seen on *The Ed Sullivan Show*. The first British show to be broadcast was on Jan. 12, when their second appearance on *Sunday Night At The London Palladium* was shown. On March 25, they appeared on *Top Of The Pops*. They visited this same show again on July 8, Dec. 3, and Dec. 9. On April 18, they appeared on ATV's *Morecambe And Wise Show*. Their first *Ready Steady Go* show, taped March 20, was aired on April 27 (this show is now available on videotape). They appeared on this show again on Oct. 16, performing live, and again on Nov. 27.

The special *Around The Beatles* was broadcast on BBC TV on May 6. Parts of this show would eventually be shown on U.S. TV. The Beatles made two appearances on *Thank Your Lucky Stars* during the year: once on July 11, and again on Nov. 21. *The Road To Beatlemania* was broadcast on ATV on July 15. *Follow The Beatles*, a show about the making of the film *A Hard Day's Night*, was shown by the BBC on Aug. 3. George made an appearance on *Juke Box Jury* on July 25, and Ringo followed him on Aug. 1.

The Beatles had appeared on various news programs in the U.S. toward the end of 1963, but the first show to feature them singing a complete song was *The Jack* with a supporting cast that included a pair of jugglers and a comedian.

The show opened with The Sons Of The Piltdown Men. They were a raucous instrumental group along the lines of Johnny And The Hurricanes and they sounded *very* loud in that small theater. As far as I am aware, no member of the group went on to make much of an impression elsewhere except bassist John Rostill who later joined Cliff Richard's Shadows and was a primarily responsible for Richard's latter day conversion to Christianity.

The Sons Of The Piltdown Men were followed by Tommy Quickly, one of Brian Epstein's least memborable discoveries. Despite his claim to be influenced by rhythm 'n' blues, Quickly sang in a wimpy pop style that, to my ears, totally lacked merit.

Beatles without words

A discography of Beatles instrumentals

by Charles Reinhart

Instrumentals have been a part of rock 'n' roll music since its very beginning. Artists such as Link Wray, Duane Eddy, and The Ventures built their entire careers around the instrumental music they created. The Beatles, as aspiring musicians, often practiced for hours to learn to play their favorite instrumentals. After all, there were no words to learn, just music. The group even played some of these songs at the earliest concert dates. Through the years, The Beatles and ex-Beatles have continned to be interested in instrumental music. It is the purpose of this article to track these instrumental works.

First, let's set up the guidelines used to determine what is and what is not listed in this discography.

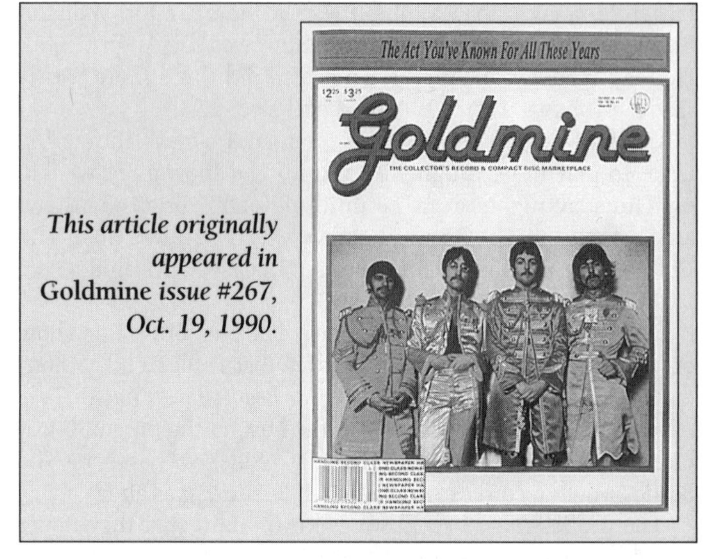

This article originally appeared in* Goldmine *issue #267, Oct. 19, 1990.

What is listed

1. Songs known to have been performed by The Beatles in concert, even if those instrumentals have never been released in commercial or bootleg form. This includes songs listed by Mark Lewisohn in his fine book, *The Beatles Live!* (Henry Holt & Company, 1986).

2. Instrumentals commercially released by The Beatles and/or ex-Beatles.

3. Instrumentals released on various bootleg recordings. This includes the songs from the soundtracks of their film projects but not released commercially.

4. Instrumental tracks for songs commercially released as vocals if these are substantially different from the released version. For instance, "Winter Rose" and "Summer's Day Song," both by Paul McCartney, have been released as instrumentals on several bootleg albums. However, neither is listed here because they are nearly identical (they may be slowed down or speeded up slightly) to the backing tracks of the vocal versions. On the other hand, an instrumental version of McCartney's "Tomorrow" is listed because it is very much different from the released, vocal, version.

5. Instrumentals by other artists that were written by a Beatle and either not commercially released by The Beatles or ex-Beatles, or, not recorded by The Beatles or ex-Beatles at all. Of course, literally thousands of instrumental versions of Beatles songs exist. It is not the purpose of this article to try to list each and every Beatles song recorded in instrumental form by some other artist.

6. Instrumentals on which a Beatle has played or been involved with in some way other than simply acting as a producer. For instance, David Hentschel's *Star*tling Music* is simply an instrumental version of Ringo's *Ringo* album, so many of the songs are not listed. However, Ringo is credited with "finger clicks" on "Step Lightly." As a result, that particular song is listed. On the other hand, Paul McCartney has recently stated that it was he who did the *Thrillington* album and not the fictitious Percy "Thrills" Thrillington. Because of this, all the songs on that album are listed in the discography.

7. For the record, some of the songs listed in this discography do have some voices in them. These may be shouts or short bursts of words at a key location. But, in their entirety, these songs are instrumental in nature. For example, George Harrison's "Zig Zag" has the words "zig" and "zig zag" repeated throughout, but it is mostly an instrumental and is treated here as such.

What is not listed

1. Material with no real lyrics but also with no real music. John Lennon's "Baby's Heartbeat" would fall into this category.

2. Songs with just a few different words, but with these words repeated, as lyrics, over and over again throughout the song. Lennon's "Scumbag" is not listed as an instrumental for this reason.

3. Songs with no real lyrics, but with a voice, or voices, heard throughout. Much of Yoko Ono's material on which John plays is not listed for this reason.

4. Untitled material is not listed. In his book, *The Beatles: Recording Sessions* (Harmony Books' 1988), Lewisohn lists "Untitled Jamming" several times. These are quite probably instrumentals, but with no known titles, they are not listed here. Included in this category are the instrumentals on the various Quarrymen rehearsal bootlegs, Lennon's One To One concert rehearsal bootlegs and the McCartney/Denny Laine session bootlegs. In all cases, the instrumental material has yet to be identified, so it is not listed.

5. Finally, there are several instrumentals on which an ex-Beatle might play, but there isn't currently enough information to establish the true facts behind the recording. For instance, George

Harrison is credited as lead guitarist on Billy Preston's *I Wrote A Simple Song* album. Preston's instrumental "Outa-Space" is on that album. However, the guitar work on the song doesn't sound at all like anything Harrison would play. Was he on this song?

The same holds true for Harrison's participation on Ravi Shankar's *Shankar Family And Friends* album. The B-side of that album is filled with instrumentals, and the album's credits do list George as having played guitar on the album. But, there's nothing that really sounds like Harrison on this side of the LP. As a result, these titles are not listed in the discography.

Now that the preliminaries are out of the way, let's take a look at some statistics concerning Beatles instrumentals.

A total of 131 instrumentals are listed in the discography. Of these 92 (70 percent) have been commercially released, 32 (25 percent) have been released on bootleg recordings, and seven (5 percent) have not been released at all at the present time. As you can see, the majority of the instrumentals recorded by The Beatles and the ex-Beatles have been commercially released, thus making them a little easier to find than their bootleg counterparts. Several of these, for example McCartney's "Zoo Gang," were available for many years only as imports but have since been released as a part of compact disc packages in the U.S.

Looking at the individual breakdown of instrumentals, we will find that only two of The Beatles' instrumentals have been released commercially. These, of course, are "Cry For A Shadow" and "Flying." Thirteen, including selections from the *Magical Mystery Tour* and *Let It Be* films, have found their way onto bootleg recordings. Interestingly enough, five have yet to be released in any form. These include four songs written and recorded by others and then covered by The Beatles: "Apache," "Guitar Boogie," "Ramrod" and "Raunchy." The Beatles' own "Winston's Walk" is the other song that has yet to be released. However, it is possible that this last song may have been released as a part of one of the Quarrymen session bootlegs. There are several unidentified instrumentals on these records, and one may be "Winston's Walk." Two other songs written and recorded by others and then performed by The Beatles have been released on bootlegs. These are Duane Eddy's "Movin' And Groovin'" and Anton Karas' "Third Man Theme."

Harrison wrote all 28 of the instrumentals he has performed, and all but one has been commercially released. "Soundstage Of Mind" is the only commercially unreleased song; however, it has been released on several bootlegs. Eighteen of his 28 instrumentals, or 64 percent, are from the soundtrack album *Wonderwall Music*.

John Lennon was involved in only six instrumentals and only one of these, "Beef Jerky," was commercially released. Two were done as a medley during the sessions for the *Rock 'N' Roll* album — "Rumble" and "Whole Lotta Love" (not an instrumental in its entirety, but Lennon plays only the introduction), and one was done with the Elephant's Memory Band during the One To One concert rehearsals: "Tequila." One of John's instrumentals, "Rock Peace," was announced by Apple as the Plastic Ono Band's new single, but it was never released and has yet to be heard.

McCartney is the most prolific of the ex-Beatles as far as instrumentals are concerned, having 50, all of which have been released in some form. Thirty-seven (74 percent) have been commercially released, while the other 13 (26 percent) have been bootlegged. McCartney wrote all of these songs with the exception of three — a TV theme ("*Crossroads* Theme"), a Christmas song ("Rudolph The Red Nosed Reggae"), and a song credited to his father, James, ("Walking In The Park With Eloise").

Ringo released only two instrumentals, both on the *Old Wave* album, which has not been commercially released in the U.S. Ringo was involved in the writing of both of these songs. One of the cowriters on both was Joe Walsh, who also produced the album and was a part of Ringo's All-Starr Band for Ringo's 1989 U.S. tour.

Harrison, McCartney, and Starr have also been involved with instrumentals by other artists. Harrison has played on 12 such recordings, while Ringo has been involved with

Wonderwall

11. Neither has written an instrumental for someone else. McCartney has written five instrumentals recorded by other artists and has played on an additional three. In addition, his "Rockestra Theme," an instrumental for McCartney himself, was recorded by Eddy, and McCartney played on the session.

Beatles Instrumentals

Notes: If a recording has been issued both commercially and as a bootleg, only the commercial release is listed. The exception would be if the two recordings are substantially different. For commercial releases, only the initial U.S. release is listed — reissues and repackagings are not listed. For bootlegged material, an effort has been made to list the recording with the best sound quality. In some cases two or three sources might be listed. But, every available release is not included. All of this is in an effort to conserve space. Many Beatles discographies are available in which other sources may be found.

TITLE	SOURCE	NOTES
Aerial Tour	Back Track (BT 6267); Unsurpassed Masters Vol. 3 (SXCD005)	Early version of "Flying"
Apache		Performed by The Beatles at 1960 concerts, but not recorded or released
Catswalk	The Cavern Tapes Circa 1962 (CT62-2)	Also recorded by The Chris Barber Band
Cry For A Shadow	The Beatles With Tony Sheridan And Their Guests (MGM 4215)	
Flying	Magical Mystery Tour (Capitol 2835)	See Aerial Tour
Guitar Boogie		Performed by The Beatles at 1957-59 concerts, but not recorded or released.
Instrumental No. 42	Get Back (GB 87 1969)	Also known as "Rocker." Was on the original, Glyn Johns *Get Back* album
Jazz Piano Song	Many *Get Back* sessions LPs	McCartney and Starr at the piano. Seen in the *Let It Be* film
Jessie's Dream	Back Track Part Two (BT 6368)	From the *Magical Mystery Tour* film
Looking Glass		Performed by The Beatles at 1957-59 concerts but not recorded or released
Movin' And Groovin'	The Quarrymen At Home (BAH 1/2)	Also known as "The Guitar Bop." Duane Eddy song
Piano Boogie	Many *Let It Be* session bootlegs	McCartney at the piano
Piano Theme	Many *Let It Be* session bootlegs	Begins the *Let It Be* film
Ramrod		Performed by The Beatles at 1958-60 concerts but not recorded or released
Raunchy		Performed by The Beatles at 1957-60 concerts but not recorded or released
Shirley's Wild Accordion	Magical Mystery Tour (Wizardo 310)	Recorded by Shirley Evans, Reg Wale, McCartney, and Starr for the *Magical Mystery Tour* film
Thinking Of Linking	The Quarrymen At Home (BAH 1/2)	
Third Man Theme	File Under (Box Top Records GN70075/70077)	
12-Bar Orignal	Unsurpassed Masters Vol. 2 (SXCD004)	Long and short versions of this are available on bootlegs. This is the long version
Winston's Walk		Performed by The Beatles at 1957-59 concerts but not recorded or released

GEORGE HARRISON

TITLE	SOURCE	NOTES
Cowboy Museum	Wonderwall Music (Apple 3350)	
Crying	Wonderwall Music (Apple 3350)	
Dream Scene	Wonderwall Music (Apple 3350)	
Drilling A Home	Wonderwall Music (Apple 3350)	
Fantasy Sequins	Wonderwall Music (Apple 3350)	
Glass Box	Wonderwall Music (Apple 3350)	
Greasy Legs	Wonderwall Music (Apple 3350)	
Greece	Gone Troppo (Dark Horse 23734)	
Guru Vandana	Wonderwall Music (Apple 3350)	
Hari's On Tour (Express)	Dark Horse (Apple 3418)	Also available on 1974 tour bootlegs
I Remember Jeep	All Things Must Pass (Apple 639)	"Jeep" is Eric Clapton's dog
In The Park	Wonderwall Music (Apple 3350)	
Love Scene	Wonderwall Music (Apple 3350)	
Microbes	Wonderwall Music (Apple 3350)	
No Time Or Space	Electronic Sound (Apple 3358)	
On The Bed	Wonderwall Music (Apple 3350)	
Out Of The Blue	All Things Must Pass (Apple 639)	
Party Seacombe	Wonderwall Music (Apple 3350)	
Plug Me In	All Things Must Pass (Apple 639)	
Red Lady Too	Wonderwall Music (Apple 3350)	
Singing Om	Wonderwall Music (Apple 3350)	
Ski-ing And Gat Kirwani	Wonderwall Music (Apple 3350)	

Sound Stage Of Mind	Various 1974 tour bootlegs	
Tabla and Pakavaj	Wonderwall Music (Apple 3350)	
Thanks For The Pepperoni	All Things Must Pass (Apple 639)	
Under The Mersey Wall	Electronic Sound (Apple 3358)	
Wonderwall To Be Here	Wonderwall Music (Apple 3350)	
Zig Zag	When We Was Fab/Zig Zag (45) (Dark Horse 28131)	

JOHN LENNON

Beef Jerkey	Whatever Gets You Through The Night/Beef Jerkey (45) (Apple 1874)	
Dirty Mac Jam	Lost Lennon Tapes Vol. 8 (Bag 5080)	Lennon with Eric Clapton, Keith Richards, Mitch Mitchell
Rock Peace		Announced by Apple for release in August 1969, not as yet released
Rumble	The May Pang Tapes (Beetle 4080)	Recorded as a medley with "Whole Lotta Love" during the session for the *Rock 'N' Roll* album
Tequila	Goodnight Vienna (DR 6975)	Recorded with Elephant's Memory during One To One concert rehearsals
Whole Lotta Love	The May Pang Tapes (Beetle 4080)	See "Rumble"

PAUL McCARTNEY

Back Seat Of My Car	Thrillington (Capitol 11642)	
Big Bop Link	Wild Life (Apple 3386)	Uncredited on LP, credited on CD
Blue Sway	The Lost McCartney Album (Sandwich GTF-222)	A few vocals appear after the halfway mark of this six-minute song, but basically instrumental
Bogey Wobble	The Lost McCartney Album (Sandwich GTF-222)	Also called "Bubbles" by some bootleggers
Bridge On The River Suite	Walking In The Park With Eloise/Bridge On The River Suite (EMI 3977)	Recorded by McCartney as The Country Hams
Castle Of The King Of The Birds	Rupert The Bear (Library 2333)	Unreleased *Rupert* soundtrack
Cohen The Wind Is Blowing	Rupert The Bear (Library 2333)	Unreleased *Rupert* soundtrack
Corridor Music	Give My Regards To Broad Street (Columbia 39613)	Incidental movie music
Crossroads Theme	Venus And Mars (Capitol 11419)	Theme for a U.K. television soap opera
Cuff Link	With A Little Luck/Backwards Traveller-Cuff Link (45) (Capitol 4559)	
Dear Boy	Thrillington (Capitol 11642)	
Eat At Home	Thrillington (Capitol 11642)	
Eleanor's Dream	Give My Regards To Broad Street (Columbia 39613)	Seven-minute instrumental from the film
Flying Horses	Rupert The Bear (Library 2333)	Unreleased *Rupert* soundtrack
Front Parlour	McCartney II (Columbia 36511)	Also available in an extended version on *The Lost McCartney Album* (Sandwich GTF-222)
Frozen Jap	McCartney II (Columbia 36511)	Also available in an extended version on *The Lost McCartney Album* (Sandwich GTF-222)
Give Ireland Back To The Irish (Version)	Give Ireland Back To The Irish/(Version) (45) (Apple 1847)	
Glasses	McCartney (Apple 3363)	
Goodnight Princess	Give My Regards To Broad Street (Columbia 39613)	On CD only, not LP
Heart Of The Country	Thrillington (Capitol 11642)	
Hey Hey	Pipes Of Peace (Columbia 39149)	Written by McCartney and Stanley Cole
Hot As Sun	McCartney (Apple 3363)	Had been performed by The Beatles in 1958-59; also, a live version by Wings is on several bootlegs.
Kreen-Akrore	McCartney (Apple 3363)	Inspired by a TV film about the Kreen-Akrore Indians of Brazil
Long Haired Lady	Thrillington (Capitol 11642)	
Loup (1st Indian On The Moon)	Red Rose Speedway (Apple 3409)	
Lunch Box/Odd Sox	Venus And Mars CD (Capitol CDP 7469842)	Also available on many bootlegs

Momma Miss America	McCartney (Apple 3363)	
Monkberry Moon Delight	Thrillington (Capitol 11642)	
Mumbo Link	Wild Life (Apple 3386)	Uncredited on LP, credited on CD
Night Out	Cold Cuts (Club Sandwich SP-11); Cold Cuts (Another, Early Version) (Sandwich PPT 0172)	
Nutwood Scene	Rupert The Bear (Library 2333)	Unreleased *Rupert* soundtrack
One Hand Clapping	One Hand Clapping (YEAH 7475)	From the unreleased 1975 Wings video of the same title
Proud Mum	Cold Cuts (Club Sandwich SP-11); Cold Cuts (Another, Early Version) (Sandwich PPT 0172)	Two versions, a long and a short
Ram On	Thrillington (Capitol 11642)	
Rockestra Theme	Back To The Egg (Columbia 36057)	Studio version
	Concerts For The People Of Kampuchea (Atlantic 7005)	Live version
Rudolph The Red Nosed Reggae	Wonderful Christmastime/Rudolph The Red Nosed Reggae (45) (Columbia 11162)	
Sea Melody	Rupert The Bear (Library 2333)	Unreleased *Rupert* soundtrack
Silly Love Songs (Reprise)	Give My Regards To Broad Street (Columbia 39613)	
Singalong Junk	McCartney (Apple 3363)	
Smile Away	Thrillington (Capitol 11643)	
Storm	Rupert The Bear (Library 2333)	Unreleased *Rupert* soundtrack
Tippi Tippi Toes (Parent's Theme)	Rupert The Bear (Library 2333)	Unreleased *Rupert* soundtrack
3 Legs	Thrillington (Capitol 11642)	
Tomorrow	Cold Cuts (Another, Early Version) (Sandwich PPT 0172)	Much different than released, vocal, version
Too Many People	Thrillington (Capitol 11642)	
Uncle Albert/Admiral Halsey	Thrillington (Capitol 11642)	
Valentine Day	McCartney (Apple 3363)	
Walking In The Meadow	Rupert The Bear (Library 2333)	Unreleased *Rupert* soundtrack
Walking In The Park With Eloise	Walking In The Park With Eloise/Bridge On The River Suite (EMI 3977)	Recorded by McCartney using the name Country Hams
Zoo Gang	Venus And Mars CD (Capitol CDP 7469842)	From the British TV series of the same name

RINGO STARR

Everybody's In A Hurry But Me	Old Wave (RCA 3233)	Canadian release
Going Down	Old Wave (RCA 3233)	Canadian release

INSTRUMENTALS WITH BEATLE INVOLVEMENT

Altar Rock	Bobby Keys (Warner Bros. K46141)	U.K. release, Harrison on guitar, Starr on drums
Appolonia (Foxtrata)	New York Connection (Ode 77033)	By Tom Scott
Bootleg	Bobby Keys (Warner Bros. K46141)	U.K. release, Harrison on guitar, Starr on drums
Catcall	(45) (Marmalade 598-005)	By The Chris Barber Band, McCartney wrote the song as "Catsall"
Command Performance	Bobby Keys (Warner Bros. K46141)	U.K. release, Harrison on guitar, Starr on drums
Crispy Duck	Bobby Keys (Warner Bros. K46141)	U.K. release, Harrison on guitar, Starr on drums
Ending Jam	The Last Waltz (Warner Bros. 3WS3146)	By The Band, not listed on LP, Starr on drums
I'm Looking For Someone To Love	Holly Days (Capitol 11588)	Denny Laine with help from McCartney
Key-West	Bobby Keys (Warner Bros. K46141)	U.K. release, Harrison on guitar, Starr on drums
Lonesome Tears	Holly Days (Capitol 11588)	Denny Laine with help from McCartney
Love In The Open Air	The Family Way (London 82007)	George Martin Orchestra; written by McCartney
Maise	Standard Time (Breaking Records BREAK 1)	Laurence Juber with McCartney on bass
Rockestra Theme	Duane Eddy (Capitol 12567)	Artist is Duane Eddy; McCartney wrote the song, played bass on this recording, and produced it
Sand And Foam	Bobby Keys (Warner Bros. K46141)	U.K. release, Harrison on guitar, Starr on drums
Smokefoot	Bobby Keys (Warner Bros. K46141)	U.K. release, Harrison on guitar, Starr on drums
Steal From A King	Bobby Keys (Warner Bros. K46141)	U.K. release, Harrison on guitar, Starr on drums
Step Lightly	Star*tling Music (Ring O'11372)	David Hentchel with Starr providing "finger clicks"
Take Away The Sadness	Work It Out (Warner Bros. 25911)	Jim Horn, with Harrison on slide guitar
Theme For Something Really Important	Duane Eddy (Capitol 12567)	Duane Eddy with Harrison on slide guitar
Theme From "The Family Way"	The Family Way (London 82007)	Recorded by the Harrison Martin Orchestra, written by McCartney
Theme From "The Honorary Consul"	(45) (Island IS 155)	Recorded by John Williams; written by Paul McCartney
Thingumybob	Yellow Submarine/Thingumybob (45) (Apple 1800)	Recorded by John Foster and some Black Dyle Mills Band; written by Lennon/McCartney; theme for U.K. TV series
Tembler, The	Duane Eddy (Capitol 12567)	Recorded by Duane Eddy with Harrison on slide guitar
Wet Hayshark	B.B. King In London (ABC 730)	B.B. King with Starr on drums

And the Grammy goes to ...

The Beatles!

by J.G. Schuberk

What do Anita Kerr, The Carpenters, Glen Campbell, New Vaudeville Band, Roger Miller, Bobby Russell and The Statler Brothers all have in common? They all have the distinction of beating The Beatles out of a Grammy Award!

Over the course of its 36-year history, the Grammy Award presentations have often been exciting and unpredictable, yet strangely inconsistent. They are responsible for elevating the careers of artists such as The Police and Bette Midler. Singers Tina Turner, Bonnie Raitt, and Natalie Cole have experienced an amazing renaissance in their respective careers after Grammy victories. On the other hand, artists such as Milli Vanilli and Rick Springfield have disappeared into musical obscurity subsequent to receiving their awards. Worse yet, classic rockers such as Jimi Hendrix, The Rolling Stones, Bob Dylan, and Elvis Presley have been practically ignored by the Recording Academy.

In the 1960s, no artists achieved more sustained critical and commercial success than The Beatles. From 1964 through 1970, the Fab Four dominated the radio charts whenever they released new records. They were showered with more entertainment awards than most of their fellow colleagues in the music world. By example, The Beatles were recipients of England's Show Business Personalities of 1963; *New Musical Express* Poll Winners in 1963 and 1964; and they scored numerous Ivor Novello Awards (presented by the British Music Industry) between 1963 and 1970. They also were the beneficiaries of countless recording industry Silver and Gold Record Awards for the sale of their records worldwide.

However, though John Lennon, Paul McCartney, George Harrison, and Ringo Starr were nominated for more than 35 Grammy Awards between 1964 and 1970, they would only win seven gramophone statuettes during that time.

The Grammy is the American music industry's highest honor. Presented annually since 1958, the Grammy Award is, according to the National Academy of Recording Arts & Sciences (NARAS), "awarded for artistic or technical achievement, not sales figures or chart positions, and the winners are determined by the votes of their peers." The chief aim of the Recording Academy is to recognize excellence and foster a greater public awareness of cultural diversity and contributions of the recording industry.

Given the artistic and technical achievements scored by The Beatles and their producer George Martin, most people might assume that the group would have routinely swept the

This article originally appeared in Goldmine issue #347, Nov. 12, 1993.

Grammy Awards during the '60s. Instead, The Beatles found themselves nowhere man when most of the awards were handed out.

Several theories have been posed as to why The Beatles did not win more Grammys during their tenure as a group. Some contend the Fab Four were too radical for the times. Perhaps the long hair, admitted drug use, controversial comments and meditation with the Maharishi were just too much for the "old guard" that dominated the 1960s Academy membership. Their musical category, rock 'n' roll, was not well recognized by the Academy in the '60s. In fact, throughout the Grammy's history, critics often accused the Academy of failing to properly recognize rock 'n' rollers. It was not until 1979 that rock music was given several of its own special categories.

Politics is perhaps the best explanation for The Beatles' failure to take home more golden gramophones. At its inception, NARAS was created by the more conservative forces within the music industry to resist the new rambunctious, degenerate rock 'n' roll music. To this day, the struggle between conservative and progressive elements within the music industry continues.

In the 1960s, the older, conservative membership had a strong foothold on voting. There were perhaps only a handful of members under the age of 30. Block voting by geographical region determined Grammy outcomes significantly, with Nashville and Los Angeles battling for their own artists. Safe ballads and love songs, over loud rock 'n' roll, was the norm in the '60s. They still are.

Nomination categories were also politicized in the 1960s. Frequent dropping, adding and changing of nomination categories caused artists to lose opportunities for nomination. In other instances, award category politics crowded certain nomination fields with nominees whose music did not properly belong.

To its credit, the Recording Academy did acknowledge the efforts of The Beatles by bestowing upon them a substantial number of nominations. Fortunately for The Beatles, who were selling records eight days a week in the '60s, winning these awards was not particularly crucial to their continued commercial success.

This article presents a year-by-year overview of The Beatles' wins, losses and nominations at the Grammys. It also includes a "Grammyography," listing Beatles and post-Beatles solo awards. So sit back and enjoy The Beatles at the Grammy Awards, commercial free. May I have the envelope, please...

Beatles Grammyography 1964-1970 and 1992

Artist	Category	Title
Beatles	Best New Artist	N/A
Beatles	Best Performance By a Vocal Group	*A Hard Day's Night*
John Lennon/ Paul McCartney	Song Of The Year (Songwriter)	"Michelle"
Paul McCartney	Best Contemporary (R & R) Solo Vocal Performance, Male or Female	"Eleanor Rigby"
Beatles	Album Of The Year	*Sgt. Pepper's Lonely Hearts Club Band*
Beatles	Best Contemporary Album	*Sgt. Pepper's Lonely Hearts Club Band*
Beatles	Best Original Score Written for a Motion Picture or TV Special (Composer)	*Let It Be*
Beatles	Hall Of Fame Award	*Sgt. Pepper's Lonely Hearts Club Band*

1964

The 1964 awards were presented April 13, 1965. The Beatles were nominated in the following categories: Record Of The Year ("I Want To Hold Your Hand"); Song Of The Year ("A Hard Day's Night," Lennon/McCartney songwriters); Best New Artist; Best Performance By A Vocal Group (*A Hard Day's Night*); Best Rock 'n' Roll Recording ("A Hard Day's Night") and Best Original Score Written For A Motion Picture Or TV Show (*A Hard Day's Night*).

The group walked away with only two awards that night, namely, Best New Artist and Best Performance By A Vocal Group. The popular mainstream hit, "The Girl From Ipanema," was deemed to be superior to "I Want To Hold Your Hand" for Record Of The Year. "Hello Dolly" took Song The Year honors, and good old *Mary Poppins* trounced *A Hard Day's Night* in the Best Original Score category.

The ceremony was aired a month later on NBC's *The Best On Record*, May 18, 1965. Although The Beatles did not appear live on the broadcast, a tape of their presentation was shown. The tape was filmed during a break in the making of the "pub scene" in *Help!* Comedian and friend Peter Sellers presented the four with their Grammy Award. Led by John Lennon, The Beatles and Sellers (never ones to let a serious ceremony spoil the party) happily spoke French-sounding gibberish into the camera and broke into the song "It's A Long Way To Tipperary."

***Help!* and its title track were both nominated for Grammys in 1965.**

1965

The 1965 awards were presented in March 1966. This was perhaps the Academy's most controversial awards year in terms of its treatment toward The Beatles. The Fabs were nominated in the following categories: Album Of The Year (*Help!*); Record Of The Year ("Yesterday," Lennon/McCartney songwriters); Song Of The Year ("Yesterday"); Best Vocal Performance ("Yesterday," McCartney); Best Performance By A Vocal Group ("Help!"); Best Contemporary (Rock 'n' Roll) Single ("Yesterday"); Best Contemporary (Rock 'n' Roll) Performance By A Group ("Help!"). The Beatles' producer George Martin was also nominated for Best Arrangement Accompanying A Vocalist Or Instrument ("Yesterday").

The theme song for this ceremony should have been titled "I'm A Loser" because that aptly describes The Beatles and producer Martin in 1965. Although nominated for nine categories, alleged ballot stuffing by the Academy's new Nashville chapter completely shut out The Beatles on this night!

MICHELLE

WORDS & MUSIC BY

JOHN LENNON & PAUL McCARTNEY

MACLEN
MUSIC,
Inc.

75¢

Perhaps the biggest mistake in Grammy history occurred in 1965 when country and western's Anita Kerr Quartet took honors for Best Performance By A Vocal Group over The Beatles. The Quartet's winning album (for all the trivia enthusiasts out there) was the unforgettable *We Dig Mancini*. Would it be a surprise to learn that Kerr was a very popular friend of the Academy's voting membership at the time? As recounted in Thomas O'Neil's book, *The Grammys — For The Record* (Penguin Books USA, Inc., 1993) Kerr was vice president of the Nashville chapter of NARAS and regularly involved herself in the affairs of the New York and Los Angeles chapters. Thus, her victory over The Beatles, though surprising to the public and news media, was probably *expected* by Nashville insiders of that era.

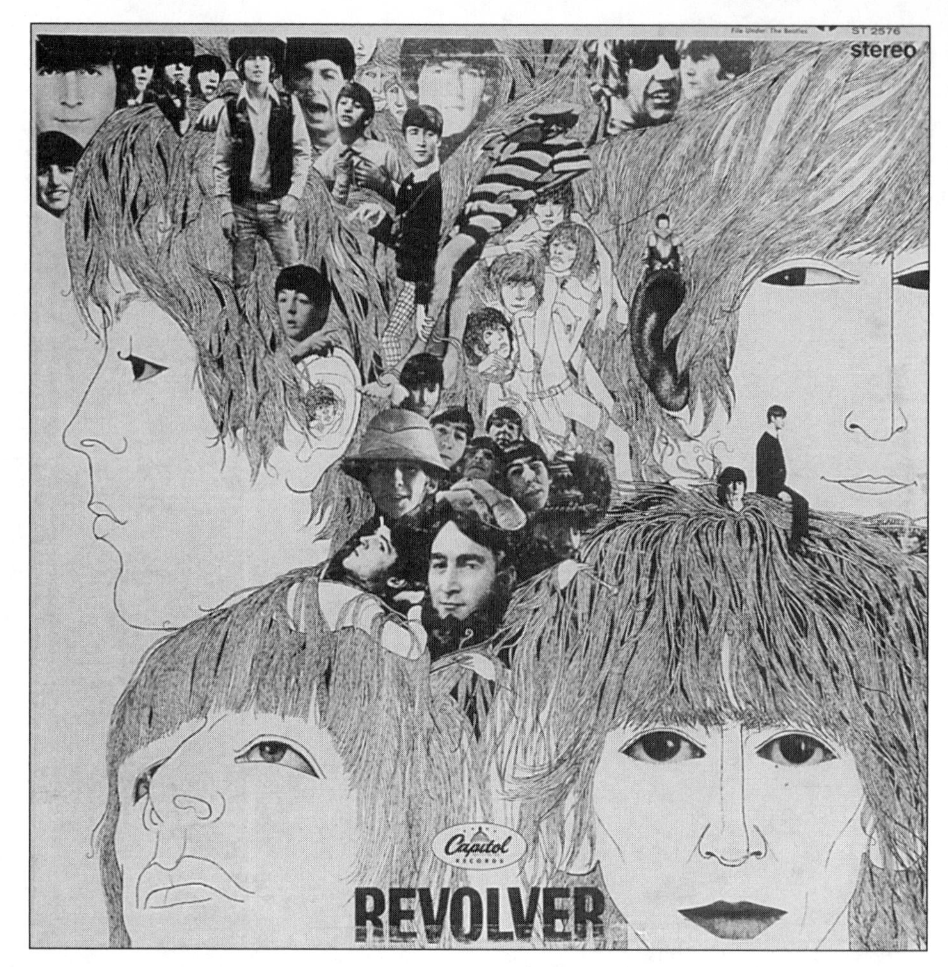

Klaus Voormann won a Grammy in 1966 for his album cover artwork on *Revolver.*

The surprises in store for The Beatles at the 1965 Awards ceremony did not stop with Kerr's victory. Another series of Nashville upsets over the Fab Four included *non*-rock singers Roger Miller and The Statler Brothers. Miller's "King Of The Road" topped The Beatles' "Yesterday" in both the Best Contemporary (Rock 'n' Roll) Single and Best Male Vocal Performance categories. And perhaps the most bizzare coup of the Nashville "mafia" was country's Statler Brothers. They were victorious over The Beatles for Best Contemporary (Rock 'n' Roll) Performance By A Group. The Statlers' winning entry was "Flowers On The Wall." Besides besting The Beatles, the Statlers finished ahead of Herman's Hermits ("Mrs. Brown"), Sam The Sham And The Pharaohs ("Wooly Bully") and The Supremes ("Stop In The Name Of Love").

Only politics and strong Nashville chapter voting could explain the placement of these country twangers into rock 'n' roll categories in the first place, especially when country and western music already had six categories designated to its own genre. As a result, Nashville's domination of the 1965 Grammys struck a dissonant chord. Beatles supporters were not the only ones disappointed. Many of the other Academy members viewed the awards that year as disproportionately balanced in favor of the Nashville clan.

1966

Awards for 1966 were handed out on March 2, 1967. The Beatles were again acknowledged through several nominations, this time successfully winning some Grammy hardware. The group and some of its collegues were up for the following categories: Album Of The Year (*Revolver*); Song Of The Year ("Michelle," Lennon/McCartney songwriters); Best Vocal performance, Male ("Eleanor Rigby," McCartney); Best Contemporary (Rock 'n' Roll) Recording ("Eleanor Rigby"); Best Contemporary (Rock 'n' Roll) Solo Vocal Performance, Male Or Female ("Eleanor Rigby," McCartney); Best Arrangement Accompanying Vocalist On Instrument (George Martin, "Eleanor Rigby"); and Best Album Cover (*Revolver*, Klaus Voormann, artist).

A Grammy was awarded to Lennon and McCartney (for "Michelle") in the prestigious category Song Of The Year, perhaps to make up for the criticism received by the Academy for snubbing The Beatles in 1965. McCartney's vocal performance on "Eleanor Rigby" also took top honors. It is interesting to note that both awards clearly reflected the voting Academy's long-standing preference for ballads and love songs over hard rock. Voormann, longtime friend of the Fabs, took the Grammy for his wonderful collage on the cover of *Revolver*.

Perhaps more than one music critic winced when the New Vaudeville Band ("Winchester Cathedral") took the trophy for Best Contemporary (Rock 'n' Roll) Recording. Not only did these one-hit wonders surpass The Beatles ("Eleanor Rigby") in this category, but they also trounced four other classic recordings as well. The four other artists overlooked by the Academy included The Association ("Cherish"), The Beach Boys ("Good Vibrations"), The Monkees ("Last Train To Clarksville") and The Mamas And The Papas ("Monday, Monday")!

Other major categories of 1966 were dominated by the "old guard" of Frank Sinatra, Ray Charles, Duke Ellington and, yes, once again, The Anita Kerr Quartet. Kerr's group took the crown for Best Performance By A Vocal Group. Unbelievable as it may seem, this was a category in which The Beatles were not even nominated in 1966!

1967

The Beatles and friends fared well at the 1967 Grammy Awards, which were presented in February 1968. *Sgt. Pepper's Lonely Hearts Club Band* won the coveted Album Of The Year and Best Contemporary Album awards. However, once again, middle-of-the-road academy voting prevented a Beatles sweep by choosing the safe 5th Dimension ("Up, Up And Away') for Best Performance By A Vocal Group and Best Contemporary Group Performance, Vocal Or Instrumental. Martin lost a bid for Best Arrangement Accompanying A Vocalist ("A Day In The Life") to Jimmie Haskell ("Ode To Billie Joe"), but his engineer Geoff Emerick did win a Grammy for Best Engineered Recording Non-Classical (*Sgt. Pepper*). Peter Blake and Jann Haworth took the award for their art direction on the *Sgt. Pepper* album cover. Also that year, Beatle buddy Ravi Shankar won the Best Chamber Music Performance award.

All in all, the 1967 Grammy Awards were remarkable in that members of the Academy were bold enough to reward The Beatles for their groundbreaking album that featured creative experimentation in concept, songwriting, music, engineering technology and its cover art. However, this nod to the cutting edge would not become a trend as the years rolled on, neither would innovation be the key to more trophies for The Beatles.

1968

The 1968 awards, given away on March 12, 1969, were marked by a return to safe, pleasant pop. The Beatles garnered four nominations, for Album Of The Year (*Magical Mystery Tour*); Record Of The Year ("Hey Jude"); Song Of The Year ("Hey Jude," Lennon/McCartney songwriters) and Best Contemporary Pop Vocal Performance, Duo Or Group ("Hey Jude"). However, once again they were shut out.

The gentle Glen Campbell (*By The Time I Get To Phoenix*) took Album Of The Year honors. The sweet sounds of Simon And Garfunkel ("Mrs. Robinson") walked off with Record Of The Year and Best Contemporary Pop Vocal Performance. The corny Bobby Russell ("Little Green Apples") was deemed best songwriter, for Song Of The Year.

A comparison between the Grammy years of 1967 and 1968 reveals that changes in category designations may have cost The Beatles an award or two. Two categories where The Beatles would likely have been favored were removed in 1968. Absent were awards for Best Contemporary Single (how about "Hey Jude"?) and Best Contemporary Album (perhaps *Magical Mystery Tour*?). Of course, we will never know the outcome for the two dropped categories. But then, there was always a possibility for the return of the amazing Anita Kerr Quartet to sweep away The Beatles' chances.

1969

The ceremony was held on March 11, 1970, just one month before McCartney would announce to the world that The Beatles had broken up forever. This time around, The Beatles and company were nominated for four awards, namely, Album Of The Year (*Abbey Road*), Best Contemporary Vocal Performance, Group (*Abbey Road*), Best Original Score Written For A Picture Or TV Special (*Yellow Submarine*, composers Lennon, McCartney, Harrison, and George Martin); and Best Engineered Recording, Non Classical (Geoff Emerick, Phillip McDonald, *Abbey Road*).

Once again, Academy voting generally embraced traditional values and more conservative music, which meant The Beatles would come up empty-handed. Blood, Sweat & Tears took Album Of The Year honors over not only *Abbey Road*, but the debut of Crosby, Stills And Nash. In an encore performance, The 5th Dimension aced The Beatles in the Vocal Performance category with the now dated "Aquarius"/"Let The Sunshine In," from the *Hair* musical. Only Geoff Emerick and Phil McDonald received an award for their engineering on *Abbey Road*.

1970

Presented on March 16, 1971, this was the first-ever live telecast of the Grammy Awards. The now-defunct Beatles pulled in five nominations for their commercial swan song album (but not the last recorded), *Let It Be*. The nominations included Record Of The Year ("Let It Be"); Song Of The Year ("Let It Be," Lennon/McCartney, songwriters); Best Contemporary Vocal Performance By A Duo, Group or Chorus ("Let It Be"); and Best Original Score Written For A Motion Picture Or TV Special (*Let It Be*, Lennon, McCartney, Harrison, Starr, composers).

The Beatles' last chance to sweep the Grammys came up short again, as they were practically shut out by the safe, soft sounds of Simon And Garfunkel and The Carpenters. The group's last Grammy award would be for Best Original Film Score. Paul McCartney surprised the audience by showing up to personally receive the award on behalf of his former bandmates. McCartney's acceptance speech consisted of a simple two words, "Thank you."

1992

By 1993, the former Beatles had been pursuing individual endeavors for some 23 years. And as everyone knows, the prospect of a Beatles reunion became moot on Dec. 8, 1980, with John Lennon's passing. Yet this fact did not stop the Academy from resurrecting The Beatles' album *Sgt. Pepper's Lonely Hearts Club Band* for its 1992 Hall Of Fame Award. The Hall Of Fame Award honors recordings of "lasting historical or qualitative significance" that were released more than 25 years ago.

The long and winding Grammy road

While the Grammy Awards remain today the most prestigious of the music industry, they were not always so generous to The Beatles. The awards are supposedly presented based upon artistic or technical achievement. Yet, given their inconsistent track record with The Beatles and other rockers, many critics might aptly present NARAS with its own Grammy for the category, Most Political Home Town Middle Of The Road, Ballad Lovers.

In recent years the Academy has begun to appreciate The Beatles in its own retroactive fashion by awarding the aforementioned Hall Of Fame Award as well as Lifetime Achievement Awards to Lennon (posthumously) and McCartney. It is anyone's guess if and when the Academy will bestow similar awards to Harrison and Starr.

The fact that the Fab Four were able to achieve such popular, commercial and critical success during their reign in the '60s (without winning more Grammys) is to their credit. However, one still has to wonder how The Beatles would have fared if Anita Kerr (and her Quartet) had never been born.

The author gratefully acknowledges assistance he received from Mrs. H.L. Schuberk in the preparation of this article.

Beginning of the end

Paul McCartney's 1970 lawsuit calling for dissolution of The Beatles

by J.G. Schuberk

For more than 20 years, fans, historians and journalists have been attempting to answer the age-old question, "Why did The Beatles break up?" Many have offered simplified answers to this complex question. Some have placed the blame on Yoko Ono's presence in the studio during recording sessions, while others have blamed the group's sense of loss and lack of direction following manger Brian Epstein's death. None of these reasons has answered the question satisfactorily. Of course, there is no simple explanation to the dissolution of the Fab Four's creative partnership.

On Dec. 31, 1970, Paul McCartney formally moved to dissolve the four-way partnership between himself and the other three Beatles and to have the court appoint a receiver to handle the group's affairs. The Application Of Dissolution titled James Paul McCartney (Plaintiff) and John Ono Lennon, George Harrison, Richard Starkey, and Apple Corps Limited (Defendants), was filed in the High Court Of Justice, Chancery Division, Group B, and was assigned case number 1970 No. 6315.

Goldmine magazine has recently obtained an exclusive copy of the complete sworn affidavit of McCartney, made in support of his Application to dissolve The Beatles. This is not simply a copy of the affidavit, it is, more importantly, the manuscript that contains John Lennon's comments and responses to Paul McCartney's statements, handwritten into the margins!

What caused McCartney to take such an extreme action, one that would impact the world as no other musical breakup ever had? What factors caused the group to drift apart both socially and creatively? And what was Lennon's personal response to the allegations made by McCartney in his application to dissolve the group?

Previously, neither fans nor historians have had the opportunity to go behind the scenes and delve into the answers to these questions. Never before have Lennon and McCartney's perspectives been fully revealed in detail.

This document is historically significant in its detailed scenario of The Beatles' breakup, as told by both of The group's principal songwriters. Lennon was undoubtedly assisting his barrister at the time, who likely instructed him to respond to McCartney's allegations by writing them in the margins. However, as the reader will see, Lennon's remarks are not

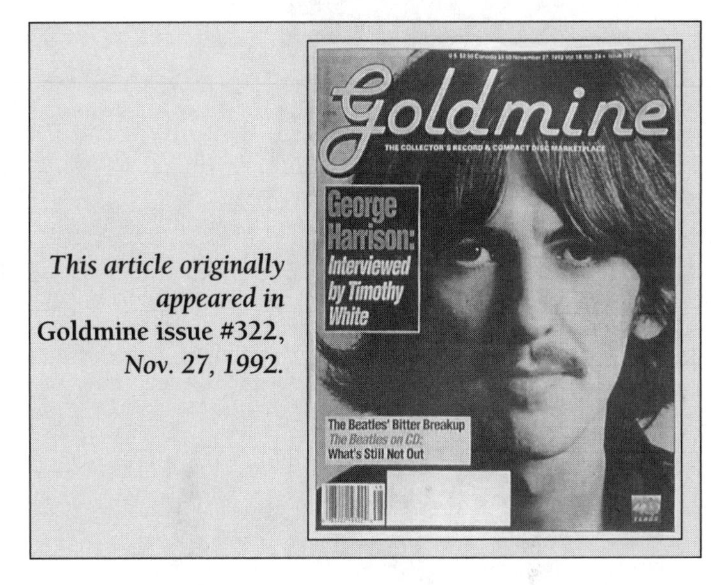

This article originally appeared in* Goldmine issue #322, *Nov. 27, 1992.

those of the witty "moptop" Lennon. On the contrary, his remarks are deadly serious.

The document was obtained by an international memorabilia expert/dealer in London in December 1991, 21 years to the month after it was drafted. The original (from which *Goldmine's* copy is directly reproduced here) was later auctioned off at Richard Wolffers Auctions, Incorporated, on June 18, 1992. Wolffers, founded in 1970, has historically offered sports memorabilia and rare stamps but recently entered the world of high-end and music-related artifacts. At the auctioneer's request, more than one autograph expert authenticated Lennon's handwriting on this rare manuscript. At auction, this intriguing piece of pop music history sold for an astounding $19,800 (including the 10 percent house premium).

McCartney begins the Affidavit by explaining the four basic reasons why he is "driven to make this application":

"(a) The Beatles have long since ceased to perform as a group,

(b) the defendants (John, George, Ringo and Apple) have sought to impose upon me a manager who is unacceptable to me,

(c) my artistic freedom is liable to be interfered with so long as the partnership continues, and

(d) no partnership accounts have been prepared since the Deed Of Partnership was entered into."

McCartney addresses the first reason by explaining that the group began to drift apart after the touring ended. He relates back to the harmonious relationship the band experienced on tour until 1965. Lennon counters this point by writing that there had been "many fights on tour about leadership."

On page three of the document, McCartney relates, "By the time that *Abbey Road* was recorded we were openly critical of each other's music, and he [John] was no longer interested in the performance of songs which he had not written himself."

As one might expect, Lennon takes issue with this statement by noting, "Paul was guilty of this for years — witness *Let It Be* [film] clips."

Both Lennon and McCartney were correct here. Neither was interested in each other's work at this stage in their careers. This was truly similar to a divorce, in that the principal "couple" had grown apart over time.

The artifact changes subjects at this point and moves onto perhaps the most central issue to the split, namely the management of The Beatles' and Apple's affairs. In a nutshell, Lennon, Harrison, and Starr had chosen Allen Klein (who had managed The Rolling Stones) to be their manager in January 1969. According to McCartney, he never assented to Klein as either his personal manager or manager for The Beatles and Apple. Instead, McCartney wanted the New York law firm of Eastman And Eastman (his father-in-law and brother-in-law) to manage his affairs.

McCartney explains on page four that, "This was the first time in the history of The Beatles that a possible irreconcilable difference had appeared between us. Hitherto we had always decided matters unanimously after appropriate discussion." In the margin, Lennon chides Paul for not warming up to Klein and writes, "He [Paul] was funny about anyone *new* including *Brian* [Epstein]!"

IN THE HIGH COURT OF JUSTICE 1970 M. No. 6315

CHANCERY DIVISION

GROUP B

BETWEEN:

JAMES PAUL McCARTNEY Plaintiff

and

JOHN ONO LENNON, GEORGE HARRISON

RICHARD STARKEY and

APPLE CORPS LIMITED Defendants

I, James Paul McCartney of 7 Cavendish Avenue, London N.W.8, the above-named plaintiff, make oath and say as follows :-

1. By a Writ of Summons issued out of this Court on December 1970 I have applied to the Court for a decree of dissolution of the partnership between me and the defendants. The partnership was formerly constituted between us for the purpose of performing in various branches of the entertainment industry as a group of musicians known as "The Beatles". By a Deed of Partnership made on 19th April 1967 between the defendants and myself the defendant company was admitted as a partner in the partnership business previously carried on by the individual defendants (to whom I shall refer by their first names or collectively as 'the other three') and myself. Thereafter the defendants and I carried on business as "Beatles and Co.' A true copy of the Deed is now produced and shown to me marked 'J.P.M. 1'. The name of The Beatles Limited was later changed first to Apple Music Limited on 17th November 1967 and then on 12th January 1968 to Apple Corps Limited (hereinafter called 'Apple').

Not only was McCartney "funny" in his failure to accept Allen Klein as his or The Beatles' manager, he openly despised and verbally attacked the man. On page six of the Affidavit, McCartney unloads a salvo of cutting barbs on Klein.

"As time went on I grew increasingly to distrust Klein on the grounds of his proneness to boast about his ability to make spectacular deals which he proved unable to fulfill; his tendency to show discord between us [Beatles] individually, by playing one off against the other; his untruthfulness; and his unscrupulous efforts to hold himself out as manager and gain commission in other fields not covered by his 'agreements.'"

From this point forward, McCartney spends the balance of the Affidavit blaming Klein and the other three for interfering with his artistic freedom and failing to provide him with any accounting of partnership proceeds. These are the last two reasons McCartney makes for filing his application.

Of special interest to music fans and scholars are the negative statements McCartney makes about Phil Spector's remixes of his songs on *Let It Be*. "I found that in the recording of my song "The Long And Winding Road," Spector had not only 'mixed' the recording, but had added strings, voices, horns and drums, and had changed the recording of my other songs considerably. This had never happened before and I regarded this as an intolerable interference with my work."

Lennon responds that this sort of thing "used to happen in earlier days." Lennon is of course correct if one considers the many stereo mixing sessions author Mark Lewisohn has documented, in which The Beatles failed to attend. As music historians will attest, there are significant differences between the stereo and mono versions of several Beatles songs. Perhaps the greatest outpouring of anger and venom is displayed at the close of the document when McCartney accuses Klein and the other three Fabs of blocking the release of McCartney's first solo album (*McCartney*). He claims that his "adversaries" were using the release date as leverage to get him to accept some of Klein's objectives on the *Let It Be* record deal with United Artists.

McCartney angrily relates, "I particularly resented the threat to my artistic freedom constituted by the attempt by the other three to stop or at least delay release of my record," to which Lennon responds in kind. "We resented the high-handed way in which his record 'suddenly' appeared, and demanding release dates with no consideration whatsoever for other Apple products."

At the time (spring 1970) The Beatles' *Let It Be* and Ringo Starr's *Sentimental Journey* were also set for release. It has been reported that ultimately Starr convinced Lennon and Harrison to allow McCartney's album to be released in April, with Starr's release coming before McCartney's, and *Let It Be* coming after McCartney's.

All in all, the document reproduced here is a very revealing and feisty portrait of Beatles history. The Beatles' wounds were long and deep, lasting for many years. There are several intriguing and intimate details found here that give fans and historians a brief snapshot into the sad state of the Lennon-McCartney-Harrison-Starr relationship in 1970.

McCartney and Lennon reportedly smoothed over a number of their differences prior to Lennon's untimely death in 1980. However, the two men never formally wrote or recorded together again after the split (save for an impromptu jam session in 1974). *Goldmine* is proud to present this exclusive, revealing document to its readers, which it believes has never before been published in its entirety.

Love calls

The inside story of John Lennon and Yoko Ono week on *The Mike Douglas Show*

by Gillian G. Gaar

During most of their time as a couple, John Lennon and Yoko Ono seemed unfamiliar with the concept of "down time." From the moment they joined forces in May 1968, the couple made a wide variety of public appearances, including live performances, art exhibits and interviews with all manner of media, compulsively recording their activities all the time.

1972 would prove to be no exception. Lennon and Ono had moved to New York City the previous September, in an attempt to gain custody of Ono's daughter, Kyoko, from her previous marriage. Within a month they appeared on *The Dick Cavett Show*, and during the rest of 1971 they worked on new music, filmed segments for their "home movie" *Imagine*, recorded the single "Happy Christmas (War Is Over)"/"Listen The Snow Is Falling," appeared in concert in Ann Arbor and at a benefit in Harlem and fraternized with political activists such as Abbie Hoffman and Jerry Rubin.

They began 1972 with another TV appearance, this time *The David Frost Show*. During the same period, they began taping a week's worth of appearances for their most high-profile TV engagement yet — *The Mike Douglas Show*.

Not only did Lennon and Ono cohost the show for a week, they also helped select the guests that appeared on the show with them. "It was a fascinating experiment in using the most conventional kind of mass media to put across the idea of John and Yoko and their friends," says Jon Wiener, author of the acclaimed book *Come Together: John Lennon In His Time*. "They weren't just being guests, pitching their own project. They ran the whole week! I don't think that's ever happened before or since. They wanted to try to get their ideas into the mainstream, into middle America, into the middle of the day! So it was an amazing idea."

The Mike Douglas Show was one of the top-rated talk/variety shows of the time, airing every weekday and catering to an audience Mike Douglas describes as "Housewives and youngsters coming home from school." The week of Feb. 14-18, 1972, this audience was confronted with an astonishing array of guests on the show not only including Lennon and Ono, but also Chuck Berry, Jerry Rubin, Black Panthers chairman Bobby Seale, consumer activist Ralph Nader, comedian George Carlin, and U.S. Surgeon General Dr. Jesse Steinfeld. The shows have been staples on the Beatles bootleg circuit for years; later, in 1996, they aired in edited versions on VH-1. Now Rhino Video has packaged the entire week's worth of unedited shows in a box set, *The Mike Douglas Show With John Lennon and Yoko Ono*.

This article originally appeared in Goldmine issue #477, Nov. 6, 1998.

In addition to the five tapes, the set also includes a hardbound booklet with liner notes, including interviews with people who worked on the show. But in the 26 years since the show originally aired, memories can change, and both Douglas and the show's executive producer, Woody Fraser, have a different take on what went on during the production and taping of the shows than the booklet's other interviewees, beginning with how Lennon and Ono came to be on the show in the first place. Though the booklet states the *Mike Douglas* staff contacted Lennon and Ono, Fraser says it might have been the other way around.

"I think they called Mike," he says. "But I can't remember exactly. I just know that somebody came in to me and said, 'What would you think of John and Yoko being on the show?' And of course we all flipped. But you know, you get a lot of that. Somebody might call up and say, 'Hey, we got Mel Gibson for a week!' And then you call back and you find out no. So I said, 'You've got make sure this is a legitimate situation.'"

The booking turned out to be legitimate, and Douglas' reaction was not surprising: "I was elated. Everybody doing a talk show wanted them!"

Most reviews of the set have focused on the audacity of Lennon and Ono airing their unconventional views in such a mainstream format. Yet *The Mike Douglas Show* was unconventional in its own way. Despite being named after the host, Fraser explains the idea behind the show was spotlighting the guests.

"When I was a kid, I used to watch all these shows, Arthur Godfrey and all these people," he says. "And if you're the guest, they're not interested in you. You're just there as a ploy for them to talk more. And so that was when I got this idea. I wanted a guy or a woman who was a total catalyst, meaning, they're going to make you look good. And it just didn't exist in those days. I wanted the host to be able to do everything: sing, dance, get hit in the face with a pie, ask a serious question. And all within the confines of one show.

"That's how I ended up with Mike, because Mike is that kind of guy," Fraser continues. "It didn't bother him to sit there day in and day out for over 20 years and make the guest the star. And that never changed. He never once said, 'I don't need the cohost, I don't want the cohost.' He never turned to me and said that. I've never been with anybody like that since."

Indeed, one of the most striking aspects of the shows is how much the guests are actually allowed to speak, engaging in bonafide conversations with Douglas, as opposed to the soundbite interview format common on most of today's talk shows.

"I think that's because of the fact that I'm one of the few good listeners left in this world!" says Douglas. "I don't think there are many of them left on television today that listen very well. Some of the best interviews on television, I hear things go by, and say, 'Whoa! Why did she let that get away?'"

Having weekly cohosts added freshness to the format, "So each Monday you get to look forward to a brand-new show, essentially," says Fraser, who adds that the show was also no stranger to controversy, bringing on guests such as Malcolm X, Jimmy Hoffa, and Martha Mitchell — the latter guest attracting the attention of the White House.

"They called Westinghouse [the show's sponsor] saying, 'Don't put this alcoholic woman on there!' and they were threatening all sorts of stuff," Fraser says. "I can't tell you what I went through with the executives and the legal department at Westinghouse. I ended up putting her on, but I do try to balance it with fun. It's not my intention to do a *Crossfire*. We were criticized by a lot of people who said, 'You're an entertainment show. You have no right to put those kinds of things on.' But it never bothered me. And the way I housed it, billed it and kept a lot of high entertainment and fun in the show, we kept the audience."

"We aimed for the variety," Douglas agrees. "I mean, television, let's face it, it's an entertainment medium. And we didn't try to book controversial things just to titillate the audience, but because we thought people were interested. Because when every time you pick up a newspaper and you're reading about a certain person, obviously people want to see that person on television because it's a whole different world. To see how they'll react to what I would say to them and all. And the fact that I would have them on in the first place; 'Why is he having so and so on the show? He doesn't seem like somebody Mike would want to talk with.'"

Both Fraser and Douglas agree their show's format was probably what enticed Lennon and Ono in the first place, though Ono's previous appearance on the show was undoubtedly another key factor. "I really don't know the genesis of how it happened or what caused them to want to do the show, other than the fact that they were fans of the show," Fraser says. "But I do believe they felt that Mike Douglas would not attack them. They looked at this show, and they saw that this is a forum. And what we said we were going to do we always delivered."

"I think they felt they would just be more comfortable with me," Douglas agrees. "They were way ahead of their time.

And much of what they said I must admit I was in total agreement with. As an example, the war in Vietnam, which I thought was a terrible, terrible mistake on our part. But you couldn't express those opinions in those days. If you did, you alienated half, or more than half, of your audience. So I couldn't express myself the way I would've liked to have. But it was interesting. And I think a lot of people watched in disbelief, first of all, never thinking that I would ever have them on a show. And secondly, some of the things he said."

Douglas himself couldn't believe some of the things the couple said, starting with their suggestions for potential guests. "When we said, 'Who would you like to have on the show?' I'll never forget it as long as I live, John said, 'The Chicago Seven,'" he says. "And everybody laughed, thinking he was joking. But he wasn't joking! He meant it!" But on Fraser's part, the variety of guests would only help present a more well-rounded view of his cohosts. "My philosophy was, if I'm going to have John and Yoko on for a week, then I want to make it as much their show as I can," he says. "So we sit with them and find out their interests. And I try to get them out of the music area: Are you interested in poetry? What else are you interested in?

"At the same time, I have to bring other things into the show," he adds. "If somebody's finished a hot movie, I have to keep that open. So it's not like Lennon and Yoko are getting a full 90 minutes. They were the biggest booking the show ever had, so everybody bent over backwards to get everybody that they wanted. However, we reached a point where the decision was, we need a little bit more balance of entertainment stuff in there. And John was fine with that. But Yoko was not fine with that. She had a definite agenda. Matter of fact, I think she was the one that really decided to do this; she was the deciding factor about them doing it. 'Cause if you were around them, you would see very quickly that she runs the show. And John was very much in love with her, and he was very concilliatory toward her. I wouldn't say he was a wimp, at all. Nobody ever said this to me, but it just became apparent that he was really kind of doing this for her."

There was also the attraction of reaching directly into the homes of a new audience (not to mention attracting a new audience to watch the show). "John and Yoko were interested not just in reaching the kids, the hip people, the rock 'n' rollers, they wanted to try to talk to everybody," says Wiener. "And they thought everybody might be interested! Or at least it was worth a try to find out. That's what never happened before. And because Lennon had the celebrity power, he was able to get the hours of TV. I don't think today anyone would get that many hours. They would have their own 12-minute segment or something like that. So it was a unique commitment on their part, breaking out of the rock 'n' roll mold, and the unique situation of Lennon's position that gave him the power to try to do this. And the couple's own interest in experimenting."

A few other concessions were in order before taping could begin. Instead of taping all the shows over the course of a week, as was usual, Lennon and Ono's schedule was such that they could only come down one day a week, so that the five shows were taped over the course of five weeks. "I would much prefer to have done it the other way," says Douglas. "It's so much easier. You build kind of a momentum, and then you have to detach yourself from it, and then suddenly here they are again. And you're going, 'Wait a minute, I've gotta get back on that planet, on that level.' You go, 'Whoa, John and Yoko today!'"

Fraser and Douglas have different memories of how the shows were taped. "We just shot on an extra day," Fraser says. "We didn't do another show the day they did theirs." Told that the Rhino booklet, and Douglas, state that a regular show and a Lennon/Ono show would be taped on one day, he concedes, "We may have done it once or twice that way because of their scheduling problems." But whatever the circumstances, Fraser agrees the work amounted to "a long tape day, 'cause there were a lot of stop downs. Though as far as everybody was concerned, they were used to working very hard. There was no hardship at all. Everybody was so excited. Everybody was walking on air. John Lennon and Yoko, please!"

Fraser explains how a day's taping was put together. "At 9 o'clock in the morning, I meet with the staff," he says. "There's a person assigned to the cohost, and there's a person assigned to the other individual guests — segment producers. Their job is to put together an interview. At 10 o'clock, rehearsal starts. And at the same time, I bring one segment producer in at a time to Mike with the cards. Everything was on cards for Mike, all the questions. And we'd run through the cards. Then Mike would go down to rehearsal about 11 o'clock."

As for rehearsals with Lennon and Ono, Fraser says, "All the problems were musical, pure and simple. We'd go in at 10 and tape at 1; that's three hours, but we really had only two and a half, because at 12:30 you've got to break down, and you've got to get everybody ready to do the show. So we'd try to get all the soundchecks done and try to get Yoko and Lennon's music stuff done. But their framework of what it takes to do a song is totally different than what it takes for us to do on a show, where we're doing a show every day, live.

"The other thing is, they may have to add musicians, bring in a conductor, add side pieces, extra musicians, then we have to make room for that, and we have to have new microphones and we have to have some lighting, and then we have to balance that sound," Fraser continues. "And to be honest, we were woefully lacking in what they would be used to having in a sound studio. So the majority of the time was spent setting up the instruments and doing soundchecks and then getting a sound balance.

"That is really the most difficult part. Especially when they're playing and singing at the same time. They have to hear themselves. Musicians and singers are nuts about hearing themselves. And also, she had to get used to our musicians, and John had to get used to our musicians. He was easy. He was very easy. She was difficult because her music is complicated and different. And she is a composer and so she wants to hear certain things. And if she can't hear the flute, then you've got to stop until you can hear the flute. Then we may hear the flute, but we can't hear the drums. I find some of her music really interesting. I call it metaphysical jazz. Metaphysical jazz-rock. But to be heard over that little television box — you didn't have the big stereo stuff like we do today.

"So we never taped on time, because we had to make sure that the music was right. Once it started, I think it only

took about two hours. But we were always late starting. But nobody ever complained, because it was John and Yoko. The audience? They would've waited until midnight! They didn't care."

There were further problems in simply deciding how many songs the couple would perform — and who would perform them. "When the deal was made, the deal was that John would perform three songs every day and she would perform one," Fraser says. "And then when they came in on the first day of taping, she rolled out three songs and he rolled out one. And of course I had to discuss with him, this was not the deal. And she did not take kindly to this. But he finally agreed he would do two and she would do two. Everything's a compromise. But that kind of set her off with an attitude for the week. All she was really interested in was playing her music. That's when I got in trouble. And then I have to go through this summit meeting to get them to change it. And she was not a happy camper. Which I guess anybody wouldn't be — she just wants to play her stuff. It's not that I think her stuff is bad. It's that you've got John Lennon. I mean, come on. You want to get as much of John Lennon as you can."

Actually, over the course of the week, Lennon and Ono performed two songs each. Lennon's performances of "It's So Hard" on Monday, Ono's "Midsummer New York" on Tuesday and Lennon's "Imagine" on Thursday, backed by the New York-based Elephant's Memory Band, were the week's strongest musical numbers. Ono also performed "Sisters O Sisters" on Wednesday, accompanied by Lennon, and the two performed "Luck Of The Irish" together on Friday. Additional music spots included Lennon and Chuck Berry performing raucous versions of "Memphis" and "Johnny B. Goode" on Wednesday and clips from the *Imagine* film: "Oh My Love" (Lennon, Tuesday), "Crippled Inside" (Lennon, Wednesday), "Mrs. Lennon" (Ono, Thursday), and "How" (Lennon, Friday).

The shows are a fascinating depiction of the meeting — and sometimes clashing — of two cultures. Ono created a number of conceptual art pieces, taking a broken cup and mending it piece by piece over the week, and starting off an "Unfinished Painting," a bare canvas guests and the audience were invited to draw on, that was supposed to be auctioned off for charity. Jerry Rubin squared off with U.S. Surgeon General Dr. Jesse Steinfeld in the show's most volatile exchange on Tuesday, when Rubin casually denounced President Nixon as a "pig," and Douglas and Steinfeld came out strongly in favor of the American mainstream. Bobby Seale, who appeared on Thursday, was much softer-spoken.

On Tuesday, Douglas naturally posed the question asked by every journalist of the era who interviewed an ex-Fab; would The Beatles ever reunite? "There's no reason why they never should do it again, but there's no reason why they should," Lennon evenly responded. Douglas also inadvertently revealed his gender/generation gap during a discussion on "women's lib," welcoming attorney Rene Uviller on the show with the comment "Very pretty attorney… I wouldn't be a bit disturbed by your bill!"

Other guests were quick to get into the spirit of things. On Monday, Ono set up her "Love Calls" piece, calling people at random to say "I love you." In the booklet, the show's bandleader, Joe Harnell, says it took an hour to complete this piece alone, as the recipients of the calls inevitably fired off an expletive and hung up — something neither Fraser or Douglas remember. "I don't recall that happening," says Douglas. "We stopped for commercial breaks. That's it. It was 90 minutes straight ahead. It's very very difficult to do it the other way. Stopping and starting over. Especially when the show's peaking and it's at a great level. We wanted to do the show as though it were a live show."

But it's clear from the video edit that a "stop tape" of some length occurred, with comedian Louie Nye eventually saving the segment, reaching a woman in Seattle who warmly thanks Nye for his "love call," saying, "And you have a nice day!" Douglas is then inspired to call David Frost, who was unavailable. There's also a clear intimacy between the guests and the audience, due to the studio's small size. "There were only about 150 people in the audience and they were only about 12-14 feet from the guests," says Fraser. "So you're really right there. It's not like you're sitting at the *Tonight Show* where there's a huge gap. You're right on them."

Wiener cites the variety of guests as a reason why the week turned out to be so successful. "Having Chuck Berry and Bobby Seale — those kind of juxtapositions were what really turned me on," he says. "That it wasn't just political rapping, talking. Everything they could think of they put on there. And Yoko's calling people up; when you just explain it, it seems kind of simple and maybe not that interesting. But when she does it, it's completely fascinating."

But Douglas admits Lennon and Ono's ideas weren't always easy to work with. "I can't say they were easy," he says. "It was a challenge. It really was. It was very challenging, what their reaction would be to certain things that we were doing. And they had to be consulted on everything we planned to do. And then their segments — on some of the things they did, I really didn't know where they were going. I had to figure it out myself while we were doing it! Like breaking the cup and putting it together. What was the meaning of this? People trying to piece their lives together or what?"

Neither does he have an answer for a more concrete question: Whatever happened to Ono's "Unfinished Painting," which evidently did not get auctioned for charity? "I really wish I could answer that question!" he laughs. "It's not in my collection of paintings, I'll tell you that!"

Douglas also had concerns about how the guest roster would gel. "You constantly worry about that," he says. "Every day you go in and you think, 'Will the chemistry be right today?' And sometimes you're terribly let down. Sometimes John and Yoko were looking at Louis Nye wondering what planet he was from. And I'm sure he was looking at them and the things they were doing. And then when they started making phone calls and telling people 'I love you,' I thought he was very funny in that segment. He was hysterical. They couldn't figure out whether he was being comedic or doing a straight thing, a straight conversation."

Things didn't always go smoothly behind the scenes either. Some conflicts are detailed in the video set's booklet, though Douglas denies Harnell's contention that the couple smoked marijuana.

"I wasn't aware of any of that," he says. "And usually I can read people when something like that is happening to them. I can see it in their eyes. You forget, I'm a former band singer! And I didn't see any of that on the show. I didn't see it in John, I didn't see it in Yoko."

But he adds, "I'll be very, very honest with you, it wasn't easy for the staff. And I heard about it all the time. They were very, she especially, I don't want to say anything to alienate anyone, but she was very rough on the staff. She made demands. And some of the things that they wanted we couldn't come up with. It was very tough. The kids were very young though, and probably fans when they arrived, and probably terribly let down at some of the behavior, but hey, listen, we live with that constantly.

"But it was worth it," he continues. "It was not like one of my normal weeks. It was entirely different. But it's great. It gets you to another level, I think. It was very challenging for me. And I think it was interesting for the viewers."

Fraser, too, agrees that there were conflicts but declines to get specific. "I will tell you that there were some people on the crew that disagreed with them politically," he says. "And [that] would be the extent of what I would want to say. But everybody did their job, and everybody will always remember that week, and everybody on the crew that talks about it, talks about it only the most glowing terms."

Except, perhaps, in Rhino's booklet.

But Fraser also points out that even people associated with the show who disagreed with the couple's views weren't immune to their star power. "They were without a doubt the biggest stars we ever had on the show," he says, "and that brought a lot of attention from people that had stopped paying attention to the show within the organization. We suddenly had executives that I hadn't seen in three years hanging around! And people taking interest in the show that never bothered me before, like censors and lawyers. And there were a lot of people, if you're a real conservative and not a music lover, that were not overly fond of John Lennon. But you know what, all those people showed up at the studio. You never saw a studio so filled in your life with people. Lot of security too."

But there was more to the show than backstage heaviness, and Douglas has no hesitation when asked to cite a high point. "The favorite moment for me, because I wasn't a part of it, I happily got to sit there like the audience, was Chuck Berry," he says. "That turned out to be the best show of the week. 'Cause it was so genuine, John's reaction. Here's the man who was responsible for the kind of music he played. Started it all. That was his idol. He was truly in awe of this man. Imagine a fellow at that level, the level of John Lennon, being in awe of anything! He was like a child with a new toy. It was so infectious just watching it."

Nonetheless, despite the lure of Lennon and Ono and their roster of friends, Douglas says the public response "was kind of mixed. A lot of the people were elated and thrilled that we had them on and thanked us for it. And others were terribly upset about it because of his views and all. I don't have to tell you that that was not the way the world was thinking at the time! But the ratings just went through the roof, because we kept our regular audience and we added to it. I used to get my hair cut in an area called Society Hill, which was a very

Rhino released a video boxed set of *The Mike Douglas Show* with John Lennon and Yoko Ono as guest hosts.

hip area. And I'd get out of my car and start walking to the shop, and I'd get, 'Yeah, cool Mike, right on!' Suddenly they knew me and called me by my first name."

One segment of the viewing public Douglas did not hear from were agents from the FBI, who took notes on the proceedings, transcribing Jerry Rubin's interview.

"It does seem ridiculous, but it is what the FBI thought their job was," says Wiener. "Jerry Rubin told jokes about Nixon. They wrote it all down. They got mixed up about a lot of things. They didn't really understand the '60s very well."

In fact, U.S. government agencies were already moving against the couple. In a memo dated Feb. 4, Senator Strom Thurmond discussed with Attorney General John Mitchell the possibility of deporting Lennon. And on Feb. 15, FBI director J. Edgar Hoover directed FBI offices around the country to keep tabs on Lennon and Ono's activities.

But at the time of *The Mike Douglas Show* tapings, the two were unaware of the impending trouble looming on horizon. "This was a fairly up time for them," Wiener agrees. "The deportation thing was beginning, but it didn't really get that heavy until later in the spring. So they weren't in legal defense mode, and I think you see that in the exuberance with which they did these shows. The decision had already been made in the Nixon administration that they were going to go after Lennon, but John and Yoko don't know it yet. So that's why they're so cheerful and happy. They're still enjoying life in New York and don't realize how much trouble they're about to be in."

But though Lennon was outspoken in his beliefs, he was hardly a revolutionary; during the *Mike Douglas* shows he repeatedly stressed that any societal change should be nonviolent in nature; he also praised the efforts of people such as Bobby Seale and Nader to organize people to help themselves. Why then was the U.S. government so threatened by his activities?

"One answer is, 'Oh, Nixon was just paranoid,'" says Wiener. "'He worried about everything.' But you have to remember that 1972 was a presidential election year. And this was the first year 18-year-olds had the right to vote, so there were going to be millions of first-time voters. And it was widely believed that young people were the basic anti-war constituency.

"But anyone that knew anything about politics knew that young voters were the least likely to vote of all age groups," Wiener continues. "So the question was, what would it take to get these new voters to go to the polls and vote, presumably against Nixon? Well, Lennon's plan, this is what the Thurmond memo was about, was a national concert tour that would mobilize young people to register to vote and to vote against the war, which meant against Nixon. This was something that Lennon's celebrity and power might be able to accomplish. And Nixon took it seriously and he was right to do so. So that's why they wanted to get rid of Lennon. Nixon abused the power of the White House against his enemies; that's what Watergate was about. And Lennon was just one of the many targets of this Watergate-style operation."

The U.S. government formally moved against Lennon in March 1972, when they filed a deportation order against him; Lennon appealed. But the escalating immigration problems hardly dampened Lennon and Ono's activities. During the rest of '72 they recorded their joint album *Some Time In New York City* and Ono's *Approximately Infinite Universe*, produced albums by the Elephant's Memory Band and David Peel and made a few concert appearances, notably the "One To One" charity shows held at Madison Square Garden on August 30; an appearance on the *Jerry Lewis Telethon* followed on Sept. 6. The *Imagine* film debuted on TV in December. Lennon even found time to appear on *The Dick Cavett Show*, insisting the government's harassment included tailing him and tapping his phone, a complaint not believed at the time.

Lennon finally won his immigration battle in October 1975, when the U.S. Court Of Appeals overturned the Immigration And Naturalization Service deportation order. He was granted permanent residency the following July. By then, it was widely known that the FBI had kept track of all of Lennon's activities during the early '70s, including his *Mike Douglas Show* appearances.

"It wasn't that great a surprise, considering what he was up to and the things he was saying," says Douglas, adding, "and that was when Hoover was alive too."

Douglas had another Beatle on his show when Ringo Starr appeared on April 17, 1978. He also invited Lennon to make a return appearance in December 1980. "We were doing a week in Honolulu," he says. "And John was booked as a guest. He'd accepted the invitation, and then called again saying, 'I'm sorry,

I'm going to have to cancel. I'm busily working on an album, and I can't get away.' He wanted desperately to get over there and do it. And two days later he was murdered. That's absolutely true. So that was terribly unfortunate."

The Mike Douglas Show was canceled in 1982, and for years the only way to see the episodes was through bootleg tapes found on the collector's circuit. Douglas himself became aware of bootlegs when a friend's son told him he'd bought tapes of his shows from a dealer in the Los Angeles area. Douglas visited the dealer and bought a tape himself, then contacted Westinghouse.

"I said, 'Are you aware this is going on?' And they of course said no." Douglas had also noted that portions of his show were being aired in foreign markets without appropriate fees being paid, such as footage of an appearance future golf star Tiger Woods made on the show when he was two years old.

"Please tell me how Nippon Television got a copy of the tape!" says Douglas. "It played everywhere on earth. And they're so cute. They admit to having played it, but they don't want to say where they got it! All kinds of things like that were happening, which I could do nothing about. The union didn't back anybody up on things like that."

The Rhino set marks the first time the shows have been commercially available in their entirety, something a writer like Wiener would have welcomed at the time he was working on *Come Together*. "Virtually anything any of The Beatles ever did somebody has collected," he says. "But it was really hard work to track down a full set of these. I ended up just getting them on audio after working for weeks answering ads in fan magazines and talking to collectors. So to have them so easily accessible is just a dream."

Douglas feels that the set's importance stands not just as an entertainment package, but as a historical document. "No question about it," he says. "Though I should really say that at the time I wasn't aware it was going to have this kind of an impact. I really wasn't. I thought, 'Well, it'll get good ratings,' but my God, people are still playing these things and people are buying them for their own libraries. So I didn't realize at the time that it would be that strong, quite honestly."

Finally, *The Mike Douglas Show With John Lennon And Yoko Ono* is important in that it chronicles an often-downplayed side of Lennon's life, his politics. Since Lennon's death in 1980, the sanctification of what Paul McCartney has called his "Martin Luther Lennon" side has tended to dismiss his political work as a fad. But, as Wiener emphasizes, "John and Yoko's involvement in politics was total. They didn't just raise money, it was their life. It was a time when if all you did was raise money for the things you believed in, you'd be a bourgeois sellout. No, the commitment was what made life meaningful, and you wanted your art and your life to be the same thing. That was what made him important."

And as to the specific shows themselves, Wiener says, "I think they're an intense and vivid example of how open he was to experimenting with communicating a political message in forms that rock 'n' rollers had never tried before. And that open experimental attitude, that willingness to try new things, especially things that seemed hopelessly conventional like daytime TV, is part of what made Lennon so interesting and so appealing."

Trivia

by Marc A. Catone

1. Which Beatles song, written by John Lennon/Paul McCartney, was inspired by an old circus poster?
2. As a group, The Beatles first came to the U.S. on Feb. 7, 1964, but one of the four had previously visited America. Name which Beatle visited the U.S. before the others, which state, when and why?
3. Name the first American rock 'n' roll artist to do a cover version of a Beatles song and name the song.
4. Which U.S. radio station is usually credited with playing The Beatles for the first time?
5. Name the individual who first asked Brian Epstein, in the latter's record shop, for a copy of "My Bonnie" by The Beatles, and when did this occur?
6. What was the first Beatles single released in the U.S. and when was it issued?
7. Who was Alfred Lacey?
8. In which U.S. city did The Beatles have to stop in mid-performance on two concert tours?
9. Name the three John Lennon/Paul McCartney compositions, recorded by The Beatles, in which no musical instruments are played by any member of the group.
10. Which Beatles song contains the traditional "Fere Jacques," as the background harmony?
11. Two members of The Rolling Stones appear on three Beatles songs. Name which members of the Stones, what songs they appeared on and what they contributed to each song.
12. Which song, written by John Lennon/Paul McCartney and recorded by The Beatles, was originally intended for Twiggy to record?

Answers

1. "Being For The Benefit Of Mr. Kite."
2. George Harrison visited his sister, Louise, in Illinois during September 1963.
3. Del Shannon did "From Me To You" in early 1963
4. WWDC of Washington, D.C., is usually credited with playing "I Want To Hold Your Hand" first in December 1963. However, if you answered that Murray the K played "She Loves You" on WINS (New York) in October 1963, give yourself a point.
5. Raymond Jones on Oct. 28, 1961.
6. "Please Please Me" was released on the Vee-Jay label on Feb. 25, 1963, to a less than enthusiastic response.
7. The actor who portrayed the gardener in The Beatles' apartment in the movie *Help!*.
8. Cleveland was the unlucky city. During the 1964 U.S. tour the concert had to be stopped due to the unruly audience, and in 1966, due to equipment problems.
9. "Eleanor Rigby," "She's Leaving Home" and "Good Night."
10. "Paperback Writer."
11. Mick Jagger was in the background of the chorus to "All You Need Is Love," and Brian Jones played the oboe on "You Know My Name (Look Up The Number)" and alto sax on "Baby, You're A Rich Man."
12. "Back In The U.S.S.R."

John Brower, promoter of Toronto Lennon concert, says Goldman's book got it all wrong

by William Ruhlmann

Central Park South at Columbus Circle in New York City has seen a few demonstrations in its day. But one of the more unusual protests may have been the vigil held by a single figure last fall when John Brower stood in front of a posh apartment building selling T-shirts emblazoned with a familiar book cover encased in the red circle and single line of the international symbol meaning "Don't."

Brower was demonstrating on a cold and rainy November day against one of the building's occupants, Albert Goldman, author of the controversial best-seller, *The Lives Of John Lennon*, and he had a special reason to be upset. Brower is featured in two chapters of the book and feels that he, and especially Lennon, were treated unfairly. While the section of the book in which Brower is featured amounts to no more than two and a half percent of the 719-page volume, it may stand as an example of the level of accuracy to be found in the rest.

This article originally appeared in **Goldmine** *issue #224, Feb. 24,1989.*

A Toronto entrepreneur (in the book, Goldman calls him "a born hustler"), Brower was a concert promoter in 1969 when he contacted Lennon in connection with the Toronto Rock 'N' Roll Revival, a stadium show featuring 1950s stars such as Little Richard. Lennon appeared at the show on Sept. 13, 1969, along with a superstar band featuring Eric Clapton, for a performance later issued as *Live Peace In Toronto*, a gold-selling, Top 10 album in 1970.

Brower and Lennon also worked on the Toronto Peace Festival, a more ambitious project that, like many festival ideas at the time, eventually foundered on problems relating to agreements with local officials and financing. 1969-1970 was the era of festivals: Woodstock had taken place in August 1969 and the disastrous Altamont show with The Rolling Stones in early December. Just as rock fans flocked to such assemblages, politicians and local citizens worried and worked to block the festivals, resulting in several abortive projects, of which the Toronto Peace Festival was one.

But in Goldman's book, the blame for the festival's cancellation is placed on Lennon. Brower, in an interview conducted at the offices of his publicist, disagreed. "I'm portrayed favorably at John Lennon's expense, which is very unfair," Brower said. "Albert Goldman seems to paint a picture of me as this boy wonder who got everything together and just wanted to please John Lennon and make everything work for him, etc., etc., which we did want to do, but that then John Lennon just turned his back on us and treated us shabbily and didn't follow through with any of his commitments, etc., which is really not true at all. [Goldman] strung together a story that seemed to indicate that John Lennon was really not behind the project at all and that he was just saying that he was and that when it came time to eventually get involved in the project that he walked away from it, which is not what happened at all."

What did happen? "Basically, John Lennon was enthusiastically supportive of the project right from the start," Brower said. "In fact, he co-created the concept of the Toronto Peace Festival, and he added a lot of the ideas to it that it was known for. And, in fact, he came to Toronto and made a lot of efforts on behalf of the festival, including going to meet the prime minister of Canada and giving a very, very long press conference and following up from England many times on the phone and just looking to do whatever he could to make the thing happen."

It wasn't Lennon that caused the project to fall through, Brower said, but problems he and his associates encountered. "We had tremendous problems with the Ontario government at the time," he said, "which was a Conservative [Party] government, as opposed to the federal government, which was Liberal [Party]. And since the prime minister of Canada was Liberal and had met with Lennon, therefore the Conservative government was against the festival, because they felt that if it was staged in Ontario it would make the Liberal prime minister look good, and they didn't want to do that.

"And let's just say that myself and several of the people working with me as my partners at the time got very filled with our own self-importance. We were very excited about the fact that we were running around representing John Lennon, and we forgot many times what we were actually supposed to be doing, and I guess a lot of our best intentions were not being really fully realized accurately. We were having a lot of internal squabbling. And he gave us every opportunity to 'Get it together, man,' so to speak, and when we finally were not able to get a site together and we were not able to consummate financing that would allow us to put the festival on in a way that John felt was most appropriate, he walked away from it. And, sure, there was great disappointment, but there was never any thought in my mind that John Lennon abandoned us for no reason or that John Lennon left us holding the bag or that John Lennon was a bad guy."

Although Brower feels that he is portrayed better than he should have been at Lennon's expense, he also noted that Goldman got the story of Brower's life wrong, too. He said that, whereas the book states that he went to California in the mid-1960s to try "to make it as a rock musician," he in fact went to go to school. And Goldman's chronology is truncated about his return to Canada. "Coming home dead broke," Goldman writes, "and with a wife and kid to support, [Brower] had borrowed some money from his rich friends and promoted this concert [the Toronto Rock 'N' Roll Revival]."

"There was like a two-year period between the time that I came back from California dead broke to the time that I put on the Toronto Rock 'N' Roll Revival," Brower said. "I didn't borrow money from my friends. I had a company that had been in business for over a year who were the biggest concert producers in the country. We had plenty of money. We'd been making money for a year and a half in the music business. And that's just an example of Goldman's kind of error of omission. He just goes from one point to another point with no regard for what really happened in between, but as best it serves his purpose to make a dramatic effect."

Brower said that when he spoke to Goldman in 1986, for what he described as 10 hours of freewheeling conversation, he had never read Goldman's other books and knew little about him. When he finally saw the result of those interviews, it came as a surprise.

"I was outraged by it," he said. "I was shocked and I was embarrassed at being in the book. It was like getting a good write-up in [Adolf Hitler's] *Mein Kampf*. Wow! Thank you, but no thanks."

Despite the inaccuracies about his own life, Brower said he did not consider suing Goldman for libel. "No," he said, "because I don't believe there's anything there that I'm libeled. I'm just having to be victim in the same sense that John was victim."

What Brower has done instead is to go into the T-shirt business and to embark on a publicity tour, activities he said have cost him $20,000.

"There are times," he explained, "when frustration gets to the point where you either do something about it at the time that you can or you always are gonna say to yourself later, 'I really should have done something about that at the time.' This, I think, was the time in my life when I really realized that I had to do something about my feelings about this book. I was flying back to Toronto, and I had finished the book a couple of days before and it was on my mind and I was just sitting on the plane looking out the window and this vision of a T-shirt came to me with the book cover on it with a red circle around it and this line through it. And I just thought, 'That is a great idea. I'm gonna make up some of these T-shirts.'"

Brower gave T-shirts to friends and then turned up at the ceremony in Hollywood awarding a star on Hollywood Boulevard to Lennon, where he attracted media and public attention that convinced him to print up more shirts and continue his campaign. But he was unable to interest merchandising companies such as Winterland Productions in handling the shirts, due to legal questions.

"This is not my license," he said, pointing at one of the shirts. "This belongs to Morrow And Company, this book cover. This is in effect a copyright infringement." Nevertheless, Brower has placed ads in several major rock-oriented publications and is selling the shirts through mail order. But he claims that making money is not the major reason for the effort.

> **"There are times when frustration gets to the point where you either do something about it at the time that you can or you always are gonna say to yourself later, 'I really should have done something about that at the time.' This, I think, was the time in my life when I really realized that I had to do something about my feelings about this book."**
>
> *—John Brower*

"So far, I have only printed up 800 of these shirts," he said. "Now, I ain't gonna make any big money on 800 shirts. So that's not the object of it. We're not looking to sell tons of these shirts. It's just not possible to get distribution or to get a reach to do that on a retail level. Nor was it ever our intention. Maybe they'll be collector's items. As far as I'm concerned, any guy that can make a T-shirt can make these up and sell them. I ain't gonna sue him. This is a free copyright. This belongs to the people. Every one that's sold and worn is gonna be a message and that's what's important.

"And if anything, maybe this could become the biggest bootlegged shirt in the world, OK? 'Cause John Brower is certainly not going to be out there trying to sell them all, and if other people want to make them, they're very simple and inexpensive to make. All we ask is that you make them on a quality shirt — that's what we're doing — because you got John Lennon's face on there. So, above all else, let's have the quality of the shirt reflect the quality of the man."

Brower noted that Yoko Ono, in a statement issued by her press representative, neither decried nor sanctioned the shirts, and he said that not only is she not receiving any money in connection with them, but that she has specifically asked that no money deriving from their sale be contributed to any charities associated with Lennon, since she wants no connection of any kind with the Goldman book. The shirts can be ordered for $12.95 from Protest Shirts, P.O. Box 756, South Laguna Beach CA 92677.

Ex-Beatles

Alone again, naturally

by Allen J. Wiener

The past year has seen a welcome number of new releases by the three surviving Beatles, and collectors, especially of the Paul McCartney variety, will have to dig deep into the old wallet and hunt among import dealers to obtain several new discs.

Most numerous are the new McCartney records, few of which were released in the United States. Collectors are already familiar with the large number of variations in releases of the *Choba B CCCP* (*Back In The USSR*) album, issued only in the Soviet Union and subsequently given away free to some members of McCartney's fan club. The album, containing the fruits of a two-day session during which McCartney ran through about 20 rock oldies, was originally released with 11 titles on board. Subsequent pressings included 13 titles. There were also some copies pressed with 12 songs. Some 13-song editions appeared in jackets listing the 11 song lineup.

The variations are far too numerous to list here; as many as 64 of them have been reported thus far. McCartney's fan club giveaway quickly drove down the prices of imported copies, originally going for as much as $200, and they are now available from some dealers for as little as $15. The 11-cut version fetches a higher price since far fewer of them were pressed, but even this version has been advertised for as little as $40. To complicate matters, excellent-appearing (and sounding) counterfeits have appeared for as little as $10. At least one bootleg CD version, *Roots — Paul Ramon*, has appeared with a few additional rare McCartney tracks added to the Soviet 13.

Purchasers of vinyl copies of McCartney's *Flowers In The Dirt LP* are already aware that they are missing one track, "Ou Est Le Soleil?," found only on the CD or cassette editions. Special 12-inch and cassette singles with three additional mixes of this song were released on both sides of the Atlantic. McCartney's first single from the album, "My Brave Face," backed with the non-album track "Flying To My Home," was released in both seven-inch and cassette formats in England and the United States.

A five-inch CD single was also released in both countries, although the U.K. release was made in May while Capitol did not release it until September in the U.S. The CD features "My Brave Face," "Flying To My Home" and two tracks from McCartney's Soviet album, "I'm Gonna Be A Wheel Someday" and "Ain't That A Shame." There were additional releases in the U.K. that did not appear in the U.S.

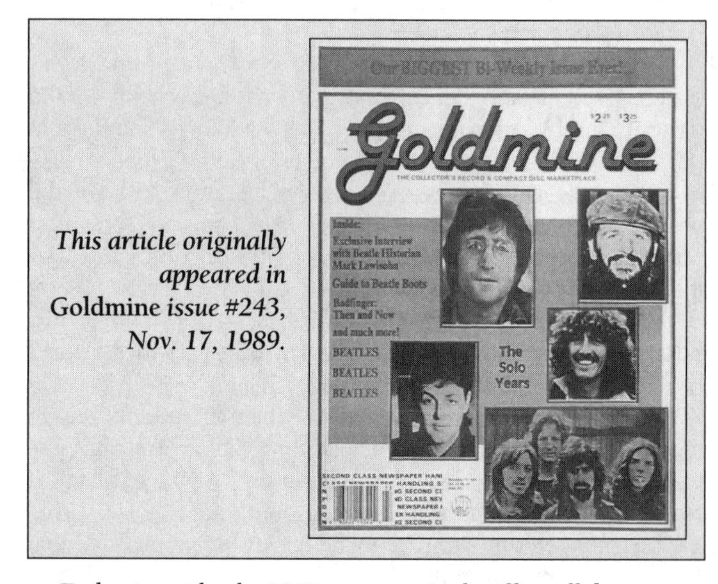

This article originally appeared in Goldmine issue #243, Nov. 17, 1989.

To begin with, the U.K. cassette single offers all four songs that appear on the CD single and features all four on both sides, while the U.S. release contains only the two found on the vinyl single. Britain also saw the release of a 12-inch single with the same four titles.

McCartney's second *Flowers* single, "This One," offered a far greater number of U.K. releases. Backed with the non-LP track, "The First Stone," it was released in the United States only on a cassette single, although both seven-inch vinyl and five-inch CD promos were distributed by Capitol. In England, by contrast, the single appeared in no less than six different formats.

In addition to the cassette single and regular seven-inch release, a second seven-inch version was released with a completely different B-side, a new version of "The Long And Winding Road" recorded by McCartney in mid-1987. This limited edition release came in a fold-open box sealed with a peel-off sticker bearing a black and white photo of McCartney and his new band. In addition to the record, the box contained six color post cards with pictures of the band members. The record was encased in the same picture sleeve as the regular seven-inch release but with the new B-side listed on the back. The CD single, and the first of two 12-inch singles, were also released. Both contained the A- and B-sides plus two more non-album tracks, "I Wanna Cry" and "I'm In Love Again." The latter title, omitted from the Soviet album, is another song from McCartney's July 1987 oldies sessions.

The second 12-inch release added yet another non-album song, "Good Sign," to the same A- and B-sides. All together, that makes 19 different titles released by McCartney in connection with his *Flowers* album, four of them unavailable in the United States.

American collectors were offered one McCartney 12-inch single with three alternate mixes of "Ou Est Le Soleil?," also released in Europe.

McCartney fans should also grab Johnny Cash's *Water From The Wells Of Home* album to get the otherwise unavailable "New Moon Over Jamaica." Cowritten by McCartney, Cash, and Tom T. Hall, the song was cut in England in June 1987 and constitutes a virtual duet by Cash and McCartney, with McCartney taking lead vocal on one verse. This is a good deal more than the usual ex-Beatle guest appearance that is most noticeable by the names on the record jacket.

McCartney is also heard sharing lead vocal with Gerry Marsden, Holly Johnson, The Christians, and Stock-Aitken-Waterman on a new recording of "Ferry 'Cross The Mersey," a special charity single released only in England on May 8, 1989, in both seven-inch and CD formats.

Other recent guest work by McCartney includes his production of The Crickets' "T-Shirt" single, production and backup work on another U.K.-only charity single, "Children In Need," and his backup work and writing credits on Elvis Costello's *Spike* album.

In addition to his successful North American tour, Ringo Starr has busied himself in recent months as a guest on several records. Late last year he appeared on the *Stay Away* album doing "When You Wish Upon A Star" as part of a medley coupled with "Desolation Theme." Earlier this year he recorded a new duet of "Act Naturally" with Buck Owens, a song each of them recorded separately in the early 1960s. The duet was released in the United States on July 5, 1989. Starr can also be heard doing one line worth of lead vocal on the fund-raising single, "Spirit Of The Forest," which features countless others as well. The record was released only as a 12-inch single in the U.S., and only in the seven-inch format in England.

The year also saw the release of a second volume of Starr's greatest hits on Rhino's *Starr Struck* album. A companion to Capitol/Apple's earlier *Blast From Your Past*, the new album features titles culled from Starr's later solo albums, including several cuts from *Old Wave*, still inexplicably unreleased in the U.S. and the U.K. There were far fewer copies of the vinyl release pressed than there were of the CD version, which adds four titles not found on the vinyl edition. The album is a welcome reminder of how many enjoyable songs Starr has recorded during his solo years and illustrates that even among his weakest albums, at least one or two decent offerings can be found. Rhino's failure to promote this album is hard to understand, especially considering the hay that could have been made of Starr's concert tour.

George Harrison, still catching his breath in the wake of his *Cloud Nine* and *Traveling Wilburys Volume I* back-to-back successes, recently worked with both Eric Clapton and Jeff Lynne on their new albums and has also reportedly been working on a new album of his own. "Cheer Down," written by Harrison and Tom Petty for Eric Clapton, was recorded by Harrison himself after Clapton rejected it, and is found on the soundtrack album from *Lethal Weapon 2*. The song also appeared on a promo five-inch CD single early in August and shortly thereafter on a seven-inch vinyl promo before finally being released in both seven-inch and cassingle formats on Aug. 28. Harrison has also guested on Petty's *Full Moon Fever* and the late Roy Orbison's *Mystery Girl* albums.

All told, a considerable assortment of new material that ought to keep Beatles collectors busily flitting from the specialty shop to the classifieds and to the bank. It's a regimen they resigned themselves to long ago and a phenomenon that shows no sign of letting up.

"They were my boys, the greatest in the world"

A chat with producer George Martin about the Fab Four

by Bill DeYoung

At age 67, George Martin is one of the longest-lived architects of rock 'n' roll. Born in London, he was an oboe player and composer of classical melodies who found steady work as a staff producer and conductor at EMI's recording studios at No. 3 Abbey Road. In the '50s and early '60s, Martin's pop successes included hits by singer Matt Monro and comedy discs by the likes of Peter Sellers, Rolf Harris, and Beyond The Fringe.

He was 36 and bored with his job when Brian Epstein presented him with The Beatles' demo recordings. Every other label in England had turned Epstein down, but Martin — with his keen ear for melody and complex harmony and an affection for warmth and humor — heard something that no one else had.

The middle part of this story is blood-familiar to every Beatles person worth his salt (or, should we say, his pepper). Martin shaped, developed, encouraged, discouraged and forged The Beatles' sound over their nearly eight-year relationship. He arranged almost every song they ever recorded, wrote all the orchestral scores (with a few exceptions) and — save the *Let It Be* debacle — is listed as producer on every single Beatles record.

Martin has written and recorded numerous instrumental works over the years (most of them Beatles-related) and, in those heady days of 1963-64 produced many, many chart-toppers for British artists (the great majority of them managed by Epstein).

After the Fabs' breakup, he went on to man the boards for America, Jeff Beck and others, and he produced a triumvirate of Paul McCartney solo albums in the '80s. Most recently, he handled production chores for the original cast album of *Tommy*, at the behest of Pete Townshend.

That's all well and good, but if Martin had never crossed paths with The Beatles (and they with him), his work with other artists would be little more than a footnote in the book of rock 'n' roll. His credits are a mile long, but one stands head, shoulders, knees and toes above the rest. He was truly the Fifth Beatle, one of the most important figures in popular music history. His contributions may never be fully absorbed.

This article originally appeared in Goldmine issue #347, Nov. 12, 1993.

Although AIR Studios, which he began in 1966 (contracting out to The Beatles and EMI until 1970) is still operational in London, its branch on the Caribbean island of Montserrat was destroyed by 1989's Hurricane Hugo.

This year, Martin supervised the digital remastering of the anthology albums, *The Beatles 1962-66* and *The Beatles 1967-70* at EMI. His Beatles work, as you'll read in this interview, is far from over.

(And no, he has no idea if or when the first four Beatles albums will be released on CD in stereo.)

Goldmine: *John Lennon used to say that when he heard a Beatles song, it automatically brought him back to the recording session, what he was playing, how he was feeling that day. Is it the same way for you?*

George Martin: Not really. Looking back at all the songs, it's a long time ago, and I purposely over the years hadn't looked back at the songs. My life has been so busy, I've tended to go on and look at tomorrow rather than today or even yesterday. And I find that you can get too obsessive about the past. I did find, however, that when I did that television program on *The*

Making Of Sgt. Pepper a couple of years ago, that of course forced me to look back and see what was going on. And it was the first time, to be honest, in all those years I'd really looked back and started thinking deeply about the past.

When I think of a song — if you play me "Paperback Writer" or "Norwegian Wood" — sometimes I will think about things. In the case of "Norwegian Wood," it immediately brings it back to a hotel in St. Moritz, where John and I had a skiing holiday together. And he wrote the song during the time there, so that's obviously very evocative. But if you take a song that doesn't have that particular kind of nostalgia, it's a kind of blur. "Fool On The Hill," I can remember how we did that... but there were so many, and there are so much of them, that it's all one sort of melting, shimmering haze.

You played piano on a lot of songs during the early years; it's particularly evident on the Hard Day's Night*–era tracks. Was that literally because no one else could do it?*

To begin with, of course, none of them knew what a keyboard was like. They were guitar players. When I first met them, I was aware that they were guitar men and I was a keyboard man. And if you're running through a new song for the first time, a guitar player will look at another guy's fingers and see the shapes. You can see what the guy's doing on the fret, and you know what chord he's playing. If you then take that guitar player, and he doesn't know anything about keyboards, what you play on the piano will be completely meaningless to him. He won't understand the chords at all. And a keyboard player, if he knows a bit about guitar, won't understand what the chords are by looking at his hands. There's a hidden language there.

So I actually said to myself, "Hey, I'm going to have to learn the guitar, because I'll need to communicate with these guys on their level." And Paul, at the same time, said the same thing to himself. He said, "I think I'll have to learn piano, to see what George is up to." Because what I used to do, whenever Paul or John sang me a song, I'd sit on a high stool and they'd play it in front of me. And I'd learn it, and I'd then go to the keyboard and I'd say, "Is it this?" and I'd play through the chords and hum the tune. And they'd say, "Yeah, that's fine, OK," and I'd know the song.

That piano sound was very distinctive.

Piano's a very useful instrument. And, of course, Paul was the one who actually took it up and learned it more quickly and more adaptably than anybody else. I mean, he's such a fine, versatile musician, he could play almost any instrument if he set his mind to it. So that by the time he got to "Lady Madonna," he was doing a bloody good solo. He couldn't possibly have done that in 1962.

And John never really mastered the keyboard. His idea of playing the piano was having a group of triads — you know, three notes that formed a chord — and just go up and down the scale with them. He could play rhythm all right on keyboard, but he wasn't very clever at doing single notes or lines.

It's been theorized that your classical music background and your work on comedy records were big factors in making the unprecedented new pop sound that you made.

I tried to turn them on to it. We did get counterpoint into their work. I remember during "Eleanor Rigby," which was quite a breakthrough in a way, when we were actually recording it I realized that one of the phrases could work against another phrase, that they hadn't designed it that way.

In other words, "Ah, look at all the lonely people" actually could come at the end of the piece. Which it does. I put it in, got them to sing it... they were knocked out by that. "Hey, yeah, those two things go together! It's great, innit? It works well." It had never occurred to them, never occurred to Paul. But that was a lesson for him. Because I'm sure that when he came to write "She's Leaving Home," that was, definitely, two lines working against each other. It was one broad melody, and another one kind of answering underneath it. He learned how to use that weaving of lines.

They were like sponges, in a way, weren't they?

They learned so quickly. But when I first met them, I had absolutely no idea at all they could write decent material. They wrote songs that were pretty awful — "One After 909" and "P.S. I Love You" and "Love Me Do" was the best of them. It was pretty rough stuff.

I didn't really blame the guy who turned them down so much. In fact, everybody turned them down, more or less, on the grounds that their material wasn't very good, I imagine.

Do you remember exactly when they stopped being your students in the studio and started pretty much calling their own shots, coming to you simply for advice?

There was no one moment. It was a gradual drift. By the time we got to a song like "Walrus" or any of John or Paul's later songs, they would have very definite ideas on what they wanted to do, which they hadn't to begin with. It was a gradual drift so that they became the teachers, almost, at the end, and I was the pupil.

SO
BAD
PAUL
McCARTNEY
Words & Music by McCartney

What I do remember, though, was that having rejected all the stuff that they had and accepting only "Love Me Do," I had actually rejected "Please Please Me," in those very early days of 1962, saying "This is no good, this song, it's very dreary. If you're going to make anything of it at all, you need to double the speed and really put some pep into it. Make something really worthwhile. Maybe use some harmonica on it." Because when they played it first to me, it was Paul singing a very kind of winsome, Roy Orbison slow ballad. Which was very dreary.

Well, they learned from that, because when I gave them "How Do You Do It" and we made a record of that, they still wanted to have their material. They said, "We've been working on 'Please Please Me.' We'd like you to listen to it." And the result was good. And that gave them an incentive, then, to do better things from that moment onward.

Had you tried that in 1968, say around "Hey Jude" time, would they have said, "Don't tell us what to do, George"?

I don't think so. I don't think they ever rejected anything I said. All of us in the studio, including Ringo, had equal voices. And the five of us would look at things and try to make things better. They were much more fruitful by this time, so that if I did have something that I didn't like... in the case of "Hey Jude" I said, "Do you think we're being a bit unwise, going on for seven minutes?" And Paul said, "No, it's there. Can you get it on a record?" I said, "I can get it on, but it's not exactly a single. DJs will fade it, won't they?" He said, "Well, let them fade it." I was being practical, and I was wrong, because he was right, because it was right that it should be seven minutes. And it always has been, ever since.

Curiously enough, Paul and I have always been good friends, and we've often had dinner with our wives and so on. And about eight years later, '78 or '79 I'd say, we were having dinner one night and Paul, at the end of it said, "By the way, I'd like you to produce my next record."

I fell apart and I said, "I'm not sure that's a good idea."

He said, "Come on! Don't be so silly! Why not?"

I said, "Because things have changed now. You're a good producer in your own right, and I don't want to spoil a beautiful friendship, thank you very much."

He laughed and said, "Why, don't you think it'll work?"

I said, "Because I don't think you will accept the direction that I have to give you as a producer."

He said, "Of course I will. We know each other too well for that. How could it not work?"

I said, "Well there's selection of songs, for a start."

"Do you want me to audition for you?!" he said, jokingly.

I said, "Not quite, Paul." But, I said, "I've got to be able to choose your songs and tell you what's good and what's bad."

And he swallowed. That had never occurred to him. By this time, all of them had got to the stage where everyone revered them so much that they hadn't quite thought anyone would dare to suggest that anything they did wasn't terribly good.

He said, "You're quite right. I've got 14 songs."

I said, "Give them to me, and I'll listen to them over the weekend. I'll tell you about them on Monday."

He rung me on Monday and said, "What about it, then?"

I said, "Well, I've listened to every one of them."

He said, "Good."

I said, "Four are great."

He said, "Four?!"

I said, "Six need a lot of work on them, and the other four you can throw away."

There was a kind of distant silence. But Paul is a sensible and honorable fellow, and he said, "All right, you and I had better talk about it, and we'd better sort them out." And we did, and we made a very happy album.

I think that people, when they become superstars, they have to have someone to tell them they're surrounded so many times by people who tell them they're the greatest thing in the world, they need to have an honest opinion. It's the emperor and his new clothes, isn't it?

Near the end of the Beatles years, did you consider yourself friends? Or was the relationship like that of an employee to an employer? This was White Album/Abbey Road *time.*

The White Album was a funny one, because at the time they came back from abroad and they all had a huge collection of songs they wanted to record. And they wanted them done all at the same time. By this time, they were four individuals with their individual songs, wanting to record them with the assistance of the other people, rather than being a group. I couldn't cope with it all at once. We were actually recording in a couple of the studios at the same time, identically. John would be in one studio, and Paul would be in another. And I was running from one place to another. I had a very able assistant by this time, a guy called Chris Thomas, who's now a first-class producer. We shared the work, so I would come in and see what he'd been doing and supervise and so on.

But it was such a frantic time, I never really worried about any sort of splits there. The real cracks appeared during *Let It Be*. That was the worst time.

With regard to The White Album, *you've said that you tried to get them to cut it down to a single-disc, 14-track album. What would you have cut out?*

That's a good question, because it's now such an accepted

***Anthology 1*, *2* and *3*, artwork by Klaus Voormann.**

album. Everyone thinks it's terrific. A lot of people say it's their favorite album. Don't forget, I was looking at it from the point of view of the songs when I heard them, rather than the songs when they were finished. I said to myself, "Let's pick the best and most commercial songs, and let's work on those. Let's forget the other ones for the moment."

I'm not saying we wouldn't have recorded those other songs, but I would like to have made a really great album out of the best of the stuff there and concentrate and work very hard on them. But they wanted everything done at once. I thought they were dissipating their energies rather than focusing them. That was my concern. There are one or two items of dross on *The White Album*.

Such as?

I haven't got the list in front of me. You'll have to read them off. Was "Bungalow Bill" on that? "Honey Pie"?

Yes, and "Revolution 9." "Birthday."

"Birthday." Well, there you go. You're picking them for me! There are songs that are not at the front rank, put it that way. From other groups they probably would be front rank, but these are my boys, they're the greatest in the world, and that's the way I saw it.

The songs that remain unreleased today: "Leave My Kitten Alone." "If You've Got Troubles," "That Means A Lot." Was there a sense while you were cutting them that they were hopeless? Or were they just culled at the end of the sessions?

There were many instances when they would come in and not get very good results. I don't remember the specific circumstances; quite often, they would be done at the tail end of sessions, or sometimes they would be done because they came into the studio and they didn't have anything else.

Would you like to see that stuff released?

Now that all the water's gone under the bridge and everybody's much older and wiser, we are actually now looking at putting out a kind of definitive, all-encompassing Beatle anthology.

They've certainly been doing it on film; the boys themselves have been collecting a hell of a lot of footage and interesting visual programming. They've got about six hours assembled so far. And toward the end of next year, or maybe 1995, there will be the beginnings of a television series of hours, probably six or seven hours. It'll be tracing the history of the boys from when they were kids right through to the dissolution in '70.

Now, there will be an accompanying series of albums which will go alongside that. But they won't be the soundtrack, because the soundtrack will be spasmodic and so on.

They will be complementary rather than identical. And for that, I'm going to delve, and I'm going to look at every source — bootlegs that are in good condition. I'm going to look at radio broadcasts, live performances, demo records, all sorts of things apart from anything else we did in the studio, and I shall collate, polish, look at, criticize, chuck away but maybe issue anything that I think is worthwhile, that actually traces their history.

The bootleg CDs that are out now, some of the stuff is pretty phenomenal.

So I understand! And where the material came from in the first place is most interesting. I'd love to know. I've heard some of it, and some of the quality is remarkably good.

You don't think anyone knows how they got out?

I think all these things will probably be incorporated in what I'm talking about. It doesn't make sense for them to go out on bootlegs, does it?

In his 1970 Rolling Stone interview, John made several disparaging remarks about Beatles recordings, what he called the "Dead Beatles sound." Did that hurt your feelings at the time?

Very much! John went through a really crazy period. I was very incensed about that interview. I think everybody was. I think he stagged off everybody, including the Queen Of England. I don't think anyone escaped his attention.

When I saw him back in L.A. some years later and we spent an evening together, I said "You know, you were pretty rough in that interview, John." He said, "Oh, Christ, I was stoned out of my fucking mind." He said, "You didn't take any notice of that, did you?" I said, "Well I did, and it hurt."

He went through a very, very bad period of heavy drugs, and *Rolling Stone* got him during one of those periods. He was completely out of it. John had a very sweet side to him. He was a very tender person at heart. He could also be very brutal and very cruel. But he went through a very crazy time. The tragedy of John was that he'd been through all that and

he'd got out the other side. And he really was becoming the person that I knew in the early days again.

I spent an evening with him at the Dakota not long before he died, and we had a long evening rapping about old times, which was marvelous. That's now my happiest memory of him, because he really was back to his own self.

You were recording Tug Of War *with Paul the day John died. Just for the record, where were you when you heard about it?*

I lived 80 miles west of London, and he [Paul] lived 70 miles south. We were both in our respective homes. It was six o'clock in the morning, and somebody rang me from America and told me the news, which was not a good way to start the day. I immediately picked up the phone and I rang Paul, and I asked if he'd heard it. He had heard it.

And after a few moments together I said, "Paul, you obviously don't want to come in today, do you?" He said, "God, I couldn't possibly not come in. I must come in. I can't stay here with what's happened. Do you mind?" I said, "No, I'm fine. I'll meet you."

So we went into AIR Studios in London. We were supposed to record that day. Of course, we didn't put down a single note, because we got there and we fell on each other's shoulders and we poured ourselves tea and whiskey and sat 'round and drank and talked. And we grieved for John all day, and it helped. At the end of the day we went back to our homes.

Now, one of the ironies and one of the bitter bits about life is that Paul, when he came out of the studio, of course was surrounded by reporters and journalists. He still was in a deep state of shock. They photographed him, and they flashed him, and they said to him the usual sort of zany and stupid reporter questions. The question was, "How do you feel about John dying then, Paul?" I don't know what you're supposed to say to that. And he looked and he shrugged and he said, "Yeah, it's a drag, isn't it?" and went off into the night.

And he was slated for that. He was mercilessly attacked, saying, "How callous can you be?" And I felt every inch for him. He was unwise, but he was off his guard. It was tough.

You recently scored Paul's song "C'Mon People." You must have a pretty good working relationship with him.

I don't produce because I'm too old and he's a good producer anyway. I don't want to produce. In fact, he's asked me if I would. But life's too short. But he had this song and he said, "Would you mind doing a bit of scoring for me?" So I listened to it and I said, "OK, why not?" and it was fun. It's nice occasionally working together. I wouldn't want to make a habit of it.

You've done a lot of remastering and CD transfer for EMT on these Beatles projects. When you get to the Phil Spector songs, "The Long And Winding Road" and that, are you ever tempted to twiddle the knobs and just wipe out those strings and choirs?

[Laughing] You bet I am! It's a silly thing, really, because that was a wounding thing. And I don't honestly think those tracks are as good as we should have made them. But hell, they were there, and they're history now. If you're a sensible bloke, you just say, "That's it." And obviously, when you're transferring to CD, it's got to be as it was when it was issued, and that's the end of it.

Maybe you'll get to change some when you do this anthology next year.

Well, you can't really change the artistic content. That would be wrong. My brief was to try and reproduce on CD what we heard on analog. That was my prime motive, to try and make it sound, on CD, with the same warmth and quality we have on analog, which is not an easy thing, by the way. So when it comes to the question of changing things, no, if I changed it, I would've re-scored it and all that kind of thing.

On the American LPs, they added all that echo and awful stuff. Did you used to hear that and throw your hands in the air?

Of course I did, but I was powerless to do anything about it. Capitol ran the roost. And they used to take the credit for it, too.

Do you know why they did those things?

Ego? I don't know! I mean, there's a guy who actually put his name on the records, saying he produced them. So you tell me. Eventually, when we do this anthology thing, then we'll go back over all those albums and make sure they're in the right order and in the original versions as well as other stuff. It'll be quite a big job, but it'll be fascinating to do. The last thing I'll ever do with The Beatles.

You think so?

I guess so. The final thing. The final solution.

So you're content with being known as The Beatles guy now?

Well, you can't escape these epithets. You get pigeonholed. Some people think I've never done anything else.

A bushel of delicious treats: Collecting Apple Records

by Tim Neely

Most people associate Apple Records with The Beatles, and rightfully so. They founded the label, and, at least in the early days, they had some say in its operation. Despite attempts to develop a diverse label roster, every new Apple record from the end of 1973 until the last original Apple release in late 1975 was by a solo Beatle.

Because of its Beatles connection, Apple is a label that some collectors try to complete. Relatively few labels are collected in this way; Sun and Philles come to mind as two more, and each of those has major rarities that may take a lifetime (and a lot of money) to find. Trying to run the entire Apple U.S. singles list from numbers 1800 to 1885, and the albums from 3350 to 3422, is by no means easy, but it can be done.

For the most part, this overview will focus on the non-Beatles material on Apple. While not as sought-after worldwide as The Beatles' material, it generally did not sell as well as The Beatles or solo releases and thus is more obscure. We'll start with the 45s from 1968 through 1975.

This article originally appeared in Goldmine *issue #492, June 4, 1999.*

The U.S. Apple singles

First of all, not every number from 1800 through 1885 was issued. The following do not exist: 1833 (allegedly reserved for a Badfinger single, "Name Of The Game"); 1846 (possibly a John Lennon or David Peel single); 1856 (maybe Elephant's Memory or Lon And Derrek Van Eaton); 1860 (scheduled for George Harrison); 1866 (another unreleased Harrison single); and 1883 (Lennon's "Slippin' And Slidin'" and "Ain't That A Shame") was never released as a stock copy.

Second, there are numbers outside the 1800s on Apple singles; all of these are by The Beatles or solo Beatles. Those in the 5000s, first issued in 1971, are reissues of Capitol originals and are, relatively speaking, not that sought-after (the originals and 1969-71 Capitol "target" label reissues are more collectible, unless there's a star on the Apple label — more on that later). The others, all in the 2000s, include two reissues (2056 and 2138) plus 2276, 2490, 2531, 2654, 2764 and 2832 (all Beatles), 2969 (Ringo Starr), and 2995 (Harrison).

That said, here are some of the tougher American Apple 45s to come across:

- Beatles records with a small Capitol logo on the back (sliced) side. The toughest to find this way is 2654 ("Something"/"Come Together"); it can bring $100 in near mint condition.
- Any Apple single with a black filled-in star on the unsliced side. These came only from the Los Angeles plant and exist on most singles through 1832, including the 5000 series reissues. Many of these also were used as promo copies in lieu of regular promos. On common titles, copies of the "starred" versions usually bring more, sometimes several times more, than the "unstarred" versions.
- 1800: "Thingumybob" by The John Foster & Sons Ltd. Black Dyke Mills Band. The A-side was credited as a Lennon/McCartney composition, though only Paul was involved. This is a $100 single in near mint.
- 1804: "Road To Nowhere" by Trash. The unstarred version is $50 in near mint, the starred version, $100.
- 1805: "Carolina In My Mind" by James Taylor. The version with "Something's Wrong" on the B-side is common. But the first issue has "Taking It In" on the flip. This is one of the rarest Apples, sporting a $300 price tag. There also is a variation of the standard version with the A-side title erroneously listed as "Carolina *On* My Mind." *{Italics ours. — Ed.}* Those can go for $30.
- 1807: "New Day"/"Thumbin' A Ride" by Jackie Lomax. His rarest Apple single, this can go for $60 in near mint for the unstarred version, $75 for the starred.
- 1854: "Liberation Special" by Elephant's Memory. A rare pressing of this exists with "Power Boogie" on the B-side rather than the more common "Madness"; that version can go for $400 in near mint condition. The regular version is about $8.
- 1883: This is the only unreleased single on Apple for which promo copies exist. (Several 45s were released only as promos and have special "PRO-" numbers; those are outside the realm of this article.) Both "Ain't That A Shame" and "Slippin' And Slidin'" exist as separate double-sided promos; each is rare and can fetch $200 in near mint condition.

The U.S. Apple picture sleeves

Relatively few Apple singles have picture sleeves. Instead, most Apple 45s came with a custom black sleeve that said either "Apple" or "The Beatles on Apple" on it. The latter sleeve can fetch $2 by itself; the former, $1.

The rarest sleeve, one that isn't even listed in the price guides, is for the Radha Krishna Temple's "Hare Krishna Mantra" (Apple 1810). Only one copy is known; an Apple completist certainly would pay into three figures for it.

Three Beatles singles on Apple had picture sleeves; any of them can fetch $100 in near mint condition. "The Ballad Of John & Yoko" (Apple 2531) is rare; the other two — "Let It Be" (2764) and "The Long And Winding Road" (2832) — are tough to find without some ring wear toward the center of the sleeve, as the former is black and the latter is white.

Otherwise, most of the sought-after Apple sleeves are by the ex-Beatles. The toughest Harrison sleeve to find is "Dark Horse" (Apple 1877, $80); the toughest Lennon is "Mother" (Apple 1827, $120); the most valuable McCartney is the version of "Mary Had A Little Lamb" that mentions its B-side, "Little Woman Love" (Apple 1851, $40); and the toughest Starr is the version of "Beaucoups Of Blues" with the catalog number erroneously listed as 1826 instead of the proper 2969 ($40).

Over the years, several warehouse finds of Apple 45s with picture sleeves have been made, depressing the value of some of them. In addition to several Lennon sleeves thus affected, it also did a number on Ronnie Spector's "Try Some, Buy Some" (Apple 1832); the sleeve is about a $10 item in near mint, about the average for a non-Beatles Apple picture sleeve.

As a guide, here are the Apple singles issued in the U.S. with picture sleeves, arranged by number, so you can determine whether the sleeve you're trying to find actually exists: 1806, 1808, 1809, 1810 (extremely rare, as noted above), 1813, 1816, 1817, 1818, 1819, 1821, 1827, 1828, 1830, 1831, 1832, 1835, 1836, 1838, 1842, 1844, 1845, 1847 (custom lyrics sleeve), 1848, 1849, 1850, 1851, 1853, 1854, 1865, 1868, 1870, 1876, 1877, 1879, 1882, 1884, 2531, 2764, 2832, 2969 (some issued with the number 1826 on them), 2995.

The U.S. Apple LPs

Just as with the singles, some of the numbers for Apple albums went unused. Those that were never issued were 3355 (slated to be *Maybe Tomorrow* by The Iveys but unissued in the States), 3356, 3366, 3374, and 3378 (possibly an unreleased Badfinger LP).

Also, when Capitol released a two-tape set of a two-LP set, each tape had a separate number, but neither number was used on the LP. The following Apple numbers were claimed that way: 3382 and 3383 (for *Fly* by Yoko Ono), 3393 and 3394 (*Some Time In New York City* by John & Yoko), 3397 and 3398 (*In Concert 1972* by Ravi Shankar), 3401 and 3402 (*Approximately Infinite Universe* by Yoko Ono), 3405 and 3406 (*The Beatles 1962-1966*), 3407 and 3408 (*The Beatles 1967-1970*).

As with the 45s, some numbers were issued outside the 3350-3422 range; again, all of these were Beatles-related. All of The Beatles' original albums, all in the 2000s, were issued with Apple labels from 1971-1975; few are sought-after compared to the original black rainbow label Capitol originals. The others are 101, 153, 383, 385 (all Beatles), 639 (Harrison's *All Things Must Pass*), 5001 (*Two Virgins*, distributed by Tetragrammaton) and 34001 (*Let It Be*, distributed by United Artists). In a separate category is 100 (*The Beatles Christmas Album*, which was only available to fan club members).

Among the more sought-after American Apple LPs include:

- Again, any with a small Capitol logo on the B-side.
- 3359, *That's The Way God Planned It* by Billy Preston. The original cover has a photo of Preston's head with his mouth open, singing. At least one wag has called this the "slow death" cover, because he appears to be in agony! The album was reissued with four full-body photos of Preston on the front. The original cover goes for $40-$50 in near mint condition.
- 3361, *Wedding Album* by John & Yoko. A boxed set with numerous inserts, the complete package is quite rare on vinyl (the eight-track tape version is much easier to find) and can go for $150 in near mint.
- 3375, *Ram* by Paul and Linda McCartney. This is a promo-only version with the "MAS" prefix, issued in mono to radio stations. It's in the same cover as the stereo version, so it's worth looking inside. This is one of the rarest of all LPs; in near mint condition, it can get $3,000 or more!
- 3387, *Straight Up* by Badfinger. The most sought-after non-Beatles Apple LP, at one time it fetched $100 or more. Its release on CD has diminished demand for the original. Still, it can get a cool $60 or so in near mint.
- 3391, *The Pope Smokes Dope* by David Peel. Another $60 or so album.
- 3396, *In Concert 1972* by Ravi Shankar. Also appearing with him is Ali Akbar Khan, who would later record with Eddie Vedder of Pearl Jam. A two-record set, this is a $50 item.
- 5001, *Two Virgins* by John & Yoko. Reproduced often, original copies of this album start at $100 in near mint and go up from there, depending on whether the bag is still there and whether the album jacket is die-cut or has photos on it.

There's much more involved in collecting Apple than I can possibly detail here. There are promos and foreign issues, varying prefixes — and I don't even include the re-activation of the label in the 1990s. Have fun!

Ex-Beatlemania!

The '70s solo chart invasion

by Casey Piotrowski

It was an amazing time. The Beatles were constantly at the top of the charts. Seemingly, every time you turned on the radio, you heard a new Beatles record. They were always in the press or on TV. Who can forget those incredible days of 1974? That's right, 1974... really, mid-1973 through mid-1975.

Because of the way they controlled pop music as a group in 1964, almost overlooked was the way they nearly duplicated (and in some ways surpassed) the feat as solo artists a decade later.

Certainly, immediately after the breakup, The Beatles' enormous popularity gave momentum to the fledgling solo careers of John, Paul, George, and Ringo. In fact, each had a #1 single million seller within 18 months of the group's breakup. But, by 1972, much of that early goodwill had dried up.

John was coming off his *Some Time In New York City* disaster, an album that peaked no higher than #33 nationally, along with the even-then politically incorrectly titled single "Woman Is The Nigger Of The World," which peaked no higher than #57 nationally (in *Billboard*) and couldn't break the top 85 in either *Cashbox* or *Record World*.

Paul was ravaged by the press for his first Wings LP, *Wildlife*, which peaked at #8 (after his first two LPs each topped the charts). And neither of his first two Wings singles could crack the American Top 20. The first, "Give Ireland Back To The Irish," was panned for being too political. The second, "Mary Had A Little Lamb," was knocked for not being political enough. George had gone two and a half years since his last studio album and 18 months since his last single and that ("Bangla Desh") failed to make the national Top 15. And Ringo had only two pop singles (though both Top 10 hits) and two specialized albums, neither of which had Beatles-esque chart numbers (the album of standards, *Sentimental Journey*, peaked at #20 and the country album, *Beaucoups Of Blues* peaked at #31) in the more than three years since the group broke up. Fans of the group had to wonder just how much each needed the others professionally, if not personally.

A modest return to form began with McCartney's "Hi, Hi, Hi" single, which peaked at #6 in *Cashbox* in February 1973. But the comeback began in earnest, ironically enough, with the first post-breakup releases from the group, the *'62-'66* and the *'67-'70* greatest hits packages. Each hit #1, though, oddly enough, not in the same national publications. (*'67-'70* reached #1 in *Billboard*, *'62-'66* in both *Cashbox* and *Record World*). This was in late May '73 but, before either album could get comfortable in the top spot, they had competition

This article originally appeared in* Goldmine *issue #477, Nov. 6, 1998.

from within the family. And that started a run on the charts that had only been seen once before.

In late May, *'67-'70* was knocked out of the top spot by McCartney's *Red Rose Speedway* which was, in turn, knocked out of the top spot by Harrison's *Living In The Material World*. Continuously, from mid-May to the end of July, a Beatles album, either from one of the group or the group as a whole, was in #1. It was something that hadn't been seen since it was done 10 years earlier by... guess who? And, in an achievement that rivaled their having the nation's top five singles in April 1964, these four albums were all in the top five of *Cashbox*'s album chart for the week ending June 23, 1973. This was something that never happened even during the halcyon days of 1964.

Meanwhile, Paul's ballad from *Speedway*, "My Love," was racing up the singles chart, hitting the #1 spot on June 2 (becoming, surprisingly, the first time a Beatle had hit the top spot in more than 18 months). It stayed there for four weeks until Paul was again knocked out of #1 by George with his "Give Me Love" single.

By the time George was falling from the Top 10, he was replaced by Paul with his "Live And Let Die" single, which would also hit #1 (in *Cashbox* and *Record World*). When the *James Bond* theme finally left the Top 10 near the end of September, it ended a string of four months when at least one ex-Beatle had a single in the Top 10. And before "Live And Let Die" dropped off the chart completely, the other ex-members of the group were about to be heard from.

Whatever Gets You Thru The Night

Words and Music by JOHN LENNON

From the album "Walls and Bridges" recorded by John Lennon on APPLE RECORDS

Distributed by

Above and below, the front and back of Wings' *Band On The Run*.

Ringo was then climbing the charts with "Photograph." As it reached the Top 10 (in *Billboard* on Nov. 10, 1973), John was climbing the charts with his "Mind Games" single, which would hit the Top 10 in both *Cashbox* and *Record World*. By the time "Photograph" reached #1 (Nov. 23, 1973), McCartney was back on the charts with "Helen Wheels." Within three weeks, the (solo) Beatles would have three records in the Top 20. In fact, with the exception of two weeks, from Oct. 27, 1973 to June 29, 1974... more than eight months, there was always at least one record from some member of the group in the Top 10, something that the group never achieved while together. During that time, besides "Photograph," "Band On The Run" and "You're Sixteen" both hit #1. "Oh My My," "Jet" and "Helen Wheels" all hit the Top 5 nationally.

The action on the album charts was no different. The *Ringo* album was in the Top 10 by its third week on the chart (Nov. 23, 1973) and was joined there by Lennon's *Mind Games* LP, followed closely by McCartney's *Band On The Run* album. By the first week in January 1974, all three solo albums were in the national Top 20. Never before (or since) had three solo projects from members of the same group charted that high simultaneously. Both *Ringo* and *Band On The Run* would peak at #1. *Mind Games* would top out at #6.

The charts had a chance to cool down a bit. (There were no singles on the charts from any of the four from Aug. 24, 1974 to Sept. 21, 1974.) But it was only the calm before another storm.

John was first out of the box with "Whatever Gets You Through The Night," which debuted on the charts on Sept. 28, 1974. It would reach #1 eight weeks later, as Paul's single, "Junior's Farm" and Ringo's first release from *Goodnight Vienna*, "Only You," and George's "Dark Horse" were also on the way to becoming major hits. On Nov. 30, 1974, all of The Beatles would have a single in the Top 40. In fact, from mid-November 1974 to mid-February 1975, a period of 13 weeks, each of The Beatles had at least one single continuously on the charts at the same time. And, during one week (Jan. 25, 1975), the four of them collectively had seven of the Top 100 singles in the country, a feat not matched since... well, you know.

It was no different on the album charts. While *Band On The Run* was concluding its phenomenal run on the charts, Lennon's *Walls And Bridges* was headed for #1, which it would reach on Nov. 16, 1974. Two weeks after Lennon's album fell from the Top 10 (Dec. 21), Ringo's *Goodnight Vienna* LP took its place, eventually peaking at #5 (in *Record World*). George's *Dark Horse* album, which would climb as high as #4, would join it in the Top 10 for the last two weeks of January 1975... the last time two members of the same band would have Top 10 albums at the same time. Within two weeks of *Dark Horse* dropping from the Top 20 (Feb. 22, 1975), John's *Rock 'N' Roll* climbed to that level on the charts on its way to #4 (in *Record World*). During the period from Dec. 21, 1974 to April 19, 1975, all four members of the group had albums continuously on the chart.

As Lennon's album left the Top 10 at the end of April, this incredible run by The Beatles, separately this time, would end. John would give us nothing new for more than five years until his tragically brief comeback. George's "This Guitar" single, released in December 1975, would fail to chart in any of the national trades. Ringo would never see the sunny side of the Top 20, either album or single charts again. Even Paul, who would have three more #1 albums in a row, couldn't get his "Letting Go" single any higher than #39 in October 1975.

But there's no taking away from what the four of them achieved during the previous 24 months. Each member of the group had at least one #1 single and one #1 album... seven #1 albums in all. Eight #1 singles in two years. Five gold singles. Eleven gold albums (again, something they couldn't match during their years together). Four more albums reaching the Top 6 nationally. Five more singles hitting the Top 5. Three more hitting the Top 10. One more hitting the Top 15. Collectively, 35 weeks in the singles Top 10 in 1973, 33 weeks in 1974. 48 weeks in the album Top 10 in 1973 (with the first album not getting there until the end of April). 42 weeks there in 1974.

And all this came during a time when radio station formats were getting fragmented and playlists getting smaller. Also, unlike 1964, each of those releases gave competition, not synergy, to the others. Each solo release would be looked upon as a new "Beatles" record and stations would hesitate adding, for example, a new Lennon record if they were already playing something from McCartney, Harrison, and Starr.

It was a tribute not only to immense popularity of these four men, but also to their immense talent. No one can make this kind of a sustained chart run on personality alone. And, looking back, much of the music that these four men produced individually during this time still ranks with the most creative and entertaining work of the era, as was the case of their work as a group 10 years before.

And, just as no group has since dominated the charts as John, Paul, George, and Ringo did in 1964, no group of individuals has since dominated the charts as John, Paul, George, and Ringo did 10 years later.

(Ed Ford and Ron Gibb contributed to this article.)

The reverse side of George Harrison's "Bangla Desh" Apple 45.

Retro News Flash
April 12, 1996, issue #410

Britain to ban The Beatles?

Amazing as it may seem, "Real Love," the new single by The Beatles, has been omitted from the playlist of BBC's Radio 1 station, which is trying to attract more younger listeners.

According to reports out of England, Beatles fans protested the decision in large numbers, accusing the station of being "ageist." Conservative member of Parliament, Harry Greenway even planned to bring the issue up for debate in the House Of Commons.

"This is a form of censorship, nothing less, and a stop should be put to it without delay," Greenway said.

A Radio 1 spokesman said the song was not chosen because it lacked merit. "It's not what our listeners want to hear," he reportedly said. "We are a contemporary music station."

The station is currently involved in a legal case with the group Status Quo, whose new single "Fun Fun Fun," recorded with The Beach Boys, was also banned from the Radio 1 playlist.

A spokesman for The Beatles said that he feared that "Real Love," already high in the charts compiled by other radio stations, would be stopped from making further progress by the Radio 1 ban.

"It's ridiculous," the spokesman said. "It's not as if The Beatles don't appeal to" Radio 1's younger audience — more than 40 percent of the people who bought the first *Anthology* album were teenagers.

Denny Laine

Talks about Moodies, McCartney and more

by Bruce Eder

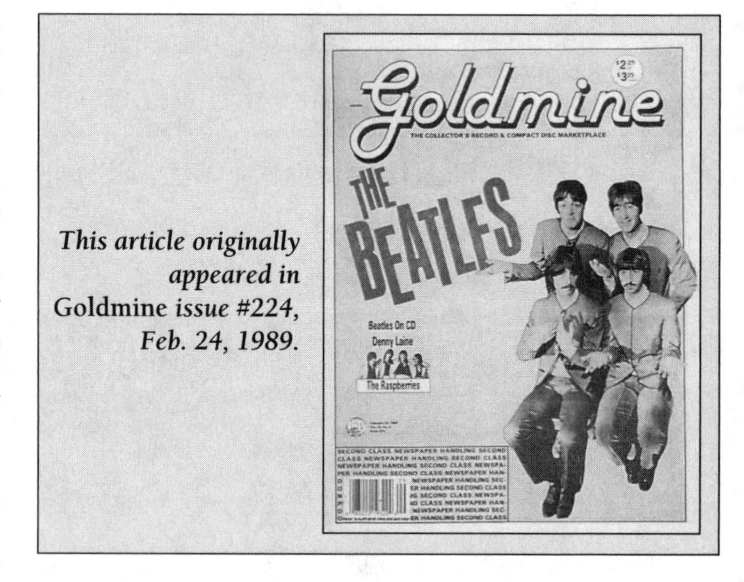

This article originally appeared in **Goldmine issue #224,** *Feb. 24, 1989.*

Denny Laine has seen it all in British rock and, unlike most other British rockers of his generation, he didn't have to wait for the birth of American rock 'n' roll to find musical inspiration.

As co-founder, lead guitarist and lead singer of the original Moody Blues (1964-66), Laine's mournful, wailing voice propelled their single, "Go Now," to the top of the charts early in 1965 and brought him within the orbit of The Beatles on two European tours and a brief stint being managed by Brian Epstein. With The Electric String Band, he was one of the most acclaimed performers to emerge in London during that psychedelic summer of 1967. His stint with Ginger Baker's Airforce at the dawn of the '70s put Laine into one of the first bands to be embraced by that newly formed fraternity of rock journalists. And as a core member of Paul McCartney's Wings from 1972 until 1979, Laine moved into that rarefied atmosphere of arena rock.

On the eve of his appearance at the New York/New England Beatles Convention at the Marriott Hotel in Trumbull, Conn., Feb. 17-19, 1989, nearly a decade after his last album with McCartney,Laine has settled comfortably into the life of a middle-aged guitarist/songwriter, still with a lot to say about McCartney, Wings, The Moody Blues and British rock.

Laine was born Brian Arthur Hayes in Birmingham, England on Oct. 24, 1944. Unlike most other British rockers of his generation, he didn't have to wait for the birth of American rock 'n' roll to find musical inspiration. Rather, Laine's first musical idol came from the world of jazz.

"I got interested in the guitar from listening to Django Reinhardt," he recalled in a recent interview.

Reinhardt, an electric jazz guitarist famed for his association with violinist Stephane Grappelli in the Quartet of the Hot Club of Paris, became a legend during the days before World War II in his performances and recordings. Years before Les Paul or Jimi Hendrix emerged as masters of the guitar's vocabulary, Reinhardt expanded its boundaries with his radical approach to jazz.

"Django Reinhardt and that whole free-form approach to jazz — the gypsy scene he was into — were my whole inspiration for taking up guitar. It was only later that Buddy Holly and rock 'n' roll came along. We were all into that, and did some skiffle playing in the '50s, and then we started listening to American rhythm 'n' blues."

By 1962 Laine was leading his own band, Denny And The Diplomats, which was heavily influenced by the sounds of Rufus Thomas, James Brown, and the heavier R&B sounds of Stax and King Records. Birmingham in those years had a home-grown music scene of its own, perhaps not as crowded or famous as the one in Liverpool but just as competitive, even if there was no local-based star-maker like Epstein.

"The Moody Blues were formed by the five of us [Laine, Mike Pinder on keyboards, Ray Thomas on harmonica, Graeme Edge on drums, and Clint Warwick on bass] from the five top bands in Birmingham," he recalled of their early 1964 origin. "We'd all been in these different groups and decided to form a group together and go south and see if we could make it in London."

"We were originally called The M & B Five. M & B was short for Mitchell's And Butler, a local brewery that sponsored our first shows together."

London was the center of the British blues revival from 1961 onward. When The Moody Blues arrived there in April 1964, they quickly found themselves in competition with some very high-powered bands, including The Rolling Stones and The Yardbirds.

MULL OF KINTYRE

WORDS AND MUSIC BY McCARTNEY–LAINE

Graham Hughes

WINGS

Laine: "We had one advantage over a lot of the competition. We got a lot of American records ahead of other people with help from a friend, James Hamilton. He was a freak DJ with an incredible record collection, and he used to get American records, demos, everything, ahead of anyone and let us hear them. The records he had that we got to hear were incredible. We got to listen to every James Brown record, every Motown record. We did a lot of them first, ahead of anyone else in London."

The Moody Blues were signed to Decca Records in 1964 and released a single titled "Lose Your Money," written by Mike Pinder, which sank without a trace despite the band's appearance, promoting it in a lip-synched performance, on the TV show *Ready, Steady, Go* (available on home video as part of *Ready, Steady, Go Vol. 3* from HBO Video). As one band member later quipped about "Lose Your Money": "We lost our money."

For their second single, however, the group chose to cover a song originally recorded by American R&B singer Bessie Banks titled "Go Now." Released at the end of 1964, "Go Now" was at the top of the British charts by the beginning of 1965 and achieved similar success in America.

The band's success with "Go Now" was immediately seized upon by their managers. From doing shows for £100 or £125 (about $300) their fee quickly went to £500 and to make sure they didn't miss any opportunity, the band was booked into ballrooms, cabarets and local dance halls as often as it was into concert halls. Meanwhile, in the studio, they thrashed about for a year after "Go Now," trying to repeat its success. "Stop From The Bottom Of My Heart" and even "Time Is On My Side" (covered at the same time the Stones did it) failed to crack the charts.

The group went through a chameleon-like evolution in its sound during 1965, doing Brown numbers such as "I Go Crazy" and smooth, elegant Motown-like songs such as "I've Got A Dream" (written by Jeff Barry and Ellie Greenwich), as well as covers of George Gershwin songs such as "Summertime." Their stage repertoire also included Willie Dixon's "Little Red Rooster" and Bo Diddley's "Bo Diddley."

Despite the soulfulness of Laine's singing and their dedication — they would frequently spend 11 hours in the studio working out a single song — they lacked the sheer, animated abandon of rivals such as The Rolling Stones and The Yardbirds. Money became a problem once the dust from "Go Now" settled, and it was realized that the band had only seen a fraction of the revenues generated by its more than one million sales in England and America.

"There wasn't any problem of funds stolen," Laine is quick to point out, however, about stories surrounding the band's early management that have circulated over the years. "We made a lot of money from that record and toured constantly for a year without a break, but we also spent a lot of money. We had a good manager in Tony Secunda.

"Later, Brian Epstein became interested in managing us, but by the time that happened in 1966, he was really only interested in The Beatles. None of his other acts really had his attention."

Oddly enough, the group began to develop a problem that was more commonly associated with its later, progressive rock incarnation — that of how to best re-create its sound on stage. Pinder had begun using a grand piano in the studio fairly early on and a Wurlitzer organ on stage, and they were one of the few groups to travel with two keyboard instruments.

Without a successful follow-up to "Go Now," however, The Moody Blues' bookings soon declined, and by the beginning of 1966 they were back on the cabaret circuit, playing for as little as £50 per night. There were also changes taking place within the band, as the quintet tried to re-establish itself.

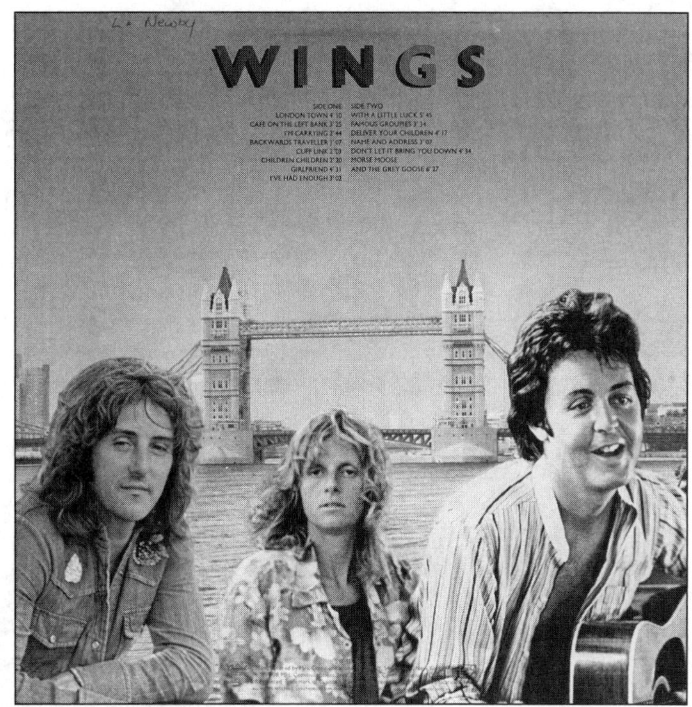

Wings' *London Town* front and back.

Early in 1966, the members arrived at a split over one of their own, according to Laine, and he found himself outvoted. "There was a vote to replace Clint Warwick [the bass player], and I voted to keep him in the band," he recalled. "When that happened, I felt that the group had changed, and I decided to leave as well."

Warwick was replaced in the band by another Birmingham-born bassist, John Lodge, while Laine's spot was taken over by Justin Hayward. After a few more unsuccessful singles, it was this incarnation of The Moody Blues that found lasting success with a much more lavish psychedelic/orchestral sound.

And what ever happened to Clint Warwick? Laine said. "He's doing all right," presumably back in Birmingham.

Laine himself has never expressed any bitterness over the way he left The Moody Blues or not being a part of their subsequent massive success. "It was an invaluable experience," he told Nick Jones in *Melody Maker* during 1967. "We saw a lot of things. We traveled all over England, we traveled all over the world. We saw America, and we lived like stars. But I was bogged down [in the band]. I stopped thinking too. The group was happy with what they'd got. Unfortunately, the public weren't."

Speaking 21 years later, Laine echoed these feelings. "The band had just changed when Clint Warwick left. I realized that. I was very happy for them [The Moody Blues] when they succeeded."

Strangely enough, even as The Moody Blues were re-emerging with their own arty new sounds in 1967, Laine himself was moving into his own realms of musical experimentation. Early in 1967, he began organizing a performing group that eventually debuted in London that year as Denny Laine And The Electric String Band. Consisting of Laine on vocals and guitar, two violins, two cellos, bass and drums, the group was hailed by *Melody Maker*'s Jones as an "exciting and creative musical plan," while Laine was called "an artist destined for enormous recognition."

The Electric String Band played fashionable clubs such as Blaises and London's UFO that summer, with a repertoire that included Laine originals such as "Say You Don't Mind" and "Ask The People." Laine himself described the new group at the time as a "rebirth" after The Moody Blues' split.

"The Electric String Band was an attempt to take a new, different idea in music and see what we could come up with," he recalled now. "We had these new, young players from The Royal Academy Of Music who were willing to try it, and it resulted in some great shows — we played some excellent shows, with Jimi Hendrix in London, during that year."

Despite critical success, The Electric String Band never recorded any albums, although they did make a single of Laine's "Say You Don't Mind" that failed to chart. A subsequent recording of the song by The Zombies' Colin Blunstone in 1972, however, made it to #15 on the British charts.

The Electric String Band in its conception and configuration preceded by four years the similarly named Electric Light Orchestra incarnation of The Move, which was another Birmingham-based band. Laine's group was just a little too early on the scene to achieve the same kind of success.

In 1968, Laine went to work under contract as a songwriter with Essex Music and began working for producer Denny Cordell (of Move fame), producing demos for Joe Cocker and Procol Harum, among many other artists.

Late that year, however, Laine was recruited by ex–Moody Blues manager Tony Secunda into a group called Balls, formed around ex-Move member Trevor Burton. Actually something of a British supergroup, Balls' lineup also included Jackie Lomax and, in its later incarnations through 1970, Steve Gibbons as well as future ELO keyboard player Richard Tandy. Laine played and recorded with Burton through four Balls lineups with little commercial success.

It was a one-shot gig during this same period that came closest to moving Laine onto the international rock scene, as

ARROW THROUGH ME

WORDS AND MUSIC BY McCARTNEY

WINGS

a member of Ginger Baker's Airforce. A 10-man group (including three drummers), Airforce was formed by Baker late in 1969 to play a single show up in Birmingham, and Laine joined as lead guitarist and singer.

"I'd known Ginger from the early days in London," he explained of his involvement in Airforce. "Back then all of the bands played the same gigs and crossed paths, and I'd met Ginger in The Graham Bond Organization. Both of us had played The Marquee Club, and we both had an interest in jazz and blues."

Airforce was an eclectic ensemble, actually formed out of the remnants of Blind Faith — with Steve Winwood on guitar, keyboards and vocals and Rick Grech on bass and violin — and Traffic, with Chris Wood on saxophone. (During this period, with Winwood moving between Blind Faith and a solo career, Traffic was on a lingering hiatus that ended when Winwood began work on the album that eventually became *John Barleycorn Must Die*). At the time, although the group's main orientation was toward African music — which Baker, as British rock's most serious drummer, had always loved — they were varied enough in their sound to accommodate all of these players. The other members, in addition to Baker on drums, included Phil Seamen and Remi Kabaka on drums and Graham Bond and Harold McNair on saxophones.

The group followed the Birmingham gig with a show at Royal Albert Hall in December 1969, and it was this second show — attracting much press attention due to Baker and Winwood's presence — that received raves from all over the world. Airforce was suddenly embraced as one of the hottest, most exciting new bands by the then-new, burgeoning rock 'n' roll press, particularly in America, where *Rolling Stone* announced the group's birth to the world in the form of an ecstatic review of the Albert Hall show.

Laine was only one member, and not even the more well-known of the two guitarists next to Winwood, but he still managed to distinguish himself in a solo spot that featured his performance of "Man Of Constant Sorrow" with Grech on electric violin.

The group decided to remain together with a few shifts in personnel during 1970 and released a studio album later in the year. (Surprisingly, though, in a manner typical of the loony nature of rock journalism in those days, the same Royal Albert Hall performances that had received such raves from concert reviewers in December 1969 were panned by record reviewers in the spring.)

Despite a high reputation and critical support, Airforce collapsed later in 1970 under the weight of public indifference. This was particularly true in the United States, where a hastily conceived American tour was canceled due to extremely poor advance ticket sales.

Balls also ended in 1970, and Laine returned to writing songs. His hiatus from the stage proved short-lived, however, when Laine was recruited in 1971 as a member of Wings, McCartney's first touring band since 1966 and his first organized band since the breakup of The Beatles early in 1970.

"I'd known Paul from the time when The Moody Blues had toured Europe with The Beatles," Laine recalled, explaining his recruitment into the band as guitarist. "He was in a very difficult position at the time he was putting Wings together, and I think one reason he wanted me was because we'd both been in groups that we'd formed and been forced out of under similar circumstances. We'd each left groups that we'd helped found under similar circumstances: He wanted someone working with him who understood what that meant.

"He was also looking for someone who had a similar attitude about playing in a group and could back him up in terms of playing, arranging, songwriting and singing."

Wings' original incarnation, which included Henry McCulloch on guitar (later replaced by Jimmy McCulloch, no relation) and Denny Seiwell on drums, got off to a rocky start with a debut release, *Wild Life*, that fared poorly in the press and on the charts. The group toured England, playing small university venues without much promotion, in an attempt to hone its sound on stage without of the glare of publicity. This strategy, attempted earlier in the decade by Eric Clapton in Derek And The Dominoes, proved just as unsuccessful for McCartney. Press reports began filtering out about Wings' seemingly unprofessional, very rough sound.

With its records under fire and its live gigs — including those on a more ambitious 1972 European tour — being savaged in the press, it seemed that the band wouldn't survive. In point of fact, it didn't. McCulloch and Seiwell were both out of the band

Selected Denny Laine Album Discography

Label/Country	Record #	Title	Year
With The Moody Blues			
London (U.S.)	428	Go Now	1965
Decca (U.K.)	4711	Magnificent Moodies	1966
Castle Communications (U.K.)	CCS 105	Collection	
With Ginger Baker's Airforce			
Polydor (U.K.)	2662 001	Airforce	1970
Atco (U.S.)	703	Airforce	1970
Polydor (U.K.)	2383 029	Airforce 2	1970
Atco (U.S.)	33343	Airforce 2	1970
With Paul McCartney and Wings			
Apple (U.K.)	7142	Wild Life	1971
Apple (U.S.)	3386	Wild Life	1971
Apple (U.K.)	251	Red Rose Speedway	1972
Apple (U.S.)	3409	Red Rose Speedway	1972
Apple (U.K.)	10007	Band On The Run	1974
Apple (U.S.)	3415	Band On The Run	1974
EMI (U.K.)	254	Venus And Mars	1975
Capitol (U.S.)	11419	Venus And Mars	1975
EMI (U.K.)	10010	Wings At The Speed Of Sound	1976
Capitol (U.S.)	11525	Wings At The Speed Of Sound	1976
EMI (U.K.)	720	Wings Over America	1976
Capitol (U.S.)	11593	Wings Over America	1976
EMI (U.K.)	10012	London Town	1978
Capitol (U.S.)	11777	London Town	1978
EMI (U.K.)	256	Wings Greatest	1978
Capitol (U.S.)	11905	Wings Greatest	1978
Columbia (U.S.)	TC 36057	Back To The Egg	1979
Denny Laine solo albums			
Wizard/Warner Brothers (U.S.)	2190	Aah Laine	1973
Wizard (U.K.)	2001	Aah Laine	1973
EMI (U.K.)	781	Holly Days	1976
Capitol (U.S.)	11588	Holly Days	1976
Scratch (U.K.)	5001	Japanese Tears	1980
Polydor (Spain)	2393 277	Japanese Tears	1981
Thunderbolt/Magnum (U.K.)	XVII	Master Suite	1988
President (U.K.)	PTLS6092	Lonely Road	1988
With Mike McGear (Mike McCartney)			
Warner Brothers (U.S.)	2825	McGear	1974
Warner Brothers (U.K.)	56051	McGear	1974

within two years, while Laine remained and ultimately became a core member of the group. His own "Say You Don't Mind" was featured in their stage shows, and in those early tours, he proved the most successful of the members in adapting to McCartney's work habits. While McCulloch was dropped from the lineup and Seiwell left when he declined to travel to Lagos, Nigeria, for the recording of *Band On The Run*, Laine's prominence increased. So, too, did his confidence in himself as an artist and he recorded the first of five solo albums, *Aah Laine*, in 1973.

By 1976, the reconstituted Wings had emerged as one of the most slickly professional arena-rock bands in the world, propelled to stardom by the hit album *Venus And Mars* and *Wings At The Speed Of Sound*. The U.S. tour that followed — later captured on the triple album *Wings Over America* and the film *Rockshow* — included a spot featuring Laine singing "Go Now," at the time when the post-Laine Moody Blues were on a five-year hiatus.

It was as a result of his exposure on this tour and the subsequent live album and the Wings album *London Town* that followed in 1978, that Laine at last emerged with a presence of his own.

In addition to writing "Mull Of Kintyre" with McCartney, which became the biggest-selling British single in history (passing The Beatles' own "She Loves You"), he became a regular songwriting contributor on the group's albums.

The scale of these live performances and the degree of attention they attracted were something Laine hadn't seen before in his career.

"The shows we played were great," he recalled, of performances before tens of thousands of fans in enormous arenas, "because we were all professional enough to handle anything that went wrong. But I prefer playing to smaller groups of people. Something was lost playing to those huge crowds."

Laine persevered, however, often over McCartney's own resistance to touring. "A lot of people don't realize that I was always working on Paul to keep the band on the road as much as possible. Paul didn't want to tour, but I kept that band going back on the road."

What finally broke Laine's enthusiasm for Wings was McCartney's drug arrest in Tokyo at the outset of the group's 1980 tour. Laine's voice still betrays anger and frustration over this incident, describing its impact.

"The Tokyo bust ended my interest in the group and doing anything further," he remembered, "because of the way it happened. We'd been planning that tour for years, and it was going to be one of the biggest and most important group of shows we ever did. And we'd worked for two years to stay clean, so there wouldn't be trouble. I'd had a couple of marijuana busts, and Paul had had his, but for two years we'd been careful, just to arrange that tour of Japan. And then, we'd spent five hours at the consulate arranging visas, telling them that we were clean and answering every question they asked us the right way.

"And then we got there, and Paul gets busted. The whole thing was stupid, incredibly stupid, and it wrecked any plans we might've had to tour anywhere. We couldn't do Europe for two years, we couldn't tour Australia, where we were supposed to play. There was nothing we could do for two years after that, and I just said, 'Enough,' and left."

Although he'd split from Wings after recording *Back To The Egg*, Laine did guest on McCartney's *Tug Of War* LP and went on to record with his fellow Wings member, drummer Steve Holly, on the appropriately named Laine album *Japanese Tears* (which also featured original Wings guitarist McCulloch and drummer Seiwell), released in 1980. This album also included re-recordings of "Go Now" and "Say You Don't Mind."

His exit from McCartney's band led to subsequent misunderstandings, however. "After I left, I started to write my memoirs," he explained, "for publication as a book. What happened was that parts of it concerning Paul were excerpted in a British paper in 1981, which printed them out of context and made it look like I was trying to exploit my years playing with Paul, which wasn't the case. A lot of people thought I was trying to cash in when that appeared, and I wasn't."

Since leaving Wings and releasing his first three solo LPs, Laine has concentrated on songwriting and working on demos, although he has also done some recording in recent years, including some work (as yet unreleased) with his old friend Ginger Baker. "Those came out very well," he remarked of those sessions, "and I'd like to see them out someday." He played a benefit concert in England called Heartbeat with George Harrison and Robert Plant in 1986.

In 1988, Laine released two new albums in England, an all-instrumental effort titled *Master Suite* and a set of modern, commercial-sounding songs called *Lonely Road*.

"These days, I'm mostly involved in songwriting, though. Basically that's what I'm about, although I enjoy playing smaller halls and clubs." He lives with his wife in Windsor, and has a home studio.

At the time of this writing, Laine planned on going to Boston to record a new album with producer Jimmy Miller. "It'll actually be two records. I have a contact with Australian EMI to do an album, and I'll be working on that too."

More than two decades after "Go Now," Denny Laine is ready to get going all over again.

Just a pair of Pussy Cats

The Lennon/Nilsson collaboration

by Dave Thompson

One night in early March 1974, John Lennon and Harry Nilsson rolled up at the Los Angeles Troubadour, steaming drunk and gratingly abusive. Lennon was particularly out of it, clothes rumpled, hair a mess and a sanitary napkin stuck on his forehead. He demanded more alcohol, the waitress refused, and the former Beatle, who had doubtless left that famous Lennon wit in the car, instead flashed angrily, "Don't you know who I am?"

"Yeah, I know," the waitress shot back. "You're an asshole with a Kotex® on his head."

John Lennon's Lost Weekend, 18 months wildcatting through the bowels of showbiz sleaze, is one of the great tales of rock 'n' roll excess, indulged in by one of the greatest excesses in rock 'n' roll history. No matter that the most scintillating retelling is to be found within Albert Goldman's masterpiece of ax-grinding malice, *The Lives Of John Lennon*; neither, as countless subsequent biographies have it, that it has since been reduced to a couple of paragraphs of Hard Love therapy. If the Lost Weekend had never existed, history would have had to invent one — and who better to enjoy it than Beatle John?

He was always a bit of a Jack The Lad. These days, it's fashionable to pin Lennon's most outrageous behavior to the flag of "cutting, acerbic wit" and to blame his victims for any offense they felt — "You just didn't understand John's humor. He's from Liverpool, you know." But that wasn't always the case. There was a time, while Lennon still lived, when he could be an obnoxious bully, a loudmouth boor and an ungracefully fading icon who hadn't made a decent record in years. Or, as another Troubadour waitress put it, after Lennon punched her in the ribs one night, "It's not the pain that hurts. It's finding out that one of your idols is a real asshole."

Lennon had arrived in L.A. in September 1973. He traveled light, girlfriend May Pang and a couple of suitcases, and though he wasn't sure what he wanted to do, he knew that this was where he wanted to do it. L.A., thousands of miles from New York and Yoko, was a playground for the rich and famous, and John was certainly both of them. The whole city, or at least that narrow band of Hollywood nightclubs where he'd be spending most of his time, was a spiritual pick-me-up that never let you down again. There he could reinvent himself; there, he could escape from whatever else he'd become.

Lennon's latest album, *Mind Games*, was on the verge of release; his next, a tribute to the rock 'n' roll records he'd loved as a kid, was in the planning stages already. Both were a long way away from the albums he'd made in the past, the cynical politicking of *Some Time In New York City*, the bitter sideswipes of *Imagine*, the savage purgative of *Plastic Ono Band*. All Lennon needed do was convince people that he meant it, that he wasn't going to go back to bed or wrap his wife up in a bag anymore.

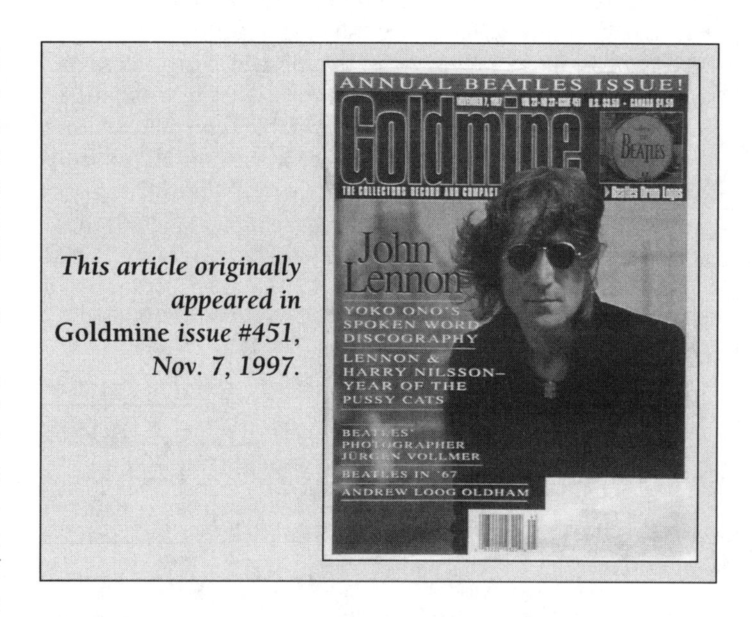

This article originally appeared in* Goldmine *issue #451, Nov. 7, 1997.

Tony King, a P.R. man schooled in the furnace of the primal Rolling Stones, was already setting the first set of wheels in motion, convincing the world that this was a kinder, gentler John than they'd seen in a long time; Phil Spector was greasing the axle of the second, hiring a crack studio session band to aid Lennon in his nostalgia-draped odyssey. And while neither project was to roll as smoothly as Lennon might have wished — *Mind Games* barely scratched the Top 10; *Rock 'N' Roll* turned into a drama of Dostoevsky-esque proportions — still they were a cakewalk compared to all he'd been through in the past and to what he'd be undergoing in the immediate future.

Albert Goldman, mastering dramatic hyperbole with a flair that makes lesser scribes blanche, credits Lennon's lost weekend to the fiendish machinations of three evil fairies. Spector was the first; music publisher Morris Levy, somewhat unexcitingly, was the third. And sandwiched in between them, the very earth trembling at the mention of its name, cities crumbling at the sound of its voice, Harry Nilsson was the second. Harry "Theme From Midnight Cowboy" Nilsson. Harry "Without You" Nilsson. "Pahl" as the man himself so memorably snorted. "Nilsson Schmilsson."

Nilsson rolled into Lennon's life like he'd just been dragged in by the cat.

"It was a time when I was really depressed and down," he admitted during interviews for the *Lost Lennon Tapes* radio series. "I was just totally down, I was looking for anyone in the world to talk to, have a drink with, be with, and I went to every bar in the town, called my friends, and there was nobody there. I started studio-hopping in case there was somebody around who was alive, and the last stop on the list was A&M and I saw this guy I recognized; I said, 'What are you working on?' He said, 'John and Phil' — Lennon and Spector. So I said 'Where are they?' He said, 'In that room,' and there was every friend I'd ever had in my life in that room. So I just hopped in, did some odds and ends, and I think I was a nice little centerpiece for them both to dance around."

The sessions, of course, eventually ground to a less than harmonious halt, but Nilsson and Lennon remained fast friends. He and May Pang were sharing a duplex suite at the Beverly Wilshire Hotel; they had the top half, Ringo Starr had the lower, and when you put the two together, it was time to hit the town. Nilsson became an inevitable third partner in a fast-expanding drunken knights of the "whose round?" table.

Those were hazy, crazy days for the rock 'n' roll cognoscenti, for those gallant soldiers whose fame offered them access to an excess they couldn't refuse. It was a time when televisions learned to fly and groupies went with fish, when Keith Moon made a solo album and a swimming pool simply wasn't a swimming pool unless it had a Rolls Royce at the bottom. Lennon and Nilsson understood this behavior intuitively, and they understood its purpose as well.

John Lennon and May Pang were sharing a duplex suite at the Beverly Wilshire Hotel; they had the top half, Ringo Starr had the lower, and when you put the two together, it was time to hit the town. Nilsson became an inevitable third partner in a fast-expanding drunken knights of the "whose round?" table.

The public, *their* public, demands entertainment. That's why it creates stars in the first place, to live out the dreams that they themselves are incapable of realizing: Presley's pink Caddy, Jimi's burning guitar, The Who's trashed hotel rooms, Foghat's... well, Foghat's whatever. So long as it went beyond the realms of normal convention, it didn't matter what the stars had or did. It was the fact that they had them and did them that counted.

But how much was too much? Lennon turning up at the Troubadour with a Kotex® on his head was one thing; turning up there with a chip on his shoulder was another. On March 13, 1974, Lennon and Nilsson were forcibly ejected from L.A.'s most famous niterie after throwing punches at the staff and hurling abuse at the headliners. Maybe "Hey, Smothers Brothers! Fuck a cow!" does deserve a prize for originality, but beating up waitresses and throwing glasses at walls was going too far.

Reporting on the fracas the following week, the British *New Musical Express* even speculated that the row might wind up in deportation. Lennon was already at loggerheads with the U.S. authorities, remaining in the country with nothing but probation and an expired visa to keep him from a long flight home. *NME* reporter Chris Van Ness continued, "when legal charges are brought against Lennon, as they almost certainly will be... he will be branded an 'undesirable alien' and deported."

As it happened, no charges were brought, but Lennon and Nilsson didn't seem to care if they had been. A couple of nights after The Troubadour incident, they provoked a near riot on a tram in Palm Springs. And in the midst of the madness, as if to justify the behavior that was now haunting the headlines, they decided to make an album together. It would be called *Pussy Cats*, Lennon determined, because that is how he and Nilsson signed themselves on the apologetic bouquet that they'd sent to The Smothers Brothers the day after The Troubadour fracas.

Lennon explained, "I was just hanging around with Ringo and Harry, we were just... hanging 'round. It became like a teenage gang only we were all 30, so one day as Harry and I sat there, I looked at him and said, 'What are we doing here? Why don't we go make a record?' Because we're playing pianos in hotel rooms, we're causing riots, we're wasting energy... so I said, 'Look kid, I'm doing nothing. Why don't I produce you?' So we went in and we made the record...."

Nilsson admitted that when the idea first surfaced, he did not take it too seriously. "[John] was out of it when he first suggested it, so I didn't pressure him or push him in any way. But a few days later he called and said, 'What songs are we going to do?' and I went, 'Jesus Christ, I think he's serious.'"

Lennon was not a recognized producer. His early recordings with Yoko, of course, were by definition self-produced, while he also took a co-credit alongside Spector for his own *Plastic Ono Band*, *Imagine* and *Some Time In New York City* albums. Just two records, however, indicated Lennon's personal studio strengths: *Mind Games*, which really wasn't very good; and David Peel's *The Pope Smokes Dope*, which was great fun to listen to but was hardly *Tubular Bells*. But of course, the marketing men who approved this new project's recording budget would hardly have worried about something like that. They would simply have studied the sales charts and done a few simple sums before deducing that if Lennon and Nilsson individually were sure-fire million sellers, then the two of them together would be a license to print money.

Of course it didn't work like that. *Pussy Cats — Starring Harry Nilsson, Produced By John Lennon* would become the worst-selling new album to bear Lennon's name on its cover since his and Yoko's *Wedding Album* a full five years before. But the accountants' loss was rock 'n' roll's gain, and *Pussy Cats* remains one of the great albums of the mid-1970s.

Fueled by an all-but-lethal combination of booze, drugs and absurdly high spirits, boasting the services of three wired-up drummers and a barrelful of revelers and pocked with some of the most gorgeously realized cover versions ever committed to wax, it is an album of dynamic extremes, each one more climactic than the last. By the time it reaches its battered finale, rocking around a war-torn clock, the listener is either exalted or exhausted (or more likely, both), and the stereo system is checking itself into Detox. *Pussy Cats* is not an album you should play in the car.

Yet it is also an album of breathtaking majesty, its finest moments matching, even outstripping, the best of either Lennon's or Nilsson's contemporary work and echoing them as well. Ghosts of the opening, despairing, cover of Jimmy Cliff's "Many

Rivers To Cross" feedback through "#9 Dream," the finest cut on Lennon's own next album; "Loop De Loop" and "Rock Around The Clock," on the other hand, prove that the rock 'n' roll session that Lennon had conducted with Spector had not quite exorcised some ghosts of their own. If, as so many critical commentaries insist, *Pussy Cats* was the sound of two mighty talents at the bottom of a pit, they still had one helluva view.

Moving into Marilyn Monroe's old house at 625 Pacific Coast Highway and booking time at Burbank Studios, Lennon and Nilsson, May Pang, and Nilsson's girlfriend Una began piecing together the gang who would double as a band on the projected album: engineer Roy Cicala, Klaus Voormann, Starr, Jim Keltner, Bobby Keys, Jesse Ed Davis, Danny Kootch, Sneeky Pete, and Ken Ascher. All of them would become shareholders in the party that started in one place when someone woke up then marched across town to wake up the other; most of them had already been involved in the abortive Spector sessions.

"I like to use the same musicians for a whole album," Lennon said at the time. "Because then they know what I'm talking about if I'm trying to explain myself to them, and I feel more relaxed. And if they've played together before, it's the next best thing to having a permanent group."

On March 28, 1974, the team set up in the studio for the first time, to assault Bob Dylan's "Subterranean Homesick Blues." It was Lennon's intention to create an album that was as spontaneous as the nightclub displays that had by now labeled him a public pariah; tracks would be restricted to no more

Harry Nilsson

than a couple of takes, a far cry from the laborious piece-by-piecing into which he'd slipped over his own last few records. Indeed, later in the sessions, when Nilsson announced he wanted to dub a snare onto the Dylan song, Lennon initially refused. There were already enough drums on the song, he said, and besides, as far as he was concerned, it was finished.

As it happened, Nilsson agreed with him entirely — it was just that he'd promised his young cousin, Doug, that he could appear on the record. Lennon finally relented (although he only allowed the youngster one take!); he knew, just as Nilsson knew, that *Pussy Cats* was already awash with percussive chaos. What difference would one more layer of noise make?

The basics of "Subterranean Homesick Blues" were completed in a day, even with two drummers (Keltner and Starr) kicking up an unholy din; even with Nilsson having to contend not only with Dylan's stream-of-something wordiness, but also with the new, savage boogie arrangement that Lennon insisted on grafting to the song.

"I like it because it's sort of mad," Lennon told DJ Tom Donahue once the song was complete, and he was right. He also pointed out "a lot of edits in it that I still hear," then invited the KSAN radio audience to "spot the edits and win an invisible T-shirt." Listen even closer, though, and you can forget the edits; forget Goldman's evil fairies. The four horsemen of the apocalypse are in there as well, uncredited auxiliaries best heard on the headphones.

The mood in the studio was wild and got wilder. Paul and Linda McCartney were in town at the time, and as the session continued on into the evening and more and more people dropped by to take part, no one was surprised when the McCartneys appeared. Three Beatles in one room — the *NME* had been laying odds on just that occurrence a mere few days before: 20 to one, a semipermanent re-formation; 15 to one, a studio reunion; two to one, a one-off new album; and four to six against, regular guest spots on each other's records. Nothing, unfortunately, about turning up in the dark of night to run through a bunch of old rock 'n' roll covers and nothing about the whole thing proving ditchwater dull.

When news of the reunion hit the streets, albeit somewhat belatedly, many fans were disappointed that no hint of it was included on the finished *Pussy Cats* album. When a bootleg of the reunion arrived, those same fans were probably glad that it hadn't.

The gathering opens with Lennon introducing a charming little number called "Never Trust A Bugger With Your Mother." Nilsson counters with "Little Bitty Pretty One," before Lennon locks everyone into a rambling attempt at completing "Stand By Me," a song he would return to when he resumed the *Rock 'N' Roll* sessions. Half rehearsal, half jam, the crowd also ran through a raucous "Lucille," "Midnight Special," "Cupid" and "Take This Hammer." There was a little bit of blues, and only one track that showed any potential or promise; a gentle "Sleepwalk" which, with some typically Lennon-esque improvisation, swiftly turned into the menacing "Nightmares."

The following evening with normalcy now restored, the gang (minus the McCartneys, of course) reconvened to attempt "Many Rivers To Cross," a song that Nilsson had long been keen to cover. Once again, the arrangement paid no attention whatsoever to the original, the classic ska ballad that made a star of Jimmy Cliff. Scaling down the beat, slowing down the tempo, it became instead a dark, brooding ballad, hooking itself around a lyric that Cliff's original barely noticed. It falls around a third of the way through the song, as Nilsson's double-tracked vocals rise in real despair... "This loneliness won't leave me alone, it's such a drag..." and where Cliff would have just carried on singing, Nilsson stops; the band stops, and for one heart-stopping moment, it is as though an elevator full of fat people has just plummeted down from the top floor. Then the song restarts, it drifts beautifully on, and when the same thing happens the next time around, it still grabs your heart in its hand.

Interviewing Lennon a few months later, KSAN DJ Tom Donahue remarked that a lot of people, himself included, were convinced that it was actually Lennon singing lead. Their voices really were similar. Lennon, however, was quick to explain, "He was singing it pretty much as he sang it, but he was holding back. So I just kept asking him for more on it, and it turned out like he did. I liked it; I knew it was going to be 'Oh, it sounds like he's doing John,' but there's a certain point when you get high, on music, whatever, when you're going to go to the same place, and there was nowhere else for him to go but there." Which kind of makes sense if you really pay attention, but it doesn't really matter. The end result still remains one of the most spellbinding performances of Nilsson's entire career.

Like Lennon, Nilsson had been planning a new album of his own in the months before *Pussy Cats* commenced; indeed, a full dozen tracks were already in the can, and Nilsson arrived at Burbank with at least a few of the songs crying out for reprieve: the plaintive, painful "Don't Forget Me," "All My Life," and the fragmentary "Mt. Elga." On April 3, work began on the first of these, a sparse recording that seated Nilsson alone at the piano, which the comically anonymous Masked Alberts Orchestra soared away behind him. (Joe Cocker would later concoct a fuller version for his 1976 album *I Can Stand A Little Rain.*)

Three Beatles in one room — the *NME* had been laying odds on just that occurrence a mere few days before: 20 to one, a semipermanent re-formation; 15 to one, a studio reunion; two to one, a one-off new album; and four to six against, regular guest spots on each other's records.

It is a delightful, delicate performance, but the rough edge that catches Nilsson's voice was not simply the choke of vicarious emotion. A few weeks before, the singer had spent a night sleeping on the beach, contracting a throat infection that wouldn't go away. Ordinarily, he would have simply followed doctor's orders and rested his voice till the problem cleared up. But ordinarily, he would not have Lennon wanting to make an album with him. Swallowing painkillers, swallowing the pain, Nilsson determined not to give in to a simple sore throat.

The roughness, which to the uninitiated sounds more like a legend-confirming drunken wastedness, is the sound of that determination.

HARRY NILSSON WAS BORN HARRY EDWARD NELSON III IN BROOKLYN, NY IN 1941 AND WILL FOREVER BE KNOWN AS ONE OF AMERICA'S FOREMOST POP SONGWRITERS! IRONICALLY, HIS TWO BIGGEST HITS WERE NOT HIS OWN COMPOSITIONS ... "WITHOUT YOU" FROM THIS 1971 RCA LP, WENT TO NUMBER ONE ON THE U.S. CHARTS AND EARNED NILSSON A GRAMMY FOR BEST MALE POP VOCAL OF 1972! IT WAS WRITTEN BY TWO OF THE MEMBERS OF BADFINGER, TOM EVANS & PETER HAM! THE OTHER TUNE MOST CLOSELY ASSOCIATED WITH NILSSON, "EVERYBODY'S TALKIN'," WAS WRITTEN BY FRED NEIL! STILL, HARRY WROTE HIS SHARE OF MEMORABLE SONGS! LONG BEFORE THE SUCCESS OF "NILSSON SCHMILSSON," HARRY WAS WORKING AWAY AT HIS CRAFT, PEDDLING SONGS AND SINGING RADIO JINGLES BY DAY WHILE MAINTAINING A NIGHT JOB AT A BANK! HIS BIG BREAK CAME WHEN PHIL SPECTOR DECIDED TO BUY A FEW OF HIS SONGS – TWO FOR THE RONETTES AND ONE FOR THE MODERN FOLK QUARTET! IN NO TIME HARRY WAS IN DEMAND AND HIS SONGS WERE BEING RECORDED BY EVERYONE ... FROM THE MONKEES TO THE YARDBIRDS TO DAVID CASSIDY! HIS TUNE "ONE" AS RECORDED BY THREE DOG NIGHT WENT TO NUMBER ONE IN 1969, AND OTTO PREMINGER HIRED HIM TO SCORE HIS 1968 FILM "SKIDOO" (HARRY EVEN APPEARED IN A CAMEO!)! HIS TELEVISION WRITING CREDITS INCLUDE THEME MUSIC FOR "THE COURTSHIP OF EDDIE'S FATHER" (HE SANG OVER THE OPENING CREDITS AS WELL!) AND A GROUP OF SONGS WRITTEN FOR THE 1971 ANIMATED SPECIAL "THE POINT" INCLUDING HIS HIT SINGLE "ME AND MY ARROW"! HIS 1972 RELEASE "SON OF SCHMILSSON" FEATURED "SPACEMAN", HIS LAST REAL HIT, AND HE FOLLOWED THAT WITH TWO THEME LP's ... A GROUP OF STANDARD POP SONGS ARRANGED AND CONDUCTED BY GORDON JENKINS APPEARED ON "A LITTLE TOUCH OF SCHMILSSON IN THE NIGHT" (1973) WITH NILSSON'S TRIBUTE TO ROCK 'N' ROLL (PRODUCED BY JOHN LENNON) "PUSSY CATS" COMING OUT IN 1974! NILSSON SUFFERED A HEART ATTACK AND EVENTUALLY DIED OF HEART-RELATED AILMENTS IN 1994.

MY FRIEND MIKE (AKA MORT) TURNED ME ON TO NILSSON WAY BACK IN THE SEVENTIES AND I'VE HAD THIS LP SINCE THEN! IT'S MY FAVORITE NILSSON LP AND THE SONG LINE-UP IS AN ECCLECTIC TOUR-DE-FORCE OF NILSSON'S TWISTED VOCALIZING! FROM THE LP'S OPENER "GOTTA GET UP" RIGHT THROUGH TO THE END YOU CAN NEVER QUITE GET COMFORTABLE WITH WHAT YOU THINK THIS ALBUM IS ABOUT! YET IT ALL SEEMS TO FIT TOGETHER SO NICELY! NILSSON IS EQUALLY CONVINCING ON THE BALLAD "WITHOUT YOU", THE GOOFY HIT "COCONUT" AND ON THE THROBBING, ALMOST FUNKY "JUMP INTO THE FIRE"*! ASTOUNDING!

Nilsson Schmilsson

☆☆☆☆☆

* MY FAVORITE!!

The sessions quickly fell into a pattern, and that despite the copious quantities of everything that the participants were imbibing.

"It was a pretty heavy drinking bunch," Nilsson remembered. While Lennon apparently excused himself from many of the late-night parties, preferring to go home with May Pang, the rest of the crew remained hell-bent hell-raisers.

"Keith Moon and Ringo, and yours truly and everybody was loaded all the time. We had a couple of limos every night to take us to the studio and back again. But we were pretty organized. We used to get there at 6, finish by 1, then we used to go back home to listen to the tapes and fall on the floor, but the bugaboo was always liquor — a combination of liquor and coke will keep you there indefinitely.

"Anyway, we'd get up and have the strangest breakfasts, pork chops and eggs in grilled something, and we never figured out what the taste or smell was, and some of us would go about our business, some of us would take a little nap, and we'd reconvene about five o'clock..."

"All My Life," one of those simple throwaway numbers that Nilsson insisted on including on every album he released, was cut on April 4, and two days later, work began on what would become one of the album's true, defining moments, a massive reworking of The Drifters' "Save The Last Dance For Me."

Already it was evident that Lennon's relative inexperience as a producer was not an obstacle. Nilsson enthused, "He's so fast and easy, 'cos when you say something that's clever or good, he'd just jump on it like it was a candy or something." He also knew when to push for perfection and when to let things slide, and 'Save The Last Dance' illustrates both extremes simultaneously.

No longer awaiting the last dance, the old Pomus/Shuman classic now was the last dance, a beautiful spiraling dirge with the Masked Alberts sweeping around Bobby Keys' gently honking sax before the song halts with a funeral drum beat of heart-stopping finality.

Nilsson himself, however, was feeling anything but summery. One of his vocal chords had now ruptured, a condition that could easily have resulted in his losing his range, or even his voice, forever. But he would not give up.

Nilsson's voice was wrecked by now, his throat red raw. When he stepped away from the microphone, it was speckled with tiny drops of blood. He refused to call a halt, however; indeed, he refused even to tell Lennon what was going on. One day, John did ask why Nilsson was holding back so much; "I'm saying, 'Where's all that doo-doo-doo stuff?' and he was going 'Kakakaka.'"

Lennon shrugged; it wasn't as if he'd never played games with his voice in the past, and besides, the croak really did seem to work, in a ragged, rough, Tom Waits sort of way. It was only much later, with the very end of the session in sight, that Lennon finally found out what was going on.

"[Harry] was going to doctors and being injected, and he didn't tell me till later that he was bleeding from the throat, else I'd have stopped the sessions!"

Which was the last thing Nilsson wanted to happen. He knew, as everyone knew, the mercurial nature of Lennon's attention span. If they didn't make the album now, they might never get 'round to doing it.

And so he soldiered on, jamming himself full of painkillers in time for his next date with the microphone, then crooning softly through the medley he and Lennon had designed around "Mt. Elga" and John's own, equally incomplete "Mucho Mungo" — a song, incidentally, that Lennon originally wrote for guitarist Jesse Ed Davis. Recorded on April 8, a faint calypso feel permeates the track, one that Lennon would again use to similar effect on his *Walls And Bridges* album; the song's key, however, was the sax refrain, a naggingly familiar snatch of melody that conjured up the same summer vacation feel as Nilsson's own lyrics were intended to.

Nilsson himself, however, was feeling anything but summery. One of his vocal chords had now ruptured, a condition that could easily have resulted in his losing his range, or even his voice, forever. But he would not give up.

All the same, arriving at the studio the following day, his heart sank when he saw what was awaiting him, the massed ranks of rock 'n' roll madness, and a grinning Lennon all ready to create the album's climax. It was party time!

With Moon joining Starr and Keltner in the drum room, three saxophonists, two guitarists and a dozen backing vocalists, The Masked Alberts Kids Chorale, the menu was as maniacal as it could get: "Loop De Loop" and "Rock Around The Clock," performed to the accompaniment of a bonanza out of bounds. Nilsson, bleeding and hoarse, threw himself into the mood as well as he could, but even the most indulgent listener, familiar with the magnificent tones of "Without You" and so on, would scarcely have recognized the clipped, choking delivery Nilsson etched into the songs... but neither would anyone have realized just how bad the singer's condition now was. Nor how difficult it must have been for him to throw in an impersonation of '50s DJ Dick "Huggy Boy" Hugg at the end.

Rock 'n' roll is made to be bellowed out loud, and Nilsson simply sounds like he's been bellowing all night, a little low in the mix, a little cracked 'round the edges and a little breathless too, as he sought to keep up with Jesse Ed Davis' lightning guitar licks. Of course it all goes on a bit too long, as most good parties tend to do, and the fast-collapsing coda that brought "Clock" to its battered conclusion registered the musicians' exhaustion. But as finales go, this one was a monster.

Like a Hollywood movie, where they film the conclusion somewhere 'round the middle, the last day of recording must have seemed anti-climactic. But Nilsson had one more song he wanted to record, and the following evening, with his voice in absolute tatters, was the ideal time to do it.

"Old Forgotten Soldier" is one of Nilsson's greatest songs. Opening, at Lennon's suggestion, to a tape of one of Hitler's speeches, it is a simple, weary lament, oozing despair, isolation and pain, a cracked blues that dissolves, as Nilsson's voice finally gave out (around the midway point, with the lyric "fired a round"), into a lonely, fading, whistle. And when the song was over, so were the sessions. Mixing, a traumatic affair as Nilsson grimaced every time he heard the

sound of his scarred, scary, voice, was completed as quickly as possible. Then, while Nilsson raced home to bed, Lennon flew to New York.

One final track would be cut before *Pussy Cats* was delivered to RCA, an afterthought as it were, to break up side two's closing barrage of rock 'n' roll numbers. "Black Sails" was recorded more than two months after the original sessions ended, on June 18, although the song itself was even older than that, dating back to an abortive movie about pirates that Nilsson had been asked to write a theme for. The movie never happened, but Nilsson loved the song and didn't want to waste it. It was a smart decision on his part.

"Black Sails" is a masterpiece of lyrical punning. While the orchestra does its damnedest to recapture the desolation of so many other rock 'n' roll sea songs, Procol Harum's "A Salty Dog" their most prominent role model, Nilsson deadpans lines that defy the music's moodiness: "black sails in the moonlight, black patch on your eye"; "you shiver your timbers baby, and I'll shiver mine"; and best of all, "you're so veiny, you probably think this map belongs to you." Eat your heart out, Carly Simon.

The album was delivered to RCA with equal panache. According to legend, the first time label head Ken Glancy got to hear it, Nilsson and Lennon were together in his office, cackling about how they'd just completed the greatest album in the history of the world. Then Nilsson pressed the "play" button, and Glancy was assailed by the three-man percussion team that opens "Loup De Loup."

His shock was only echoed by the music press. Condemned as a self-indulgent mess, hammered for its slapdash chaos, shot through with criminally barely realized moments of vague inspiration, *Pussy Cats* had to contend not only with its makers' own reputations, but also with its makers' old friends as well — 1974 was the year in which McCartney finally stopped making records that he liked and produced one that the critics liked as well, *Band On The Run*. So far as the reviews were concerned, there was no competition, and the charts reflected the mismatch.

Despite being released in both regular stereo format and as a top-end-of the market Quadradisc, *Pussy Cats* itself could reach no higher than a lowly #60 in the U.S.; in Britain, it didn't even make the Top 75. Three singles, "Many Rivers To Cross," "Subterranean Homesick Blues" and "Don't Forget Me," slipped out unnoticed; and as if to add insult to injury, great swathes of the album have since been appended to sundry John Lennon bootlegs, where they masquerade as demos for some unknown Ringo Starr project!

But neither Lennon nor Nilsson ever regretted their efforts, and though *Pussy Cats* remains an overlooked episode in both men's illustrious careers, it was an immensely important one nevertheless.

"Whatever Gets You Through The Night," the song that would return Lennon to the #1 slot in America later in the year, was written during the *Pussy Cats* sessions; indeed, according to Lennon, speaking in a Canadian radio interview that fall, "We wrote the song together, so I put it on my album, and Harry of course wanted to sing it, because he'd been part of it, so he sang the harmonies." The pair also collaborated on "Old Dirt Road," Nilsson dropping in lyrical contributions while Lennon composed on piano, and once Lennon settled in the studio to work on what became *Walls And Bridges*, Nilsson remained ensconced alongside him.

Today, of course, both Lennon and Nilsson are dead. So are several of the musicians who worked alongside them through the *Pussy Cats* sessions. Yet of all the records that they made, *Pussy Cats* remains the one that has the most life in it, a raucous, raunchy, remarkable life that has utterly defied the passing of time. Dig it out and crank it up — you can hear how much fun everyone was having leaking out of the grooves; you can feel it in the vibrations that rattle the speakers off the wall.

And when the wind's in the right direction, you can probably smell it as well. Because, just as Nilsson affirmed a few years back, "We were all so blitzed. All of the time."

It shows.

Klaatu

The magical mystery band

by Mark Hershberger, Jaimie Vernon and Dave Bradley

Many bands would sell their souls to be compared to The Beatles. Klaatu, that mysterious Canadian group, went one step further. They were not only compared to The Beatles, they were rumored to *be* The Beatles recording anonymously. Indeed it was quite an honor, but it also turned out to be the deathblow to their career as a group.

Klaatu was a three-piece band that had its origins in the late 1960s when John Woloschuk, Dee Long, and Terry Draper played in a number of Toronto-based bands together. There was Whitemail, which later evolved into Mudcow, and by 1972, had split up altogether. Draper went to work in a Toronto record store, but Woloschuk and Long continued to record together with a new name, Klaatu, during downtime at Toronto Sound, which was run by the engineering/production team of Terry Brown and Doug Riley. The name came from the classic sci-fi film *The Day The Earth Stood Still*. The members of Klaatu were very big fans of the sci-fi genre and chose the name of the alien character of that movie as their band name.

Brown bankrolled the production of Klaatu's recordings under a lucrative (for the time) development deal. Woloschuk and Long released a couple of singles as Klaatu on the GRT label in 1973 with session drummer Penti "Whitey" Glan before they realized that they needed a permanent percussionist in order to continue as a group. Draper rejoined his old bandmates for their 1974 single "California Jam," which was released on Daffodil Records in Canada and on Island Records in the U.S.

At this stage of their career, there was no secrecy and no hiding of their identities at all. In fact, in November 1974, the band appeared as Klaatu on the Canadian television show *Keith Hampshire's Music Machine*, lip-synching to that latest single, "California Jam," and "True Life Hero."

"True Life Hero" itself popped up as the final single for the financially troubled Daffodil Records label in mid-1975. Daffodil president, Frank Davies, was trying his best to "manage" Klaatu, who were one of the few financially rewarding aspects of his label. He began scouting for a major label deal for the band. There were a couple of roadblocks set up by Klaatu themselves that made it a bit difficult for Davies to promote the band. The members of Klaatu did not want to appear in public, play live or give any interviews in support of an album. They wanted the music to speak for itself. As a group, they were tired of seeing over-hyped, talentless media babies climbing the charts based on their "image" and not their music.

Capitol Records met with Davies and Brown, liked what they heard of the band, and in an unprecedented move, signed the band without ever meeting the members or seeing them perform. Capitol Records knew the music that they were hearing was outstanding — they would worry about how to promote the group later. As it turned out, the promotion took care of itself. In August 1976, the debut LP *Klaatu* was released (known as *3:47 EST* in Canada). The album contained no names or pictures of the group members and no writing credits. The LP sleeve simply said, "Produced by Klaatu" and "All selections composed by Klaatu." The cover artwork was stunning: a large rising sun covering virtually the entire LP cover, with a border of plants and vegetation. The artist, Ted Jones, would go on to paint three more album covers for Klaatu, each one a breathtaking landscape. The album, however, failed to make any headway as far as sales and chart success were concerned. By the end of the year, the band had put the release behind them and began concentrating on a second album, *Hope*. In January 1977 the band flew to England to have the London Symphony Orchestra add to the arrangements. The album was to become a "concept" album with a "space" theme and a more progressive sound than their debut LP.

This article originally appeared in Goldmine issue #503, Nov. 5, 1999.

In March 1977, Klaatu, not completely happy with the finished product but under a contractual deadline, reluctantly turned the tapes over to Capitol Records. This is when their careers took a major turn. Some say for the better — some were not so sure. Steve Smith, a music journalist from the Providence, R.I., *Journal*, had declared that the album called *Klaatu* from the previous year could very well be The Beatles recording together again. He had written an article titled "Could Klaatu Be

The Beatles? Mystery Is A Magical Tour" that fueled the interest of countless thousands of Beatles fans worldwide.

Almost overnight the demand for Klaatu's debut album skyrocketed. It started in the northeast United States and mushroomed from there. Canada and Australia media also joined in on the "Klaatu is The Beatles" hysteria. Sales of the first album were going through the roof, so Capitol Records decided that they would not release *Hope* right away. They wanted to soak the marketing capabilities of The Beatles rumor for all it was worth. Yes, Capitol Records was going to perpetuate the rumor and yes, even though the band members were not altogether happy that the rumor had started, they did realize that they were selling a ton of records because of it, and so they stayed "in the closet" so to speak.

Initially, there were very few individuals inside Capitol Records or the music business in general that had any clue to the identities of Klaatu, and this helped to keep the mystery alive for a number of months. During this time, Klaatu decided to completely rework their yet-to-be-released album *Hope*, adding to and changing some vocals and adding a number of synthesizer overdubs to augment some weak orchestral passages. The end result was a stunning concept album of legendary proportions. By the summer of 1977, The Beatles rumor was dying out as more and more people started to realize that this was not The Beatles recording together again but simply a mystery band with a couple of songs that were "Beatles-like."

One of Klaatu's most popular songs, a track off the debut LP called "Calling Occupants Of Interplanetary Craft," caught the attention of pop duo The Carpenters, who decided to cover it on their *Passages* album. Karen Carpenter's voice was perfect for the song, and the single charted worldwide in October 1977, bringing even more acclaim to this still–mystery group called Klaatu.

Klaatu's second album, the reworked *Hope*, was released in September 1977 to critical acclaim. Unfortunately, the record-buying public was riding the disco wave and could not be bothered with a concept album of progressive pop by a band that was once rumored to be The Beatles. They just were not buying it. It remains a legendary LP in progressive rock circles.

At this point in their careers, Klaatu were a bit unsure of their musical direction. Their first album contained mostly straight-ahead rock and pop tunes, and it sold very well (with the help of The Beatles rumor of course). The band wanted to remain anonymous, but at the same time, they needed to sell some records in order to continue to make a living as Klaatu. They decided that the third record was going to be more of a straight-ahead pop record. In mid-1978, *Sir Army Suit* was born. The name of the album came from one of the album's songs — "Silly Boys." "Silly Boys" is actually the backing tracks from their first seven-inch single in 1973 (and later re-recorded for their debut) played backward. The idea was a stroke of genius.

Klaatu live in 1981, from left: Dee Long, guitar, and Terry Draper, keyboards.

Klaatu Discography

by Mark Hershberger

Singles

Label/Label #	A-side/B-side	Year
GRT 1233-18	Anus Of Uranus/Sub-Rosa Subway	1973
GRT 1233-20	Doctor Marvello/For You Girl	1973
Daffodil DIL 1057	California Jam/Doctor Marvello	1974
A&M/Island IS 011- A/B	California Jam/Doctor Marvello	1974
Daffodil DIL 1066	True Life Hero/Anus Of Uranus	1975
Daffodil/GRT DIL 1216-1073	Calling Occupants Of Interplanetary Craft/Sir Bodsworth Rugglesby III	1976
Daffodil/GRT 1216-1075	Calling Occupants Of Interplanetary Craft/Sub-Rosa Subway	1977
Capitol 4412	Calling Occupants Of Interplanetary Craft/Sub-Rosa Subway	1977
Daffodil 1216-1077	We're Off You Know/Around The Universe In 80 Days	1977
Capitol 4516	We're Off You Know/Around The Universe In 80 Days	1977
Daffodil DFS 1079	Dear Christine/Older	1978
Capitol 4627	Dear Christine/Older	1978
Daffodil/Capitol DFS 1080	Juicy Luicy/Perpetual Motion Machine	1979
Daffodil/Capitol DFS 1081	A Routine Day/Silly Boys	1979
Daffodil DFS 1083	Knee Deep In Love/Dog Star	1980
Capitol 4866	Knee Deep In Love/Dog Star	1980
Daffodil/Capitol DFS 1085	I Can't Help It/Sell Out, Sell Out	1980
Daffodil/Capitol 72865	The Love Of A Woman/At The End Of The Rainbow	1981
Daffodil/Capitol 72871	December Dream/Maybe I'll Move To Mars	1981
Capitol 72876	A Million Miles Away/I Don't Want To Go Home	1982
Polydor–Germany 887 899-7 Y	Woman/Woman (instrumental)	1988

Albums

Label/Label #	Title	Year
Daffodil/GRT 9216-10054	3:47 EST	1976
Capitol ST 11542	3:47 EST	1976
Daffodil/GRT 9216-10057	Hope	1977
Capitol ST 11633	Hope	1977
Daffodil SBA 16059	Sir Army Suit	1978
Capitol SW 11836	Sir Army Suit	1978
Daffodil SBA 16060	Endangered Species	1980
Capitol ST 12080	Endangered Species	1980
Daffodil/Capitol ST 6487	Magentalane	1981
Daffodil	Klaasic Klaatu	1982

Compact Discs

Label/Label #	Title	Year
Capitol–U.S. CDP 7 97800 2	Klaatu (3:47 EST)/Hope (*two LPs on one CD*)	1989
Justin/MCA JEMD 9	3:47 EST	1990
Justin/MCA JEMD 13	Hope	1990
Attic/MCA ACD 1374	Peaks	1993
Attic/MCA 24122	Sir Army Suit/Endangered Species (*two LPs on one CD*)	1994
Attic/MCA 700 550009-2	3:47 EST	1994
Attic/MCA 700 550013-2	Hope	1994
Permanent Press–U.S. PPCD 52701	Magentalane	1995
Si-Wan–Korea SRMC 4046	Magentalane	1995
EMI–Canada E2 72438 36961 23	Magentalane	1996

They decided to take "Anus Of Uranus" and turn the master tape around, play it backward and add additional instruments. The lyrics would simply be whatever the backward lyrics to "Anus" sounded like to them. A featured line in the song translates as "Ah, sir army suit, you're psychic"; the inner sleeve even shows the lyrics to "Silly Boys" printed backward. Despite the attempts to make a more commercial-sounding pop record with three singles and Canada's first animated video for the song "A Routine Day," *Sir Army Suit* was another failure sales-wise. Radio was not going to support the "mystery" band theme any longer. The rumor was old hat and the music was not what was hot on the radio of the day.

Capitol Records was getting tired of the secret identity of the band as well — especially in light of it not working as a marketing tool for them any longer. They still believed that the band was good and marketable, but they now wanted the band to do it Capitol's way or not at all. Capitol wanted to recoup their investment from two consecutive flop albums, so they took control of the entire recording process for album number four.

From left: Dee Long; Terry Draper; Mike Gingrich, a member of Klaatu's touring band; and John Woloschuk.

Klaatu were put in the hands of producer Christopher Bond (Hall & Oates), who was in charge of selecting songs to be recorded. These were Klaatu original compositions as before, but the band were not going to have the say in which songs would appear on the album. Bond flew the band to Los Angeles to stay for four months in late 1979/early 1980. He also hired studio musicians Lee Sklar and Ed Greene to play bass and drums, respectively, on the album, while Bond himself played a number of guitar parts. As it ended up, Draper did not even appear on the album, and Woloschuk and Long were relegated to vocals and minor instrumental parts as session players on their own album. The resulting album, 1980's *Endangered Species*, was released and went almost immediately to the delete bin because of administrative changes going on at Capitol at the time. Capitol had invested more time and money into Klaatu, hired a well-known producer, brought in studio musicians to play the songs and then deleted the album upon release. There was no promotion, no press, and subsequently, no sales.

The only interesting thing about the album was that for the first time, there were songwriting credits listed as Long, Woloschuk, and Tome. Were these the members of Klaatu?

To further confuse the issue, there was a note at the end of the liners that talked about endangered species and the status of declining wildlife. The note was signed Terry Draper, Dee Long, and John Woloschuk. So now we have a different threesome, this time with a Draper and no Tome. The album also contained an address to write to the band.

Anyone who had purchased the album before it was deleted and who had taken the initiative to write to the band, received a nice package in return, usually containing fan-type material and information, but, more important, it contained an 8x10-inch picture of the band with their names. The band indeed was Terry Draper, Dee Long, and John Woloschuk. Finally!

Dino Tome, it turns out, was a good friend and songwriting partner of Woloschuk and not a member of Klaatu.

Capitol had pretty much given up on Klaatu at this point. Soon after the *Endangered Species* album was released, the band was released from their contract with Capitol in the U.S.

Klaatu was not willing to finish their recording career on a bad note. They did not want their swan song to be *Endangered Species*. The album itself is not bad by any means, but they did not like the fact they were not in control of the recording process. Klaatu then negotiated a deal with Capitol's field office in Canada. Capitol Canada agreed to finance and release the fifth LP on the condition that the band would publicly reveal their identities and go on tour in support of the album. Klaatu reluctantly agreed but only under the condition that the album would be recorded in their own studio, Long's E.S.P. Studio, and that they would have complete control over the recording. The band's fifth and final studio album, *Magentalane*, was released in late 1981 to coincide with their first and only Canadian tour. The album was vintage Klaatu, a mix of the styles from the first four albums, a wistful swan song. *Magentalane* was released only on vinyl

Klaatu's debut album.

and only in Canada (and Mexico) with a limited run of 25,000 copies. This explains why many Americans thought the band had packed it in after *Endangered Species*.

The first leg of the tour in November and December 1981 was spent as the opening act for a popular Canadian band called Prism. With Draper acting as the frontman and keyboardist, Woloschuk on keyboards and lead vocals, and Long on vocals, guitar, and keyboards, Klaatu was augmented by keyboardist Gerald O'Brien (Surrender, The Hunt), bassist Mike Gingrich (Toronto), and drummer Gary McCracken (Max Webster).

Klaatu virtually stole the show from Prism at every performance, which was another nail in the coffin for Prism's then-spiraling career. After that initial leg of the tour, Klaatu booked a number of club gigs as the headliner. Eventually, the cost of keeping six musicians on the road with little support from the record label led to the band calling it quits in August 1982. There would be no more touring; there would be no more Klaatu.

After nine years as a band and five studio albums, Klaatu had run out of gas and out of support. Their manager, Davies, released a posthumous "best of" LP called *Klaasic Klaatu* in December 1982.

The members of Klaatu went their separate ways. Draper tried his hand in a duo with vocalist Jacqui Kroft but could not attract any label interest. He then retired from music and started his own business as a roofing contractor. Woloschuk used his music-based street education and a subsequent reschooling to become an accountant to the Toronto music industry. And, in the strangest twist of fate known to the music world, Long ended up as a digital editor at George Martin's AIR Studios in London (and yes, he did meet Paul McCartney!). This was actually the only real connection that Klaatu ever had to The Beatles.

In 1988, Klaatu reunited briefly to record a song to be used as part of a soundtrack to a German TV show called *Tatort*. The song was written by Paul Vincent Gunia and was called "Woman." It was released on a limited basis on Polydor in Germany only. This reunion was short-lived and really just a one-off production in order to pay some outstanding, protracted legal bills.

A "real" Klaatu reunion was scheduled to take place in 1991. A new CD compilation of Klaatu's hits called *Peaks* was planned to include several new Klaatu compositions. Long left England to return to Canada specifically for the project, but the label responsible for the reissue of their back catalog failed to finance the new recordings and the idea was scrapped. A breach of contract soon followed. While Davies and the band searched frantically for a new label for Klaatu's CD reissues, Long and Draper began working together in a new recording facility dubbed Second Sun in Unionville, producing a number of local acts just to make ends meet. Though the new songs never came to be, reissue of the Klaatu back catalog on CD hit full stride in 1994 on Attic Records in Canada — including the "best of" disc called *Peaks*.

A full Klaatu resurgence began in 1995 when Permanent Press Records in the United States was the first American label to issue *Magentalane* on CD. A Korean company, Si-Wan Records, followed suit for the Pacific Rim, followed by EMI Canada in 1996. The CD began climbing the charts in the Pacific Rim with the single "December Dream" going Top 10 in some areas. This prompted Draper (writer of "December Dream") to dust off the vocal chords and the keyboards and begin writing and recording again. Draper, in collaboration with Klaatu album cover artist Jones, issued the children's album *Can You Pretend?* (on cassette only) and an accompanying activity kit in 1996. After getting his feet wet in children's music, Draper released *Light Years Later* in February 1997 on Bullseye Records in Canada while Permanent Press did the same, with bonus tracks for the U.S. market. The CD was a mix of old and new Draper songs with one track, "Winter In Peru," an actual Klaatu recording left over from the *Magentalane* sessions. Draper introduced this new CD with two live performances, his first since 1982. These shows were recorded and later released as a limited edition multimedia enhanced CD called *Live.... Years Later: From The*

Klaatu's *Sir Army Suit.*

'Cue To The 'Shoe.

Currently Draper is promoting the reissue of *Can You Pretend?* on CD with eight bonus tracks. Upcoming projects include a second solo release and work on solo albums by Dr. John Baird and Maureen Leeson, among others.

Long, guitarist for Klaatu, has spent the last few years as a computer software programmer. He has been creating graphics software and has recently been working on a music sampling software tool called the De-Sampler. Bullseye Records is about to release a Long double CD set called *Been Here Before*, which will include unreleased Long material and demos spanning the years between his tenure at ESP Studio and AIR London with Martin.

And lastly, Woloschuk, Klaatu's main songwriter and vocalist, has continued his career as an accountant in the greater Toronto area. He has opened up to the Klaatu fan base in recent years and has even given a lengthy interview on his recollections of the Klaatu years. The entire interview, as well as a ton of information about the band, can be seen at the official Klaatu web site at www.klaatu.org/klaatu.

All of Klaatu's albums have been released on CD and have recently been deleted. Currently the band is negotiating a new licensing deal to reissue the CDs once more with the anticipation of bonus tracks and enhanced packaging. The only CD still in print is their fifth and final album *Magentalane*, which is available through Permanent Press Records in the U.S. The solo CDs from Draper and Long are available through Bullseye Records of Canada at www.bullseyecanada.com with distribution through Indie Pool www.indiepool.com/bullseye.

There is also a new tribute CD out on Bullseye Records called *Around The Universe In 80 Minutes... A Tribute To Klaatu*, which features 19 indie power pop and prog rock bands covering the best of Klaatu.

The rumors have long since been forgotten, but the music lives on.

The Rutles: Turn left at Greenland

by Dave Thompson

Britain, 1964. Harold Wilson's Labour Government had just been returned to power with their promises of a brave new society, forged in the white heat of technological revolution. The winter following the coldest winter since weather records began was over, and London was beginning to swing again.

In the coffee bars of Soho, the last generation of surly young mod was preparing to meet its media maker and perish on the sands of Bank Holiday Brighton, and "oop north," four lads from Liverpool were about to visit an American named Ed Sullivan. It was all a long way from Rutland.

Rutland is one of the great jokes in British geography. The smallest county in the country, it existed in a kind of political no-man's land between the wealthy shoe farmers of Northants and the poor soccer players of Leicester, unparalleled in its pointlessness. By 1974, it had ceased to exist, the victim of the then-incumbent Conservative Government's attempts to rig the forthcoming election by concentrating all its most loyal supporters in one place. They failed, and amid the jubilation that followed, Rutland was forgotten.

But it was there, amid the scheming squires of Rutland's rural heartland, that another four lads, Dirk McQuickly, Ron Nasty, Barrington Womble, and Stig O'Hara, had a dream, a dream that would see them take on all comers, conquer the world and still be home in time for tea.

They were, of course, The Rutles, and as the entire Western world braces itself once again to meet the full force of Rutlemania head on, only one man dares to speak out against them. One man remains unconvinced that this is "the reunion of the century," that it might well be "the most significant event in modern western culture," that it represents any of the many other laudatory labels with which excited commentators have greeted the most eagerly awaited incident in yours or anyone else's entire lifetime. The Rutles are back, and Spiggy Topes doesn't care.

Spiggy Topes?

"Oh God, I remember Spiggy Topes," muses a puzzled but nicely greying mop-topped Nasty, following a brief silence during which it was plain he didn't have a clue who Topes was. "But he didn't really exist, did he?"

Britain, 1964. Harold Wilson's Labour Government had just been returned to power with their promises of a brave new society, forged in the white heat of technological revolution. The winter, the coldest winter since records began was over, and London was beginning to swing again. Et cetera et cetera. But this time, the coffee bars of Soho are hosting a group of journalists, staffers at the satirically inclined *Private Eye* magazine, who have cast a jaundiced eye over the current pop scene and decided to lambast it in the only way they can.

This article originally appeared in* Goldmine *issue #425, Nov. 8, 1996.

"We will form our own pop group," announces a laconic Peter Cooke (the same). "Their singer will be named Spiggy Topes," insists a compendious William Rushton. "They will be called The Turds," continues a sententious Richard Ingrams. "And they will not exist," choruses an epigrammatic everyone else. "But that won't stop us writing about them."

Spiggy Topes And The Turds were great. Long hair, yeah yeah yeah, everything a real band did, The Turds would do better, or at least, funnier. They even made a record, released through *Private Eye*, and today it's worth absolutely zillions on the collector's market.

And though it's true that they were never more than figments of some writers' imagination, remember all those lonely housewives who send wreaths to the funerals on *As The World Turds*... sorry, *Turns*. Figments can and often do become fact in many peoples' minds. And for millions of lifelong Turd fans, neither convinced nor perturbed by subsequent claims that they've wasted three decades digging a dream, Topes (who may or may not have been modeled upon a marginally popular singing star named Lennon, and is, therefore, probably dead) lives forever.

And Spiggy hates The Rutles.

Which makes sense.

"The Rutles? They stole everything from The Turds. Even the first three letters of their name. They stole their look, their sound, their songs, their instruments, their trousers. That movie they did. That wasn't their story, it was The Turds.' Those songs. They just took songs we wrote, mucked around with the chords a bit, changed a few words. It was daylight robbery, and they didn't even have the decency to wait until it was dark."

He leafs through The Rutles' discography as though it were a catalog of war crimes: "Those record jackets. All ours. Those movies. We made them first. Spelling out an album title in semaphore. We did that. 'A Hard Day's Rut?' 'A Hard Day's Turd.' 'Judy In Disguise With Rutles?' 'Lucy In The Lavvy With Turds.' Need I go on? No, but I will."

And he does, growing ever more obscene, ever more obstreperous, ever more obscure, until it becomes apparent (even to the horde of middle-aged secretaries who gathered around this rather sad, pathetic spectacle in the heart of London's cardboard city in the vague hope that someone might be having embarrassing convulsions) that the poor old rocker is off his rocker.

It is, indeed, a far cry from the swish Uptown hotel in New York City, where Nasty and Barry Wom are holding court to the American press. It's just as sad and just as pathetic, and the gathered horde of secretaries is just as middle-aged. But if these men have convulsions, it's art. And if things get embarrassing, they just take the party elsewhere.

"I'd forgotten about this side of it," Nasty sighs as he gazes up at two pendulous beasts (giraffes, probably, or maybe tall llamas) and contemplates his forthcoming schedule of interviews and video shoots. "All we wanted to do was write some songs."

"Turn left at Greenland," deadpans Wom. "Or was that a different question?"

The Rutles' story, of course, needs no retelling, although few authors who are paid by the word can resist doing so anyway.

Nasty and McQuickly met, literally bumped into one another, in 1959. Discovering a mutual interest in alcohol, they became drinking partners first, songwriting partners later.

Theirs was a tempestuous relationship. According to the recently published book *The Day Ron Met Dirk* (Flightless Arctic Bird Books, 1995), by the time they formed their first band, The Quarrelmen, they had already fallen out three times, twice with each other and once through a window.

But they persevered, and by 1960, with guitarist O'Hara, drummer Womble and a fifth member remembered simply as Leppo now in tow, The Quarrelmen had become The Rutles.

It is from these formative months that the earliest known live recording of The Rutles, a raw version of "I Got You Under My Skin," dates. According to Nasty, "It was taped at the Leicestershire Hunt Ball, where everybody is talking all the way through it." There are, he claims, "a lot of musicians-only type jokes in it," but still, it remains an inauspicious start.

Much confusion still surrounds the band's choice of name.

According to one popular legend, they arrived at The Rutles by throwing darts at a map of the United States (still a popular pastime in Britain, where a well-supported National America Impaling League, the NAIL, continues to lobby for it to become an Olympic event) but never spiked anything better than Bay City. So then they threw darts at each other.

Another tale insists that the band simply followed the prevalent fashion in provincial English cities and named themselves after a popular sport, in honor of Buddy Holly's backing band The Crickets. This theory falters on the absence of any popular sports involving rutting.

Neither was the band named for its home county, Rutland. In fact O'Hara, speaking for the first and, it is believed last time in his entire musical career, invented the name, taking it from the Latin word "ruta," meaning unpleasant, and the French "les," meaning the.

It was an appropriate choice. As musicians, as songwriters, as human beings, The Rutles were unpleasant, so unpleasant that by 1961, they had been deported to Germany, only to be deported back again six months later.

In the interim, however, they had changed beyond recognition. No longer five foul-mouthed leather-clad yobs, The Rutles returned to England four foul-mouthed leather clad yobs. Leppo had disappeared. (He later resurfaced on a Robyn Hitchcock album, with his new band, The Jooves.)

It was in Germany, too, that The Rutles learned to be a band. With a repertoire highlighted by well-loved classics such as "Goose Step Mama," The Rutles served their musical apprenticeship on the Reeperbahn in Hamburg, plying the same sordid circuit as sired so many of British rock's bastard offspring: Hans Smith, the lovechild of a Mancunian roadie and a large-breasted fraulein named Helga; Wolfgang Brown, illegitimate heir to both the Rochdale-based Brown's Guitars And Suppositories empire *and* a fortune cookie factory in Dusseldorf; and many more.

Another tale insists that the band simply followed the prevalent fashion in provincial English cities and named themselves after a popular sport, in honor of Buddy Holly's backing band The Crickets. This theory falters on the absence of any popular sports involving rutting.

"Ah, those torrid Teutonic nights," Topes fondly reminisces. "They were a religious order founded during The Crusades who adopted an Augustine lifestyle and pledged themselves both to fight the fees of the Christian faith and to give succor to sick and wounded pilgrims." Unfortunately, his historical erudition is utterly irrelevant, and The Rutles' tale continues uninterrupted.

It was only shortly after their return home that The Rutles came under the benevolent gaze of one Leggy Mountbatten, a Bolton-born retail chemist who, in the coy parlance of the day, was immediately taken by the young Rutles' trousers.

Again, truth and fiction have become irrevocably intertwined; the apocryphal and the apothecary are completely indistinguishable. What is certain, however, is that Mountbatten was alerted to The Rutles' existence by a young woman who entered his store to enquire after a "certain remedy for shingles."

Mountbatten innocently misunderstood her, and convinced she was looking for a "certain melody on single," he began scouting the clubs and dives of the English music scene in the hope that he might find it. It was the first in the catalog of atrocious misunderstandings, spoken and written, that would shape The Rutles' future career.

Another popular misconception involves Mountbatten's sexuality. His own mother, interviewed for the television documentary, insinuated that "he was always very interested in young men" and had in fact first encountered The Rutles "in a dark cellar."

This thread was to be followed by numerous subsequent authors. Indeed, according to the late (or at least, very tardy) Albert Goldman's unpublished biography of Nasty, *Nasty*: "The very thought of The Rutles' trousers was sufficient to restore to the unipedal pharmacist the limb which fate, and a Nazi mine, had deprived him of two decades previous. At times like that, the normally lopsided Leggy did not know the meaning of the word 'limp.'"

Goldman received his information in the back streets of Bolton. Unfortunately, he misheard it. Leggy wasn't "promiscuous and gay." He was prematurely grey.

According to Wom, too, the true story is more piquant than picturesque; a truth, incidentally, that Wom himself only came to appreciate through his own personal misfortune.

Following the breakup of The Rutles, Wom spent a year in bed for tax purposes, then became two separate hairdressers.

He enjoyed a highly successful career, only for the whole thing to blow up following what he calls "a freak hairdressing accident involving my left leg and some hot rolling tongs."

The accident left him emotionally unable to face returning to the salon life, and after a brief but equally disastrous flirtation with motor racing ("his thumbs were too big for the buttons, and he crashed all his cars against the skirting boards"), Wom retired. Today he lives in the castle in Cambridge.

Wom's professional alter-ego, John Halsey, has also been forced to abandon the career he loved. Working with the British rock band Patto in the early 1980s, "Halsey" was involved in what he also describes as "a freak accident involving my left leg and a motor car." Today he lives in The Castle in Cambridge.

"Now I'm Leggy," the affable landlord of that delightful public house smiles wryly, and he admits that if trousers do hold any unusual fascination for him, it is only that he'd like to be able to wear them properly again. He speculates vaguely that Mountbatten, whose retirement to a teaching post in Australia was the first nail in The Rutles' own coffin, felt the same way.

"Or maybe he didn't. I really can't remember."

Leg injuries, of course, are a terrible subject to joke about, but Wom, like his fellow Rutles, is adamant that this time around the legends who have grown up around the band must be punctured. Cleaning, or at least polishing, Leggy's oft-muddied reputation (not to mention his wooden leg), is only the first order of business.

Besides, the man knew his trousers.

Under Mountbatten's proud tutelage, The Rutles were transformed. The leather jackets and scruffy shoes that had once been their pride and joy were replaced by smart suits, their hair was cut and their inseams measured. By the time Mountbatten was

ready to launch The Rutles onto a stagnant British music business, their trousers were already the talk of the town.

Music publisher Dick Jaws was the first man to spot The Rutles' potential, signing up the band "for the rest of their natural lives" and much of any unnatural lives they might lead as well. A former costermonger who had dabbled in the garment trade toward the end of one of the wars, Jaws told the makers of the 1978 Rutles documentary, "I liked the trousers right away," Mountbatten's plans were already bearing fruit.

Signing to the customarily moribund Parlourphone label, The Rutles' first single, "Rut Me Do," became a minor hit in the bleak and bitter winter of 1962. But it was with the release of "Please Rut Me," early in the new year, that Rutlemania really hit.

Andrew Loog Oldham, brilliant, young and soon-to-become manager of The Rolling Stones, remembers:

"I was in Birmingham with Mark Wynter for the [television program] *Thank Your Lucky Stars*, and as we walked in, we were confronted by four monstrous metal hearts that the props men were staring at in disbelief. What were they going to do with them?

"Anyway, Mark ran through a quick rehearsal, did his bit as confidently and gracefully as ever, and then it was time for the filming to start, and at the foot of the bill, the metal heart boys, four kids with tightly buttoned gray suits, fringes which flopped to their eyelids, a left-handed bassist and a fab new waxing called "Please [word indistinct] Me." They were called The Beatles," Substitute the word "Rut" for "Beat," and Oldham might well have been somewhere else entirely on that historic evening in January 1963, when the phenomenon known today as Rutlemania first burst upon a startled nation.

The hits began piling up. "She Ruts You," "Twist And Rut," The Rutles were unstoppable. Their first album was recorded in less than 20 minutes, their second, claims their official biography, took even longer. The movies *A Hard Day's Rut* and *Ouch* packed picture houses all over the world.

The Rutles had the Midas touch. They wrote a song for the fledgling Rolling Stones ("It was horrible," reminisced Mick Jagger. "We never bothered to record it"), and at one point, they had 19 hits in the British Top 20, with 19 more in the 10 below that. An unprecedented 73 million people watched their U.S. television debut, and they became the first pop group ever to play the cavernous Che Guevara Stadium.

They were so big that even the French, universally renowned as the one nationality that doesn't like anything if there's a chance of anyone else being interested, fell for them. Among the greatest of all Rutles rarities is a French language version of "Baby, Let Me Be," poorly translated as "Baby, S'il Vous Plats." "It's very childish," Nasty chuckles, "with schoolboyish vulgar lyrics which, if you translate them back, should provoke an oafish grin."

The Rutles were even scheduled to perform before Queen Elizabeth II at the Royal Variety Performance, possibly the most prestigious support slot in the entire pop calendar. The boys were reportedly heartbroken when the Queen canceled and chose to sit the evening out in the Royal Box. Cynics, of course, reckoned she was simply scared of being blown off stage.

Controversy could not touch them. In 1964, Church leaders alleged that The Rutles were promoting youth promiscuity by incorporating the invitation to "rut," archaic agricultural slang for wild and abandoned fornication, into their song titles. They pointed to the rising incidence of pregnancy in young adult females as an example of the band's pernicious influence.

"Is it any coincidence," demanded one arch Bishop, "that these Rutles are worshipped almost exclusively by women in the 18 to 36 age group? Precisely the same age group which is foisting its demon spawn children upon a society which already has enough months to feed?"

The Rutles responded with their biggest hit yet, the innocent love song "Hold My Hand." There was not a rut in sight.

Neither was the band affected by the much publicized revelation that Nasty, the most consistently eligible bachelor around town, was already married, particularly when the journalist responsible for breaking the story admitted that Ron's entire wedded life was a misprint and the correct word was "harried."

Indeed, by the time The Rutles became embroiled in the greatest scandal of their entire careers, the whole "We are bigger than God" debacle, misprints, typos and spelling mistakes had become so much a part of their life that there were at least three Rutles tribute bands on the scene who took their names from these unfortunate errors, and a fourth called precisely that.

Neither were these bands simply unimaginative session hacks trying to ride someone else's coattails to success. The Misprints, The Typos, and The Spelling Mistakes all went on to become leading progressive rock bands of the early 1970s, carving out an admirable niche with their skilled blending of rock and classical music, while Precisely That are best known for their attempt to sue Pearl Jam for stealing their name and best remembered for not actually having a case.

As Judge Pilkington-Orifice remarked in his summing up, "One cannot claim damages for copyright infringement simply because one forgot to have one's ears syringed." He then awarded them $10 million for spilling courtroom coffee on their laps, adding, "The trauma must have been unimaginable, I'd imagine."

The same can be said for the so-called God scandal. Interviewed by an American journalist ("Of course it was an American," interjects Topes, "Never trust a nation who can't pronounce tomato"), Nasty was quoted not only as saying "The Rutles are bigger than God," but also, "God has never had a hit record."

Outraged religious types, of course, were even more outraged. Rutle record burnings were staged all across the land of the free, preachers spoke out against these evil young Englishmen and even the young Bill Clinton got in on the act, refusing to inhale until The Rutles issued a formal apology.

Fortunately for the future of American politics, Nasty was swift to soothe the troubled waters, informing the nation that he had said "Rod" (as in Stewart) not "God," (as in The Almighty), a reference to a raspy young and distinctly un-Scottish singer, who had not at that point had a hit single. Clinton duly inhaled, and the free world was saved. Hurrah!

1966 was a watershed year for The Rutles, initially when Dirk invented, and patented, the world's first Aquatic Storage Area, but also when the band itself announced it would no longer be playing live.

"Quite honestly, their records stink," McQuickly said of the-then very young and certainly not-yet-up-and-coming American band. "Plus they sound like R.E.M."

Unfortunately, nobody heard him. Whether they wanted to or not, The Rutles had played their last gig.

The band took advantage of this unexpected layoff by returning to the studio to complete their latest album, *Travolta.*

The title, apparently, came to McQuickly in a dream, together with an accompanying tale of a deaf, dumb and blind disco-dancing champion who is directed off the bus at the wrong stop and promptly becomes the biggest star in the world. The world itself, however, was not yet ready for a Rutles concept album, and the story was abandoned in favor of another clutch of disconnected songs.

But The Rutles never lost sight of that initial vision, the idea of an album of related themes, and the following year, they released what remains their masterpiece and quite possibly the most influential record in the entire history of the universe, the epochal *Sergeant Rutter's Only Darts Club Band.*

It was "a millstone in the history of popular music," the band's official biography trumpets, and today, the album's combined worldwide sales are so high that for many serious Rutles collectors, it is not enough to simply own examples of each of the manifold pressings and variations.

A true fan also possesses the names and addresses of everybody who has ever owned a copy of this legendary record, usually in triplicate. (There are now computer programs available that store and sort this information by anything up to 17 different categories, including "color of owners' curtains.")

Yet even this album was not without its attendant problems. The front cover, a collage of several dozen well-known personages whom The Rutles admired, underwent a number of changes before the familiar gathering of celebrities, stars and political refugees was arrived at, with the original lineup including at least three men wanted for burglary in the American Midwest, two of the lesser-known suspects in the century-old Jack The Ripper murders, and Jef, a talking mongoose who haunted a farmhouse on the Isle Of Man in the early 1930s.

"That was one of Harry Price's cases," explains Topes. "Price was what today's generation would call a ghostbuster and was probably the most respected psychic investigator of his age. He investigated Jef very thoroughly and ultimately described the whole affair as a bafflingly pointless hoax. Some people, though, remain unconvinced by his findings." It was these doubts that ultimately deterred The Rutles from including Jef on the album sleeve.

"We don't think he exists," McQuickly told a press conference. "But if he does, we'd need his written permission to include his photograph, and everybody knows that mongooses can't write."

"Mongeese, surely?" asked Barry.

"No, I think it's mongooes." (Excerpted from "The Secret Rutles Interviews," copyright and right to copy asserted by Jeffrey Juliarmpit, 1995.)

Mongooses, or indeed mongeese, were not the only problem with which The Rutles had to contend that summer, however. Visiting the U.S. the previous year, the boys had been introduced to the joys of recreational tea drinking by the bardic Bob Dylan.

Soon, Rutles' HQ was the site of orgiastic tea parties, with many guests combining their tipples into a lethal Darjeeling and Cookies cocktail.

Donovan, The Beach Boys and some band from Liverpool were so impressed by tea that they actually relocated to India temporarily to learn ancient brewing techniques, while Who drummer Keith Moon hit even greater headlines with his invention of the world's first mobile teabag.

"You fill a Rolls Royce with tea," he explained, "then drive it into the swimming pool."

And though tea was, and remains, a legal stimulant throughout most of the world, the possibility that the English national drink could be implicated in anything so sordid as sex and rock 'n' roll mortified the establishment. The forces of Law and Order, or whatever that show is called, were swift to respond.

With the undercover Jayne Mansfield Brigade choreographing a series of well-publicized busts, the British pop aristocracy was in uproar. From the mightiest stars (Nasty was loudly arrested by the infamous but so aptly named Detective Inspector Brian Plant), to the lowliest has-been (that Lennon chap again), the long arm of the law spent the summer tapping shoulders, a campaign that climaxed when Rolling Stones Mick Jagger and Keith Richards were sentenced to jail, despite not even having had any tea in the house at the time of their arrest!

Then there were the muffled lyrical oddities that turned up in The Rutles' songs and may have sounded like "alas, poor Stig, I buried him in a well," "while my guitarist gently sleeps"... But the crowning evidence came with the widely published newspaper story that claimed that O'Hara had been killed in a flash fire in a waterbed store and replaced by a waxwork.

It was in the midst of this turmoil that The Rutles suffered their most devastating blow. Mountbatten decamped to Australia, and for the first time, the group was trouserless.

"Leggy bought them all," a despondent Dirk announced. "I don't know what we're going to do now."

"Turn left at Greenland?" asked Barry. "Oh sorry, wrong question. Again."

The Rutles' decline was merciless. So was the quality of their trousers, and so was Ron Decline, the American businessman whom they recruited to oversee their sartorial affairs.

An ill-advised sojourn with the Surrey mystic Arthur Sultan left The Rutles mystically addled and their public simply mystified.

A television special, *Tragical History Tour*, was broadcast to widespread public opprobrium, an emotion that lightened only when 85 percent of the public realized they didn't know what opprobrium meant.

A cartoon adventure movie based around The Rutles' *Yellow Submarine Sandwich* hit left even the most tea-tripping audience baffled and bemused. And an attempt to form their own record company, Rutle Corps, would leave the band at the mercy of every entrepreneurial charlatan on the block.

Only their music did not suffer. That, and the insane loyalty of their fans.

In 1969, an American (why is it *always* Americans?) student, obviously gifted with considerably more spare time than dodging the draft should normally afford one, determined that if you played *Sgt. Rutter's* title track backward, you could hear McQuickly (or was it Nasty?) sing, "Stig has been dead for ages, honestly."

It was true, of course, that O'Hara had not spoken since that tumultuous afternoon nine years previous, when he christened the band that would conquer the world. It was also true that he had not been seen for some time and had not moved for some time before that. But dead? Who could believe that?

Our American friend, for a start. Emboldened by his initial discovery, he made more.

The best-known clues are all too well known to bear much repetition. First came the visual puns pertaining to obscure Mesopotamian funeral rites. Then there were the muffled lyrical oddities that turned up in The Rutles' songs and may have sounded like "alas, poor Stig, I buried him in a well," "while my guitarist gently sleeps" and, most famously of all, "happiness is a warm bun." But the crowning evidence came with the widely published newspaper story that claimed that O'Hara had been killed in a flash fire in a waterbed store and replaced by a waxwork.

Indeed, according to a recent book, *Turn Me On, Dear Man* (Esteemed Cultural Ink, 1994), a further 734 clues can be unearthed from the collected ephemera of The Rutles' career, including the fact that the book's very title is a clue: *Turn Me On*, of course, is an anagram of "Rut No Men," and if one follows the then-popular belief that Mountbatten was gay (or grey) but assumes that the silent O'Hara was not, then something fairly cosmic and not a little scary can possibly be deduced.

There is more, but Topes, at least, is quick to dismiss it. "We had our own dead guy hoax. The Rutles just stole it from us."

However, he also admits that had The Turds released an untitled double album in a plain, one-color sleeve, full of songs about disemboweling dolls and sexy sadists, "We might have had some psychopathic American (see? It's *always* Americans! What's the matter with you people?) cult leader on our case as well, so I guess you can't blame them."

In fact, the now hopelessly drunken Topes is confusing The Rutles with Willy's Rats, British author Mick Farren's fictional account of a rock 'n' roll band whose own late 1960s career was blighted by just such an occurrence but who were, in fact, modeled loosely on an unholy cross between The Rolling Stones and Farren's own real life band, The Deviants.

The end for The Rutles came in 1970. Progressive in-fighting, usually over whose round it was next and whether the caddy should be refilled with Constant Comment or Sleepy-Time, saw all four band members quit the group, normally without telling each other, while bidding to out-do one another in the Unsuitable Wives stakes.

Financial wranglings at Rutle Corps, meanwhile, brought some of the most ferocious legal minds in the entertainment business to bear on the band's hopelessly tangled circumstances. And McQuickly's number nine dream of reinventing The Rutles as a half-baked bar band who'd simply go out and play old rock 'n' roll standards, although adequately documented by the *Let It Rot* film and movie, was doomed to failure when the band realized that none of them knew the chords to "Don't Worry Kyoko."

In December 1970, The Rutles' own biography concludes, "Dirk sued Stig and Nasty, Barry sued Dirk, Nasty sued Stig and Barry, and Stig sued himself accidentally. It was the end of an era."

Or was it? Wom and McQuickly, both operating under their post-Rutle pseudonyms of "John Halsey" and "Ollie Halsall," worked together regularly through the 1970s, most famously alongside John Otway and with Mike Patto's band, Patto.

Nasty, having adopted the infantile pseudonym of Neil Innes (it rhymes, of course, with Real Guinness, a reference to the popular drink of Irish renown), would also revisit The Rutles, linking with McQuickly's other alias, the humorously slothful sounding "Eric Idle," in a series of popular television comedies.

The first, *Do Not Adjust Your Set*, saw the "Innes" character's extra-curricular Bonzo Dog Plastic Ono DooDah Band supply jocular musical interludes around the "Idle" character's anarchic comedy routines, and it is surely mere coincidence that one of the Bonzo Band's songs, the hit "I'm The Urban Spaceman," was written by legendary left-handed Liverpudlian bassist Apollo C. Vermouth.

When the *DNAYS* cast reconvened as *Monty Python's Flying Circus*, "Innes" joined them as their in-house musical mastermind, and it is itself ironic that few of that long-running show's millions of fans, watching "Idle" and "Innes" at work, were aware that they were actually witnessing a historic reunion of the Nasty/McQuickly team that once shaped an entire generation.

What was now becoming an extremely long-running joke ran even further when "Idle" and "Innes" teamed up for *Rutland Weekend Television*, a half-hour British comedy series that thought it was an entire network, compensating for its brevity by constricting even its most popular shows down to a few minutes in length (are you listening, Fox?).

One of these shows, highlighted on an accompanying soundtrack album, recalled the delirious days of Rutlemania and how the "presenters" must have laughed when nobody got the real joke. Nobody, that is, except for Topes.

"I knew what they were up to. I knew it was them. The thing was, we'd already done that, pretended to have a TV station, pretended to be someone else, then done a show about ourselves. But we never let anyone see it, because we knew they'd rip us off. And we were right."

Such shenanigans continued throughout the 1970s, but the individual Rutles continued moving ever further away from their birthright. Unimpressed even by the wave of nostalgia that accompanied the release of The Rutles' documentary, they refused to break cover, preferring the comparative anonymity of their new identities.

"Innes, for instance, went on to a remarkable solo career before moving into British children's television; "Idle" turned to movies and more television; while "Rikki Fataar," the frankly absurd and faintly obscene name adopted by O'Hara (it is an anagram of KAKA FART, followed by a bunch of letters that don't seem to mean anything), chose to bury (clue #587) himself in session work.

Even more excitingly, he did so with such success that one of his own former employers, Al Jardine of American barber-

crucial member, might easily find their name jokingly bastardized by insensitive critics; the Moon-less Who performing "Triophenia," for example, or the post-Brian Stones becoming the Rolling Jonesless. Other possibilities doubtless abound. The Rutles, though, remain The Rutles, and pray God (or Rod) they always will.

Neither does their reemergence today compromise that immortality. Although the three surviving Rutles have shot a video, have contemplated touring and openly admit that there's actually very little they will not do to cash in on their own past, they are adamant that there will be no multihour television documentaries, no six-disc anthologies of unreleased material, no re-recording absent friends' home demos.

There will, however, be a new album of old songs, thrown together from a box full of outtakes and hyped to the heavens in hope of a hit.

Attempting to leave a more permanent record of themselves than having simply imprinted their image on the brains of a generation, The Rutles' final act as a group was to gather together a heap of unreleased and sometimes uncompleted songs and bury them in a time capsule. These tracks, unheard and unknown, would eventually take on legendary proportions among Rutles collectors. They were referred to, simply, as "the *Archaeology* tapes."

This is not the first time that their retrieval and release has been mooted. Several of the tracks, for instance, have already seen the light of day on Nasty's *Innes Book Of Records* album, while one of those same songs even made it onto network American television.

"Shangri-La," a track which, despite rumors to the contrary, was not written for any other bandmate's son and only employs a five minute "la-la-la-la" type fade out because Nasty didn't have any other outros handy. It was performed by "Innes" on *Saturday Night Live* in the mid-1970s!

But still, The Rutles' own versions remained stubbornly unavailable, eluding even the attentions of industry and bootleggers alike. Throughout the 1970s, for example, numerous attempts were made to bring The Rutles back together, climaxing with 1978's wildly successful Rutles documentary.

An accompanying soundtrack album, compiling highlights from throughout The Rutles' career, went silver, and such was the accompanying excitement that Nasty, McQuickly, and O'Hara were all presented with silver discs inscribed to their respective aliases! Only "John Halsey" received a correctly annotated award, and laughs:

shop legends The Beach Boys ("Fataar" appears on their *Holland* album), cornered him during the recent reunion celebrations and announced, "Hey Rikki, I never knew you were a Rutle." O'Hara, aghast that his cover had been so rudely blown, promptly fled and was last seen touring with Boz Scaggs. Or Bonnie Raitt.

"Halsey" also lapsed into comparative anonymity, particularly after the injuries he sustained in that terrible car accident; and finally, sadly, McQuickly's other alias, "Ollie Halsall," passed away four years ago. His loss is one from which the surviving Rutles agree they will never recover.

An even greater mark of respect, however, is the dignity displayed by the media when referring to the group today. Other quartets, returning to the fray so tragically shorn of one

"Everybody who's seen it, it hangs in my son's bedroom, looks at it and goes, 'Who's that? Who's Barry Wom?' My one and only trophy," he grimaces, "and it's got the wrong bloody name on it."

Ah, that droll Rorie humor!

In the face of such success, the demand for more Rutles was deafening.

The Rutles, however, didn't want to know, mainly, says Nasty, because they couldn't actually remember where the *Archaeology* tapes had been buried. It took the fortuitous nose of Barry's dog to unearth them from their resting place, and with the time capsule idea having been conveniently overlooked, well, you know the rest.

"Anything 20 years ago is being tugged out again," Ron Nasty reflects, "and I suppose of all the comeback bands, The Rutles are the ones who are most poised to be able to send themselves up."

He admits that the reunion idea was not The Rutles' own. "No, I didn't think of it myself, but people rang up and said 'Well, why don't you do something?' So we did.'"

The decision was not, however, taken precipitously. Shortly after the release of the documentary, The Rutles found themselves embroiled in a lengthy, and particularly ugly publishing dispute, battling claims that their entire repertoire had been pillaged from another band's — and amazingly, it wasn't The Turds! Even more amazingly, it was a battle that they ultimately lost.

Topes remains speechless on the subject, and it's clearly one that Nasty, too, dislikes hearing too much about. "It's funny," he muses. "Musicians like to make music, they like people to hear the music, and if a lot of people like the music and want to buy it, it accumulates a lot of money. And this attracts the wrong kind of people, who have the power to take the money away.

"A lot of people who've heard the soundtrack album would say that this is an unfair thing to do, and I would tend to agree with them. But it's like being back in the school playground, you're the new boy and some big boys come and take your packed lunch, and you can't go to the teacher because they'll beat you up, so you just have to bite that one."

For Nasty, the defeat was the end. "I responded by throwing down my teddy and kicking it and leaving the music business."

Still, what goes around comes around. Two years ago, a song that "Innes" wrote for Monty Python's *Live At Drury Lane* album, "The Idiot Song," was casually rehashed for the hit single "Whatever," by Oasis, a British band to whom the epithet "The New Rutles" could now very accurately be applied.

Nasty admits, "Somebody drew it to my attention, but then I found out that I didn't own the song, EMI did. Or Sony, or someone. But they drew Oasis' attention to it, and now I've taken it back, or at least the bit that was mine, and incorporated it into 'Shangri-La.'"

And emboldened by this experience, fears that someone might be eyeing his next packed lunch are among the last things on Nasty's mind.

"'People have expressed concern, 'Are you sure you won't be hammered again?' and I hope I won't be. But there's no way of knowing, and I really don't think there's any material here you could really say is like any other song."

On sonic evidence, the vast majority of the *Archaeology* tapes date from the latter part of the band's existence, a belief that Nasty can only vaguely confirm. Still, it is undeniable that the opening track, "Major Happy's Up And Coming Once Upon A Good Time Band," is little more than a sketchy rewrite of the classic "Sergeant Rutter," and Ron doesn't deny it.

"It's the same reason as putting on the suits and the wigs. We wanted a little curtain raiser that nodded to the history of The Rutles, and at the same time establish that we are something else in a parallel universe. Huge concepts to open up with."

"Rendezvous" was originally at least partially written during Nasty's Bonzo Dog days, while another cut, "We've Arrived (And We're Here To Prove It)" opens with a roaring jet engine before developing into a spot-on recreation of Jan And Dean in Red Square. And "Back In '64" reflects gently on the past through the rose-tinted eyes of an old man, old and losing his hair, many years from now. When we were Pre-Fab indeed!

There are also, says Ron, several tributes to Dirk's "Halsall" persona. "We miss him horribly, and it's nice to put out some tracks with him on them. 'We've Arrived' was a mucking about song which never saw the light of day before, and there's another one called 'She's Left You.'"

"Halsall" also stars on one of several tracks that the band intends reserving for a forthcoming single, handling lead vocals on a previously unreleased version of "It's Looking Good," a cut from The Rutles' 1966 *Rubbery Mole* album.

But his finest moment, perhaps, is the backing track to "Unfinished Words," an incomplete demo that the band faithfully restored during the preparation of *Archaeology*.

Nasty rambles, "I listened to it, and when the others came, I said, 'Do you remember this one?' and no one could remember what it was. It must have been one that was half finished, so I came up with a tune for it, then I realized I wouldn't have time to write any proper lyrics, so I remembered [the old songwriter's trick] of just singing things like 'scrambled eggs,' simply to get the pattern of the words down, so I thought I'd do that."

He is adamant, incidentally, that the lyric "unfinished words, flying like birds," has absolutely nothing to do with Lynyrd Skynyrd's greatest hit. Or anybody else's. "I just put that in as a lazy rhyme."

So, just how momentous is The Rutles' re-formation?

"Not very," says Ron Nasty. "We'll probably dress up a bit in the grey wigs and suits, and probably not, because we want to keep our own identity. We're not pretending to be anything else any more, it's The Rutles in their own right, whatever that is. George Harrison [the famed Indian mystic who didn't write "He's So Fine"] said a nice thing the other night when I asked him about it. He said, 'Why not? It's all part of the soup.' And it is. It's there."

"Not very," says Topes. "They only did it because we were thinking about it."

And "not very," says the old man who's been nursing half a pint of lager in the corner for the last two hours. "Given the choice between a Rut and a Turd, I'd go for a Turd any day," he says. "Rutting's for the youngsters."

Yeah yeah YEAH!

Bringing The Beatles to a manageable size

by Chuck Miller

These days, to say someone is "a Beatles Collector" is almost like saying they collect everything associated with the Renaissance. So much has been written and recorded about the Fab Four, they have become a musical and historical genre unto themselves. Because of this, many collectors are finding special areas within The Beatles universe on which to focus their collections. A collector of Beatles concert tickets, for example, might pass up a near mint copy of *Revolver* for a ticket stub from The Beatles' Kansas City concert. Someone who collects teen mags with Beatles covers might still be searching for the issue where John made his "bigger than Jesus" statement.

Such collections almost invariably focus on The Beatles' impact on history and on the recording industry, doing things no other artist or band had done at the time. Tony Pavick of Pittsburgh, Pa., focuses on finding Beatles records that were released in the 10-inch, 78 rpm format.

Beatles 78s?

Well, there was that pre-Beatles Quarry Men acetate of "That'll Be The Day"/"In Spite Of All The Danger," but only one copy survives today (Paul McCartney owns it; don't think he's selling it right now). And although American 78s had died out by 1958, the format remained alive in countries where that type of phonograph was still the predominant record player. India, for example, continued to produce 78s into the late 1960s — including a series of Beatles 78s on Parlophone. "The more unusual, sometimes unique aspects of record collecting fascinate me," said Pavick. "So the presence of these recordings pressed in the mid-60s in a format that was gone in the western world by 1961 is an eye-opener. To further that thought, that the recordings would be by musicians who 'changed the face of rock music forever' simply astounds me. Plus, any standard issue 78 that made it out in the '60s just has to be a treat."

His web page (http://members.aol.com/agp78/index.html) has plenty of Indian Beatles 78 scans, as well as a discography. It also contains a rare photo of The Quarry Men 78 label. "Given the existence of The Beatles on 78," said Pavick, "one has to wonder if other EMI groups made it onto shellac. I have heard that The Beach Boys may have shown up on an Indian 78. And just to make life interesting, could a Decca 78 of The Rolling Stones be outside the realm of possibility?"

For some collectors, The Beatles' *Yesterday And Today* has its own fascination. The "butcher" cover, showing The Beatles posing with meat and doll heads, combined with Capitol's knee-jerk reaction to replace the cover with a generic photo, is still one of the most talked-about and collected albums among Beatles fans.

Robert York, of Tacoma, Wash., not only collects butcher covers, but he also sells and trades with other collectors. "I've been a big fan of The Beatles since 1964. As far as I'm concerned, Beatle collecting pretty much started with the butcher.

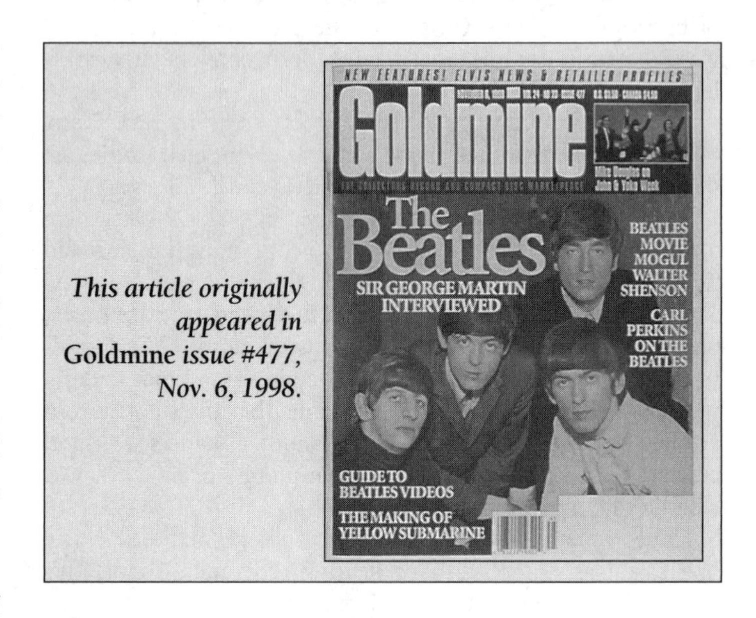

This article originally appeared in Goldmine *issue #477, Nov. 6, 1998.*

This album was something that, if you knew what to look for, you could own a unique collectible and a piece of history. From a collector's point of view, this release wasn't a planned mistake to capitalize on the collectibles market. Sure, The Beatles had 'long' hair, but other than that, they sang relatively 'decent' songs and ballads. Previous albums and 45 sleeves all had innocent stage shots and portrait graphics, so when the 'meat and doll parts' album graphic came out, America wasn't ready for this type of artwork, especially from a group of musicians considered innocent 'teen idols.' If this graphic came out today, no one would care. It's nothing compared to some of the graphics that have been put out in the decades following the 1960s."

After trying to find more information on butcher covers through the Internet, York set up a site of his own (www.eskimo.com/~bpentium/butcher.html), which is also a meeting point for other butcher collectors. "The butcher is such a pivotal piece of history that I thought it would be great to collect as much information as possible and put it all together at one location, along with pictures and resources on how to find and collect them. I've had the pleasure over the years of connecting many sellers to buyers. I do it for the love of the hobby and to keep The Beatles' legend alive for the next generation of fans and collectors."

For York, the most joy he gets out of collecting butcher covers is selling one to someone who has never owned one.

"The excitement they have knowing one is flying their way brings back memories of when I got my first copy. Butcher collecting isn't limited to vinyl records and discs. There is also memorabilia associated with this album including alternate photos, covers, buttons, original written articles, matches, tapes, foreign discs, compact discs, posters, slicks, magazines, bootlegs etc. Many of these items can be seen at Mitch McGeary's butcher cover site (www.rarebeatles.com/album2/discog/discog.htm). Mitch has been collecting for more than 25 years and is one of the leading authorities on everything butcher related."

For many kids who were too young to purchase Beatles music, there was another place where the music could be found — on Saturday mornings, as part of ABC's cartoon lineup. Darren English of Pakenham, Victoria, Australia, is a Beatles/Badfinger collector who specializes in finding copies of those Saturday morning cartoons. He has also amassed artists' models, animated cels and internal memos from King Features Studios, the company that created The Beatles cartoons.

"These are about the first TV shows I remember. I remember very little from the early '70s," said English, "so for me the 'toons are a link back to when I was a kid. I first saw them when I was four or five (1972-1973). I managed to track down some tapes of the 'toons a few years back. Now my kids love them as well. It is a real sharing experience I feel."

The Internet also allows some Beatles niche collectors to showcase their best pieces. Our final site comes from Canadian Steve Clifford, who has built a virtual Beatles museum for his collection. His web site, "All You Need Is Louvre," (www3.islandnet.com/~scliffor/beatles/museum/museum.htm) has some very interesting Beatles goodies, and they're just a click away. You can check out some of the seven-inch picture sleeve scans he's acquired over the years, some of the *Yellow Submarine* promotional toys or even some of the buttons and souvenirs associated with The Beatles. Perhaps these pictures will inspire future Beatles collectors or give some collector a new avenue to search through in finding Beatles history.

If you have any questions about your music collections, please drop a card or a letter to: *Goldmine*, Attn: *Collectormania!*/Chuck Miller, Krause Publications, 700 East State Street, Iola WI 54990. Or you can send an e-mail to Collectormania@krause.com. Hope to hear from you soon!

Retro News Flash
Sept. 24, 1999, issue #500

Still-sealed first state stereo butcher cover fetches $38,500

by Tim Neely

The highest price ever paid for a record at auction? Try $38,500.

That's how much a bidder paid for a still-sealed copy of the stereo "first state" *Yesterday And Today* butcher cover at the Aug. 4-5 Good Rockin' Tonight auction. Only seven copies of this album that have never been opened are reliably known to exist.

In this case, I know whose album it was before it was in this GRT auction, and I believe, based on my trust of the former owner, it's exactly as it was in 1966. But one of the problems with still-sealed albums is that they can be resealed and passed off as authentic period pieces, which is why I tend to be hesitant in paying a premium for a still-sealed album. That's also why I won't list a still-sealed album as the world's most valuable in one of my price guides, as a competitor has.

Let me use an analogy from coin collecting here: "Proof" is a state of manufacture, not a condition; as a result, many reputable coin dealers don't use "proof" as a condition. They'll say a coin was manufactured as a proof but also give it a grade. Proof coins often are subject to many of the same environmental and handling factors as non-proof coins. Similarly, still-sealed is a state of manufacture, not a condition. A still-sealed album can have a cut-out notch, which automatically knocks the cover down to VG+ or VG++ at best. The cover can have ring wear if it is improperly stored. And you don't know what the record will sound like or even if it's been properly pressed.

Anyway, in most cases, I'll open it to hear that pristine sound as it was meant to be heard. (Several years ago I bought a still-sealed Philles pressing of *A Christmas Gift For You*. It even still had a price tag on the shrink wrap. I promptly unsealed it and played it. What a great listening experience!)

I'll still list the stereo version of the original *The Freewheelin' Bob Dylan* with the four banned songs as the #1 most collectible piece on the albums list until near mint, opened stereo copies of the first-state butcher cover start fetching something close to what this still-sealed copy did.

By the way, a mono first-state butcher cover, also sealed, went for $13,750, by far the most ever paid for a mono copy of this album.

It was 20 years ago today...

The (Ex-) Beatles in 1974

by Gillian G. Gaar

When The Beatles split officially in 1970, their breakup was widely regarded as the end of an era. But as each ex-Fab broke off into his own career, the "solo Beatle" era was just beginning. Four years after the split, the activities of each member of the group still attracted great media attention, and their hold on the charts was nearly as strong as it had been when The Beatles were together. Throughout 1974, aside from a three-week period from Sept. 28 to Oct. 12, there was an album by one of The Beatles in the Top 40; singles by the solo Fabs were also in the Top 40 charts for most of the year, except for a two-and-a-half month period from August to mid-October.

The names of John Lennon, Paul McCartney, George Harrison, and Ringo Starr also turned up frequently in the press for both personal and professional reasons. Starr and McCartney enjoyed the acclaim generated by their 1973 efforts, *Ringo* and *Band On The Run*, respectively. Harrison became the first solo Beatle to undertake a full-length U.S. tour. Lennon brawled in public while embroiled in his "lost weekend" period in Los Angeles but saw the year out on a more positive note, with a successful new album in the charts and a rare live appearance before a Thanksgiving audience.

Starr initially spent 1974 watching singles from his most successful album, *Ringo* (released in November 1973), storm their way up the charts. "Photograph" (cowritten by Starr and Harrison), b/w Starr's own "Down And Out" (released Sept. 24, 1973), had peaked at #1 in November. Dec. 3, 1973, saw the release of "You're Sixteen" (originally recorded by Johnny Burnette), b/w "Devil Woman," which reached #1 on Jan. 26, 1974. Hot on its heels came "Oh My My" (cowritten by Starr and Vini Poncia) b/w another Starr composition, "Step Lightly," released on Feb. 18, and peaking at #5 in April. Ringo had reached #2 in the album charts in late 1973.

The "Ringo and guest stars" formula proved to be so successful, Starr went back into the studio that summer to try it again on *Goodnight Vienna*. The album was released on Nov. 18, preceded by the single, "Only You (And You Alone)" (originally recorded by The Platters) b/w Starr's "Call Me" on Nov. 11; the album would peak at #8, the single at #6, both in January 1975.

Lennon assisted Starr on three of the album's tracks, writing and recording a demo of the title track (which was released as the album's third single), recording a demo of "Only You" and playing piano and supervising the recording of the song, also playing "All By Myself." Longtime friend Harry Nilsson contributed his composition "Easy For Me," in addition to providing backing vocals throughout the album.

This article originally appeared in Goldmine issue #374, Nov. 25, 1994.

Goodnight Vienna proved to be a pleasant musical outing, if less inventive than *Ringo*. The title track was a paler copy of "I'm The Greatest," and Starr's cover of Roger Miller's "Husbands And Wives" was a bit too maudlin to be enjoyably tongue-in-cheek. But the album did have its high points, most notably the reworking of "Only You" and Hoyt Axton's "No No Song," in which Starr playfully swears off marijuana, cocaine and alcohol.

Starr was also involved in various projects with Nilsson during the year. Starr and Nilsson were credited with "overall production" on the *Son Of Dracula* soundtrack album, recorded in 1972 but not released until April 1, 1974 on the RCA subsidiary Rapple. The album was a combination of film dialogue and songs by Nilsson, including "Daybreak," which was released as a single on March 25, with Starr on drums and Harrison on cowbell, b/w "Down." The film itself (which featured Nilsson, and Starr as "Merlin The Magician") had its premiere on April 19 in Atlanta, Ga., at the same cinema where *Gone With The Wind* had its premiere in 1939. Starr also played drums on Nilsson's *Pussy Cats* album (produced by John Lennon).

In addition, Starr drummed on Jimmy Webb's *Land's End* album, recorded during the summer of 1973 and released on June 3, 1974 and adopted the pseudonym "Billy Shears" for his appearance on Ravi Shankar's *Shankar Family And Friends* (which began recording in April 1973 and was produced by Harrison) and on Harrison's *Dark Horse* album.

All in all, 1974 was destined to be one of Starr's most successful years as a solo artist, as he opened and closed the year with an album in the Top 10 and a single in the Top 20. It was an impressive record from the ex-Beatle most people assumed would be the least successful when the group split.

Harrison was involved in a number of different ventures during 1974, not the least of which was launching his own label, Dark Horse (distributed by A&M), in May, thus becoming the first solo Beatle to have his own label. The label's first releases were singles by Splinter ("Costafine Town"/"Elly May"), released in Sept. 13 in the U.K, followed by Splinter's *The Place I Love* and Shankar's *Shankar Family And Friends* on Sept. 20 (in the U.S., Shankar's single was released Nov. 6 and the album Oct. 7; Splinter's single was released Nov. 7 and the album Sept. 25).

Harrison had produced Shankar's album and played guitar under the name "Hari Georgeson." He also produced Shankar's "Music Festival From India" concert, held in London on Sept. 23. The concert was filmed and recorded for Dark Horse, but nothing from the event was ever released.

In September, Harrison began recording his own album. Though struck with a bout of laryngitis, he persevered, and the first single from the sessions, "Dark Horse"/"I Don't Care Anymore," was released on Nov. 18. This was followed by the release of "Ding Dong, Ding Dong"/"I Don't Care Anymore" on Dec. 23, with the *Dark Horse* album released on Dec. 9 (featuring a retouched school photo of Harrison from his Liverpool Institute days). The "Dark Horse" single would peak at #15 in January 1975, with "Ding Dong" peaking at #36 in February; the album itself would peak at #4 in February.

Dark Horse was an up-tempo rock offering, opening with the bouncy instrumental "Hari's On Tour (Express)." But what the album lacked was a strong hit. "Ding Dong" may have been a contender, but its seasonal theme limited its appeal during the other 11 months of the year. Harrison's spiritual interests were reflected in the cover art and songs such as "It Is He (Jai Sri Krishna)," but *Dark Horse* also

touched on Harrison's personal unhappiness. His marriage to former model Pattie Boyd recently ended when she took up with Harrison's friend Eric Clapton, and in a weird twist Harrison invited both to contribute backing vocals to his cover of the Everly Brothers song "Bye Bye Love."

Harrison would later marry Olivia Arias, whom he met when she worked at A&M and later served as a secretary for Dark Horse Records. Outtakes/alternate versions from the album sessions can be found on *Onothimagen*, *By George*, and *Somewhere In Utopia*.

But Harrison's biggest undertaking of the year was a 44-date U.S. tour (two additional dates in Cleveland were canceled due to a snowstorm). It was interesting that Harrison would be the first solo Beatle to go on a full U.S. tour, since he had been the member of the group most resistant to touring. But the anticipation on the part of the U.S. fans to see an ex-Beatle again quickly soured. Harrison's voice had not totally recovered from the exertions of recording and became further strained on the tour, leading critics to dub the show "Dark Hoarse."

Harrison also opened his show with a lengthy set from Shankar and irritated fans with his religious commentary (asking crowds to chant "the holy name of the Lord") and altering words in sacrosanct Beatles songs to reflect his own beliefs: "In my life, I love you more" from the Lennon-penned song "In My Life," became "In my life, I love God more." Other Beatles numbers Harrison performed included "While My Guitar Gently Weeps" (which was altered to "gently smiles"), "For You Blue" and "Something."

The '74 tour was documented on bootlegs such as *George Harrison 1974*, *Live In Vancouver*, *Let's Hear One For Lord Buddha*, *On Tour 1974*, *George Harrison: Baton Rouge*, *Chicago 11 30 74*, *Last Live Concert*, *Excerpts From Three Major Concerts* and the CDs *Hari's On Tour* and *Washington '74*. An appearance on the U.K. radio program *Rock Around The World*, with Harrison performing "I Don't Care Anymore," "Far East Man" and "Awaiting On You All," was documented on *Onothimagen* ("I Don't Care..."), *Somewhere In Utopia* ("Far East Man" and "Awaiting...") and *By George* (all three numbers).

But though the tour did have its memorable moments — Harrison became the first Beatle to meet a U.S. president when he had lunch with Gerald Ford and his son Jack on Dec. 13 while in Washington, D.C. (Harrison's father, Shankar, and longtime associate Billy Preston also attended the lunch) — it proved to be a discouraging experience, and Harrison would limit himself to one-off appearances until his 1992 tour of Japan.

Like Starr, McCartney basked in the success of his achievements in 1973, which saw the release of the album generally acknowledged as the finest of his solo career, *Band On The Run* (released on Dec. 5, 1973). The album's first single, "Jet"/"Mamunia," was released on Jan. 28, 1974, though in less than a month it would be reissued with a new B-side, "Let Me Roll It"; on March 30 the single would peak at #7. The album's second single, "Band On The Run"/"Nineteen Hundred And Eighty Five," was released on April 8 and hit the top of the charts two months later, on June 8.

Sparked by the success of the single, *Band On The Run* also reached #1 on three separate occasions: April 13, June 8 and again on July 1. Amazingly, the album remained in the Top 20 during the first eight months of the year, finally slipping

DARK HORSE
Words and Music by GEORGE HARRISON
Recorded on EMI Records Limited by
GEORGE HARRISON
GEORGE HARRISO
DARK HORSE
PRODUCED BY GEORGE HARRISON
CHARLES HANSEN
GANGA PUBLISHING B.V.

out of the Top 40 on Sept. 28. By the end of the year, *Band On The Run* had sold six million copies worldwide, two million of those in the U.S. The album also won two Grammy Awards: for Best Pop Vocals Performance By A Duo, Group Or Chorus, and Best Engineered (Non-Classical) Recording.

McCartney's first major recording venture of the year was working on his brother Michael's album, **McGear* (the pseudonym Michael adopted when he became a performing artist), with sessions beginning in January. Perhaps because it was his brother's record, McCartney felt freer to indulge his off-the-wall sense of humor that's rarely evident in his own solo work. Except for the opening Bryan Ferry cover, "Sea Breezes," McCartney wrote or cowrote all of **McGear*'s songs, in addition to producing and playing on the album.

He brought the rest of Wings along as well, with his wife Linda, Denny Laine, departed Wings drummer Denny Seiwell and future Wings guitarist Jimmy McCullough all appearing on the album. As one of rock's classic "undiscovered" records, **McGear* should be of interest to anyone with an interest in the work of either McCartney brother.

**McGear* was released on Warner Bros. Oct. 14, with the first single, "Leave It" b/w a non-album track, "Sweet Baby," released Oct. 28, though unfortunately neither the album nor the single found much success. McCartney also produced a single for his brother's group Scaffold, "Liverpool Lou" b/w "Ten Years After On Strawberry Jam" (the B-side cowritten by Paul and Linda), released May 24 on Warner Bros. (July 29 in the U.K.)

Once work on **McGear* was completed, McCartney set about finding replacements for guitarist Henry McCullough (no relation to Jimmy) and Denny Seiwell, who had both quit Wings prior to recording sessions for *Band On The Run*. McCartney held auditions in April for a drummer, eventually choosing Geoff Britton, though Britton's stay in the band was destined to be short-lived. In June, McCartney tapped Jimmy McCullough to formally join the band on guitar, and the new lineup went to Nashville for recording sessions, which were also filmed for a documentary to be titled *One Hand Clapping* (the documentary was never released but has made the rounds in collector's circles for years).

McCartney also took time out to write the song "Let's Love" for Peggy Lee, in addition to producing the number (which would become the title track of Lee's next album and the album's first single, both released in October).

The first songs to be released from the Nashville sessions appeared on the single "Junior's Farm"/"Sally G," released on Nov. 4 (the group appeared on the BBC series *Top Of The Pops* later in the month performing the song) and which reached #3 on Jan. 11, 1975; the jaunty song was inspired by Junior Putnam, who put Wings up at his ranch during their stay in Nashville. Nine days later, the single was reissued, with A- and B-sides reversed, and the new A-side, the country and western "Sally G," peaked at #39 in late February.

A more unusual single was "Walking In The Park With Eloise"/"Bridge Over The River Suite," released on Dec. 2 and credited to the "Country Hams." The A-side was written by McCartney's father, the leader of a jazz band during the 1920s in Liverpool. Chet Atkins and Floyd Cramer rounded out the rest of the Hams' lineup. The single did not chart, thus making it one of the rarest McCartney singles.

Other songs recorded during Nashville sessions include "Hey Diddle," "Wide Prairie," "Send Me The Heart" and "Proud Mum"; the first song appears on the bootlegs *Cold Cuts*, *Hot Hits And Cold Cuts (Second Mix)* and all four (with "Diddle" in a different mix) on *Cold Cuts, Another Early Version* and *Hot Hits And Cold Cuts*. "Send Me The Heart," with a new Laine vocal, also appears on his solo album, *Japanese Tears*, in addition to the bootleg *Suitable For Framing*. Songs from the *One Hand Clapping* film appear on the bootleg of the same title, in addition to *And All The Rest*, *Classified Document* and the *All The Rest* CD.

In November, work began on Wings' next album, *Venus And Mars*, though McCartney had been recording demos as early as mid-1974 (which can be found on the EP *Rock Show*; fall recordings appear on the boot *Venus*). Final sessions for the album would be held in New Orleans and Los Angeles during early 1975, at which time Britton would be dismissed. Meanwhile, McCartney finished 1974 with a live appearance, when he and Linda contributed backing vocals to "Mine For Me" at Rod Stewart's Nov. 27 concert at the Odeon Cinema in Lewisham (a song McCartney had written for Stewart); the performance was broadcast the following year on the TV program *Midnight Special* and appears on the bootleg *Oriental Nightfish*.

McCartney's other recording appearances released during the year included bass and backing vocals on *Thornton, Freadkin And Unger And The Big Band's Pass On This Side* album on the track (and single) "God Bless California" (recorded in 1971), backing vocals on James Taylor's *Walking Man* album ("Rock 'N' Roll Is Music Now," "Let It All Fall Down") and synthesizer and backing vocals on Adam Faith's *I Survive* LP.

For John Lennon, 1974 meant further battles with the Immigration and Naturalization Services (INS). Lennon had been plagued by deportation orders since he and his wife, Yoko Ono, had their visa extensions canceled on March 6,

1972. Ono was granted "permanent resident" status a year later (on March 23, 1973), but Lennon's deportation order was still on appeal. Lennon's first legal maneuver in 1974 was petitioning the Queen for a royal pardon of his 1968 drug conviction in January; his request was denied. In March, he asked for a temporary restraining order to delay the INS Appeals Board ruling; this request was denied on May 1.

In July, the heat was turned on again as the INS denied Lennon's October 1973 appeal and ordered that he leave the U.S. in 60 days; Lennon again filed an appeal. But the tide began to turn the next month, when Nixon resigned on Aug. 8. In late August, Lennon testified in Federal Court that the Nixon administration wanted to deport him because of his antiwar activities, not because of his drug conviction, and in November he requested permission to question immigration officials about the reasons behind his deportation. His request would be granted in January 1975, offering the first sign of light at the end of the tunnel; in October of that year, the INS deportation order would be overturned.

Lennon's claims that he was facing extreme government harassment gathered increasing public support during the year, especially in the wake of Nixon's resignation. On Dec. 5, *Rolling Stone* printed a copy of a memo, dated Feb. 4, 1972 (little more than a month before the Lennons' visa extension was canceled), from Senator Strom Thurmond to then-Attorney General John Mitchell, suggesting that Lennon be deported as an "undesirable alien." Lennon's lawyer, Leon Wildes, also uncovered information showing how the INS had allowed persons convicted of more serious crimes, including rape and murder, to stay in the U.S.

Lennon's other major problem in his personal life during 1974 grew out of his separation from Ono in October 1973. Lennon had left New York and relocated to Los Angeles, where he planned to record an album of rock 'n' roll hits with Phil Spector producing. Sessions for what would be appropriately titled *Rock 'N' Roll* began soon after Lennon's arrival in L.A., but quickly degenerated into chaos, as the participants indulged freely in drugs and drink.

Before things totally ground to a halt and Spector absconded with the tapes, Lennon managed to record "You Can't Catch Me," "Sweet Little Sixteen," "Bony Moronic," "My Baby Left Me," "Angel Baby To Know Her Is To Love Her," "Be My Baby" and "Here We Go Again," a number cowritten with Spector. Bootlegs featuring material from this period include *You Should'a Been There*, *Winston O'Boogie*, *The May Pang Tapes*, *The Toy Boy*, and the CDs *Dreaming Of The Past*, *Yer Blues* and *Watching The Wheels*.

By 1974, Lennon had settled into a house in Santa Monica and spent the first part of the year carousing with Starr, Nilsson, Keith Moon and any other rock stars in the vicinity who were up for nonstop partying. "It was a pretty hectic period, pretty wild," Lennon told Andy Peebles in 1980. "It sounds funny in retrospect, but it was pretty miserable."

The best-known incident from Lennon's "lost weekend" period came on the night of March 12, when Lennon and Nilsson were thrown out of a Smothers Brothers show at the Troubadour Club after heckling the performers. Lennon was also charged with assaulting a waitress, but the charges were later dropped. Lennon and Nilsson later sent flowers to The Smothers Brothers with an apology.

Still determined to do something productive, Lennon tried to quell the nonstop partying atmosphere by undertaking production of Nilsson's next album (in addition to writing the song "Mucho Mungo" for Nilsson — on the album the song was part of a medley with the folk song "Mt. Elga"). Sessions began in March, and the album, ultimately called *Pussy Cats*, was released Aug. 19. One evening's session was particularly memorable, when Paul and Linda McCartney turned up; the resulting jam was documented on the bootleg *A Toot And A Snore In '74* — the last time the Lennon/McCartney team played together. Bootlegs featuring demo takes of "Mucho Mungo" include *Yin Yang*, *Johnny Moondog* and the CDs *Lost Sleepy Blind Lemon Lennon* and *Look At Me*.

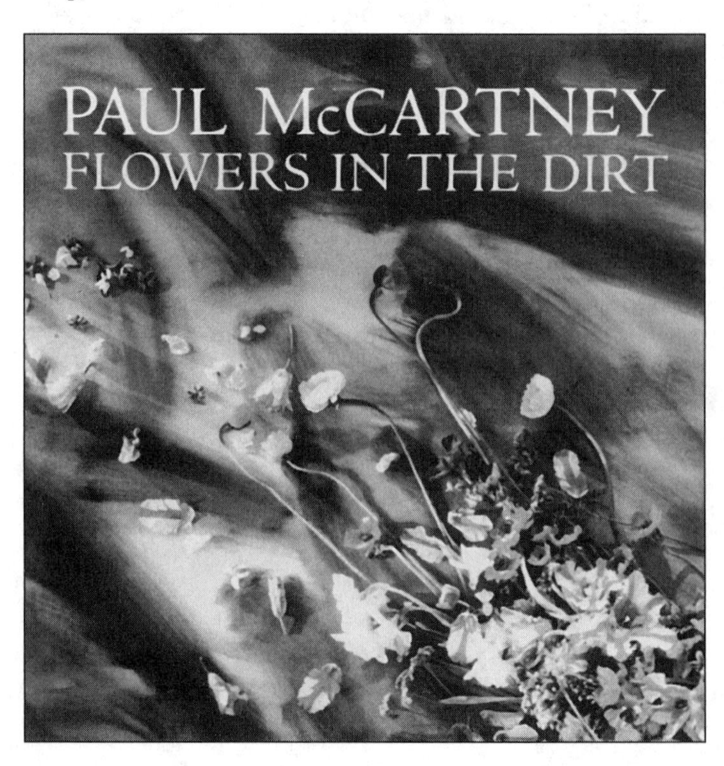

In addition to helping Starr on *Goodnight Vienna*, Lennon also contributed guitar and backing vocals to "Lucy In The Sky With Diamonds" with Elton John, recording at Caribou Ranch in Colorado during the summer. Demos of *Goodnight Vienna* can be found on the bootleg of the same name and *Johnny Moondog*, while Lennon's demo of "Only You" is on *Classified Document Volume Three* and the *Yer Blues* CD. Elton John released "Lucy" as a single in November, b/w Lennon's "One Day At A Time."

In July, Lennon began preparations for his own album, *Walls And Bridges*, returning to New York to record it. Nilsson, Jesse Ed Davis and longtime friend and associate Klaus Voormann were among those who appeared on the album, but two of the most notable guests were Lennon's son Julian, who played drums on "Ya Ya," and Elton John, who sang on "Surprise, Surprise (Sweet Bird Of Paradox)" and was given "star" billing on "Whatever Gets You Through The Night," on which he played organ and piano in addition to singing. John made Lennon promise that he would appear on stage with him should the song make it to #1, and Lennon readily agreed, not believing the song would accomplish the feat "in a million years" (perhaps because he'd also stated the song was "one of my least favorites"). Another song recorded during these sessions, "Move Over Ms. L," would appear as the B-side to "Stand By Me," released in 1975.

Though Lennon later described the album as "the work of a semi-sick craftsman," *Walls And Bridges* was not without its high points. "Whatever... " burst with commercial appeal, "Bless You" was a lovely ballad to Ono which hinted at reconciliation, and "#9 Dream" was a mesmerizing and haunting tune. Still, an unmistakable air of sadness does hang over the album, which opens with Lennon moaning, "Somebody please, please help me/You know I'm drowning in a sea of hatred," skipping to the lament "Scared" and closing with "Nobody Loves You (When You're Down And Out)."

The album's cover featured some of Lennon's childhood paintings, cut into three strips, so that the inside picture,

close-ups of his face, could be flipped over to make different faces. Lennon also adopted a number of pseudonyms spread throughout the credits, not only his familiar "Dr. Winston O'Boogie," but also "Rev. Thumbs Ghurkin," "Kaptain Kundalini" and "Booker Table And The Maitre D's," a playful move considering it was his own album.

"Whatever Gets You Through The Night"/"Beef Jerky" was released Sept. 23 (credited to John Lennon With The Plastic Ono Nuclear Band), followed by the release of *Walls And Bridges* Sept. 26. Asked about the title by journalist Ray Coleman, Lennon replied, "Walls you walk into and bridges you cross over. Deep stuff!"

Promotion of the album used an ad campaign featuring Lennon's eyes appearing on different items branded with the slogan "Listen To This T-Shirt," "Listen To This Picture Record," "Listen To This Press Kit" and so on. The photographer for the album, Bob Gruen, also took a number of dramatic shots of Lennon on a rooftop wearing a "New York City" T-shirt and flashing the peace sign in front of the Statue Of Liberty (while wearing a *Walls And Bridges* promo item, "Listen To This Button"). It has since become one of the most-often seen photos of Lennon.

On Nov. 16, both the single and the album topped the charts (with "Night" becoming Lennon's first #1 single). Twelve days later, Lennon kept his promise to Elton John and appeared at John's Thanksgiving Day concert on Nov. 28 at Madison Square Garden, after rehearsing together Nov. 24. The two performed Lennon's current hit, "Whatever Gets You Through The Night," "Lucy In The Sky With Diamonds" and "I Saw Her Standing There," which Lennon introduced as "a number of an old, estranged fiance of mine called Paul." Ono was in the audience and met with Lennon backstage after the show — the beginning of their reconciliation; within two months, Lennon would move back into the Dakota apartment building with Ono.

"I Saw Her Her Standing There" was first released as the B-side to John's "Philadelphia Freedom" single, released Feb. 24, 1975. All three numbers appeared on a variety of foreign EPs released in 1981 but would not be released in the U.S. until their inclusion on the four-CD set *Lennon*, released in 1990. A rehearsal of "I Saw Her Standing There" appeared on the bootleg *The Toy Boy*.

Lennon nearly made another live appearance less than a month after joining Elton John on stage. On Dec. 20, he planned to appear with George Harrison during his second show at Madison Square Garden, the final show of Harrison's tour. But the two had an argument over signing a form relating to Beatles business, and the appearance never came off — on stage anyway, for by the time the show ended, the two had made up and were interviewed together at Harrison's hotel for radio station KHJ.

The next *Walls And Bridges* single, "#9 Dream"/"What You Got," was released Dec. 16 and reached #9 in February 1975. Rehearsals and alternate versions from the *Walls And Bridges* sessions have appeared on the bootlegs *Something Precious And Rare* (LP and CD), *Off The Walls* and the CDs *Watching The Wheels, Yer Blues, Look At Me, Dreaming Of The Past, My Love Will Turn You On, Gone From This Place* and *Serve Yourself* (Lennon's solo work has of course also been documented on *The Lost Lennon Tapes* series). The only official release of *Walls And*

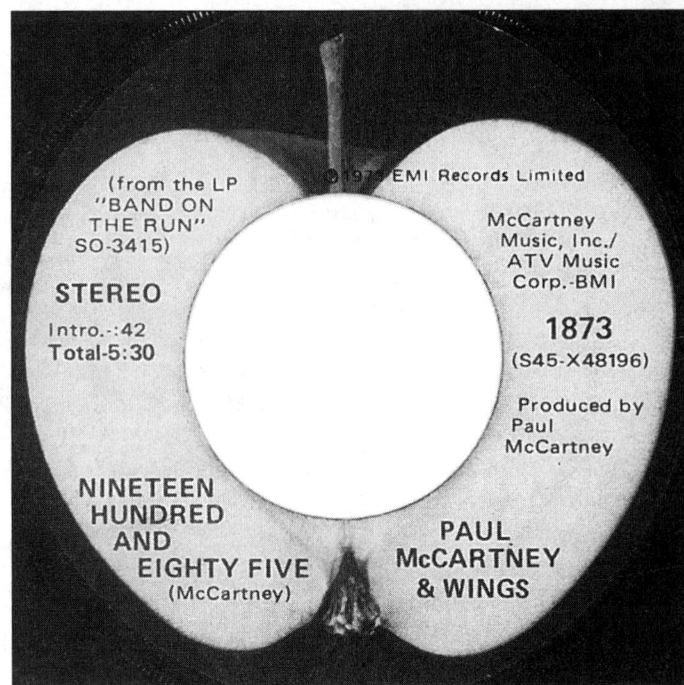

Bridges outtakes would come with the release of *Menlove Ave.*, released in 1986 and including the songs "Old Dirt Road," "Bless You," "Scared," "Steel and Glass" and "Nobody Loves You (When You're Down And Out)."

Meanwhile, on Oct. 21, Lennon had returned to the studio, planning to salvage the *Rock 'N' Roll* album. After getting hold of the tapes he'd recorded with Spector the previous year and listening to them, Lennon realized there was little material that could be used. In fact, only three songs from the Spector sessions would appear on *Rock 'N' Roll*: "Sweet Little Sixteen," "You Can't Catch Me" and "Bony Maronie." So over the next five days, Lennon ordered a batch of new songs: "Just Because" (using the instrumental backing from the Spector sessions but recording a new vocal), "Stand By Me," "Be-Bop-A-Lula," a medley of "Rip It Up"/"Ready Teddy," "Ain't That A Shame," "Do You Want To Dance," "Slippin' And Slidin,'" "Peggy Sue," another medley of "Bring It On Home To Me"/"Send Me Some Lovin'" and an instrumental version of "Ya Ya" at Record Plant East.

The album stood as a good testament to the music that inspired Lennon, but he took it one step further, perceiving it as the conclusion of a chapter of his life. When recording "Just Because," he began improvising a monologue toward the end of the song, concluding with the lines, "This is Dr. Winston O'Boogie, saying goodnight from Record Plant East in New York... goodbye." As he told interviewer Andy Peebles, "Something flashed through my mind as I said it — 'Am I really saying farewell to the business?' I thought, 'Is this some sort of cosmic thing? Here I am with this old picture of me in Hamburg in '61 [referring to the striking cover shot by Jurgen Vollmer], and I'm saying farewell from Record Plant, and I'm ending as I started, singing this straight rock 'n' roll stuff.'"

But the saga of *Rock 'N' Roll* was not quite over. One of Lennon's intentions in doing the album was to settle a dispute with music publisher Morris Levy, who'd threatened to sue Lennon for pinching a line from a Chuck Berry's "You Can't Catch Me" and using it in "Come Together" (the offending line being "Here come old flat-top"). Lennon agreed to record three numbers from Levy's catalog on his next album, and as a sign of good faith, gave Levy rough tapes of *Rock 'N' Roll*. But Levy, possibly irritated that Lennon's next album had been *Walls And Bridges* and not *Rock 'N' Roll*, issued the tapes on the Adam VIII label, under the name *John Lennon Sings The Great Rock & Roll Hits* (a.k.a. *Roots*) on Feb. 8, only available through mail order. The track listing ran: "Be-Bop-A-Lula" "Ain't That A Shame," "Stand By Me," "Sweet Little Sixteen," "Rip It Up"/"Ready Teddy," "Angel Baby," "Do You Want To Dance," "You Can't Catch Me," "Bony Moronic," "Peggy Sue," "Bring It On Home To Me"/"Send Me Some Lovin'," Slippin' And Slidin'," Be My Baby," "Ya-Ya" and "Just Because."

Lennon sued successfully to have the album withdrawn, and *Rock 'N' Roll* was rush-released on Feb. 17; in addition to the songs having varying mixes and lengths, "Angel Baby" and "Be My Baby" were dropped from the album. "Angel Baby" would eventually be released on *Menlove Ave*. Other numbers from the *Rock 'N' Roll* sessions that appeared on *Menlove Ave.* included "Here We Go Again," "Since My Baby Left Me" and "To Know Her Is To Love Her." Aside from its appearance on *Roots*, "Be My Baby" remains unreleased.

Lennon also made a number of interesting guest appearances on radio and TV during the year. On May 17 and 18, he was a guest DJ for Philadelphia radio station WFIL, appearing as part of a station fund-raising effort, and other guest DJ stints included appearances Sept. 27 on KHJ (excerpts can be heard on *Snap Shots*, *Broadcasts* and *Stereo Walk*) and Sept. 28 on New York station WNEW. Lennon also appeared on *Monday Night Football* alongside Howard Cosell on Dec. 9 (documented on *Come Back Johnny*).

There were also signs during 1974 that The Beatles years were winding down and being transformed into myth. On Oct. 28, Allen Klein would lose his case against Harrison, Lennon, and Starr; in early 1975 The Beatles & Co. partnership would be formally dissolved. Mark Lapidos' Beatlefest, the longest-running American Beatles convention, would hold its first con

Sept. 7 and 8. The first stage show based on The Beatles story, *John, Paul, George, Ringo... And Bert* would open in London on Aug. 14 (after its original run in Liverpool).

Another tongue-in-cheek look at the Fab Four had its debut on BBC-TV's *Rutland Weekend Television* show, during which Eric Idle and Neil Innes presented the original "Rutles" sketch. An excerpt from the sketch would run on *Saturday Night Live* in 1976 and the idea would be expanded into the spoof documentary *All You Need Is Cash*, which would air in 1978.

Even today, news of the solo Beatles' activities, or one of the many "reunion" rumors, is sufficient to generate headlines and soundbites. But most important, the music of George Harrison, John Lennon, Paul McCartney, and Ringo Starr, individually and collectively, is still selling in impressive quantities and is still regarded as among the best music in rock history. For a musician, that's the best legacy the passage of time can offer.

Retro News Flash

Nov. 22, 1996, issue #426

Beatles sue to stop Republic Of Chad stamp sales

by Lloyd A. de Vries

The three surviving former Beatles, along with Yoko Ono, have filed a lawsuit demanding that stamps depicting the band issued last December be withdrawn from sale in the United States.

Their attorney describes the Republic Of Chad stamps issued late in 1995 showing The Beatles as "bootleg merchandise which is hiding behind the fact that small Third World countries put a seal of approval on them."

Yoko, Paul, George, and Ringo aren't actually the plaintiffs in the lawsuit: Apple Corps Ltd., The Beatles' marketing operation, is the entity taking legal action. But Ono, McCartney, Harrison, and Starr own Apple.

The nine stamps depicting The Beatles were produced for the Republic Of Chad by the International Collectors Society of Owings Mills, Md., which bills itself as "the largest and most-respected stamp collector society in the world."

"Shock and disappointment," was the reaction from ICS co-owner Scott Tilson. "All of us here have been longtime Beatles fans. They were our idols... we've grown up and lived with [their music]."

"It's really incredible, because most people and most personalities consider it a once in a lifetime honor and achievement to be pictured on a postage stamp," said Tilson.

An ICS attorney in Newark, where the federal lawsuit was filed last April, says the four will have to give depositions in the case. "They'll have to come in and sing their tune factually, and melodiously, supporting their positions," Donald A. Robinson told the Associated Press.

Apple's attorney, Paul Licalsi, calls that threat a "litigaton tactic" but says the four are willing to do so if ordered. "They're very, very serious about protecting their rights and protecting their fans."

Chad is neither the only nation selling stamps showing The Beatles, nor the only country represented by ICS.

"The vast, vast bulk of whatever stamps these countries print are sold in the United States and hawked as collector's items," says Licalsi. "I don't believe The Beatles are any kind of cultural icons in Tanzania. This is pure profit and a rip-off of Beatles fans and a rip-off of The Beatles."

The Beatles' lawsuit charges the International Collectors Society with copyright infringement and violating licensing laws and that only a minimal number of the stamps are actually sold in Chad or the country allegedly issuing the stamps.

Another ICS attorney claims The Beatles improperly registered some copyrights and abandoned their rights to others.

Tilson said ICS has no plans to withdraw the stamps from sale in the U.S., as demanded by the lawsuit.

"Absolutely not. In fact, with all this uproar, all our phones have been ringing off the hook. And those who have been lucky enough to get one of these limited editions will have something that will be highly treasured in the future."

George Harrison

Dark Horse Records

by Charles Reinhart

More than a year before The Beatles' Apple label released its final U.S. record, George Harrison had begun work on his own record label, Dark Horse. Harrison founded Dark Horse on May 25, 1974, with Dennis Morgan as its director of operations. Harrison was determined not to allow his new label to fall into the same traps that had brought Apple to the brink of disaster. He would keep the label's artist roster small and not spend fortunes on anyone with the nerve to just approach the label. The plan wasn't perfect, but it has worked well enough to keep the label alive and active for more than 14 years.

At first, Harrison signed a contract with A&M Records to distribute Dark Horse. His first artists were people he knew and respected as musicians. Ravi Shankar had been his mentor. He had recorded for Apple with Harrison producing and playing on his recordings. The group Splinter consisted of Bob Purvis and Bill Elliott. Elliott had done the lead vocals on the Apple release "God Save Us," and the duo had worked on the soundtrack of the Harrison film, *Little Malcolm And His Struggle Against The Eunochs*.

Harrison took a personal interest in each artist. Both of their debut albums were recorded at F.P.S.H.O.T., Harrison's home studio. Harrison also produced and played on sessions. Harrison even recorded a special interview album (his only Dark Horse album to be released under the A&M contract) to promote the label and the releases of Shankar and Splinter. Harrison was interviewed for the promo disc by Chuck Cassell. Songs by Shankar and Splinter were included on the disc.

The hard work and promotion appeared to pay off when *Shankar Family & Friends* and Splinter's *The Place I Love* both entered *Billboard's* album chart, and Splinter's single, "Costafine Town," entered the singles chart. But that success was short-lived. Of 10 other singles released, only one, "Sweet Summer Music," by Attitudes, made the charts. Two other singles, "From Us To You" and "Tell Me Why," both by The Stairsteps, did appear on *Billboard's* Bubbling Under chart. No other A&M-distributed albums or singles made a chart appearance.

The biggest hope for the Dark Horse label seemed to be a record by George Harrison. But his contract with EMI didn't expire until early 1976. A&M had hoped to release Harrison's first Dark Horse album, *Thirty-Three And 1/3* on his 33 1/3 birthday, July 26, 1976. However, Harrison had a bout with hepatitis and was unable to complete the album on time. A&M saw this as the perfect opportunity to get out of its contract with Dark Horse. The label's performance had been less than spectacular, and A&M couldn't see any value in continuing to

This article originally appeared in** Goldmine **issue #209, July 29, 1988.

release and promote new material. A&M sued Harrison. Harrison sued A&M. The suits were quickly settled out of court with both parties agreeing to end the contract.

With an ex-Beatle involved, getting a new distribution deal was easy. Dark Horse was soon signed to Warner Brothers. Part of the deal with Warner Brothers called for all of the A&M Dark Horse albums and singles to be taken out of print, thus making them instant collector's items. Less than four months after the last A&M release, Warner Brothers released Harrison's single, "This Song," and the album, *Thirty-Three And 1/3*.

During its first two years with Warner Brothers, Dark Horse issued albums and singles by Attitudes, Keni Burke, and Splinter. None of the material charted. From 1979 through the present, Harrison has been the only Dark Horse artist. His chart success, although sometimes disappointing, has more than made up for the lack of success of the other artists.

Not including Harrison, seven artists have recorded for Dark Horse. The group Attitudes released two albums and five singles for the label in the United States. Attitudes consisted of Jim Kellner (drums), Paul Stallworth (bass), Danny "Kootch" Kortchmar (guitar), and David Foster (keyboards). All had been top session musicians before forming the group. Keltner had often done work for Harrison and Starr. Except for "Drink My Water" and "Foster's Frees," all of the songs on both of their Dark Horse albums were published by Harrison's Ganga Publishing, B.V. Ringo Starr played drums on "Good News," a single from their second album of the same name. Attitudes'

George Harrison during the filming of *The Magical Mystery Tour.*

The first artist signed to the fledgling Dark Horse label was Ravi Shankar. Harrison was involved in the recording of both Shankar albums as producer and musician. Despite promotional work by Harrison, *Shankar Family & Friends* only managed a three-week stay on the *Billboard* album chart, reaching only as high as #176. The single, "I Am Missing You," was a U.K. hit but failed to make the U.S. charts.

Except for Harrison himself, Splinter was the most productive of the Dark Horse artists. Three albums and six singles by the group were released in the United States. Their first album, *The Place I Love*, peaked at #81, spending 14 weeks on the chart. Their single, "Costafine Town," was on the chart eight weeks and peaked at #77. Only Harrison had albums or singles that reached higher chart positions. All three albums were recorded at F.P.S.H.O.T. with Harrison acting as producer, coproducer, and executive producer, respectively. All songs written by Splinter were published by Ganga Publishing, B.V. Harrison also played on various tracks on their first and second albums under the aliases Hari Georgeson, Jai Raj Harisein, and P. Roducer.

The Five Stairsteps, a group made up of the Burke siblings, Alohe, Dennis. Clarence Jr., James, and Kenny, had been hitting the charts since 1966. In 1970, their version of the John Lennon/Paul McCartney song "Dear Prudence" made the pop and soul charts. After Alohe left the group, the "five" was dropped from their name and they were signed to Dark Horse. Although their album failed to make the charts, their two singles did "bubble under" for several weeks. Billy Preston played the T.O.N.T.O. keyboard system on their album.

"Sweet Summer Music" was a small hit (six weeks on the chart, peaking at #94) when it was first released in 1976.

Keni Burke, who had also recorded for Dark Horse as a member of The Stairsteps, recorded one album and two singles for the label. Harrison had no personal involvement in the project.

The first American group to sign with Dark Horse was Jiva. The members of the group were Michael Lanning (guitar, lead vocals), James Strauss (bass), Thomas Hilton (guitar), and Michael Reed (drums). The group's single, "Something Goin' On Inside L.A.," was very Beatles-esque and even mentioned Ringo and his hit, "Only You." Although Harrison was not involved with Jiva's album, his friend Gary Wright did the keyboard work for them.

Henry McCullough, a former member of Paul McCartney's band Wings, recorded just one album for Dark Horse. There was no Harrison involvement.

Despite a valiant attempt at promoting new talent, Dark Horse's top artist has always been Harrison. All five of his albums have charted, including *Cloud Nine*, which went to #1. Of his 11 singles, seven have made the charts, including the #1 hit "Got My Mind Set On You." (Note: As of this writing, "This Is Love," Harrison's latest single, has not entered the charts, although it is likely to do so.) If you judge a label's success by the number of hits it has, then Dark Horse must be a success. If you judge a label by its longevity, then Dark Horse has been a success. Dark Horse has outlasted hundreds of labels, including Apple and Ringo's Ring O' Records. With Harrison's recent return to hit form, the label's future appears very bright.

All Those Years Ago

Words and Music by *GEORGE HARRISON*

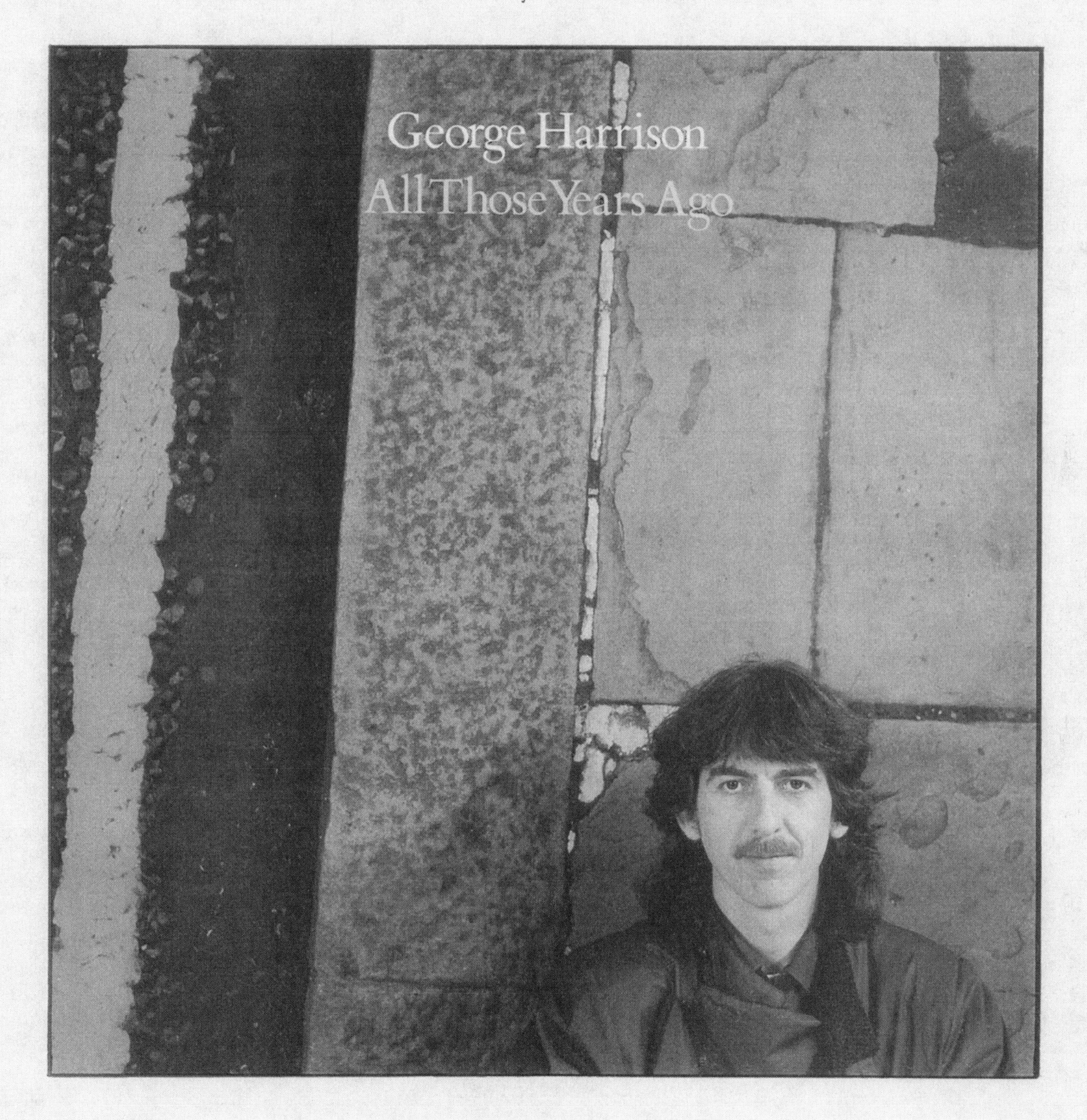

Recorded by

George Harrison

on

DARK HORSE RECORDS

Dark Horse Records Discography

by Charles Reinhart

Record #	Title	Artist	Year
Singles			
10001	I Am Missing You/Lust	Ravi Shankar	1974
10002	Costafine Town/Elly-May	Splinter	1974
10003	China Town/Haven't Got Time	Splinter	1975
10004	Ain't Love Enough/The Whole World's Crazy	Attitudes	1975
10005	From Us To You/Time	Stairsteps	1975
10006	Something Goin' On Inside L.A./Take My Love	Jiva	1976
10007	Which Way Will I Get Home/ What Is It	Splinter	1976
10008	Honey Don't Leave L.A./Lend A Hand	Attitudes	1976
10009	Tell Me Why/Salaam	Stairsteps	1976
10010	After Five Years/Halfway There	Splinter	1976
10011	Sweet Summer Music/If We Want To	Attitudes	1976
8294	This Song/Learning How To Love You	G. Harrison	1976
8313	Crackerbox Palace/Learning How To Love You	G. Harrison	1977
8404	Sweet Summer Music/Being Here With You	Attitudes	1977
8452	In A Stranger's Arms/Good News	Attitudes	1977
8439	Round And Round/ I'll Bend For You	Splinter	1977
8474	Shuffle/From Me To You	Keni Burke	1977
8522	Keep On Singing/Day	Keni Burke	1978
8523	Motions Of Love/I Need Your Love	Splinter	1978
8763	Blow Away/Soft-Hearted Hana	G. Harrison	1979
8844	Love Comes to Everyone/Soft Touch	G. Harrison	1979
49725	All Those Years Ago/Writing's On The Wall	G. Harrison	1981
49785	Teardrops/Save The World	G. Harrison	1981
0410	All Those Years Ago/Teardrops *(reissue)*	G. Harrison	1981
29864	Wake Up My Love/Greece	G. Harrison	1982
29744	I Really Love You/Circles	G. Harrison	1983
28178	Got My Mind Set On You/Lay His Head	G. Harrison	1987
28131	When We Was Fab/Zig Zag	G. Harrison	1988
27913	This Is Love/Breath Away From Heaven	G. Harrison	1988
Albums			
22001	The Place I Love	Splinter	1974
22002	Shankar Family & Friends	Ravi Shankar	1974
22003	Jiva	Jiva	1975
22004	2nd Resurrection	Stairsteps	1976
22005	Mind Your Own Business	Henry McCullough	1975
22006	Harder To Live	Splinter	1975
22007	Music Festival In India	Ravi Shankar	1976
22008	Attitudes	Attitudes	1976
3005	Thirty-Three And 1/3	G. Harrison	1976
3021	Good News	Attitudes	1977
3022	Keni Burke	Keni Burke	1977
3023	Two Man Band	Splinter	1977
3255	George Harrison	G. Harrison	1979
3492	Somewhere In England	G. Harrison	1981
1-23734	Gone Troppo	G. Harrison	1982
9 25643	Cloud Nine	G. Harrison	1987
Special Items			
9 25643-2	Cloud Nine *(CD)*	G. Harrison	1987
9 25643-2	Cloud Nine *(promo; G. Harrison silhouette silk-screened on CD)*	G. Harrison	1987
928178-4	Got My Mind Set On You/Lay His Head *(cassette single)*	G. Harrison	1987
928131-4	When We Was Fab/Zig Zag *(cassette single)*	G. Harrison	1988
PRO-CD-2846	Got My Mind On You *(promo CD single)*	G. Harrison	1987
PRO-CD-2924	Cloud Nine *(promo CD single)*	G. Harrison	1988
PRO-CD-3068	This Is Love *(promo CD single)*	G. Harrison	1988
PRO-A-949	All Those Years Ago *(promo 12-inch single)*	G. Harrison	1981
PRO-A-1075	Wake Up My Love *(promo 12-inch single)*	G. Harrison	1982
PRO-A-2845	Got My Mind Set On You *(promo 12-inch single)*	G. Harrison	1987
PRO-A-2885	When We Was Fab *(promo 12-inch single)*	G. Harrison	1988

John Lennon (1940-1980)

by Rick Whitesell

Often it takes a great shock to jar us into reflection, into stopping long enough to take stock of what is really happening around us in the world. On Dec. 8, 1980, a lot of us were certainly shocked and depressed to learn that John Lennon had been gunned down in front of the Dakota Hotel in New York City. And while the media sought to wrench every emotion (and dollar, of course) from us — with special programming, tributes, magazines, buttons, etc. — it seems that the public was not sidetracked from the main issue here.

The point of the Lennon murder, if a "point" can be derived from an act of such senselessness, is that no matter how talented, charismatic or legendary an artist becomes in the music field, they're still human. There is nothing wrong with admiring an artist's talents, but there is something wrong when an artist is forced to live the life of a prisoner, as Elvis Presley was; or when an artist's attempt to live a normal, above-ground existence is rewarded with death, as in John Lennon's case. One reason fans took Lennon's murder so badly was that everyone knew where he lived, and there was always a small pack of devoted followers waiting for him to come or go from the Dakota, and yet Lennon was the sort of gentleman who always displayed infinite patience with his fans, signing autographs and shaking hands.

Lennon's death made me think hard about what we, who write about music and musicians, are about. John Lennon, to be sure, ushered in a new era when he and The Beatles began giving interviews during the '60s; today, it is common practice for a publication like *Rolling Stone* to print every new "star's" outlook on social and political subjects (and the lesson learned from reading some of those interviews is that an artist can make fantastic music and not be qualified in the least to address any issue intelligently!). Certainly, one reason for this is that when reporters asked John Lennon's opinion on virtually any subject, his responses were intelligent, frequently witty, and well-worth hearing. But instead of letting the constant media attention go to his head, Lennon often expressed himself in ways that indicated his concern with the conditions that had elevated four boys from Liverpool to a pedestal from which they swayed a society with even the most insignificant gesture or action. The controversial statement Lennon made about The Beatles being more popular than Christ offended many, but who could deny that the machinery of our communications media put The Beatles under a brighter spotlight than any other figure or group before them?

I'm not sure The Beatles loved the attentive adulation. Many people saw Paul McCartney interviewed the day after Lennon's death, and when he appeared to be detached and

This article originally appeared in Goldmine issue #57, February 1981.

off-handed in this comments, they were quick to condemn his "insensitivity" to the tragedy. Few looked beyond what they saw on their television screens, though, to note the insensitivity of the media. Is it terribly humane to subject a human being to a wall of jabbing microphones and impersonal interrogators under any circumstances? Should Paul McCartney be expected to bare his most personal feelings to us, simply because some fans feel their love for an artist gives them the right to pry?

How did it happen, I hope this suffering was small
Tell me every detail, I've got to know it all.

Phil Ochs' line from "Crucifixion" seems particularly appropriate in the wake of Lennon's death.

One of the most unsettling and macabre sidelights of Lennon's murder was that his alleged killer, Mark Chapman, seems by all accounts to have been a fan of The Beatles, and particularly Lennon. It seems that Lennon's assassin found more excitement in Lennon's life than his own; while this may be true of many fans, who look for what they lack in the lives of their idols, it seems that one man's obsession went over the edge of sanity.

John Lennon's death made me look at myself, as big a "fan" of music and artists as can be found. If I didn't love doing it, I certainly would do something other than editing *Goldmine* and writing sporadically for other publications; as all *Goldmine* staff writers know all too well, great fortunes will not be made by most of us in this field. But there is something about music that makes us want to spread the word, share our enthusiasms with others.

For me, there is little I enjoy more than listening to Sam Cooke sing or seeing Bruce Springsteen perform on stage or discovering a hot aircheck of Alan Freed beating the pulp out of a phone book during a Roy Milton record. These are just my individual preferences; everyone reading this has their own, undoubtedly. And for all of us, there are probably a few artists that we've followed and listened to so long that we feel we "know" them... or when we meet them and perhaps shake their hands or get their autographs, it makes us feel great for a week.

But — whether a musician is a former star whose hits stopped coming years ago, or whether he or she is at their peak — no one should forget for a moment that they're just people, doing their job and trying to keep on keepin' on... like all the rest of us. After Lennon's death, I read over back issues of *Goldmine*; I guess I was a bit afraid that maybe I'd find that this magazine was just another, albeit smaller than most, insensitive periodical that exploited others' creative skills for profit.

Fortunately, I can objectively say that my considered opinion is that we've successfully aspired to do something more than that. Our interviews and stories cover virtually every kind of popular, rock-related musical style imaginable, but the coverage is bound together by the fact that our writers really have enthusiasm for their subjects. More important, I noted that our writers approach their writing with a scholarly attitude oriented toward chronicling pop music history; yet, they have consistently done so with a sense of humor — and more important, some compassion for the people interviewed for these stories. And when our writers shove microphones under someone's nose, the line of questioning doesn't extend past music. While we're thorough in our search for accuracy and truth, *Goldmine* has never invaded someone's privacy to give readers a vicarious thrill or two. What's more, I don't think our readership is looking for that.

Over the years, I've met or written people whose main collecting interest, and personal passion, was the music and memorabilia of The Beatles. As a group and as individuals, The Beatles' impact was profound on a whole generation, myself included; but for the serious fans, the tragedy of John Lennon's death has hit much harder and deeper. To those readers, I express my sympathy; more than one person has told me that this event was equivalent to the loss of a close family member, and when one considers the degree to which some of us grew up with The Beatles providing a sort of "soundtrack," that makes perfect sense.

But I have no sympathies for the off-center individuals who have gained appreciably through the exploitation of John Lennon (or Elvis Presley, or any other artist, for that matter) — when that exploitation takes on the ghoulish insensitivity exemplified by *The New York Post* cover photo of John Lennon lying face-up in his coffin. Frankly, I felt nauseous to watch certain parts of the media exploit Lennon in death as they'd done in life, as if to them there were no real difference. I did note that the public was having less tolerance for those who would turn sincere emotions into sheer profit and can only hope the trend continues.

After John Lennon died, many people asked me what *Goldmine* would do in reaction. And aside from this unusually long editorial, I've lived up to my reply: nothing special. We really don't have to; throughout our existence, John Lennon's name cropped up constantly in both the editorial and advertising sections of *Goldmine* — commensurate, I'd say, with his greatness as an artist. And that will certainly continue to be the case, as new listeners become aware of his music as a solo artist and as a Beatle, perhaps for the first time.

For the majority of us who read and write *Goldmine* each month, John Lennon provided us with many hours of enjoyment in the years he created music. There just doesn't seem to be any point to dwelling on the fact that, because of a senseless act, that creative mind has been silenced.

John Lennon remembered

Goldmine readers were asked to submit their memories of what they were doing and feeling the night John Lennon was murdered 20 years ago. We appreciate all who sent us letters and regret that space did not allow all of them to be reprinted here.

On Dec. 8, 1980, I spent much of the evening doing some early (for me) Christmas shopping. I was in a great mood. I had just had a great time shopping with some good friends, it was the holiday season, and of course John Lennon had just released *Double Fantasy*, his first new album in five years.

The Beatles, both as a group and as individuals, had been a big part of my life ever since that fateful night nearly 17 years earlier when my life was changed by a certain telecast of *The Ed Sullivan Show* on Feb. 9, 1964. I had all the records, read most of the books and magazine articles and spent much time thinking about and discussing those Four lads from Liverpool.

When I got home that night, I listened to the first side of Jackson Browne's *Hold Out* album, which was one of my favorites at the time. At the end of side one, I flipped my amplifier's selection switch from "Phone" to "Tuner." It was at that moment that I got one of the great shocks of my life. The announcer on one of my favorite rock stations said, "John Lennon has been shot. We don't know much more about it than that, but John Lennon has been shot and is apparently dead."

I froze. I remember exactly where I was standing in my bedroom and what went through my mind at that moment. John Lennon DEAD? It was impossible. And from a gunshot? That didn't make sense either. Rock stars died from drug overdoses or alcohol problems. They didn't get shot. And on top of that, this was one of the BEATLES: Who would want to shoot a Beatle? None of this made any sense. But as the evening wore on and my radio supplied the horrible details as they became available, the sad reality set in. John Lennon was dead. It was a night I'll never forget.

It's been nearly 17 years since that tragic night. It seems strange, but as much time has passed since John's death as had passed between that first time I saw him on *The Ed Sullivan Show* and the night he died. It doesn't seem like it.

The last 17 years have seen many changes in the world. One of the most amazing is the surviving three Beatles putting aside their differences to give us the fantastic wealth of audio and video material known as *The Anthology*. There were even two new songs that Paul, George, and Ringo helped John to posthumously finish, giving the world the first new Beatles songs in more than 25 years. Sad to say, the life of John Lennon was prematurely cut short on that December night in 1980. But he lives on through the legacy of his music, a great gift to be enjoyed forever.

— *Michael Rinella*
Peoria, Ill.

This article originally appeared in Goldmine issue #451, Nov. 7, 1997.

I remember how I learned about John Lennon's death, a very unpleasant memory. Since I started work very early, I would go to bed by 10 p.m. The next morning I did what I always did, turn the radio on as I was getting ready for work. In hushed tones I heard two announcers talking (it was WMCA-AM in New York), one of whom said something like, "Did he come to New York to kill him?" to which the reply was, "We don't know yet."

It sounded bad. My first thought was that something terrible had happened to Mayor Koch. But about a minute later I found out. Driving into work I was stunned with disbelief. It was one of the most difficult days I've ever had.

— *Gary Wilbur*
New Hyde Park, N.Y.

I heard about John Lennon's death at 1 in the morning on my car radio. Having gone to bed early on the night of Dec. 8, I hadn't heard any news. As I began my nightly routine as a carrier for the *Arkansas Democrat*, I switched on the radio to get a little night music, only to hear the shocking news that former Beatle John Lennon was shot to death in New York City.

I couldn't think; I couldn't breathe. I had to talk to someone. The nearest pay phone was in the tiny town of Thornton. I woke my wife, Pam, from a sound sleep, although she didn't complain. She too was a Beatles fan and couldn't believe the news.

After a while, I knew I had to regain my composure and finish my route. My '75 Comet had only AM radio, and I spent the rest of the night feverishly spinning the dial as I drove, trying to get every scrap of information I could. John's *Imagine* album had helped me get through a lonely time as a college freshman in 1972, and every time I heard the song "Imagine" that night, I felt as if an important part of my past had withered and died.

At home the next morning, I continued my scramble for knowledge of what had happened, switching from *Good Morning America* to *Today* and back again, trying to understand it all. I had John's single, "(Just Like) Starting Over," but "hadn't gotten around" to buying *Double Fantasy*. I asked Pam to get it for me. She found it at the local Wal-Mart. It was the last copy. I suppose the after-death buying frenzy had begun.

Perhaps death is not necessarily all-conquering. I think John, wherever he is, appreciates that his former bandmates paid tribute to him with two new Beatles songs. The four of them are still together, in a sense, and always will be. In that same mode, John Winston Lennon will be with the rest of us forever.

— *Dale Waldrop*
Fordyce, Ark.

I first heard about the shooting of a man "identified as former Beatle John Lennon" on a *Sports Update* program airing at the time on a local television station in New York. This short, two-minute or so program aired nightly at 11:30 p.m. right after syndicated reruns of *M*A*S*H*. The sportscaster had no further information.

I immediately turned to *Monday Night Football* and heard Howard Cosell report the horrifying news that it was indeed John Lennon who was shot and that he was "dead on arrival." So what? you might say. Millions of people found out about the tragedy via the dramatic mouth of Mr. Cosell. Well, let me introduce two interesting wrinkles into the picture. At the time I was writing for and editing a local entertainment magazine. And as a music critic, I was sent many records by the record companies to review. In mid-to-late November, I received the "(Just Like) Starting Over"/"Kiss Kiss Kiss" 12-inch plus the *Double Fantasy* LP.

I had immediately listened to the 12-inch, but I kept putting off John and Yoko's new album in lieu of stuff I had in my possession longer — an unfortunate habit that has grown out-of-control over the years since my wife and I started to have kids. In a sense, I was "saving" *Double Fantasy* — John's recorded comeback after five long years — for the "perfect time."

Thus, I never listened to the album until after John was killed. And I've never forgiven myself for this and am extremely jealous of people who had the foresight (?) to put the damn thing on the turntable as soon as it came out.

What this all means is I never had the opportunity to hear these new songs in the context they were originally meant to be heard, e.g., "Beautiful Boy (Darling Boy)" ("I can hardly wait to see you come of age" and "Life is what happens to you while you're busy making other plans"); "I'm Losing You" ("So what the hell am I supposed to do?, just put a Band-Aid® on it?, and stop the bleeding now"); "Cleanup Time" ("The gods are in the heavens, the angels treat us well, the oracle has spoken, we cast the perfect spell"); "Hard Times Are Over" ("It's been very rough, but it's getting easier now, hard times are over, over for a while"); etc. etc. etc.

The other ironic thing about this whole mess was that I was, at the time, in the midst of writing a long monthly series for the magazine on the music of The Beatles and the solo Beatles. After doing a nine-part series on The Beatles as a group, I then dove into a multi-part series on the music of John, Paul, George, & Ringo. After dealing with first Ringo, then George, then Paul, I saved John for last since I had always felt his solo material was the most impressive. After dealing with his early experimental work with Yoko as well as the *Live Peace In Toronto 1969* LP in a chapter or two, my segment on *The Plastic Ono Band* album hit the streets on Dec. 3, 1980.

The sad thing about all this was that I wrote each part of the entire Beatles/solo Beatles series month-to-month, like a serial, so after Dec. 8 I now had to write the rest of the John Lennon portion — eight or nine more parts — knowing John had died. It certainly affected my point of view, though I tried not to let it alter my critical thinking.

— *Martin E. Horn*
South Plainfield, N.J.

I was a 25-year-old apprentice electrician working the midnight shift at the old Pontiac Motor Division complex in Pontiac, Mich., on Dec. 8, 1980. This is the place that made GTOs during The Beatles' tenure from 1964 through 1970.

My shift in the trade school started at 10:30 p.m. and was totally uneventful for the first two hours. Sometime after midnight my friend Gary came walking in and said, "Did you hear John Lennon has been shot?" Knowing that Gary was a practical joker, I blurted out, "Bullshit!!!" Gary stared at me without a smile and replied: "I'm not kidding you, man. They say he's dead!"

I ran to the nearest radio and the instant I turned it on, the announcement of John's death was heard. I had a lot of quiet nights working the midnight shift back then, but that night was the quietest of them all. We were all in our 20s and it hit us like a ton of bricks because we had grown up with The Beatles.

When Keith Moon died in '78 and John Bonham died in early '80, I would morbidly joke that drummers have to die in threes, meaning that Ringo or Charlie Watts would be the next to die. I had no idea that by the end of 1980, one of The Beatles would actually leave us.

— *Carl Johnson*
Lake Orion, Mich.

Yesterday and today

The Beatles' butchered cassettes

by Mark Wallgren

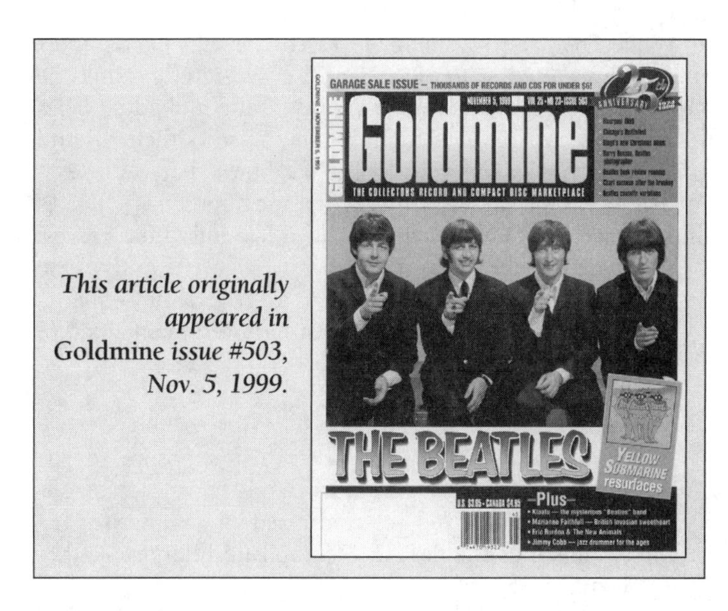

This article originally appeared in Goldmine issue #503, Nov. 5, 1999.

For Beatles fans not readily familiar with the cassette versions of the group's albums, the initial encounter often proves rather alarming. The official cassette version of nearly every Beatles album differs quite substantially in its song sequencing when compared against the playing order of the original vinyl LP and currently available compact disc of the same title.

Closer inspection of The Beatles' cassette catalog reveals that severe alterations in album sequencing have occurred on both sides of the Atlantic ever since the group's catalog first began appearing on cassette tape in the late '60s. In fact, of The Beatles' 12 formal British studio albums, only one, *Sgt. Pepper's Lonely Hearts Club Band*, accurately corresponds on cassette with the song lineup of the original LP.

The original British albums

As far as The Beatles have always been concerned, the British albums represented the official manner in which these recordings were intended to be listened to. Of course, most fans realize that outside of Great Britain, seldom were the group's recorded works presented in the form intended. From the moment Beatlemania exploded throughout the world in 1964, the chief concern of manager Brian Epstein and EMI Records focused on maximizing profits. This attitude quickly surpassed the group's own hope of maintaining any serious degree of artistic control over the manner in which the majority of their recordings were released around the world. As a result, album titles, cover art, song selection and sequencing was for the most part left up to EMI executives in each territory — a move that left an untold number of worldwide Beatles album variations in its wake.

The American albums

Nowhere was this policy practiced to a greater degree than in the U.S., where Capitol Records gave The Beatles' album catalog a complete overhaul. This process artificially increased the total number of available Beatles LPs for the American market (e.g. typically, the U.K. albums contained 13 or 14 tracks each, whereas Capitol usually restricted the number of songs per album to 11, thereby allowing the label to stretch the contents of the first seven British LPs into no less than 11 American albums between 1964 and 1966.)

Although it was not uncommon during this period for The Beatles themselves to take occasional verbal swipes at Capitol's "repackages" during American press conferences, interviews and even as they performed on stage, the truth is that the group and its management had actively participated in this practice from the very beginning, regularly providing Capitol with advance tapes of songs not yet released in Britain in order to meet the frenzied demand of the U.S. market. To their credit, Capitol seemed more than willing to allow "the boys" some venting of their artistic resentment over this practice, as both sides quietly slipped off to the deposit line at the bank.

The Beatles on cassette

Capitol Records had introduced the first Beatles cassettes in late 1967, two years after the label began issuing the group's albums on eight-track tapes. During the next 15 years, the two tape formats would compete for sales dominance in the world of portable prerecorded music, where the primary destination was the automobile tape player. By its very design, the eight-track tape was never regarded as the ideal means by which to seriously listen to an album.

On the other hand, the prerecorded cassette offered listeners the best hope of duplicating the album listening experience as it was originally intended. As far as fans of The Beatles were concerned, it seemed logical to assume that the two-sided cassette would be able to easily replicate the contents of the vinyl LP sans any of the mechanically dictated musical aberrations inherent to the eight-track tape format. Alas, as would be the case with their British cousins, the cassette versions of the American albums rarely duplicated the sequencing of the original LPs. Incredibly, Capitol's repackaged Beatles LPs were further repackaged for their release on cassette.

The main reason behind this move was presumably rooted in economics. When manufacturing cassettes, record companies significantly reduce their costs by keeping the overall length of the audiotape to a bare minimum. Whereas vinyl LPs are pressed on 12-inch-sized discs regardless of the amount of music contained on either side, the actual length of audiotape necessary in producing a cassette is determined solely by the longest running side of the album. Therefore, if the total running time of the two sides of the cassette can be aligned as closely as possible, there is less wasted blank tape on either side. This fractional elimination of raw tape stock translates into a fractional financial savings that takes on far greater significance when multiplied by the millions of cassettes sold each year. Unfortunately for The Beatles, the record company's desire to increase the bottom-line profit margin on the audiotapes was achieved by sacrificing the group's artistic intentions.

While The Beatles' catalog on cassette appears in an almost universally altered state of sequential confusion, it should be noted that the overwhelming majority of the individual Beatles' solo releases on cassette accurately mirrors their LP and CD counterparts. The very few solo albums that were resequenced on tape underwent only the most minor of changes and, for the most part, included only a handful of the earliest titles released, mainly during 1969 and 1970. The bulk of the ex-Beatles' tape catalog was left intact to reflect the sequencing of the original LP, a situation that has been maintained to the present day.

The British cassettes

For many fans in the U.S., their first exposure to the group's British cassettes came with the 1978 release of *The Beatles Collection*, a boxed set comprised of The Beatles' 12 studio albums plus the new U.K. compilation *Rarities*. Rather than manufacture its own tape edition of the set, Capitol heavily imported copies of the royal blue faux-leather boxed cassettes from EMI in England. At the time, LPs were handily outselling cassettes six-to-one, and sales of the vinyl set far outdistanced the tape version, leaving the vastly different album sequencing featured on the U.K. cassettes largely unnoticed. However, that situation soon changed forever with the dramatic increase in the sale of prerecorded cassettes, which occurred during the 1980s.

For many second- and third-generation Beatles fans who purchased their Beatles albums during the '80s and early '90s, they most likely did so on cassette rather than vinyl LP. According to official RIAA (Recording Industry Association Of America) figures, the cassette achieved its status as the dominate tape format in 1980, when it surpassed sales of the eight-track tape for the very first time.

Three years later, in 1983, cassettes accomplished the once-impossible feat of dethroning the venerable vinyl LP. For the nine-year period of 1983-1991, cassettes far outsold all other forms of prerecorded music (cassettes registered more than 3.3 billion units sold compared to only 937 million vinyl LPs during this run), clearly establishing itself as the format of choice for an entire generation of music buyers. In contrast, sales of the LP declined rapidly, and by 1993, the LP accounted for less than 0.3 percent of all prerecorded music sales.

The Beatles on compact disc

In 1987 Capitol Records issued The Beatles' album catalog on compact disc, consisting of the group's 12 studio albums as released in England, plus *Magical Mystery Tour*. At the same time, Capitol formally added the first seven British albums to its official U.S. Beatles vinyl and cassette catalogs. This was all part of a larger plan on behalf of Apple to bring the entire Beatles album catalog into uniformity on a worldwide basis. Not surprisingly, the release of The Beatles' music on compact disc coincided with an unprecedented growth that witnessed industry-wide sales of the CD triple in number between 1986 and 1988.

In 1989, legal settlements involving a complicated and lengthy series of lawsuits between Apple, EMI and Capitol Records were successfully achieved. One consequence of these settlements gave Apple control over all present and future Beatles recordings, including authorized reissues and previously unreleased material. It also gave Apple veto power over any Beatles compact disc product suggested by Capitol and EMI.

As the '90s began, and with vinyl no longer a serious sales factor in the U.S. marketplace, Capitol's deletion of the entire Beatles LP catalog drew little attention except among the hardcore collectors. In 1992, the CD surpassed the cassette as America's preferred choice for prerecorded music. Throughout the remainder of the decade, sales of the compact disc continually increased, while those of the cassette declined dramatically. In 1997, sales of albums on compact disc totaled more than 753 million units for the year (representing a 70 percent share of the market) while cassettes fell to their lowest annual tally since 1981, dropping to 172 million units (18 percent market share). This rapid decline in overall market share recalls the similar demise of the eight-track tape at the start of the '80s and the vinyl LP at the beginning of the '90s, and it would seem to suggest that the days of the prerecorded music cassette appear to be numbered.

Tomorrow never knows

One month prior to the release of *The Beatles Anthology* in the fall of 1995, Capitol Records announced that it would no longer accept orders for the American Beatles albums on cassette. These cassette titles had remained in print even beyond the deletion of their vinyl counterparts. In the aftermath, only one American-compiled tape was allowed to remain in the active catalog, *The Beatles — 20 Greatest Hits* (today, this tape stands as the only U.S. Beatles album presently available on cassette but not on compact disc).

With the deletion of the American Beatles cassettes complete, Apple had at long last brought the group's official catalog into line on both sides of the Atlantic, although given Apple's degree of concern and attention to the matter, it is extremely difficult to comprehend why on earth the group's official catalog of cassettes is allowed to remain in print with track sequencing that in no way reflects that of the original albums. Not even the digital remastering of the entire catalog in 1987 (for release on compact disc) resulted in any realignment of the pre–*Sgt. Pepper* cassettes, neither among any of the post–*Magical Mystery Tour* titles.

Today, more than 10 years after The Beatles' album catalog first appeared on compact disc, the group's cassettes remain in the same severely altered state. Given the tremendous popularity of the cassette during this period, it is quite disturbing to consider the possible number of fans who may be completely unaware that the sequencing on their tapes does not match that of the original albums.

It would certainly be interesting to learn whether or not the individual Beatles are aware of these discrepancies and what their reactions might be. Given the group's considerable degree of involvement with every phase of the recent *Anthology* project, it is obvious that the surviving members hold their recorded legacy in extremely high esteem, not the least of which concerned the final track selection and sequencing of the three *Anthology* albums. In fact, their personal involvement led to at least one very well-publicized event surrounding the *Anthology 2* album.

Production of *Anthology 2* was already underway in early 1996 when Paul McCartney voiced serious second-thoughts concerning the previously approved sequencing of disc one of the two-CD set. McCartney reportedly felt so strongly about bringing "I'm Down" forward in the lineup (from the sixth track position to the third) that he personally insisted to EMI that the lineup had to be revised before the album could be released. This seemingly minor change of musical heart eventually cost McCartney more than $1 million, a sum he was forced to forfeit from his personal share of the group's royalties in order to cover the added production expenses incurred by EMI, which reportedly scrapped two and a half million CD booklets already printed with the original track listing.

Thirty years after the first Beatles cassettes were introduced, the cassette tape itself may not survive as a viable music format into the new millennium. If it does, however, Apple should consider bringing The Beatles' cassettes into sequential harmony with the group's compact discs, a decision that would finally allow listeners of the audiotapes the opportunity to share in the magic of The Beatles' music as it was originally meant to be experienced.

How the cassettes compare, track by track

by Mark Wallgren

The following tables provide a track-by-track comparison in the sequencing of the original vinyl LP (and currently available CD) and cassette tape of the group's official album catalog. Differences between U.S. and U.K. cassettes of the same title are also noted. Prefixes and catalog numbers are provided for both the original and more recent tape designations. All tapes listed are the U.S. editions issued by Capitol Records unless otherwise noted.

***Please Please Me* (Capitol-Parlophone C4J-46435)**

Few true Beatles fans are likely to be very pleased the first time they endure this cassette. In short, the commercially released tape is a radically jumbled-up mess bearing little resemblance to the original track lineup of the LP (and current compact disc) with no less than 12 of the album's 14 songs appearing in a dramatically altered playing order. The massive swapping of tracks reduced the imbalance between the LP sides from a minute and a half down to four seconds, but at what price was this profit-minded feat achieved in genuine artistic terms?

Original LP/Compact Disc	Capitol-Parlophone Cassette
Side one (17:09)	**Side one (16:25)**
1. I Saw Her Standing There	1. Misery
2. Misery	2. Chains
3. Anna (Go To Him)	3. P.S. I Love You
4. Chains	4. Do You Want To Know A Secret?
5. Boys	5. I Saw Her Standing There
6. Ask Me Why	6. Ask Me Why
7. Please Please Me	7. Baby It's You
Side two (15:37)	**Side two (16:21)**
1. Love Me Do	1. Please Please Me
2. P.S. I Love You	2. Love Me Do
3. Baby It's You	3. A Taste Of Honey
4. Do You Want To Know A Secret?	4. There's A Place
5. A Taste Of Honey	5. Anna (Go To Him)
6. There's A Place	6. Boys
7. Twist And Shout	7. Twist And Shout

***With The Beatles* (Capitol-Parlophone C4J-46436)**

With a difference of just over two minutes in the length of the original LP sides, EMI's tape wizards once again relied heavily upon their calculators to reduce the running time on each side of the reconstructed cassette to close within 10 seconds of one another. To achieve this, the LP's first two songs were moved to the start of side two on the tape, while the remainder of the tracks were so severely rearranged that the cassette bears virtually no relationship to the sequencing of the original album.

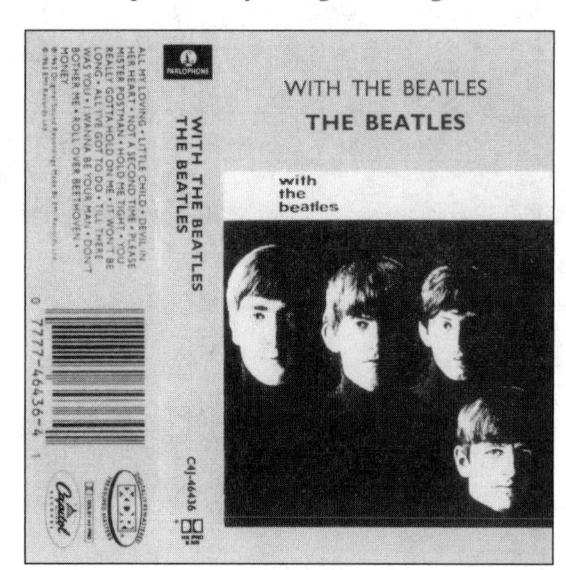

Original LP/Compact Disc	Capitol-Parlophone Cassette
Side one (15:39)	**Side one (16:47)**
1. It Won't Be Long	1. All My Loving
2. All I've Got To Do	2. Little Child
3. All My Loving	3. Devil In Her Heart
4. Don't Bother Me	4. Not A Second Time
5. Little Child	5. Please Mister Postman
6. Till There Was You	6. Hold Me Tight
7. Please Mr. Postman	7. You Really Gotta Hold On Me

Side two (17:45)	Side two (16:37)
1. Roll Over Beethoven	1. It Won't Be Long
2. Hold Me Tight	2. All I've Got To Do
3. You Really Gotta Hold On Me	3. Till There Was You
4. I Wanna Be Your Man	4. I Wanna Be Your Man
5. Devil In Her Heart	5. Don't Bother Me
6. Not A Second Time	6. Roll Over Beethoven
7. Money (That's What I Want)	7. Money

A Hard Day's Night (Capitol-Parlophone C4J-46437)

When The Beatles and producer George Martin originally sequenced the group's first soundtrack album, it was decided that the soundtrack tunes would comprise side one (the label on side one of the LP included the subtitle *Songs From The Film* A Hard Day's Night), while the non-soundtrack numbers would appear on side two. Not only does the cassette randomly intersperse soundtrack tunes with non-soundtrack selections, but even the album's distinctive opening title track (featuring George Harrison's legendary opening 12-string guitar chord) was relocated to the beginning of side two on the tape. In the end, only two of the album's 13 numbers remain in their original slots on the cassette.

Original LP/Compact Disc	Capitol-Parlophone Cassette
Side one (16:33)	**Side one (15:35)**
1. A Hard Day's Night	1. I Should Have Known Better
2. I Should Have Known Better	2. When I Get Home
3. If I Fell	3. I'll Be Back
4. I'm Happy Just To Dance With You	4. I'm Happy Just To Dance With You
5. And I Love Her	5. Tell Me Why
6. Tell Me Why	6. Any Time At All
7. Can't Buy Me Love	7. I'll Cry Instead
Side two (13:57)	**Side two (14:55)**
1. Any Time At All	1. A Hard Day's Night
2. I'll Cry Instead	2. Can't Buy Me Love
3. Things We Said Today	3. Things We Said Today
4. When I Get Home	4. If I Fell
5. You Can't Do That	5. And I Love Her
6. I'll Be Back	6. You Can't Do That

Beatles For Sale (Capitol-Parlophone C4J-46438)

Of the group's first seven albums, this is the only cassette wherein the opening number matches that found on the original LP. Otherwise almost every remaining track on the album has been resequenced in an effort to trim the difference in playing time between the sides from 1:05 down to just 13 seconds on the cassette. Rumor has it that the person at EMI responsible for the sequencing of The Beatles' cassettes is also credited with having invented the shuffle-play mode featured on many of today's compact disc players.

Original LP/Compact Disc	Capitol-Parlophone Cassette
Side one (16:34)	**Side one (17:13)**
1. No Reply	1. No Reply
2. I'm A Loser	2. Baby's In Black
3. Baby's In Black	3. Eight Days A Week
4. Rock And Roll Music	4. I Don't Want To Spoil The Party
5. I'll Follow The Sun	5. I'll Follow The Sun
6. Mr. Moonlight	6. What You're Doing
7. Kansas City/Hey Hey Hey	7. Honey Don't
Side two (17:39)	**Side two (17:00)**
1. Eight Days A Week	1. I'm A Loser
2. Words Of Love	2. Everybody's Trying To Be My Baby
3. Honey Don't	3. Rock And Roll Music
4. Every Little Thing	4. Mr. Moonlight
5. I Don't Want To Spoil The Party	5. Words Of Love
6. What You're Doing	6. Kansas City/Hey Hey Hey
7. Everybody's Trying To Be My Baby	7. Every Little Thing

Help! (Capitol-Parlophone C4J-46439)

As with the group's prior soundtrack release, it was the desire of The Beatles and producer George Martin to place all numbers from the film on the first side of the album, with the non-movie songs comprising side two. When it came time for EMI to prepare the cassette version of this album, it is difficult to understand why any changes were even deemed necessary. To begin with, there was only a 23-second difference in the playing time of the two LP sides. Even after a massive readjustment of the entire running order, EMI was only able to trim an additional eight seconds. Only the album's closing number remained undisturbed on the cassette, although the LP and tape departments could not seem to agree on the spelling of its title.

Original LP/Compact Disc	Capitol-Parlophone Cassette
Side one (17:22)	**Side one (17:18)**
1. Help!	1. I Need You
2. The Night Before	2. Another Girl
3. You've Got To Hide Your Love Away	3. I've Just Seen A Face
4. I Need You	4. Yesterday
5. Another Girl	5. The Night Before
6. You're Going To Lose That Girl	6. Ticket To Ride
7. Ticket To Ride	7. Act Naturally
Side two (16:59)	**Side two (17:03)**
1. Act Naturally	1. Help!
2. It's Only Love	2. You've Got To Hide Your Love Away
3. You Like Me Too Much	3. It's Only Love
4. I've Just Seen A Face	4. You Like Me Too Much
5. Yesterday	5. Tell Me What You See
6. Dizzy Miss Lizzy	6. Dizzy Miss Lizzie

Rubber Soul (Capitol-Parlophone C4J-46440)

Hailed by many rock critics as a remarkable step beyond the usual collection of hit singles that typically comprised most popular rock 'n' roll albums of its day, *Rubber Soul* has gained a far greater degree of respect with the passage of time. Unfortunately, those sentiments fell by the wayside when EMI prepared the cassette version of this album. Reducing the difference in the length of the two sides from 1:08 to a more profitable eight seconds clearly outweighed any of the group's artistic aspirations. Meanwhile, through the first six British-based Beatles cassettes, a pattern had emerged, wherein the first track of the LP was almost always moved to the beginning of side two on the tape, while the last song on the album was allowed to remain in place.

Original LP/Compact Disc	Capitol-Parlophone Cassette
Side one (18:28)	**Side one (17:58)**
1. Drive My Car	1. Norwegian Wood (This Bird Has Flown)
2. Norwegian Wood (This Bird Has Flown)	2. You Won't See Me
3. You Won't See Me	3. Think For Yourself
4. Nowhere Man	4. I'm Looking Through You
5. Think For Yourself	5. Nowhere Man
6. The Word	6. Michelle
7. Michelle	7. Wait
Side two (17:20)	**Side two (17:50)**
1. What Goes On	1. Drive My Car
2. Girl	2. If I Needed Someone
3. I'm Looking Through You	3. What Goes On
4. In My Life	4. Girl
5. Wait	5. In My Life
6. If I Needed Someone	6. The Word
7. Run For Your Life	7. Run For Your Life

Revolver **(Capitol-Parlophone C4J-46441)**

Perhaps no other original British Beatles album suffers as much from EMI's rearrangement on cassette as does *Revolver*. Considered by many fans and critics alike to be one of The Beatles' finest releases (many consider it the group's absolute best) the cassette version of the album is almost unrecognizable compared to the original vinyl pressing or compact disc. This time out, EMI reversed its previous trend by transferring the first song from side two of the LP over to side one, where it now opens the tape. Meanwhile, the album's original leadoff track was buried deep within the first side of the cassette. Incredibly, side two of the tape was resequenced so as to begin with no less than four McCartney numbers in a row, despite the fact that there aren't even two McCartney lead vocals presented back-to-back anywhere on the original LP! For those keeping score, the original playing time difference of the two LP sides was reduced from 2:07 down to 25 seconds, no doubt earning someone at EMI the title of Member Of The Order Of The British Empire (MBE) along the way.

Original LP/Compact Disc	Capitol-Parlophone Cassette
Side one (18:33)	**Side one (17:17)**
1. Taxman	1. Good Day Sunshine
2. Eleanor Rigby	2. And Your Bird Can Sing
3. I'm Only Sleeping	3. Doctor Robert
4. Love You To	4. I Want To Tell You
5. Here, There And Everywhere	5. Taxman
6. Yellow Submarine	6. I'm Only Sleeping
7. She Said, She Said	7. Yellow Submarine
Side two (16:26)	**Side two (17:42)**
1. Good Day Sunshine	1. Eleanor Rigby
2. And Your Bird Can Sing	2. Here, There And Everywhere
3. For No One	3. For No One
4. Doctor Robert	4. Got To Get You Into My Life
5. I Want To Tell You	5. Love You To
6. Got To Get You Into My Life	6. She Said, She Said
7. Tomorrow Never Knows	7. Tomorrow Never Knows

Sgt. Pepper's Lonely Hearts Club Band **(Capitol 4XT-2653/C4-46442)**

To their credit, neither EMI nor Capitol elected to alter the running order of a single track on this album, albeit the running time of the LP's two sides just happened to already fall within 10 seconds of one another. This is the first album in The Beatles' currently available cassette catalog to retain the original playing order of both the LP and CD.

Magical Mystery Tour **(Capitol 4XT-2835/C4-48062)**

Perhaps owing to the fact that this particular album was originally compiled by Capitol Records for release in the U.S. this cassette remains completely faithful to the sequencing of the original LP, despite a difference or more than a minute and a half in the playing time of side one (19:04) beyond that of side two (17:30).

The Beatles (The White Album) **(U.K.: Parlophone-Apple TC PCS 7067/8) (U.S.: Capitol-Apple 4XW-160, 161/C-4 160, 161)**

In Britain, EMI managed to squeeze all 30 tracks of the double LP onto a single, extended-length cassette, while in the U.S. Capitol opted to release a double-tape set. In order to seek comparable running lengths for both sides of their single cassette, EMI had to make considerable changes in the running order of the original lineup, especially among the songs that appeared on sides three and four of the LP. As a result, only about half of the British cassette manages to vaguely resemble the original album. For all of their work, EMI did succeed in reducing the difference in playing time for each side from 52 seconds down to only four seconds.

Original LP/Compact Disc	Parlophone-Apple Cass.(U.K. only)
Sides one and two (46:22)	**Side one (46:46)**
1. Back In The U.S.S.R.	1. Back In The U.S.S.R.
2. Dear Prudence	2. Dear Prudence
3. Glass Onion	3. Glass Onion
4. Ob-la-di, Ob-la-da	4. Ob-la-di, Ob-la-da
5. Wild Honey Pie	5. Wild Honey Pie
6. The Continuing Story Of Bungalow Bill	6. The Continuing Story Of Bungalow Bill
7. While My Guitar Gently Weeps	7. While My Guitar Gently Weeps
8. Happiness Is A Warm Gun	8. Martha My Dear
(Side two of LP, CD continues)	**(Side one of U.K. tape continues)**
9. Martha My Dear	9. I'm So Tired
10. I'm So Tired	10. Blackbird
11. Blackbird	11. Piggies
12. Piggies	12. Rocky Raccoon

13. Rocky Raccoon	13. Don't Pass Me By
14. Don't Pass Me By	14. Why Don't We Do It In The Road?
15. Why Don't We Do It In The Road?	15. I Will
16. I Will	16. Julia
17. Julia	17. Long Long Long

[NOTE: On part one of the U.S. Capitol double cassette, side one closes with "Blackbird" as the last song following "While My Guitar Gently Weeps." "Happiness Is A Warm Gun" moves to become the first track on side two preceding "Martha My Dear." The remainder of sides one and two correspond to the original LP.]

Sides three and four (47:14)	**Side two (46:50)**
1. Birthday	1. Everybody's Got Something To Hide Except For Me And My Monkey
2. Yer Blues	2. Sexy Sadie
3. Mother Nature's Son	3. Helter Skelter
4. Everybody's Got Something To Hide Except For Me And My Monkey	4. Revolution 1
5. Sexy Sadie	5. Honey Pie
6. Helter Skelter	6. Savoy Truffle
7. Long Long Long	7. Goodnight
(Side four of LP, CD continues)	**(Side two of U.K. tape continues)**
8. Revolution 1	8. Happiness Is A Warm Gun
9. Honey Pie	9. Birthday
10. Savoy Truffle	10. Yer Blues
11. Cry Baby Cry	11. Mother Nature's Son
12. Revolution No.9	12. Cry Baby Cry
13. Goodnight	13. Revolution No.9

[NOTE: On part two of the U.S. Capitol double cassette, "Revolution 1" follows "Long Long Long" at the close of side three. "Sexy Sadie" is moved to the beginning of side four ahead of "Honey Pie." The remaining tracks correspond to the original LP.]

Yellow Submarine (U.K.: Parlophone-Apple TC PCS 7070) (U.S.: Capitol-Apple 4XW-153/C4-46445)

Not only does the cassette version of this soundtrack album fail to mirror the original LP, but the American and British cassettes themselves differ from one another in both content and sequencing. Faced with the fact that side one of the LP clocked in nearly four minutes longer than side two, Capitol chose to add a seventh Beatles track to the album, placing "Lucy In The Sky With Diamonds" at the beginning of side two on the U.S. cassette. In Britain, EMI's answer to this same dilemma was merely to remove "All Together Now" from side one of the album and place it at the start of side two on the tape, where it now preceded George Martin's instrumental score.

Original LP/Compact Disc	Parlophone cassette (U.K. only)
Side one (22:00)	**Side one (19:47)**
1. Yellow Submarine	1. Yellow Submarine
2. Only A Northern Song	2. Only A Northern Song
3. All Together Now	3. All You Need Is Love
4. Hey Bulldog	4. Hey Bulldog
5. It's All Too Much	5. It's All Too Much
6. All You Need Is Love	
Side two (18:13)	**Side two (20:26)**
1. George Martin instrumental score	1. All Together Now
	2. George Martin instrumental score

Abbey Road (Capitol-Apple 4XT-383/C4-46446)

The Beatles' last-recorded studio LP was also one of their most critically acclaimed and immensely popular. Even so, the album's opening number, "Come Together," was swapped straight across for the first song on side two, "Here Comes The Sun," in order to reduce the imbalance in playing time between the sides from two and a half minutes down to no more than four seconds on the cassette. Of course, this also meant that George Harrison's two major contributions to the album were now sequenced back-to-back at the very beginning of the tape.

Meanwhile, the remainder of the LP's original playing order was preserved.

Let It Be (U.K.: Parlophone-Apple TC PCS 7096) (U.S.: Apple-United Artists ART 2001) (U.S.: Capitol-Apple 4XW-11922/C4-46447)

Phil Spector was not the only one who worked overtime in overhauling *Let It Be*. Side one of Spector's final product ran almost three and a half minutes longer than did side two, necessitating further rearrangement by EMI before the British cassette managed to reduce that difference to nine seconds. Across the ocean, Apple's original 1970 cassette release as distributed in the U.S. by United Artists retained the LP's original playing order fully intact. When rights to the soundtrack album reverted to Capitol in the late '70s the label immediately went to work, displacing "I Me Mine" from side one over to the beginning of side two.

Original LP/Compact Disc	Parlophone-Apple cass. (U.K. only)
Side one (19:20)	**Side one (17:40)**
1. Two Of Us	1. Two Of Us
2. I Dig A Pony	2. I Me Mine
3. Across The Universe	3. One After 909
4. I Me Mine	4. Across The Universe
5. Dig It	5. Dig It
6. Let It Be	6. Let It Be
7. Maggie Mae	

[NOTE: On the Capitol U.S. reissue cassette, "I Me Mine" is dropped from side one and appears as the opening track on side two. Beyond this, the remainder of the Capitol cassette is the same as the original LP.]

Side two (15:51)	**Side two (17:31)**
1. I've Got A Feeling	1. Maggie Mae
2. One After 909	2. Dig A Pony
3. The Long And Winding Road	3. I Got A Feeling
4. For You Blue	4. The Long And Winding Road
5. Get Back	5. For You Blue
	6. Get Back

Capitol's American cassettes

Although many American Beatles fans still hold a deep affection for Capitol's original U.S. Beatles albums, it should be pointed out that the cassettes rarely matched the sequencing as featured on the vinyl LPs. Unlike their British counterparts, the powers-that-be at Capitol Records appeared to follow no particular criteria or discernible pattern when preparing The Beatles' albums for release on audiocassette. While several U.S. Beatles LPs were resequenced for cassette, others faithfully duplicated the sequencing of the original albums. Ultimately, while some tapes reduced the difference in running time between the two sides of the album to only a few seconds, other titles were allowed to retain a playing-time imbalance of as much as three full minutes. In at least one instance, Capitol's resequencing of the cassette actually increased this difference!

***The Beatles' Second Album* (Capitol 4XT-2080/C4-90444)**

To bring the two sides of the cassette to within 14 seconds of one another, Capitol took the second song from side one on the LP, "Thank You Girl," and moved it to the end of side two on the cassette. Otherwise, the remaining tracks appeared in their original LP playing order.

***Something New* (Capitol 4XT 2108/C4-90443)**

When Capitol's third Beatles album was prepared for cassette release, the staff seemingly adopted the lead already employed by their counterparts at EMI in Great Britain, no doubt working overtime to bring the two sides of the tape to within four seconds of one another. To accomplish this, only three of the 11 tracks remained in their original LP positions.

Original LP	Capitol cassette
Side one (13:14)	**Side one (12:43)**
1. I'll Cry Instead	1. I'll Cry Instead
2. Things We Said Today	2. When I Get Home
3. Any Time At All	3. Matchbox
4. When I Get Home	4. Tell Me Why
5. Slow Down	5. And I Love Her
6. Matchbox	6. I'm Happy Just To Dance With You
Side two (11:09)	**Side two (12:39)**
1. Tell Me Why	1. Things We Said Today
2. And I Love Her	2. Any Time At All
3. I'm Happy Just To Dance With You	3. Slow Down
4. If I Fell	4. If I Fell
5. Komm Gib Mir Diene Hand	5. Komm Gib Mir Diene Hand

***Beatles '65* (Capitol 4XT 2228/C4-90446)**

Apparently not satisfied with the fact that there was only a two-second differential in the playing times of the LP (side one runs 13:21, side two runs 13:19), Capitol's tape department elected to swap each side's original closing numbers, moving "Everybody's Trying To Be My Baby" from the end of side one to the end of side two, while bringing "Mr. Moonlight" from the end of side two forward to close out the first side of the cassette. The end result actually increased the difference in the two sides of the tape by 10-fold, to 21 seconds. Apparently someone inside the Capitol Tower was unclear on the concept. The remainder of the cassette follows the track order found on the original LP.

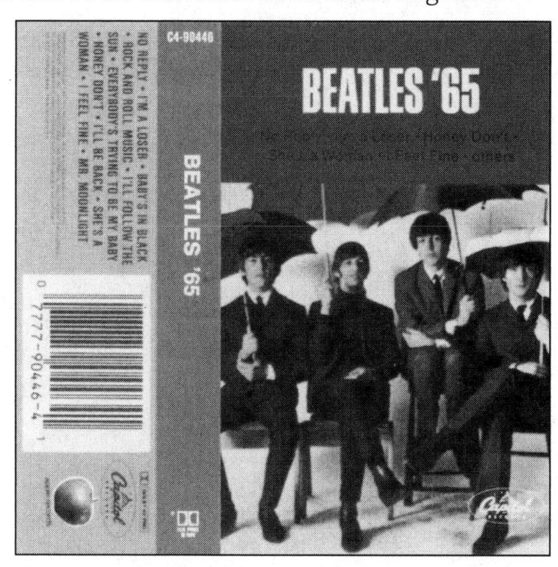

***The Early Beatles* (Capitol 4XT-2309/C4-90451)**

For the cassette tape version of Capitol's contractually reworked reissue of Vee-Jay Records' *Introducing The Beatles*, the majority of tracks featured on side one of the LP were moved to side two on the cassette and vice-versa. Additionally, the two numbers that originally closed the first side of Capitol's LP were resequenced to open the cassette. By the time Capitol was finished tinkering with the contents, not even one of the album's 11 tracks appeared in its original slot.

Original LP	Capitol cassette
Side one (14:56)	**Side one (12:47)**
1. Love Me Do	1. Boys
2. Twist And Shout	2. Ask Me Why
3. Anna (Go To Him)	3. Please Please Me
4. Chains	4. P.S. I Love You
5. Boys	5. A Taste Of Honey
6. Ask Me Why	6. Do You Want To Know A Secret?
Side two (10:35)	**Side two (13:02)**
1. Please Please Me	1. Love Me Do
2. P.S. I Love You	2. Twist And Shout
3. Baby It's You	3. Anna (Go To Him)
4. A Taste Of Honey	4. Chains
5. Do You Want To Know A Secret?	5. Baby It's You

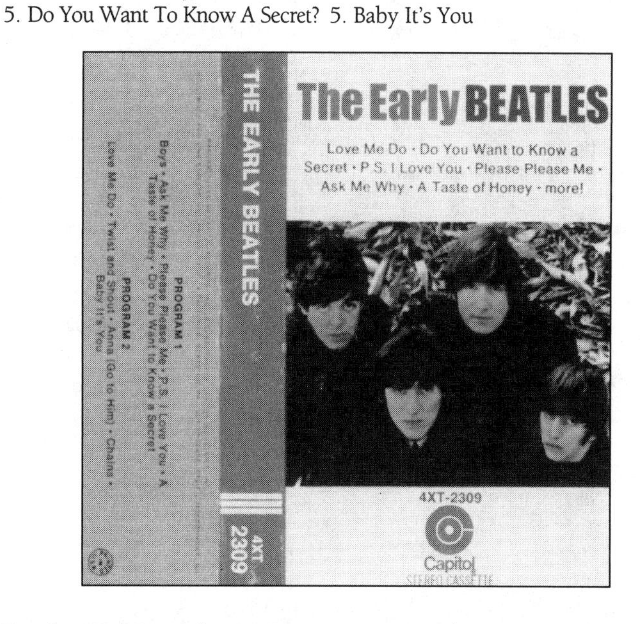

***Beatles VI* (Capitol 4XT-2358 / C4-90445)**

Capitol's patented "secret formula" for preparing a Beatles LP for release on cassette: First, take the second and third tracks from side one of the LP and place them at the start of side two on the cassette. Second, remove the opening and closing numbers from side two of the album and add them to the end of side one. Next, bring the remaining tracks on side one forward, while at the same time sliding the leftover songs on side two further back in the running order until they close out the second side of the tape. Voilá! Instant Beatles cassette! Only "Kansas City/Hey Hey Hey" remained untouched in its original pole position.

Original LP	Capitol cassette
Side one (14:47)	**Side one (14:01)**
1. Kansas City/Hey Hey Hey	1. Kansas City/Hey Hey Hey
2. Eight Days A Week	2. Bad Boy
3. You Like Me Too Much	3. I Don't Want To Spoil The Party
4. Bad Boy	4. Words Of Love
5. I Don't Want To Spoil The Party	5. What You're Doing
6. Words Of Love	6. Every Little Thing

Side two (12:37)
1. What You're Doing
2. Yes It Is
3. Dizzy Miss Lizzie
4. Tell Me What You See
5. Every Little Thing

Side two (13:23)
1. Eight Days A Week
2. You Like Me Too Much
3. Yes It Is
4. Dizzy Miss Lizzie
5. Tell Me What You See

Yesterday And Today (Capitol 4XT-2553/C4-90447)

Before its release on cassette, the infamous "butcher" cover album was hacked around a little more. By moving the last three songs found on side one of the LP to the start of side two on the cassette and by taking the final two selections from the second side of the album and placing them at the end of side one on the tape, Capitol was able to reduce the original differential of the two sides (2:56) down to only 20 seconds.

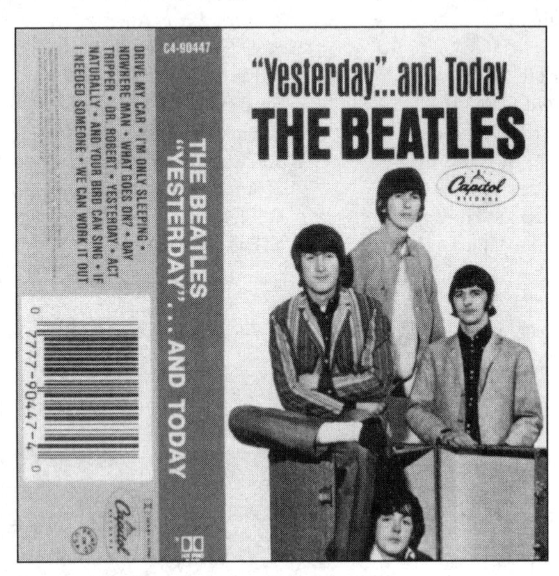

Original LP

Side one (14:48)
1. Drive My Car
2. I'm Only Sleeping
3. Nowhere Man
4. Dr. Robert
5. Yesterday
6. Act Naturally

Side two (11:52)
1. And Your Bird Can Sing
2. If I Needed Someone
3. We Can Work It Out
4. What Goes On?
5. Day Tripper

Capitol cassette

Side one (13:55)
1. Drive My Car
2. I'm Only Sleeping
3. Nowhere Man
4. What Goes On?
5. Day Tripper

Side two (13:35)
1. Dr. Robert
2. Yesterday
3. Act Naturally
4. And Your Bird Can Sing
5. If I Needed Someone
6. We Can Work It Out

Hey Jude (Capitol-Apple 4XT-385/C4-90442)

For reasons unknown to anyone outside of the Capitol Tower, the original sides of the LP were flip-flopped for their release on cassette. Whereas the songs on the LP essentially ran in chronological order of release (i.e. 1964-1969), the presentation on cassette obviously did not.

Original LP

Side one (16:00)
1. Can't Buy Me Love
2. I Should Have Known Better
3. Paperback Writer
4. Rain
5. Lady Madonna
6. Revolution

Side two (16:59)
1. Hey Jude
2. Old Brown Shoe
3. Don't Let Me Down
4. The Ballad Of John & Yoko

Capitol-Apple cassette

Side one (16:59)
1. Hey Jude
2. Old Brown Shoe
3. Don't Let Me Down
4. The Ballad Of John & Yoko

Side two (16:00)
1. Can't Buy Me Love
2. I Should Have Known Better
3. Paperback Writer
4. Rain
5. Lady Madonna
6. Revolution

The Beatles/1962-1966 (Capitol-Apple 4X2K-3403/C4-97036)
The Beatles/1967-1970 (Capitol-Apple 4X2K-3404/C4-97039)

When these double LPs were first released in 1973, they each appeared on single, extended-length cassettes in the U.S. Twenty years later, when the "red" and "blue" albums were officially issued on compact disc, Apple insisted that the original single cassettes be deleted and replaced with a pair of twin-tape sets. Despite this change in packaging, the sequencing of both remained faithful to the original albums.

Love Songs (4X2B-11711)

The first two sides of the double vinyl LP became side one on the extended-length cassette, while sides three and four served as the second side of the audiotape. Sequencing remained true to the LP with only two exceptions: "Yes It Is" (which appeared as the 13th track of the LP, closing out side two) was switched with "It's Only Love" (the 15th track of the LP, the second song on side three), the former now appearing on side two of the cassette, the latter at the end of side one. This exchange brought the two sides of the tape to a final running length within one minute of one another.

Rock 'N' Roll Music Volume 1 (Capitol 4N-16020)
Rock 'N' Roll Music Volume 2 (Capitol 4N-16021)

In the fall of 1980, the original double-album set was reissued as two separate single albums, both in LP and cassette formats. For reasons undisclosed, side one of the LP became side two of the cassette, and vice-versa. This reversal of the sides was performed on both tape volumes.

20 Greatest Hits (Capitol 4XV-12245)

The audiocassette retained the sequencing of the vinyl LP with one minor adjustment: "Penny Lane" was moved from its position as the last track on side one of the LP to become the first track on side two of the cassette.

And in the end...

The remaining Beatles cassette titles in Capitol's U.S. catalog presented the sequencing of the songs exactly as they had appeared on LP. These included the cassette releases of the following albums: *Meet The Beatles*, *A Hard Day's Night* (U.S. version), Help! (U.S. version), *Rubber Soul* (U.S. version), *Revolver* (U.S. version) and the compilation/reissues: *Reel Music*, *The Beatles Rarities*, and *The Beatles At The Hollywood Bowl*. Curiously, *The Beatles' Story* (Capitol STBO 2222) never appeared on cassette (or any other prerecorded tape format).

(Author's note: Special thanks to the RIAA Recording Industry Association Of America, Inc. for their kind assistance in providing the sales data presented in this article.)

Back to the future

Beatles 45 sleeves in the '90s

by Charles Szabla

The heyday of the 45 rpm picture sleeve is gone. Never again will we see the proliferation of those seven-inch beauties. They graced the record buyers' presence for 50 glorious years. By 1989 the production of sleeves had all but disappeared. But the death toll has not yet rung for the picture sleeve. There are still a handful of major label record companies that release singles and an even smaller number that accompany those records with picture sleeves. Among the artists still releasing seven-inch vinyl with sleeves include The Beatles, The Rolling Stones, Pearl Jam, Janet Jackson, and Mariah Carey.

1994 saw the release of *The Beatles Live At The BBC*. In conjunction with the disc's release came a seven-inch extended play that featured the songs "Baby It's You," "I'll Follow The Sun," "Devil In Her Heart" and "Boys." On the front of the picture sleeve was a photo of the band leaving the BBC studios after one of their performances. This is an example of a sleeve that was not as much designed to reflect a specific concept but instead following the lead set by the image selected.

The original photograph was a black and white print. To emphasize the archival nature of the recordings and the period in time it was taken, the image was treated in an deep sepia-toned manner using four-color process. This picture was used on all recorded formats and promotional material in order to present a powerful presentation for the graphic identity.

The presentation of John, Paul, George, and Ringo together was in keeping with the picture sleeve tradition set by Capitol and Apple for The Beatles. It was a standard visual device to always show the four mates photographically on all commercially released sleeves while the band was together. An effort was made to use a concert shot when The Beatles were touring. This was a method that helped promote the live appearances of the band.

It wasn't until The Beatles broke up and the reissues started appearing that this tradition was interrupted. "Got To Get You Into My Life" was the single and sleeve pulled from the 1976 album *Rock 'N' Roll Music*. The picture sleeve was based on the album art and was not a photo of the band but an illustration of them circa 1964. 1976 also saw the release of "Ob-La-Di, Ob-La-Da," which echoed the stark simplicity of *The White Album* and featured no photos at all. The sleeves were even machine numbered just as the album was.

The Anthology series of three double-CD sets brought with them two singles with picture sleeves for "Free As A Bird" and "Real Love." Both were intended for use as teasers for the second and third *Anthology* releases. There was no expectation for the singles to create any revenue on their own but instead to spur interest, excitement and sales for the CDs. The job of conceptualizing and designing the *Anthology* series was handled by The Team, a London design firm, and Richard Ward is the lucky one to handle the Apple account.

This article originally appeared in* Goldmine *issue #477, Nov. 6, 1998.

Ward's association with The Beatles began with George Harrison. Their relationship began through a book Ward had cowritten titled *Fairground Art*. The book documented the history of amusement park imagery from rustic 19th-century fairs, through the Art Deco period of the '30s, to today's high-tech amusement parks and carnivals. A mutual friend of Ward and George gave Harrison a signed copy of *Fairground Art* as a gift. Harrison was so impressed with the book, he contacted Ward directly to express his admiration. This eventually led to Ward designing Harrison's 1992 release, *Live In Japan*. The Japanese-influenced brush painting of Harrison was part of the entire concept created by Ward.

The image used on the "Baby It's You" EP had not been previously published commercially, while the studio shot of The Beatles shown on the "Real Love" picture sleeve had been used in the past. This time the group photo was outlined, which means to eliminate the background from the main image, and then placed on a mechanically produced flat color. The back of the sleeve was the same canvas stretcher theme that was meant to link all of the *Anthologys* together. Ward stated, "The original concept was relating it all to a work of art, like a painting on canvas, which they [The Beatles] liked."

"Free As A Bird" received a high promotional push as a Beatles "reunion." The song was recorded by John Lennon in demo form but never finished, and in 1994 the tape was entrusted to

Paul McCartney, Harrison, and Ringo Starr. With the help of Jeff Lynne as coproducer, the three remaining Beatles added vocals and instrumentation to the basic Lennon track thus creating a "new" Beatles tune.

In a conversation with Ward he states, "There were many different concepts considered" for the "Free As A Bird" picture sleeve, "but it didn't make sense to show old photos of the band since this was essentially a new recording of The Beatles."

"I had this sort of mad idea that I went through a whole variety of abstracts and illustrative ideas as well as old photos, but then I had this thought that this was originally John Lennon's. Now this guy's a brilliant artist, so I then put it to Apple and they said, 'Have a go and see if the guys will buy it.' So I then contacted Yoko and she supplied me with a selection of drawings that in her eyes would fulfill this particular brief. She came back with about six drawings, some of which had not been seen before, of which she preferred three of them."

Having seen those three, Ward selected the one he felt best reflected the song's message. Mockups were produced and sent to Ringo, Paul, and George. They all liked the idea and felt it would be a nice way of signaling John's presence and to demonstrate the respect and love they have for him.

No manipulation of the original drawing was made. Rick simply took the image and put it onto a canvas background to graphically tie it in with the *Anthology*. Luckily, the drawing was rendered on a white background, which made it easy to reproduce cleanly and in its original form.

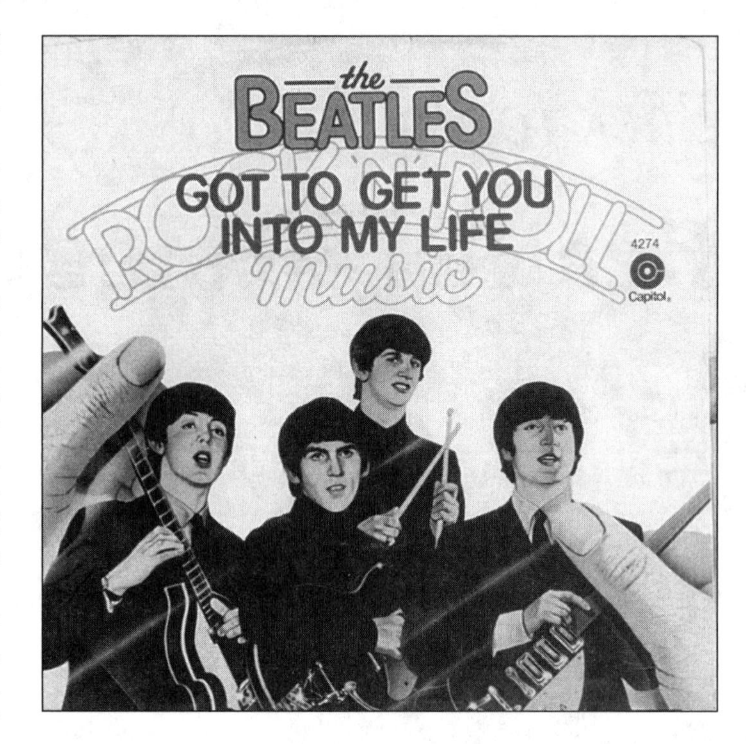

Future Beatles releases seem inevitable, but for now The Beatles appear "anthologied out." But the Nov. 3 release of the Lennon four-CD boxed set holds promise for another exciting batch of unreleased material. We can hope a single with a picture sleeve is included in Capitol's plans.

Retro News Flash

January 28, 2000, issue #508

Harrison stabbed; attacker believes Beatles are witches

by Chuck Miller

George Harrison spent New Year's weekend in a hospital, recovering from various stab wounds received from a deranged attacker. The former Beatle and his wife Olivia were attacked in their home Dec. 30, 1999, by Michael Abram, a 33-year-old father of two who is currently charged with two counts of attempted murder.

Police reports say Abram broke into the Harrison estate at Henley-on-Thames, an upper-class suburb outside of London. Once Abram got past the maximum security, he attacked Harrison with a seven-inch knife, stabbing the ex-Beatle several times in the chest. One of those stab wounds collapsed his right lung; another wound landed barely an inch from Harrison's heart.

Olivia, who had also been attacked, stopped her husband's assailant by hitting him on the head with a heavy table lamp. Both Harrisons then struggled with Abram until police arrived at the mansion.

According to the Liverpool *Echo* newspaper, Abram's mother Lynda said that her son was mentally unstable and had become obsessed with Beatles lyrics. She also said that Abram had spent time in a psychiatric ward but was kicked out after he attacked a nurse at the facility.

"He takes all music literally," said Lynda to the *Echo*. "It is The Beatles at the moment, but a few weeks ago it was Oasis. He hates [The Beatles] and even believes they are witches and takes their lyrics seriously."

On Jan. 1, 2000, the 56-year-old singer was discharged from Harefield Hospital in west London and returned with his wife to his 120-room castle at Henley-on-Thames.

A week earlier, another obsessed fan broke into Harrison's Hawaii estate, making herself at home until police arrived to take her away. The burglar, Christine Keleher, is currently charged with first-degree burglary and fourth-degree theft.

The attack comes 19 years to the month that Mark David Chapman, another deranged fan obsessed with The Beatles, murdered John Lennon outside a New York City apartment complex.

(Compiled from various Associated Press, Bloomberg and Reuters wire sources.)

Yoko Ono

Her controversial recording career

by Gillian G. Gaar

Say that Yoko Ono ranks as one of the most misunderstood recording artists of our time and you'll be opening yourself up to misunderstanding as well. Few performers have generated such hatred in their lifetime, a hatred that appears to stem more from personal, rather than artistic, dislike. Certainly one can understand the confusion critics must have felt in 1970 listening to Yoko Ono/Plastic Ono Band without any punk/new wave frame of reference in which to place it. Yet by the 1980 release of *Double Fantasy*, critics were not only praising her music, some found it more in tune with the times than that of her collaborator's, John Lennon.

Whatever the era, Ono's work has provoked extreme opinions, and there were as many positive comments about her music in 1970 as there were critical jibes in 1980. But Ono used music and recording as part of an exploratory artistic process, constantly defining and redefining her artistic vision, creating songs that told stories, painted abstract pictures or just plain screamed.

Ono was born in 1933 and came from wealthy parents, splitting her childhood between America and her native Japan. She left studies at Sarah Lawrence College to live in New York City with her first husband and gradually worked her way into the city's burgeoning avant-garde scene, creating "happenings" out of her "instructional poems" ("Throw a stone into the sky high enough/so it will not come back"). As was to happen with her music, her work met with mixed receptions from the critics. But she continued to create art and in 1966 was invited to participate in a "Destruction In Art" symposium in London. Her appearance generated good reviews (the *Financial Times* called her performance "uplifting") and she was asked to assemble an exhibit for London's Indica Gallery, whose owners included John Dunbar (then married to Marianne Faithfull) and Peter Asher (one half of Peter & Gordon). It was on the show's preview night, Nov. 9, 1966, that she met Lennon.

Though interested in one another from the start, it wasn't until May 1968 that John and Yoko joined forces, both personally and profesionally. During their first night together, they made experimental tapes that would become *Unfinished Music No. 1: Two Virgins*, an album of avant-garde "noise" released in November 1968. The record pined more notoriety for its cover, which featured front and rear shots of John and Yoko in the nude. Though pressed on the Beatles' Apple label, EMI refused to distribute the album, leaving that duty to Track Records in the U.K. and Tetragrammation in the U.S., who shipped the LP in a plain brown wrapper. *Two Virgins* is now one of the rarest Apple records; counterfeits have a stark white cover (the original was off-white) and a green-

This article originally appeared in Goldmine issue #188, Oct. 9, 1987.

ish-gold wrapper instead of brown. The album was also reissued in the U.S. in 1985.

By the time of their meeting, John had divorced his wife, Yoko had divorced her second husband and the two began an active recording career. The Beatles' *White Album*, released in November 1968, had several contributions from Yoko: backing vocals in "The Continuing Story Of Bungalow Bill" and "Birthday," and a John and Yoko collaboration on the aural collage "Revolution No.9." Next, the two appeared on The Beatles' 1968 Christmas flexi-disc (a special gift for Beatles Fan Club members). Their next album was on the short-lived Zapple label, released April 1969 in the U.K., May in the U.S., *Unfinished Music No. 2: Life With The Lions*. Though lacking the controversial cover of *Two Virgins*, the contents still mystified the public, consisting of the heartbeat of John and Yoko's child (which Yoko later miscarried), Yoko reading press clippings about their activities, and their first public performance together at Cambridge University in March 1969.

In July 1969, John released his first solo single, "Give Peace A Chance," with Yoko's "Remember Love" on the flip, inaugurating a tradition of John A-side/Yoko B-side singles (all future records until 1980 on the Apple label). October 1969 saw the release of John's "Cold Turkey" single with Yoko's "Don't Worry Kyoko (Mummy's Only Looking For A Hand In The Snow)" on the flip. The *Wedding Album* followed, released in October in the U.S., November in the U.K., packaged in a deluxe box that featured photos, posters, a booklet of pictures and clippings and a photo of a slice of wedding cake. This box set was reissued in Japan in the late

POWER TO THE PEOPLE

JOHN LENNON/PLASTIC ONO BAND

MUSIC SALES LTD., 78 Newman Street, London, W.1. 20p

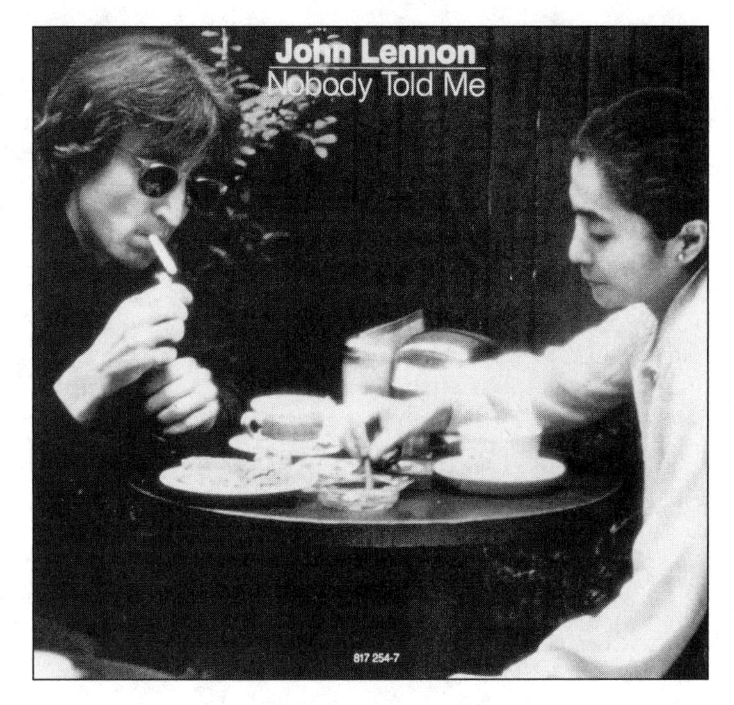

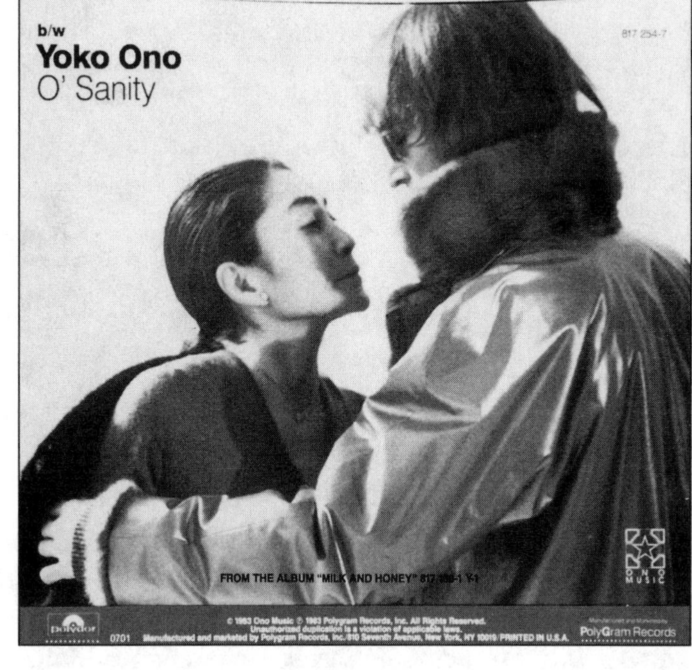

'70s. The two ended 1969 with two December releases, the 1969 Beatles Christmas flexi-disc and the album *Live Peace In Toronto*, a live LP of their spur-of-the-moment performance at Toronto's "Rock 'n' Roll Revival Show" with Eric Clapton, Klaus Voormann, and Andy White. Original issues of the album also included a 16-page calendar.

The next record was Lennon's "Instant Karma!" single backed with Ono's "Who Has Seen the Wind?" released in February 1970. Their next single, released in the U.S. only, did not appear until December 1970; Lennon's "Mother" backed with Ono's "Why" were each taken from *John Lennon/Plastic Ono Band* and *Yoko Ono/Plastic Ono Band*, respectively, both albums also released in December. The screaming and vocal ranting that would provide the starting point for countless punk groups in 1976 was generally slammed by the critics in 1970. Apple also released an album containing all seven of The Beatles' Christmas flexis in December 1970.

In March 1971 John's "Power To The People" single was released, with Yoko's "Open Your Box" as the flip in the U.K.; censorship problems forced the two to substitute "Touch Me" (from *Yoko Ono/Plastic Ono Band*) as the U.S. B-side ("Open Your Box" would resurface on *Fly* as "Hirake"). The two then cowrote, produced and performed on "God Save Us"/"Do The Oz" along with Bill Elliot as a benefit single for the *Oz* magazine obscenity trial, released on Apple in July 1971. September 1971 saw the U.S. release of Yoko's *Fly* LP (released in Britain in December) along with her first solo single, "Mrs. Lennon"/"Midsummer New York" (released in September in the U.S., October in the U.K.). Another John and Yoko 45 was released that December in the U.S., "Happy Christmas (War Is Over)"/"Listen, The Snow Is Falling" (not released in the U.K. until November 1972). Original issues of the single were pressed on green vinyl and featured a special photo label.

In January 1972, a second single was pulled from *Fly* for U.K. release only, "Mind Train"/"Listen, The Snow Is Falling." April saw the U.S.-only release of "Woman Is The Nigger Of The World" backed with Yoko's "Sisters O Sisters." Both were from the double LP *Some Time In New York City*, released in June in the U.S., September in the U.K. (original copies had a photo label and petition insert). In November 1972, Yoko released a third solo single, in the U.S. only, "Now Or Never"/"Move On Fast." Both songs were from *Approximately Infinite Universe*, released in January 1973 in the U.S., February in the U.K. A second single from the LP, "Death Of Samantha"/"Yang Yang," was released in February in the U.S., May in the U.K. At this time, John and Yoko separated and did not collaborate musically until 1980.

Yoko's next single, released in September 1973 in the U.S. only, was "Woman Power"/"Men, Men, Men," from *Feeling The Space*, released that November. November also saw the U.K.-only release of "Run, Run, Run"/"Men, Men, Men." There were also three Japan-only releases in 1973, the LP *Welcome (The Many Sides Of Yoko Only)*, containing previously released material, and the single "Josei Joi Banzai"/"Josei Joi Banzai (Part 2)." This was followed by another Japan-only release in 1974 (on the Odeon label), "Yume O Motou (Let's Have A Dream)"/"It Happened."

There were no new Yoko releases until 1980, though in October 1975 Apple released *Shaved Fish*, a John Lennon "greatest hits" collection, with a snippet of "Give Peace A Chance" and "Happy Christmas" (which had Yoko on backing vocals). In 1976, Polydor released *The Beatles Tapes* in the U.K. only, a double album of interviews by David Wigg; John and Yoko are interviewed on side one. Meanwhile, John and Yoko had reunited, John had received his green card allowing him resident status in the U.S., and the two finally gave birth to a child, Sean Ono Lennon. Both then retired from the music world, John concentrating on raising his son and Yoko attending to their business affairs.

In the summer of 1980, it was announced that John and Yoko had returned to the recording studios. That October, John's "Starting Over" backed with Yoko's "Kiss, Kiss, Kiss" was released on Geffen Records, and the album *Double Fantasy* followed in November. The LP had John and Yoko

alternating tracks, and the critics singled out Yoko's "new wave" sound as being especially accessible. Sales of the album soared after John's tragic death in December, and two more singles were released (following the John A-side/Yoko B-side pattern), "Woman"/"Beautiful Boys" (released in January 1981) and "Watching The Wheels"/"I'm Your Angel" (released in March 1981). Yoko also released a solo single in February 1981, "Walking On Thin Ice"/"It Happened," released as a seven- and 12-inch single and a special cassette single, with the additional track "Hard Times Are Over" (from *Double Fantasy*) on the latter two. The single was Yoko's first solo chart hit, reaching #33 in the *Billboard* charts and #13 in *Billboard*'s Disco Club Play chart.

In June 1981 Yoko released *Season Of Glass*, which again featured a controversial cover, this time a shot of John's blood-stained spectacles. Yoko made no apologies for the photo, stating "If people can't stomach the glasses, I'm sorry. There was a dead body. There was blood... that's the reality... People are offended by the glasses and the blood? John had to stomach a lot more." Yoko's anger permeated the tracks on the LP with a mixture of sadness and hostility, punctuated by gunshots (the opening of "No, No, No") and curses ("You bastards! Hate us, hate me... we had everything!" from "I Don't Know"). The LP reached #49 in the U.S. charts. August saw the U.S.-only release of "No, No, No"/"Will You Touch Me," released in seven- and 12-inch formats. In September another U.S.-only single was released, "Goodbye Sadness"/"I Don't Know Why."

There were no new Yoko releases until 1982, by which time she'd left Geffen and signed with Polydor. "My Man"/"Let The Tears Dry" was released in November in the U.S., December in the U.K., from the album *It's Alright*, released shortly after the single in each country. Geffen also released *The John Lennon Collection* in November 1982, with a full version of "Give Peace A Chance" and "Happy Xmas." "Happy Xmas" was also released as a single backed with "Beautiful Boys" in seven- and 12-inch formats (the latter a promo-only release). In February 1983 a second single was released from *It's Alright* in the U.S. only, "Never Say Goodbye"/"Loneliness," in seven- and 12-inch formats (the latter with extended versions of each song).

In December 1983, Polydor released *Heart Play*, an interview album from John and Yoko's lengthy *Playboy* interviews in late 1980. January 1984 saw the release of *Milk And Honey*, the intended follow-up to *Double Fantasy*, with a similar sequencing of John/Yoko alternating tracks, also released as a picture disc. There were three singles from the LP, "Nobody told Me"/"O' Sanity" (released in January 1984), "I'm Stepping Out"/ "Sleepless Night" released in the U.S. only, and "Borrowed Time"/"Your Hands," released in the U.S. and U.K. with a special 12-inch release in Britain that included a poster and the additional track, "Never Say Goodbye." In addition, Polydor released *Every Man Has A Woman Who Loves Him* in 1984, a compilation album with artists as varied as Lennon, Elvis Costello, Roberta Flack, and Rosanne Cash covering different Yoko songs. A biography, *Yoko Ono: Then & Now* was also released as a video, featuring interviews and clips from her video work.

Yoko's "Hell In Paradise" single (backed with an instrumental version of the song) was released in October 1985 in both seven- and 12-inch formats, the 12-inch featuring an extended mix of the song. The 12-inch hit #16 in *Billboard*'s Disco Sales chart and #12 in the Club Play chart. The song was from Yoko's *Starpeace* album, released in 1985. This was followed in 1986 by the ill-fated *Starpeace* tour, where poor ticket sales generated the usual mix of positive and negative critical jibes.

1986 also saw the release of *John Lennon Live In New York City* on record (Capitol) and video, a live documentation of John and Yoko's One To One benefit performances in 1972. As well as singing backup, Yoko performs two numbers on the video, "Sisters O Sisters" and "Born In A Prison." John and Yoko's "home movie" *Imagine* was also released in 1986, with two songs from *Fly*, "Don't Count The Waves" and "Mrs. Lennon" (the original *Imagine* film also included Yoko's

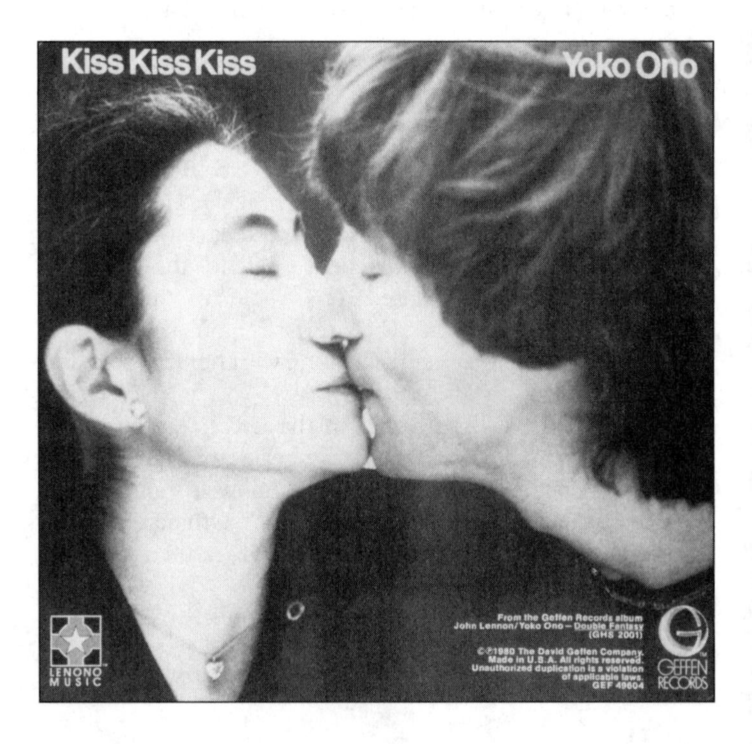

John Lennon and Yoko Ono, at Philharmonic Hall in Manhattan, 1971. Ono was directing one of her humorous performance pieces from the front row of the audience.

"Mind Train" and "Midsummer New York"). Yoko's last record, released in April 1986 in the U.S. only, was a 12-inch single with two remixed of "Cape Clear" (from *Starpeace*) and a remix of "Walking On Thin Ice."

Since John's death, Yoko and her music have gained a grudging respect, though, she says, "Did the world have to lose John for people to change their opinion of me? It's unreal. If it brought John back, I'd rather remain hated."

One can see the roots of the new wave in seminal recordings such as *Yoko Ono/Plastic Ono Band*, and the assimilation of her avant-garde stance into the mainstream Top 40 makes her hit singles "Walking On Thin Ice" and "Hell In Paradise" sound almost conventional. Yoko has always mixed her artistic influences into her music, which is why pop music critics have frequently decried her music. But this lack of acceptance is what gives Yoko's music its edge, sometimes harsh and grating, sometimes sweeping and mysterious, but always something that elicits a strong reaction from the listener, the true end of any artistic endeavor.

Yoko Ono

A spoken-word discography

by Gillian G. Gaar

Defying all expectations, the '90s have proved to be Yoko Ono's decade of vindication. 1992 saw the release of *Onobox*, the critically acclaimed six-CD box set that offered an overview of Ono's musical career. Three years later came *Rising*, Ono's first album of new material since 1985's *Starpeace*, another hit with critics and fans. And the good notices continued into 1996, when Ono embarked on a successful (and largely sold-out) tour of the U.S. and Europe.

Now Rykodisc, the label that released *Onobox*, has undertaken the most ambitious task yet in dealing with Ono's substantial catalog; reissuing Ono's first three album collaborations with John Lennon (*Unfinished Music No. 1: Two Virgins*; *Unfinished Music No. 2: Life With The Lions*; *Wedding Album*), her seven solo albums (*Yoko Ono/Plastic Ono Band*; *Fly*; *Approximately Infinite Universe*; *Feeling The Space*; *Seasons Of Glass*; *It's Alright*; *Starpeace*), and one previously unreleased album (*A Story*). Much of this material is being released for the first time on CD, and as an added incentive, each CD includes bonus tracks. Every CD is also individually numbered.

Ono said that Rykodisc had always planned on reissuing her albums after testing the waters with *Onobox*. "When they approached me to do *Onobox*, they wanted to retain the rights to put out individual albums later," she explained. "But I didn't know what 'later' meant. I thought probably they'd forgotten the idea. And then they came back."

All the material included in *Onobox* was remastered for that set, and the new CDs have been remastered again. "I thought it really is important to remaster very carefully," Ono says. "In the box set, I couldn't put in music like the *Two Virgins*, *Life With The Lions*, or *Wedding Album* stuff, because Rykodisc said 'Only six CDs.' And even that was giving me a lot! And so when I started to remaster, I was remastering the early ones [first], *Two Virgins* and all that. And I realized that the music had a lot of avant-garde touch to it. It's very, very difficult for people to remaster without me overseeing it very carefully. So this time around I decided to really get into the remastering."

Goldmine has covered Ono's music and career in previous issues (Oct. 9, 1987, May 1, 1992 and July 19, 1996). As a result, this interview focuses on Ono's thoughts regarding each Rykodisc reissue.

Unfinished Music No. 1: Two Virgins
Original Label: Tetragrammaton (U.S.)/Track (U.K.)
Original Release Date: Nov. 11, 1968(U.S.)/ Nov. 29, 1968 (U.K.)

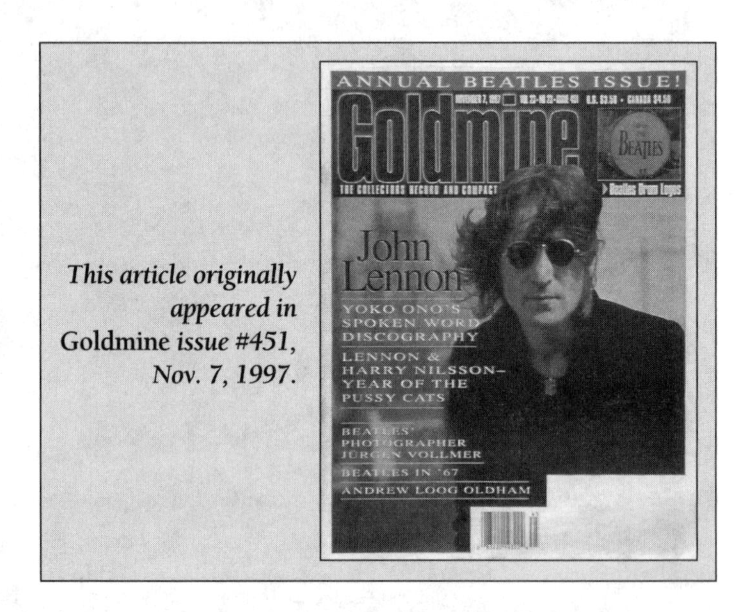

This article originally appeared in* Goldmine *issue #451, Nov. 7, 1997.

Bonus Track: "Remember Love" (B-side to "Give Peace A Chance")

Notes: Ono and Lennon are the sole musicians on the album, which was recorded in Lennon's home studio in May 1968. The album was notorious for the cover picture of Ono and Lennon in the nude.

This was your first musical collaboration with John. What was that like?

Well, in hindsight, I was a very nervous person and John's a very nervous person.

And when I was invited into his living room, he was saying, "So, we can do two things. We can just sit here and chat. Or we can go upstairs and make music. Which do you think?" And of course I saw that for me it would be easier to make music with somebody rather than small talk. It sounded like an easier situation. And then we started to make music. It was fun; it was that original concept of playing music, the word "play." That's a very important aspect of music, I think, instead of getting so serious that it's contrived. So we were just playing music, let's put it that way. It was nice.

Were you thinking of releasing it at the time?

No, no, definitely not until much later when we were living together. We were playing it to Paul [McCartney], and Paul would say some nice things, very civilized! And we went, "Well, we think we can put it out." And John was looking at Paul like, "What are you going to say?" kind of thing. So we put it out. The music part was all right, but the

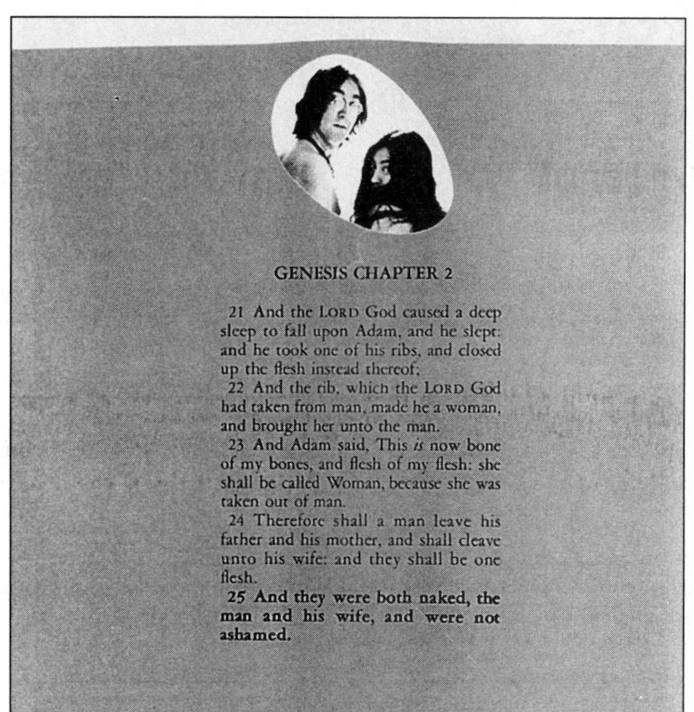

***Two Virgins*, front and back. Reissue.**

cover, I don't think that the other three liked the idea! "Are you really going to?"

Whose idea was the cover shot?

John wanted to do it as the cover, so you can say it's John's idea. John photographed it too. The concept of standing together naked, I had a filmic idea about it, but I didn't think of putting it on the cover of the record!

Did you have reservations about doing it?

No, not at all. I immediately thought it was a great idea. And it was very strange because, great idea? What was I thinking! John had somebody set it up so that he could [take the picture] automatically with a switch, and then he kicked everybody out, and we took off our clothes. We were shy people. And it's very strange to say "shy" because we were about to show our nakedness to the whole world! So what is with kicking everybody out and taking the photo? But that's how we did it.

Did you anticipate the fuss it would cause?

No. From my point of view, I was in the artistic community where a painter did a thing about rolling a naked woman with blue paint on her body on a canvas; nakedness was part of the event "happening" kind of thing that was going on at the time. The only difference was that we were going to stand together, which I thought was very interesting, instead of always exploiting women's bodies. This was, we are together, man and woman. And also it wasn't a sexy scene; it was just standing straight. I liked that concept. And that's why I had this filmic idea about us standing naked and being filmed in a way that we're part of nature or something like that. But John's idea about putting it on an album cover, wow! That was very good.

Now that you were working with John, what were your thoughts about being more in the mainstream?

I didn't think the quality of the music was something that we had to worry about. I thought it was nice and wild and not contrived at all. There were some very interesting things that we were doing; I felt that in the avant-garde I was doing that kind of thing. But there's a certain kind of contrivedness in the avant-garde; already avant-garde was kind of established. And there was a kind of contrivedness that was coming in. And this [album] was going back to the primitiveness that I thought was very important. I was a rebel. In the avant-garde, I was busy rebelling against avant-garde! So when I met John it was really great to team up and kind of stick our tongue out to the avant-garde. But of course it was sticking our tongue out to the other mainstream circle of people, which I never thought of. For me, it was just sticking my tongue out to the avant-garde, my colleagues.

Unfinished Music No. 2: Life With The Lions
Original Label: Zapple Original
Release Date: May 26, 1969 (U.S.)/May 9, 1969 (U.K.)
Bonus Tracks: "Song For John," "Mulberry" (both previously unreleased, circa 1968)

Notes: Ono and Lennon provide most of the music and vocals. Outside musicians appear on the live track "Cambridge 1969." Other tracks are recorded at Queen Charlott's Hospital, London, November 1968.

Was this album your way of sending a message to the public? The cover shots (depicting the two leaving a police station after being arrested and in the hospital at the time of Ono's miscarriage) make it look like you were living under siege.

Well, we were! But we weren't feeling that we were living under siege. We were busy creating new ideas and we were excited by the ideas. That, and the fact that we were in love with each other, all that was so exciting. So the kind of thing that was happening — by the way, we were in the hospital when we were arrested — was like a dream, you know? It's like something that was happening outside of us. We were busy thinking about all these ideas that are coming into our heads.

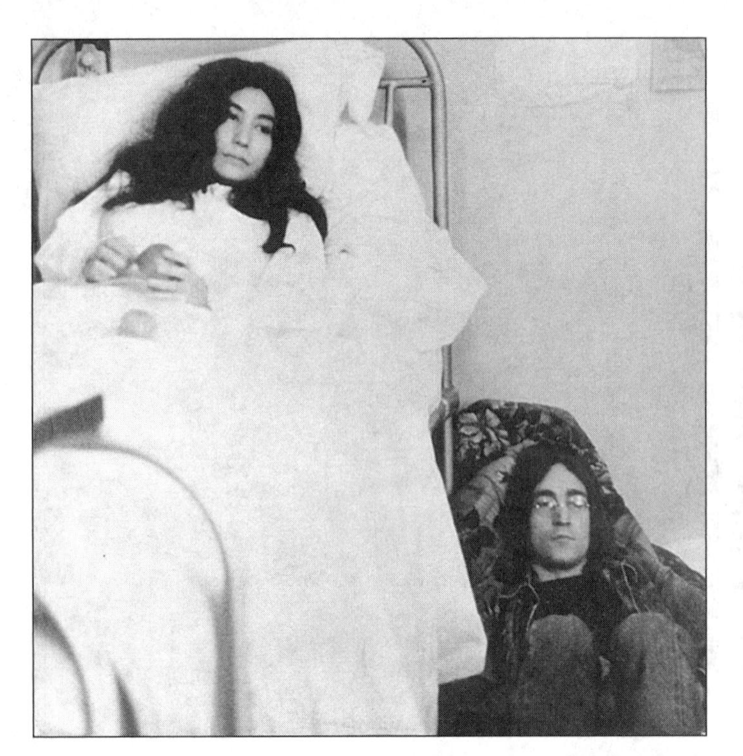

***Life With The Lions* front and back.**

When did you decide to start recording in the hospital?

I think in the hospital the main thing that we were thinking of was making this film called *Rape* [in which a woman is "raped" by the constant scrutiny of the film camera]. And the concept of the film, the theme of the film, the instructions of the film, was created before I went into this strange, exploitative atmosphere. In other words, I made the instructions before John and I got together. Isn't that weird? That I would think of a filmic idea like that without knowing what I'm going to get into? And when I saw the film after John's passing, because I had to put it in some festival somewhere, I got chills. I was describing the life I was going to be in without knowing it. But in *Life With The Lions*, I think what John is doing is very interesting. "Radio Play," that's his idea. The scratch, scratch in the track, it's like the real disco scratch, the beginning of that. So there was a lot of creative things we were doing at the time, and a fearlessness that was created because we were together and we were in love. Creative things that we could never even have created if we were not together. In other words, John might have done it, but he would not have put it out as a record. Or John might have done it without thinking that he could ever put it out. The idea came because we were together.

Did the album begin like Two Virgins*, with no initial thought of releasing it?*

It was bits and pieces that we made, small short moments. Like "Baby's Heartbeat" was taken when the baby was still alive and kicking and we were happy. And so when we started the record together we wanted to throw that in.

"Two Minutes Silence" — we know where that title came from!

In "Two Minutes Silence," we sent a tribute to John Cage in a way. Cage did "4:33," and the title was the timing, the time. And he was saying the music is the sound that comes in, the sounds that come in during the silence, like environmental sounds, that was the music. So we were going to make a piece called "Two Minutes Silence," and we were giggling, because we did the opposite, which was we made it totally dead silence! Like, this is the real silence, baby! So we were just being rebellious.

As usual.

But nobody knew about John Cage. And the ones who knew about Cage, they were like, "This has been done before." They didn't get the humor of it.

People miss a lot of the humor in your work.

Exactly.

"Cambridge 1969" documents your performance in Cambridge, England on March 2, 1969. Did you rehearse for the performance at all?

No, no, no, Cambridge asked me to come and do it before they knew about John and me. When we got together, there's a few appointments I missed because we were so involved with each other. But John was saying, "Call them back, call them back," so I said, "OK, I'll call back," and I said, "Yes, I will come." And then John was saying, "Say that you'll bring your own band." "OK. I'm bringing my own band." And my own band turns out to be just John. It was fun.

Wedding Album

Original Label: Apple

Original Release Date: Oct. 20, 1969 (U.S.)/Nov. 7, 1969 (U.K.)

Bonus Tracks: "Who Has Seen The Wind?" (B-side to "Instant Karma!"); "Listen The Snow Is Falling" (B-side to "Happy Xmas [War Is Over]"); "Don't Worry Kyoko (Mummy's Only Looking For Her Hand In The Snow)" (previously unreleased, from the same tape as "Song For John" and "Mulberry," the *Lions* bonus tracks)

Notes: Ono and Lennon are the sole musicians, though "Amsterdam" includes comments from other people during

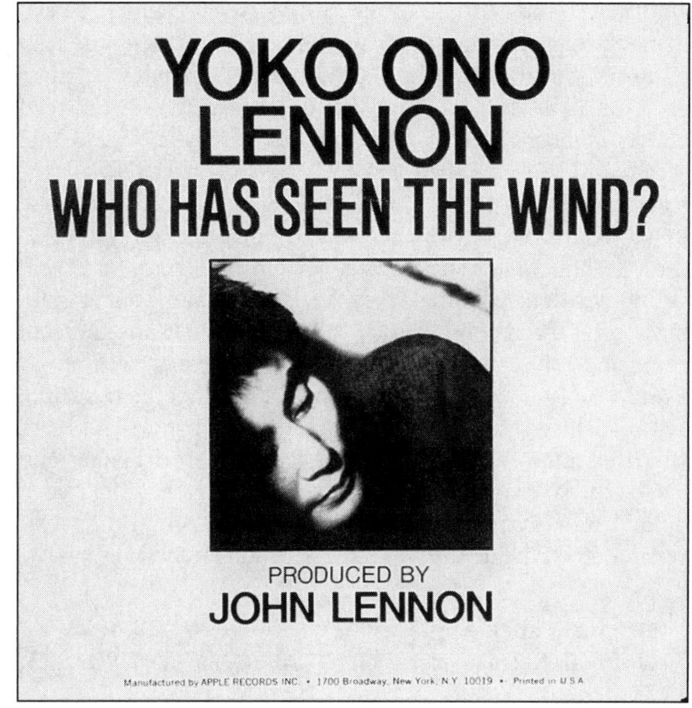

the interview segments. "John & Yoko," recorded at Abbey Road Studios April 22, 1969.

Was this record meant as a "thank you" to the public?

Sharing, that was the word we thought of.

How did you decide what to put on it?

We did all these things and then we thought, "Well, why not a wedding album?" "Amsterdam" is to do with the bed-in.

And then the other side is "John & Yoko."

Screaming! John! Yoko! But I think that's music. I mean, that's how I formalized it. In other words, the heartbeat is the beat of rock, right? So we put our own heartbeats there as the beat of the music. And it starts with a kind of pianissimo and goes on to crescendo and approaches largo, and it goes into a faster rhythm and then it goes into a big fortissimo kind of thing. I mean, we did it right! And then most people just ignored the form, the musical form. "They were just screaming!"

But you also did songs like "Who Has Seen The Wind?"; why were those overlooked?

They're just ballads, it's not anything controversial. It's almost like saying, "Wow, Bill and Jill have married for 30 years!" That doesn't become news, you know what I mean? But "They split," or "They killed each other," that's news!

So if you'd done a ballad and screamed at the end, that would've got more notice.

Well, we didn't do it for that, we did it for the art's sake.

Yoko Ono/Plastic Ono Band
Original Label: Apple
Original Release Date: Dec. 20, 1970 (U.S. and U.K.)
Bonus Tracks: "Open Your Box" and "Something More Abstract" (both *Plastic Ono Band* outtakes); "The South Wind" (previously unreleased, recorded in New York, early '70s)

Notes: Musicians include Ringo Starr, Klaus Voormann; Ornette Coleman appears on the track "AOS." Other tracks recorded at Abbey Road Studios, October 1970.

This album was recorded at the same time as John Lennon/Plastic Ono Band. *Was it difficult working on two albums at once?*

It was really not a factor. I'm one of those people who's thinking about 20 different things and doing 20 different things at the same time. That's a norm for me. It was fine. It was in fact very exciting. I didn't get equal time, mind you. It was done on the side. And then after I was done — I think John has mentioned this in *Lennon Remembers* or something — I had a few snips of takes, and OK, I'll make something out of it. One night was dedicated to doing that, and I was doing it, and John was fascinated. And he got into the game too. And he loved it and we finished it by dawn, meaning the collage part of it, doing things with the tape.

Did the songs come out of jams? Did you do more than one take of a song like "Why'?

No, no, no. It was just one take, And then I did editing, things like that, juggled around. But I wanted to create a feeling of a jam. And they're good aren't they? They're having fun I think.

It sounds very energized.

It was very punky.

It sounds like a very DIY punk thing, recorded quickly.

Very.

Did it take a couple of days to record?

No, it was just one afternoon. It was one afternoon, and there were a few little other tracks that were lying around. Little strips of this and that. And then I had some soundtracks, sound effect records and things like that. And I put it together.

So many of the "lyrics" are one word. Did you feel the feelings you were trying to express couldn't be put into words?

Yes, that too. I was telling John about this famous actress

who was considered one of the best by George Bernard Shaw, that era. She was such an incredible actress that she just read numbers, but the way she recited numbers people started to cry. And I was talking about that to John, saying, "I can read phone numbers and make people cry," and he was saying, "Yeah, I'd like to see that happen." And so I said, "OK, I'll just read this newspaper, look, this article here, 'No Bed For Beatle John.'" And that's how I did "No Bed For Beatle John," just to show to him what I mean. That anything can be a song. And "Why" was done with that spirit. I was being daring about making a song that is one word. It can be said in many different ways, and it just makes something else. And when we put out *Plastic Ono Band*, a month later John was listening to the radio, saying, "Ah! They picked up on it! They heard yours and that's why this artist is doing that!" The critics were laughing and maybe the whole world was laughing, but the artists picked it up and were inspired by what we did and they did their own version, so on that level I think we were communicating.

Fly

Original Label: Apple

Original Release Date: Sept. 20, 1971 (U.S.)/Dec. 3, 1971 (U.K.)

Bonus Tracks: "Between The Takes" (*Yoko Ono/Plastic Ono Band* outtake); "Will You Touch Me?" (previously unreleased, circa early '70s)

Notes: Musicians include Starr, Voormann, and Eric Clapton. Recorded at Ascot (Ono and Lennon's English estate) and The Record Plant, New York City, summer 1971.

Your songs started to have a more conventional structure now.

Well, *Fly* is still very unconventional stuff. What about "O Wind"? There are many different types of music in there. "Open Your Box," that was controversial. It's called "Hirake," but that was to hide from the censorship! It was already censored, so we just slipped it in like that. But *Fly* has more [conventional] songs as well. I had a few songs, and John was saying, "Why don't you put them out as an album?" "OK, we'll do that." So it happened like that. Up to then, it was always like I'm doing a strip of this, a strip of that, here and there. And they're all sitting on the shelf. And then we string it together and make it into a record.

Why did you decide to make it a double album?

Because there was enough material for a double album.

When did you start working on the album?

There was no "working" on the songs at all up to then. Like "Midsummer New York," I wrote it, and then we went into the studio and we did long hours of John's songs and I was just sitting there. And when everybody was tired and it was two o'clock in the morning, John said, "OK, we'll round it up now, we did a good job. Oh, by the way, there's a song that Yoko thought of this morning. Can we just try that?" "OK, we'll try it." It was like that. And I just got on the platform and started singing. I sang it twice, one I sang it like normal, and then one I was fooling around and doing like Elvis or something. And John said, "That's the one, it sounds good." And I didn't even rehearse!

Was that frustrating, working that way?

Well, I thought it was normal. I mean, here's this big John Lennon, so I didn't think anything of it. No, it's not like I didn't think anything of it. I think it was almost like I was enjoying the challenge, maybe, that I can just do it like that. I guess!

Turning the negative into a positive. Tell me about "Mrs. Lennon."

I wrote it in Ascot. Ascot life was strange! It reminded me of *Citizen Kane*. I'm sitting there and I see this retired colonel

Plastic Ono Band performing on *Top Of The Pops*.

who was our gardener, coming from far, far away in the distance, in the huge garden, just walking very slowly. And I'd think, 'What is he doing?' And then I'd hear that he was downstairs; I'd hear little whispers, the sound of voices. And then the maid coming up and saying, "The colonel left these flowers for you, Mrs. Lennon." "Oh, thank you." Uh-huh. Mrs. Lennon! It was like that.

How did you feel dealing in an artistic realm where things like chart placings are important?

There were always people who were just interested in the commercial side. And I think that John treaded on the edge, where he could be commercial and also say something meaningful. It's a very tricky thing. I think he was more artsy than commercial in some ways. And in my case, I think that now I'm finally coming to a point where I can see that OK, there's some people who really want to hear my music. And that's that. That's how I feel about it. I don't think OK, am I going in the Top 10 or something like that. I don't feel that way. And that's fine. There's a bunch of people like that, writers, composers. We're just doing it for the fun of it and trying to create something that they feel OK about.

Yet here you were creating a new style of music that was largely not appreciated at the time. Was that difficult to deal with?

Yeah, I was totally surprised that they didn't understand it. I was very naive. I'm thinking, "Wow, what is this that they don't understand it at all and are just saying that it's screaming?" But that's how you gradually get through and start to create a different kind of awareness. I mean, talk about not understanding in the beginning. The Beatles, because they had a Liverpool accent, people didn't understand them at all. Now it sounds like a joke; everybody understands them. So the ears changed; their ears tuned up for it. And now, like *Plastic Ono Band*, nobody thinks that I'm just screaming. They know that I was doing some interesting notation. So that's how it keeps changing and widening the horizon of music, how much you can do. And it's fun to do that.

Approximately Infinite Universe

Original Label: Apple

Original Release Date: Jan. 8, 1973 (U.S.)/Feb. 16, 1973 (U.K.)

Bonus Tracks: "Dogtown" (Previously unreleased, circa early '70s) "She Gets Down On Her Knees" (previously unreleased, circa 1974)

Notes: Elephant's Memory provide the musical backing; recorded at The Record Plant and Butterfly Studios, New York City, October-November 1972.

It seems like you had an explosion of songwriting during this period, recording Some Time In New York City *in March 1972,* Approximately Infinite Universe *in October 1972, and* Feeling The Space *in April 1973. What sparked that?*

I don't know. Words were flowing and just kept coming to me. All this notation, the music and the words, they were just coming to me, that's all. And I kept wanting to put them out. And each time I'd go to the studio, I'd think of another song. Each one of them could've been triple albums! And I didn't want to do that. And so I kept some songs in the file. So I go in for the next album, and I bring some songs from the file out, and it just goes on.

The songs were also becoming more openly feminist.

You see, what happened to me, when I was brought up in several places, I never thought that I was being deprived; there was no "You're a woman, so don't study," kind of attitude. That was not there. And when I was in America, it was fine too. And then I go to England, and suddenly I'm in this family of Apple, shall we say. And I'm suddenly facing a situation like when the boys are discussing things, all the women are in the kitchen, chatting. Like the kind of situation that you see in the 18th century. And I'm thinking, "What is this? Wait a minute, wait a minute! Aren't we in the 20th century?" I suppose the crowd, the environment that I had been in, was privileged in a sense, whether it's college or going to New York City; it's this kind of artistic crowd. So I never encountered a situation like that, where that was going on. But I was again privileged, because John would not do that to me. So I'm the only woman who would be in the living room. But then I felt badly about it. And I would go back and forth, between the kitchen and the living room. And then I thought all the stuff that I went through was not so much John doing it but the people around him. Then in one of the interviews I said, "Women are the niggers of the world," and that became like "OK, we're going to write a song about it." The first feminist song was "Sisters O Sisters," and then "Woman Is The Nigger Of The World," lyrically John and I wrote it together. But the music was John's. I suppose if I could not express myself in song at the time, whether it was "Mrs. Lennon" or "Death Of Samantha" or whatever, John would have had a very difficult irritable partner sitting there! Like an out of job guy or something. So it was very good that instead of repressing myself and pushing my anger inside or taking it out on John or something, they all came out as songs. Which is great! Because I was feeling good about all the songs coming out. And John was a very understanding and encouraging partner because he's an artist too. And he appreciated the work, so I think he was amused and inspired as well. So it was good. It was like a dialogue was going on.

Why weren't those themes in earlier songs?

In the beginning, I was being a little bit polite, I suppose. Like John was saying when he was a child and he wanted to write things in his diary, Mimi would always look into it, so he would start to write in gobbledygook and that's how his expressions became surreal. It's a bit like that. I was tiptoeing around a bit. "Open Your Box," that's a hint. And "Don't Worry Kyoko," "Mrs. Lennon." "Why," "Why Not." It's all a message of, "So, what's happening?"

Was it a big deal to have so many feminist songs on the records?

It was a very feminist time. There were a lot of feminists who were really coming out and speaking out. But some feminists almost ignored me, though there's sections of feminists who were very nice to me too. But the idea was that I was a wife of a rich man. They were more interested in career women. In general, there was a criticism about feminists ignoring the housewives. And I fit that category of being a housewife; "Oh, John Lennon's a powerful person and she's just a wife." And then they were talking about Lesbian Nations and all that kind of thing, and I thought that was very interesting, but at the same time, being heterosexual, they felt that I was compromising by being with a man. So I kind of fell in between all that stuff. But even now, I think it was important for me to be true to myself and stand up for being a woman who goes through all the experiences of being a woman, in a sense of having had to cope with a guy, or men. Because 50 percent of the population is women, but the other half is men. And it's better that we reach out or cope with each other.

You tried to address both sides, being a feminist, but also sympathetic to men.

Or caring about another human being.

Like on "I Want My Man To Rest Tonight."

"I Want My Man" was controversial in the sense that the sisters didn't like it so much; "What is that?" But I felt that way, because of the love that I had for John. But also I felt the other way "I'm A Witch" [on *A Story*] is a song that I couldn't put out then, because I'm saying, "I'm a witch, I'm a bitch." But strangely, this Top 10 song, one of the women [Meredith Brooks] is singing "I'm a bitch"! Oh! It came to a point that now we can say, "I'm a bitch," it's great! But when you said, "Weren't you upset that you had to do things on the side," I think that's what most women went through, or shall we say most housewives went through. And that's how it was. And when you say "housewives" you can include people like writers in the old days, like the woman who wrote *Uncle Tom's Cabin* [Harriet Beecher Stowe]; she said that she used to write it in the morning when the kids were asleep or something like that. That's the tradition of women in a way. In the end, maybe it'll be totally a different society where most babies are made in an incubator or something like that. But as it stands now, the fact that women have babies, that is the thing that really makes a difference in our position, with men and women. Even though we demand, "OK, you better take care of the kid too," that's different from this instinctive connection you have with the child. It becomes like, "OK, there's that big connection, there's nothing you can do about it, you're stuck with it." And from the guy's point of view, they can make an effort, but they don't have to. They can say goodbye and go to another country or something. So that is the thing that we have to really face and cope with, that situation.

Thurston Moore said he liked seeing you and John on The Mike Douglas Show *in 1972 because it was the first time he'd seen a man talk about feminism.*

Yeah, it's great, isn't it? All sisters were doing it in their own way. Each sister was doing it in her own way, to change the world, to change the concept, the basic concept of what it is to be a woman and a man in this society. And that was my gift to the sisters and therefore to the world. The fact that I turned John on to understanding what women go through.

Had you moved beyond recording songs in one take by this point?

I think it was almost like one take, most of them. One of the reasons being because there were so many songs. And I would say, "Can we do this too? Can we do this too?"

"OK, we'll do it..." It was a bit like that.

So you wanted to get it done before the band got fed up and wanted to leave.

Yeah, well, they were wanting to leave already! From the beginning! So we did all the stuff pretty quickly.

Tell me about "Death Of Samantha."

I think we did it maybe twice, but the first one was better. I'm one of those people like, there are guitarists that you say, "OK, do you want to do a solo here?" and he just goes and it's brilliant. And then he can never match that again. And then there's another kind of guitarist who does it over and over again and they're much better then. There's two kinds of artists, I think. But anyway, the first take was pretty good. Because my emotion was in it.

What inspired the song?

Well, this was a situation that was sort of famous, I think. George McGovern lost the election [in 1972] and that night at Jerry Rubin's place they had a party. And John was getting a little bit high, and by the time that we went to the party he was very high. And then he just took a girl and pulled her into the next room, and we're hearing all this noise and everything, and everybody's trying to pretend like they weren't listening to it. And then someone was putting a record on and putting it a bit loud so that maybe that would erase the noise. And I'm just sitting there and everybody's looking at me or saying something like, "Well, you do understand how much we love him. He's our hero. You know that." Or something like, "Don't get too upset about this, you've got to understand, this is rock 'n' roll." And I'm turning pale and I'm just sitting there. It was a very painful moment. In hindsight, I understand he was drunk, but at that point it was a shock. And of course he was shocked too in a way. And he felt very badly; he wrote the song called "Aisumasen" — "I'm Sorry." I was just kind of frozen for a while. And then we were going to go to the studio. And John went in another room, and this whole "Death Of Samantha" just came to me. And I was writing it like crazy on paper, and I just started saying, "OK, give me E minor, OK, let's go" or something, and I started singing. And then John came into the room and he said, "Oh! Do I have to hear this!" So he was surprised. But my emotion was totally into it.

Feeling The Space

Original Label: Apple

Original Release Date: Nov. 2, 1973 (U.S.)/Nov. 23, 1973 (U.K.)

Bonus Tracks: "I Learned To Stutter"/"Coffin Car" (previously unreleased, speech excerpt and live performance at the First International Feminist Planning Conference at Harvard University, Cambridge, Mass., June 1973); "Mildred, Mildred" (previously unreleased, circa early '70s)

Notes: Musicians include David Spinozza and Jim Keltner. Recorded at The Record Plant, New York City, spring-summer 1973.

You were the sole producer on Feeling The Space*; what did that mean as far as working on the album?*

It was OK. You were saying, "How come that you were getting more feminist, the songs?" and I'm just thinking about it. I think John went through a soul search [at the time]. The first soul search he had about feminism is the fact that the whole world was attacking me and the way I was treated by people around him. He realized that it was unfair to me, because he understood that I was an artist of a certain caliber. And he said, "If you were a guy, this would not have happened." At one point, finally, he said, "OK, why don't we just tell the world that you are actually a guy!" So that was the first soul search, thinking, "Wow, what

women go through, that's too much." And I think the next soul search was to find out that he was not a kind of man who was caring about that, he was also a macho guy. So then he felt totally sympathetic to women, sympathetic to me, with a lot of feeling of guilt about what I had to go through. And so while he was becoming more and more understanding about things, it was easier for me to express our position, the woman's position. If I did it at the time that we just met — my presence was pretty feminist anyway — but I think that at the time, expressing it in a very artsy way was probably appropriate. And then I started to express it more definitely, which was the right moment when he started to come around. I wasn't pushing him to the edge when he wasn't ready. And this was not calculated, it just happened that way. And with *Feeling The Space*, up to then it was like him saying, "OK, we'll go in to the studio. And I'm going to do this or that. And then if we have time we'll do one of your songs." There was that attitude. Though I thought it was very good of him to even think of giving me a chance to do something. Because the macho atmosphere, especially in the rock world, most people around us were thinking, "Why would he do that? Why would he even take her to the studio? Most wives have to sit at home just counting the hours or cooking the porridge or something, so he'll come back and eat the porridge." So I thought it was very big of him to do that, in that kind of tradition. And he was steeped in that tradition. It was a very big step for him. And then, in *Feeling The Space*, I had so many songs, I didn't know what to do. I wasn't going to say, "OK, I'm going to go to the studio by myself." But it was like he sussed it; "She's got all those songs, and she's itchy, so she's going to go to the studio." He became ready to give me a space like that, which was very, very big of him. And so I went to the studio and I just did it. By then he knew that I could just do it.

Did being the sole producer help you better realize your vision?

It was a very interesting experience in the sense that I was still coping with very macho musicians. But I would come home with a rough mix and John would be waiting, and he would listen to it and he would make comments.

Was that the first time you'd worked with session musicians?

Yeah, this was the first time I worked with session musicians, that's for sure.

Was that OK?

It was OK in a sense that they were very professional.

Do you think they were into your music?

Not necessarily. But they were professional musicians of the highest caliber. So they probably did it out of pride. They wanted to do a good job. And probably they were thinking, "Well, we're too good for Yoko." I don't know what they were thinking, but there was that attitude. And when remix time came, they were concerned about their playing, and so we'd push up the guitar or we'd push up the bass or we'd push up this, that and the other, and the voice was sacrificed. There was a little bit of that. But I did think, "This is really amazing. Somebody's giving me a chance now." All those things were happening. And when you listen to those songs on *Feeling The Space*, you know how I was treated in the studio. Though it was my session, I was the producer, I was paying for the whole thing, but their attitude was I don't know. A little bit like, "Why do we have to do this for Mrs. Lennon?" kind of attitude.

That's ironic considering they were recording songs like "Woman Power."

I think maybe that's why they didn't like it! That happened with Elephant's Memory too, on *Approximately Infinite Universe*. Elephant's Memory were very macho guys, and they have to play these songs? When I'm saying "What A Bastard The World Is" or something. Of course I can understand that they weren't very happy about it. But I know that their girlfriends, they were all sitting there, and they started to get into it. And the album communicated to them, I think. I hope.

Tell me about "Woman Power."

Oh, you like that one?

Yeah, I really like that beginning groove.

I was just inspired to write it. And the fact that it became so good was because with "She Hits Back" and "Woman Power," John liked them so much he said, "OK, do you just want to let me come to the studio, like a regular session musician, and I'll do a solo for 'Woman Power' and 'She

Hits Back'?" And I said, "Sure, that's fine." So he came and he did those solos. And the "Woman Power" solo is really great. It's the kind of solo that those session musicians who were playing then wouldn't have played. The session musicians for *Feeling The Space* were mostly jazz-oriented. John understood all that, and he wasn't commenting or anything like that, but he said, "'Woman Power,' you need my solo. Let me do it, let me do it." And he just came to the studio — "Hi, here I am. Let me do it." And he just did it, then left. Very professionally. John was a perfectionist! And so once he felt that the women were not getting a chance, he wanted to do everything right. And he was very helpful. He was proud of that particular solo in "Woman Power," and we all loved it. It was great.

Was the live bonus track taken from a whole performance?

Well, this was funny too. It was the First International Woman's Conference in Cambridge, and I was invited. And so I went, naturally, with John. Whenever there was a woman's meeting or something I'd say, "Look, I'm going to bring my husband, 'cause he's a friend, he's a partner. And I want a guy to participate in the feminist movement." And that wasn't too popular among the feminist people — "Really bringing a guy?" But the other side of it was that these very macho feminist women liked John of course. "Wow, John Lennon's coming! OK, fine." It's a very complex feeling they had. Shouldn't they be disdaining the fact that this guy's coming? But actually, their hearts are jumping a little. And so at this feminist meeting, I took John with me. And they wanted me to do a concert, so I did maybe six, 10 songs, I don't remember how many. And John was my accompanist. He played the guitar. And we have a little shot of video towards the end of that concert. It's beautiful. He was just trying to stay in the background.

A Story
Original Label: None
Original Release Date: None
Bonus Tracks: "Anatanio Te/Your Hands," "Extension 33" (previously unreleased, circa mid-late '70s); "Now Or Never" (previously unreleased, recorded live in Budapest, Hungary, March 14, 1986)

Notes: Musicians include David Spinozza and Hugh McCracken. Recorded at The Record Plant, New York City, in early 1974.

A Story *was also featured in a different version on* Onobox; *is this one an alternate version or the definitive version?*

This one is "the story." When I put it in *Onobox*, I couldn't put everything in. I also wanted to put "We're All Water" in [from *Some Time In New York City*], I wanted to put "Namyohorengekyo" in, "Yume O Moto," was in for Japan, and "Josei-Joi Banzai" was important too. So stuff like "She Gets Down On Her Knees," it's interesting the way I changed it on *Season Of Glass*, but because we had to get it on the *Season Of Glass* CD [the *No, No, No* disc on *Onobox*] I dropped that. That kind of thing. So I dropped a few songs.

Was it something you felt you had to record?

No, I didn't feel that way. This is what happened with *A Story*. A lot of songs on *A Story* were already there when I did *Feeling The Space*. Because one, I'd go in with a set of songs. But then when I'm recording, I get inspired and write other songs. So it was going on and on a bit. *Feeling The Space* I thought would be a double album, definitely. And then I realized, "Whoops!" I think I was even advised by the record company, "Don't do that." We all felt one of the reasons that *Fly* and *Approximately Infinite Universe*, especially *Approximately Infinite Universe*, didn't fly — didn't fly! — was because they were double albums. So let's keep it a single. And I was thinking that's really important, because *Feeling The Space* is a message album. So it's important that it circulates. And so there were songs left; naturally I wanted to go in again. And after *Feeling The Space*, well, almost in the middle of *Feeling The Space*, there was a little... I don't know how to put it. There was a little kind of seven-year itch or something.

"Whenever there was a woman's meeting or something I'd say, 'Look, I'm going to bring my husband, 'cause he's a friend, he's a partner. And I want a guy to participate in the feminist movement.' And that wasn't too popular among the feminist people — 'Really bringing a guy?' But the other side of it was that these very macho feminist women liked John of course. 'Wow, John Lennon's coming! OK, fine.'"

— Yoko Ono

You mean the separation of you and John?

Well, the separation didn't start until after *Feeling The Space*. But there was that feeling of "OK, I'm getting to be strong." And John was feeling suffocated. And I felt that everybody was saying I was the possessive one who wanted to keep John under my thumb, and that was not true at all. I wasn't trying to do that. I was thinking, "Don't they know that maybe it's suffocating for me to be the wife of a famous guy like John?" So I thought, "This is a time that we should separate and look into ourselves and see what's going on." And so the separation happened, and I immediately went into recording *A Story*. It was like that. It was that kind of time.

Why wasn't the album released?

I was thinking, "OK, I'm going to release this." But before that happened, John and I came back together. It was a very romantic coming back together. We were enjoying the fact that we didn't burn bridges, and so it was more important to concentrate on being together. And I knew that the press would be very mean and everything. Well, they were always mean to me. But bringing this record out was not that important. And it would have been subjected to a lot of "Was this inspired by the separation?" So I thought, "No, I'm just going to shelve it."

Until Onobox *came about I didn't even know you'd been recording an album.*

Well, it was not the most earth-shattering news at the time. So I'm sure very few people caught it.

I didn't know "Hard Times Are Over" [which appeared on Double Fantasy*] was from that period.*

Isn't that amazing? I'll tell you how that was inspired. It was a song inspired by the fact that John and I, after *Approximately Infinite Universe* — so that would be 1973, spring, around that time — went cross-country to Ohio and then to L.A. Cross-country in a car. And the car stopped at Salt Lake City and John and I were just standing on the corner of the street. And we just looked at each other. And that's when the song came about! I think there's something about that in the song, the lyrics. So that was another song floating around from the *Feeling The Space* era, though it didn't fit *Feeling The Space*, so I didn't put it there. "The leaves are shining in the sun/And I'm smiling inside/You and I watching each other on a street corner... Hard times are over/Over for a while." You know what this hard time was?

What?

Drugs. And this cross-country trip was to shake it. We were going to withdraw. And we were withdrawing while we were going cross-country. Can you imagine that? It was a station wagon, Peter Bentley, our assistant was driving, and we were trying to get off drugs. And it was really frightening! So we're standing on a corner looking at each and saying, "OK, we're going to get off drugs, it's great!'

I'd heard about that trip, but I didn't know if was true that you were kicking drugs.

No, we were kicking drugs. Which is fine. I don't think that's a bad story, kicking drugs.

Season Of Glass

Original Label: Geffen

Original Release Date: June 8, 1981 (U.S.)/June 12, 1981 (U.K.)

Bonus Tracks: "Walking On Thin Ice" (single); "I Don't Know Why" (previously unreleased, recorded Dec. 9, 1980)

Notes: Musicians include Hugh McCracken and Tony Levin; Sean Lennon contributes a spoken-word piece. Recorded at The Hit Factory, New York City, early 1981.

Was it inhibiting to think this album would be seen as your response to John's death?

That's another thing that's so funny. People say, "What did you think when you were going to do a bed-in?' I never expected any reaction in the way it happened. Being an artist, you get an idea, and you go with it. And you just make something. You don't think, "Well, this is going to be considered my response to John's death." I never thought that way. It's just the fact that I was frantic and I was going crazy, and I had to work, that's all. I just had to work. If I didn't work, if I didn't do music, I couldn't have survived. My mind was just about at the edge, you know?

Courtney Love said that about returning to touring after her husband Kurt Cobain killed himself.

I totally understand that. I totally understand that. "Walking On Thin Ice," the video, I made it in January, and some critic was saying, "When was this made?" as if I did something wrong, that I should just be crying in the apartment or something. That notion of, "A widow should not be doing this." I think that it's so devastating to go through that kind of experience, that a widow should be allowed to do anything. Not to hurt people or anything like that, but to get over it. To survive. To rescue their sanity. And everybody's watching her. It was really weird. It was like a week from when John died, and some friends, because I couldn't eat anything, kept saying, "OK, we are going to take you to this pizza place, so get dressed. We're not going to let you just sit in bed like this." And I got dressed. And I was wobbling, but I went to the pizza place. And it's not like I could eat, but just sitting with them was nice. And that was in the news like something I shouldn't be doing! It was an outrageous thing that I did! I was really thankful to the friends who did stuff for me. Not because I wanted the pizza, it just put my mind off what I was in. And in the same way, I made *Season Of Glass*.

Where did the songs come from?

Most from *A Story*. And then I wrote "No, No, No." And I wrote "I Don't Know Why."

I like the sequence of "I Don't Know Why," "Extension 33" and "No, No, No." They work well together. And "Extension 33" was seven years old by then.

Isn't that amazing. "Goodbye Sadness" was from a long time ago too. I wrote it when we were separated. John was in L.A. and people were calling me and saying, "You have to come and take care of him because we can't deal with him."

John was in a stupor or something. At first I said, "I'm not coming. Because all this time you guys were thinking I was the baddie who was holding him and all that. Now you've got him, OK? Just deal with it!" But then I got worried about John. And also John wanted me to come. So I went to L.A. and it was fine. And on my way back from L.A., I was in a plane by myself and I was intensely writing "Goodbye Sadness" just like I wrote "It's Alright" later. Goodbye sadness, I don't want any more sadness, this is crazy.

Was "Mind Weaver" new?

"Mind Weaver" was called "Mind Fucker" first! I wrote it when John was still around in 1980. And I was saying, "I don't know what to do about this 'Mind Fucker,' we can't put out a song called 'Mind Fucker'!" So I changed it a little.

"Even When You're Far Away."

"Even When You're Far Away" was written when we were separated, and the funny thing was, while I was writing "Even When You're Far Away," he was writing "Bless You." And so we were both very sad that we were away. But also we were expressing love for each other. It was sad but strange times.

"Nobody Sees Me Like You Do."

"Nobody Sees Me Like You Do" could've been on *Double Fantasy*. John loved the chord sequence. He was telling everybody, "Don't you like this chord sequence? Isn't that great?" He was just bragging about his wife. He had that side.

"Turn Of The Wheel"

"Turn Of The Wheel" was 1974.

"Dogtown"' we know is from an earlier period.

Way earlier, right. I was in Bank Street when I wrote that. That's '71 or '72.

I always liked the "Peas porridge hot" lines.

I did that kind of thing in "Carman" as well [on *Approximately Infinite Universe*]. I like using children's rhymes and changing it around so it's like a distorted children's rhyme.

"Silver Horse."

"Silver Horse" could've got in on *Double Fantasy*. John loved that song. We were going to put it in and we didn't. "Don't Be Scared" was from that era too. They could've gone into *Double Fantasy*, but they were never recorded.

"I Don't Know Why."

This is a very strange song. The bonus track is an a capella tape [of the song]. What happened was, the day after John's death there were 2,000 people outside and my bedroom was right there. The window was closed because it was winter. But when you play this tape, you first of all hear some car horns and things like that, but then you hear this kind of "aaah!" like the sound of the people. And the reason is because I was just sitting there at night by myself on the bed. And suddenly this whole song came through me, all with the chords and everything. And when I don't write it down or put it on a cassette tape quickly, I just forget songs. So I wobbled out of the bed and I got a cassette tape and I put "I Don't Know Why" on the tape.

"Will You Touch Me."

A long time ago. That was written because a Japanese singer came to me and said she wanted a song from me. And so I made it that song. And then I recorded it later, to send it to her, like a guide. A demo.

"She Gets Down On Her Knees" is an older song. "Toyboat."

"Toyboat" was then. "Toyboat" was like "I don't know what to say, help me out, help me out, please somebody help me out! I'm drowning!"

"Mother Of The Universe."

"Mother Of The Universe" I was writing when John was still around. And I did show it to him. I showed it to him on the piano. But it was just on the piano then. And so I recorded it on *Season Of Glass*.

What was it like working on the album?

With *Season Of Glass* I was very lucky that Phil Spector [the album's original producer] was there. Phil did it in a way that he does; he's like a king and he does everything the way he wants to. And the musicians just take it. And I started to feel like, "Phil is brilliant, but he has his own way, and it was going to be the 'wall of sound.'" And *Season Of Glass* was not a wall of sound kind of album in my mind. It could've been a wall of sound, beautiful, I love you, etc. album, and I'm sure that he was working on that. So he did all the basic tracks with me, and I thought, "From here on, it's going to be lots of overdubs, etc., and it will become the wall of sound." So at that point I explained to him about the vision I had, and that's when we parted. On very good terms. He understood what I wanted to do, though he didn't agree with it — he said, "You don't want success" or something. He might have been right! But I went for the artsy. So we parted in a good way. And the musicians were really gung ho in making this album well. Because they were the musicians from *Double Fantasy*, and we had a rapport and also feeling the loss and all that. So it was all done very well.

Tell me about "Walking On Thin Ice," one of your best-known songs.

John and I went to Chicago, and I saw Lake Michigan, and it was so huge and so incredibly large. Somebody was saying,

"As large as an ocean!" And I just remembered that. And when I was watching Lake Michigan, I even almost saw this girl just walking there, walking across the lake. So that's how it came about.

What about the rest of the lyrics? "I'm paying the price for throwing the dice in the air."

"Walking On Thin Ice" is how I felt about our life at the time. It wasn't easy for both of us, because we were happy about each other, and the family, especially, was getting all right. But still, John had a side that he gets very depressed about his life sometimes. And he was like that from when he was a young kid. And I was a bit depressed, too. It was finally getting to us about the fact that they don't accept us as what we are.

And here you were about to re-enter public life with the release of Double Fantasy.

Yeah.

So there was an uneasiness in addition to excitement about the album.

Yeah. I was looking back at my whole life. Why I went to London was understandable, because I was invited. And then I got involved in this situation, and as a person, as an individual, I was so humiliated from beginning to end as got involved with John. Every corner that I turn was like humiliation, humiliation. And then not just as a person, but as a career woman, I think that was a very bad career move, probably! So I'm just looking at my life and I said, "Well, I just threw the dice in the air. That's the price I'm paying." So, it's that kind of thing.

But, of course, there's another side. The songwriter side. "Walking on Thin Ice" OK, ice, dice, twice. There's that side, too.

It's Alright

Original Label: Polydor

Original Release Date: Nov. 29, 1982 (U.S.)/Dec. 10, 1982 (U.K).

Bonus Tracks: "Beautiful Boys" (previously unreleased, circa mid-late '80s); "You're The One" (previously unreleased, recorded August-Sept. 1980)

Notes: Musicians include Paul Shaffer. John and Sean Lennon make brief spoken appearances. Recorded at The Hit Factory, New York City, spring-summer 1982.

Season Of Glass, It's Alright, *and* Starpeace *were the only albums you recorded during the '80s. Why didn't you record as many as in the '70s?*

Well, now I not only had to cope with being a mother, but being a widow. Most widows, suddenly they have to do the business, but in my case I was doing the business before that. But the business became extremely complex. It's a very strange situation.

A widow goes through a terrible time, not just being sad about the loss, but you don't know how much a widow is taken advantage of. I was lucky that I was doing business; usually, the widow suddenly is put in the position where she has to do the business, and she's not ever done it before, so then she has to rely on people who might necessarily not be trustworthy. It's a very hard situation you go through. And in my case, whatever I did, when I did the *Starpeace* world tour [in 1986], not only did they knock the tour, they were writing up saying, "She's wasting John's money doing these things." That's so mean, isn't it? However I use my money for whatever I want to use, that's none of their business.

It's like you can't win whatever you do.

Exactly. What I'm saying is, why didn't I make more albums? I was simply shut up. I mean people shut me up in some ways. And I went along with it, because I had too much to do, and I felt that protecting the family was the first thing that I should think about. My health. Sean's health, you know?

You worked with session musicians through the '80s. Did that work against the music?

Yeah, there's that. It was getting more and more difficult. I'll tell you what happened. It's to do with who you have and how they sympathize with what you're trying to do. With *It's Alright*, I didn't particularly feel that the musicians understood what I was trying to do. Most of the stuff I did with synthesizers, and I was making it into an interesting synthesizer trip. And there was some interesting stuff that I did sound-wise; I would make a sound combining the cello sound and a violin sound or something like that. Each sound is made out of several different instruments or two instruments at least. So that when you hear it, you think, "Is that a bass?" So it's that weird kind of unworldly feeling about it. [In remastering] I found out that I was very good in laying down everything that I wanted to put in the tracks. But that was a time when there was a bomb scare. It was the time that we found out about all the betrayal of friends; it's all in David and Victoria Sheff's "The Betrayal Of John Lennon," the *Playboy* article. "It's Alright" is a song that I made when there was a bomb scare — "Don't go to the studio, it's very dangerous, and don't stay in the Dakota because it's dangerous. You have to get a hotel room." So Sean and I were put in a hotel room, and I asked them to get me a piano. Because at least it was a security blanket. And that's when I banged on the piano and made the song "It's Alright."

Like you were trying to send a message to yourself.

Yes, exactly. Because it wasn't all right at all. So, I laid down everything and by the time that I was remixing, I went a bit slack about it. So this time, to make sure that *It's Alright* is all right, I went back to the multitrack tapes and listened to it. And everything was there. So I fixed it up. Everything was there, but a lot of it wasn't used. So when you hear it now, I think you would feel it totally differently.

So the album was your reaction to everything going on around you.

Yeah. Now, when I went back to the studio, I realized how sane I was. I was really, again, trying to create new sounds. And the reason why I made each song so complex in terms of the overdubs — someone said there's like 80 tracks or something like that — the reason for that was because I wanted to really seep into, just drown in music. That's where I wanted to put my attention. Because otherwise I would have gone crazy.

I like "Never Say Goodbye"; it's a very positive song, but the overdubbing gets carried away to the point where it sounds sinister.

Yeah, I wanted to get carried away with all different kinds of the weaving of the sound. It's an album that was meant to come out again, I think. To have me go back and remaster it and have it come out again to just give it a chance.

Starpeace
Original Label: Polydor
Original Release Date: Oct.-Nov. '85 (U.S.)/Nov. 22, 1985 (U.K.)
Bonus Tracks: "Imagine" (previously unreleased, recorded live in Budapest, Hungary, March 14, 1986)
Notes: Musicians include Robbie Shakespeare, Sly Dunbar, and Tony Lennon. Sean Lennon and Nona Hendryx contribute vocals. Recorded at Right Track Recording, New York City, spring-summer 1985).

> **"And around *Starpeace*, I was really getting very, very tired. It was catching up on me, the fact that I lost John. That happens, I understand, with many people, that when you lose somebody, you block it or something. In my case, I didn't block it, I was just crying all the time. But still, later, it hits you in a very bad way. It becomes more lonely."**
>
> ***— Yoko Ono***

Tell me about Starpeace.

After *It's Alright*, I was concerned about Sean. If John and I, both of us, weren't there, what would happen to Sean? So I was praying that I would stay alive until he's 18. Survival was the first issue for me and Sean at the time. And around *Starpeace*, I was really getting very, very tired. It was catching up on me, the fact that I lost John. That happens, I understand, with many people, that when you lose somebody, you block it or something. In my case, I didn't block it, I was just crying all the time. But still, later, it hits you in a very bad way. It becomes more lonely. The feeling is so strong that "It did happen, it actually did happen, and I'm alone." And it was very, very bad. Very, very bad.

I was all ready to go into the studio with the album *Starpeace*. I wrote all the songs, I typed up all the lyrics, I put chords on it and everything. It was like a booklet already, a thick booklet of songs, And I thought, "Well, I'm going to go in." And then somebody suggested that I get a name producer; DJs might not want to play my songs, but they would play them because of the producer. So there was one producer that we thought would be a good one. And he came and I played all the songs on the piano. And he said, "This is like a Broadway play or something. You have it all, already every chord and every note and every word." And he said he's used to going in with a big group and they don't even have chords, maybe just a half a sentence or something. And they go in and he can participate in the creation of it. And this would be just bringing out the song exactly the way I composed it. So it's not very challenging. So he said, no, he wasn't taking the job.

Next was Bill Laswell and he said he'd do it. And so we did it. Usually, even when I have somebody else coproducing, I'm usually on top of things. But with this, I was, "OK, I'm just going to leave it to you. Let me be the singer; you prepare it and I come in, and I just sing." It was a little bit more than that, my participation, but it shows that I was kind of sad about the whole situation. And the stuff that I would usually say to musicians — "No, I don't want you playing that way" — I did a little bit of that, but I kind of let it go. So this time, I listened to it and I thought, "Oh, I let this happen?" The good songs were messed up a bit, not because Bill Laswell is a bad producer, but there was miscommunication. He didn't know what I wanted because I simply didn't say very much, I suppose. And if I said it, he probably didn't understand it.

So this time, *It's Alright* and *Starpeace* are the two albums I really had to work very hard to bring back to what I would have liked.

Tell me about "Cape Clear."

"Cape Clear" was originally called "Teddy Bear." It was inspired when my daughter [Kyoko] was still with me, when she was about five years old.

We were in either Montreal or Amsterdam. After the bed-in, we had to go downstairs, rush rush into the car, and just when we were rushing into the car, she said, "Where's my teddy bear?" And we couldn't go back to pick it up. We just got in the car and John said, "Look, I'll get you another teddy bear." And she was crying and saying, "No, no, no, that was my teddy bear." And I felt totally devastated, sorry for her, and saw exactly what she meant. But because people were crowding around the car, and some of them were trying to climb up the car, it was a very intense situation. There was no way that John could say, "OK, I'm going to get your teddy bear. Just wait. I'll go upstairs." So we left; the car started to move and she was still crying, and I felt so bad.

The song was inspired by that. In a way, now it was me. I lost my teddy bear. And you know, the double entendre was, teddy bear, rocker. So I called it "Teddy Bear" and then I thought, "Cape Clear" is better; it was much more than just a teddy bear.

Final Thoughts

Are you working on another new album?

I have a few songs that I'm writing. *Rising* was going to be a double album, and then Sean and all the musicians were saying, "This is going to be a triple!" and that's when I woke up and said, "No, no, no, it's going to be a single." So there's a lot left there, and also there's some new songs, so I want to go in, but I don't know when. I'll see what happens.

Is Sean going to work on an album?

For Sean, I think the next thing is not going to be just helping Mommy or helping another band; I think he's going to go in to do his own. And I think that's really great. I think it's a healthy thing to do. And if he makes that decision, that'd be great.

The '90s have been a good decade for you, with your old music getting rediscovered, and the success of Rising.

It's amazing, isn't it? But you see, because the first full albums that come out, except for *Yoko Ono/Plastic Ono Band*, are really so avant-garde. I know that the kids, Sean's friends, that generation, they're exchanging CDs that they privately made or something, and they're really pretty far out. So those kids will probably enjoy them, but other than that, I think people are still, "Oh dear, is this what it was?" They're like that, I think!

Ringo Starr

The Fab 4/4

by Robyn Flans

There was excitement in the air Feb. 9, 1964. Like millions of others across the United States (perhaps you) I settled in front of the TV to watch the much anticipated American debut of The Beatles on *The Ed Sullivan Show*. My youthful reaction to these four strange moptops, however, came in a burst of laughter, which got me booted from the room by my sister and her boyfriend. I'll never know what compelled me to beg for forgiveness, re-enter the room and watch them, but I'm glad I did. My life changed that night; so too did rock 'n' roll and maybe the character of life in this country. How many musicians since that day, 24 years ago, have admitted they wouldn't be doing what they do had it not been for The Beatles?

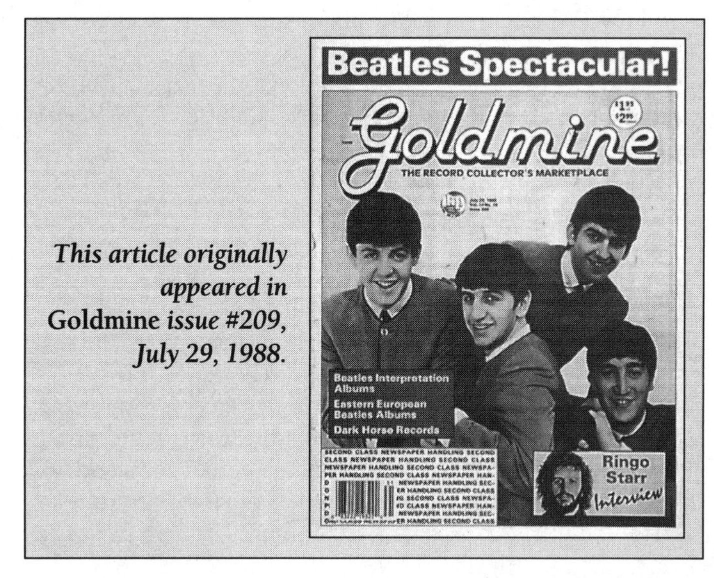

This article originally appeared in Goldmine *issue #209, July 29, 1988.*

The impact made by Paul McCartney, John Lennon, George Harrison, and Ringo Starr may forever be impossible to explain, but the fact that they altered the course of music and changed sociological norms from fashion to morals to attitudes cannot be denied. First it was little things like hair — the barbering profession must have really hit the skids as of Feb. 10 — and later on it was bigger things such as war and drugs. People listened to what The Beatles had to say. The Beatles became, for millions all over the world, not merely an object of affection or a group of talented entertainers, but an obsession to be emulated and idolized — a lifestyle.

Their greatest impact was, of course, musically. They challenged the field and made experimentation acceptable. Before them, there was no such thing as "growth" when one spoke of a rock 'n' roll artist. The idea was just to keep getting hits, and when you stopped doing that, your time was up. Few artists challenged the hit-making process by altering a proven formula; that was commercial suicide. The Beatles never sat still, from start to finish, and whatever they did worked. They were gifted with talent, charisma and everything else it took to become a phenomenon the like of which hadn't been seen before or and hasn't since.

They even altered the almighty music business itself. Before them, it was the record companies, the producers, the publishers who came first, who determined who and what was a hit. The Beatles largely took hold of their own destiny instead; they decided what they would sing and how they would look, and nobody was going to tell them otherwise. Within a couple of years after their initial burst of success, they were even responsible for the album taking over from the single as the dominant format in which rock was heard.

For this Beatles fan, their effect was such that it determined my profession; without The Beatles, it is unlikely that I would be a music journalist. Needless to say, one of my dreams as such was to interview a member of The Beatles. When I expressed that desire to a drummer named Jim Keltner a few years ago, he made that dream come true by arranging for me to meet with Ringo Starr for an interview with *Modern Drummer* magazine.

Walking into his rented Beverly Hills house, I was nervous. I had been warned by other reporters that Ringo was not receptive to talking about The Beatles, that he was temperamental and difficult. I was worried that if he were indeed like that, it might damage my feelings for the music that had played such a large part in my childhood and has remained with me since. Ringo always seemed so lovable, the Beatle who kept out of the bickering at the end and just wanted to play his drums.

But that was an occupational risk I had to take. I'm sure there are many among us who have met a long-admired celebrity, only to be disappointed by finding out what he or she was really like away from the image. A tainted personal impression of a musical artist can forever sour the artist's music in one's mind.

But Ringo was nothing like the description I had gotten from others. He was warm, sincere and witty. Sitting in his garden, he spoke about The Beatles and anything else I wanted to know, to my heart's content. The transcript of that interview, minus some of the more technical questions about drumming which he answered for *Modern Drummer*'s readers, follows.

Today, incredibly, Ringo Starr is without a record contract. He has been for several years; his last album, 1983's *Old Wave*, was not even released in America. That's a sad commentary, considering just who this man is. But rather than set a down tone for an interview with a man who's brought happiness to so many and whose own demeanor always seems so cheery, let's just lead off by saying... heeeeere's RINGO!

Goldmine: *Why drums?*

Ringo Starr: I tried everything else. Originally, my grandfather and grandmother were very musical and played mandolin and banjo, and we had a piano, which I used to walk on as a child. Being an only child and a spoiled brat, my mother would let me do most things, so I used to walk on the piano but never actually learned it. Then when I was seven, my grandfather brought me a mouth organ, which I never got into either, and then they died and I sort of ended up with the banjos but never got into that.

Drums were just the ones I always felt an affinity with. At 13, in the hospital, we used to play on the little cupboard next to the bed, and then once a week, they had a band to keep us occupied, since we were in there for a year. So they fetched this band around and this guy would have these big green, yellow and red notes, and if he pointed to the red note, you would hit the drum, or the yellow was the cymbal or the triangle, and things like that. It was a percussion band, but it was just to keep us entertained while we were in bed.

They used to come once a week to the hospital, and we used to knit and do all stuff like that, anything to keep us occupied. So in the hospital, I wouldn't play in the band unless I had the drum. When I came out, it was always the only instrument I wanted. So at 16, I bought a $3 bass drum, made a pair of sticks out of firewood and used to pound that, much to the joy of all the neighbors. I couldn't really play; I used to just hit it. Then I made a kit out of tin cans, with little bits of metal on the snare. Flat tins were the cymbals, and a big biscuit tin with some depth in it was the tom, and a shallow biscuit tin was the snare drum, and so forth.

Then my stepfather, Harry Graves, who came from the south of England (we're from the north), went down to see his family one Christmas, and one of his uncles was selling a kit of drums for £12 [roughly $30]. It was a great old kit — a great trap and all the wood blocks and everything — so I had that. I got that kit in January 1958. There were two problems, though. One, I didn't have a car to carry it and, two, I wasn't in a band. But in February, one month later, I joined a band, although I couldn't play. Nobody knew, though, because they couldn't play well, either. We were all just starting out playing. It was the skiffle days in 1958 in England.

What was the name of the band?

It was called The Eddie Clayton Skiffle Group. The guy next door used to play guitar, a friend of mine used to play tea-chest bass, and we played "Hey Lidy Lidy Lo" and all the skiffle songs. We used to play for the men at lunch hour in the factory. It was mainly if you had an instrument, you could join a band. It didn't matter if you could play. But my problem was I was always traveling on the bus, so I couldn't carry the kit.

Then we started auditioning, and we did every audition in the world, every free show we could do. We had no sense of time, so we'd start with the count of "one, two, three, four," and then it would be like an express train because we'd get faster and faster and faster. People were just dropping like flies on the dance floor because it was like, "Can't you slow it down, can't you slow it down?"

So we did a lot of free shows. In that band, I didn't really need the full kit, but I always wanted to play it. Anyway, I got the kit, and I set it up in the back bedroom like a professional, thinking, "I'll practice and everything." I only did that one night and we had all the neighbors yelling "shurup [shutup], get out of here," because we were in very close proximity to everyone else. So I never practiced since that day, except with a band. I made all the mistakes on stage, as it were.

Did you have any drum idols?

No, the only drum record I ever bought was Cozy Cole's "Topsy," parts I and II. I used to like Gene Krupa, although I never bought any of his records. It was that type of drumming, though, heavy kind of tom-tom stuff, and Cozy Cole was another tom-tom person. But I was never really into drummers and I never did solos. I hated solos. I wanted to be the drummer within the band, not the frontman. The longest solo I ever did was 13 bars.

I read somewhere, though, that part of the reason you changed your last name was that in the beginning, they wanted to bill your solo time as "Starr Time."

We used to have "Starr Time" when I had the solo spot about two years later with Rory Storm And The Hurricanes. We all were professional, as it were. The difference is that they pay you for playing. That's the only difference in being a professional from being an amateur.

What was your first professional job?

On the first professional gig, they offered me 10 shillings, which was about a dollar and a half in those days, and the guy got so drunk at the end of the night that he didn't pay us anyway. We were really down about that, but it was the first paying gig. We [The Eddie Clayton Band] had done all the auditions and won a few competitions and stuff like that but also still worked in the factory.

Then I joined a couple of other bands, a skiffle group, and I ended up with Rory Storm, which was basically a skiffle group, but we were going rock. We were the first band to be thrown out of The Cavern for playing rock 'n' roll because it was a jazz club. The only thing we used to have different was that our lead guitarist used to come out of a radio. That was his amp. He used to plug into this little radio on stage, so suddenly we were too rock 'n' roll for this jazz club, and they threw us off the stage. It was all in good fun at the time.

When did you join up with Rory Storm?

1959. In 1960, we all decided to leave our jobs and go real professional, where that's all we'd do. So I left the factory.

That must have been a major commitment, the money being so poor in that business, particularly at that time.

It was a major commitment, but it was all I wanted to do. The family said, "It's all right as a hobby, but keep the job."

"You'll never make a living by being a musician."

My mother still thinks that to this day, I think: "It's all right as a hobby, son." Anyway, this is a roundabout way of saying how the names came about. We decided to go away to play Butlin's Holiday Camp in England, which is a camp where people go for two weeks' holiday. So when we went professional and bought the red suits and the shoes and everything, we all thought we'd change our names, because show biz means changing your name. That's what's so great about it; you can call yourself anything you like, like Zinc Alloy.

So the guitarist called himself Johnny Guitar, and in the end, I think because we're English, we all picked cowboy names like Ty Hardin, Lou O'Brien, Rory Storm, and Ringo Starr, because of the rings, which I always wore then. But then, to get back to your point, I used to do a 20-minute spot with vocals. I used to sing songs, because we used to do hours, so anyone could sing, play a solo or anything. The guitarist would do a couple of guitar numbers, then the singer would come on, and then I'd do a couple of numbers, and that's why it was called "Starr Time." So I'd do "Let's Twist Again," "Hully Gully," "Sticks And Stones," a Ray Charles number, and a couple of other numbers like that. God, it's all so long ago. I was even doing "Boys" in those days.

So you never did any drum solos?

I never did any drum solos, no. Never have, never wanted to — even at the beginning. While we were still at this holiday camp, we used to play in The Rockin' Calypso, but on Sunday, the big night, they had a big theater there, and they'd have name acts, and the local people working there would be on the bill. So we were working with The Happy Wanderers, an English street band with a big walking bass drum, trumpet, clarinet, and they were like a walking jazz band. They

used to walk around the streets of London playing songs, and then the guy would walk around with the hat. They became very well known. At the end of the show, it used to get to the solo and I used to let their drummer take the solo on the bass drum: "boom, boom, boom, boom." I would never do the solo, even then. Never liked them. So anyway, that's when we got our names.

Why did you grow up with such a fascination for the American West?

As children in England, your cowboys were great heroes to us. To an English kid, a cowboy was a fascinating thing, you know, in his leather waistcoat and his black gloves and all of that, so that's part of it.

Had rock come into the picture yet in England?

Rock 'n' roll was very big here, and Elvis was out in 1957. We're talking about '59 and '60, so we were just getting into rock and away from the skiffle stuff. We suddenly got amplifiers and played different songs. Rock was coming in, and that's where I went. That was my direction. I was purely rock 'n' roll. Drummers or musicians were either going for jazz or rock.

There used to be coffee shops and things like that in those days, and we'd sit around, and I used to get so mad at the drummers who wanted to play jazz because I was just strictly rock 'n' roll. I always felt it was like rats running around the kit if you played jazz, and I just liked it solid. So we'd have these great deep discussions about drums. It was all so exciting then. It's still exciting, but...

Were you a drum fanatic in those days?

No, just a rock fanatic, but my instrument was drums. I never wanted to play anything else. But I also wanted every other drummer to play rock. I didn't want them to play anything else [laughs]. "You've got to be kidding. Just rock! Listen to it. Get into it." There was more emotion in rock than in jazz. We went through jazz, in my opinion, just listening to it. I went through it in one week and knew I had had enough of that. Rock never ceases to make me happy when it's good.

How far into your Rory Storm gig were you when you came in contact with The Beatles?

I was playing with Rory about 18 months or two years. We'd all played the same venues and, at the time, Rory And The Hurricanes used to be top of the bill. There'd be all these other bands on and occasionally, The Beatles would play. It ended up that they were the only band I ever watched because they were really good, even in those days. One morning, I was in bed, as usual; I don't like getting up in the day because I live at night. So a knock came at the door, and Brian Epstein said, "Would you play a lunchtime session at The Cavern with The Beatles?" And I said, "OK, OK, I'll get out of bed," and I went down and played. I thought it was really good. I thought the band was good, and it was great for me to play.

Were they different from other bands playing at the time?

Yeah, they were playing better stuff. They were doing very few of their own songs then, but they were doing really great old tracks: Shirelles tracks and Chuck Berry tracks, but they did it so well. They had a good style. I don't know; there was a whole feel about Paul, George, and John. And Pete, it's no offense, but I never felt he was a great drummer. He had sort of one style, which was very good for them in those years, I suppose, but they felt, I think, that they wanted to move out of it more. So I just played the session and then we went and got drunk and then I went home.

So it was a one-shot deal.

It was a one-shot, but we knew each other. We met in Germany when Rory played there and so did The Beatles, but we didn't play with each other. There was heavy competition because we used to play weekends, 12 hours a night between the two bands, and we'd try to get the audience in the club, so there was a lot of competition. And then, at 4 a.m. or 5 a.m. in the morning set, if The Beatles were left on, I'd usually still hang around because I was drunk, asking them to play some sort of soft sentimental songs, which they did. So basically, they were at one club and we were at another club and we ended up at the same club. That's how we sort of said hello. We never played with each other, but then out of the blue, Brian came and asked me to play.

Was that an audition for you from their standpoint?

No, Pete wasn't well or something, so they needed a drummer for the session and asked me, or asked Brian to ask me. So I went and played and that was all there was to it. This went on for about six months, where every couple of weeks I'd play, for whatever reasons. Then there was talk about me joining, and I was asked if I would like to. I said, "Yeah" and then went away with Rory to play this holiday camp again because it was good money for three months, and we just played what we wanted.

A 1961 concert poster.

About five weeks into this three-month gig, Brian called and asked if I would join The Beatles. I said, "Yeah, I'd love to. When?" He called me on a Wednesday and he said, "Tonight." I said, "No, I can't leave the band without a drummer. They'd lose a six-week gig, which they have left to go." So I said I'd join Saturday, which gave Rory the rest of the week to find a drummer.

Why did you choose to join The Beatles if both bands, in essence, were starving young bands?

Well, I'd rather starve with a better band, and I felt The Beatles were a better band. By then, we weren't actually starving. We were making, not great money, but enough to live on. And The Beatles were making a bit more; they were coming up real fast. But I loved the band so much. I thought it was a better band and I thought I had done everything our band could do at the time. We were just repeating ourselves. So it was time to move on again, and that's why. And I liked the boys as well as the music.

So you joined them that Saturday.

I left Saturday, played on Saturday night and it was in every newspaper. There were riots. It was OK when I just joined in and played a gig and left, but suddenly I was the drummer. Pete had a big following, but I had been known for years in Liverpool, so I had quite a following too. So there was this whole shouting match, "Ringo never, Pete forever," and "Pete never, Ringo forever." There was this whole battle going on, and I'm just trying to drum away.

But they got over it, and then we went down to make a record. I'm not sure about this, but one of the reasons they also asked Pete to leave was George Martin, the producer, didn't like Pete's drumming. So then, when I went down to play, he didn't like me either, so he called a drummer named Andy White, a professional session man to play the session. But George has repented since [laughs]. He did come out one day saying it, only when he said it it was 10 years later. In the end, I didn't play that session. I played every session since, but the first session, he brought in a studio drummer.

There were two versions of the first tune ["Love Me Do"], one where White plays and one where you play.

You're right. There are two versions. I'm on the album, and he's on the single. You can't spot the difference, though, because all I did was what he did, because that's what they wanted for the song.

{According to Bruce Spizer's Songs, Pictures And Stories Of The Fabulous Beatles Records On Vee-Jay *and* The Ultimate Beatles Encyclopedia *by Bill Harry, White's version appears on the* Please Please Me *album and Starr's version was used for the first pressings of the single (red label). Later pressings of the single (black label) feature White.*

— Ed.}

I heard that Ron Richards handed you a tambourine.

Yeah, and told me to get lost. I was really brought down. I mean, the idea of making a record was real heavy. You just wanted a piece of plastic. That was the most exciting period of records — the first couple of records. Every time it moved into the 50s on the charts we'd go out and have dinner and celebrate. Then when it was in the 40s, we'd celebrate. And we knew every time it was coming on the radio and we'd all be waiting for it in cars or in someone's house. We wouldn't move for that three minutes.

And then, of course, the first gold disc and the first #1! But like everything else, when you've had five #1s, one after the other and as many gold discs as you can eat, it's not boring, but it's just that the first couple of records were so exciting. I think they are for everybody. It's like sweets every day, though. You get used to it.

So I was really brought down when he had this other drummer, but the record came out and made it quite well, and from then on I was on all the other records, with my silly style and silly fills. They used to call it "silly fills."

Who?

Everyone used to sort of say, "Those silly fills he does."

And yet, it turned drumming around for a lot of people.

But we didn't know that then. Everyone put me down — said that I couldn't play. They didn't realize that was my style and I wasn't playing like anyone else — that I couldn't play like anyone else.

How did it come to be that Martin allowed you to play the second session?

I think I drove him mad, because we rehearsed for the next record and I had a tambourine in one hand and maracas in the other and played the kit with them. George was just flabbergasted. I didn't have a stick in my hand. I just had a tambourine and maracas, and I was hitting the cymbals and smashing the tom with the maracas, so he thought he'd better do something about it. So he said, "Well, if you use sticks, I'll let you play."

He never said that really, but I think he just thought I'd gone mad, so he'd better please me and let me play on the next record. And from then on, I played, except for "Back In The U.S.S.R.," which Paul played on because I wasn't there. We just carried on from there, and then it got to where John and Paul were always the writers and the bass player and rhythm guitar, and George was getting some notice as a lead guitarist, but I was still getting, "He's all right," so it was a bit of a put-down at the time.

Let's talk about sessions. How much creative input were you allowed, and how much did Martin dictate?

Well, at the beginning, George Martin dictated a certain amount, and then it was John and Paul's writing to consider. See, what helped me a lot was that I had three frustrated drummers around, because everyone wants to be a drummer for some reason. John could play and Paul could play and George could play, but they each had one standard style. We all have one standard style, but they only had one sort of groove, where I have two or three.

John and I used to have, not arguments, but discussions, because we'd be playing all these records and he'd say, "Like that," and I'm saying "But John, there's two drummers on there," and he could never hear there were two drummers. They'd play stuff with two drummers on it and the three of them each had their own idea of what the drummer should do, and then I

An early promo shot of The Beatles.

had my idea. So all I would do was combine my idea, their three ideas, and the ideas of the two drummers on a record. They got what they were given, and it worked. But that helped me to play. Also, the long hours in Germany, you know, you soon get your act together.

So we were playing and making these records, and then we sort of got free-form rock in our own way, though it was a lot tighter than acid rock because we had songwriters and we did songs and didn't just jam. We went through a lot of changes on records. Then in '68, I got the kit with the calf skins and that changed everything. Then it really became tom-tom city because of the calf and wood.

When you're touring, everyone thanks God that the plastic heads were invented because you're playing outside in the heat, or the wet, or whatever, and skins are very hard to handle. But since '66, we were in a controlled environment, in the studio, so the temperature was always the same and you could deal with calf. You can't deal with them outside, although drummers have for thousands of years. So plastic heads were a godsend on the road, but then when we were just in the studio, I ordered this kit and I had calf skins put on.

"We could play in any town or country in the world and get the same response, but only the four of us would know if we played any good, and that was very seldom because we couldn't hear. So you're getting the same response for a bad gig and it wasn't any help. You only wanted applause if you did something that worked, so we decided to go into the studio. It was pointless playing on stage anymore."

— Ringo Starr

To backtrack even further: I'd had this kit that my stepfather got for £12. It was a great old kit, but it was old-fashioned. I joined a band when I was 18, and in my silliness, thought. "I want a new kit." So I bought an Ajax kit, which is an English company. It was a black pearl kit, about £47, roughly $125, complete with a pair of sticks. "You can take it away and play it" — it was one of those. You had everything you needed.

Then one of the band got a car so we could carry the kit, because in the old days, as I was saying, we were on the bus, so you couldn't take a kit. I would only take a snare drum, a hi-hat and cymbal and beg all the other drummers for their kits. Some of them wouldn't give them to me, so I'd just have to play with a snare. I never like to let the kit out, either, unless I know the person. You never let anyone use the snare. The only two times I ever lent a snare, it was broken. And it takes a long time to get it to how you want it to sound. I would understand others not lending the kit, but I thought they were real mean.

One time, I remember a guy asking me if he could use my kit and I said, "Well, can you play?" And he said, "Yeah, I've been playing for years," and if you can imagine, a guy gets on your kit and puts his foot on the beater of the bass drum pedal and thinks it's a motorbike starter, kick starting. So I just went over and grabbed him off the kit and threw him off stage. It blew me away! The man never played in his life, and he thought it was a motor bike. That was one time I lent the kit out.

So you had this Ajax set.

Right up to The Beatles, and then we were getting new instruments and things and I wanted a new kit. I wanted a Ludwig kit. It was good, for their own good and my good, because while we were touring, of course, they would give me a couple of free kits because I was a Ludwig drummer. I used to play that mini-kit on stage. Couldn't hear a thing! But it was good for me to get behind because I'm not that tall, so I looked bigger with a small kit, so at least you could see me.

But it didn't matter much what you sounded like in concert, did it?

No. That's why we stopped.

Harrison said that he felt the response to The Beatles was some sort of hysterical outlet for people. The four of you must have sat around and conjectured as to what the hell was going on. That had to be mind-blowing.

Well, we enjoyed them getting their hysterical needs out because no one came to listen to our gigs. They bought records to listen to. They just came to scream and shout, which was fine, but after four years, I was becoming such a bad player because I couldn't hear anything. Because of the noise going on, all I had to do was just constantly keep the time, so we'd have something to follow.

If you look at films, you'll see I'm looking at their mouths — I'm lip-reading where we're up to in the song because I couldn't hear the amps or anything. We were becoming bad musicians, so we had the discussion about it. Besides, we could play in any town or country in the world and get the same response, but only the four of us would know if we played any good, and that was very seldom because we couldn't hear. So you're getting the same response for a bad gig and it wasn't any help. You only wanted applause if you did something that worked, so we decided to go into the studio. It was pointless playing on stage anymore.

I guess I wonder what you thought. I mean, that response had never happened before.

I don't know. The media and the madness of the time, I guess. Things were very dead just up to when we came out and that was just part of what we did.

So on stage, you were absolutely reading lips at that point?

Yeah, just to find out where we were up to in the song and just carrying a beat. So then we went back into the studio where we could get back to playing with each other again, because we'd do the same 12 numbers every night and we'd do a 30-minute show. That seems amazing now, because Bruce Springsteen does four hours. He still has the best show I've seen in the last 10 years, and I only watched two hours of that, and it was enough. But every group does at least an hour and a half, and Bruce, who is the extreme, does four hours.

We did a 30-minute show, and if we didn't like the place, we'd play a bit fast and do it in 25 minutes. We were getting real despondent playing live, so we went into the studio for months and months. It got us playing again and exploring a lot of avenues of the technology of the studio, which compared to now, was Mickey Mouse.

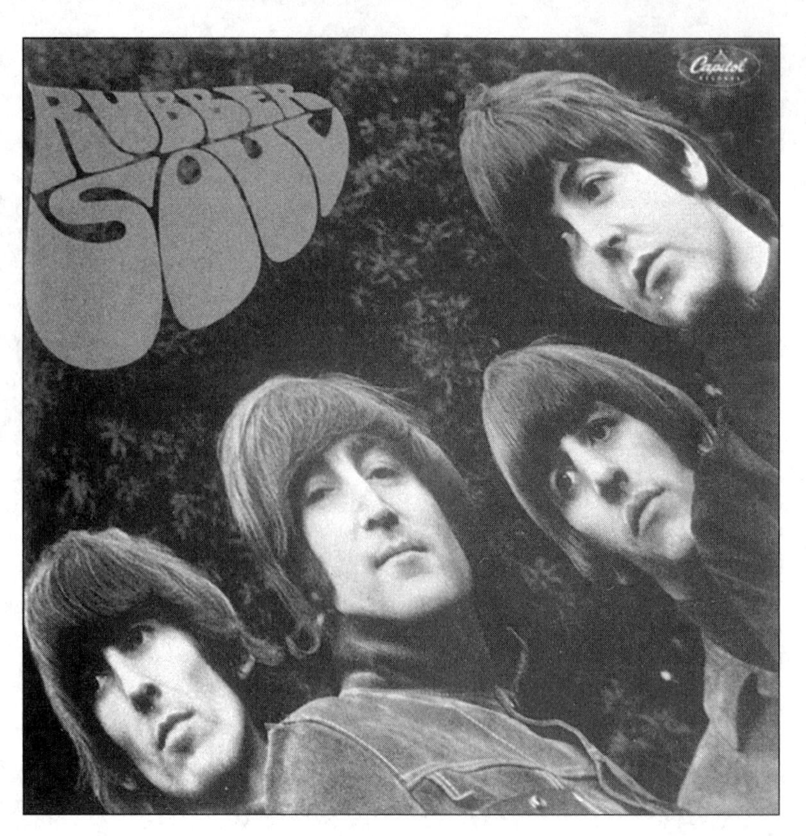

Eight-track was a big deal then.

And we didn't have one. We begged for one because we did everything on four-track up to *Pepper* [*Sgt. Pepper's Lonely Hearts Club Band*] and four-to-four, but EMI was technically a very, very good studio with their engineers and electronic wizards. When we went four-to-four, to go tape-to-tape, there's usually a loss, but the loss was so slight, because their engineers were technically so good that no one missed it. You can't miss it anyway because the public didn't know what they were missing, so they only got what they got. But we put the drums through phasers and things like that.

How did you feel about all that?

It was great, because it worked with the tracks we were doing and it was magic. Just like magic. And we put it through the Hammond speaker and it goes 'round and 'round, whatever that's called, and just tricks like that. We put the guitar through something going backwards and it was all experimental madness to us, but it was in the form of a song. It wasn't us just freaking out, playing, which we did quite a lot, but we never released any tapes like that.

And you knew you wouldn't have to reproduce it on stage anyway.

We knew we weren't going out on stage and it ended up, like on *Pepper*, that if we wanted to go out, we'd have to take an orchestra with us. But no one was interested in going out. We were only interested in making records. So that was exciting, the sound we could get. And then the group broke up. So I started playing with a lot of other people. One year I did Leon Russell, Stephen Stills, B.B. King, and Howlin' Wolf, which was good for my head. After being in one band so long, suddenly playing with such a diverse group of people was good for me.

I wondered if during The Beatles, you ever felt you wanted to get out and do something else.

No, never did. That was always good enough for me. I never played any other sessions. I only did a few, like Jackie Lomax and a couple of other people. But then it was exciting when the group had split and I just started playing with a lot of people. In 1970, England was the place everyone wanted to make albums, so I played a lot of different sessions, like with Jimmy Webb and Harry Nilsson.

After The Beatles, I heard that you really felt that you didn't want to play drums anymore, for a while at least.

It wasn't that I didn't want to play drums. I didn't know what to do with my life. I'd been playing with the band for so long and suddenly it ended. I just sat there wondering what to do with my life, because I wasn't a producer and I wasn't a writer.

To backtrack for a second: The White Album. *I read that you left for about a week.*

I left for two weeks. I felt I wasn't part of the group. I felt that the other three were really together and close and I wasn't part of the group, so because of that feeling, I felt I wasn't playing well. I went around to John, knocked on the door and said, "I'm leaving the band, man. You three are really close and I'm getting out." And he said, "I thought it was you three." So I went around to Paul and said the same thing: "I'm leaving; I'm not playing well because you three are real close and I'm not in the band anymore." And he said, "I thought it was you three." I said, "Well, I don't know who it is, but I'm going on holiday," and I went to Sardinia for a couple of weeks to clear my head. That's when they made "U.S.S.R.," which I wasn't on. Then I came back to *The White Album*, which I felt, for me, was a better album than *Pepper* for the group.

Why do you say that?

Well, we were much more like a band. We're like session players on *Pepper*, using all those orchestras and sound effects. I mean it was good fun, but I felt we were getting more like a group on *The White Album* again, though it was a double album, and double albums give too much information for me, anyway. But that and *Abbey Road*, besides *Rubber Soul*, are a few of the finest albums.

The music became a lot more sophisticated, and I'm sure you were called on to do more sophisticated kinds of things.

Never. You got what you got. I don't know if it got more sophisticated. I don't think you'd call *The White Album* sophisticated, but I enjoyed it more than *Pepper*, which you could call sophisticated. But you'd only call that sophisticated because of what you put on top, the brass section and such. The idea behind *Pepper*, which never got fully realized, was that it was going to be a whole show, but we only got into two tracks and then we made it just a regular album.

A show as far as a concept album or something to take on the road?

Just a concept album of a show, and we segued from *Sgt. Pepper* into the next track with the cheer, and there's Billy

Shears, and then we did it for two tracks and we got bored with that and just made another album. *The White Album* was not to do tricks. It was for us to get together, I felt, and play together as a group, which is what we were, and best at.

I read that Paul had been very critical of your playing on The White Album *before you left for two weeks, and that's one of the reasons you left.*

No, I left for the very reason I told you. I thought I just had to go away and straighten my head out because it was getting too silly. And while I was away, I got telegrams from John saying, "The best rock 'n' roll drummer in the world," and when I came back, George had the whole studio decorated with flowers. So Paul may have been pissed off. I don't know. He never did anything. But he never actually said to me, "That's not good," or whatever, so I don't know where that rumor came from. He was never that critical.

Dispelled that rumor.

I've never read that one, even [laughs]. I've read most of them. There was a guy in New York who said he played on everything. All that bull has gone down. You have to let those things pass. Some drummer in New York wanted to make a name for himself and said he played on everything, and I never played on anything. So what was I doing? I know on some sessions I wasn't all there, but I wasn't off completely away.

Obviously, John and Paul were the most integral portion of what went on in the studio.

It was their songs.

But what would happen? Take us through a typical session, or even a song.

Well, what would happen is that someone would say, "Well, I've got this," because it was very early on that John and Paul didn't write together. It was their own songs, and then a lot of them would start as jams and someone would put lyrics to them; like "Helter Skelter" was a full-on jam, and "Birthday," just to mention jams where we had nothing when we went in. Other songs would have a verse and a chorus and they'd finish them, or anyone could shout a line and if the line was good, they'd use it. The roadies, the tea lady, if anyone had a line, it would be used.

It was always open like that, and always the best line would be used. It wouldn't matter who said it. No one had the ego big enough to say, "I have to write this," not all the time; I mean, they wrote 90 percent finished songs, but not musically, because they could only use what we could play. "Birthday" was one case. "They say it's your birthday," do you know that track?

Of course.

We went over to Paul's and came back and wanted to do a sort of rowdy rock 'n' roll track because Little Richard had freaked us out yet again, so we just took a couple of chord sequences and played them sort of raucous and loud and there was a newspaper on the floor and it was about someone's birthday. So Paul started singing and we all just hopped on behind him. That's how that came about, but we never went in with anything. We just went in and I sat behind the kit and they stood behind their instruments and that came about like that.

On the finished tunes, would you get called into the session, come in and listen to the tune and just supply what you felt was right?

No. On the finished tunes, they'd sit at the piano and play them. Then we'd go through several different changes of how we all felt it should be done. Mainly, the writer had the definite idea, but if anyone did anything to change it and it was good and moved into a place they enjoyed, that's how it would be. There was a lot of open-mindedness. There were very few tracks with the definite idea, "This is how it has to be." Mostly, if someone came up with anything that was different and worked, then everyone would go along with it.

In those days, for a drummer to have that kind of creative allowance was somewhat unusual.

Well, I was allowed to create anything I could as long as it worked, and it was the same with the guitar or the bass or the piano. It was all the same, but the difference was that it had to fit around their song.

"'Helter Skelter' was a full-on jam, and 'Birthday,' just to mention jams where we had nothing when we went in. Other songs would have a verse and a chorus and they'd finish them, or anyone could shout a line and if the line was good, they'd use it. The roadies, the tea lady, if anyone had a line, it would be used."

— Ringo Starr

What about when you began to write?

First of all, I used to rewrite Jerry Lee Lewis B-sides and not really know it. I just put new words to all the songs. It took me years to fetch a song in because I, as much as anyone else, was in awe of our two writers, who I felt were the best writers around. So I'd write my little songs and I'd be embarrassed to fetch them in because of John and Paul.

So then I started fetching them in and they'd all be laughing on the floor, "Oh, you've rewritten 'Crazy Arms,'" or something. So then I started writing a bit more, like, "I listen for your footsteps coming up the drive," some song I wrote, don't know the title any more ["Don't Pass Me By"]. That was the first one that we did of mine. But they used to write songs for me, tailor-made, because they knew my range and it was like a personality thing I used to put across. Or then I'd pick the country song, because I always liked country and western: "Boys" I had done for years, then they started writing songs just for me. Then I started writing my own, and then I wrote "Octopus' Garden." I always mention "Octopus' Garden."

That was the first one you were proud of, really, wasn't it?

Well, it was so silly.

That was written on your holiday in Sardinia?

Yeah. We were on this boat and they offered us this meal and we'd ordered fish and chips, and the fish came and I said, "What's that?" There were legs and things. And the guy said,

07150 / $1.25

photograph

RINGO STARR

07150 / PHOTOGRAPH—RINGO STARR

apple single 1865

Richoroony Ltd.
Harrisongs Ltd. registered as Harrisongs Music Ltd.
and Startling Ltd. Music Companies

"Oh, it's octopus," and being English and food-wise, that blew me away. "Are you kidding? Octopus? You've got be to crazy. Nobody eats that. Tentacles? It's not fish. It's jet-propelled."

Then I got talking to the captain, and he was telling me the story of octopuses building gardens under the sea. They find shiny rocks and tins and whatever and they build these gardens, and I found it fascinating. I was just sitting on the pier one day and I wrote "Octopus's Garden" for me and the children. And some days you really feel like you'd like to be there, under the sea, in an octopus's garden, because it gets a bit tough out here, and it was as a tough period then. So I felt it would be very nice to be real quiet under the ocean.

Was the breakup gradual? I presume it didn't happen in just one day.

No, the breakup came because everyone had ideas of what he wanted to do, whereas everyone used to have ideas of what we would do, as a group. Then we weren't really fulfilling John's musical ambitions or Paul's or George's, or my own, in the end, because it was separate. We weren't working for one aim, just the one band. Everyone wanted to do other things as well. So you could see it coming but like everything else, we all held it off for a while.

Then it just got too silly and we had a meeting about what everyone wanted to do. You can't keep a band together. We never did it for the money. We did it for the playing. I mean, the money is very nice, but we were players first. As anyone will tell you, if we had wanted, we could have just carried on and made fortunes, but that was not our game. Our game was actually making music. So it became too strange, because there was a lot of stuff I didn't want to play on that I felt just wasn't exciting anymore.

Can you be specific?

Well, John is the easiest to talk about. He wanted to do stuff which was avant-garde in its way. Besides, I had no place being on it, and I wasn't on some of it. He wanted to do that more than play with the group, and Paul wanted to do another thing, and George was wanting something else.

What did you want?

Well, I just wanted to play really good music — not that any of it is bad. I enjoyed the group thing, and then people wanted to do other things, which could have included us if we had wanted to. But half the time, we didn't want to get involved with certain tracks because it just wasn't what we were there to do as a group. We were there to do it individually, but not as a group. So the regression started about '68 and it was over by '70. So that was the end of that, and I did feel lost, as we talked about before.

I would imagine it was an adjustment personally, but did you feel lost musically?

Well, I'd never played with a better band, you see, so I think that's the loss I felt.

Where does one go from the best?

It's not even just the best. A lot of it was telepathy. We all felt so close. We knew each other so well that we'd know when any of us would make a move up or down within the music, and we'd all make it. No one would say anything or look at each other. We'd just know. The easiest word is telepathy. The band worked so well, and we were four good friends a lot of the time. But like any four friends, we had rows and shouted and disliked each other for a moment.

Then it ended, and I started playing sessions and had a really good time, but I was just playing. You can play with any band, but that band was something special to me, and it's never been like that again. I've had great sessions, great tracks, but it's never been like that, and you can't expect that if you walk into a studio and play someone's session. You're strangers.

We had all lived together so close. We knew each other so well that it crossed over into the music. We knew exactly what the other was doing. That's even the wrong way to explain it. We just knew that the chemistry worked! The excitement! If things were just jogging along and one of us felt, "I'm going to lift it here," it was just a feeling that went through the four of us and everyone lifted it or everyone lowered it, or whatever. It was just telepathy. When I do sessions now, I'm playing the best I can, and some sessions are really great. But I've never played on anyone's album all the way through, because I always felt it was boring, so I'd do three or four tracks.

Can you define what you think is a good drummer?

Yeah, me. It took me a long time to think of myself like that, but I am probably the best rock drummer.

Why do you say that?

Because I play with emotion and feeling, and that's what rock is. Rock is not reading, and I'm not putting reading down, although it's something that I don't do and something I never wanted to do. I did have one lesson in the old days and the guy wrote all those dots on the paper, but I felt it wasn't the way I wanted to play. I only wanted to play, and some days it's a real bummer for people, because if I'm on a downer, I still have to play, and you only get what's in my soul at the time. But that's life. We all make a choice. A lot of session guys can go in and read and play five different sessions a day, totally different types of music. He just reads it and plays it, but that's a different musician to me.

There was never a time where you felt you should have lessons or you'd like to take lessons?

Only in the very early days when I first got the kit, because you think that's what you should do. So I had one lesson and realized that wasn't what I should be doing.

Did you play along with records?

No, I never practiced in my life. I just practiced one day and then joined a band and made every mistake I could on stage.

That's incredible.

Well, it was easier then. I don't know if it was easier then, but it seems like it was. Now, you've got to be an amazing player to get a job, even in the local band that plays a Bar Mitzvah. You've got to read and play.

As I told you before, back then if you had an instrument, you were in a band. That was how easy it was when I started. And a month after I had the kit, I had one lesson, gave that up, practiced once in the back room and joined a group and I've played with groups ever since. I think it's better for you. Well, I don't know if it's better for you, but it was for me.

I have a son who is a drummer, who played for three years, three hours a day, practicing with headphones on to records and to himself, but that's his style. He plays a totally different style from me, and he plays, not better, but technically he can do more than I can do. And he's interested in all those words they keep mentioning like flams and paradidtiles and things like that, which I never understood.

So you really feel that what made you special was that you worked from your gut emotion?

Well, I think that the drums are an emotional instrument and there's no melody. It's not like you can sit in a room with a guitar or piano and play. It's only "boom-boom-boom" or "ratta-tat-tat," and there's no real melody there. That's why I dislike solos. I don't care which drummer does a solo. It's not melodic, and he just has an ego problem.

When did you decide to make your first solo album?

After the breakup, I was sitting around, wondering what to do with myself. I had done a few sessions, but it was the end of that gig and I was wondering what to do next. I realized I had to do something, so I ran and did a standard album. I did all tracks I was brought up with at the parties at the house: "Sentimental Journey" and "Stardust" and all those '40s tunes.

Was Sentimental Journey *really a gift to your mother?*

Yeah. It was a gift for her, and it got me off my ass. So I did that, and then I was working on George's album and he flew Pete Drake in because Pete had done something with [Bob] Dylan's album and they were friends. I lent Pete my car, and he noticed I had a lot of country cassettes in the car. I told him I liked country music. So he said, "Well, why don't you do a country album?"

And I said, "I'm not going to live in Nashville for six months," which was how long The Beatles would be there to make an album. He said, "Are you kidding? We did Bob's album in two days." I was blown away, even though The Beatles' first album took 12 hours, but it had been so long ago my memory had failed. So I said, "OK, I'll come over next week and we'll do an album." And we did the album in three days. It was just all to get me moving.

I did the *Sentimental Journey* album and then the Nashville album [*Beaucoups Of Blues*], and then Harry Nilsson called me. Harry and I had been invited to present some Grammy awards, so I thought, "I'm not going to fly all the way to America just to present a Grammy award and then go home. Why don't I do some sessions in Nashville again?" So I phoned Richard Perry, who I had met in England while playing on some sessions for Harry, and said, "Why don't we do some sessions while we're in Nashville?" Then he called back saying, "Well, why don't you leave Nashville and fly to L.A. and we'll do some sessions there?"

So I figured I'd make two weeks out of it, and that's how the *Ringo* album came about. I came into L.A. just to do the album, and it just happened that John had flown into L.A. and George was in L.A. I was making an album, and we're all friends even if we had split up, so I said, "Have you got any songs, boys?" and John said, "Yeah, I've got a song," so I said, "Well, come and play." So he came down, and I asked George if he had one and he came down, and then I called Paul in England and said, "You can't be left out of this" — like it was the big deal of his life — so we came to England and did the track. That's how that came about. It was all accidental, not planned.

How did you feel, suddenly becoming the focal point of a project in an album that revolved around you?

It was really good. Before that, we had had the two singles, which George had produced, "It Don't Come Easy" and "Back Off Boogaloo," which were #1. I had written them and George finished them. So that was exciting, and I was getting excited about the business again as a solo career, so I was back in the music trade as a solo. It just took time for me to get used to the idea, because I had never been a solo artist. I had always been in a band, since drummers are usually in the band.

Are there specific recordings you are particularly proud of?

There's different styles, though it's the one attitude. I still think the finest stuff I did was on "Rain." "Rain" is, to me, my all-time favorite drum track.

Why?

Because of what I did; wherever my head was at the time. It is a vague departure for me. And *Abbey Road*, and there's lots of things in between — bits here and bits there. "Get A Woman," by B.B. King, I felt I played some real solid drums on that. "A Day In The Life," I felt the drums were as colorful as the song and the guitars. There's one, "It's been a long time..." ["Wait"]. That has really fine tom-tom work on it.

It's fine on everything, really, but some of them knock me out. And it took me a while to listen to Beatle records without going through the emotions of the day: how we felt, what was going on, who was saying hello to who.

After we broke up, it took me a couple of years to really listen. You know, you'd make the record and really enjoy making it, and when it was finished, you'd enjoy listening to it in the studio and enjoy having it at home as a piece of plastic in a sleeve, but then I would never play them again. Only in the last several years could I listen to them as tracks. And you can also look back and see the stages you were going through or you went through.

What about highlights, playing or personal?

There's too many. Well, there's high and high. How high do you want to get? You know what I'm saying? As an act, which we were, the *Palladium* or *The Ed Sullivan Show*, because they were definite moves in a career. I always thought, though we played music, we still wanted to be the biggest band in the world. Not that we knew it would be a monster, but we knew we were aiming somewhere, and the only degree of saying it is popularity. And we did become the most popular group on earth, so there's all those moves.

But like the "Rain" session, where something just comes out of the bag, that just arrives, that's exciting. It's not a conscious thing. It just happens, and some sessions can get exciting. Musically, sometimes you would be blown away with what came out, but not every time. Other times you did the best you could and if it worked, great. But sometimes a lot of magic, a lot of magic, just came out of the blue, and it comes out for everybody. To play with three other people, any other people, when it works is when everyone is hitting it together — no one is racing, no one's dragging, the song is good or the track is good and the music is good, and you're all just hitting it together.

If you're not a musician, I don't know if you'll understand that, when just three, four, 10 of you, a 100-piece orchestra, hit it together for as much time as you can — because there's very few times it goes through the whole track. Never mind the whole album — there's magic in that that is unexplainable. I can't explain what I get from that. It's getting high for me. Just a pure musical high.

How does someone maintain his perspective on being a human being when the world has made him larger than life?

I think you're born with it. Also, at certain periods, I did go over the edge and believe the myth, but I had three great friends who told me, "You're fooling yourself."

But weren't they going over the edge as well?

Yes, but they had three friends, too, to tell them they're fooling themselves. It's not that we actually all did it at once.

During all the talk about a Beatles reunion and all of that, was there ever a time when you thought if you got together for a night that...

Well, we did. The four of us never got together, but at certain times after the breakup, three of us got together.

Was that magic still there?

Well, we looked at each other and smiled. It was interesting. Now, it's impossible to put it all back together, of course, but I don't think any of us really thought we'd get back together. Everyone got too busy. No matter how much money they offered us, we never did it for the money, then or now. Then, when we were doing it in the '60s, and when they were offering us $50 million in the '70s, it wasn't an incentive to play. Money is no incentive for musicians. It's nice to have, but it's not enough.

I think it was John and Paul who said they felt that spark couldn't be re-created. I wondered whether you agreed or how you felt.

I don't believe that. I think, had the four of us gotten down and played, that spark would have been there. But the reasons would have been different, and that was the difference.

What kind of effect would you say The Beatles, the fame, all that, has had on you today?

I don't know. It's hard to say where I'd be if it hadn't happened. But it did, so I'm exactly where I feel I should be. Does anybody know what he would have done if he hadn't been doing what he did do at the time he was doing something? It's impossible to tell.

The difference would be that you wouldn't be interested in talking to me if I had just been playing some little club somewhere. But whether I would have been a different human being... it's hard to tell. I'm sure I must have changed, but would I have changed had I gone through a whole different type of life? I don't know. The effect it all had from being born to today and everything that went on in between is that we're here in the garden, trying to say hello.

Fixing some holes

Recent guest appearances, unconfirmed sightings and a dubious theory or two

by Belmo and Thomas Ramon

One aspect of Beatles collecting that can be a source of frustration as well as fascination is the category of "Beatles For Others And Guest Appearances." Let's call it FOGA for short.

A great deal of detective work is required to track down these elusive compositions for other artists and guest appearances on the recording of others. More often than not, these important musical works go unheralded, unannounced and unnoticed. Accordingly, collectors must be vigilant and resourceful if they are to possess a complete portfolio.

Harry Castleman and Walter Podrazik were the first to compile an accurate FOGA discography in their acclaimed series of books (*All Together Now*, *The Beatles Again* and *The End?*) However, a number of years have passed since their last book appeared, and an update of these releases has been long overdue.

This is only a start, intended to fix a few holes and foster discussions... about who was Ersel Hickey? Which Donovan songs did Paul McCartney play on? And where the heck did "Sitar Man" come from? There is certain to be missing data — and, possibly, incorrect information. Readers are therefore urged to write either the authors or *Goldmine* with their additions and corrections. Please note that this list neither includes multiple releases of tracks nor featured appearances on "various artists" releases, i.e., Artists Against Apartheid or Ferry Aid, which do not qualify as FOGA.

This article originally appeared in Goldmine *issue #295, Nov. 15, 1991.*

More clues for you all — Recent discoveries, 1965-1984

Unidentified Donovan Tracks, produced by Mickie Most.

It has been known for some time that Paul McCartney is one of the revelers on the "Mellow Yellow" single, released in October 1966. But while being interviewed for his World Tour program, McCartney revealed that he had played bass "on a few [Donovan] tracks around 'Mellow Yellow.'" That these tracks appear on the actual *Mellow Yellow* LP, U.S. Epic 26239, is unlikely, however, as Donovan seems to have employed a stand-up bass player for the sessions.

"Dear Delilah" and "The Dead Boot," performed by Grapefruit, written by George Alexander, "Produced by Terry Melcher" (assisted by Executive producers, John Lennon and Paul McCartney), "Arranged by Bill Shepheard" (assisted by McCartney). U.K. 45, RCA 1656, January 1968.

"Lullabye," performed by Grapefruit, written by George Alexander, produced by Terry Melcher, again assisted by Lennon and McCartney U.K. 45 [?], 1968.

"Elevator" and "Yes," performed by Grapefruit, written by George Alexander (A-side) and John Perry (B-side), "Produced by Apple Music Ltd." U.S. 45, Equinox E-70005, May 1968.

John Lennon and Paul McCartney's involvement with this unremarkable quartet was surprisingly heavy. Lennon actually named the band (from a book by a favorite author of his, Yoko Ono), Apple published their music, and the two Beatles helped produce their singles and promotional films. What's more, a demo for "Lullabye" was found in Lennon's archives. (Westwood One actually trumpeted "Lullabye For A Lazy Day" as a lost Lennon/McCartney demo when first publicizing their *Lost Lennon Tapes* series. As such, the lyrics were subsequently quoted in *Musician* magazine, although it was pointed out that the song had not been up to the pair's usual standards.) Although these recordings are quite interesting, Grapefruit's songs are indeed pale Lennon/McCartney imitations, and a the phasing in the world — which Lennon and McCartney seem to have employed — could not turn these pretenders into the real thing.

"Carolina In My Mind," performed and written by James Taylor, produced by Peter Asher. U.S. Apple single 1805,

December 1968. Also appears on U.S. LP *James Taylor*, Apple SKAO 3352.

'Sweet Baby' James recently revealed that while McCartney provided the *White Album*–style bass, George Harrison was participating as an uncredited backup singer. Additionally, Taylor now says, his line about the "Holy Host Of Others" was intended as a reference to the Fabs.

"Charity Bubbles" and "Goose," performed by The Scaffold, written by Mike McGear and Roger McGough, produced by Norrie Paramor and Tim Rice. U.K. single, Parlophone R 5784, June 1969.

Brother Paul McCartney contributes the prominent lead guitar, played in a style similar to that which he employed on the oft-booted "Watching Rainbows" jam.

"Penina," performed by Jotta Herre, written by Paul McCartney. Holland 45, Philips 369 002 PF, July 18, 1969.

Apparently, there are two "official" recordings of this song, as McCartney simultaneously gave the song to both the Portuguese singer Carlos Mendes, and the Dutch/Portuguese band, Jotta Herre. In late 1968, McCartney was vacationing at the south Portugal home of writer Hunter Davies, and the exchange took place in a night club, following a late-evening jam session. Although recorded independently, both versions premiered on the same day, with Mendes' recording appearing on a Portuguese 45, Parlophone QMSP 16459.

"Hare Krishna Mantra" and "Prayer To The Spiritual Masters," performed by the Radha Krishna Temple (London), arranged by Makunda Das Adhikary, produced by George Harrison. U.S. 45, Apple 1810, August 1969.

Harrison's involvement with the recording of these tracks is well documented, of course, but according to Srila Prabhupada's authorized *Every Town And Village* biography, another Beatle was present. While the Radhas sang, it reports, Paul and Linda McCartney operated the recording console. Harrison played organ, and "afterwards, dubbed in the bass guitar and other voices."

"Let It Be," performed by Aretha Franklin, written by John Lennon/Paul McCartney, produced by Jerry Wexler [?]. U.K. 45, Atlantic Records, May 1970.

In early 1969, McCartney gave the emerging First Lady Of Soul a recording of The Beatles performing "Let It Be," along with the first option to release the song. She ultimately issued this surprisingly restrained interpretation, but not before The Beatles' original recording had come out in early 1970.

"Roll It Over," performed by Derek And The Dominoes, produced by Phil Spector. B-side of U.S. single "Tell The Truth," Atco 6780, September 1970.

According to legend, this single was available for one day only — Sept. 14, 1970 — before being pulled from the market. Previous discographies cite Harrison's guitar contribution to the Spector-produced version of "Tell The Truth," but Hari's long-rumored guitar and vocal contributions to "Roll It Over" have only recently been confirmed. The track displays the spirit and intensity of the *Layla* LP, both of which are surprisingly absent from the A-side.

Once bootlegged as a "1972 Clapton-Harrison outtake" "Roll It Over" recently resurfaced on Clapton's *Crossroads* boxed set.

"I'm Your Spiritual Breadman," performed by Ashton, Gardner And Dyke, with help from "Sir Cedric Clayton, guitar" And "George O'Hara Smith, electric swivel guitar." Written by Tony Ashton, produced by Ashton, Gardner And Dyke. Appears on U.S. LP *Ashton, Gardner And Dyke*, Capitol ST 563,1970.

Harrison's contribution to this track goes beyond the previously cited "guitar," as the album jacket acknowledges that "Breadman" was "kneaded and leavened by George Harrison" (In fact, it was once rumored that Harrison helped compose the song). Harrison owed Tony Ashton and Roy Dyke a favor at the time, as the two musicians had been featured extensively on *Wonderwall* — and because Apple Records had rejected their previous band, The Remo Four.

Of additional interest, *Ashton, Gardner And Dyke* features an Ashton paean to "Sweet Patti O'Hara Smith," in which he professes his love for the wife of a "best friend." Could John Lennon have been referring to Harrison and his lovely "Layla" when he penned "You've Got To Hide Your Love Away"?

"Tandoori Chicken," performed by Ronnie Spector, written and produced by George Harrison and Phil Spector. Appears on the U.S. 45, Apple 1832, April 19, 1972.

The air was thick with marijuana smoke, and "a great big bottle of wine" was changing hands, but Ronnie Spector was not having a good time. According to her *Be My Baby* autobiography, she hated "Try Some, Buy Some" and was equally unimpressed by its proposed B-side, "Tandoori Chicken," improvised on the spot by producers Phil and Harrison. Still, she was glad to see old friend John Lennon, who stopped by to offer support — and to join in on the raucous "Tandoori" backing vocals.

"Bored As Butterscotch," performed and produced by Mike McGear, written by "McGear/McGough/Friend." U.K. album *Woman*, Island ILPS 9191, April 1972.

The McCartney melody gave this one away — and made it the stand-out track on his brother's LP.

"One Day At A Time," performed by Elton John, written by John Lennon, produced by Gus Dudgeon. B-side to U.S. single "Lucy In The Sky With Diamonds," MCA 40344, November 1974.

While Dr. O'Boogie's contribution to the A-side is significant — and well-documented — he also plays guitar, albeit imperceptibly, on "One Day At A Time."

"Tomorrow" and "Crowds Of You," performed by Kate Robbins, "Produced by Del Newman, Production by MPL." U.K. single. Anchor ANC 1054, June 1978.

McCartney helped produce this recording for relative Kate, who later sang on *Press To Play*. Released on June 30, 1978, this heavily orchestrated cover of the Broadway hit, written by Martin Charnin and Charles Strouse, hinted that McCartney missed his sessions with Mary Hopkin. The flip, "Crowds Of You," is a Kate Robbins composition. Of note, Del Newman had previously arranged the strings on two songs from *Adam Faith*, the 1974 album featuring uncredited McCartney contributions.

"Girlfriend," performed by Michael Jackson, written by Paul McCartney, produced by Quincy Jones. From the U.S. LP *Off The Wall*, Epic FE 35745, 1979.

According to his *Moonwalk* autobiography, this song was originally intended for Michael Jackson. McCartney played the song for him on piano at a party during Wings' 1976 American tour. Jackson was duly flattered but overwhelmed, unable to fully appreciate the song in the somewhat chaotic atmosphere. Several years later, when Quincy Jones was preparing to produce *Off The Wall*, he pulled out McCartney's *London Town* and told Jackson that he had the perfect song for him. The gloved one knew fate when he saw it. Some critics have suggested that Jackson and Jones improved the song with their arrangement, but McCartney's original, longer version is superb as well, with its Smokey Robinson–influenced bridge.

Another day — 1985-1991

"California Calling," performed by The Beach Boys, produced by Steve Levine. Appears on the U.S. LP *The Beach Boys*, Caribou BFN 39946, June 1985.

Ringo sits in with the Beach Boys, playing drums and timpani.

***Water*, soundtrack for the Hand Made film, "Featuring Songs by Eddy Grant, Eric Clapton, George Harrison, and Mike Moran," produced by Mike Moran. U.K. LP, London. Filmtrax Year 2, August 1985.**

Includes: "Celebration." performed by Jimmy Helms, written by Harrison/Moran; "Focus Of Attention," performed by Jimmy Helms, written by Moran/Clement/Harrison; and "Freedom," performed by "Billy Connolly/Chris Tummings and the Singing Rebels Band," written by Eric Clapton and Ian La Frenais.

A movie is Hand Made in the Caribbean, providing Harrison and pals with the excuse to write and play some reggae. Harrison helped write two, though the songs bear little resemblance to your typical Harisong, and played guitar on Clapton's "Freedom" while Starr drummed. "Freedom" is performed live in the film, with a mix that accents the Clapton/Harrison backup vocals. "Freedom" and "Celebration" were coupled together on the U.K. 45, Audiotrax 10.

"Children Of The Sky," written, produced and arranged by Mike Batt. Appears on the U.K. LP *The Hunting Of The Snark*, Adventure Records SNARK 1, and on the 45, Adventure Records, ARK 1, September 1986.

Inspired by the poetry of Lewis Carroll, the *Snark* album by Womble Mike Batt boasts a bona fide "all-star cast." Sir John Gielgud and John Hurt share the role of narrator, while Roger Daltrey, Art Garfunkel, Julian Lennon and other singers are backed by the London Symphony Orchestra. Even so, Harrison's brief but joyous slide solo is the best part of the single.

"Talk Don't Bother Me," performed, written and produced by Alvin Lee. Appears on the U.S. LP *Detroit Diesel*, 21 Records 7 90517-1, 1986.

This average white blues track is enlivened by Harrison's burning slide solo. The lineup is Alvin Lee, lead vocal, guitars, drums, bass; Tim Hinckley, Hammond organ; George Harrison, slide guitar.

"Back In The U.S.S.R.," performed by The Beach Boys, written by Lennon/McCartney. Appears on the U.S. mail order LP *Fourth Of July: A Rockin' Celebration Of America*, December 1086.

"It's Beatlemania," Mike Love declares as Ringo Starr joins The Beach Boys to play drums on a spirited "Back In The USSR." The song was recorded live during The Beach Boys' July 4, 1984 concert on the Mall in Washington, D.C.

***Tana Mana*, performed by The Ravi Shankar Project, written and arranged by Ravi Shankar, produced by Shankar, Frank Serafine, and Peter Baumann. U.S. LP Private Music 20161-P, April 1987.**

Harrison plays "auto harp synthesizer" and, according to Alan Clayson's Harrison biography, *The Quiet One*, supplies the "throaty" vocal on the title track, sung in Hindi. The album was recorded at FPSHOT (Harrison's Friar Park Studio, Henley-on-Thames) during the making of *Cloud 9*. Tracks include: "Chase," "Tana Mana," "Village Dance," "Seven And 10-1/2," "Friar Park," "Romantic Voyage," "Memory Of Uday," "West Eats Meat," "Reunion" and "Supplication."

"Rockestra Theme," performed by Duane Eddy, written and produced by Paul McCartney. Appears on the U.S. LP *Duane Eddy*, Capitol 12567, June 1987.

Back from the Egg, this instrumental track is revived in the Duane Eddy style — and it works. McCartney plays bass and howls, working alongside Harrison buddy Jim Horn. The track was issued as a single in the U.K. and was used for a time on *Entertainment Tonight* as incidental music.

"Theme For Something Really Important," performed by Duane Eddy, written and produced by Jeff Lynne; and "The Trembler," performed by Eddy, written by Ravi Shankar and Lynne, produced by Lynne. Appears on the U.S. LP *Duane Eddy*, Capitol 12567, June 1987.

Some pleasant, understated Harrison slide perfectly complements the patented Duane Eddy style. Of additional interest here, Eddy played on two unreleased *Cloud 9* tracks while touring Friar Park.

***Alvin Lee*, U.K. LP on Epic.**

Beatles Book reported that Harrison played guitar on this 1987 release but provided no further details.

"Come Away Death," written by Shakespeare/McCartney/Doyle, from the Riverside Theatre production of *Twelfth Night*. Broadcast on BBC television *Shakespeare* series (PBS in America) in early 1988.

He has written with John Lennon, Elvis Costello, Stevie Wonder, and now... William Shakespeare. Pat Doyle had recently become managing director of the Renaissance Theatre Company when he was given an advance tape of "Once Upon A Long Ago," along with McCartney's assurance that they could do with — it as they pleased. Doyle slowed the tempo and added a counter melody on top of the original chorus. McCartney was pleased upon hearing his haunting melody married to more deserving lyrics — and so were the critics.

***Give A Little Love*, performed by various artists. Executive producer Lon Van Eaton. U.S. CD, COMIN INC. CMN 1187-002, January 1988. Includes "Get Happy," performed by "Derrek," written by Lon and Derrek Van Eaton, produced by Klaus Voormann, and "Sweet Music," performed by "Derrek," written by Lon and Derrek Van Eaton, produced by George Harrison.**

Lon and Derrek Van Eaton's *Brother* LP, recorded with the assistance of fellow Apple artists George Harrison and Ringo Starr, received glowing reviews. Their second LP, issued by A&M, also earned favorable notices. By the time they began their subsequent album, the talented singers and multi-instrumentalists had established impeccable credentials as studio session players, appearing on *Ringo*, *Dark Horse* and *Rotogravure*. Incredibly, however, they were not given the opportunity to complete their own album.

This noteworthy release from 1988 includes two tracks from the duo's final A&M sessions, described today by Derrek Van Eaton as "the best things we ever did." "Getting Better" is a bouncy remake of the classic *Sgt. Pepper* track, recorded without assistance from any of the song's original performers, while the infectious "Get Happy" features Starr on drums and percussion. "Sweet Music," the gorgeous Harrison-produced single from 1972, again with Starr on drums, is also part of this collection. Assembled to help raise funds for the Boy Scouts Of America, limited copies of the rare CD and album are still available from Music For A Better World, 1-800-733-5193.

"Love's A State Of Mind," performed by Slyvia Griffin, produced by Chris Thomas. U.K. 45, Rocket Records BLAST 7, May 1988.

Chris Thomas played harpsichord on "Piggies" while helping to produce *The White Album*, and Harrison "rushed" to repay the favor, adding his distinctive guitar to this recording some 20 years later.

"T Shirt," performed by The Crickets, written by Jim Imray, produced by Paul McCartney. U.S. 45, Epic 34-087028, September 1988. Also appears on the U.S. LP, *T-Shirt*, Epic 44446.

"T Shirt" is the song that won the MPL-sponsored "Buddy Holly Song Contest." It's not bad, and The Crickets sound happy to be recording anything. McCartney sings backup and adds some perky piano riffs.

"(I Don't Wanna) Hold Back," performed by Gary Wright, written by Robert Brookins/Wright, Produced by Wyn Davis and Wright. Appears on the U.S. LP *Who Am I*, Cypress Records YL 0111, September 1988.

"I don't want to hold back this feeling," Wright sings, but even an old friend's economical guitar lines can't inject the missing "feeling" into this smooth but unsuccessful grab for "adult contemporary" FM radio play.

"New Moon Over Jamaica," performed by Johnny Cash, written by Paul McCartney/Johnny Cash/Tom T. Hall, produced by McCartney, "additional recording and remix by Jack Clement." Appears on the U.S. LP *Water From The Wells Of Home*, Mercury 834 778 1, October 1988.

Apparently, the three songwriters got together by chance while vacationing in Jamaica. And although we might have expected more from this formidable partnership, their song evokes the friendly, laid-back atmosphere in which it was written. In addition to playing bass, McCartney shares the lead vocals with Cash. Hamish Stuart and Chris Whitten contribute to the instrumental backing, and Linda McCartney joins forces with singers June Carter and Tom T. Hall. There may have been an outtake from this session, for it was reported at the time that Cash had also planned to cover McCartney's "Man We Was Lonely."

"Oh Lord, Oh Why," performed and produced by Jim Capaldi, written by P. Trim/J.M. Bouchar. Appears on U.S. LP *Some Come Running*, Island 91024 1, November 1988.

George Harrison and Eric Clapton briefly trade licks in the middle of a song that sounds as if it could have been an outtake from the *All Things Must Pass* sessions. The ex-Beatle defers to the ex-Domino during the fade, however, letting

Clapton steal the recording with his fiery licks. Harrison appears in a promotional video for the track.

"Children In Need" and "Children In Need (instrumental)," performed by Spirit Of Play, written by Craig Mathieson/Nicky Hopkins, produced by Paul McCartney and Spirit Of Play. U.K. 45, Release Records KIDS 1988, December 1988.

This is one of those songs that sounds instantly familiar, because the chorus is Similar to Pink Floyd's "Bring The Boys Back Home." Spirit Of Play is Craig Mathieson, vocals; Woody Woodmansey, drums; and Nicky Hopkins, piano, keyboards. McCartney plays bass and provides the appropriate anthemic production, Ken Wilson plays lead guitar, and the Greenfields School Choir sings. The instrumental B-side is pleasant — even though it turns into George Harrison's "Can't Stop Thinking About You," on which Hopkins played, during the fade. And it is good to hear McCartney and Hopkins playing together after all these years.

"Veronica" and "Pads, Paws And Claws," performed by Elvis Costello, written by McCartney/MacManus, produced by Costello, Kevin Killen, T-Bone Burnett. Appears on the U.S. LP *Spike*, Warner Brothers 9 25848, February 1989.

Two great songs from the potentially immortal songwriting team. And as if that isn't enough, McCartney's bass on "Veronica" is brilliant.

"...This Town..." performed and written by Elvis Costello, produced by Costello, Kevin Killen, T-Bone Burnett. Appears on the U.S. LP *Spike*, Warner Brothers 9 25848, February 1989.

Although they weren't in the same studio at the same time, D.P.A. MacManus created a musician's "dream team" by getting Paul McCartney and Roger McGuinn to individually tape their Rickenbacker bass and 12-string guitar parts. Jim Keltner plays drums.

"A Love So Beautiful," performed by Roy Orbison, written and produced by Jeff Lynne. Appears on the U.S. LP *Mystery Girl* Virgin 91058, February 1989.

Nelson Wilbury helps out his brother, Lefty, by adding a track of acoustic rhythm guitar.

"I Won't Back Down," performed by Tom Petty, written by Petty and Jeff Lynne, produced by Lynne with T.P. and Mike Campbell. Appears on the U.S. CD *Full Moon Fever*, MCA D-6253, March 1989.

Harrison sings backup and plays acoustic guitar on the first single from Petty's greatest hit, *Full Moon Fever*. The video features two additional surprise guests: Starr, who "stick synchs" to Phil Jones' original drum track, and Harrison's psychedelic Fender of *Magical Mystery Tour* and 1974 U.S. Tour fame (played mysterioso-ously during Mike Campbell's Harrison-influenced solo).

"Run So Far," performed by Eric Clapton, written by George Harrison, produced by Russ Titelman. Appears on U.S. CD *Journeyman*, Reprise 9 26074-2, 1989.

This pleasant, country-tinged number grows on the listener, as do the mellow Clapton/Harrison harmonies and Harrison's always tasteful guitar. When it came out in 1989, it made one want to hear more... a wish that was answered several months later with the release of the various artists CD, *Nobody's Child — Romanian Angel Appeal*, Warner Brothers 9 26280. With *Nobody's Child* came "That Kind Of Woman," enabling fans and music lovers to enjoy the first of two Harisongs that had been left off of *Journeyman*. "Cheer Down," written by Harrison and Petty and later re-recorded by Harrison for the *Lethal Weapon 2* soundtrack, was the second.

"Leave A Light On," performed by Belinda Carlisle, written by Rick Nowels/Ellen Shipley, and "Deep Deep Ocean," performed by Belinda Carlisle, written by Billy Steinberg/Tom Kelly/Amy Sky, produced by Rick Nowels. Appears on U.S. LP *Runaway Horses*, MCA 6339, 1989.

Well, why not? The Go-Go's sounded a lot like the "girl groups" who influenced The Beatles in the early '60s, and Belinda Carlisle has an appealing voice. Harrison plays some excellent and prominent slide on the hit single, "Leave A Light On," MCA53706, and provides the "atmosphere" on "Deep Deep Ocean" by multitracking the lush 12-string guitar and bass parts.

"Amerika," performed by David Peel and The Lower East Side with Yoko Ono, written by David Peel, produced by John Lennon and Ono, 1989.

Recorded after the sessions for *The Pope Smokes Dope* had been completed, this repetitious song deserves its status as an outtake. When released on Peel's Orange Records, ORA 8374 S, the liner notes stated that Yoko Ono had "suggested that a single be made of 'Amerika.'" Yoko wails throughout the recording; her voice is multitracked near the end.

"Act Naturally," performed by Buck Owens and Ringo Starr, written by Morrison/Russell, produced by Jerry Crutchfield and Jim Shaw. Appears on the U.S. LP *Act Naturally*, Capitol C 1 92893, 1989.

While the single, Capitol B-44409, was credited to the duo, on the album Starr is a guest. He shares the lead vocals with Owens on this track recorded at Abbey Road Studios.

"That Kind Of Woman," performed by Gary Moore, written by George Harrison, produced by Moore and Ian Taylor. Appears on the U.S. CD *Still Got The Blues*, Charisma 2-91369, as a bonus track, March 1990.

Hot stuff. This is the George Harrison who wrote and sang "Savoy Truffle." The horns are tight, Moore's playing is tough and Harrison adds some great backup vocals and slide parts. Moore said he had heard the Clapton demo — or more likely, the finished track, which was not yet slated for release — before asking for permission to record his version. Harrison must have been pleased with the results, as it earned Moore a spot on the *Wilburys III* album. (Moore plays the scorched-earth solo on "She's My Baby.") Harrison later dubbed the guitarist "Ken Wilbury."

"While My Guitar Gently Weeps," performed by the Jeff Healey Band, written by George Harrison, produced by Ed Stasium. Appears on the U.S. CD *Hell To Pay*, Arista ARCD 8632, and on the U.K. 45, Arista 113 622, May 1990.

Harrison's contribution is more symbolic than substantive, as the track was pretty much finished when a tape was flown across the Atlantic so that Harrison could add an acoustic rhythm track and backup vocal.

***Armchair Theatre*, performed and produced by Jeff Lynne, U.S. LP and CD, Reprise 9 26184, June 1990. Includes: "Every Little Thing," written by Lynne; "Lift Me Up," written by Lynne; "September Song," written by Maxwell Anderson and Kurt Weill; and "Stormy Weather," written by Ted Koehler and Harold Arlen.**

With Harrison's prominent slide guitar and vocals, the two standards and the sterling "Lift Me Up" could be tracks from a one of his own albums. In fact, Lynne's vocals throughout the album often sound as if they are Harrison's, taken down a

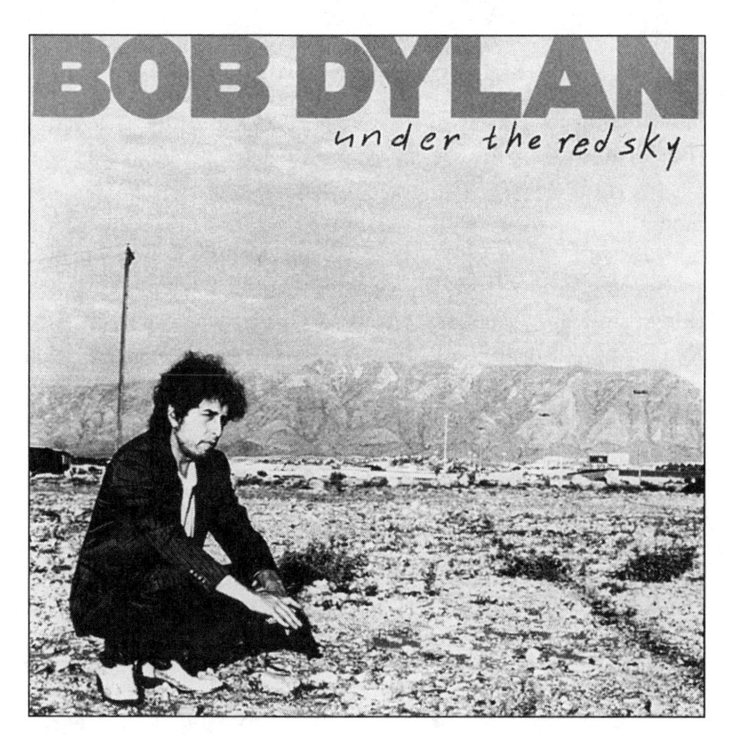

key or two. Perhaps if one played the vinyl version of *Armchair Theatre* at a slightly faster speed, it would actually turn into a George Harrison album.

"Take Away The Sadness," performed by Jim Horn, written by Richard Tandy/Horn, produced by Larry Knechtel and Horn. Appears on the U.S. CD *Work It Out*, Warner Brothers 25911-2, July 1990.

Beautifully played guitar and sax — and a pleasant melody — don't quite rescue this song from its overly lush, "designer jazz" improvisation. The personnel are George Harrison, solo slide guitar; Jim Horn, soprano sax; Michael Rhodes, bass; Paul Lem, drums; and Larry Byrom, electric rhythm guitar. Of note: Jeff Lynne and Tom Petty play and sing (without Harrison) on the album's spirited Lynne-penned title track.

"Dance The Do," performed by Mike McGear, written by McCartney/McGear, Produced by Paul McGear. Appears as the bonus track on U.S. CD **McGear*, Rykodisc RCD 10192, 1990.

An alternate take of the 1975 UK single is included on the CD reissue of the excellent **McGear* album. Of course, "Dance The Do" wasn't much of a song to begin with, but the performance is interesting, with McCarthy on Moog synthesizer and Jimmy McCullough on guitar. Too bad Mike forgot about the excellent "Leave It" B-side, "Sweet Baby," which would have been much more at home on the **McGear* CD.

"Under The Red Sky," performed and written by Bob Dylan, produced by Don Was, David Was, and Jack Frost. Appears on the U.S. CD *Under The Red Sky*, Columbia CK 46794, September 1990.

After attending sessions for *Under The Red Sky*, guitarist Slash from Guns N' Roses said he was disappointed by the real-life Bob Dylan (and, in particular, his inability to offer specific suggestions on instrumentation). Still, Slash told *Rolling Stone* it had been a rewarding experience because he was able to meet George Harrison, who played some "fucking awesome slide guitar." The ex-Beatle does so on one of the better tracks, along with an interesting cast that includes Waddy Wachtel, guitar; Al Kooper, keyboards; Don Was, bass; and Kenny Aronoff, drums.

"Lu Le La," performed by Vicki Brown. Appears on the European LP, *About Love And Life*, label unknown, late 1990.

She sang with Liverpool's Vernon Girls (who played some dates with the early Beatles) and later shared lead vocals with George Harrison on his unreleased theme song for "Shanghai Surprise." Prior to her death on June 6, 1991, she was a successful cabaret singer in Europe, although this doesn't make it easier to find *About Love And Life*, with Harrison's guitar contribution to "Lu Le La."

"Hurdy Gurdy Man" (longer version), performed by Donovan, composed by Donovan Leitch and George Harrison. Appears on U.K. CD *Donovan Rising*, Permanent Records PERM CD 2,1990.

For several years now, Donovan has been telling concertgoers how Harrison improvised the lyrics for one verse in the Maharishi's camp, while the other Beatles, Mike Love, and Mia Farrow watched. Producer Mickie Most deleted the verse in the studio, however, as he felt it made the song too long to be commercial. Most may have been correct, for the studio version of the song stands up better today than most other Donovan hits. Still, Donovan has recently restored the missing verse in concert, and it appears on this 1990 import CD.

"Fame '90," performed by David Bowie, written by Lennon/Bowie/Alomar, produced by Bowie and Harry Maslin. Appeared in the U.K. in seven formats, all on EMI: FAME 90, FAMEPD 90, FAMES 90, 12FAME90, 12FAMES 90, TCFAME 90 and CDFAME 90. Several of these are available on the bonus disc included with Bowie's *Young Americans* CD reissue, and the basic remix appears in the U.S. on the *Changes-Bowie* CD, Ryko RCD 20191.

A great track is remixed for the *Pretty Woman* movie soundtrack, but why?

"Bein' Angry" and "Walkin' Nerve," performed and written by Nils Lofgren, produced by Kevin McCormick and Lofgren. Appear on the U.S. CD, *Silver Lining*, Rykodisc RCD 10170, March 1991.

If they're "bein' angry," why do they sound bored? Starr sings backup on the song, and his "I Wanna Be Your Man" growl could have improved the track. But we never hear it. Andy Newmark handles the drumming chores, while Billy Preston plays organ. On "Walkin' Nerve," Starr is the drummer, and he proves he can still "whack the skins" with the best of 'em. But good drumming is not enough to make a good song. Curiously, Starr makes another of his cameos in the video for the album's single, "Valentine," along with Bruce Springsteen, even though Newmark played drums on the actual recording.

"If Not For You," performed and written by Bob Dylan. Appears on the U.S. CD set, *Bootleg Series, Volumes 1-3*, Columbia 47382, March 1991.

From the famous May 1, 1970, session, Harrison and Dylan make their way through a tentative "If Not For You." Harrison works out his guitar part as he goes and does not sing. Of course, both would record superb versions on their own a few months later, and they would rehearse the number as a duo backstage at Madison Square Garden, captured briefly in the *Bangla Desh* movie. A young Charlie Daniels plays bass while Russ Kunkel drums.

"So Like Candy" and "Playboy To A Man," performed by Elvis Costello, written by McCartney/MacManus, produced by Mitchell Froom, Kevin Killen and D.P.A. MacManus. Appears on the U.S. CD *Mighty Like A Rose*, Warner Brothers 2-26575, May 1991.

These songs were once slated for *Flowers In The Dirt*, but when McCartney changed his mind, Costello took them for his own. Costello then started fresh, duplicating the original McCartney/Costello harmonies and getting T-Bone Wolk and Jerry Scheff to provide the McCartney-esque bass figures. Jim Keltner plays drums, Marc Ribot guitar, while Larry Knechtel, Mitchell Froom and Benmont Tench pound a variety of keyboards. "So Like Candy" is a gem, as are the majority of the McCartney/Costello collaborations, and "Playboy To A Man" is fun. Still, it would be interesting to hear McCartney's original studio versions. There's one heck of a bootleg waiting to be released someday.

***Liverpool Oratorio*, performed by the Royal Liverpool Philharmonic Orchestra, written by Paul McCartney and Carl Davis, produced by John Fraser, executive producer Paul McCartney. U.S. CD *Angel*, October 1991.**

School motto of the Liverpool Institute, "Non nobis solum sed toti mundo nati," inspires an ambitious 97-minute classical piece. (Translated into English, the motto proclaims, "Not for ourselves alone but for the whole world were we born"). Soloists Dame Kiri Te Kanawa, Sally Burgess, Jerry Hadley, and Willard White perform the work with the renowned Royal Liverpool Philharmonic Orchestra, Royal Liverpool Philharmonic Choir, and Choristers of Liverpool Cathedral. Carl Davis conducts. The oratorio is built around eight movements: "War," "School," "Crypt," "Father," "Wedding," "Work," "Crises" and "Peace."

You won't see me — Recordings left in the can

Two George Harrison originals, recorded by Marianne Faithfull and produced by George Harrison. Unreleased.

In *The Quiet One* biography, it is reported that Harrison actually helped Faithfull record two Harisongs during the early Apple era. Author Alan Clayson writes, "[Harrison] also submitted songs from his growing portfolio for [Mary Hopkin's] and Paul's consideration. Two of these were tried by Marianne Faithfull under the supervision of George, who perhaps saw her as a more worldly Hopkins."

One of these songs may have been mentioned in Hunter Davies' *The Beatles* biograpy. According to that author, Faithfull had asked Harrison to write something like "Within You Without You" for her, and he had let Davies watch as he worked on the song, which contained lyrics about "grapefruit eyes" and "artichoke hearts."

McCartney composition for actress Jessie Matthews.

Unreleased, possibly never recorded, first announced in 1969.

Abbey Road Studios tour.

"Careless And Free" an unidentified Jimmy Webb song, recorded by Mary Hopkin "at Paul's request." Unreleased.

Reported in *New Musical Express*, Aug. 15, 1970. Perhaps these will turn up on the forthcoming Apple CDs.

"Gotta Sing Gotta Dance," performed by Twiggy, written by Paul McCartney. Unreleased.

This may never have made it to the recording studio (apart from McCartney's performance for his *James Paul McCartney* television special). But *NME* reported in 1973 that McCartney had written this song for the former model — and that he was planning to write additional material for a 90-minute television special she was planning.

Interesting to note, in early 1968, Lennon and McCartney had promised to write the music for a proposed Apple film starring Twiggy. It was to have been titled *The Wishing Tree*.

***Born To Boogie*, soundtrack for film about T Rex, produced and directed by Ringo Starr, 1972. Now available in the U.K. on video from EMI's Picture Music International.**

Starr and Elton John jam with Marc Bolan and percussionist Mickey Finn on "Tutti Frutti" and "Children Of The Revolution." The performances were filmed in the Apple Studio.

"My Old Pal" written and performed by Carl Perkins, produced by Paul McCartney. Unreleased.

Will we ever hear this song from the *Tug Of War* sessions? According to Perkins, McCartney said he'd produce the song if Carl didn't mind Linda singing backup. "I don't care if all of England sings on it," Perkins claims to have replied. Linda said at the time that the song had reminded Paul of his friendship with Lennon and that it was the first thing that enabled Paul to cry following the tragedy.

Unfinished Paul McCartney/Peter Gabriel collaboration.

In 1986, Gabriel announced that he and Paul were working together on a song for Amnesty International's "International Day Of Peace." The song was not completed.

McCartney/Carla Lane animal rights song. Unreleased, may not exist.

Although Carla Lane told an interviewer that she had written an animal rights song "with the McCartneys," she may have meant "Linda McCartney." Lane — the writer of British TV's acclaimed *Bread* series — is a good friend of the Macs, and she has written at least one song, "The White-Coated Man," with Linda. Both Linda and Paul have guested on *Bread*, and it was through Lane that Paul was introduced to Carl Davis, co-composer of the *Liverpool Oratorio*.

"Shelter Of Your Love," performed by Alvin Lee, written by Harrison/Lee. Unreleased.

This title is mentioned in *The Quiet One*. The year of origin is unspecific, and it may have been recorded by Harrison rather than Lee.

Tell Me If You Can — Rumors and unconfirmed sightings

"I've Just Fallen For Someone," performed by Johnny Gentle.

This section is off to a bad start with its first entry, as it comes from a very unreliable source, the infamous Albert Goldman. This necrophiliac posing as a biographer "reports" that Johnny Gentle needed a middle eight when he played this song for Lennon during their now historic 1960 tour of Scotland, and that the Silver Beatle contributed a melody and lyrics on the spot. Allegedly — a word that applies to nearly everything in Goldman's tome — Gentle used Lennon's uncredited contribution when he recorded the song for the B-side of an unidentified Parlophone single in early 1962.

"Tell Me If You Can," composed by Tony Sheridan and Paul McCartney.

A more reliable source than Goldman, Tony Sheridan claims to have written this song with McCartney when they were working together in Hamburg. Furthermore, he recorded a version without McCartney's endorsement in 1964. Sheridan recently revived the song on European radio, singing: "Tell me if you can/Could there ever be another man/Who loves you like I do?/Tell me if you can.

"Tell me if you care/or is it just another love affair?/I really want to know/Tell me if you can.

"There is something/I wanna say to you/There ain't nothing/I wouldn't do for you."

"Yesterday," performed by Marianne Faithfull, composed by John Lennon and Paul McCartney, arranged and produced by Mike Leander. Appears on the U.S. LP *Go Away From My World*, London PS 452.

On Nov. 2, 1965, Faithfull taped a performance of "Yesterday" for the Granada Television special, *The Music Of Lennon And McCartney*. Her version was then edited and pieced together with McCartney's *Ed Sullivan* performance to create a "duet." Nine days later, McCartney attended the session for Faithfull's cover, and it's unlikely that the famed workaholic could have sat quietly and watched. However, it's hard to tell what McCartney's contribution to the lush arrangement for piano, chorus and strings might have been.

Of historic note, this session let McCartney see Mike Leander at work; Leander was subsequently asked to arrange "She's Leaving Home" for the *Sgt. Pepper* LP.

"Bluebirds Over The Mountain," written by Ersel Hickey, performed by The Beach Boys, produced by Bruce Johnston and Carl Wilson. U.S. single, Capitol 2360, December 1968. Appears on U.S. album, *20/20*, Capitol SKAO 133,1969.

This minor hit (#61 in *Billboard*) was once rumored to be a McCartney composition. Northern Songs published the music in Britain (as it had with Peter And Gordon's "Woman"). And Ersel Hickey sounds like a pseudonym if ever there was one. *{He is, in fact, a '50s rockabilly singer.}* McCartney certainly could have dashed off the light, breezy song in a matter of minutes. Of note: The B-side also presented a mystery at the time of its release. its co-composer was not credited, although Dennis Wilson had paid Charles Manson for writing the bulk of "Never Learn Not To Love."

"Labio Dental Fricative," recorded by Vivian Stanshall. U.K. single, Liberty lf 10520.

In its Feb. 21, 1970, edition, *Disc And Music Echo* reported that Bonzo Dog Band member Vivian Stanshall had recorded this track with Bo Diddley and Neil Innes... and possibly... Eric Clapton and McCartney. McCartney had worked with the Bonzos before, of course, but this would be one of his rare collaborations with Clapton.

"Fields Of St. Etienne," performed by Mary Hopkin, written by Gallagher/Lyle, produced by Paul McCartney. Released as the B-side to Hopkin's "Qué Será Será" single, U.S. Apple 1823, June 1970.

While discographies acknowledge that McCartney produced this gentle antiwar track, no mention is made of his subtle harmony vocal in the final chorus.

***New Morning*, performed and written by Bob Dylan. U.S. album, Columbia KC 30290, October 1970.**

This is most likely another of Bob Dylan's dreams, but he recently said that Harrison "may" have played on this album. Dylan was probably recalling the one-day session that took place earlier in 1970 — at which time the pair did run through "If Not For You" (see entry above). The session is not believed to have provided any of the material for *New Morning*.

***The Whale*, written and performed by John Tavener, U.S. LP, Apple SMAS 3369, November 1970.**

Starr may appear in a minor role-as one of the speaking voices — on this recording. When *The Whale* was first being issued, *Billboard* reported that Starr was a featured vocalist. Several years later, Starr demonstrated his attachment to this recording by reissuing it on his own Ring O' label.

***Raga*, soundtrack for a film about Ravi Shankar, produced by George Harrison. U.S. LP, Apple SWAO 3384, December 1971.**

Damn it, "Frenzy And Distortion" is The Beatles. Harrison and McCartney sing, and The Byrds-like instrumentation was not multitracked by Ravi. So maybe it's not on the EMI logs, but if you can't believe your ears.... The album's liner notes — stating, "Indian music has inspired many western creative composers, but in most cases one finds a distorted version of the sound and music of India" — certainly hint that this track had more to do with the album's "Western" producer than with Shankar.

"Tell The Truth" and "Dearest I Wonder," performed by Bobby Whitlock, produced by Whitlock and Andy Johns. From the U.S. LP *Raw Velvet*, ABC Records 50131, 1972.

George Harrison is said to be the "friend" who plays bass on these two tracks. The guitarist and drummer are identified, cleverly, by "domino" graphics, hinting that these could be outtakes from the *Layla* sessions. (They sound nothing like the more polished material that makes up the bulk of this album and were probably included only to remind listeners of Whitlock's illustrious then-recent past.)

Background vocals are by D.M. — Dave Mason, most likely. Harrison may also contribute second lead. Of greatest interest here, however: "Dearest I Wonder" was written by Whitlock and... Paula Boyd!

"The Flying Saucer Song," performed, written and produced by Harry Nilsson. Appears on the U.S. LP *Sandman*, RCA APLI 1031, 1976.

Starr is said to have had a hand in "writing" this number, which mainly consists of a repetitious rap between two drinking buddies, very much in the Nilsson/Starr tradition. The song was copyrighted in 1974, when rumor has it the pair collaborated. All other selections on the *Sandman* album are copyrighted 1975. Starr's name comes first on the back cover's "Special Thanks" list, and he "appears" in Klaus Voormann's inside cover illustration.

***Gone Too Long*, performed by Don Nix, "Produced by Don Nix (with spiritual guidance from George Harrrison)." U.S. LP *Cream* CR 1001, 1976.**

Who knows what this means? Nix was one of many backup singers at Bangla Desh, and Harrison may have repaid the favor by helping out with this standard mid-70s fodder. The album was recorded in a number of locations, however, ranging from France to Muscle Shoals, and it seems highly unlikely that Harrison would have accompanied Nix on his world travels. The track listing is as follows (Nix is the composer unless otherwise stated): "Goin' Thru Another Change," "Feel A Whole Lot Better" (Gene Clark), "Gone Too Long," "Backstreet Girl" (Jagger/Richards), "Rollin' In My Dreams," "Yazoo City Jail," "Harpoon Arkansas Turn Around," "Forgotten Town," "A Dernain (Until Tomorrow)" (Nix/Denimal).

***The Honorary Consul*, movie soundtrack performed by John Williams, produced by Stanley Myers and Richard Harvey.**

McCartney's excellent instrumental theme, released on the 1983 U.K. single, Island IS/155, most likely comprises the extent of his contribution to the soundtrack. However, in his World Tour program, McCartney notes that he "played guitar on John Williams' soundtrack," hinting that he may have attended other sessions for the project. The movie was retitled *Beyond The Limit* for American release.

"Bullshot," theme from another Hand Made film performed by Less Larry Smith, 1986. Unreleased on record.

Harrison is said to have helped with the lyrics and production for this song which is very much in the Hoagy Carmichael style of Harrison's later "Hottest Gong In Town." He definitely sings on the recording, as confirmed in Geoffrey Giuliano's *Dark Horse* biography.

***Blind Faith*, produced by Jimmy Miller, reissue on import CD, RSO Records 825 094-2 YH, 1990.**

L'Angelo Mysterioso is rumored to play on the two bonus tracks, "Exchange And Mart" and "Spending All My Days." According to legend, Harrison was actually asked to join Blind Faith but declined.

"Good Golly Miss Molly," performed by Little Richard, produced by Jeff Lynne. Promo CD single, label unknown, 1991.

Starr may have been the drummer on this remake of the Little Richard classic, produced by Lynne for the *King Ralph* soundtrack.

Things to come. Starr plays drums on two new CDs from his new label, Private Music — the first is by Taj Majal, produced by Skip Drinkwater, the second by Johnny Guitar Watson. Harrison played guitar at a session for Siobham Fahey, produced by Dave Stewart. McCartney was planning to contribute a song (possibly with Elvis Costello) to the next NRBQ album, and he'd been asked to produce a Happy Mondays cover of the Scaffold's "Thank U Very Much."

Retro News Flash

March 29, 1996, issue #409

Beatles turn down megabucks for tour

Paul McCartney, George Harrison, and Ringo Starr have said thanks but no thanks to an offer to regroup for a tour. A group of American and German businessmen reportedly offered the "Threetles" $225 million to perform 22 concerts in Japan, the U.S. and Europe. McCartney said that they turned down the offer because they would not perform live without John Lennon, despite having recently reunited in the studio to create "new" Beatles music from unfinished Lennon demo recordings. The Beatles have been approached with multi-million-dollar reunion offers several times since their breakup in 1970.

Conversation with Ringo

by Allen J. Wiener

While his distinctive backbeat on Beatles records is legendary — always on time, never a beat ahead or behind — the bulk of Ringo Starr's solo work is not generally well known. Most of it has been critically maligned, sometimes brutally so. To be sure, Ringo's solo career has had its share of ups and downs. He has scored a total of seven *Billboard* Top 10 singles, five of them in the Top 5 and two #1s. Three more reached the Top 40. He has had five Top 40 albums, including 1973's *Ringo*, which reached #2 in *Billboard* (#1 in *Cash Box* and *Record World*), and on which all four Beatles appeared.

Unfortunately, all of his subsequent efforts have been measured against that mega-hit. While none of them ever matched it, a few were given less credit than they deserved. That is particularly true of his 1983 release *Old Wave*, largely a collaboration with Joe Walsh. It was not released in England or the United States but did appear in many other countries, including Canada and Germany.

Starr would be the first to admit that several of his solo efforts were just plain lousy, lacking originality or inspiration. How much of the blame can be placed on Ringo's long bout with alcoholism is difficult to judge, but it clearly played a significant part in his professional undoing.

He had begun his solo career with two offbeat albums. *Sentimental Journey* (Apple, 1970) was a collection of cover versions of standards, mostly from the 1940s. *Beaucoups Of Blues* (Apple, 1970), cut in Nashville, was a venture into country 'n' western music, long a favorite form of his and a project that must have been dear to his heart. Neither effort was very successful among rock enthusiasts, although *Sentimental Journey* reached #22 in *Billboard*. His landmark *Ringo* album came next (Apple, 1973), followed by the successful and entertaining *Goodnight Vienna* (Apple, 1974).

Things began going wrong with *Ringo's Rotogravure* (Atlantic, 1976), a weak imitation of the previous two albums and the first under his new contract with Atlantic. The bottom really fell out with *Ringo The 4th* (Atlantic, 1977), a bizarre misfire aimed at the disco market. *Bad Boy* (Portrait, 1978) was a slight improvement with a few good songs, but far more weak ones. The album even includes "A Man Like Me," a simple rewrite of "A Mouse Like Me" from the children's album *Scouse The Mouse*, released only in England in 1977.

Starr seemed to bounce back with *Stop And Smell The Roses* (Boardwalk, 1981), cut mostly in 1980 and including contributions by former Beatles Paul McCartney and George Harrison. The album was not well received critically and barely cracked *Billboard's* Top 100, reaching only as far as #98. Then came *Old Wave* (RCA and Boardwalk, 1983). Then came nothing but scattered guest appearances.

This article originally appeared in* Goldmine *issue #310, June 12, 1992.

A new album was recorded early in 1987 with Chips Moman at that producer's 3 Alarm Studio in Memphis. Two years later Ringo blocked release of the album, claiming that his work was of inferior quality due to excessive use of alcohol during the sessions. Starr noted that he had not played drums on the album himself and that he viewed Moman's planned release as an attempt to cash in on the then-successful "All-Starrs" tour. The album remains unreleased.

In October 1988 Ringo and his wife, actress Barbara Bach, checked into an Arizona alcohol rehabilitation center for six weeks. After completing treatment, Ringo publicly admitted that he had wasted a good chunk of his life and squandered much of his career due to a virtual lifetime of alcohol dependency. Although a number of things worked against a revitalization of his career, he was determined to get back to work any way he could.

Lacking a record deal, he assembled a supergroup comprising Clarence Clemons, Walsh, Dr. John, Levon Helm, Rick Danko, Billy Preston, Jim Keltner, and Nils Lofgren and took his show on the road. Fronting his own group for the first time, "Ringo Starr And His All-Starr Band" played 32 North American dates before enthusiastic crowds during July-September 1989. A short seven-show swing through Japan followed.

Despite the release of an entertaining live concert album and video, a new record contract eluded Starr until March 1991, when he signed with the Private Music label. Working with four producers (Jeff Lynne, Don Was, Phil Ramone, and Peter Asher), Starr cut 16 songs during 1991, culling 10 of them for *Time Takes Time*, his first studio album to be released in nine years. More than a little reminiscent of *Ringo*, *Time Takes Time* is both infectious pop-rock and a gentle message about the hard knocks life inevitably has in store and the foolishness of wasting the time it takes to cry over them.

The album is supported by a new tour of North America and Europe beginning in June, with Ringo heading up a new "All-Starr" band. The new lineup includes Lofgren and Walsh, both holdovers from the 1989 tour, and new additions Dave Edmunds, Todd Rundgren, Burton Cummings, Tim Cappello, Timothy B. Schmit, and Ringo's son, Zak Starkey.

The following interview with Ringo took place in his New York hotel suite following a lively press conference at Radio City Music Hall. Before the press, Ringo had displayed the same wit, charm and humor that disarmed America early in 1964 when he shared the platform with his three former bandmates. Although suffering from a slight cold, he remained equally good humored throughout the interview.

Goldmine: *Did you have any specific objective in mind when you entered the studio to begin work on* Time Takes Time?

Ringo Starr: Initially, it was, "Let's go and make an album. Let's do some songs." I went in with Jeff [Lynne] and we did four tracks. Then I went in with Phil Ramone and did three tracks with him. The tracks were good, but it didn't make any real sense.

Nothing to really hold it together?

No. So then we did some tracks with Don Was, and that sort of helped straighten it out a bit because then there were three attitudes. Then the record company [Private Music] actually sent Peter Asher in and I said, "Sure," because he's done some really great stuff. And then it started to feel that we were really making a record. Then we went back in with Don and did some more tracks. Then we remixed the other stuff so that it then felt like an album.

Since you did work with four producers, was there a lot of shifting of gears because you suddenly had a new producer who did things differently than the last one? You've mentioned that Phil Ramone brought a "New York approach" to his sessions.

Well, I loved that with Phil. I mean, I never worked with him before, though we've bumped into each other. Actually, every producer I worked with I loved. [laughing] You know, "Let's do it like this, let's do it like that." We sort of had to straighten it out in the end, but I had a lot of fun with everybody.

And it plays through as a unified piece now.

It does now because of the remixes on Phil's and Peter's, and Jeff mixed his own.

Is there anything symbolic in the title?

Just that it's really good for me to hear. Just that time takes time, and you have to learn if you want to do anything.

A line from the first song on the album, "Weight Of The World" [also the first single], jumped out at me: "You either kiss...

[Reciting along] "the future or the past goodbye." All of the songs have something in them for me, even if I didn't write them.

There seems to be several points where that theme reappears, like "Don't Go Where The Road Don't Go."

Well, that's one that I wrote, so it certainly says what it says.

I think it says, "Now those friends have all disappeared."

We have a lot of fair-weather friends, you know. And that song, because I wrote it, was relating to me because there's been a mighty change in me, thank God, from being totally derelict. But it's not heavy, you know?

Things do change; rock 'n' roll has changed. This is the first time that we have a generation of rock 'n' roll stars who are over 40.

Well, we're the only ones who were there. I think that the kids now are not playing rock 'n' roll; they're playing smash 'n' grab. [laughs]

There seem to be two markets divided by age.

I found with my kids, though, that they all went through their own situation, then they played everything I'd listened to. And then they keep that, and then play their own situation again. I don't know if I was the same because I don't think that I had the choices they have. Johnnie Ray was my first real hero, after Gene Autry, the singing cowboy. What a great voice.

But I think it changed when Bill Haley came out.

Well, that's what I was getting to. Bill Haley: I was a fan of his because of his rock 'n' roll. I was 14 at the time. But even he seemed like your dad when Elvis came. Elvis was the one who actually turned my head around. I knew Chuck Berry, and Carl [Perkins], and all of those guys as well. They were coming through. And I was into the blues and all of that. But Elvis actually did it for me.

You mentioned at the press conference announcing your new record and tour that there were 15 or 16 songs in all that were cut for this album, so there's some stuff that got left out, including "Don't Be Cruel."

"Don't Be Cruel" is out on the CD5, so there'll be a few bonus tracks along the way.

Can you give a little background on "Angel In Disguise"? Did Paul [McCartney] start it?

Paul wrote it and then gave it to me to finish, which I did, and I recorded it with Peter Asher. And it just needed something. I didn't know what it was, and I don't know if Peter knew what it was. We have to say no to some tracks, you know? One that I wrote isn't on the album, "Everyone Wins," the most positive song. But, it didn't make it for the album. It just didn't happen.

You've said that you're not interested in putting out leftover tracks, and that if they weren't good enough at the time they won't get better with age. Sometimes they're omitted for that reason, other times you just don't have room.

There's none of these that I would absolutely say never comes out. In fact, up to two-and-a-half weeks ago, "Everyone Wins" was on the album. And we changed it. You know, you're putting your best shot out here. It's my best shot, so I even have to take myself off if I want to be honest. But, it may sneak back later.

Was that the first time you'd ever written anything with Paul?

Well, we didn't really write it together. He'd sent me the tape with his two verses and a chorus, and I just did the last verse in my own way.

You're listed as the author of [The Beatles'] "Don't Pass Me By."

I am the author of "Don't Pass Me By."

But there's a tape of a BBC interview [recorded July 14, 1964 for Top Gear*] where you and Paul noted that the two of you were working on your song "Don't Pass Me By."*

You sure that wasn't George?

No, I'm pretty sure it was Paul.

OK. Well, I don't remember Paul working on it. Paul would have said that as the band was working on it; he wasn't working on it as the writer.

Author's note: The actual radio dialogue was comic banter typical of the group at that time, with Ringo being asked about his songwriting. The following is an excerpt from that interview:

Ringo: I've written a good one, ya see, but no one seems to want to record it.
Paul: No.
Ringo: Oh, Paul may record it on a...
Paul: No.
Ringo: Yes, Paul, you promised!
Paul: No, the thing is, I was doing the tune for you to sing it.
Ringo: No, I don't want to sing it. You sing it.
Paul: [begins reciting lyrics to "Don't Pass Me By."]

Goldmine: *It's funny. That title keeps coming up. On the day that The Beatles were actually recording that in the studio [June 1968], Kenny Everett taped a very famous interview that actually was released by Apple in Italy, and John is saying, "We're working on Ringo's track."*

[laughs] Yeah, but that's when we were working on the tracks, not writing it. They didn't help me at all writing it.

How did you get to do the song "You Never Know" [from the film Curly Sue*]? It wasn't part of the album, but you did it during those sessions.*

Somebody called and said, "We've got this song that's to go with this movie. We've spoken to the director, John Hughes, and he thinks it's a great idea. Would Ringo do this song?" And I said yes. I'm in the studio, I'm working again, I was off that Sunday. They put it together and I went in and did it. But they did tell me it was going to be at the beginning of the movie, not right at the end. I've not seen the movie, but I think the song was actually to set up the movie, but they didn't use it [until

the end]. I don't know what happened. But those things happen, you know. You do it and then things change. I'm not going to cry about it; it's on to the next round.

A lot of people were really struck by your remake of "I Call Your Name," recently done as a video [videotaped for May 5, 1990, Liverpool Lennon benefit concert]. That's not out on a record. Any chance?

I don't own it. I did it for that specific reason and I gave it to the charity and that was it. I don't know if they'll ever do anything with it. I might do it on tour, though.

Speaking of the tour, Walsh is in the band again. When I saw your show last time [1989], I expected you guys to do "In My Car." Both of you recorded it and you wrote it together.

We felt we might. You've got so much material to choose from. Everyone I've been doing the interviews with says, "Why didn't you do that?" "Why didn't you do this?" So they're just picking one track that they actually like, but we have to do it the way we feel it will be great for the show and, in my case, what I want to do.

Will you hold some songs in readiness in case you want to change the song lineup?

Up to now we're saying the rest of the boys get three songs, possibly four, and I'll get the bulk again, about eight to 10. But it depends on how long they go. Until we get to the rehearsals, we can't shape it in any way. So, what we've done for each other — like Todd [Rundgren] put four songs on a tape, Burton [Cummings] put four on a tape, and everyone's done that. So, at least we'll have heard them.

We'll practice at home, not that I ever do, but, sure, some people do. And when we get to the show, we'll see what actually works. One of the most amazing trips on the last tour was that we tried "Back Off Boogaloo" [during some early shows on the tour]. We tried it this way and that way, but it just did not work live. We even had Dr. John on a snare drum. It just didn't happen. I mean, things don't happen. That was one of them. Now, we might try it this time and it clicks. We don't know. It's funny what happens out there.

How will you get the songs together?

We've just passed each other the [demo] tapes [of the songs each band member will do]. Todd knows the four songs Burton, Nils [Lofgren] and Dave [Edmunds] are thinking about, so it's not like we hit rehearsal the first day and "this is it." We all have some sort of idea, so that's why we can rehearse in two weeks. Possibly Todd has the most complicated of any of the songs, and that's not that complicated.

In 1985 EMI was set to put out an album of unreleased Beatles songs called Sessions.

What songs are they? They're not songs. There's no songs.

Well, there are some titles that were never released. Some sounded like they had probably never been finished.

Well, it's like putting "Yesterday" out with its original title, "Scrambled Egg." I don't understand that these are songs. As far as I know, there are no songs that didn't come out.

Well, there's one of yours, "If You've Got Trouble."

[singing] "You've got your trouble, then do-do-da-do."

Right. You got it.

Yeah, well that's a song that we just didn't do, didn't finish it.

Fans are obsessed with this. You just can't ignore the fact we want to know, "What's that one? And that one."

Well, after me screaming, "There's no songs," there is that one. But what else is there?

Well, there are some others, like "How Do You Do It?," which the group apparently didn't want to do and did it reluctantly because George Martin insisted. There's "That Means A Lot," done during Help!

Well, you've made an absolute liar out of me. And you're right!

This is what you get from collecting.

This will stop me being a "know-all."

Now that the lawsuit between EMI and Apple has been settled there are reports that the way is finally clear for this stuff to come out; the BBC tracks, for example.

I like the BBC tracks because I think they're really worthwhile. They're live and we were playing really well because that's when we were playing every night.

And there are lots of unreleased songs there.

Sure. We had to do eight tracks a night, including ones we hadn't done.

So we might see those come out?

I believe the problem with the BBC tracks is that they've only got a second-generation tape. They're still looking for the first generation.

There was a recent report that George Martin is trying to work with the original tapes.

George Harrison is trying to work with them also. We're waiting for the tape. I like my cassette [laughs]. It's cool.

What do you think of Beatles songs or any rock 'n' roll standards being used in television commercials?

I don't particularly like to hear the Nike one. But I had nothing to do with that. Talk to Yoko, not me.

That's actually John's recording [of "Instant Karma"] on that.

Yes, but I'm not on it. And he's not here to discuss it anymore.

I was also appalled to see that there is now a line of John Lennon eyeglasses.

I know nothing about that. I'm trying to get in charge of my own life.

It doesn't sound like you're very strongly in favor of it.

No, I'm not, really.

What about censorship and putting labels on records warning parents about lyrics?

This happens every 10 years. This madness happens where people try to sue people saying that their children jumped out the window because this record said something. I just think that it's totally silly. The kids will get it anyway. If your parents are censoring you, your pal's parents aren't censoring him. It goes down. It's like, "Rock 'n' roll is the devil's music!" And you had all that madness. It's gone on forever. I take very little notice of it, actually. Everyone wants to censor somebody. It just gets on my nerves.

Back in 1980 when you were working on Stop And Smell The Roses, *George [Harrison] produced a couple of tracks for you: "Wrack My Brain" and "You Belong To Me." The story is that there was an early version of the song that later became "All Those Years Ago," which was George's tribute to John, and your drum track is on that. Was there an earlier version of the song entirely? Perhaps with a different title and different lyrics?*

Not that I recall. No. You'll have to talk to [George]. I don't know.

Similarly, John apparently made demos of four songs that he gave to you shortly before he died that he thought would be good for you.

Yeah, they gave me some of John's songs after he died. But I couldn't do them. I was not interested then. I mean, if he had given them to me it would be a different situation. But he did not give them to me. They were given to me later and I couldn't deal with it at that time. They said, "John felt these would be good for you."

You can hear John say, "This is for Ringo" on the demos. I think they were "Life Begins At Forty," "Nobody Told Me" and "I Don't Wanna Face It."

Sure. But it was too late for me to do them.

You've cowritten three songs on Time Takes Time, *all with Johnny Warman, who was responsible for the "Spirit Of The Forest" charity single. You hooked up with him through Ring O' Records?*

Yeah, because he used to be on the label. We've kept in contact ever since. Besides being a writer and a rock 'n' roll musician he's also a health freak. So, we'd work out and write. He'd come and stay with me in Monte Carlo. In the mornings we'd get up and go running and stretching and working out. In the afternoons and evenings we'd sit around writing, then go and have dinner, and we'd start the whole thing again the next day.

"Runaways" really stands out on the album. It's a change of pace. What were you trying to say in that?

I watched a program on kids who'd run away. But, it was mainly a program on the parents trying to find them and just how devastated they are. And the dreams that the kids have, like to go to London and it's all going to be cool, and "I'll be free." So many of them end up raped, pillaged and burned. They just want to run away from home. I wanted to do that too when I was 16. And hundreds and hundreds of them are doing it today. They run away to Hollywood, they run away to New York. And these are the caves of steel. I just put it in this science fiction form. It's still about runaways, but in a science fiction attitude.

How do you write? Do you play the piano or guitar?

I still play three chords on the piano and I still play three chords on the guitar. That's how I do it. With Johnny, he was holding the guitar. In the early days when I would write "Photograph," or whatever, then I would give it to George [Harrison], who would actually put the real chords in. But I would have written it on the three chords, and he would put the passing chords in.

You knew where you wanted to go.

Sure. You just make it real. Not that we couldn't have done it on those three chords [laughs], but he knows a few more, which makes it sound better.

Do you write from time to time when inspiration hits you?

It's just started again. I've written very little. I've got a couple of pieces — I call it "bits" — of me just on my own with the guitar. I just sit down, and if it comes, it comes.

It's not just because you've got an album coming up and you have to sit down and do a couple of songs? It might happen any time?

Any time. It's not just because I'm working. It's not like I'm never going to write now until the next album. If anything happens, it happens.

Record collectors are frequently surprised at how many records are issued in one country but don't come out in others.

Well, you know, Amsterdam is the capital of bootleg records.

That's a different matter entirely. I'm talking about things that are issued.

Oh, you're talking about real stuff.

Yeah. Like, The White Album *[The Beatles, 1968] only came out in mono in England, never here. If you listen to it, it's like listening to a different album.*

Of course it is. It's a mono mix.

"Don't Pass Me By," for example, plays through much faster. Or maybe it was slowed down on the stereo. The question is, were you guys aware at the time that this sort of thing was going on?

I wasn't. I was not aware. I don't know if the others were aware.

In preparing the Sgt. Pepper *album The Beatles themselves worked on the mono mix but reportedly were not even there when the stereo version was mixed.*

Well, that's not true. I remember being there for a lot of the stereo mixes. Because we were having fun making the horses gallop across the room. Things like that.

There's a report that during the '60s Paul made a special little Christmas album just for the other members of the group and gave one to each of you, with only four copies ever pressed. Do you remember receiving one?

No. I don't have mine. But I do have some acetates that just have The Beatles playing the blues on them that no one else has.

Some people think that it was a mistake to ever make albums in the first place. In the '50s, stars seemed to want to get one great song recorded that might have a shot at the Top 10. Now you have to record an entire album, and singles are pulled off the album.

Yes, but you've forgotten that period in between when you made the single and you made the album. That's what we did. We made it totally separate. We always ended up with more tracks over in America, so that's how they could make these compilation crazy albums.

But do you think the music has suffered because artists have to do a whole album, whereas they might have had a great single?

Yeah, but who would put the money behind the great single? The return is not enough. It's economics again. It's nothing to do with music.

Things have changed. In those days, kids had enough money to buy the 50-cent single.

Most of them only had enough to buy the single. And when you toured, you only toured to sell records. You didn't go on the road to make any money. They paid your expenses and you got a few dollars, but the main aim was to keep promoting that record because people were buying lots of records in those days.

The last time you went on tour [1989] you didn't have an album to promote, which is very unusual these days. Why did you opt for the tour?

I didn't opt for it. That was the actual situation of life. I didn't have anything, but I wanted to go out. [Promoter] David Fishof came up with this idea and asked, "Do you want to put a band together and go on tour?" And I said yes. And then I thought, "Shit, who would I go with?" That's how the concept came. We'll just go out and give them all the hits we can. With Levon [Helm], Dr. John, Billy [Preston] and Joe [Walsh] and everyone it just became the concept — let's go and give them the hits. It was a revue, really. As one promoter said, it was like listening to his past flash between his ears [laughs].

How did you like playing in Japan? You did a short leg there.

A short leg of Japan; that's enough. It was good. The kids were good and the reaction was good, but that was enough, thank you.

Who were some of the early rockers, other than Elvis, who most influenced you? I know you've mentioned Jerry Lee Lewis.

Jerry Lee was my hero and Clyde McPhatter.

I always thought that you guys heard the Big Joe Turner songs or the Hank Williams songs through Jerry Lee Lewis' cover versions.

Hank Williams was my hero. We had the original records. We came from Liverpool, which was a port, and all those guys who went to sea used to bring all the records in. At one point Liverpool — maybe it still is — was the capital of country 'n' western music in England.

Trivia

by Charles Reinhart

1. Paul McCartney's girlfriend through much of the '60s was Jane A ____.
2. The group B ________ was originally known as The Iveys.
3. The Beatles and Gerry & The Pacemakers once played as a single band at the Litherland Town Hall using the name B _________.
4. Patti Harrison's maiden name was B ___.
5. Maureen Starkey and Yoko Ono once shared the last name C __.
6. The D ____ label auditioned The Beatles on Jan. 1, 1962, but did not give them a contract.
7. Linda McCartney's maiden name was E ______.
8. The Beatles' road manager was Mal E ____.
9. Bill H ____ was the editor of *Mersey Beat*, which published many Beatles stories.
10. Dick J ____ was the music publisher who helped The Beatles set up Northern Songs.
11. John Lennon's mother's first name and also the name of a Beatles song: J _____.
12. Bert K ________ produced The Beatles' first recording session in Germany.
13. Although Paul McCartney didn't want him, the other three Beatles hired Allen K ____ as their manager.
14. The first two Beatles films were directed by Richard L _____.
15. John Lennon was raised by his Aunt M ___ Smith.
16. The Beatles were once known as Johnny & The M _______
17. John Lennon and Paul McCartney once performed together as the N ___ Twins.
18. The screenplay for *A Hard Day's Night* was written by Alun O ___.
19. Cynthia Lennon's maiden name was P ______.
20. Billy P ______ received billing on the label of The Beatles' "Get Back."
21. John Lennon first used reversed tape segments on the song "R ___."
22. The Beatles' first manager, the one who booked them in Germany, was Allan W _______.
23. Before changing it to Ono, John's middle name was W ______.
24. John Lennon and Yoko Ono's *Life With The Lions* album was released on the Z _____ label.

Answers

1. Asher
2. Badfinger
3. Beatmakers
4. Boyd
5. Cox
6. Decca
7. Eastman
8. Evans
9. Harry
10. James
11. Julia
12. Kaempfert
13. Klein
14. Lester
15. Mimi
16. Moondogs
17. Nurk
18. Owen
19. Powell
20. Preston
21. Rain
22. Williams
23. Winston
24. Zapple

The long and winding road: The making of The Beatles' video *Anthology*

by Gillian G. Gaar

When *The Beatles Anthology* debuted on television in the fall of 1995, Beatles fans the world over were generally amazed at the scope of the series and dazzled at the wealth of rare and previously unseen footage. And the experience was heightened by the fact that what we saw on TV was only the *Cliff Notes* version of the story and an even longer version would follow on video. Now, almost a year later, the landmark Beatles *Anthology* video box set is here, serving up 10 hours — longer by more than half what was aired on ABC. And it's already been a sales success, entering *Billboard*'s Top Music Videos chart at #1, and the Top Video Sales chart at #3 — impressive for a set with a suggested retail price of $159.95.

This article originally appeared in Goldmine issue #425, Nov. 8, 1996.

For the most part, the extra footage doesn't result in entirely new sequences, but rather in extended sequences. For example, in the TV version, only "Till There Was You" was presented from The Beatles' *Royal Variety Show* appearance in 1963; on video, you also get "From Me To You" and "Twist And Shout." Ditto the Washington, D.C., concert in February 1964; on TV, only "She Loves You" was aired. On video, you also get "I Saw Her Standing There" and "Please Please Me." Which isn't to say that there aren't any brand-new sequences. A lot more promos are shown, from "I Want To Be Your Man" and "Please Mr. Postman," to the Chiswick House versions of "Paperback Writer" and "Rain." There's home footage of The Beatles' trip to Greece in July 1967, when they contemplated buying an island retreat. And there are many more comments from The Beatles themselves, especially about drugs. Surprising to note, there are also a few clips from the TV show not in the video series.

But one of the most fascinating aspects of the *Anthology* is how it documents more than just The Beatles' story. It's also the story of the music industry as a whole: how rock 'n' roll mutated into pop and then turned into rock, how rock bands were granted the autonomy to write their own material, how the music video was born, how marketing came to be as important (in some cases more so) to the industry as music is. It's more than the story of one group; it's the story of an entire generation's coming of age.

It's this element that makes the story particularly interesting, even though the video *Anthology*, like the TV show, gets off to a slow start. Tape one (which takes you from The Beatles' individual births to "Please Please Me" topping the chart) suffers, largely because there's little moving footage to document this period. Consequently, more time is spent on The Beatles' influences; they cite Big Bill Broonzy, Frankie Laine, Lonnie Donnegan, and Jimmie Rodgers, to name a few. What's often forgotten about The Beatles is that they were part of the first generation to be influenced by rock 'n' roll. Consequently they were the first to rework it while it was still fresh; it was the first and last time there was no "revival" of some previous rock era in progress. As a result, they got to play with new musical concepts before they'd hardened into clichés.

Tape two covers 1963, the year Beatlemania broke in Britain. It's amusing to hear producer George Martin admit his initial lack of faith in The Beatles' songwriting abilities — "There was much doubt on my part whether they could ever write a hit song" — which thankfully proved to be a groundless fear. An increasing number of promo films are featured, including a version of "This Boy" that has Paul McCartney looking surprisingly nervous, and a version of "I Wanna Be Your Man" that features some hilariously inept miming. This was standard promo fare for the time; most films had the group simply miming their hit single on a stage. "Scopitones," promo films made for specially designed jukebox-type machines, were also being made at the time and varied the format by having the group mime in different settings (a film for The Exciters' "Tell Him" had the group in a zoo). Within a year, The Beatles would take this format to the next level.

Tape three covers the hectic six-month period from February to July '64, when the group played dates in eight countries, made their landmark appearance on *The Ed Sullivan Show*, thus conquering America, and made their feature film debut, *A Hard Day's Night*. Richard Lester's innovation with the promo-film format is readily seen in the excerpt of "Can't Buy Me Love," especially when compared to The Beatles' earlier promos. The editing is much quicker, and for the first time, The Beatles are not miming. As a result, the sequence has an artistic edge lacking in other contemporary promos. And once it was shown The Beatles were open to such techniques, the way was paved for future efforts such as the Chiswick House setting for "Paperback Writer" and "Rain," not to mention the surreal touches in "Strawberry Fields Forever" and "Penny Lane."

Tape four continues up to the Shea Stadium gig in the summer of '65. Dissatisfaction with Beatlemania had already crept in. In the previous tape, George Harrison expressed his annoyance at The Beatles' lack of control over their lives, specifically referring to demands that the group not cancel their '64 European tour due to Ringo Starr's being hospitalized to have his tonsils removed. "I really despised the way we couldn't make a decision for ourselves," he says (for his part, Starr recounts how he couldn't keep from smoking, even immediately post-operation). Now, drug use accelerates, once Bob Dylan introduces the group to marijuana ("I thought I got the meaning to life that night," says McCartney), but it's as much out of boredom with the continual touring as anything else. In Hamburg, the group had popped amphetamines until they were "frothing at the mouth" in

order to adhere to the grueling performing schedule. Now, they were smoking dope to anesthetize themselves from the madness of Beatlemania.

Underscoring John Lennon's admission that the group was "smoking marijuana for breakfast" during this period is Harrison's comment regarding the filming of the "Buckingham Palace" sequence in *Help!*: "We were doing that scene for days," he says (actually it was only a day and a half). But Starr later points out that the use of pot and, later, acid had a positive impact on the development of the group's songwriting; he also adds later that the group rarely used drugs in the studio, because the music made while under the influence "was absolute shit."

McCartney told writer Allan Kozinn he considered The Beatles' interviews for the *Anthology* to be "pretty frank." Yet he especially is somewhat coy during his interviews, as when he recounts the genesis of "Yesterday," saying at the time he was living "in a little flat at the top of a house." Actually, he was living with the family of his then-girlfriend, Jane Asher. While not exactly an example of censorship, it is indicative of how the group has an interest in tidying up elements of their image, more bizarrely in the case of the cover for the "Real Love" single, which airbrushed out the cigarettes the group was holding in the original shot. Similarly, McCartney plays down the stage business of Lennon's facial grimaces as "irreverent humor," while Harrison bluntly states it was Lennon's impersonation of a spastic. They pull more punches in the later years; while the viewer clearly gets the idea that the group was tired of each other, there's little examination of the business differences that also helped to tear the band apart.

Tape five opens with coverage of the band's first Shea Stadium appearance and continues through the Japanese concerts in the summer of '66. One highlight is the near-complete performance — five out of six songs — from The Beatles' Aug. 1, 1965, appearance on *Blackpool Night Out*; the sixth, "Act Naturally," appears on the previous tape. Tape six covers the group's transition from live band to studio group, opening with their disastrous experience in the Philippines, continuing through the release of *Sgt. Pepper's Lonely Hearts Club Band*, closing with the Greece home-movie footage.

Tape six also covers the "bigger than Jesus" controversy, but there's no mention of another American-oriented controversy of the time — the fuss over the *Yesterday And Today* "butcher cover." There's an amusing sequence from the group's '66 appearance at Shea (which Harrison didn't even remember playing) when a determined reporter is seen pushing fans to admit they're not interested in The Beatles anymore:

"Tell me the truth, are you really a Beatles fan or are you here because it's the right thing to do?" "I love The Beatles!" "I bet there's a group you like better now." "No, I don't like any group better than The Beatles." "Honestly, aren't The Beatles on their way out?" "I don't think so."

One surprise is learning how little regard most of the group had for *Sgt. Pepper*. Starr makes the wry observation that "I did learn to play chess on it," referring to his downtime in the studio. "It wasn't that spectacular when you look back on it," says Lennon, while Harrison calls it, "A bit tiring, a bit boring. Generally, I didn't really like that album much. I was losing interest in being fab at that point." Yet if anything confirmed the wisdom of The Beatles' decision to

> **"Generally, I didn't really like that album much. I was losing interest in being fab at that point."**
>
> *— George Harrison, on* Sgt. Pepper

quit touring, it was this inventive album. Subsequent albums such as *The Beatles* and *Abbey Road* clearly illustrate the heights the group could reach once they'd freed themselves from the rigors of touring.

Tape seven covers the year between the "All You Need Is Love" broadcast and the installation of Apple Records at 3 Savile Row in London, along with all-too-brief clips from promo films of various Apple artists. Appropriately, tape eight, which covers the breakup of The Beatles, opens with a discussion of Starr's defection from the group during the recording of *The Beatles* (interestingly, later in the tape, he speculates that the band "could've carried on" instead of breaking up). By the time the group does split in 1970, the music industry has become a completely different business from what it was when The Beatles entered it a mere eight years before. Beatlemania had changed the business as much as it had changed the personal lives of John, Paul, George, and Ringo. The "Free As A Bird" video is shown at the end.

Bob Smeaton was part of the team who worked on *The Beatles Anthology* since the early '90s, as series director/writer. He explains how his role differed from that of Geoff Wonfor's, the *Anthology*'s director, by saying, "Geoff's main role was he dealt with the guys on a one-to-one basis. After I'd put the program together, he would speak to George, Paul, and Ringo. Also, Geoff was responsible for how the interviews looked — the cameras and setting up the interviews. Even though I did 50 percent of the interviews, I was more or less responsible for the contents of the programs and actually what went in there, whereas Geoff was more or less in charge of how the thing looked overall."

The 10-hour edit of the current *Anthology* is actually very close to the first cut the team came up with. "Neil [Aspinall head of Apple Corp. and the *Anthology*'s executive producer] was great," Smeaton says. "He said, 'Make this thing as long as it needs to be. If it works at two hours long, make it a two-hour program, if it works at six hours, make it six, if it works at 12 hours, make it 12.' So the first rough cut that we did ran for about 12 hours. The guys looked at that, and there was some stuff where they said, 'Look, I think you're digging a bit too deep into stuff which might not be of interest to people.' So I said, 'Right, we'll take out some bits that maybe went into too much detail.' And we got it down to 10 hours, which they seemed happy with."

One of the greatest challenges the team was faced with was selecting what material to use out of a huge archive. During The Beatles' touring years in particular, hundreds of local TV stations around the world filmed press conferences, stage shows or simply the sight of the group arriving at yet another airport. As Smeaton says, "We could've had press conferences for six hours! There was so much stuff, it's not a lie. We had a room full of stuff. This thing could've run forever."

The contemporary interviews with the group played a key role in determining what footage was used. "What we did was, I would write up a pre-synopsis for each program, knowing the areas which I wanted to cover," Smeaton says. "And then when we interviewed the guys, judging from what they said in the interviews, that very much dictated what footage that we'd use. If they mentioned a lot about a certain gig, we'd use that footage. And also by stuff unearthed on tape with John talking; if John talked about something, we would spend a lot of time on that."

Still, the fact that the archive of Lennon material, though large, was necessarily limited, meant there were holes left in the story. "A lot of people said, 'You didn't spend a lot of time talking about Stu Sutcliffe.'" says Smeaton. "But we only had one bit of audio, which was pretty crappy, of John talking about Stu. If we'd unearthed some footage or audio of John talking about Stu, then we would've spent a lot more time on him and his dying and that. But because there wasn't anything on John talking about Stu, we didn't feel it was right to have the other guys talking about him, who weren't as close to him as John was. So we let John dictate a lot of the decisions with the stuff that he'd said in his interviews."

Smeaton says he was never told to avoid any particular topic in interviews. "They never ever said, before we started talking to them, 'We don't want to talk about that.' There were certain areas that when we mentioned them, they would go a bit quiet. And you'd get the vibe that this isn't something that they wanted to talk about. But they never actually came out up front and said, 'We don't want to talk about X.'"

But having said that, Smeaton then goes on to describe an instance that sounds like "the guys" saying, "We don't want to talk about X": "Like the Maharishi and the Mia Farrow thing [the Maharishi was alleged to have made sexual advances toward Farrow during The Beatles' stay in Rishikesh, India, in 1968]. George did a big thing on that. He said, 'Look Bob, it's bullshit, that whole thing. You shouldn't even pay lip service to it, because if you do, you're saying that it's true. That thing didn't happen, despite what people have said. I was there. And if you put that sort of stuff in there, all you're doing is sensationalizing something. If you talk about something, people think it really happened. If you leave it, people eventually will think, 'Well, it must've been this thing which was built up over the years.' And that was the same with a lot of things."

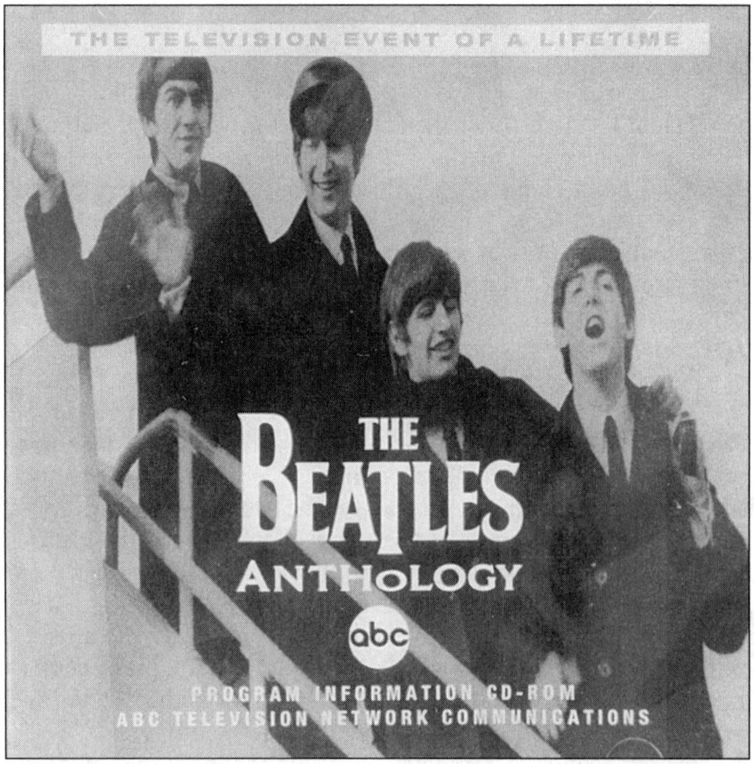

A promo CD-ROM from *The Anthology* tv special.

So, instead of using the *Anthology* as a platform to shatter certain myths, The Beatles' logic was to not discuss certain topics at all, out of the fear that "once you put it out in the open, this whole big thing gets built up around it," as Smeaton says. This explains some critics' complaints that the *Anthology* didn't dig deeply enough into controversial areas in The Beatles' story; rather than confront them, The Beatles would say nothing. Smeaton also reveals the great extent to which Aspinall influenced the making of the series. As the team prepared rough cuts, they were screened for Aspinall first, "And Neil would say maybe, 'I don't think the guys would be happy with that.' When Neil was happy with it, then we'd show it to the guys all at the same time, and we'd collate all their comments and have a list of everybody's comments, the three guys and Yoko. And then we'd change stuff." Thus, The Beatles could be said to be approving Aspinall's view of what the series should be.

Eventually, a degree of self-censorship entered the process. "It was hard, because I don't think that we would normally do something that we thought that people wouldn't approve of or wouldn't like," Smeaton admits. "But by the time we'd been on the thing for three years, we had a good idea of stuff which they wouldn't like. We'd think, 'Hang on, I know that Yoko's going to have a problem with that,' or George or Ringo or Paul is. So by the end of it, we'd got to know the guys pretty well in order to not have to change that much stuff 'cause we were second-guessing them to a certain extent."

But there were limitations on what the group could change. "The order was that George couldn't change something that Paul said," Smeaton explains. "George could only change something which George said. Or we couldn't have Yoko saying, 'I don't like what Ringo says there.'" Hearing what their fellow bandmates said also resulted in surprises for the group. "When we got the three of them in together, and I showed them film, George would say to the others, 'I didn't realize that you thought that about me!'" says Smeaton. "That was strange. That was one of the reasons we didn't get the three of them in there at once [for interviews] more often, 'cause — I've said this loads of times — if you're sat next to somebody, and someone's asking you questions about that person, you're not going to be as honest as what you would be if that person was in the other room. So we got The Beatles' story from George's angle, and from Paul's and Ringo's and John's."

Much was made of the fact that the *Anthology* marks the first time The Beatles have told their story "in their own words." What was not realized at the time was that this still meant you'd be getting only one side of the story, which, though admittedly from the inside, would not necessarily be the "definitive version" touted by the ads. That The Beatles wanted to accentuate the positive in the

Anthology was made clear by McCartney's statement to Kozinn, "People tend to remember The Beatles with a pleasant feeling." So when the group saw that the team making the *Anthology* did in fact remember — and document — the less-pleasant aspects of the story, changes were mandatory.

"The first cut that we did had a lot of negative stuff in there about the breakup of the band," Smeaton says. "And they said, 'Hang on a minute, people are going to be left with this memory, which would be a negative memory. Let's leave them with something as upbeat as it can be under those circumstances. Rather than make people looking at it in years time think, 'The Beatles was a terrible thing. It was really acrimonious. We don't want to make it like that. Let's celebrate the thing rather than make it look like it was World War Three.'" Even though it was at time. But basically, they had the final say. If they didn't like something, that would change, because they were the guys who were making it. They got the film they wanted. They got the stuff they wanted in there, and stuff they didn't want in there wasn't in there 'cause they wanted to keep it very upbeat."

Part of the group's reasoning for keeping the series "upbeat" was undoubtedly because the rancor of the final years was still hard to relive, even more than 20 years later. "I think that's what they thought when they were making this thing," says Smeaton. "They were turning around going, 'Oh, we're going through this again! The painful stuff we went through. You're digging it up! You're putting this stuff in! All the crying bad stuff, like Paul and John fighting.' I know that George was pissed off with The Beatles thing really early on. George is saying in 1965 he was sick of being a Beatle. Paul would still be a Beatle in 1996, 'cause Paul was quite happy. George was the one who was the most reluctant to get involved in the *Anthology*. He didn't really want to. I'm sure he was doing it because the other guys wanted to do it. In his first interviews, he wasn't opening up."

But actually, the *Anthology* allowed Harrison and Starr, long considered the "secondary" Beatles in light of the Lennon/McCartney partnership, the chance to come into their own, both as individuals and as members of The Beatles. "Paul has talked about The Beatles so much anyway," says Smeaton. "Every time he gets interviewed the subject comes 'round to The Beatles getting back together or whatever. Whereas I think with George and Ringo it happened to a lesser extent, 'cause George didn't want to talk about The Beatles. He'd talk about them under duress. But I think in the end it was like, 'Right, let's get it all out. We're only going to do this once, so let's try and do it right, and let's everybody be happy with it at the end of the day.' I think that was where they were going."

Smeaton also feels working on the *Anthology* "was part of the healing process," for the group. "I'm sure you'd have never got George and Paul in the same room in 1970," he says. "But you do get them in the same room in 1995 and 1996. I think that had we not done the *Anthology*, the guys would never have got back together again and done the 'Free As A Bird' track and the 'Real Love' track."

Besides The Beatles, the only other people to be interviewed for the *Anthology* were Neil Aspinall, George Martin, and Beatles publicist Derek Taylor. "That wasn't my decision or Geoff Wonfor's decision," says Smeaton. "That was Neil's decision. You've got to have George Martin in there, that's an obvious one. And Neil has never been interviewed before. Neil was the Fifth Beatle. He was there all the way through, and he's still there now! So we thought, well, Neil has got to be in there. Because people have heard about this guy, Neil Aspinall, but you never see him! And Neil is the one person who never left The Beatles from when he started working for them and never let them down. He never sold his story, he didn't do a book. We could've made a program about Neil on his own. Because he's been there, he's seen it all, he was there through all that crap that was going on with Apple, and he's still there now."

Smeaton's rationale for Taylor's inclusion is less clear. "Derek is great value, he's really entertaining and we thought we could have somebody who wasn't 'attached' but who saw them as an outsider. Whereas Neil was very much in the inner circle, and George Martin was standing on the border of that circle, Derek was just outside of it." Yet Smeaton admits Taylor was underused. "Derek had some great stories. He told us a load of stuff. But we didn't use a lot. We had to limit the amount of times that we had Derek in there. I think for Beatles fans it's good to hear what Derek's got to say, but we had to focus on the guys. We had to realize that it had to be the four guys in the main with comments from George, Derek, and Neil." Considering that Taylor's appearances in the series are few and add little insight of the story, it would perhaps have been better if they were eliminated entirely in favor of additional Beatles footage. A more extensive interview could also have worked, though it would then have invited the obvious question of where the interviewee line was drawn and why other people with equally interesting stories weren't included.

"I'm sure you'd have never got George and Paul in the same room in 1970, but you do get them in the same room in 1995 and 1996. I think that had we not done the *Anthology*, the guys would never have got back together again and done the 'Free As A Bird' track and the 'Real Love' track."

— Bob Smeaton

The opening is one of the most effective sequences in the *Anthology*, starting with a close-up of The Beatles logo on Starr's drum, pulling back to reveal The Beatles themselves playing together (from the opening sequence of *Help!*), and pulling back still further until The Beatles disappear and the words *The Beatles Anthology* loom above them, as if they've been dwarfed by their own legend. The *Anthology* team designed their own opening sequence first. "We had a really long 10-minute sequence for the opening," says Smeaton. "And when it was made into a TV program, it was like 10 minutes and we haven't even got to the start of the show yet! So a company in England called LambieNairn were brought in to do something which was more to the point. We had a chat with them and said, "Look, we want something that's simple and people that want to read into it can read into it what they want." I think it worked. It was good to see the band getting overtaken by the whole Beatle thing."

As far as putting the series together, one complaint that has arisen is that "new" promos have been created by editing together different versions or by adding outtake material, as in the case of "Rain" (the former) and "I Am The Walrus" (the latter), when some would have preferred to see the promos in their original state. Smeaton explains this approach was used because simply presenting a series of original promos would have been too easy. "I'm sure some people would've looked at it and said, 'So, one version of "Rain," which is just the promo anyway. This is a bit of a rip-off.' And with "Rain," there are like five different versions of it, right? So we couldn't have put five different versions of "Rain" on the videos — though I'm sure some people would've liked that. So we thought we'd pick the best shots out of it and give people a bit of a mixture. We spent a lot of time hunting out extra shots to give people something different to what they've seen before. And it's the same with "I Am The Walrus." It would be very easy to take "Walrus" from the movie and just put that in. But we hunted out through scraps of film and actually found some extra shots to put in there, just to make it a bit more interesting. For us, for the program makers, we though it'd be good to give people something extra, rather than stuff that they had seen before."

"Free As A Bird" picture sleeve.

"And as regards to cutting from studio versions to live versions, it was just a case of trying to keep it interesting," Smeaton continues. "I'm sure that some Beatles fans would've liked to have had the straight video running through. But I'm sure that other people would've turned 'round and said, 'We bought this video and all it is is a collection of pop promos.' So we wanted to make it more than just that. That's why we cut in extra shots, we put in bits which might seem off-the-wall, just to say to people, look, it isn't a cut-and-paste job where we stuck in a load of videos to make the thing up to running time. We paid a load of money for I think it was about 30 seconds of "Strawberry Fields," which somebody shot on their home-movie camera. Which cost Apple a load of money. It would've been very easy just to do the promo in there. But Neil was saying, 'No, we'll give people something extra. Rather than give them something which they might have a scratched bootleg copy of. We'll give them stuff they haven't seen before.' But I'm sure we'll still get people who'll turn 'round and say, 'I would've rather just seen one version of 'Rain.'"

Smeaton points out that the team was well aware of what material was available on the collector's circuit and that an effort was made to present such material in the best possible condition.

"The Washington, D.C., concert has been out there for years, but the quality of the material was really shitty and didn't look that good," he says. "So Apple went to great expense to get the film cleaned up, and it looks so much better. Rather than just sticking it in — 'Oh, just put it out, we'll bump it up, stick it on the tape and send it out there' — they went to a lot of expense and trouble to clean the thing up and make it look good. 'Cause this program could easily have been made in a year, but Apple spent a lot of time on it. Us guys spent a lot of time trying to make it as best as we can. People were saying, 'Why didn't you run the Shea Stadium concert for the length of one of the videos and just have the guys talking about the gig?' But then you would've got people who turned 'round saying, 'Hang on, all this is is the Shea Stadium concert with a few comments scattered through it.' So we were very aware of them wanting to do the best job possible."

Smeaton also reveals that some subjects, though not directly addressed, were alluded to, specifically in the case of Brian Epstein's homosexuality. After discussing Epstein's death, a montage of clips of The Beatles' manager is shown. But the choice of song used for the sequence, "You've Got To Hide Your Love Away," comes across as a homophobic slap at Epstein's sexuality (not to mention the song's already been featured in the *Help!* sequence). Smeaton says the song is meant to refer to Epstein's sexuality, though not in a negative way. But he adds that Harrison himself didn't like the use of the song.

"George said, 'You can't use that song. Why are you using that song?'" says Smeaton. "And we said, 'Well, there was a rumor somewhere down the line that John wrote it for Brian — got to hide your love away, Brian. Now, nowhere in the film did anybody say that Brian was gay, because at the time, we're trying to stay in the '60s. Being gay wasn't a thing you broadcast. So that was a veiled sort of comment that we know Brian was gay. And this track is a track which might have been written as a veiled comment about Brian from John. And also it's a beautiful song. And it seemed to tie in good with those images of Brian.

"George still didn't like it," Smeaton continues. "He wasn't that happy with it. But Yoko was happy with it and Ringo was and Paul was, and it worked well. There was stuff in there where George would turn 'round and say, 'Oh, we don't want to say that in *Let It Be*, arguing about going on the roof. I hate that! I hated that period!' And we would say, 'Yeah, but the fans want to see it. They've never seen it before, George.' And it was painful. But sometimes it's the painful stuff which people want to see."

> **"When I had to cut the thing down for the Americans, it was a nightmare! We'd spent three and a half years putting this piece of work together, where we thought we hit all the bases, we've covered all the areas which need to be covered. And then suddenly it was, 'OK, you've got to lose five and a half hours of it!' And it was like, 'Hang on a minute, you can't cut this thing down.' So I had a lot of dark nights when I had to lose a lot of stuff."**
>
> ***— Bob Smeaton***

His work on the *Anthology* gave Smeaton a different perspective on what it was like to be a part of one of the greatest entertainment phenomenons of the century.

"I thought that being in The Beatles must've been the greatest thing in the world," he says. "To have that fame and everything that you could want from life. But you lose a little bit of that human element in yourself by being public property all the time. And they spent so much time incarcerated with each other, eventually they all wanted to go off and do different things. They'd taken it as far as they could go and they wanted to do something different.

"Like George says, it got to the point where they were only staying together for the fans instead of for themselves," Smeaton continues. "I think Paul probably got to the point where he was sick of being the one who was trying to keep the thing going, when John was off with Yoko and George wanted to do his thing. He thought, 'Hang on a minute, nobody wants to do this except me. So let's let the thing take its natural course, and let's just break it up. We've got to have a life.' I think they wanted to get away from it, to try and be normal people for a while. Even though they couldn't, because The Beatles got bigger after they fell apart."

Nonetheless, he was impressed with how the "Threetles" have remained "regular guys. I know people who've had one hit record who I've interviewed before and they're impossible, these people. But you sit with Ringo or George or Paul, and you're talking to these guys who have really been through it and they're still as normal as you can possibly be having been through that stuff."

The nature of the project changed when the *Anthology* was sold to television.

"When we started out making this thing, it was for Beatles fans," Smeaton explains, "so people would stop ringing up Apple and saying, 'When are we going to see Shea Stadium? When are we going to see the outtakes from *Magical Mystery Tour* and *Let It Be*?' So we made it for Beatles fans, but suddenly it became a TV show. So we had to halve it and make it for the average viewer, who really wasn't that interested in the fact that Billy Preston turned up halfway through *Let It Be* and played some keyboards on 'Get Back.' Certain people were saying we shouldn't cut the thing, it should go out on TV running at the original length. But the TV stations wouldn't have it."

Making cuts for the U.S. broadcast was particularly difficult for Smeaton, given that the U.S. version was half an hour shorter than the U.K. version.

"When I had to cut the thing down for the Americans, it was a nightmare!" Smeaton says. 'We'd spent three and a half years putting this piece of work together, where we thought we hit all the bases, we've covered all the areas which need to be covered. And then suddenly it was, 'OK, you've got to lose five and a half hours of it!' And it was like, 'Hang on a minute, you can't cut this thing down.' So I had a lot of dark nights when I had to lose a lot of stuff. And I was thinking The Beatles' fans, when they see this, they'll be saying, 'Why didn't they mention this? Why isn't that in?"

But seeing the full-length version makes you appreciate how well the U.S. edit was handled. Far from there being huge gaps in the story, the TV *Anthology* hit on all the major points of The Beatles' career and offered enough promo clips and rare footage to keep it engaging. In speaking to *Goldmine* in 1995, Smeaton said he preferred the TV version, though this year he admitted his preference was due to the fact that 'I was so Beatled-out. I'd seen this thing so many times. Sometimes I'd sit through it and I'd think, 'Here we go again, we've got 25 minutes on *Magical Mystery Tour*.' I was so sick of it!

"Sometimes, if someone sits you down to a 12-course meal, it all looks beautiful, but maybe you would just like a starter and a main course," Smeaton continues. "So I think at the time I wanted just a starter and the main course. Then you've got people saying, 'Where's the coffee and where's the hors d' oeuvres?' and all this stuff. It's going to come later! It's all been kept back in the fridge, so to speak. But you know, I did like the TV version. I think the TV version worked really well for people who wanted to watch it as a TV program. I'd say, 'The TV versions work. They're nothing to be embarrassed about.' I know that we're going to get feedback of people saying that we've missed stuff, but look what we've got you, we've made a really good TV program."

Though last year Smeaton had said, "Anybody that watches it will really enjoy the show, even if they're not music fans; they'll still get something out of the program," he now says, "I think if people didn't like The Beatles, they wouldn't have liked the programs. But we didn't make it to try and win over the people who didn't like The Beatles anyway."

Still, the critical reception in some quarters was surprising, even from those who weren't Beatles fans. Instead of the *Anthology* being critiqued on its own merits as a documentary, the very idea that The Beatles' story was worth retelling was offensive to critics at media outlets ranging from *Enter-*

tainment Weekly to a local Seattle paper aimed that the 20-something market, that dismissed The Beatles as a band "more boring than The Beach Boys."

"We expected that," Smeaton says. "Derek Taylor had said to us fairly early on, 'Guys, there will be stuff falling from a great height which will be landing on your head. And it'll be smelly.' We knew that there would be a backlash. Some people don't want to live in the past. But even when The Beatles were out there, actually doing it, people were slagging them off, people disliked them. Like now, a band like Oasis, people are slagging them off — 'They're spoiled!' It's the same with The Beatles. We could never have dreamed that you would have got 100 percent support from people. There'll always be people — 'Ah, these bunch of old fogies sat round reminiscing.' Well, people have been wanting this thing for years and years and years, and we've made it for those people."

Of course, Beatles fans had their own complaints about the TV series, as they will about the video series. In addition to the creation of "new" promos, there are also several instances where a promo is jarringly interrupted by comments from one or more of the group (as in the case of the "Hey Jude" promo). With the knowledge that there's so much footage in the *Anthology* archives, why waste valuable screen time re-creating Starr's inept turn at the helm of a yacht in Miami in 1964, repeating shots from the '65 *Hollywood Bowl* performance both at the beginning of tape four and in the *Hollywood Bowl* sequence, having McCartney perform a contemporary rendition of "Eleanor Rigby" for no clear purpose or having endless footage of circuses as a backdrop for "Being For The Benefit Of Mr. Kite"? Given the choice, some fans might have opted instead for having more of Lennon and McCartney's press conference for Apple in New York in May 1968, to mention just one sequence that could have been extended. Other fans will of course have their own ideas of which parts of the series should have been expanded.

One area of the series that might have been expanded concerned the group's early years, with the discovery of the earliest known footage of The Beatles in performance, playing a Valentine's Day show in 1961 at Liverpool's Cassavona club.

"We'd heard it was out there, but we'd never actually seen it," Smeaton says. "It came up just before we finished [the videos]. And we looked at it with a view to buying it, but it just didn't look good, and it didn't have any sound on it. I think had it had sound on it, Apple would have definitely bought it and put it in there. But it wasn't that great, and we didn't think it was worthwhile busting the bank for some footage which wasn't that great. People would find footage and think they'd found the Holy Grail. Someone said, 'Oh, there's rare footage of them playing in Hamburg. It's out there.' We were looking all over for it. We got these Beatles bootleg guides and tried to find stuff, but it didn't exist. I'm sure that one day, somebody will find some footage of John and Paul meeting at the Woolton village fete and it'll be worth a million dollars!"

"I'm glad that the thing's actually going to see the light of day and that people will realize we had actually covered all those areas and all those songs," Smeaton adds. "When the *Anthology* aired in the states, we got a lot of feedback, people saying, 'You missed this, you missed that, you didn't have 'Eleanor Rigby' in there, 'Penny Lane' wasn't in there,' all this sort of stuff. So we were saying, 'Yeah, but you've got to view the TV program as being like the EP or the single.' The video is the album, so to speak. There's so much material in there."

As for future releases from Apple, Smeaton admits, "There's a load of stuff which never actually saw the light of day. When the guys got together up at George's place we used some of the stuff where they sat round talking and when George is playing ukulele in the courtyard. There's at whole load of that stuff. They played some old Beatles songs, like "Thinking Of Linking" and that sort of stuff. They did a whole load of rock 'n' roll songs. And we shot a load of stuff at *Abbey Road* with the three guys and George Martin, which was fantastic.

"But when you see the three of them playing together, now, it felt very much like, "Where's John?" Smeaton continues. "That's why we tried to stay away from having the three guys in there too often. 'Cause once you had them together, you think, 'There's somebody missing from the equation.' When you had them individually, it wasn't as evident that John wasn't around anymore, and we're using old recordings or tapes or whatever. So I think that was a conscious decision. But I'm sure that somewhere down the line, that stuff will come out, because people will find out about it and start saying, 'What about that session that they did up at George's place?'

"I'm sure Apple'll do something else, if Neil can find the energy and the enthusiasm to go through this all again," Smeaton concludes. "Cause it's been a nightmare for some people. Especially for Neil, for Neil to suddenly open up this Pandora's box and have those three guys and Yoko on the phone to him again, it was a brave decision to go into it. 'Hang on, can I handle this? Do I want to do this?' But he loves the band. That's what it all comes down to. He had a great time. And he knew that people wanted to see it. And the thing was made for Beatles fans, basically."

And for Beatles fans, there's still some good news: the "Magical History Tour" isn't quite over yet. The success of all the *Anthology*-related releases will undoubtedly have an impact on the likelihood of even more previously unreleased material escaping from the Apple Corp. vaults.

The last hurrah of the Fifth Beatle

As he retires from producing, Sir George Martin remembers his time with the Fab Four

by Ken Sharp

If there's anyone who can legitimately lay claim to the mantle of "Fifth" Beatle, it's George Martin. Martin's unparalleled production expertise coupled with his profound talents as a musician, arranger and conductor helped catapult The Fab Four to unprecedented waves of worldwide success.

Born in London in 1926, Martin has been an integral force in the musical scene for almost 50 years. Classically trained at The Guildhall School Of Music, Martin parlayed his education into a job as assistant to Oscar Preuss, EMI Parlophone record chief. After Preuss retired in 1955, Martin was elevated to head of Parlophone where he worked with such disparate acts as Peter Sellers, Shirley Bassey, Stan Getz, Sir Malcom Sargent, and Sophia Loren.

Prior to his involvement with The Beatles, Martin had a rich and diverse career, working in the fields of classical, comedy, jazz and light pop. His exemplary work with the legendary British comedy troupe "The Goons" further cemented Martin's reputation — especially impressing John Lennon in particular.

But the course of Martin's life inexorably changed — as it did for four lads from Liverpool — on June 6, 1962. This was the fateful date Martin first met The Beatles at a recording audition for Parlophone Records held at London's Abbey Road Studios. Impressed more with the group's cheeky charm and charisma than their musical talents, (George Harrison even criticized the producer's tie!), Martin signed the group to Parlophone, in the process making inarguably the smartest A&R move in recording history.

Not only a wonderfully talented producer and arranger, Martin was also a trusted friend to The Beatles, an ally that could shape their wondrous sonic visions into reality. An experienced musician, Martin often lent his talents to Beatles recordings — his masterful baroque piano break on "In My Life" are among his impressive contributions to the group's vast body of work. Martin's inventive and majestic orchestral work beautifully graced such Beatles gems as "Yesterday," "Penny Lane," "Strawberry Fields Forever," "Eleanor Rigby," "Within You, Without You" and many more. Though he was 14 years older than the eldest Beatle (Ringo), Martin's freewheeling experimental spirit matched the whims and desires of The Beatles themselves, all coalescing into the creation of

This article originally appeared in Goldmine issue #477, Nov. 6, 1998.

such avant-garde mini-masterpieces as "Tomorrow Never Knows," "I Am The Walrus," "A Day In The Life," and "Strawberry Fields Forever."

While it's his long-standing connection with The Beatles that is most widely known, Martin is also responsible for working/and or producing a stellar and diverse range of artists including Pete Townshend, Badfinger, Jeff Beck, Aerosmith, The Bee Gees, Cheap Trick, America, Cilia Black, Gerry & The Pacemakers, P.J. Proby, and Billy J. Kramer & The Dakotas to name but a few.

Most recently, Martin oversaw *The Beatles Anthology* collections and worked with former Fabs Paul McCartney and Ringo Starr on their *Flaming Pie* and *Vertical Man* CDs respectively.

Capping off an extraordinary career, Martin has compiled his last recording project, *In My Life* (MCA Records). Slated for release on Oct. 20, the collection is a joyous celebration of Martin's illustrious and remarkable 48-year career. This compendium of Beatles songs as interpreted by the famed producer's friends and heroes includes stars such as Sean Connery, Phil Collins, Jim Carrey, Goldie Hawn, Robin Williams, Bobby McFerrin, Jeff Beck, and Celine Dion.

Goldmine sat down with the ever-charming Sir George Martin for an all-encompassing career retrospective touching

on his musical beginnings, his days with the Fab Four and his final musical statement, *In My Life*.

Goldmine: *With the tragic passing of Linda McCartney, I'd like you to share your memories of her.*

George Martin: Linda was a very good friend and a lovely woman. She was so special. Apart from being a beautiful woman, she was very, very kind and loving to everybody. Very self-effacing. Amongst Beatles fans she sometimes became not loved very much because of her presence in Paul's band. But that wasn't her doing, that was Paul's doing always. And she was uncomfortable with that. But she did it because she loved him. They were inseparable. Her loss to him is really quite unimaginable. I think it will take a long while for him to get over it. The cruelest thing was everybody thought that she had beaten it. Everybody thought she was OK. And it suddenly turn-tailed and reversed and killed. I think it's awful. We were all very, very saddened by what happened.

How is Paul managing?

He is managing but only just. It's a tough time for him. It will take him a while, I think. When I get back I hope to see him again. He's very well supported by his kids, all of them are very supportive, but it's a tough thing. He's so alone now.

Why are you retiring?

Well I'm not actually retiring, I'm just not making any more records.

Let's talk about the In My Life *record and why you chose it to be your final musical statement.*

Well, for the past few years I've been aware that I've got to finish. My hearing has been going. I've just about held onto it by my fingertips to do this one. Giles [Martin's son] has been very helpful to me. He's been my right arm and my ears as well. But having decided to make a final record, my thought was to write a complete album of new material. And there are two items on this of mine. But then I thought, "Who the hell's going to listen to this anyway?" [laughs]. And that would be really self-indulgent. And I can do that any time to please my own ego. I didn't want to inflict that on the people. So I thought, "What will they expect of me?" And of course I'm so connected with The Beatles that there was something there. I didn't want to make another wallpaper music thing, but I would just do something that I would enjoy doing. So we embarked on making an album that would be fun to do, fun for myself and for the performers and hopefully fun for the people who listen to it. And certainly it's done that. I was just going to have a few friends on and then I extended that by saying, "Well, let it be friends and heroes. People I haven't met, people I've always admired." I was encouraged by this because one of the few people that I had started to approach who I hadn't met before, they were very enthusiastic and seemed to like the idea.

Who was the first person you approached to be involved?

I think it was Jim Carrey. Anyhow, the reception was astonishing. These characters are pretty big people. When I began working with people they were all very enthusiastic. In the case of Jim, I was looking for somebody to do "I Am The Walrus." I wanted to have that on the album. And it needed somebody who could be clever enough to get their tongue around those very difficult lyrics and sing them very well.

Jim Carrey interestingly sings each verse with a different character voice and inflection.

He's got a very good voice. I was surprised by how good he was. He came over to England to work and he brought a whole gang of people who sat in the back of the control room while we did it. And of course he fooled around a helluva lot.

> **"We embarked on making an album that would be fun to do, fun for myself and for the performers and hopefully fun for the people who listen to it. And certainly it's done that. I was just going to have a few friends on and then I extended that by saying, 'Well, let it be friends and heroes.'"**
>
> *— George Martin*

We filmed most things. There's actually a documentary about the making of the record which will be coming out in November, just after the record comes out. After a while I had to turn off the cameras because he was playing to the cameras so much. But we had such great fun. Giles and I were with him the other day, and he said it was one of the most enjoyable things he's ever done in his life.

It seems John Lennon could be a pretty zany person at times, and he probably would have appreciated Carrey's comic interpretation.

Yeah, I think so. The lyrics on "I Am The Walrus" are pretty weird. I mean who the hell knows what they mean? "Crab a locker fish wife..." what does that mean? But to John it was just word poetry. John's version wasn't a funny version, it was just John, and John wasn't trying to be humorous. It was just his interpretation of what he liked in his kooky way. But he loved making up words. I often think that Lennon got his inspiration from Bob Dylan and Bob Dylan got his inspiration a lot from Dylan Thomas, the Welsh poet. I think there's a bit of Lewis Carroll, "Jabberwocky" style, making it pormento words, compressing two words into one. So John's lyric writing is very interesting.

Your choice of Beatles songs is unique, not all the standards, such as "Yesterday."

Deliberately. Paul said to me, "You've got a hell of a lot of Lennon songs on this album." [laughs] And I said to him, "Well, Paul you did all the ones that people like hearing. You've done all of the very, very popular ones, things like 'Michelle' and 'Fool On The Hill,' 'Hey Jude,' 'Yesterday.'" If you look at the performances of Lennon/McCartney songs, you will find that a good 70 percent of them if not more are Paul McCartney compositions because people want to hear those rather than John's. John once said to me, "Look, let's face it George, I don't expect to walk into a bar in Spain and hear someone whistling 'I Am The Walrus.'" And that summed it up. That's why I went for the ones I did. I would have liked to have done "Glass Onion," for example. They're interesting. I put in a few of Paul's as well.

Have Paul, George, and Ringo heard the record?

None of them have said to me, "You've made a fantastic record," but they've all liked what they've heard. Ringo was with me at the launch of the record in England. He was very enthusiastic. They've all known what I've been doing.

You produced the Jeff Beck album Blow By Blow *and you had him cover "A Day In The Life."*

Jeff and I have been mates for a long time although we haven't worked together for a long time. But we've talked about working together and never got around to it. And Jeff came to see me when I was working on the *Anthology* at Abbey Road. And it so happens that the day he came in Paul was already there listening to stuff that I'd selected for him to hear. It was then, in front of Paul, where we talked about him doing a track for the album. And Jeff said to me, "Can I choose the track?" And I said, "Sure, if you want to." And he picked "A Day In The Life."

He covered The Beatles' "She's A Woman" on the Blow By Blow *album.*

That's right. It was good track, wasn't it? He used "the bag" on that. Anyhow, you could have knocked me sideways when he chose to do "A Day In The Life." I thought he would have chose to do something like "Yer Blues." When he did it, I was very pleased to hear what he'd done.

Goldie Hawn's version of "A Hard Days Night" is interesting, as she croons the song.

I've always adored Goldie Hawn, ever since she was in her 20s. I remembered she could sing, and she'd been one of my idols. I wasn't sure if she would go for this. I hadn't met her. And we contacted her and met up and got on like a house on fire. She said she would come over to England to record it, which was lovely, but she didn't because she was offered a film to direct and she had to do that. I had to come to Texas, in fact, to record her. To do it, I explained to her I wanted a nightclub version of it, slow, sexy, moody. I said, "Think of Peggy Lee, think of Marilyn Monroe and think of yourself as well." And so I booked a jazz trio — piano, bass and drums — in a little studio in Austin, Texas. We spent an afternoon together and that was it. I was delighted by what she did. We had a nice dinner in the evening, and she flew off in one direction and I flew off in another. I brought the tapes back to England and overdubbed a better backing. She had a very good sense of what I was looking for. She put in quite a lot of her own style.

I wanted to speak about your two compositions that appear on the record.

Right. Well, the first one is the "Pepperland" one. The reason I put that in is *Yellow Submarine* was a pretty important piece of film for me. I'd already done some film work, but it was the first major film that I'd done and it was a very difficult thing to do and very rewarding. We made that animated feature in a year from start to finish, which is incredibly quick. Disney takes two years for most of them. In order to do this I had to work very close with the director writing music as he was animating. I would exchange my music with him and he would exchange his animation as we went along. I'd work on reel four and reel seven and so on. All pickle-dee, pickle-dee, I'd obviously had the whole script and sometimes the reels would be empty with just storyboards. And I would write descriptive music that would fit, really like free writing. He said, "I trust you. Just do what you can. We have not time for anything else." I wrote over an hour of music to go with the film.

Wasn't "The Pepperland Suite" a hit?

Yes, in Brazil, it was a big hit and high in the charts. So I thought, getting back to the record, let's bring back "The Pepperland Suite." I put together a very small selection of items from

that. I thought that was very worthwhile doing. The second one was a theme that I thought of quite a few years ago just after John died. I was in Montserrat, my island — it's a beautiful place, and I thought of this tune and thought of the way it should be done and orchestrated it. Then I put it aside and forgot about it. It's one of things that you can't use, you can't put it on an album out of the blue. I thought if I get asked to do a picture and it needs a good, moody, slow theme, that'd be useful. Then when I wanted to do the last track which was rather a serious track with Sean Connery ("In My Life"), a very dangerous track to do. I thought, "Let me link these two things up because my piece can act as an introduction, a prelude if you like, into 'In My Life.'" "In My Life" is such a personal song for me because part of it is me anyway, part of it is my writing with the solo in the middle which happened originally, and the words are so evocative of what my life is all about. I've been lucky all my life working with the greatest of people, and I've had great fun. I've really had a marvelous time. And I'm very grateful to all those people, a lot of them aren't with us anymore, "some are dead some are living, in my life, I've loved them all." And those words meant so much to me that I wanted them to be spoken, not sung. I couldn't have them sung because no one could sing them better than John. By speaking it, it brings out the meaning of the words. It is dangerous territory, but I wanted to have a very memorable voice and Sean Connery has one of the most identifiable voices in the world.

Previously, in 1964 you worked with Peter Sellers doing some spoken-word versions of Beatles songs.

Doing spoken-word that is humorous is no problem. It's when you start getting serious. I did a lot of stuff with Sellers of course. We did "Hard Day's Night." Have you heard all the other ones like "She Loves You"?

Yes, it's hilarious. Were there any heroes that you did not approach? Brian Wilson comes to mind.

Brian? Well indeed, he's not really a perfomer as such. He's a great writer and a great thinker. I was with Brian last year because I have a television series that hasn't come out here called *The Rhythm Of Life*, three one-hour shows, a series where I'm talking about music which aired on BBC One. I've been going around the world talking to people. I've had people in the classical world as well as people like Paul McCartney, Billy Joel, Elton John, Celine Dion, and also Brian Wilson. I went down to his house and chatted to him about his work. It's so nice to see him coming back to life again. He's got two babies now and he's very happy. And he's creating again, which is great. We've managed to get permission to get a copy of his old masters, and we went into a studio and opened them up. Like I did with "Pepper." I dissected them, listened to all the tracks and put them back together again. He was so excited by this. I asked him, "Haven't you done this?" And he said, "I haven't heard this stuff since we recorded it," "God Only Knows" and "Good Vibrations." And I tore them apart and said, "Brian, tell me what this track is?" And he said, "Oh, that's an instrument called a theremin." And it was extraordinary how he came to life with that.

Tell us about your musical beginnings at Guildhall School Of Music and how that background influenced your later work.

Well, I was very similar to both John and Paul in a way where I wasn't taught music to begin with. I just grew up feeling music and naturally making music. I can't remember a time where I wasn't making music on the piano. I was running a band by the time I was 15.

What was the name of the band?

[laughs] Very corny but I thought it was fantastic. The first one was a four-piece and then it became a five-piece. When it was a four-piece I called it "The Four Tune Tellers." [laughs] And then it became "George Martin And The Four Tune Tellers." Very clever. And I had T T's on the stands in front. We made quite a little bit of money as well. And then the war intervened, and by the time I was 17 I was in the Fleet Air Arm, which is part of the Royal Navy. We flew off carriers and we were fliers in the Navy. That was the tall end of the war. I was four years in the service, I was 21 when I came out. Having managed to evade Japan, I was all right. And I had no career. A professor of music who befriended me, he'd received from me during the war various compositions that I'd painfully put together. I went to see him and he said, "You must take up music." I said, "How can I? I'm not educated. I've never had any training." He said, "Well, get taught. I'll arrange it for you." He arranged an audition for me to play some of my work to the principal of the Guildhall School Of Music And Drama, which is a college in London. And he said, "We'll take you on as a composition student." And I got a government grant for three years to study. I started composition, conducting and orchestration, and I took up the oboe. I took up the oboe so I could make a living playing some instrument. You can't make a living playing the piano. I just played piano naturally. I wasn't taught. I didn't take piano as a subject, because I didn't see any future in it. I didn't rate myself as being a great pianist. I could never see myself making a living at it. I wanted to be a film writer. So that's what happened. I was trained and I came out and I would work playing the oboe in different orchestras in the evenings and sometimes afternoons in the park, that kind of thing. I was a jobbing oboe player.

Do you still play?

No. [laughs] I don't think I could now. I took a job during the day to make some extra money, that was in the music department at the BBC. Then out of the blue I got a letter from someone asking me to go for an interview at a place called Abbey Road. So I cycled along there and the guy said, "I'm looking for someone to help me make some classical recordings, and I gather you can do this." Because I was a woodwind player and educated by now, I got the job of producing the classical baroque recordings of the Parlophone label. And I got hooked. Gradually this guy who was running the label gave me more and more work to do. I started doing jazz records, orchestral, pop of the period — it wasn't rock. Over a period of five years I worked as his assistant gradually doing more and more. By the time the five years was up I was virtually doing everything. And five years later in 1955, he retired. He was 65 years old and he left. I thought somebody was going to be brought in over me because I was in my 20s still. But to my astonishment I was given the job of running the label. I was the youngest person ever to be given that job.

I'm surprised you didn't try to sign The Four Tune Tellers.

[Hearty laughs] Exactly. And that was the beginning of my work with Parlophone.

Prior to your work with The Beatles, you worked in many different musical idioms. How did that impact your production skills? It seemed you were very willing to be experimental in your work with The Beatles.

Oh absolutely. But I always was experimental even before The Beatles came along. One of the records I made was an electronic record called "Ray Cathode," which was collaborating with the BBC radiophonics people. I made a lot of what I call "sound pictures" with actors and comedians because it was fun to do. I'm a person who gets bored quite easily, and I don't like doing the same thing over and over again. Once I was running the label I didn't earn much money, but I did have freedom to do what I wanted to do.

Discuss your approach toward string arrangements. Your work on Beatles songs such as "Strawberry Fields Forever," "Eleanor Rigby" and "Glass Onion" is extraordinary.

The writing of the parts is me and the requirements is them. It varied between John and Paul. Paul was generally quite articulate with what he wanted. Mostly we would sit down at the piano together and play it through and work out how it would sound. Paul still doesn't know how to orchestrate, but he knew what he wanted and would give me ideas and I would say, "You can't do that," or "You can do this." We'd talk about it, talk it through. John would never take

Entry door to Abbey Road Studios, front shot.

Un successo mondiale dei **BEATLES**

Eleanor Rigby

Testo italiano di **MOGOL**

Testo originale e Musica di
J. LENNON - P. McCARTNEY

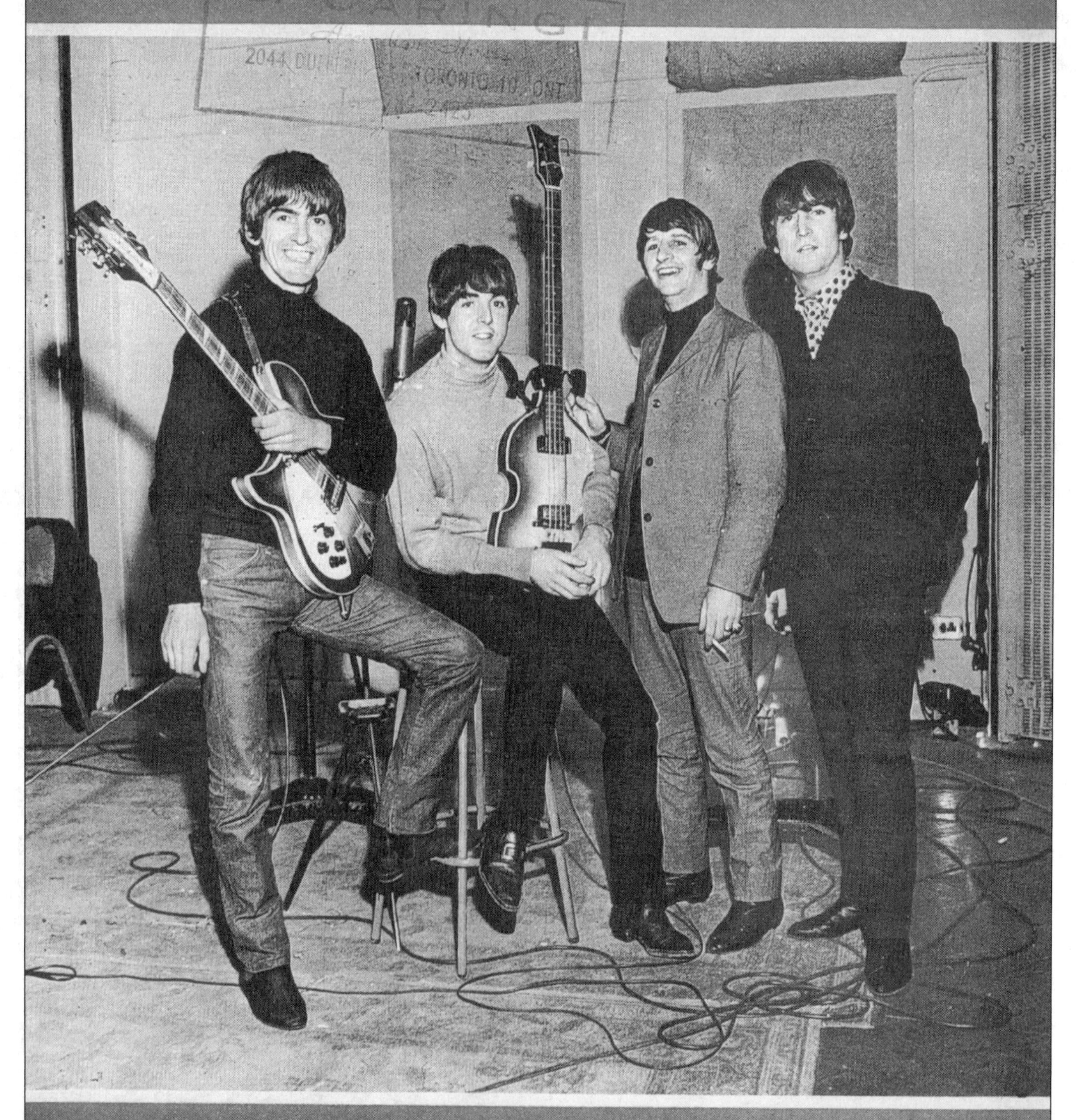

edizioni musicali **RITMI E CANZONI** milano

At the *Yellow Submarine* premiere in Liverpool in 1999, Sir George Martin answered some questions for the press before going inside The Philharmonic Hall.

that kind of attention. John was less articulate and much more full of imagery. He would have ideas which were difficult to express. It was quite difficult for me to interpret. One of the problems was getting inside his brain and find what he really wanted. Quite often he would say, "You know me. You know what I want." In the case of "I Am The Walrus," when I first heard that he just stood in front of me with a guitar and sang it through. But it was weird. I said to him, "What the hell am I going to do with this, John?" And he said, "I'd like for you to do a score and use some brass and some strings and some weird noises. You know the kind of thing I want." But I didn't, but I mean I just went away and did that.

Didn't you hire The Mike Sammes Singers for that?

Yes, that was a surprise for him. He didn't know that. I thought, "Well, let's do this because it adds to it." I had a group of singers called The Michael Sammes Singers who were pretty corny people. They were very good at reading what you wrote. If you wrote something, they could pretty much sing it instantaneously. They were very good. In the score you've got the directions for them where they have to shout or all the glasses, the up and downs and the ha ha ha's and hee hee hee's and so on. And when we ran it through and John heard it, he fell about laughing and thought it was so funny. So that's why "Walrus" was such an important song to put on the album.

What is the orchestral arrangement that you did for The Beatles of which you're most proud? "Strawberry Fields Forever" is a wild score.

The Beatles wanted something unusual. Although at the core of it is orchestration that I liked to do. I liked to have clean orchestration. I've got various theories about orchestration. I don't think the human brain can take it too many notes at once. For example, when you're listening to a fugue of Bach or someone and you hear the first statement and the second one joins it, you can catch hold of that all right and then the third one comes in and it starts to get more complicated. Any more than that and then it becomes a jumble of sound. You can't really sort out what is what.

Tell us about the time you tried to turn John Lennon onto a piece of classical music.

He went back to my flat one night. We had dinner and were rapping away. We were talking about different kinds of music. I wanted to play him one of my favorite pieces of classical music. It was the *Deathless* and *Fairy Suite Number Two* by Ravel which is a gorgeous piece of music. It lasts about nine minutes, and he sat through it patiently. I mean, it's one of the best examples of orchestration you can get, because it's a swelling of sound that is just breathtaking. And he listened very patiently and said, "Yeah, it's great. The trouble is by the time you get to the end of the tune you can't remember what the beginning's like." And I realized it was too stretched out for him to appreciate in one go. He couldn't assimilate it. He was so used to little sound bites. A lot of people are nowadays. It's the curse of advertising and television that we are now tuned to little jingles that we can connect to and recognize right away. And we can't listen to anything longer than that, so consequently the way people write sometimes is to connect together a lot of little jingles, which is not maybe the best way of doing things.

For a long time when asked about unreleased Beatles material you would state that it was all "rubbish" and there was nothing worth issuing. Working on Anthology 1, 2 *and* 3 *disproved that.*

I was convinced that there was nothing in the vaults that people hadn't heard that was worthwhile. But I was thinking like singles. Is there a great song that people hadn't heard? No, there's not a great song that people hadn't heard, there's little bits of rubbish. But what did emerge is I was given a brief by EMI, who asked me to put together stuff that would reflect the visual *Anthology* that wouldn't be a soundtrack but like an accompaniment or a companion. I thought the only way to do that is to see what there is. And I started listening and I found that there were different versions of songs that people would be interested in. The more I listened, the more I was convinced that people would want to have an analysis of what's gone. In order, admittedly, to give me more material, I would then put in things like "Eleanor Rigby" without the voices to show you the construction of it. Conversely, "Because" without the accompaniment to show you the beauty of the voices, that kind of thing. And I thought, "OK, I'm spinning things out a bit here," but I think it's valid.

The unreleased George Harrison song "You Know What To Do" was quite a treat. You listen to that an then something like "I Need You" and "Savoy Truffle" and George kind of blossomed all at once.

He did blossom, didn't he? To begin with, most of the songs he did were rubbish.

What was the first song George wrote where your ears perked up and you thought, "He's gotten much better as a writer"? I like "I Need You."

[sings chorus of "I Need You"] Nice little song. I remember the song I hated most of all, "Only A Northern Song." "Taxman" wasn't bad, typical George bitching about the world. Really, the one that I thought was better than any of

those was "Here Comes The Sun." I mean that was the first time he showed real cleverness in a song. From "Here Comes The Sun" onwards everything he did was pretty good.

On Anthology *you showed not only the musical side of the band but the zany side like "And Your Bird Can Sing," where John and Paul are cracking up doing the vocal.*

Isn't that super? [laughs] They were stoned out of their minds, of course, but it was also very funny. When I played it to Paul when I discovered it, I'd forgotten about it. We actually fell around laughing listening to it, too. We had marvelous times. We had such fun in the studio. I have such happy memories. John was very funny. John would do impersonations and send-ups of people, sometimes quite cruel but always very very funny.

In the '70s, John vacillated between loving and hating his days with The Beatles.

John went through some very bad times, like the *Let It Be* sessions. Later on he got pretty into drugs. During his time with May Pang, he admits it was a year and a half lost weekend.

Hypothetically, if John were still alive would he have gotten involved with Anthology *and recorded with Paul, George, and Ringo?*

I think he would have taken part in it. I think he would have been very active in putting it together 'cause John actually was an obsessive collector anyway. He would keep almost anything. I think he would have done it. John actually regained himself at the end, which was lovely. It was just too tragic having got back to himself that he was killed.

When you met up with John in the '70s he would tell you if he had the chance he would re-record every Beatles song. Could you understand where he was coming from?

It's a funny thing. When John said this to me originally was when we were spending an evening together, and it shook me to the core when we were talking about old things and he said, "I'd love to do everything again." To me that was just a horror. And I said, "John, you can't really mean it. Even 'Strawberry Fields'?" And he said, "Especially 'Strawberry Fields!'" I thought, "Oh shit, all the effort that went into that." We worked very hard on that trying to capture something that was nebulous. But I realized that John was a dreamer. In John's mind everything was so beautiful and much better than it was in real life. He was never a person of nuts and bolts. The bitter truth is music is nuts and bolts. You've got to bring it down to horse hair going over a bit of wood, people blowing into brass tubes. You've got to get down to practicalities.

How about you, George, is there one Beatles song you wish you could redo?

Would I like to do something again? No, I wouldn't want to do anything again. I'm not a person to look back, although having said that on this album I'm doing that. But I'm not trying to do anything better than what we did. I don't honestly think I could do anything better than what we did. I think what we did was right. It becomes solidified with time. You can't imagine any other way of doing it. You get surprised if you hear someone doing something that does work. When Joe Cocker came out with "With A Little Help From My Friends," I thought that was great, but that wouldn't have worked with Ringo. So the answer is I'd rather leave it to history, thanks.

When Paul, George, and Ringo recorded the two new Beatles songs, "Free As A Bird" and "Real Love," did they ask you to be involved?

I kind of told them I wasn't too happy with putting them together with the dead John. I've got nothing wrong with dead John, but the idea of having dead John with live Paul and Ringo and George to form a group, it didn't appeal to me too much. In the same way that I think it's OK to find an old record of Nat King Cole's and bring it back to life and issue it, but to have him singing with his daughter is another thing. So I don't know, I'm not fussy about it, but it didn't appeal to me very much. I think I might have done it if they asked me, but they didn't ask me.

Did you enjoy Jeff Lynne's production of "Free As A Bird" and "Real Love"?

I thought what they did was terrific. It was very, very good indeed. I don't think I would have done it like that if I had produced it.

What would you have done differently?

Well you see, the way they did it, you must remember, the material they had to deal with was very difficult. It was a cassette that John had placed on top of his piano, played and sang. The piano was louder than the voice and the voice wasn't very clear, and the rhythm was all over the place. So the way they tackled it was first of all they tried to separate the voice and the piano, not very successfully. Then they tried to put it into a rigid time beat so they could overdub easily other instruments. So they stretched it and compressed it and put it around until it got to a regular waltz control click, and then they were done. The result was, in order to conceal the bad bits, they had to plaster it fairly heavily, so what you ended up with was quite a thick homogenous sound that hardly stops. There's not much dynamics in it. The way I would have tackled it if I had the opportunity would have been the reverse of that. I would have looked at the song as a song and got The Beatles together and say,

"What can we do with this song?" bearing in mind we have got John around as well somewhere. I would have actually have started to record a song and I would have dropped John into it. I wouldn't have made John the basis of it. So where possible I would have used instruments probably and we would then try and get his voice more separate and use him for the occasional voice so it would become a true partnership of voices. Whether that would be practical or not I don't know. This is just theoretically the way I would tackle it.

You did some beautiful scoring for Paul on his recent album, Flaming Pie, *especially your orchestral work on "Somedays" and "Beautiful Night."*

Oh thank you. I worked on "Great Day" and "Calico Skies" too. On Ringo's new album I did a score for him too ("I'm Yours"). Paul I know very well. When he came along doing *Flaming Pie*, the stuff he was demonstrating for me was pretty good. I think it's the best album he's done in a long time. He asked me if I would collaborate with him. I said, "Choose something you think I can be helpful on." He actually gave me the numbers and said, "Would you like to do this?" It's always a challenge with Paul because you're on your mettle to try and do something that he won't be disappointed in. He was very pleased with "Beautiful Night" and the others too. On "Calico Skies" it was just a question of production. There was no real arrangement really, very, very simple. I enjoyed working with him very much as I always do.

After The Beatles broke up there were quite a score of "power pop" bands who mined a Beatles-esque sound, such as Badfinger and The Raspberries. Were you aware of this power pop movement?

I worked with Badfinger [orchestral score for "Money"/"Flying"], but I didn't actually produce them. Geoff Emerick worked with them. I was aware of all this. It was inevitable that The Beatles would spawn imitators and emulators. People wanted to be like The Beatles. So there's nothing wrong with that.

Still do.

Still do. How are you Liam? [laughs]. In an oblique way I worked with another group who had much more individuality but they weren't dissimilar with The Beatles, and they were America. America were like an American version of The Beatles, but they had their own homespun kind of songs. They were all good guitar players and all good singers and harmony singers. So there was that kind of illusion there. But I don't find anything wrong with people, providing they don't imitate. I think that Oasis have made a mistake in being so close to The Beatles and admitting. Noel actually said to me if he'd been born 20 years earlier he would have been Paul McCartney. Noel is a good songwriter — you can't knock him in that respect. I think he would have made it anyway regardless.

You worked with the power pop band Cheap Trick and produced their All Shook Up *album. Why did you get involved with them?*

I liked them. [laughs] I like Cheap Trick. It was a different thing. It's part of the business of liking to do different things and not get stuck in one groove. So I would try everything. I had one little assay into heavy rock, which was a terrible mistake, UFO. Cheap Trick I enjoyed very much.

What's your take on Badfinger? It seemed being on Apple Records got them tagged as Beatles wannabees when they had much more to offer.

> **"It's always a challenge with Paul because you're on your mettle to try and do something that he won't be disappointed in. He was very pleased with 'Beautiful Night' and the others too. On 'Calico Skies' it was just a question of production. There was no real arrangement really, very, very simple. I enjoyed working with him very much as I always do."**
>
> ***— George Martin***

I thought they were very good. It was a terrible tragic thing, all of that, the suicides and the ripping-offs that went on. It was terrible. It was all the seamy side of our business. They were a good group and they should have survived and they should have come through and been brilliant. But they didn't and they were one of the victims, I'm afraid. I don't remember working with them, although I did. It's difficult to remember everything after 48 years. [laughs] What did you have for breakfast on Tuesday the 19th of June, 1945? [laughs]

Can you assess the instrumental talents of The Beatles?

Paul's the most talented instrumentally in that he could play very good guitar. He was probably the best guitar player in the group. Of course he played bass guitar — he could tackle almost anything. He played very good drums too. His bass playing is wonderful. He was irritatingly good to other people. Sometimes he would put up the backs of the other guys 'cause he would get on the drums and tell Ringo what to do, and Ringo would get a bit irked by it. John was good, but he was careless. John was a gut man, and if it happened it happened and if it didn't he would fling the guitar across the room and say, "Get me a better one." John hated tuning his guitar, for example, such a mundane thing. He would get good sounds, good ideas. Some of his riff ideas were terrific. George was the painstaking one. He would be brilliant after 45 years. He would assemble his work. I used to think he used to assemble his recordings like a guy in Turkey making a carpet. He would work away in every room and every little inch would be detailed and beautiful. But it would take time and he would overdub and he'd track and correct and so on. He's a very good guitar player, of course.

How is George doing, with the reports of him having throat cancer?

He's OK. He did have a very serious cancer of the throat. We've all been having problems, one or the other from time to time. With Derek Taylor dying as he did. Derek and George were very close to each other. Derek was incredibly brave because he struggled with his cancer and went into remission for a while and then it came back. Worked all the while, he was very cheerful through this. It was extraordinary. And of course Linda and George being attacked himself and Ringo's ex-wife dying. But George is fine now. I saw him at Linda's memorial. He came over and spoke to us, and I'll try and get together with him when I get back. I've been awfully busy. I haven't been around much.

We can't forget Ringo.

Ringo is a sweet guy. As you know he's given up booze and cigarettes. He's too clean for words. He and his wife Barbara are such sweet people. And as a drummer he is unique. He's not a great technical drummer if you measure him against someone like Steve Gadd or Jeff Porcaro — he wouldn't be able to play like that. But he has a unique sound. When you hear Ringo, you know it's Ringo. There's no one else. He contributed an enormous amount to The Beatles' sound with his distinctive-sounding drums. Enormously supportive, he was always there. Apart from his drumming he would be the catalyst. His opinions counted. If John was doing something a bit dubious and Ringo would say, "That's crap, John," John would take it out. He wouldn't get angry, he would accept it.

In the '60s, did any of the other major British bands such as The Who, The Kinks, The Small Faces, or The Rolling Stones attempt to have you produce them?

They didn't approach me, mainly because I was so damn busy. I really couldn't have worked any harder than I did. All of the people from Brian's [Epstein] stable came along. I was just about able to cope with those and very little more. I had a tremendous roster of artists. But going back to Ringo again, one of the essential things about his drumming is he took infinite pains on getting the tone of his drums right. He tuned assiduously and got them exactly right. He was intently interested in the way that we recorded, so he would come and listen and say, "I'd like to hear more space on this one."

The drum sound changed on Revolver.

He had a lot of influence on that. He would put his input in. He would come up to the control room and talk to Geoff Emerick and try to get it to sound better. He was very keen on their sound.

You did work later in your career with another major '60s band, The Bee Gees. How would you characterize their talents?

Terrific songwriters. I remember going to meet with them in The Bahamas when we were talking about doing the *Sgt. Pepper* film, and they played me the tracks that they just recorded for a new film that nobody had ever heard about called *Saturday Night Fever*. I couldn't quite connect what I was hearing with the guys that I knew because it was so hip. I was looking at Barry and Maurice and Robin and I was saying it was a great dance sound. It could have been Motown, it was so good. I asked, "Have you done this? It's fantastic. You've got big hits here." I was enormously impressed. What was good about them was they weren't just writing good songs, but they were writing good production ideas into the songs the way that they were putting it together and the guitar work. Barry is very, very talented, and the others also contribute quite a bit too.

Lastly, it's been more than 15 years since Paul McCartney's Tug Of War *album was released. What are your memories of working with Paul on that record, acclaimed by many as one of Paul's best solo records?*

With *Tug Of War* the way it started was funny because we'd always been good friends and had dinner from time to time. One night we all went out to dinner. Paul and Linda were staying at their flat in town. I dropped them off and we said our good-byes. Just as I was about to drive off, Linda nudged Paul and then Paul ran through and knocked on the window. I thought we'd left something behind. He said, "I forgot something." And I said, "What is it?" He said, "Would you like to produce my next album?" [Laughs] I said, "Paul, we've been together all night and you give me a sledgehammer like that. We'd better talk about it." I said, "I'll ring you. We've got to talk about this, Paul, because I'm not sure how it's going to work." And he said, "Why?" I said, "Because for eight years or more you've been making very, very good records. You're a very good record producer. What do you need me for?" He said, "I think it would be a good idea." I said, "You may not like it." He said, "Well, why not?" I said, "Because I don't think you'll like being told what to do." He said, "We know each other so well it won't be a problem." So

> **"We got Stevie [Wonder] up. He agreed to come to Montserrat. We had a great time there.... He looked through the glass of our control room and said, 'Isn't that a beautiful sunset?' He also brought out the very first Linn drum machine, and it went wrong. He said to get the engineer to open the box and that he could fix it. I said, 'Are you sure?' So he opened up the lid and he said, 'Now switch it on.' And I said, 'Stevie, there are 440 volts running through there.' And he said, 'I know, but I can't fix it unless it's on.' And there he was in the live chasis, and I expected to have a fried Stevie Wonder at any minute and he fixed it. He's an amazing man."**
>
> *— George Martin*

I said, "OK, all right, if you want to try it. What about the songs?" And he said, "What do you mean, what about the songs?" I said, "Well, I'll need to have a look at them and judge them first of all." And he said, "Well, you mean I'll have to audition for you?" And I said, "Well, the material is pretty important." So he said OK and gave me about 14 songs he had on tape. I listened to them over the weekend and we met up on Monday. He said, "What do you think of them?" I said, "Four are great." He said, "Four?" And I said, "Of the other 10, six need a lot of work and the other four you should just throw away." He kind of gulped and said OK. He was a bit miffed, but you see it was necessary. It was vital. It's no good working with someone and being a yes man. You've got to be honest about it. He knows I'm always honest, so that was it. Working with Paul from that moment on, once we established the ballpark area, was a delight, an absolute delight. He did revise all the six songs that needed working on. "Ebony & Ivory" was one of them. We got Stevie [Wonder] up. He agreed to come to Montserrat. We had a great time there. We'd generally work from two in the afternoon 'til about seven, we'd have a break for dinner and then we'd work until about midnight. He would spend the following morning on the beach with the kids. Ringo came out, Stevie Wonder came out. He looked through the glass of our control room and said, "Isn't that a beautiful sunset?" [laughs] He also brought out the very first Linn drum machine, and it went wrong. He said to get the engineer to open the box and that he could fix it. I said, "Are you sure?" So he opened up the lid and he said, "Now switch it on." And I said, "Stevie, there are 440 volts running through there." And he said, "I know, but I can't fix it unless it's on." And there he was in the live chassis, and I expected to have a fried Stevie Wonder at any minute and he fixed it. He's an amazing man. And dear Carl Perkins. He's never been to the West Indies in his entire life. I put him in a bungalow down by the beach. I rang him the next morning to see if he slept OK. And he said, "Man, I thought I'd died and gone to heaven." He was a lovely man. When he did our Montserrat show in September for the victims of Montserrat, I purposely didn't ask anyone from America because I didn't want to pay expenses for anybody. I only asked people from England because I wanted every penny to go to those victims. And Carl rang up and said, "I want to come and do this for you." I said, "Carl, honey, I'd love you to but we can't pay expenses." And he said, "I'll come anyway." And so did Jimmy Buffett. They paid their own way to come over. And Carl turned up in his winkle-picker blue suede shoes. He really did have them.

Conspicuous by their absence

How The Beatles dominated the music charts — after they broke up

by Casey Piotrowski

The Beatles' predominance in American rock 'n' roll in the '60s? Oh, yeah, I heard something about that. The 23 #1 singles? Not bad. The 16 #1 albums? Worth a mention. Had all Top 5 singles in America in April 1964. Probably beginner's luck.

Obviously, what The Beatles did during those magnificent seven years before their breakup was remarkable. But don't forget, during all that time, The Beatles were there, selling their music as well as making it. They toured, made movies, had TV and radio appearances and, eventually, produced music videos. Seemingly, they always had time for an interview or a photo op. (Try finding a music magazine from that time that didn't feature a piece on The Beatles.) There was always a steady stream of great new product being released.

But how their success as a group continued after their breakup may be an even greater achievement. Remember, after 1970, all "new" Beatles product consisted of either repackages (Beatles fans who bought *Reel Music* enjoyed the privilege of getting "And I Love Her" for the seventh time) or the group's own second choices.

Frequently, those packages would have to compete with usually good, often great, new solo releases from the group's members. Instead of John, Paul, George, and Ringo celebrating their past, the four of them have spent the best part of the last 30 years throwing rocks at the group's legacy and at each other. That's hardly the best way to promote your catalog. Still, the public knew much better. It is the fans' loyalty and the quality of the group's work that has made The Beatles the most successful music act not only from 1964 to 1970 but, arguably, from 1970 to today as well. Without question, they have enjoyed more success after their breakup than any other act.

Consider the following: Since the invention of the longplay record, only 11 acts (besides The Beatles) have had as many as five #1 albums. The Beatles have had that many #1 albums since they broke up (*'62-66*, *'67-70* and all three volumes of *Anthology*). Along with that, three other Beatles packages (*Hollywood Bowl*, *Live At The BBC* and *Rock 'N' Roll Music*) peaked at #2. Using that as the yardstick, over the last 30 years, only Paul McCartney (in all the permutations of his solo career), with 10, and The Rolling Stones, with nine, have charted more albums as high as the disbanded Beatles. (And we're not counting two more #1 albums — *Let It Be*, new recordings released after the group's breakup and *The Beatles Again* (*Hey Jude*), which held #2 the week the group split.) In fact, discounting the new reunion recordings from the Eagles and Fleetwood Mac, no band has had even one archival release hit #1 — much less five of them. If we stretch that point to include solo artists, only two of them have had albums reach #1 after their deaths — Janis Joplin (*Pearl*) and, predictably enough, John Lennon (*Double Fantasy*).

This article originally appeared in Goldmine issue #503, Nov. 5, 1999.

In their native England, it was more of the same. Both *Hollywood Bowl* and *Live At The BBC* hit #1, as did the five other titles that reached #1 in America, giving The Beatles seven #1 albums in their homeland after their split. (Three more albums, *Love Songs*, *20 Greatest Hits* and *Rock 'N' Roll Music* also hit the Top 10.) In the past three decades, only four other artists (McCartney, Queen, ABBA, and David Bowie) hit #1 more frequently than The Beatles did after they broke up!

A couple more quick notes about their post-breakup albums. The Beatles hit #1 three times in one year with the release of *Anthology 1*, *2* and *3*. Only Elvis Presley, who did it in 1960, and The Beatles themselves, who had four #1 albums in 1964 and three #1's in 1965, 1966 and 1970, hit the top spot on the album chart that many times in one year. (They would have done it in 1969, too, but *Yellow Submarine* was blocked from #1 by *Abbey Road*.) No other band has had three albums debut at #1 (which all three volumes of *Anthology* did).

As for singles, The Beatles have had four major hit singles since their breakup. (We're not counting "The Long And Winding Road," which was already in pre-release when McCartney announced his intention to leave the group.) In order of their release, they include "Got To Get You Into My Life" which peaked at #3, "The Beatles Movie Medley" (#12), "Free As A Bird" (#6) and "Real Love" (#10). No other band has hit the Top 10 even once after their breakup.

Even reunion efforts from other bands failed to do much. The Eagles' terrific "Get Over It" could do no better than #15.

Fleetwood Mac, with a tour and a #1 album to support them, couldn't chart either of the wonderful singles from *The Dance* ("Silver Springs" and "Landslide").

Only three solo artists had major hits after their passing — Janis Joplin ("Me And Bobby McGee," hitting #1), Jim Croce ("Time In A Bottle" hitting #1, "I've Got A Name" hitting #10 and "I'll Have To Say I Love You In A Song" peaking at #12) and, of course, John Lennon ("Woman" hitting #1, "Nobody Told Me" hitting #5 and "Watching The Wheels" hitting #10). But the chart success of those artists pretty much stopped not long after their deaths. The Beatles have had at least one major hit in every decade since their breakup.

(In Britain, "Movie Medley" hit the Top 10. So did "Yesterday," finally released as a single there in 1976. "Love Me Do" finally became a Top 5 there with its 20th anniversary release in 1982. "Baby It's You," from *Live At The BBC*, hit #7 in 1993. Both "Free As A Bird" and "Real Love" hit the Top 5 in 1996. That gave The Beatles six Top 10 singles in the U.K. after they split.)

As for gold singles, the recent certification of "Got To Get You Into My Life" gave The Beatles three singles released after their breakup to go gold. No other disbanded group has even one. As for departed solo artists, Elvis Presley (with "Way Down" and "My Way") has two. Lennon, Joplin, and Croce have one each.

Speaking of 24-carat hardware, while together The Beatles earned 19 gold albums. They've earned 20 more gold albums with packages released after their breakup. In fact, every package Capitol has issued since the group's split has gone at least gold; most have gone platinum. The *'62-66* and *'67-70* packages have earned the RIAA's new diamond certification with sales of more than 10 million units each. *Rock 'N' Roll Music* has gone gold three different ways — as a double album and as two single albums.

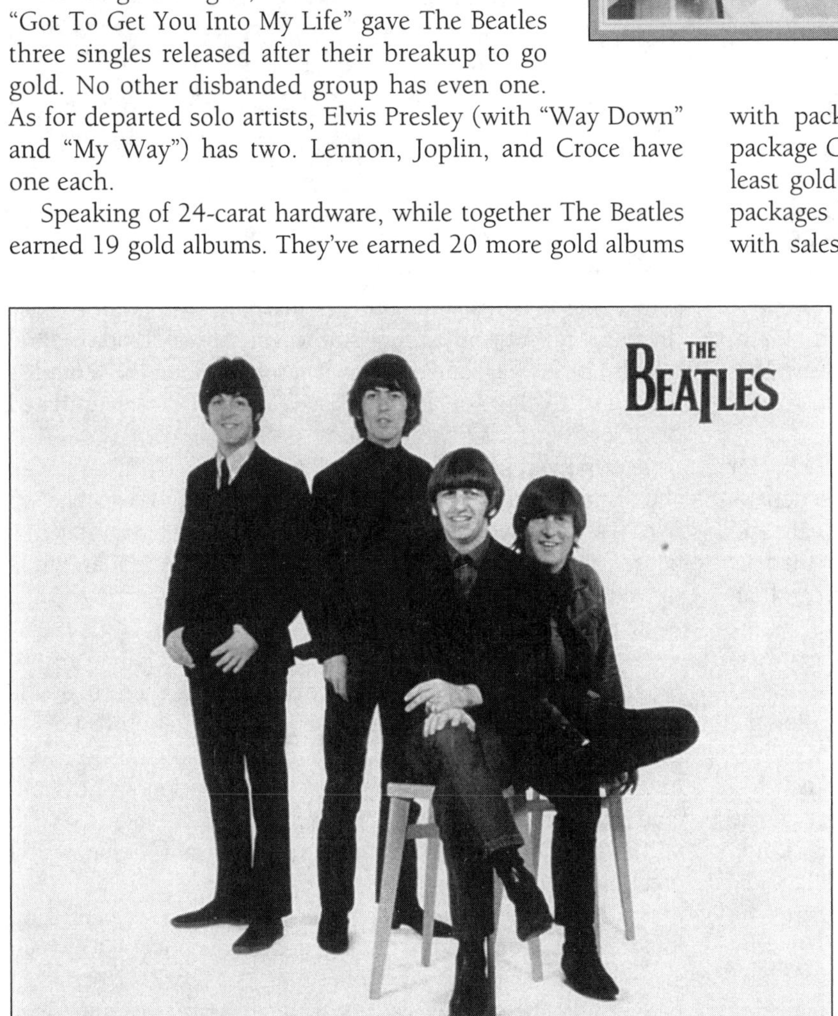

In the last 30 years, as record sales have exploded, more than 20 artists have earned at least 21 gold albums. It's a list wide enough to include The Rolling Stones, Elton John, Barbra Streisand, George Strait, and Kiss.

Still, for The Beatles — who spent much of the last three decades not speaking to one another, much less working together — to average one gold album every 15 months for 30 years after they've broken up is staggering!

All in all, they haven't done badly. While the artists who followed in the '70s, '80s and '90s worked intently to perfect their art and then feverishly to sell it, The Beatles just about matched them stride for stride while pretty much doing nothing.

This part of The Beatles' history — where they threw away their crowns but remained kings nonetheless — is overlooked. Though it doesn't contribute to the body of their work, it does add to the legacy of their popularity. It offers more proof that The Beatles didn't just fill our ears, they also filled our hearts.

(Thanks to Ed Ford and Gil Perez for contributing to this article.)

Linda McCartney

Remembering a photographer, an activist, a musician and above all, a survivor

by Dave Thompson

In December 1995, Linda McCartney revealed that she was undergoing treatment for breast cancer.

It was a stunning revelation. Linda had always preached that positive thinking and a vegetarian diet would lead to good health and a long life, but rumors concerning Linda's health had been flying for months. Now, as she dropped completely out of public view, they flew even faster. It would be nine long months before husband Paul was finally able to quell public fears when he announced that his wife had made a full recovery, a revelation that was quickly heralded among the most inspiring medical stories of the age.

No longer simply the plucky fighter whose ability to withstand the slings and bows of critical and public distaste had at least earned her the world's admiration, Linda was now a survivor as well, someone who could combat the most horrific odds and make it through. Her battle with cancer alone was one of colossal bravery. Added to the long campaign of other battles she had fought and won, it became one of absolute inspiration, the courage to keep going, whatever the odds.

But this apparent happy ending was not to be. In March, the cancer was found to have spread to Linda's liver. Less than a month later, she died on the McCartneys' ranch near Tucson, Ariz.

Linda Louise Eastman was born on Sept. 24, 1942. Her mother, Louise, was heir to the Cleveland Linders department store chain; her father Lee was a Harvard graduate and show business copyright lawyer; and the family divided its time between homes in Scarsdale, East Hampton and an apartment on Park Avenue. Visitors to the Eastman home included actor Hopalong Cassidy and songwriters Hoagy Carmichael, Tommy Dorsey, and Jack Lawrence — who composed "Linda" (later recorded by Jan And Dean) for the six-year old-girl in return for legal work by Lee.

Linda was, she admitted, "the black sheep of the family." Childhood piano lessons were abandoned in the face of the headstrong child's objections, and by her late teens, Linda was regularly playing truant from school in Scarsdale. Neither would her attendance record improve when she enrolled at exclusive Sarah Lawrence College in nearby Bronxville (coincidentally, Yoko Ono's alma mater). She took off from there as well, to attend Alan Freed's all-day rock 'n' roll shows in New York.

In 1960, Linda enrolled at Princeton, studying art and history. She was dating a geophysics student, Melvin See, soon

This article originally appeared in **Goldmine issue #465,** *May 22, 1998.*

to become her husband, but the marriage was doomed. See dreamed of continuing his studies in Africa; Linda would travel no further afield than Tucson, where the couple's daughter Heather was born on Dec. 31, 1963. Linda initiated divorce proceedings shortly after.

It was in Tucson, however, that Linda first realized what she wanted to do with her life. Arizona, she said, "opened up my eyes to the wonder of light and color," and having taken a course in art history at the University Of Arizona, Linda moved on to a course in photography, presented by Hazel Archer at Tucson Art Center.

She returned to New York in 1964, landing a job as receptionist at *Town And Country* magazine. It was there that one morning's mail delivery brought an open invitation to photograph The Rolling Stones aboard a boat on the Hudson River. Linda took it for herself, arrived at the reception and discovered she was the only photographer there.

"That got my name around," she later said. "That was a great piece of luck."

Resigning from her receptionists' desk, Linda set herself up as a freelance photographer, a precarious role but one to which she seemed ideally suited. Combining the rebelliousness that had so often helped her get her own way with a genuine love for meeting people, Linda learned that if she couldn't bully her way into a commission, she could cajole instead. Soon she was traveling as far afield as California, to work with The Beach

Boys, and Austria, photographing The Beatles during the making of *Help!* She cowrote one of the first serious books of the rock generation, 1967's *Rock And Other Four Letter Words*, and when Bill Graham opened the Fillmore East in New York, Linda became house photographer.

In May 1967, Linda arrived in London to photograph Traffic, and on May 15, Jimi Hendrix's manager, Chas Chandler, took her out to the Bag O'Nails nightclub to see Georgie Fame And The Blue Flames. Paul McCartney was seated at the next table.

Thus began one of the most remarkable courtships and love stories in rock history, a 30-year partnership during which the couple were apart just once, the nine days that Paul spent in a Japanese jail cell.

It was not always a bed of roses. Alongside Ono, Linda found herself the media scapegoat for The Beatles' demise, a role that her subsequent involvement in McCartney's solo career did not diminish. Almost unanimously, the world's press mercilessly scorned the music that the couple would make together, the string of albums that ran from 1971's *Ram* through to 1976's *Wings At The Speed Of Sound* (with *Band On The Run* an honorable exception). Linda's onstage contributions to Wings were cast as intolerable aberrations within what could have been a great rock 'n' roll band.

Yet Linda weathered the storm, just as she had weathered so many in the past, and by the 1980s, with Wings disbanded and Paul himself an increasingly unpredictable talent, Linda's involvement in his music was not only accepted, it was often even praised. Maybe the world was not yet ready for the Linda McCartney solo album that astute listeners to Paul's "Oobu Joobu" radio series compiled from broadcast outtakes, but it wasn't calling for her head either. In the minds of his critics as well as his fans, the only partnership in the ex-Beatle's life that mattered now was the one that the world had spent so long trying to sunder.

No longer the scheming groupie who stole away the heartthrob of millions or the musical incompetent who bewitched and bedraggled a genius, Linda was now accorded unreserved respect by Paul's fans, love by his peers. And if that was the least of her accomplishments, she would already have been a remarkable woman. Of course it wasn't. As a mother, she ensured that the couple's four children grew up completely untouched by the oppressive heat of superstardom. As a wife, Paul himself admitted, Linda kept his feet firmly on the ground. And as an ecological campaigner, she raised the profile of that debate higher than it had ever been before.

It was Linda who involved Paul in recording a series of "radical" messages for the animal welfare organization PETA (People For The Ethical Treatment Of Animals); it was Linda who was called to the phone whenever local animal welfare groups needed an emergency home for an injured animal. And of course, it was Linda who persuaded Paul — and a great many other people too — to give up eating meat. Indeed, speaking in the aftermath of Linda's death, Paul insisted that the best tribute anyone could pay his wife's memory would be to turn vegetarian.

Photographer and author, songwriter and musician, ecological campaigner and animal rights activist, Linda McCartney was one of the most remarkable women of her generation, one who deliberately pitted herself against the harshest odds and came out on top every time. As a teenager struggling to make her name in the world of rock photography, as the onstage partner of one of the most famous musicians in the world, as a vegetarian voice in a carnivorous society, Linda was irrepressible and continued to be so to until her death. Just weeks before she died, she announced to the world, "I'm back"; just days before the end, she was horseback riding with her family.

"She was just different," Paul said of the first time he met the brash American blonde. "The others were girls — she was a woman. I just went for her in a big way, and that was it. We've never looked back."

In the wake of Linda's death, looking back is all that Paul, and the couple's countless fans and admirers can do — look back on a life that may have ended tragically early but that was crammed with living nonetheless.

Ringo Starr

A sentimental rock 'n' roll journey

by Ken Sharp

After the Beatles split in 1970, Ringo Starr was at an artistic crossroads. Unlike his fellow bandmates who were creative giants, Starr's initial attempts at songwriting met with modest success. Through the 1970s, Ringo experienced a roller coaster ride of success and failure as a solo artist. For every triumph such as his singles "It Don't Come Easy" and "Photograph" and his *Ringo* and *Goodnight Vienna* albums, all exemplary pop/rock efforts, there were infinitely lesser artistic moments such as his sub-par *Bad Boy* and *Ringo's Rotogravure* records — uneven recordings that mirrored Ringo's ever worsening substance abuse problems.

In the late 1980s, Ringo and wife, actress Barbara Bach, met their problems head-on, entering rehab and finally emerging clean and sober. It was the moment Ringo conquered his demons that his artistic and creative aspirations truly blossomed.

Hard to believe, but in the past several years Ringo has been the most active of the former Beatles, issuing several critically acclaimed solo albums — *Time Takes Time* and *Vertical Man* — and embarking on a series of successful live concert tours with his ever-changing lineup of All-Starrs.

Last year, Ringo became the first Beatle to perform in Russia. His new *Storytellers* album is a delight, showcasing a splendid collection of material spanning his entire career. Ringo And His All-Starr Band is currently on an American tour, with plans for a U.S. summer jaunt with Foreigner also on the bill.

Goldmine caught up with Ringo for a revealing conversation spotlighting his new *Storytellers* album, an overview of his solo career and much more.

Goldmine: *I attended your recent club gig at The Bottom Line. That must be your first club show in many, many years.*

Ringo Starr: Yeah, it was. I don't remember when the last club gig was unless you call Billy Bob's in Texas a club, which has 4,000 people. But that [The Bottom Line] was the first sort of club I've played in 40 years. No, not 40, maybe 30. I loved it. It was great to have people that close to you.

Let's talk about some of the songs that appear on your new CD, Storytellers, *starting with "Don't Pass Me By." You cowrote "What Goes On" in The Beatles, but isn't "Don't Pass Me By" the first complete song you ever wrote?*

Well "Don't Pass By" was the first song I'd written that we recorded. I'd written other songs, but as I said in the *Storytellers* show, they were always other people's songs, I just rewrote the words. I used to say that I was rewriting Jerry Lee Lewis' B-sides. It was just a thrill. I remember writing it at the piano at this home in England that we were living in at the time. Then for me and 'til this day, it's still magic when I write a song and get together with other musicians and we record it and it turns into the track. It's still a mindblower for me, that process.

This article originally appeared in* Goldmine *issue #487, March 26, 1999.

With "Don't Pass Me By" and much of your work, there's a distinct country thread. How did you first get into country music, and who are some your favorites?

Oh there's so many. Hank Snow, Buck Owens. Merle Haggard, Ernest Tubb, sort of the old boys in the country school. I come from Liverpool, which is a port, so a lot of neighbors went to sea. In fact, Liverpool is sort of the capital of country music in England. So I just came by it naturally, sailors who would play the records. You'd go by someone's house to visit someone, and his brother was in the Navy and had these records. And I just instantly liked country music.

Is Hank Snow still one of your favorite singers?

Oh sure. I was just playing the other day "The Golden Rocket." But so is Ernest Tubb and lots of other old country guys.

"Back Off Boogaloo" was a surprise choice to play live on TV.

Oh you mean on *Letterman*? We were going to do "King Of Broken Hearts" from the *Vertical Man* album and their management, as I said on the show, wondered if we could do something a little livelier because its 11, 12 at night [laughs]. So we thought, "Let's run down 'Back Off Boogaloo' because it's on the *Storytellers* album anyway."

The song was influenced by Marc Bolan?

Yes, it was because he'd come for dinner. And he spoke like that. Not every line out of his mouth, but you would say,

"Would you like some gravy?" and he'd say, "Oooh, back off!" [laughs]. Or he'd call you a boogaloo for some reason. Those words just stuck in my head. When I went to bed that night the melody and the words, "Back off boogaloo, what do you think you're gonna do?" came in my head. It was all there. I ran downstairs to tape it so I wouldn't forget it. Many nights you think you've got a song and [you say], "I'll get up in the morning and I'll write it down then." But you don't stand a chance in hell 'cause it's gone. So this time I thought I'm gonna get up and do it. None of the tapes were working, but in the end I got some batteries together and got it down, thank God.

You directed Marc Bolan's film Born To Boogie.

Yeah. We were good friends. At that time I was running Apple Films, and I did two movies, the *Born To Boogie* with Marc, and I did the Dracula movie with Harry Nilsson, *Son Of Dracula*. So I was sort of keeping it musical as well as movies. And so I said to Marc, "You do the concert, and I'll take care of everything else, the cameras and everything." And that's how we did the deal. If we made a dollar, we split it 50/50.

Ever since you've become sober, you've been amazingly productive, the most productive in fact out of the three Beatles. In the late '70s, if you were asked about touring you would have said, "No way."

I attribute it to being healthy and you have energy. You wanna put it somewhere. In my case I put it behind the drums.

The first time you ever played "Octopus' Garden" live was at The Bottom Line show. What took so long getting it into the set?

Every tour I do, I do "Yellow Submarine," and I didn't really want to do sort of novelty songs. "Yellow Submarine" and "Octopus' Garden," I always felt it was just too much. So I chose to do "Yellow Submarine" because in all honesty it is the bigger song. And so I end the first half of my show every night with "Yellow Submarine." And so when we were putting the set together for *Storytellers*, not only did you want to do songs that were interesting, you always wanted to do them with ones that had a story [laughs]. And "Octopus' Garden" certainly had the story. During the recording of *The White Album* I left The Beatles. I went on holiday. We were lent this yacht and we ordered lunch and the guy presented us with octopus and french fries. And we thought, "What the hell is that?" And then the captain proceeded to tell me that afternoon that octopus actually go 'round the sea bend [singing] "resting their head" [laughs] and picking up shiny coral and stones and actually putting a garden around their cave. I just thought that was so beautiful and I happened to have a guitar there and wrote the song.

Yachts must be good luck for your creativity. You wrote another great song of yours on a yacht, "Photograph."

"Photograph" was written in Spain. I was doing the movie *Blindman*. And then I finished it on a yacht in Cannes at The Cannes Film Festival with George [Harrison].

Did you come up with music and he helped finish it up?

I write the melody and the lyrics for the first two verses and a chorus. And then George used to help me on the last verse so I could end the damn thing [laughs]. I've got a song that I wrote called "Three Ships In The Harbor," and it has 43 verses. Like a Bob Dylan song... [laughs] And at one time I gave it to Harry Nilsson to edit and he got it down to I think 10 or 11 verses, and I still haven't recorded it of course.

It'll probably turn out to be a 20-minute song.

Yeah, if we ever do it. You know, you've got songs, and sometimes the day you write it isn't the day you need to record it. You can record it later. So maybe one day "Three Ships In The Harbor" will be out there. Who can tell?

"It Don't Come Easy" is arguably your signature song as a solo artist. You've mentioned that Harrison helped out even though he's not listed as a cowriter. Did he help you with that song?

Yes he did. George wrote some of the last verse. He produced the track too. He produced the original version of "Photograph," and then Richard Perry did it for the *Ringo* album.

Is Stephen Stills playing guitar on "It Don't Come Easy?"

You know, I couldn't tell you. He could be, because Stephen and I at that time had become real friendly. I played on his first solo album. And he also produced a track on the *Stop And Smell The Roses* album. So we bumped into each other over the years. We spent more time together in the '70s.

"La De Da" is particularly Beatles-esque. It's a shame you never got a chance to film that video at Shea Stadium as originally planned.

Oh yeah. You're in the hand of God. I mean you set up your whole video shoot and it rains. It's like Woodstock. There's no amount of chanting that could stop the rain. So we had to make do with the time we had. "La De Da" started in a very weird way because it was just an expression when something would break down on the board or an amp or something. And because we were there recording Mark [Hudson] occasionally would get fraught. "Oh, got to get it together, gotta fix it!" And I said, "La de da," you know, the man will come when he comes to fix it. We're not electricians. And that's how it started. Then with him, Dean Grakall and myself it turned into the song. It was just that expression of "la de da," it turned into the expression no matter what happened. You have bands today like Oasis, and in the early '70s you had groups like The Raspberries and Badfinger emulating The Beatles' melodic sound.

I'm curious, were you a fan of these groups and power pop music in general?

See, I support any musician who's out there doing their gig. I really do. The line I draw is what records I have in my home, but I always support the musicians to do whatever they feel, whether it's power pop or whatever.

Did you like power pop bands such as The Raspberries and Badfinger?

Yeah. Badfinger. Is that power pop? I would never have known — it's all pop to me. Badfinger were good. They were on the Apple label, so it's always more interesting when you know the people.

Pete Ham and Tom Evans of Badfinger sang background vocals on "It Don't Come Easy." Pete played on Blindman *as well.*

Yeah. They would hang out.

How do you remember Pete Ham — he was a major talent who took his own life.

He was a major talent. Both of those boys decided they'd had enough, which was a shame, really. My memory of them was nice guys, just two really nice guys. The band was good. Paul produced them.

On Vertical Man, *you recorded the album in a very small studio. That atmosphere and the comfortableness brought out an outstanding album.*

I think everything you're saying about the atmosphere came about because we were in that room, Mark's studio in Santa Monica. We weren't in this so-called major studio with the red light and all the glass and the drummer's two miles down the hall with the separation. There was no real separation. The only real separation we had was the drums were in the cupboard. But when we would record the tracks, the guitarist and the bass player were in there with me. They would directly inject. If anybody said anything, the drum mikes were open. If you really wanna listen, you'll find a lot of chat in there [laughs]. You know it was like what you were saying about The Bottom Line show. Having the people in your face, that's what it's all about really. Being on stage, the energy comes down to the audience, and you get the energy back. And when you're in this room — nobody was more than six feet away from me — it's the way to play.

When you stopped playing live with The Beatles, you'd occasionally jump on stage and play with someone — The Band, Jerry Lee Lewis. When you started touring again with the All-Starr Band, did it click in your head where you said, "Geez, I shouldn't have waited this long. This is fun?"

Well, yes, I should have done it a lot earlier, but I didn't, so too bad, I can't worry about that. But I'm making up for it now, I really am. I've got two bands going, The All-Starr Band and The Roundheads. I'm like a schizoid now.

The Roundheads were very impressive backing you at The Bottom Line. Any chance of touring with them in the future?

The Roundheads are an excellent band. Well, you know the thing with The All-Starr Band is we need all those other hits around, that's the deal with that. But I'd have no qualms to tour with The Roundheads. I just don't want to be in the front all the time. I wanna get back on the kit and just play with other people instead of just being a frontman.

In 1970, you released two solo albums, Sentimental Journey, *an album of standards, and* Beacoups Of Blues, *a country record. There was also talk that you were working on an avant-garde album with Maurice Gibb.*

No, it didn't happen. It was a little movie actually that we were working on. It was like *The Chase*. We had one camera between us and we'd chase each other all round the area in Britain where we were both living in at the time [laughs]. We went into the studio, and I just overdubbed all the sound effects from the movie *Yellow Submarine*.

There was a period of time in the '70s when you were the most commercially successful of all the Beatles.

Yeah, '74 was the *Ringo* time. That and *Goodnight Vienna* are still my biggest solo albums. But then the bottom dropped out and the records that followed, *Ringo The 4th*, *Rotogravure*, *Bad Boy*, among them weren't nearly as good. I think the bottom dropped out 'cause I was dropping out — that was the deal. My energies were not into making records. I would make records, but there was no energy to promote it or take care of it and make sure that it was what I wanted to do. You know, it was my own fault. I felt other people might know better.

You're always asked about your favorite drum work with The Beatles.

"Rain," that's my best work.

I wanted to know if you could choose your favorite drum work on your solo albums?

Oh I don't know. I don't play the drums so people can look at it and go, "Wow, that was really cool!" I just play them the best I can.

"Drumming Is My Madness" is quite good.

Well, drumming is my madness [laughs].

For your solo records in the '70s, you often recorded with a second drummer, often Jim Keltner, why?

That started by accident because of the Bangladesh concert, which we played for George. And Jim was on it also. That was the first time I played with two drummers, and I just loved it so much. Then we got to do the *Ringo* album and the *Goodnight Vienna* album. And also when we got to New York to do the album, *Ringo The 4th* that Arif [Mardin] produced, suddenly we had Steve Gadd around. I think a bit of that was a union situation as well in those days. You can sing because no one can do that for you, but I think it was something about taking the job away from an American musician.

Your drum work was not only tight but could be very adventurous. The ending of "Strawberry Fields" showcases some wild off-the-wall tribal drumming. Was that work you enjoyed as well?

You know, what you're talking about just happens. There was no plan for that. I can play basic patterns and the freedom is the fills. To move it to where you can put it in a different space as a drummer, especially with The Beatles, only came at the end because the songs were so set up that there was two verses, a chorus, a verse, a middle eight and a chorus and something like that. Then at the end we'd all be allowed to blow our tops, which we did. And we still did that under three minutes [laughs].

You truly blossomed as a drummer on Revolver. *Did the vast improvement in sound inspire you?*

Yeah. Also I think we decided we could finally hear the bass drum on our records. If you listen to the early ones there's no sign of the bass drum, just like the snare and cymbals. So the recordings were getting better and you would play differently because you could hear it.

Has songwriting become easier for you since you first began?

Well, I enjoy writing with other people more than sitting there on my own [laughs]. I think it's more fun. It's always more fun to hang out with another human being anyway.

How do you know if collaboration will work with another writer?

You don't know. When we started the *Vertical Man* album with Mark and Dean, I just invited them over to see if it would work. And we had so much fun. We were just laughing — it was just fun. We were writing some serious songs, some real songs. But we were having joy with it, there was no torture. So that's how we decided to carry on and complete the album, *Vertical Man*. We had no plans to make an album when we started writing together. We'd write a few songs and we'd go to Mark's studio to demo them. And then a couple of hours into the demo we were going, "Why are we demoing? Let's make a record and just get it now."

"King Of Broken Hearts" is a should-have-been-a-hit from Vertical Man.

Well it came out as a single and it sunk. But they're gonna push it again in January [1999].

How was the song written? And discuss enlisting Harrison to play the beautiful slide guitar work.

The song was written by four guys in a room who can write you a million love songs [laughs], sad and happy ones. Once we got the song and melody and the feel of it, there was only one guitar on it. Mark and I were in London when he did the George Martin strings on "I'm Yours." Then we went to Paul's to do "What In The World" and "La De Da." *{Paul played bass and did backing vocals. — Ed.}* And I went to visit George with a cassette and played "King Of Broken Hearts" to him. At that moment he was busy with his own life and wasn't so interested in being on the record. And then when we got the "King Of Broken Hearts" track, I called him like a month later. His was the only guitar that I wanted on that track. He plays such beautiful guitar with such emotion that it was the only one I wanted. I said, "I've gotta have George on this." And so anyway I called him and spoke to him — I was in L.A. at the time, and he was in London. And he said, "Oh, send it over then." Which we did and he just did the finest job. All his emotion comes out of that guitar. And so the track was really brilliant, but he doubled that with feelings.

Can you cite any of your solo work that deserves reappraisal from fans?

I think they should listen to the *Ringo* album and the *Vertical Man* album.

Old Wave *is quite good.*

I like that too. That's the one Joe Walsh produced. We did that in England, and everyone was going, "Oh, that's new wave." So we thought we'd have a bit of fun and call it *Old Wave* [laughs]. And we have that 18-year-old picture of me on the cover with the big haircut [laughs]. It's a big wave.

Where was that photograph taken?

That was taken at a holiday camp in England called "Butlins."

Included on the new John Lennon Anthology *are several guide tracks with John singing lead on songs he wrote for you or found for you to record — "I'm The Greatest," "Goodnight Vienna" and "Only You." What are your recollections of those sessions with John?*

We always used to do that. It was great! Besides, it's easier for me if someone's singing the song to play to them because I play with the singer. You can feel where it needs bringing up or bringing down or whatever I feel at the time. John was always great fun to have in the studio and great energy. And I'd known him, so it was always relaxing. Then I'd have to go and do the vocals after him of course. And he'd be in the booth with me and he'd just be willing you on. You know, "Come on, let's go!" It was just great energy and great support.

So obviously you've heard these tracks with him singing on it once again?

Oh yeah. They're great! He was the best. I loved John. He was fine singer, a fine musician and he was a fine friend.

Last question, how do you look back on your record label, Ring O' Records, and some of the artists such as David Hentschel and Graham Bonnett?

I tried my best. I thought, "We'll form a label." No one will have to beg. I put the artists on it, but I ended up being in the board room too much being bored. Business. That's definitely something musicians shouldn't do, have their own record labels. I think because we're creative, we're not businessmen. Or at least that's in my case. There were some good people on the label. Then we closed it down and opened it up again with Bobby Keyes and people like that. It just didn't work. My head was just being beaten up at the end.

Mark Hudson

The legends in his own mind: Funny stories about being the "Fifth Beatle"

by Ken Sharp

You grew up loving The Beatles, formed The Hudson Brothers, a power pop band who emulated them, and now it's come full circle — you're writing and producing a real Beatle, Ringo.

Mark Hudson: It blows my mind. I said to Ringo, "The reason I started playing drums was because of you." When anyone asks me to sit down and play the drums, I can only play like Ringo. If they want Steve Gadd or anyone fancy, they better call someone else. I play the song. It's one thing I learned listening to the Beatle records, if you're the drummer, you play the song. End of story.

I think that's what the greatness of Ringo is. Drummers such as Russ Kunkel and Jim Keltner and a lot of those guys all came from that school. That's what Ringo gave to rock 'n' roll.

Ringo Starr [in same room as Hudson, screaming]: Yeah! Yeah!

Mark, are you pushing Ringo to do more Roundhead gigs?

Yeah, I'm pushing him to do more Roundheads gigs. This is what my big dream would be. If he could do Ringo And The Roundheads and throw in a Joe Walsh. Now Joe's gonna do "Rocky Mountain Stench" and "Funky Forty what-ever." Rich could go back and play the drums or be off stage having some tea.

Ringo: I won't be off stage!

Mark Hudson: Well then come up and play, ya bastard! [laughing]

Ringo: [laughing] All right.

Mark Hudson: When we did *Storytellers* show, it was the addition of Joe Walsh which gave The Roundheads a fatter sound, as well as he's got his own legacy as Joe Walsh and as an Eagle to do stuff.

Were you somewhat intimidated working with a Beatle?

No. To me, I was always the "Fifth" Beatle in my own head. So when I got a chance I just took over in my own sick mind where John would have left off. [imitates John], "OK Ring, here we go, thanks for coming," and we would just rock away. And now and then I'd turn around and hear this infectious sound that Ringo's got and the way that he plays like nobody else. While we were playing I would go, "Oh my God, I'm playing with a Beatle!" And it would hit me and I would snap back and become Marky again.

You and Ringo went over to London to work with Paul McCartney and George Martin on tracks for Vertical Man. *George Harrison contributed slide guitar to "King Of Broken Hearts." Did you work with him as well while you were there?*

No, George was down on his own, he's got that [imitates George] "Send it to me, I'll do it on my own, man."

Share the experience of going to Paul's studio "The Mill" and working with him on "What In The World" and "La De Da?"

It was a two-hour ride down and I got to spend the night 'cause I was doing a Hanson record at the time, a Hanson Christmas album. Ringo said, "Come down, stay at my flat, and we'll come get you in the morning and we'll go down to Paul's." There I am staying at Ringo's house in Ringo's bed, this beautiful wooden bed with all these stars and owls on it. First thing I did was I called my brother Brett and went, "Brett, you'll never guess where I am." And he went, "Where?" I said, "I'm in Ringo's bed." And he went "With Ringo?" And I went, "No, you idiot!" And I told him all about it. Brett was the bass player in The Hudson Brothers, sort of a "Paul McCartney with bigger lips" sort of look-alike. I said, "Guess where I'm going tomorrow?" And he said, "Where?" I went, "Paul's house." "What!?" Then I said, "I gotta go," and I acted like the phone was breaking up with static and I hung up on him. [laughs] Just to screw with his head. But on the whole ride down there, I must admit that I was a bit anxious.

You'd met Paul before.

Oh yeah. I had met Paul before, and my brothers and I were invited to one of his parties in the '70s held on the Queen Mary. We actually knew John [Lennon].

Did you know Ringo back in the '70s as well?

Oh sure. We were represented by the same attorney, Bruce Grakall, and we would be at functions together. We all knew each other, but there was never a question of working together. It was like, here we are. Everyone was pretty much messed up. So it did come full circle.

Did Paul mention The Hudson Brothers when you saw him?

Oh sure. He goes [imitates Paul] "Ah, the singing Hudsons!" And I went "Yeah," and we reminisced about meeting on the boat and all sorts of stuff. Anyhow, we spent the day at the studio with Paul. He was great. He was very, very generous. There was a big food spread. It was weird because as soon as he got with Ringo, me being a guy on the outside watching, it was like *Hard Day's Night* with crows' feet. There they were and their relationship — it was just incredible. Finally when I got down to the musical part, Geoff Emerick was engineering. As soon as Paul picked up the Hofner [bass] it wa like magic beginning to happen. He said to me, [imitates Paul] "I need to learn the chords, man," and he went, "Here," and gave me John's Gibson [guitar], the acoustic. There we were like back-to-back, him playing the Hofner and me playing the acoustic and him looking at a chord chart of a song that Ringo and I had written ["What In The World"]. And I was just thinking to myself [talks in whisper and meek voice] "Please, someone take a picture now!"

Did they?

No. It will forever be imprinted in my head, which is good enough.

So Paul played bass on "What In The World" and sang background vocals on that and "La De Da?"

Yes. It was a full-day session. It was so great 'cause all my life whenever I'd be singing background with my brother Bill or Brett, they would be McCartney and I'd be John and we'd shake heads as we'd be singing the "oohs." So we're singing background and all of a sudden I look over my headphones and next to me it's Paul singing. It was just like, give me a break!

You also worked with George Martin, who did the strings for the song "I'm Yours."

Yeah and that was beautiful. He was such a lovely, classy man. On "King Of Broken Hears," when Graham Prescott — who is a George [Martin] guy — and George [Martin] was there for the whole session, there's this part where I wanted the cellos to do a certain thing. And George went, "Mark, you look perplexed, is there something that you want?" I didn't know how to say it, but I said something like I was hoping that the cellos could sort of fall down like ah, ah... I was stuttering. And George looked over his glasses and said, [imitates George Martin] "You mean more Walrusy?" And I went, "Yeah, yeah, that's it." And he went out himself and re-miked the cellos. He is unbelievable.

Have you been working with Ringo on any new material?

Yes, when I was in London last time we started writing some Christmas songs. And constantly on the phone he'll call me up while he's on his treadmill going [imitates Ringo speaking while he's out of breath] "Mark, listen to this," and he'll come up with an idea. One of the Christmas songs we wrote is called "Christmas Eve." There's another one called "Dear Santa."

Why Christmas songs?

Because we both love Christmas and plan on doing a Christmas release next year. It'll be Ringo And The Roundheads. We're gonna record a Christmas record next year and God willing another studio album.

The lineup is the same as the Storytellers show?

Yes. It's me, Simon Kirke on drums. Gary Burr on guitar, Joe Walsh, Jim Cox on keys, Steve Dudas on guitar, Jack Blades on bass and Scott Gordon on harmonica if necessary.

I saw the Ringo And The Roundheads show at The Bottom Line and heard that it was even better than the Storytellers *performance a day later.*

It was. There was a bit more anarchy at The Bottom Line. You really got to feel the audience. When we did *Storytellers* it was a bit more reserved. The executives had their best friends there who were executives, and they were a bit more reserved. And it was a different kind of pressure. But when we did *Hard Rock Live* we kicked some ass, and we just did *Letterman* and were kicking some butt on that one too. We're a band to be reckoned with. If I can just get Ringo to say, "Yeah, I'll go out with The Roundheads plus Joe," I think that would probably be enough. It's so easy for me to do this stuff because it's so much a part of who I really am.

The Vertical Man *CD is perhaps Ringo's best studio effort since the* Ringo *album.*

Thanks, that means a lot. I was actually talking to Doug Fieger from The Knack — great guy. And he said to me, "Marky, *Vertical Man* is the best album Ringo's ever done — it's better than the *Ringo* album." And coming from a guy like him was cool.

As a producer, it seems you knew exactly what needed to be brought out of Ringo. You weren't afraid of allowing the album to have Beatles-esque touches.

Yeah. It was sort of weird. We were at Paul's house, and when we played him the song "What In The World," Paul looked at him and said, "Hey you know Ring, this is sort of Beatlelish." And Ringo went, kind of insecure, "Yeah I know, I've been saying that to Mark." And then Paul leaned over to him and said, [imitates Paul] "You're a fucking Beatle, man." And we all started laughing. It was so great. "You are a Beatle!"

Tell me about your other current projects.

Well I've just finished producing Timothy B. Schmitt from the Eagles, a solo record. It's great. He was a joy to work with as a human. Great pop roots, and his voice is just incredible. I loved that. There's some talk of me maybe doing the next Hanson record. But getting back to Ringo, what's weird about all of this stuff is that I came close to producing him 10 years ago with Lee DeCarlo, who engineered *Double Fantasy*. And we got really really close to doing it and the deal fell through, and so it didn't happen. This one was very casual. Ringo said to come up and write, and we wrote and it worked out great. You can sense the joy in the songs on *Vertical Man*, you really can.

Beatles Price Guide & Apple Records Numerical Listing

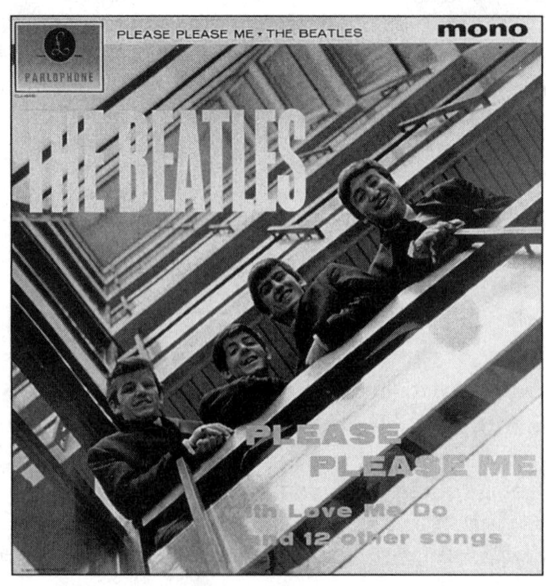

BEATLES, THE

Also see PETE BEST; GEORGE HARRISON; JOHN LENNON; PAUL McCARTNEY; YOKO ONO; RINGO STARR; SUZY AND THE RED STRIPES; TRAVELING WILBURYS.

12-Inch Singles

(NO LABEL)

Number	Title (A Side/B Side)	Yr	VG	VG+	NM
(no #) [DJ]	Merry Christmas and Happy New Year	1965	125.00	250.00	500.00
—Promo item from KYA Radio, San Francisco; B-side is blank					

45s

APPLE

Number	Title (A Side/B Side)	Yr	VG	VG+	NM
Promo-1970 [DJ]	Dialogue from the Beatles' Motion Picture "Let It Be"	1970	15.00	30.00	60.00
2056	Hello Goodbye/I Am the Walrus	1971	7.50	15.00	30.00
—With star on A-side label					
2056	Hello Goodbye/I Am the Walrus	1971	2.50	5.00	10.00
—Without star on A-side label					
2056	Hello Goodbye/I Am the Walrus	1975	5.00	10.00	20.00
—With "All Rights Reserved" disclaimer					
2138	Lady Madonna/The Inner Light	1971	7.50	15.00	30.00
—With star on A-side label					
2138	Lady Madonna/The Inner Light	1971	2.50	5.00	10.00
—Without star on A-side label					
2138	Lady Madonna/The Inner Light	1975	5.00	10.00	20.00
—With "All Rights Reserved" disclaimer					
2276	Hey Jude/Revolution	1968	3.75	7.50	15.00
—Original: With small Capitol logo on bottom of B-side label					
2276	Hey Jude/Revolution	1968	2.50	5.00	10.00
—With "Mfd. by Apple" on label					
2276	Hey Jude/Revolution	1975	5.00	10.00	20.00
—With "All Rights Reserved" disclaimer					
2490	Get Back/Don't Let Me Down	1969	2.50	5.00	10.00
—Original: With small Capitol logo on bottom of B-side label					
2490	Get Back/Don't Let Me Down	1969	2.50	5.00	10.00
—With "Mfd. by Apple" on label					
2490	Get Back/Don't Let Me Down	1975	5.00	10.00	20.00
—With "All Rights Reserved" disclaimer					
2531	The Ballad of John and Yoko/Old Brown Shoe	1969	2.50	5.00	10.00
—Original: With small Capitol logo on bottom of B-side label					
2531	The Ballad of John and Yoko/Old Brown Shoe	1969	2.50	5.00	10.00
—With "Mfd. by Apple" on label					
2531	The Ballad of John and Yoko/Old Brown Shoe	1975	5.00	10.00	20.00
—With "All Rights Reserved" disclaimer					
2531 [PS]	The Ballad of John and Yoko/Old Brown Shoe	1969	25.00	50.00	100.00
2654	Something/Come Together	1969	25.00	50.00	100.00
—Original: With small Capitol logo on bottom of B-side label					
2654	Something/Come Together	1969	2.50	5.00	10.00
—With "Mfd. by Apple" on label					
2654	Something/Come Together	1975	5.00	10.00	20.00
—With "All Rights Reserved" disclaimer					
2764	Let It Be/You Know My Name (Look Up My Number)	1970	3.00	6.00	12.00
—Original: With small Capitol logo on bottom of B-side label					
2764	Let It Be/You Know My Name (Look Up My Number)	1970	2.50	5.00	10.00
—With "Mfd. by Apple" on label					
2764	Let It Be/You Know My Name (Look Up My Number)	1975	5.00	10.00	20.00
—With "All Rights Reserved" disclaimer					
2764 [PS]	Let It Be/You Know My Name (Look Up the Number)	1970	25.00	50.00	100.00
2832	The Long and Winding Road/For You Blue	1970	5.00	10.00	20.00
—Original: With small Capitol logo on bottom of B-side label					
2832	The Long and Winding Road/For You Blue	1970	2.50	5.00	10.00
—With "Mfd. by Apple" on label					
2832	The Long and Winding Road/For You Blue	1975	5.00	10.00	20.00
—With "All Rights Reserved" disclaimer					
2832 [PS]	The Long and Winding Road/For You Blue	1970	25.00	50.00	100.00
5112	I Want to Hold Your Hand/I Saw Her Standing There	1971	7.50	15.00	30.00
—With star on label					
5112	I Want to Hold Your Hand/I Saw Her Standing There	1971	2.50	5.00	10.00
—Without star on label					
5112	I Want to Hold Your Hand/I Saw Her Standing There	1975	5.00	10.00	20.00
—With "All Rights Reserved" disclaimer on label					
5150	Can't Buy Me Love/You Can't Do That	1971	7.50	15.00	30.00
—With star on A-side label					
5150	Can't Buy Me Love/You Can't Do That	1971	2.50	5.00	10.00
—Without star on A-side label					
5150	Can't Buy Me Love/You Can't Do That	1975	3.75	7.50	15.00
—With "All Rights Reserved" disclaimer on label					
5222	A Hard Day's Night/I Should Have Known Better	1971	7.50	15.00	30.00
—With star on A-side label					
5222	A Hard Day's Night/I Should Have Known Better	1971	2.50	5.00	10.00
—Without star on A-side label					
5222	A Hard Day's Night/I Should Have Known Better	1975	3.75	7.50	15.00
—With "All Rights Reserved" disclaimer					
5234	I'll Cry Instead/I'm Happy Just to Dance with You	1971	7.50	15.00	30.00
—With star on A-side label					
5234	I'll Cry Instead/I'm Happy Just to Dance with You	1971	2.50	5.00	10.00
—Without star on A-side label					
5234	I'll Cry Instead/I'm Happy Just to Dance with You	1975	3.75	7.50	15.00
—With "All Rights Reserved" disclaimer					
5235	And I Love Her/If I Fell	1971	7.50	15.00	30.00
—With star on A-side label					
5235	And I Love Her/If I Fell	1971	2.50	5.00	10.00
—Without star on A-side label					
5235	And I Love Her/If I Fell	1975	3.75	7.50	15.00
—With "All Rights Reserved" disclaimer					
5255	Matchbox/Slow Down	1971	7.50	15.00	30.00
—With star on A-side label					
5255	Matchbox/Slow Down	1971	2.50	5.00	10.00
—Without star on A-side label					
5255	Matchbox/Slow Down	1975	3.75	7.50	15.00
—With "All Rights Reserved" disclaimer					
5327	I Feel Fine/She's a Woman	1971	7.50	15.00	30.00
—With star on A-side label					
5327	I Feel Fine/She's a Woman	1971	2.50	5.00	10.00
—Without star on A-side label					
5327	I Feel Fine/She's a Woman	1975	3.75	7.50	15.00
—With "All Rights Reserved" disclaimer					
5371	Eight Days a Week/I Don't Want to Spoil the Party	1971	7.50	15.00	30.00
—With star on A-side label					
5371	Eight Days a Week/I Don't Want to Spoil the Party	1971	2.50	5.00	10.00
—Without star on A-side label					
5371	Eight Days a Week/I Don't Want to Spoil the Party	1975	3.75	7.50	15.00
—With "All Rights Reserved" disclaimer					
5407	Ticket to Ride/Yes It Is	1971	7.50	15.00	30.00
—With star on A-side label					
5407	Ticket to Ride/Yes It Is	1971	2.50	5.00	10.00
—Without star on A-side label					
5407	Ticket to Ride/Yes It Is	1975	3.75	7.50	15.00
—With "All Rights Reserved" disclaimer					
5476	Help!/I'm Down	1971	7.50	15.00	30.00
—With star on A-side label					
5476	Help!/I'm Down	1971	2.50	5.00	10.00
—Without star on A-side label					
5476	Help!/I'm Down	1975	3.75	7.50	15.00
—With "All Rights Reserved" disclaimer					
5498	Yesterday/Act Naturally	1971	7.50	15.00	30.00
—With star on A-side label					
5498	Yesterday/Act Naturally	1971	2.50	5.00	10.00
—Without star on A-side label					
5498	Yesterday/Act Naturally	1975	3.75	7.50	15.00
—With "All Rights Reserved" disclaimer					
5555	We Can Work It Out/Day Tripper	1971	7.50	15.00	30.00
—With star on A-side label					
5555	We Can Work It Out/Day Tripper	1971	2.50	5.00	10.00
—Without star on A-side label					
5555	We Can Work It Out/Day Tripper	1975	3.75	7.50	15.00
—With "All Rights Reserved" disclaimer					
5587	Nowhere Man/What Goes On	1971	7.50	15.00	30.00
—With star on A-side label					
5587	Nowhere Man/What Goes On	1971	2.50	5.00	10.00
—Without star on A-side label					
5587	Nowhere Man/What Goes On	1975	3.75	7.50	15.00
—With "All Rights Reserved" disclaimer					
5651	Paperback Writer/Rain	1971	7.50	15.00	30.00
—With star on A-side label					
5651	Paperback Writer/Rain	1971	2.50	5.00	10.00
—Without star on A-side label					
5651	Paperback Writer/Rain	1975	3.75	7.50	15.00
—With "All Rights Reserved" disclaimer					
5715	Yellow Submarine/Eleanor Rigby	1971	7.50	15.00	30.00
—With star on A-side label					
5715	Yellow Submarine/Eleanor Rigby	1971	2.50	5.00	10.00
—Without star on A-side label					
5715	Yellow Submarine/Eleanor Rigby	1975	3.75	7.50	15.00
—With "All Rights Reserved" disclaimer					
5810	Penny Lane/Strawberry Fields Forever	1971	7.50	15.00	30.00
—With star on A-side label					
5810	Penny Lane/Strawberry Fields Forever	1971	2.50	5.00	10.00
—Without star on A-side label					
5810	Penny Lane/Strawberry Fields Forever	1975	3.75	7.50	15.00
—With "All Rights Reserved" disclaimer					
5964	All You Need Is Love/Baby, You're a RicMan	1971	7.50	15.00	30.00
—With star on A-side label					
5964	All You Need Is Love/Baby, You're a Rich Man	1971	2.50	5.00	10.00
—Without star on A-side label					
5964	All You Need Is Love/Baby, You're a Rich Man	1975	3.75	7.50	15.00
—With "All Rights Reserved" disclaimer					
58348	Baby It's You/I'll Follow the Sun//Devil in Her Heart/Boys	1995	—	2.00	4.00
—All 4 tracks from BBC sessions					
58348 [PS]	Baby It's You/I'll Follow the Sun//Devil in Her Heart/Boys	1995	—	2.00	4.00
58497	Free as a Bird/Christmas Time (Is Here Again)	1995	—	2.00	4.00
—Small center hole; all with large hole were "dinked" somewhere other than when manufactured and have little, if any, value					
58497 [PS]	Free as a Bird/Christmas Time (Is Here Again)	1995	—	2.00	4.00
58544	Real Love/Baby's in Black (Live)	1996	—	—	3.00
—Small center hole; all with large hole were "dinked" somewhere other than when manufactured and have little, if any, value					
58544 [PS]	Real Love/Baby's in Black (Live)	1996	—	—	3.00

APPLE/AMERICOM

Number	Title (A Side/B Side)	Yr	VG	VG+	NM
2276/M-221	Hey Jude/Revolution	1969	75.00	150.00	300.00
—Four-inch flexi-disc sold from vending machines; "Hey Jude" is edited to 3:25					

Number	Title (A Side/B Side)	Yr	VG	VG+	NM
2490/M-335	Get Back/Don't Let Me Down	1969	250.00	500.00	1000.
	—Four-inch flexi-disc sold from vending machines				
2531/M-382	The Ballad from John and Yoko/Old Brown Shoe	1969	200.00	400.00	800.00
	—Four-inch flexi-disc sold from vending machines				
5715	Yellow Submarine/Eleanor Rigby	1969	1000.	1500.	2000.
	—Four-inch flexi-disc sold from vending machines				

ATCO

Number	Title (A Side/B Side)	Yr	VG	VG+	NM
6302	Sweet Georgia Brown/Take Out Some Insurance On Me Baby	1964	50.00	100.00	200.00
6308	Ain't She Sweet/Nobody's Child	1964	12.50	25.00	50.00
	—With "Vocal by John Lennon" on left of label				
6308	Ain't She Sweet/Nobody's Child	1964	15.00	30.00	60.00
	—With "Vocal by John Lennon" under "The Beatles"				
6308 [PS]	Ain't She Sweet/Nobody's Child	1964	125.00	250.00	500.00
	—Sleeves with black and green print are reproductions				

ATLANTIC

Number	Title (A Side/B Side)	Yr	VG	VG+	NM
OS-13243	Ain't She Sweet/Sweet Georgia Brown	1983	2.50	5.00	10.00
	—"Oldies Series"				

BACKSTAGE

Number	Title (A Side/B Side)	Yr	VG	VG+	NM
1112 [DJ]	Like Dreamers Do/Love of the Loved	1982	6.25	12.50	25.00
	—Promotional 45 from "Oui" magazine				
1122 [DJ]	Love of the Loved/Memphis	1983	6.25	12.50	25.00
	—Promotional picture disc				
1133 [DJ]	Like Dreamers Do/Three Cool Cats	1983	6.25	12.50	25.00
	—Promotional picture disc				
1155 [DJ]	Crying, Waiting, Hoping/Take Good Care of My Baby	1983	6.25	12.50	25.00

BEATLES FAN CLUB

Number	Title (A Side/B Side)	Yr	VG	VG+	NM
(1964)	Season's Greetings from the Beatles	1964	75.00	150.00	300.00
	—Tri-fold soundcard				
(1965)	The Beatles Third Christmas Record	1965	20.00	40.00	80.00
	—Flexi-disc				
(1965) [PS]	The Beatles Third Christmas Record	1965	25.00	50.00	100.00
(1966)	Everywhere It's Christmas	1966	37.50	75.00	150.00
	—Postcard				
(1967)	Christmastime Is Here Again	1967	37.50	75.00	150.00
	—Postcard				
(1968) H-2041	The Beatles 1968 Christmas Record	1968	15.00	30.00	60.00
	—Flexi-disc				
(1968) H-2041 [PS]	The Beatles 1968 Christmas Record	1968	17.50	35.00	70.00
(1969) H-2565	Happy Christmas 1969	1969	10.00	20.00	40.00
	—Flexi-disc				
(1969) H-2565 [PS]	Happy Christmas 1969	1969	15.00	30.00	60.00

CAPITOL

Number	Title (A Side/B Side)	Yr	VG	VG+	NM
2056	Hello Goodbye/I Am the Walrus	1967	7.50	15.00	30.00
	—Original: Orange and yellow swirl, without "A Subsidiary Of"... in perimeter label print; publishing credited to "Maclen" (we're not sure which came first)				
2056	Hello Goodbye/I Am the Walrus	1967	7.50	15.00	30.00
	—Original: Orange and yellow swirl, without "A Subsidiary Of"... in perimeter label print; publishing credited to "Comet" (we're not sure which came first)				
2056	Hello Goodbye/I Am the Walrus	1968	12.50	25.00	50.00
	—Orange and yellow swirl label with "A Subsidiary Of" in perimeter print				
2056	Hello Goodbye/I Am the Walrus	1969	15.00	30.00	60.00
	—Red and orange "target" label with Capitol dome logo				
2056	Hello Goodbye/I Am the Walrus	1969	5.00	10.00	20.00
	—Red and orange "target" label with Capitol round logo				
2056	Hello Goodbye/I Am the Walrus	1976	—	3.00	6.00
	—Orange label with "Capitol" at bottom				
2056	Hello Goodbye/I Am the Walrus	1978	2.00	4.00	8.00
	—Purple label; label has reeded edge				
2056	Hello Goodbye/I Am the Walrus	1983	—	3.00	6.00
	—Black label with colorband				
2056	Hello Goodbye/I Am the Walrus	1988	—	2.50	5.00
	—Purple label; label has smooth edge				
2056 [PS]	Hello Goodbye/I Am the Walrus	1967	25.00	50.00	100.00
P 2056 [DJ]	Hello Goodbye/I Am the Walrus	1967	62.50	125.00	250.00
	—Light green label promo				
2138	Lady Madonna/The Inner Light	1968	7.50	15.00	30.00
	—Original: Orange and yellow swirl, without "A Subsidiary Of"... in perimeter label print				
2138	Lady Madonna/The Inner Light	1968	12.50	25.00	50.00
	—Orange and yellow swirl label with "A Subsidiary Of" in perimeter print				
2138	Lady Madonna/The Inner Light	1969	15.00	30.00	60.00
	—Red and orange "target" label with Capitol dome logo				
2138	Lady Madonna/The Inner Light	1969	5.00	10.00	20.00
	—Red and orange "target" label with Capitol round logo				
2138	Lady Madonna/The Inner Light	1976	—	3.00	6.00
	—Orange label with "Capitol" at bottom				
2138	Lady Madonna/The Inner Light	1978	2.00	4.00	8.00
	—Purple label; label has reeded edge				
2138	Lady Madonna/The Inner Light	1983	—	3.00	6.00
	—Black label with colorband				
2138	Lady Madonna/The Inner Light	1988	—	2.50	5.00
	—Purple label; label has smooth edge				
2138 [PS]	Lady Madonna/The Inner Light	1968	25.00	50.00	100.00
2138 [PS]	Lady Madonna/The Inner Light	1968	5.00	10.00	20.00
	—"Beatles Fan Club" insert that was issued with above sleeve. Originals are glossy.				
P 2138 [DJ]	Lady Madonna/The Inner Light	1968	50.00	100.00	200.00
	—Light green label promo				
2276	Hey Jude/Revolution	1976	—	3.00	6.00
	—Orange label with "Capitol" at bottom				
2276	Hey Jude/Revolution	1978	2.00	4.00	8.00
	—Purple label; label has reeded edge				
2276	Hey Jude/Revolution	1983	—	3.00	6.00
	—Black label with colorband				
2276	Hey Jude/Revolution	1988	—	2.50	5.00
	—Purple label; label has smooth edge				
2490	Get Back/Don't Let Me Down	1976	—	3.00	6.00
	—Orange label with "Capitol" at bottom				
2490	Get Back/Don't Let Me Down	1978	2.00	4.00	8.00
	—Purple label; label has reeded edge				
2490	Get Back/Don't Let Me Down	1983	—	3.00	6.00
	—Black label with colorband; "Get Back" replaced by LP version as on Let It Be				
2490	Get Back/Don't Let Me Down	1988	—	2.50	5.00
	—Purple label; label has smooth edge; "Get Back" replaced by LP version as on Let It Be				
2531	The Ballad of John and Yoko/Old Brown Shoe	1976	—	—	—
	—Orange label with "Capitol" at bottom; should exist, but not known to exist				
2531	The Ballad of John and Yoko/Old Brown Shoe	1978	—	3.00	6.00
	—Purple label; label has reeded edge				
2531	The Ballad of John and Yoko/Old Brown Shoe	1983	—	3.50	7.00
	—Black label with colorband				
2531	The Ballad of John and Yoko/Old Brown Shoe	1988	—	3.00	6.00
	—Purple label; label has smooth edge				
2654	Something/Come Together	1976	—	3.00	6.00
	—Orange label with "Capitol" at bottom				
2654	Something/Come Together	1978	—	3.00	6.00
	—Purple label; label has reeded edge				
2654	Something/Come Together	1983	—	3.00	6.00
	—Black label with colorband				
2654	Something/Come Together	1988	—	2.50	5.00
	—Purple label; label has smooth edge				
2764	Let It Be/You Know My Name (Look Up My Number)	1976	—	3.00	6.00
	—Orange label with "Capitol" at bottom				
2764	Let It Be/You Know My Name (Look Up My Number)	1978	2.00	4.00	8.00
	—Purple label; label has reeded edge				
2764	Let It Be/You Know My Name (Look Up My Number)	1983	—	3.00	6.00
	—Black label with colorband				
2764	Let It Be/You Know My Name (Look Up My Number)	1988	—	2.50	5.00
	—Purple label; label has smooth edge				
2832	The Long and Winding Road/For You Blue	1976	—	3.00	6.00
	—Orange label with "Capitol" at bottom				
2832	The Long and Winding Road/For You Blue	1978	2.00	4.00	8.00
	—Purple label; label has reeded edge				
2832	The Long and Winding Road/For You Blue	1983	—	3.00	6.00
	—Black label with colorband				
2832	The Long and Winding Road/For You Blue	1988	—	2.50	5.00
	—Purple label; label has smooth edge				
4274	Got to Get You Into My Life/Helter Skelter	1976	—	3.00	6.00
	—Original: Orange label with "Capitol" at bottom, George Martin's name not on label				
4274	Got to Get You Into My Life/Helter Skelter	1976	2.50	5.00	10.00
	—Orange label with "Capitol" at bottom, George Martin's name is on label				
4274	Got to Get You Into My Life/Helter Skelter	1978	—	3.00	6.00
	—Purple label; label has reeded edge				
4274	Got to Get You Into My Life/Helter Skelter	1983	—	3.00	6.00
	—Black label with colorband				
4274	Got to Get You Into My Life/Helter Skelter	1988	—	2.50	5.00
	—Purple label; label has smooth edge				
4274 [PS]	Got to Get You Into My Life/Helter Skelter	1976	—	2.50	5.00
P-4274 [DJ]	Got to Get You Into My Life (mono/stereo)	1976	10.00	20.00	40.00
P-4274 [DJ]	Helter Skelter (mono/stereo)	1976	10.00	20.00	40.00
4347	Ob-La-Di, Ob-La-Da/Julia	1976	2.00	4.00	8.00
	—Original: Orange label with "Capitol" at bottom				
4347	Ob-La-Di, Ob-La-Da/Julia	1978	2.00	4.00	8.00
	—Purple label; label has reeded edge				
4347	Ob-La-Di, Ob-La-Da/Julia	1983	—	3.00	6.00
	—Black label with colorband				
4347	Ob-La-Di, Ob-La-Da/Julia	1988	—	2.50	5.00
	—Purple label; label has smooth edge				
4347 [PS]	Ob-La-Di, Ob-La-Da/Julia	1976	2.00	4.00	8.00
	—Sleeves are individually numbered; very low numbers (under 1000) can fetch premium prices				
P-4347 [DJ]	Ob-La-Di, Ob-La-Da (mono/stereo)	1976	10.00	20.00	40.00
4506 [PS]	Girl/You're Going to Lose That Girl	1977	3.75	7.50	15.00
	—Sleeve for a single that was never pressed				
P-4506 [DJ]	Girl (mono/stereo)	1977	50.00	100.00	200.00
	—Promo only; all colored vinyl versions are counterfeits				
4612	Sgt. Pepper's Lonely Hearts Club Band-With a Little Help from My Friends/A Day in the Life	1978	2.00	4.00	8.00
	—Original: Purple label; label has reeded edge				
4612	Sgt. Pepper's Lonely Hearts Club Band-With a Little Help from My Friends/A Day in the Life	1983	—	3.00	6.00
	—Black label with colorband				
4612	Sgt. Pepper's Lonely Hearts Club Band-With a Little Help from My Friends/A Day in the Life	1988	—	2.50	5.00
	—Purple label; label has smooth edge				
4612 [PS]	Sgt. Pepper's Lonely Hearts Club Band-With a Little Help from My Friends/A Day in the Life	1978	5.00	10.00	20.00
P-4612 [DJ]	Sgt. Pepper's Lonely Hearts Club Band-With a Little Help from My Friends (mono/stereo)	1978	10.00	20.00	40.00
B-5100	The Beatles' Movie Medley/Fab Four on Film	1982	12.50	25.00	50.00
	—Stock copy; not officially released, but some got out by mistake				
B-5100 [PS]	The Beatles' Movie Medley/Fab Four on Film	1982	5.00	10.00	20.00
PB-5100 [DJ]	The Beatles' Movie Medley/Fab Four on Film	1982	6.25	12.50	25.00
B-5107	The Beatles' Movie Medley/I'm Happy Just to Dance with You	1982	—	2.50	5.00

Number	Title (A Side/B Side)	Yr	VG	VG+	NM
B-5107 [PS]	The Beatles' Movie Medley/I'm Happy Just to Dance with You	1982	—	2.50	5.00
5112	I Want to Hold Your Hand/I Saw Her Standing There	1964	10.00	20.00	40.00
—First pressing credits "Walter Hofer" as B-side publisher					
5112	I Want to Hold Your Hand/I Saw Her Standing There	1964	8.75	17.50	35.00
—Second pressing credits "George Pincus and Sons" as B-side publisher					
5112	I Want to Hold Your Hand/I Saw Her Standing There	1964	7.50	15.00	30.00
—Third (and all later) pressings credit "Gil Music" as B-side publisher					
5112	I Want to Hold Your Hand/I Saw Her Standing There	1968	15.00	30.00	60.00
—Orange and yellow swirl label with "A Subsidiary Of" in perimeter print					
5112	I Want to Hold Your Hand/I Saw Her Standing There	1969	6.25	12.50	25.00
—Red and orange "target" label, round logo					
5112	I Want to Hold Your Hand/I Saw Her Standing There	1969	15.00	30.00	60.00
—Red and orange "target" label, dome logo					
5112	I Want to Hold Your Hand/I Saw Her Standing There	1976	2.50	5.00	10.00
—Orange label, "Capitol" logo on bottom					
5112	I Want to Hold Your Hand/I Saw Her Standing There	1978	3.75	7.50	15.00
—Purple label					
5112	I Want to Hold Your Hand/I Saw Her Standing There	1984	—	2.50	5.00
—20th anniversary reissue; black print on perimeter of label (1964 pressings are white)					
5112	I Want to Hold Your Hand/I Saw Her Standing There	1994	—	2.50	5.00
—30th anniversary reissue; has "NR-58123" engraved in record's trail-off area					
5112 [PS]	I Want to Hold Your Hand/I Saw Her Standing There	1964	25.00	50.00	100.00
—Die-cut, crops George Harrison's head in photo					
5112 [PS]	I Want to Hold Your Hand/I Saw Her Standing There	1964	25.00	50.00	100.00
—Straight cut, shows all of George Harrison's head					
5112 [PS]	I Want to Hold Your Hand/WMCA Good Guys	1964	500.00	1000.	2000.
—Giveaway from New York radio station with photo of WMCA DJs on rear					
5112 [PS]	I Want to Hold Your Hand/I Saw Her Standing There	1984	—	3.00	6.00
—Same as 1964 sleeve except has "1984" in small print, and Paul McCartney's cigarette is airbrushed out					
5112 [PS]	I Want to Hold Your Hand/I Saw Her Standing There	1994	—	2.00	4.00
—Same as 1964 sleeve except "Reg. U.S. Pat. Off." has periods (1964s do not). Also came with a plastic sleeve with a "30th Anniversary" and UPC stickers (add 25%)					
5150	Can't Buy Me Love/You Can't Do That	1964	7.50	15.00	30.00
—Original: Orange and yellow swirl, without "A Subsidiary Of"... in perimeter label print					
5150	Can't Buy Me Love/You Can't Do That	1964	2000.	3000.	4000.
—Yellow vinyl (unauthorized); value is conjecture					
5150	Can't Buy Me Love/You Can't Do That	1964	1000.	1500.	2000.
—Yellow and black vinyl (unauthorized); value is conjecture					
5150	Can't Buy Me Love/You Can't Do That	1968	12.50	25.00	50.00
—Orange and yellow swirl label with "A Subsidiary Of" in perimeter print					
5150	Can't Buy Me Love/You Can't Do That	1969	6.25	12.50	25.00
—Red and orange "target" label, dome logo					
5150	Can't Buy Me Love/You Can't Do That	1969	15.00	30.00	60.00
—Red and orange "target" label, round logo					
5150	Can't Buy Me Love/You Can't Do That	1976	—	3.00	6.00
—Orange label with "Capitol" at bottom					
5150	Can't Buy Me Love/You Can't Do That	1978	3.75	7.50	15.00
—Purple label					
5150 [PS]	Can't Buy Me Love/You Can't Do That	1964	200.00	400.00	800.00
—One of the rarest Beatles picture sleeves. Numerous counterfeits exist; if in doubt, see an expert.					
B-5189	Love Me Do/P.S. I Love You	1982	—	2.50	5.00
—Original: Orange and yellow swirl label, black print					
B-5189	Love Me Do/P.S. I Love You	1983	—	3.00	6.00
—Black label with colorband					
B-5189	Love Me Do/P.S. I Love You	1988	—	2.00	4.00
—Purple label; label has smooth edge					
B-5189 [PS]	Love Me Do/P.S. I Love You.	1982	—	2.50	5.00
PB-5189 [DJ]	Love Me Do (same on both sides).	1982	3.75	7.50	15.00
5222	A Hard Day's Night/I Should Have Known Better.	1964	7.50	15.00	30.00
—Original: Orange and yellow swirl, without "A Subsidiary Of"... in perimeter label print; first version credited both "Unart" and "Maclen" as publishers					
5222	A Hard Day's Night/I Should Have Known Better.	1964	7.50	15.00	30.00
—Orange and yellow swirl, without "A Subsidiary Of"... in perimeter label print; second version credited only "Maclen" as publishers					
5222	A Hard Day's Night/I Should Have Known Better	1968	12.50	25.00	50.00
—Orange and yellow swirl with "A Subsidiary Of"... on perimeter print in white					
5222	A Hard Day's Night/I Should Have Known Better	1968	25.00	50.00	100.00
—Orange and yellow swirl with "A Subsidiary Of"... on perimeter print in black					
5222	A Hard Day's Night/I Should Have Known Better	1969	15.00	30.00	60.00
—Red and orange "target" label with Capitol dome logo					
5222	A Hard Day's Night/I Should Have Known Better	1969	5.00	10.00	20.00
—Red and orange "target" label with Capitol round logo					
5222	A Hard Day's Night/I Should Have Known Better	1976	—	3.00	6.00
—Orange label with "Capitol" at bottom					
5222	A Hard Day's Night/I Should Have Known Better	1978	3.75	7.50	15.00
—Purple label					
5222 [PS]	A Hard Day's Night/I Should Have Known Better	1964	25.00	50.00	100.00

Number	Title (A Side/B Side)	Yr	VG	VG+	NM
5234	I'll Cry Instead/I'm Happy Just to Dance with You	1964	10.00	20.00	40.00
—Original: Orange and yellow swirl, without "A Subsidiary Of"... in perimeter label print					
5234	I'll Cry Instead/I'm Happy Just to Dance with You	1968	15.00	30.00	60.00
—Orange and yellow swirl label with "A Subsidiary Of" in perimeter print					
5234	I'll Cry Instead/I'm Happy Just to Dance with You	1969	17.50	35.00	70.00
—Red and orange "target" label with Capitol dome logo					
5234	I'll Cry Instead/I'm Happy Just to Dance with You	1969	5.00	10.00	20.00
—Red and orange "target" label with Capitol round logo					
5234	I'll Cry Instead/I'm Happy Just to Dance with You	1976	—	3.00	6.00
—Orange label with "Capitol" at bottom					
5234	I'll Cry Instead/I'm Happy Just to Dance with You	1978	3.75	7.50	15.00
—Purple label					
5234 [PS]	I'll Cry Instead/I'm Happy Just to Dance with You	1964	37.50	75.00	150.00
5235	And I Love Her/If I Fell	1964	7.50	15.00	30.00
—Original: Orange and yellow swirl, without "A Subsidiary Of"... in perimeter label print; publishers listed as "Unart" and "Maclen"					
5235	And I Love Her/If I Fell	1964	7.50	15.00	30.00
—Original: Orange and yellow swirl, without "A Subsidiary Of"... in perimeter label print; publishers listed as "Maclen" only					
5235	And I Love Her/If I Fell	1968	12.50	25.00	50.00
—Orange and yellow swirl with "A Subsidiary Of"... on perimeter print in white					
5235	And I Love Her/If I Fell	1968	18.75	37.50	75.00
—Orange and yellow swirl with "A Subsidiary Of"... on perimeter print in black					
5235	And I Love Her/If I Fell	1969	5.00	10.00	20.00
—Red and orange "target" label with Capitol dome logo					
5235	And I Love Her/If I Fell	1969	15.00	30.00	60.00
—Red and orange "target" label with Capitol round logo					
5235	And I Love Her/If I Fell	1976	—	3.00	6.00
—Orange label with "Capitol" at bottom					
5235	And I Love Her/If I Fell	1978	3.75	7.50	15.00
—Purple label					
5235 [PS]	And I Love Her/If I Fell	1964	30.00	60.00	120.00
5255	Matchbox/Slow Down	1964	7.50	15.00	30.00
—Original: Orange and yellow swirl, without "A Subsidiary Of"... in perimeter label print					
5255	Matchbox/Slow Down	1968	12.50	25.00	50.00
—Orange and yellow swirl label with "A Subsidiary Of" in perimeter print					
5255	Matchbox/Slow Down	1969	15.00	30.00	60.00
—Red and orange "target" label with Capitol dome logo					
5255	Matchbox/Slow Down	1969	5.00	10.00	20.00
—Red and orange "target" label with Capitol round logo					
5255	Matchbox/Slow Down	1976	—	3.00	6.00
—Orange label with "Capitol" at bottom					
5255	Matchbox/Slow Down	1978	3.75	7.50	15.00
—Purple label					
5255 [PS]	Matchbox/Slow Down	1964	37.50	75.00	150.00
5327	I Feel Fine/She's a Woman	1964	7.50	15.00	30.00
—Original: Orange and yellow swirl, without "A Subsidiary Of"... in perimeter label print					
5327	I Feel Fine/She's a Woman	1968	12.50	25.00	50.00
—Orange and yellow swirl label with "A Subsidiary Of" in perimeter print					
5327	I Feel Fine/She's a Woman	1969	5.00	10.00	20.00
—Red and orange "target" label with Capitol dome logo					
5327	I Feel Fine/She's a Woman	1969	15.00	30.00	60.00
—Red and orange "target" label with Capitol round logo					
5327	I Feel Fine/She's a Woman	1976	—	3.00	6.00
—Orange label with "Capitol" at bottom					
5327	I Feel Fine/She's a Woman	1978	3.75	7.50	15.00
—Purple label					
5327 [PS]	I Feel Fine/She's a Woman	1964	20.00	40.00	80.00
5371	Eight Days a Week/I Don't Want to Spoil the Party	1965	7.50	15.00	30.00
—Original: Orange and yellow swirl, without "A Subsidiary Of"... in perimeter label print					
5371	Eight Days a Week/I Don't Want to Spoil the Party	1968	12.50	25.00	50.00
—Orange and yellow swirl label with "A Subsidiary Of" in perimeter print					
5371	Eight Days a Week/I Don't Want to Spoil the Party	1969	15.00	30.00	60.00
—Red and orange "target" label with Capitol dome logo					
5371	Eight Days a Week/I Don't Want to Spoil the Party	1969	5.00	10.00	20.00
—Red and orange "target" label with Capitol round logo					
5371	Eight Days a Week/I Don't Want to Spoil the Party	1976	—	3.00	6.00
—Orange label with "Capitol" at bottom					
5371	Eight Days a Week/I Don't Want to Spoil the Party	1978	3.75	7.50	15.00
—Purple label					
5371 [PS]	Eight Days a Week/I Don't Want to Spoil the Party	1965	6.25	12.50	25.00
—Die-cut sleeve					
5371 [PS]	Eight Days a Week/I Don't Want to Spoil the Party	1965	18.75	37.50	75.00
—Straight-cut sleeve					
5407	Ticket to Ride/Yes It Is.	1965	7.50	15.00	30.00
—Original: Orange and yellow swirl, without "A Subsidiary Of"... in perimeter label print					
5407	Ticket to Ride/Yes It Is.	1968	12.50	25.00	50.00
—Orange and yellow swirl with "A Subsidiary Of"... on perimeter print in white					
5407	Ticket to Ride/Yes It Is.	1968	25.00	50.00	100.00
—Orange and yellow swirl with "A Subsidiary Of"... on perimeter print in black					
5407	Ticket to Ride/Yes It Is.	1969	15.00	30.00	60.00
—Red and orange "target" label with Capitol dome logo					
5407	Ticket to Ride/Yes It Is.	1969	5.00	10.00	20.00
—Red and orange "target" label with Capitol round logo					
5407	Ticket to Ride/Yes It Is.	1976	—	3.00	6.00
—Orange label with "Capitol" at bottom					
5407	Ticket to Ride/Yes It Is	1978	3.75	7.50	15.00
—Purple label					
5407 [PS]	Ticket to Ride/Yes It Is	1965	25.00	50.00	100.00
B-5439 [PS]	Leave My Kitten Alone/Ob-La-Di, Ob-La-Da	1985	12.50	25.00	50.00
—Sleeve for a record that was never released, not even as a promo					
5476	Help!/I'm Down	1965	7.50	15.00	30.00
—Original: Orange and yellow swirl, without "A Subsidiary Of"... in perimeter label print					

Number	Title (A Side/B Side)	Yr	VG	VG+	NM
5476	Help!/I'm Down	1968	12.50	25.00	50.00
—Orange and yellow swirl with "A Subsidiary Of"... on perimeter print in white					
5476	Help!/I'm Down	1968	25.00	50.00	100.00
—Orange and yellow swirl with "A Subsidiary Of"... on perimeter print in black					
5476	Help!/I'm Down	1969	15.00	30.00	60.00
—Red and orange "target" label with Capitol dome logo					
5476	Help!/I'm Down	1969	5.00	10.00	20.00
—Red and orange "target" label with Capitol round logo					
5476	Help!/I'm Down	1976	—	3.00	6.00
—Orange label with "Capitol" at bottom					
5476	Help!/I'm Down	1978	3.75	7.50	15.00
—Purple label					
5476 [PS]	Help!/I'm Down	1965	18.75	37.50	75.00
5498	Yesterday/Act Naturally	1965	7.50	15.00	30.00
—Original: Orange and yellow swirl, without "A Subsidiary Of"... in perimeter label print					
5498	Yesterday/Act Naturally	1968	12.50	25.00	50.00
—Orange and yellow swirl with "A Subsidiary Of"... on perimeter print in white					
5498	Yesterday/Act Naturally	1968	25.00	50.00	100.00
—Orange and yellow swirl with "A Subsidiary Of"... on perimeter print in black					
5498	Yesterday/Act Naturally	1969	15.00	30.00	60.00
—Red and orange "target" label with Capitol dome logo					
5498	Yesterday/Act Naturally	1969	5.00	10.00	20.00
—Red and orange "target" label with Capitol round logo					
5498	Yesterday/Act Naturally	1976	—	3.00	6.00
—Orange label with "Capitol" at bottom					
5498	Yesterday/Act Naturally	1978	3.75	7.50	15.00
—Purple label					
5498 [PS]	Yesterday/Act Naturally	1965	25.00	50.00	100.00
5555	We Can Work It Out/Day Tripper	1965	7.50	15.00	30.00
—Original: Orange and yellow swirl, without "A Subsidiary Of"... in perimeter label print					
5555	We Can Work It Out/Day Tripper	1968	12.50	25.00	50.00
—Orange and yellow swirl label with "A Subsidiary Of" in perimeter print					
5555	We Can Work It Out/Day Tripper	1969	15.00	30.00	60.00
—Red and orange "target" label with Capitol dome logo					
5555	We Can Work It Out/Day Tripper	1969	5.00	10.00	20.00
—Red and orange "target" label with Capitol round logo					
5555	We Can Work It Out/Day Tripper	1969	500.00	1000.	1500.
—Red and white "Starline" label (mispress)					
5555	We Can Work It Out/Day Tripper	1976	—	3.00	6.00
—Orange label with "Capitol" at bottom					
5555	We Can Work It Out/Day Tripper	1978	3.75	7.50	15.00
—Purple label					
5555 [PS]	We Can Work It Out/Day Tripper	1978	15.00	30.00	60.00
5587	Nowhere Man/What Goes On	1966	6.25	12.50	25.00
—Original: Orange and yellow swirl, without "A Subsidiary Of"... in perimeter label print; composers of B-side listed as "John Lennon-Paul McCartney"					
5587	Nowhere Man/What Goes On	1966	12.50	25.00	50.00
—Orange and yellow swirl, without "A Subsidiary Of"... in perimeter label print; B-side composers listed as "Lennon-McCartney-Starkey"					
5587	Nowhere Man/What Goes On	1968	12.50	25.00	50.00
—Orange and yellow swirl label with "A Subsidiary Of" in perimeter print					
5587	Nowhere Man/What Goes On	1969	15.00	30.00	60.00
—Red and orange "target" label with Capitol dome logo					
5587	Nowhere Man/What Goes On	1969	5.00	10.00	20.00
—Red and orange "target" label with Capitol round logo					
5587	Nowhere Man/What Goes On	1976	—	3.00	6.00
—Orange label with "Capitol" at bottom					
5587	Nowhere Man/What Goes On	1978	3.75	7.50	15.00
—Purple label					
5587 [PS]	Nowhere Man/What Goes On	1966	10.00	20.00	40.00
B-5624	Twist and Shout/There's a Place	1986	—	2.50	5.00
—Black label with colorband					
B-5624	Twist and Shout/There's a Place	1988	—	2.50	5.00
—Purple label; label has smooth edge					
P-B-5624 [DJ]	Twist and Shout (same on both sides)	1986	3.75	7.50	15.00
5651	Paperback Writer/Rain	1966	6.25	12.50	25.00
—Original: Orange and yellow swirl, without "A Subsidiary Of"... in perimeter label print					
5651	Paperback Writer/Rain	1968	12.50	25.00	50.00
—Orange and yellow swirl with "A Subsidiary Of"... on perimeter print in white					
5651	Paperback Writer/Rain	1968	25.00	50.00	100.00
—Orange and yellow swirl with "A Subsidiary Of"... on perimeter print in black					
5651	Paperback Writer/Rain	1969	15.00	30.00	60.00
—Red and orange "target" label with Capitol dome logo					
5651	Paperback Writer/Rain	1969	5.00	10.00	20.00
—Red and orange "target" label with Capitol round logo					
5651	Paperback Writer/Rain	1976	—	3.00	6.00
—Orange label with "Capitol" at bottom					
5651	Paperback Writer/Rain	1978	3.75	7.50	15.00
—Purple label					
5651 [PS]	Paperback Writer/Rain	1966	18.75	37.50	75.00
5715	Yellow Submarine/Eleanor Rigby	1966	6.25	12.50	25.00
—Original: Orange and yellow swirl, without "A Subsidiary Of"... in perimeter label print; print on perimeter is white					
5715	Yellow Submarine/Eleanor Rigby	1966	12.50	25.00	50.00
—Orange and yellow swirl, without "A Subsidiary Of"... in perimeter label print; print on perimeter is yellow (mispress)					
5715	Yellow Submarine/Eleanor Rigby	1968	12.50	25.00	50.00
—Orange and yellow swirl label with "A Subsidiary Of" in perimeter print					
5715	Yellow Submarine/Eleanor Rigby	1969	5.00	10.00	20.00
—Red and orange "target" label with Capitol dome logo					
5715	Yellow Submarine/Eleanor Rigby	1969	15.00	30.00	60.00
—Red and orange "target" label with Capitol round logo					
5715	Yellow Submarine/Eleanor Rigby	1976	—	3.00	6.00
—Orange label with "Capitol" at bottom					
5715	Yellow Submarine/Eleanor Rigby	1978	3.75	7.50	15.00
—Purple label					
5715 [PS]	Yellow Submarine/Eleanor Rigby	1966	25.00	50.00	100.00
5810	Penny Lane/Strawberry Fields Forever	1967	6.25	12.50	25.00
—Original: Orange and yellow swirl, without "A Subsidiary Of"... in perimeter label print; "Penny Lane" time listed as 3:00					
5810	Penny Lane/Strawberry Fields Forever	1967	7.50	15.00	30.00
—Orange and yellow swirl, without "A Subsidiary Of"... in perimeter label print; "Penny Lane" time listed as 2:57					
5810	Penny Lane/Strawberry Fields Forever	1968	12.50	25.00	50.00
—Orange and yellow swirl label with "A Subsidiary Of" in perimeter print					
5810	Penny Lane/Strawberry Fields Forever	1969	15.00	30.00	60.00
—Red and orange "target" label with Capitol dome logo					
5810	Penny Lane/Strawberry Fields Forever	1969	5.00	10.00	20.00
—Red and orange "target" label with Capitol round logo					
5810	Penny Lane/Strawberry Fields Forever	1976	—	3.00	6.00
—Orange label with "Capitol" at bottom					
5810	Penny Lane/Strawberry Fields Forever	1978	3.75	7.50	15.00
—Purple label					
5810 [PS]	Penny Lane/Strawberry Fields Forever	1967	25.00	50.00	100.00
P 5810 [DJ]	Penny Lane/Strawberry Fields Forever	1967	75.00	150.00	300.00
—Light green promo; most copies have an extra trumpet solo at the end of "Penny Lane"					
P 5810 [DJ]	Penny Lane/Strawberry Fields Forever	1967	150.00	300.00	600.00
—Light green promo; a few copies have no trumpet solo at the end of "Penny Lane"					
5964	All You Need Is Love/Baby, You're a Rich Man	1967	6.25	12.50	25.00
—Original: Orange and yellow swirl, without "A Subsidiary Of"... in perimeter label print					
5964	All You Need Is Love/Baby, You're a Rich Man	1968	12.50	25.00	50.00
—Orange and yellow swirl label with "A Subsidiary Of" in perimeter print					
5964	All You Need Is Love/Baby, You're a Rich Man	1969	18.75	37.50	75.00
—Red and orange "target" label with Capitol dome logo					
5964	All You Need Is Love/Baby, You're a Rich Man	1969	5.00	10.00	20.00
—Red and orange "target" label with Capitol round logo					
5964	All You Need Is Love/Baby, You're a Rich Man	1976	—	3.00	6.00
—Orange label with "Capitol" at bottom					
5964	All You Need Is Love/Baby, You're a Rich Man	1978	3.75	7.50	15.00
—Purple label					
5964 [PS]	All You Need Is Love/Baby, You're a Rich Man	1967	10.00	20.00	40.00
P 5964 [DJ]	All You Need Is Love/Baby, You're a Rich Man	1967	62.50	125.00	250.00
—Light green label promo					
S7-17488	Birthday/Taxman	1994	12.50	25.00	50.00
—Black vinyl "error" pressing					
S7-17488	Birthday/Taxman	1994	—	2.00	4.00
—Green vinyl					
S7-17688	She Loves You/I'll Get You	1994	—	2.00	4.00
—Red vinyl					
S7-17689	I Want to Hold Your Hand/This Boy	1994	—	2.00	4.00
—Clear vinyl					
S7-17690	Can't Buy Me Love/You Can't Do That	1994	—	2.00	4.00
—Gren vinyl					
S7-17691	Help!/I'm Down	1994	—	2.00	4.00
—White vinyl					
S7-17692	A Hard Day's Night/Things We Said Today	1994	—	2.00	4.00
—White vinyl					
S7-17693	All You Need Is Love/Baby You're a Rich Man	1994	—	2.00	4.00
—Pink vinyl					
S7-17694	Hey Jude/Revolution	1994	—	2.00	4.00
—Blue vinyl					
S7-17695	Let It Be/You Know My Name (Look Up My Number)	1994	—	2.00	4.00
—Yellow vinyl					
S7-17696	Yellow Submarine/Eleanor Rigby	1994	—	2.00	4.00
—Yellow vinyl					
S7-17697	Strawberry Fields Forever/Penny Lane	1994	—	2.00	4.00
—Red vinyl					
S7-17698	Something/Come Together	1994	—	2.00	4.00
—Blue vinyl					
S7-17699	Twist and Shout/There's a Place	1994	—	2.00	4.00
—Pink vinyl					
S7-17700	Here Comes the Sun/Octopus's Garden	1994	—	2.00	4.00
—Gold/orange vinyl					
S7-17701	Sgt. Pepper's Lonely Hearts Club Band-With a Little Help from My Friends/A Day in the Life	1994	—	2.00	4.00
—Clear vinyl					
S7-18888	Norwegian Wood/If I Needed Someone	1995	12.50	25.00	50.00
—Green vinyl; 1,000 pressed, given by Collectors' Choice Music to buyers of Beatles reissue LPs					
S7-18889	You've Got to Hide Your Love Away/I've Just Seen a Face	1996	—	2.00	4.00
—Gold/orange vinyl					
S7-18890	Magical Mystery Tour/The Fool on the Hill	1996	—	2.00	4.00
—Yellow vinyl					
S7-18891	Across the Universe/Two of Us	1996	—	2.00	4.00
—Clear vinyl					
S7-18892	While My Guitar Gently Weeps/Blackbird	1996	—	2.00	4.00
—Blue vinyl					
S7-18893	It's All Too Much/Only a Northern Song	1996	—	2.00	4.00
—Blue vinyl					
S7-18894	Nowhere Man/What Goes On	1996	—	2.00	4.00
—Green vinyl					
S7-18895	We Can Work It Out/Day Tripper	1996	—	2.00	4.00
—Pink vinyl					
S7-18896	Lucy in the Sky with Diamonds/When I'm 64	1996	—	2.00	4.00
—Red vinyl					
S7-18897	Here, There and Everywhere/Good Day Sunshine	1996	—	2.00	4.00
—Yellow vinyl					

Number	Title (A Side/B Side)	Yr	VG	VG+	NM
S7-18898	The Long and Winding Road/For You Blue	1996	—	2.00	4.00
—Blue vinyl					
S7-18899	Got to Get You Into My Life/Helter Skelter	1996	—	2.00	4.00
—Gold/orange vinyl					
S7-18900	Ob-La-Di, Ob-La-Da/Julia	1996	—	2.00	4.00
—Clear vinyl					
S7-18901	Yesterday/Act Naturally	1996	—	2.00	4.00
—Pink vinyl					
S7-18902	Paperback Writer/Rain	1996	—	2.00	4.00
—Red vinyl					
S7-19341	Norwegian Wood (This Bird Has Flown)/If I Needed Someone	1996	—	—	3.00
S7-56785	Love Me Do/P.S. I Love You	1992	—	2.00	4.00
S7-56785	Love Me Do/P.S. I Love You	1992	7.50	15.00	30.00
—Small pressing on red vinyl "by mistake"					
72133	Roll Over Beethoven/Please Mister Postman	1964	12.50	25.00	50.00
—Orange and yellow swirl; Canadian release that was heavily imported to the U.S.					
72144	All My Loving/This Boy	1964	12.50	25.00	50.00
—Orange and yellow swirl; Canadian release that was heavily imported to the U.S.					
72144	All My Loving/This Boy	1971	25.00	50.00	100.00
—Canadian number with U.S. labels (red and orange "target" label)					
7PRO-79551/2 [DJ]	Love Me Do/P.S. I Love You	1992	6.25	12.50	25.00
7PRO-79551/2 [PS]	Love Me Do/P.S. I Love You	1992	6.25	12.50	25.00
CAPITOL STARLINE					
6061	Twist and Shout/There's a Place	1965	30.00	60.00	120.00
—Green swirl label					
6062	Love Me Do/P.S. I Love You	1965	30.00	60.00	120.00
—Green swirl label					
6063	Please Please Me/From Me to You	1965	30.00	60.00	120.00
—Green swirl label					
6064	Do You Want to Know a Secret/Thank You Girl	1965	30.00	60.00	120.00
—Green swirl label					
6065	Roll Over Beethoven/Misery	1965	30.00	60.00	120.00
—Green swirl label					
6065	Roll Over Beethoven/Misery	1971	7.50	15.00	30.00
—Red and orange "target" label					
6066	Boys/Kansas City	1965	20.00	40.00	80.00
—Green swirl label					
6066	Boys/Kansas City	1971	7.50	15.00	30.00
—Red and orange "target" label					
6278	I Want to Hold Your Hand/I Saw Her Standing There	1981	5.00	10.00	20.00
—Originals have blue labels					
6279	Can't Buy Me Love/You Can't Do That	1981	2.00	4.00	8.00
—Originals have blue labels					
6281	A Hard Day's Night/I Should Have Known Better	1981	2.00	4.00	8.00
—Originals have blue labels					
6282	I'll Cry Instead/I'm Happy Just to Dance with You	1981	2.00	4.00	8.00
—Originals have blue labels					
6283	And I Love Her/If I Fell	1981	2.00	4.00	8.00
—Originals have blue labels					
6284	Matchbox/Slow Down	1981	2.00	4.00	8.00
—Originals have blue labels					
6286	I Feel Fine/She's a Woman	1981	2.00	4.00	8.00
—Originals have blue labels					
6287	Eight Days a Week/I Don't Want to Spoil the Party	1981	2.00	4.00	8.00
—Originals have blue labels					
6288	Ticket to Ride/Yes It Is	1981	2.00	4.00	8.00
—Originals have blue labels					
6290	Help!/I'm Down	1981	2.00	4.00	8.00
—Originals have blue labels					
6291	Yesterday/Act Naturally	1981	2.00	4.00	8.00
—Originals have blue labels					
6293	We Can Work It Out/Day Tripper	1981	2.00	4.00	8.00
—Originals have blue labels					
6294	Nowhere Man/What Goes On	1981	2.00	4.00	8.00
—Originals have blue labels					
6296	Paperback Writer/Rain	1981	2.00	4.00	8.00
—Originals have blue labels					
6297	Yellow Submarine/Eleanor Rigby	1981	2.00	4.00	8.00
—Originals have blue labels					
6299	Penny Lane/Strawberry Fields Forever	1981	2.00	4.00	8.00
—Originals have blue labels					
6300	All You Need Is Love/Baby You're a Rich Man	1981	2.00	4.00	8.00
—Originals have blue labels					
CAPITOL/EVATONE					
420826cs	All My Loving/You've Got to Hide Your Love Away	1982	2.50	5.00	10.00
—Flexi-disc issued as giveaway by The Musicland Group; "Musicland" version					
420826cs	All My Loving/You've Got to Hide Your Love Away	1982	5.00	10.00	20.00
—Flexi-disc issued as giveaway by The Musicland Group; "Discount" version					
420826cs	All My Loving/You've Got to Hide Your Love Away	1982	6.25	12.50	25.00
—Flexi-disc issued as giveaway by The Musicland Group; "Sam Goody" version					
420827cs	Magical Mystery Tour/Here Comes the Sun	1982	2.50	5.00	10.00
—Flexi-disc issued as giveaway by The Musicland Group; "Musicland" version					
420827cs	Magical Mystery Tour/Here Comes the Sun	1982	5.00	10.00	20.00
—Flexi-disc issued as giveaway by The Musicland Group; "Discount" version					
420827cs	Magical Mystery Tour/Here Comes the Sun	1982	6.25	12.50	25.00
—Flexi-disc issued as giveaway by The Musicland Group; "Sam Goody" version					
420828cs	Rocky Raccoon/Why Don't We Do It in the Road?	1982	2.50	5.00	10.00
—Flexi-disc issued as giveaway by The Musicland Group; "Musicland" version					
420828cs	Rocky Raccoon/Why Don't We Do It in the Road?	1982	5.00	10.00	20.00
—Flexi-disc issued as giveaway by The Musicland Group; "Discount" version					
420828cs	Rocky Raccoon/Why Don't We Do It in the Road?	1982	6.25	12.50	25.00
—Flexi-disc issued as giveaway by The Musicland Group; "Sam Goody" version					

Number	Title (A Side/B Side)	Yr	VG	VG+	NM
830771 X	Till There Was You/Three Cool Cats	1983	—	3.00	6.00
—Flexi-disc issued as giveaway with a book					
1214825cs	German Medley	1983	15.00	30.00	60.00
—Flexi-disc given away by House of Guitars in New York					
CICADELIC/BIODISC					
001	A Hard Day's Night Open End Interview	1990	3.75	7.50	15.00
—Limited edition of 700; lower numbers increase value substantially					
001	A Hard Day's Night Open End Interview	1990	7.50	15.00	30.00
—"Records Etc." pressing					
002	Help! Open End Interview	1990	—	2.50	5.00
002 [PS]	Help! Open End Interview	1990	—	2.50	5.00
COLLECTABLES					
1501	I'm Gonna Sit Right Down and Cry Over You/Roll Over Beethoven	1982	—	—	3.00
1501 [PS]	I'm Gonna Sit Right Down and Cry Over You/Roll Over Beethoven	1982	—	—	3.00
1502	Hippy Hippy Shake/Sweet Little Sixteen	1982	—	—	3.00
1502 [PS]	Hippy Hippy Shake/Sweet Little Sixteen	1982	—	—	3.00
1503	Lend Me Your Comb/Your Feets Too Big	1982	—	—	3.00
1503 [PS]	Lend Me Your Comb/Your Feets Too Big	1982	—	—	3.00
1504	Where Have You Been All My Life/Mr. Moonlight	1982	—	—	3.00
1504 [PS]	Where Have You Been All My Life/Mr. Moonlight	1982	—	—	3.00
1505	A Taste of Honey/Besame Mucho	1982	—	—	3.00
1505 [PS]	A Taste of Honey/Besame Mucho	1982	—	—	3.00
1506	Till There Was You/Everybody's Trying to Be My Baby	1982	—	—	3.00
1506 [PS]	Till There Was You/Everybody's Trying to Be My Baby	1982	—	—	3.00
1507	Kansas City-Hey Hey Hey Hey/Ain't Nothing Shakin Like the Leaves on a Tree	1982	—	—	3.00
1507 [PS]	Kansas City-Hey Hey Hey Hey/Ain't Nothing Shakin Like the Leaves on a Tree	1982	—	—	3.00
1508	To Know Her Is To Love Her/Little Queenie	1982	—	—	3.00
1508 [PS]	To Know Her Is To Love Her/Little Queenie	1982	—	—	3.00
1509	Falling in Love Again/Sheila	1982	—	—	3.00
1509 [PS]	Falling in Love Again/Sheila	1982	—	—	3.00
1510	Be-Bop-a-Lula/Hallelujah I Love Her So	1982	—	—	3.00
1510 [PS]	Be-Bop-a-Lula/Hallelujah I Love Her So	1982	—	—	3.00
1511	Red Sails in the Sunset/Matchbox	1982	—	—	3.00
1511 [PS]	Red Sails in the Sunset/Matchbox	1982	—	—	3.00
1512	Talkin' Bout You/Shimmy Shake	1982	—	—	3.00
1512 [PS]	Talkin' Bout You/Shimmy Shake	1982	—	—	3.00
1513	Long Tall Sally/I Remember You	1982	—	—	3.00
1513 [PS]	Long Tall Sally/I Remember You	1982	—	—	3.00
1514	Ask Me Why/Twist and Shout	1982	—	—	3.00
1514 [PS]	Ask Me Why/Twist and Shout	1982	—	—	3.00
1515	I Saw Her Standing There/Can't Help It "Blue Angel"	1982	—	—	3.00
—B-side is actually "Reminiscing"					
1515 [PS]	I Saw Her Standing There/Can't Help It "Blue Angel"	1982	—	—	3.00
1516	I'll Try Anyway/I Don't Know Why I Do (I Just Do)	1987	2.50	5.00	10.00
—Despite label credit to The Beatles, both are Peter Best recordings					
1517	She's Not the Only Girl in Town/More Than I Need Myself	1987	2.50	5.00	10.00
—Despite label credit to The Beatles, both are Peter Best recordings					
1518	I'll Have Everything Too/I'm Checking Out Now Baby	1987	2.50	5.00	10.00
—Despite label credit to The Beatles, both are Peter Best recordings					
1519	How'd You Get to Know Her Name/If You Can't Get Her	1987	2.50	5.00	10.00
—Despite label credit to The Beatles, both are Peter Best recordings					
1520	Cry for a Shadow/Rock and Roll Music	1987	—	2.50	5.00
—Despite label credit to The Beatles, B-side is a Peter Best recording					
1521	Let's Dance/If You Love Me Baby	1987	—	3.00	6.00
—Despite label credit to The Beatles, A-side is a Tony Sheridan solo recording					
1522	What'd I Say/Sweet Georgia Brown	1987	—	3.00	6.00
—Despite label credit to The Beatles, A-side is a Tony Sheridan solo recording					
1523	Ruby Baby/Ya Ya	1987	—	3.00	6.00
—Despite label credit to The Beatles, both are by Tony Sheridan without the Fab Four					
1524	Why/I'll Try Anyway	1987	—	3.00	6.00
—Despite label credit to The Beatles, B-side is a Peter Best recording					
DECCA					
31382	My Bonnie/The Saints	1962	7500.	11250.	15000.
—By "Tony Sheridan and the Beat Brothers"; black label with color bars (all-black label with star under "Decca" should be a counterfeit)					
31382 [DJ]	My Bonnie/The Saints	1962	1000.	2000.	3000.
—By "Tony Sheridan and the Beat Brothers"; pink label, star on label under "Decca"					
EVA-TONE					
830771X [DJ]	Til There Was You/Three Cool Cats (both on same side)	1983	—	3.00	6.00
—Red plastic flexidisc; issued as giveaway with a Beatles price guide					
MGM					
13213	My Bonnie (My Bonnie Lies Over the Ocean)/The Saints (When the Saints Go Marching In)	1964	10.00	20.00	40.00
—The Beatles with Tony Sheridan; no reference to LP on label					
13213	My Bonnie (My Bonnie Lies Over the Ocean)/The Saints (When the Saints Go Marching In)	1964	12.50	25.00	50.00
—The Beatles with Tony Sheridan; LP number on label					
13213 [DJ]	My Bonnie (My Bonnie Lies Over the Ocean)/The Saints (When the Saints Go Marching In)	1964	75.00	150.00	300.00
—The Beatles with Tony Sheridan					
13213 [PS]	My Bonnie (My Bonnie Lies Over the Ocean)/				

Number	Title (A Side/B Side)	Yr	VG	VG+	NM
	The Saints (When the Saints Go Marching In)	1964	30.00	60.00	120.00
—The Beatles with Tony Sheridan					
13227	Why/Cry for a Shadow	1964	37.50	75.00	150.00
—The Beatles with Tony Sheridan					
13227 [DJ]	Why/Cry for a Shadow	1964	62.50	125.00	250.00
—The Beatles with Tony Sheridan					
13227 [PS]	Why/Cry for a Shadow	1964	100.00	200.00	400.00
—The Beatles with Tony Sheridan					
OLDIES 45					
#149	Do You Want to Know a Secret/Thank You Girl	1965	3.75	7.50	15.00
#150	Please Please Me/From Me to You	1965	3.75	7.50	15.00
#151	Love Me Do/P.S. I Love You	1965	3.75	7.50	15.00
#152	Twist and Shout/There's a Place	1965	3.75	7.50	15.00
SWAN					
4152	She Loves You/I'll Get You	1963	150.00	300.00	600.00
—Semi-glossy white label/red print; "Don't Drop Out" not on label					
4152	She Loves You/I'll Get You	1963	162.50	325.00	650.00
—Flat white label/red print, "Don't Drop Out" not on label					
4152	She Loves You/I'll Get You	1963	162.50	325.00	650.00
—Semi-glossy white label/red print, "Don't Drop Out" on label					
4152	She Loves You/I'll Get You	1963	150.00	300.00	600.00
—Semi-glossy white label/blue printing					
4152	She Loves You/I'll Get You	1964	10.00	20.00	40.00
—Black label, silver print, "Don't Drop Out" not on label					
4152	She Loves You/I'll Get You	1964	7.50	15.00	30.00
—Black label, silver print, "Don't Drop Out" on label					
4152	She Loves You/I'll Get You	1964	12.50	25.00	50.00
—Black label, silver print, "Produced by George Martin" on both labels					
4152	She Loves You/I'll Get You	1964	12.50	25.00	50.00
—Black label, silver print, "Produced by George Martin" on only one label					
4152	She Loves You/I'll Get You	196?	5.00	10.00	20.00
—Black label, silver print, "Don't Drop Out" not on label, smaller numbers in trailoff area					
4152	She Loves You/I'll Get You	196?	12.50	25.00	50.00
—White label, red or maroon print, same as above					
4152 [DJ]	She Loves You/I'll Get You	1963	125.00	250.00	500.00
—Thick print, no "Don't Drop Out" on label					
4152 [DJ]	She Loves You/I'll Get You	1963	112.50	225.00	450.00
—Thin print, "Don't Drop Out" on label					
4152 [DJ]	She Loves You/I'll Get You	1963	125.00	250.00	500.00
—Flat white label, no "Don't Drop Out" on label					
4152 [DJ]	I'll Get You (one-sided)	1964	200.00	400.00	600.00
4152 [PS]	She Loves You/I'll Get You	1964	30.00	60.00	120.00
4182	Sie Liebt Dich (She Loves You)/I'll Get You	1964	37.50	75.00	150.00
—White label, "Sie Liebt Dich (She Loves You)" on one line					
4182	Sie Liebt Dich (She Loves You)/I'll Get You	1964	37.50	75.00	150.00
—White label, "(She Loves You)" under "Sie Liebt Dich," narrow print					
4182	Sie Liebt Dich (She Loves You)/I'll Get You	1964	37.50	75.00	150.00
—White label, "(She Loves You)" under "Sie Liebt Dich," wide red print					
4182	Sie Liebt Dich (She Loves You)/I'll Get You	1964	43.75	87.50	175.00
—White label, "(She Loves You)" under "Sie Liebt Dich," wide orange print					
4182 [DJ]	Sie Liebt Dich (She Loves You)/I'll Get You	1964	100.00	200.00	400.00
—White label, "(She Loves You)" under "Sie Liebt Dich"					
4182 [DJ]	Sie Liebt Dich (She Loves You)/I'll Get You	1964	112.50	225.00	450.00
—White label, "Sie Liebt Dich (She Loves You)" on one line					
TOLLIE					
9001	Twist and Shout/There's a Place	1964	12.50	25.00	50.00
—Yellow label, green print, "tollie" lowercase					
9001	Twist and Shout/There's a Place	1964	12.50	25.00	50.00
—Yellow label, black print, "TOLLIE" stands alone					
9001	Twist and Shout/There's a Place	1964	12.50	25.00	50.00
—Yellow label, black print, black "tollie" in box					
9001	Twist and Shout/There's a Place	1964	15.00	30.00	60.00
—Yellow label, black print, purple "tollie" in box					
9001	Twist and Shout/There's a Place.	1964	12.50	25.00	50.00
—Yellow label, black print, black "TOLLIE" in thin box					
9001	Twist and Shout/There's a Place.	1964	18.75	37.50	75.00
—Yellow label, black print, "TOLLIE" in brackets					
9001	Twist and Shout/There's a Place.	1964	15.00	30.00	60.00
—Yellow label, blue print					
9001	Twist and Shout/There's a Place.	1964	20.00	40.00	80.00
—Yellow label, purple print					
9001	Twist and Shout/There's a Place.	1964	20.00	40.00	80.00
—Yellow label, green print, "TOLLIE" uppercase					
9001	Twist and Shout/There's a Place.	1964	15.00	30.00	60.00
—Black label, silver print					
9008	Love Me Do/P.S. I Love You.	1964	12.50	25.00	50.00
—Yellow label, black print (any logo or print variation)					
9008	Love Me Do/P.S. I Love You.	1964	12.50	25.00	50.00
—Yellow label, blue/green print					
9008	Love Me Do/P.S. I Love You.	1964	15.00	30.00	60.00
—Black label, silver print					
9008 [DJ]	Love Me Do/P.S. I Love You.	1964	100.00	200.00	400.00
9008 [PS]	Love Me Do/P.S. I Love You.	1964	37.50	75.00	150.00
UNITED ARTISTS					
SP-2357 [DJ]	A Hard Day's Night Theatre Lobby Spot	1964	500.00	1000.	1500.
UAEP 10029 [DJ]	A Hard Day's Night Open End Interview	1964	500.00	1000.	1500.
ULP-42370	Let It Be Radio Spots	1970	400.00	800.00	1200.
VEE JAY					
(no #) [PS]	We Wish You a Merry Christmas and a Happy New Year	1964	20.00	40.00	80.00
—Used with any Vee Jay or Tollie Beatles single in 1964-65 holiday season					
Spec. DJ No. 8	Ask Me Why/Anna	1964?	5000.	7500.	10000.
—One of the more controversial items in Beatles collecting, but it is nonetheless authentic					

Number	Title (A Side/B Side)	Yr	VG	VG+	NM
498	Please Please Me/Ask Me Why	1963	800.00	1200.	1600.
—Misspelled "The Beattles"; number is "#498"					
498	Please Please Me/Ask Me Why	1963	750.00	1125.	1500.
—Misspelled "The Beattles"; number is "VJ 498"					
498	Please Please Me/Ask Me Why	1963	800.00	1200.	1600.
—Correct spelling; number is "#498"					
498	Please Please Me/Ask Me Why	1963	300.00	600.00	900.00
—Correct spelling; number is "VJ 498"; thick print					
498	Please Please Me/Ask Me Why	1963	1000.	1500.	2000.
—Correct spelling; number is "VJ 498"; brackets label					
498 [DJ]	Please Please Me/Ask Me Why	1963	550.00	825.00	1100.
—Misspelled "The Beattles"					
522	From Me to You/Thank You Girl	1963	150.00	300.00	600.00
—Black rainbow label; "Vee Jay" in oval					
522	From Me to You/Thank You Girl	1963	300.00	600.00	900.00
—Black rainbow label; "VJ" in brackets					
522	From Me to You/Thank You Girl	1963	200.00	400.00	800.00
—Plain black label					
522 [DJ]	From Me to You/Thank You Girl	1963	125.00	250.00	500.00
581	Please Please Me/From Me to You	1964	12.50	25.00	50.00
—Black rainbow label, oval logo					
581	Please Please Me/From Me to You	1964	11.25	22.50	45.00
—Plain black label with two horizontal lines					
581	Please Please Me/From Me to You	1964	18.75	37.50	75.00
—Plain black label, brackets logo					
581	Please Please Me/From Me to You	1964	18.75	37.50	75.00
—Yellow label					
581	Please Please Me/From Me to You	1964	40.00	80.00	160.00
—White label					
581	Please Please Me/From Me to You	1964	62.50	125.00	250.00
—Purple label					
581	Please Please Me/From Me to You	1964	15.00	30.00	60.00
—Plain black label, "VEE JAY" stands alone					
581	Please Please Me/From Me to You	1964	16.25	32.50	65.00
—Plain black label, "VJ" stands alone					
581	Please Please Me/From Me to You	1964	15.00	30.00	60.00
—Black rainbow label, brackets logo					
581	Please Please Me/From Me to You	1964	15.00	30.00	60.00
—Plain black label, oval logo					
581 [DJ]	Please Please Me/From Me to You	1964	200.00	400.00	600.00
—White label, blue print; "Promotional Copy" on label					
581 [DJ]	Please Please Me/From Me to You	1964	300.00	600.00	900.00
—White label, blue print; no "Promotional Copy" on label					
581 [PS]	Please Please Me/From Me to You	1964	1250.	1875.	2500.
—Special "The Record That Started Beatlemania" promo-only sleeve					
581 [PS]	Please Please Me/From Me to You	1964	125.00	250.00	500.00
587	Do You Want to Know a Secret/Thank You Girl	1964	12.50	25.00	50.00
—Black rainbow label, oval logo					
587	Do You Want to Know a Secret/Thank You Girl	1964	16.25	32.50	65.00
—Plain black label; "Vee Jay" in oval					
587	Do You Want to Know a Secret/Thank You Girl	1964	16.25	32.50	65.00
—Plain black label; "VJ" in brackets					
587	Do You Want to Know a Secret/Thank You Girl	1964	16.25	32.50	65.00
—Plain black label; "VJ" stands alone					
587	Do You Want to Know a Secret/Thank You Girl	1964	12.50	25.00	50.00
—Plain black label; "VEE JAY" stands alone					
587	Do You Want to Know a Secret/Thank You Girl	1964	11.25	22.50	45.00
—Plain black label with two horizontal lines; "VJ" in brackets					
587	Do You Want to Know a Secret/Thank You Girl	1964	16.25	32.50	65.00
—Yellow label					
587	Do You Want to Know a Secret/Thank You Girl	1964	10.00	20.00	40.00
—Black rainbow label, brackets logo					
587 [DJ]	Do You Want to Know a Secret/Thank You Girl	1964	150.00	300.00	600.00
587 [PS]	Do You Want to Know a Secret/Thank You Girl	1964	30.00	60.00	120.00
(NO LABEL)					
MBRF-55551	Decade	1974	—	—	—
—A clever bootleg of radio spots for the Beatles' back catalog, compiled without authorization by two former Capitol employees.					

7-Inch Extended Plays

Number	Title (A Side/B Side)	Yr	VG	VG+	NM
CAPITOL					
SXA-2047 [PS]	Meet the Beatles	1964	150.00	300.00	600.00
—With all jukebox title strips intact (deduct 33 percent if missing, deduct less if material is there but not intact)					
SXA-2047 [S]	(contents unknown)	1964	100.00	200.00	400.00
—33 1/3 rpm, small hole jukebox edition					
SXA-2080 [PS]	The Beatles' Second Album	1964	150.00	300.00	600.00
—With all jukebox title strips intact (deduct 33 percent if missing, deduct less if material is there but not intact)					
SXA-2080 [S]	(contents unknown)	1964	100.00	200.00	400.00
—33 1/3 rpm, small hole jukebox edition					
SXA-2108 [PS]	Something New	1964	150.00	300.00	600.00
—With all jukebox title strips intact (deduct 33 percent if missing, deduct less if material is there but not intact)					
SXA-2108 [S]	(contents unknown)	1964	100.00	200.00	400.00
—33 1/3 rpm, small hole jukebox edition					
EAP 1-2121	Roll Over Beethoven/This Boy//All My Loving/ Please Mr. Postman	1964	25.00	50.00	100.00
EAP 1-2121 [PS]	Four by the Beatles	1964	75.00	150.00	300.00
PRO-2548/9 [DJ]	Open End Interview with the Beatles	1964	200.00	400.00	800.00
—33 1/3 rpm, small hole. Authentic copies have colorband along outside of label.					
PRO-2548/9 [PS]	Open End Interview with the Beatles	1964	250.00	500.00	1000.
—Contains script for interview. Authentic copies are glossy and have a die-cut thumb tab.					
PRO-2598/9 [DJ]	The Beatles Second Album Open End Interview	1964	200.00	400.00	800.00
—33 1/3 rpm, small hole; interview plus three songs from the LP					

Number	Title (A Side/B Side)	Yr	VG	VG+	NM
PRO-2598/9 [PS]	The Beatles Second Album Open End Interview	1964	250.00	500.00	1000.
—Contains script for interview					
R-5365	Honey Don't/I'm a Loser//Mr. Moonlight/ Everybody's Trying to Be My Baby	1965	20.00	40.00	80.00
R-5365 [PS]	4-By the Beatles	1965	50.00	100.00	200.00

POLYDOR

Number	Title (A Side/B Side)	Yr	VG	VG+	NM
PRO 1113-7 [DJ]	Ain't She Sweet/Cry for a Shadow//My Bonnie/ The Saints	1994	6.25	12.50	25.00
PRO 1113-7 [PS]	Backbeat	1994	6.25	12.50	25.00
—Picture sleeve for above sampler					

VEE JAY

Number	Title (A Side/B Side)	Yr	VG	VG+	NM
1-903	Misery/Taste of Honey//Ask Me Why/Anna	1964	10.00	20.00	40.00
—Black rainbow label, oval logo					
1-903	Misery/Taste of Honey//Ask Me Why/Anna	1964	31.25	62.50	125.00
—Plain black label, oval logo					
1-903	Misery/Taste of Honey//Ask Me Why/Anna	1964	31.25	62.50	125.00
—Black rainbow label, brackets logo, "Ask Me Why" in much larger print					
1-903	Misery/Taste of Honey//Ask Me Why/Anna	1964	22.50	45.00	90.00
—Black rainbow label, brackets logo, all titles the same size					
1-903	Misery/Taste of Honey//Ask Me Why/Anna	1964	50.00	100.00	200.00
—Plain black label, brackets logo					
1-903	Misery/Taste of Honey//Ask Me Why/Anna	1964	37.50	75.00	150.00
—Plain black label, "VEE JAY" stands alone					
1-903 [DJ]	Misery/Taste of Honey//Ask Me Why/Anna	1964	100.00	200.00	400.00
—White and blue label, all titles the same size					
1-903 [DJ]	Misery/Taste of Honey//Ask Me Why/Anna	1964	75.00	150.00	300.00
—White and blue label, "Ask Me Why" in much larger print					
1-903 [PS]	Souvenir of Their Visit to America	1964	15.00	30.00	60.00
—Cardboard sleeve					
1-903 [PS]	Souvenir of Their Visit to America	1964	4000.	6000.	8000.
—"Ask Me Why/The Beatles" plugged on promo-only sleeve					

Albums

APPLE

Number	Title (A Side/B Side)	Yr	VG	VG+	NM
SBC-100 [M]	The Beatles' Christmas Album	1970	100.00	200.00	400.00
—Fan club issue of the seven Christmas messages; very good counterfeits exist					
SWBO-101 [(2)]	The Beatles	1968	37.50	75.00	200.00
—Numbered copy; includes four individual photos and large poster (included in value); because the white cover shows ring wear so readily, this is an EXTREMELY difficult album to find in near-mint condition					
SWBO-101 [(2)]	The Beatles	1975	17.50	35.00	70.00
—With "All Rights Reserved" on labels; title in black on cover; photos and poster of thinner stock than originals					
SWBO-101 [(2)]	The Beatles	197?	15.00	30.00	60.00
—Un-numbered copy; includes four individual photos and large poster (included in value)					
SW-153 [P]	Yellow Submarine	1969	12.50	25.00	50.00
—With Capitol logo on Side 2 bottom. "Only a Northern Song" is rechanneled.					
SW-153 [P]	Yellow Submarine	1971	5.00	10.00	20.00
—With "Mfd. by Apple" on label					
SW-153 [P]	Yellow Submarine	1975	6.25	12.50	25.00
—With "All Rights Reserved" on label					
SO-383	Abbey Road	1969	18.75	37.50	75.00
—With Capitol logo on Side 2 bottom; "Her Majesty" is NOT listed on either the jacket or the label					
SO-383	Abbey Road	1969	10.00	20.00	40.00
—With Capitol logo on Side 2 bottom; "Her Majesty" IS listed on both the jacket and the label					
SO-383	Abbey Road	1969	5.00	10.00	20.00
—With "Mfd. by Apple" on label; "Her Majesty" is NOT listed on the label					
SO-383	Abbey Road	1969	5.00	10.00	20.00
—With "Mfd. by Apple" on label; "Her Majesty" IS listed on the label					
SO-383	Abbey Road	1975	6.25	12.50	25.00
—With "All Rights Reserved" on label					
SO-385 [DJ]	The Beatles Again	1970	4000.	6000.	8000.
—Prototypes with "The Beatles Again" on cover; not released to the general public					
SW-385	Hey Jude	1970	10.00	20.00	40.00
—Label calls the LP "The Beatles Again"; record is "SO-385" (this could be found in retail stores as late as 1973)					
SW-385	Hey Jude	1970	6.25	12.50	25.00
—Label calls the LP "The Beatles Again"; record is "SW-385"					
SW-385	Hey Jude	1970	18.75	37.50	75.00
—With Capitol logo on Side 2 bottom; label calls the LP "Hey Jude"					
SW-385	Hey Jude	1970	5.00	10.00	20.00
—With "Mfd. by Apple" on label; label calls the LP "Hey Jude"					
SW-385	Hey Jude	1975	6.25	12.50	25.00
—With "All Rights Reserved" on label; label calls the LP "Hey Jude"					
SKBO-3403 [P]	The Beatles 1962-1966	1973	7.50	15.00	30.00
—Custom red Apple labels. "Love Me Do" and "I Want to Hold Your Hand" are rechanneled; "She Loves You," "A Hard Day's Night," "I Feel Fine" and "Ticket to Ride" are mono; "From Me to You," "Can't Buy Me Love" and everything else is stereo.					
SKBO-3403 [P]	The Beatles 1962-1966	1975	12.50	25.00	50.00
—Custom red Apple labels with "All Rights Reserved" on labels					
SKBO-3404 [B]	The Beatles 1967-1970	1973	7.50	15.00	30.00
—Custom blue Apple labels. "Hello Goodbye" and "Penny Lane" are mono, all others stereo.					
SKBO-3404 [B]	The Beatles 1967-1970	1975	12.50	25.00	50.00
—Custom blue Apple labels with "All Rights Reserved" on labels					
SPRO 11206/7 [EP]	Anthology 2 Sampler	1996	37.50	75.00	150.00
—Promo-only collection sent to college radio stations					
C1-8-31796 [(2)]	Live at the BBC	1994	12.50	25.00	50.00
AR-34001	Let It Be	1970	6.25	12.50	25.00
—Red Apple label; originals have "Bell Sound" stamped in trail-off area, counterfeits do not					
C1-8-34445 [(3)]	Anthology 1	1995	10.00	20.00	40.00
—All copies distributed in the U.S. were manufactured in the U.K. with no distinguishing marks (some LPs imported directly from the U.K. have "Made in England" stickers, which can be removed easily)					
C1-8-34448 [(3)]	Anthology 2	1996	10.00	20.00	40.00
C1-8-34451 [(3)]	Anthology 3	1996	7.50	15.00	30.00
C1-97036 [B]	The Beatles 1962-1966	1993	6.25	12.50	25.00
—Custom red Apple labels; red vinyl; all copies pressed in U.K; U.S. versions have a bar-code sticker over the international bar code on back cover. "Love Me Do," "Please Please Me," "From Me to You" and "She Loves You" are mono; all others are stereo.					
C1-97039	The Beatles 1967-1970	1993	6.25	12.50	25.00
—Custom blue Apple labels; blue vinyl; all copies pressed in U.K.; U.S. versions have a bar-code sticker over the international bar code on back cover					

APPLE FILMS

Number	Title (A Side/B Side)	Yr	VG	VG+	NM
KAL 004 [DJ]	The Yellow Submarine (A United Artists Release)	1969	1000.	1500.	2000.
—One-sided LP with radio spots for movie					

APPLE/CAPITOL

Number	Title (A Side/B Side)	Yr	VG	VG+	NM
(no #) [(10)]	The Beatles Special Limited Edition	1974	300.00	600.00	1200.
(no #) [(17)]	The Beatles 10th Anniversary Box Set	1974	1000.	1500.	2000.
ST 2047 [P]	Meet the Beatles!	1968	10.00	20.00	40.00
—With Capitol logo on Side 2 bottom					
ST 2047 [P]	Meet the Beatles!	1971	5.00	10.00	20.00
—With "Mfd. by Apple" on label					
ST 2047 [P]	Meet the Beatles!	1975	6.25	12.50	25.00
—With "All Rights Reserved" on label					
ST 2080 [P]	The Beatles' Second Album	1968	10.00	20.00	40.00
—With Capitol logo on Side 2 bottom					
ST 2080 [P]	The Beatles' Second Album	1971	5.00	10.00	20.00
—With "Mfd. by Apple" on label					
ST 2080 [P]	The Beatles' Second Album	1975	6.25	12.50	25.00
—With "All Rights Reserved" on label					
ST 2108 [S]	Something New	1968	10.00	20.00	40.00
—With Capitol logo on Side 2 bottom					
ST 2108 [S]	Something New	1971	5.00	10.00	20.00
—With "Mfd. by Apple" on label					
ST 2108 [S]	Something New	1975	6.25	2.50	25.00
—With "All Rights Reserved" on label					
STBO 2222 [(2) P]	The Beatles' Story	1968	12.50	25.00	50.00
—With Capitol logo on bottom of B-side of both records					
STBO 2222 [(2) P]	The Beatles' Story	1971	7.50	15.00	30.00
—With "Mfd. by Apple" on labels					
STBO 2222 [(2) P]	The Beatles' Story	1975	10.00	20.00	40.00
—With "All Rights Reserved" on labels					
ST 2228 [P]	Beatles '65	1968	10.00	20.00	40.00
—With Capitol logo on Side 2 bottom					
ST 2228 [P]	Beatles '65	1971	5.00	10.00	20.00
—With "Mfd. by Apple" on label					
ST 2228 [P]	Beatles '65	1975	6.25	12.50	25.00
—With "All Rights Reserved" on label					
ST 2309 [P]	The Early Beatles	1969	10.00	20.00	40.00
—With Capitol logo on Side 2 bottom					
ST 2309 [P]	The Early Beatles	1971	5.00	10.00	20.00
—With "Mfd. by Apple" on label					
ST 2309 [P]	The Early Beatles	1975	6.25	12.50	25.00
—With "All Rights Reserved" on label					
ST 2358 [P]	Beatles VI	1969	10.00	20.00	40.00
—With Capitol logo on Side 2 bottom					
ST 2358 [P]	Beatles VI	1971	5.00	10.00	20.00
—With "Mfd. by Apple" on label					
ST 2358 [P]	Beatles VI	1975	6.25	12.50	25.00
—With "All Rights Reserved" on label					
SMAS 2386 [P]	Help!	1969	10.00	20.00	40.00
—With Capitol logo on Side 2 bottom					
SMAS 2386 [P]	Help!	1971	5.00	10.00	20.00
—With "Mfd. by Apple" on label					
SMAS 2386 [P]	Help!	1975	6.25	12.50	25.00
—With "All Rights Reserved" on label					
ST 2442 [S]	Rubber Soul	1969	10.00	20.00	40.00
—With Capitol logo on Side 2 bottom					
ST 2442 [S]	Rubber Soul	1971	5.00	10.00	20.00
—With "Mfd. by Apple" on label					
ST 2442 [S]	Rubber Soul	1975	6.25	12.50	25.00
—With "All Rights Reserved" on label					
ST 2553 [P]	Yesterday and Today	1969	10.00	20.00	40.00
—With Capitol logo on Side 2 bottom					
ST 2553 [P]	Yesterday and Today	1971	5.00	10.00	20.00
—With "Mfd. by Apple" on label					
ST 2553 [P]	Yesterday and Today	1975	6.25	12.50	25.00
—With "All Rights Reserved" on label					
ST 2553 [S]	Yesterday and Today	1971	6.25	12.50	25.00
—With "Mfd. by Apple" on label; all 11 tracks are in true stereo. Check for a triangle in the record's trail-off area.					
ST 2576 [S]	Revolver	1969	10.00	20.00	40.00
—With Capitol logo on Side 2 bottom					
ST 2576 [S]	Revolver	1971	5.00	10.00	20.00
—With "Mfd. by Apple" on label					
ST 2576 [S]	Revolver	1975	6.25	12.50	25.00
—With "All Rights Reserved" on label					
SMAS 2653 [S]	Sgt. Pepper's Lonely Hearts Club Band	1969	10.00	20.00	40.00
—With Capitol logo on Side 2 bottom					
SMAS 2653 [S]	Sgt. Pepper's Lonely Hearts Club Band	1971	6.25	12.50	25.00
—With "Mfd. by Apple" on label					
SMAS 2653 [S]	Sgt. Pepper's Lonely Hearts Club Band	1975	6.25	12.50	25.00
—With "All Rights Reserved" on label					
SMAL 2835 [P]	Magical Mystery Tour	1969	10.00	20.00	40.00
—With Capitol logo on Side 2 bottom; with 24-page booklet					
SMAL 2835 [P]	Magical Mystery Tour	1971	5.00	10.00	20.00
—With "Mfd. by Apple" on label; with 24-page booklet					
SMAL 2835 [P]	Magical Mystery Tour	1975	6.25	12.50	25.00
—With "All Rights Reserved" on label; with 24-page booklet					

Number	Title (A Side/B Side)	Yr	VG	VG+	NM
ATCO					
33-169 [M]	Ain't She Sweet	1964	50.00	100.00	200.00
33-169 [M-DJ]	Ain't She Sweet	1964	250.00	500.00	1000.
—White label promo					
SD 33-169 [P]	Ain't She Sweet	1964	100.00	200.00	400.00
—Tan and purple label; all four Beatles tracks are rechanneled					
SD 33-169 [P]	Ain't She Sweet	1969	125.00	250.00	500.00
—Yellow label					
AUDIO RARITIES					
AR-2452 [M]	The Complete Silver Beatles	1982	3.75	7.50	15.00
—Contains 12 Decca audition tracks					
AUDIOFIDELITY					
PD-339 [M]	First Movement	1982	7.50	15.00	30.00
—Contains eight Decca audition tracks; picture disc					
PHX-339 [M]	First Movement	1982	3.00	6.00	12.00
—Contains eight Decca audition tracks					
BACKSTAGE					
2-201 [(2) M]	Like Dreamers Do	1982	10.00	20.00	40.00
—Gatefold package, individually numbered (numbers under 100 increase value significantly)					
2-201 [(2) M]	Like Dreamers Do	1982	12.50	25.00	50.00
—Non-gatefold package					
BSR-1111 [DJ]	Like Dreamers Do	1982	12.50	25.00	50.00
—White vinyl promo in white sleeve					
BSR-1111 [DJ]	Like Dreamers Do	1982	12.50	25.00	50.00
—Gray vinyl promo in white sleeve					
BSR-1111 [(3) M]	Like Dreamers Do	1982	15.00	30.00	60.00
—Two picture discs (10 of 15 Decca audition tracks on one, interviews on the other) and one white-vinyl record (same contests as musical picture disc)					
BSR-1111 [(3) M]	Like Dreamers Do	1982	25.00	50.00	100.00
—Same as above, except colored-vinyl LP is gray					
BSR-1165 [PD]	The Beatles Talk with Jerry G.	1982	6.25	12.50	25.00
—Picture disc					
BSR-1175 [PD]	The Beatles Talk with Jerry G., Vol. 2	1983	6.25	12.50	25.00
—Picture disc					
CAPITOL					
(no #) [(18)]	The Beatles Collection Platinum Series	1984	200.00	400.00	800.00
BC-13 [(14)]	The Beatles Collection	1978	62.50	125.00	250.00
—American versions have "EMI" and "BC-13" on box spine; imports go for less					
SWBO-101 [(2)]	The Beatles	1976	7.50	15.00	30.00
—Orange label; with photos and poster					
SWBO-101 [(2)]	The Beatles	1978	7.50	15.00	30.00
—Purple label, large Capitol logo; with photos and poster (some copies have four photos as one perforated sheet)					
SWBO-101 [(2)]	The Beatles	1983	10.00	20.00	40.00
—Black label, print in colorband; with photos and poster (some copies have four photos as one perforated sheet)					
SW-153 [P]	Yellow Submarine	1976	3.00	6.00	12.00
—Orange label					
SW-153 [P]	Yellow Submarine	1978	2.50	5.00	10.00
—Purple label, large Capitol logo					
SW-153 [P]	Yellow Submarine	1983	3.75	7.50	15.00
—Black label, print in colorband					
SJ-383	Abbey Road	1984	7.50	15.00	30.00
—New prefix; black label, print in colorband					
SO-383	Abbey Road	1976	3.00	6.00	12.00
—Orange label					
SO-383	Abbey Road	1978	2.50	5.00	10.00
—Purple label, large Capitol logo					
SO-383	Abbey Road	1983	3.75	7.50	15.00
—Black label, print in colorband					
SJ-385	Hey Jude	1984	7.50	15.00	30.00
—New prefix; black label, print in colorband					
SW-385	Hey Jude	1976	3.00	6.00	12.00
—Orange label (all Capitol label versions call the LP "Hey Jude")					
SW-385	Hey Jude	1978	2.50	5.00	10.00
—Purple label, large Capitol logo					
SW-385	Hey Jude	1983	12.50	25.00	50.00
—Black label, print in colorband					
ST-8-2047 [P]	Meet the Beatles!	1964	125.00	250.00	500.00
—Capitol Record Club edition; black label with colorband					
ST-8-2047 [P]	Meet the Beatles!	1969	50.00	100.00	200.00
—Capitol Record Club edition; lime green label					
ST 2047 [P]	Meet the Beatles!	1964	37.50	75.00	150.00
—Black label with colorband; "Beatles!" on cover in tan to brown print. "I Want to Hold Your Hand" and "This Boy" are rechanneled, the other 10 tracks are true stereo					
ST 2047 [P]	Meet the Beatles!	1964	18.75	37.50	75.00
—Black label with colorband; "Beatles!" on cover in green print					
ST 2047 [P]	Meet the Beatles!	1969	10.00	20.00	40.00
—Lime green label					
ST 2047 [P]	Meet the Beatles!	1976	3.00	6.00	12.00
—Orange label					
ST 2047 [P]	Meet the Beatles!	1978	2.50	5.00	10.00
—Purple label, large Capitol logo					
ST 2047 [P]	Meet the Beatles!	1983	3.75	7.50	15.00
—Black label, print in colorband					
T 2047 [M]	Meet the Beatles!	1964	50.00	100.00	200.00
—Black label with colorband; "Beatles!" on cover in tan to brown print					
T 2047 [M]	Meet the Beatles!	1964	25.00	50.00	100.00
—Black label with colorband; "Beatles!" on cover in green print					
ST-8-2080 [P]	The Beatles' Second Album	1964	125.00	250.00	500.00
—Capitol Record Club edition; black label with colorband					
ST-8-2080 [P]	The Beatles' Second Album	1969	75.00	150.00	300.00
—Capitol Record Club edition; lime green label					
ST 2080 [P]	The Beatles' Second Album	1964	25.00	50.00	100.00
—Black label with colorband. "She Loves You," "I'll Get You" and "You Can't Do That" are rechanneled					
ST 2080 [P]	The Beatles' Second Album	1969	10.00	20.00	40.00
—Lime green label					
ST 2080 [P]	The Beatles' Second Album	1976	3.00	6.00	12.00
—Orange label					
ST 2080 [P]	The Beatles' Second Album	1978	2.50	5.00	10.00
—Purple label, large Capitol logo					
ST 2080 [P]	The Beatles' Second Album	1983	3.75	7.50	15.00
—Black label, print in colorband					
T 2080 [M]	The Beatles' Second Album	1964	45.00	90.00	180.00
ST-8-2108 [S]	Something New	1964	75.00	150.00	300.00
—Capitol Record Club edition; black label with colorband					
ST-8-2108 [S]	Something New	1969	37.50	75.00	150.00
—Capitol Record Club edition; lime green label					
ST-8-2108 [S]	Something New	1969	75.00	150.00	300.00
—Longines Symphonette edition (will be stated on label); lime green label					
ST 2108 [S]	Something New	1964	20.00	40.00	80.00
—Black label with colorband					
ST 2108 [S]	Something New	1969	10.00	20.00	40.00
—Lime green label					
ST 2108 [S]	Something New	1976	3.00	6.00	12.00
—Orange label					
ST 2108 [S]	Something New	1978	2.50	5.00	10.00
—Purple label, large Capitol logo					
ST 2108 [S]	Something New	1983	3.75	7.50	15.00
—Black label, print in colorband					
T 2108 [M]	Something New	1964	37.50	75.00	150.00
STBO 2222 [(2) P]	The Beatles' Story	1964	37.50	75.00	150.00
—Black label with colorband. Some of the musical snippets are rechanneled.					
STBO 2222 [(2) P]	The Beatles' Story	1969	12.50	25.00	50.00
—Lime green label					
STBO 2222 [(2) P]	The Beatles' Story	1976	5.00	10.00	20.00
—Orange label					
STBO 2222 [(2) P]	The Beatles' Story	1978	5.00	10.00	20.00
—Purple label, large Capitol logo					
STBO 2222 [(2) P]	The Beatles' Story	1983	10.00	20.00	40.00
—Black label, print in colorband					
TBO 2222 [(2) M]	The Beatles' Story	1964	50.00	100.00	200.00
ST 2228 [P]	Beatles '65	1964	20.00	40.00	80.00
—Black label with colorband. "She's a Woman" and "I Feel Fine" are rechanneled.					
ST 2228 [P]	Beatles '65	1969	10.00	20.00	40.00
—Lime green label					
ST 2228 [P]	Beatles '65	1976	3.00	6.00	12.00
—Orange label					
ST 2228 [P]	Beatles '65	1978	2.50	5.00	10.00
—Purple label, large Capitol logo					
ST 2228 [P]	Beatles '65	1983	3.75	7.50	15.00
—Black label, print in colorband					
T 2228 [M]	Beatles '65	1964	30.00	60.00	120.00
ST 2309 [P]	The Early Beatles	1965	25.00	50.00	100.00
—Black label with colorband. "Love Me Do" and "P.S. I Love You" are rechanneled.					
ST 2309 [P]	The Early Beatles	1969	10.00	20.00	40.00
—Lime green label					
ST 2309 [P]	The Early Beatles	1976	3.00	6.00	12.00
—Orange label					
ST 2309 [P]	The Early Beatles	1978	2.50	5.00	10.00
—Purple label, large Capitol logo					
ST 2309 [P]	The Early Beatles	1983	6.25	12.50	25.00
—Black label, print in colorband					
T 2309 [M]	The Early Beatles	1965	50.00	100.00	200.00
ST-8-2358 [P]	Beatles VI	1965	125.00	250.00	500.00
—Capitol Record Club edition; black label with colorband					
ST-8-2358 [P]	Beatles VI	1969	100.00	200.00	400.00
—Capitol Record Club edition; lime green label					
ST 2358 [M]	Beatles VI	1983	3.75	7.50	15.00
—Black label, print in colorband; plays in mono despite label designation					
ST 2358 [M]	Beatles VI	1988	20.00	40.00	80.00
—Purple label, small Capitol logo; plays in mono despite label designation					
ST 2358 [P]	Beatles VI	1965	20.00	40.00	80.00
—Black label with colorband; with "See label for correct playing order" on back cover					
ST 2358 [P]	Beatles VI	1965	18.75	37.50	75.00
—Black label with colorband; with song titles listed in correct order on back cover. "Yes It Is" is rechanneled.					
ST 2358 [P]	Beatles VI	1969	10.00	20.00	40.00
—Lime green label					
ST 2358 [P]	Beatles VI	1976	3.00	6.00	12.00
—Orange label					
ST 2358 [P]	Beatles VI	1978	2.50	5.00	10.00
—Purple label, large Capitol logo					
T 2358 [M]	Beatles VI	1965	30.00	60.00	120.00
—With "See label for correct playing order" on back cover					
T 2358 [M]	Beatles VI	1965	25.00	50.00	100.00
—With song titles listed in correct order on back cover					
MAS 2386 [M]	Help!	1965	37.50	75.00	150.00
SMAS-8-2386 [P]	Help!	1965	100.00	200.00	400.00
—Capitol Record Club edition; black label with colorband; no "8" on cover					
SMAS-8-2386 [P]	Help!	1965	150.00	300.00	600.00
—Capitol Record Club edition; black label with colorband; with "8" on cover					
SMAS-8-2386 [P]	Help!	1969	50.00	100.00	200.00
—Capitol Record Club edition; lime green label; no "8" on cover					
SMAS-8-2386 [P]	Help!	1969	100.00	200.00	400.00
—Capitol Record Club edition; lime green label; with "8" on cover					

Number	Title (A Side/B Side)	Yr	VG	VG+	NM
SMAS-8-2386 [P]	Help!	197?	175.00	350.00	700.00
—Longines Symphonette edition; with "Mfd. by Longines" and "8" on cover					
SMAS 2386 [P]	Help!	1965	18.75	37.50	75.00
—Black label with colorband. Has incidental music by George Martin. "Ticket to Ride" is rechanneled.					
SMAS 2386 [P]	Help!	1969	10.00	20.00	40.00
—Lime green label					
SMAS 2386 [P]	Help!	1976	3.00	6.00	12.00
—Orange label					
SMAS 2386 [P]	Help!	1978	2.50	5.00	10.00
—Purple label, large Capitol logo					
SMAS 2386 [P]	Help!	1983	3.75	7.50	15.00
—Black label, print in colorband					
ST-8-2442 [S]	Rubber Soul	1965	75.00	150.00	300.00
—Capitol Record Club edition; black label with colorband					
ST-8-2442 [S]	Rubber Soul	1969	50.00	100.00	200.00
—Capitol Record Club edition; lime green label					
ST-8-2442 [S]	Rubber Soul	1969	62.50	125.00	250.00
—Longines Symphonette edition (will be stated on label); lime green label					
ST 2442 [S]	Rubber Soul	1965	15.00	30.00	60.00
—Black label with colorband					
ST 2442 [S]	Rubber Soul	1969	10.00	20.00	40.00
—Lime green label					
ST 2442 [S]	Rubber Soul	1976	3.00	6.00	12.00
—Orange label					
SW 2442 [S]	Rubber Soul	1978	2.50	5.00	10.00
—Purple label, large Capitol logo					
SW 2442 [S]	Rubber Soul	1983	3.75	7.50	15.00
—Black label, print in colorband					
T 2442 [M]	Rubber Soul	1965	30.00	60.00	120.00
ST-8-2553 [P]	Yesterday and Today	1966	75.00	150.00	300.00
—Capitol Record Club edition; black label with colorband					
ST-8-2553 [S]	Yesterday and Today	1969	37.50	75.00	150.00
—Capitol Record Club edition; lime green label; all 11 tracks are in true stereo! (We don't know if the same is true of the black label version.)					
ST 2553 [P]	Yesterday and Today	1966	4000.	6000.	8000.
—"First state" butcher cover (never had other cover on top); cover will be the same size as other Capitol Beatles LPs					
ST 2553 [P]	Yesterday and Today	1966	500.00	750.00	1000.
—"Second state" butcher cover (trunk cover pasted over original cover)					
ST 2553 [P]	Yesterday and Today	1966	375.00	750.00	1500.
—"Third state" butcher cover (trunk cover removed, leaving butcher cover intact); cover will be about 3/16-inch narrower than other Capitol Beatles LPs; value is highly negotiable depending upon the success of removing the paste-over					
ST 2553 [P]	Yesterday and Today.	1966	20.00	40.00	80.00
—Trunk cover; black label with colorband (all later variations have the trunk cover). "I'm Only Sleeping," "Dr. Robert" and "And Your Bird Can Sing" are rechanneled.					
ST 2553 [P]	Yesterday and Today.	1969	10.00	20.00	40.00
—Lime green label					
ST 2553 [P]	Yesterday and Today.	1976	3.00	6.00	12.00
—Orange label; it's possible that this and all future pressings have all 11 tracks in true stereo, but we don't know.					
ST 2553 [P]	Yesterday and Today.	1978	2.50	5.00	10.00
—Purple label, large Capitol logo					
ST 2553 [P]	Yesterday and Today	1983	3.75	7.50	15.00
—Black label, print in colorband					
T 2553 [M]	Yesterday and Today	1966	2000.	3000.	4000.
—"First state" butcher cover (never had other cover on top); cover will be the same size as other Capitol Beatles LPs					
T 2553 [M]	Yesterday and Today.	1966	250.00	500.00	1000.
—"Second state" butcher cover (trunk cover pasted over original cover)					
T 2553 [M]	Yesterday and Today.	1966	400.00	800.00	1200.
—"Third state" butcher cover (trunk cover removed, leaving butcher cover intact); cover will be about 3/16-inch narrower than other Capitol Beatles LPs; value is highly negotiable depending upon the success of removing the paste-over					
T 2553 [M]	Yesterday and Today.	1966	37.50	75.00	150.00
—Trunk cover					
ST-8-2576 [S]	Revolver.	1966	100.00	200.00	400.00
—Capitol Record Club edition; black label with colorband					
ST-8-2576 [S]	Revolver.	1969	30.00	60.00	120.00
—Capitol Record Club edition; lime green label					
ST-8-2576 [S]	Revolver.	1973?	50.00	100.00	200.00
—Capitol Record Club edition; orange label (a very late issue, as Capitol Record Club closed in 1973)					
ST 2576 [S]	Revolver.	1966	25.00	50.00	100.00
—Black label with colorband					
ST 2576 [S]	Revolver.	1969	10.00	20.00	40.00
—Lime green label					
ST 2576 [S]	Revolver.	1970	75.00	150.00	300.00
—Red label with "target" Capitol at top (same design as lime green label)					
ST 2576 [S]	Revolver.	1976	3.00	6.00	12.00
—Orange label					
SW 2576 [S]	Revolver.	1978	2.50	5.00	10.00
—Purple label, large Capitol logo					
SW 2576 [S]	Revolver.	1983	3.75	7.50	15.00
—Black label, print in colorband					
T 2576 [M]	Revolver.	1966	50.00	100.00	200.00
2653	Sgt. Pepper's Lonely Hearts Club Band Cut-Out Inserts.	1967	—	—	3.00
2653	Sgt. Pepper's Lonely Hearts Club Band Special Inner Sleeve.	1967	3.75	7.50	15.00
—Red-pink psychedelic sleeve only issued with 1967 (mono and stereo) editions					
MAS 2653 [M]	Sgt. Pepper's Lonely Hearts Club Band	1967	75.00	150.00	300.00
SMAS 2653 [S]	Sgt. Pepper's Lonely Hearts Club Band	1967	25.00	50.00	100.00
—Black label with colorband					
SMAS 2653 [S]	Sgt. Pepper's Lonely Hearts Club Band	1969	12.50	25.00	50.00
—Lime green label					
SMAS 2653 [S]	Sgt. Pepper's Lonely Hearts Club Band	1976	3.00	6.00	12.00
—Orange label					
SMAS 2653 [S]	Sgt. Pepper's Lonely Hearts Club Band	1978	2.50	5.00	10.00
—Purple label, large Capitol logo. Many copies from 1978 had a "The Original Classic" sticker on shrink wrap; it was added at the time of the release of the bomb movie version of Sgt. Pepper. Double the value if the sticker is still there.					
SMAS 2653 [S]	Sgt. Pepper's Lonely Hearts Club Band	1983	3.75	7.50	15.00
—Black label, print in colorband; some of these had "The Original Classic" stickers, too. Add $10 to value if it is there.					
MAL 2835 [M]	Magical Mystery Tour	1967	75.00	150.00	300.00
—With 24-page book bound into center of gatefold					
SMAL 2835 [P]	Magical Mystery Tour	1967	25.00	50.00	100.00
—Black label with colorband; with 24-page booklet. "Penny Lane," "Baby You're a Rich Man" and "All You Need Is Love" is rechanneled, as is the second half of "I Am the Walrus" (every "stereo" version of "Walrus" is this way)					
SMAL 2835 [P]	Magical Mystery Tour	1969	12.50	25.00	50.00
—Lime green label; with 24-page booklet					
SMAL 2835 [P]	Magical Mystery Tour	1976	3.00	6.00	12.00
—Orange label; with 24-page booklet					
SMAL 2835 [P]	Magical Mystery Tour	1978	2.50	5.00	10.00
—Purple label, large Capitol logo; this edition did not come with booklet					
SMAL 2835 [P]	Magical Mystery Tour	1983	3.75	7.50	15.00
—Black label, print in colorband; no booklet					
SKBO-3403 [P]	The Beatles 1962-1966	1976	5.00	10.00	20.00
—Red labels					
SKBO-3403 [P]	The Beatles 1962-1966	1976	7.50	15.00	30.00
—Blue labels (error pressing)					
SKBO-3404 [B]	The Beatles 1967-1970	1976	5.00	10.00	20.00
—Blue labels					
SPRO-8969	Rarities	1978	12.50	25.00	50.00
—Purple label, large Capitol logo; part of the U.S. box set The Beatles Collection (BC-13)					
SKBO-11537 [(2)]	Rock 'n' Roll Music	1976	6.25	12.50	25.00
SMAS-11638	The Beatles at the Hollywood Bowl	1977	5.00	10.00	20.00
—Originals with embossed title and ticket on front cover					
SMAS-11638	The Beatles at the Hollywood Bowl	1980	3.75	7.50	15.00
—Second pressing without embossed title and ticket					
SMAS-11638	The Beatles at the Hollywood Bowl	1989	10.00	20.00	40.00
—With UPC code on back cover					
SMAS-11638 [DJ]	The Beatles at the Hollywood Bowl	1977	125.00	250.00	500.00
—Advance tan label promo in plain white jacket					
SKBL-11711 [(2) P]	Love Songs	1977	5.00	10.00	20.00
—With booklet and embossed, leather-like cover. "P.S. I Love You" and "Yes It Is" are rechanneled.					
SKBL-11711 [(2) P]	Love Songs.	1988	7.50	15.00	30.00
—With booklet, but without embossed cover					
SEAX-11840 [PD]	Sgt. Pepper's Lonely Hearts Club Band.	1978	5.00	10.00	20.00
—Picture disc; deduct 25% for cut-outs					
SEBX-11841 [(2)]	The Beatles.	1978	12.50	25.00	50.00
—White vinyl; with photos and poster (with number "SEBX-11841" on each)					
SEBX-11842 [P]	The Beatles 1962-1966.	1978	10.00	20.00	40.00
—Red vinyl					
SEBX-11843 [B]	The Beatles 1967-1970.	1978	10.00	20.00	40.00
—Blue vinyl					
SEAX-11900 [PD]	Abbey Road.	1978	10.00	20.00	40.00
—Picture disc; deduct 25% for cut-outs					
SW-11921 [P]	A Hard Day's Night.	1979	3.00	6.00	12.00
—Purple label, large Capitol logo					
SW-11921 [P]	A Hard Day's Night	1983	3.75	7.50	15.00
—Black label, print in colorband					
SW-11921 [P]	A Hard Day's Night	1988	6.25	12.50	25.00
—Purple label, small Capitol logo					
SW-11922	Let It Be	1979	3.75	7.50	15.00
—Purple label, large Capitol logo; with poster and custom innersleeve					
SW-11922	Let It Be	1983	3.75	7.50	15.00
—Black label, print in colorband; add 33% if poster is included					
SW-11922	Let It Be	1988	6.25	12.50	25.00
—Purple label, small Capitol logo; add 20% if poster and custom innersleeve are included					
SN-12009 [DJ]	Rarities	1979	75.00	150.00	300.00
—Green label; withdrawn before official release; all known copies have a plain white sleeve					
SHAL-12080 [B]	Rarities	1980	5.00	10.00	20.00
—Completely different LP than 12009; black label with colorband. First pressing says that "There's a Place" debuts in stereo (false) and that the screaming at the end of "Helter Skelter" was a "classic Lennon statement" (it's actually Ringo).					
SHAL-12080 [B]	Rarities	1980	3.75	7.50	15.00
—Same as above, with errors deleted and "Produced by George Martin" added to back cover					
SV-12199	Reel Music	1982	2.50	5.00	10.00
—Standard issue with 12-page booklet					
SV-12199 [DJ]	Reel Music	1982	10.00	20.00	40.00
—Yellow vinyl promo; numbered back cover with 12-page booklet					
SV-12199 [DJ]	Reel Music	1982	5.00	10.00	20.00
—Yellow vinyl promo; plain white cover with 12-page booklet					
SV-12245 [P]	20 Greatest Hits.	1982	5.00	10.00	20.00
—Purple label, large Capitol logo. "Love Me Do" and "She Loves You" are rechanneled, the other 18 tracks are stereo					
SV-12245 [P]	20 Greatest Hits.	1983	5.00	10.00	20.00
—Black label, print in colorband					
SV-12245 [P]	20 Greatest Hits.	1988	6.25	12.50	25.00
—Purple label, small Capitol logo					
SN-16020	Rock 'n' Roll Music, Volume 1.	1980	2.50	5.00	10.00
SN-16021	Rock 'n' Roll Music, Volume 2.	1980	2.50	5.00	10.00
C1-46435 [M]	Please Please Me	1995	3.00	6.00	12.00
—New prefix; Apple logo on back cover					

Number	Title (A Side/B Side)	Yr	VG	VG+	NM
CLJ-46435 [M]	Please Please Me	1987	5.00	10.00	20.00
—Black label, print in colorband; first Capitol version of original British LP					
CLJ-46435 [M]	Please Please Me	1988	6.25	12.50	25.00
—Purple label, small Capitol logo					
C1-46436 [M]	With the Beatles	1995	3.00	6.00	12.00
—New prefix; Apple logo on back cover					
CLJ-46436 [M]	With the Beatles	1987	5.00	10.00	20.00
—Black label, print in colorband; first Capitol version of original British LP					
CLJ-46436 [M]	With the Beatles	1988	6.25	12.50	25.00
—Purple label, small Capitol logo					
C1-46437 [M]	A Hard Day's Night	1995	3.00	6.00	12.00
—New prefix; Apple logo on back cover					
CLJ-46437 [M]	A Hard Day's Night	1987	5.00	10.00	20.00
—Black label, print in colorband; first Capitol version of original British LP					
CLJ-46437 [M]	A Hard Day's Night	1988	6.25	12.50	25.00
—Purple label, small Capitol logo					
C1-46438 [M]	Beatles for Sale	1995	3.00	6.00	12.00
—New prefix; Apple logo on back cover					
CLJ-46438 [M]	Beatles for Sale	1987	5.00	10.00	20.00
—Black label, print in colorband; first Capitol version of original British LP					
CLJ-46438 [M]	Beatles for Sale	1988	6.25	12.50	25.00
—Purple label, small Capitol logo					
C1-46439 [S]	Help!	1995	3.00	6.00	12.00
—New prefix; Apple logo on back cover					
CLJ-46439 [S]	Help!	1987	5.00	10.00	20.00
—Black label, print in colorband; first Capitol version of original British LP					
CLJ-46439 [S]	Help!	1988	6.25	12.50	25.00
—Purple label, small Capitol logo					
C1-46440 [S]	Rubber Soul	1995	3.00	6.00	12.00
—New prefix; Apple logo on back cover					
CLJ-46440 [S]	Rubber Soul	1987	5.00	10.00	20.00
—Black label, print in colorband; first Capitol version of original British LP					
CLJ-46440 [S]	Rubber Soul	1988	6.25	12.50	25.00
—Purple label, small Capitol logo					
C1-46441 [S]	Revolver	1995	3.00	6.00	12.00
—New prefix; Apple logo on back cover					
CLJ-46441 [S]	Revolver	1987	5.00	10.00	20.00
—Black label, print in colorband; first Capitol version of original British LP					
CLJ-46441 [S]	Revolver	1988	6.25	12.50	25.00
—Purple label, small Capitol logo					
C1-46442 [S]	Sgt. Pepper's Lonely Hearts Club Band	1988	6.25	12.50	25.00
—New number; purple label, small Capitol logo					
C1-46442 [S]	Sgt. Pepper's Lonely Hearts Club Band	1995	3.00	6.00	12.00
—With Apple logo on back cover					
C1-46443 [(2)]	The Beatles	1988	12.50	25.00	50.00
—New number; purple label, small Capitol logo; with photos and poster (some copies have four photos as one perforated sheet)					
C1-46443 [(2)]	The Beatles	1995	5.00	10.00	20.00
—With Apple logo on back cover					
C1-46445 [P]	Yellow Submarine	1988	6.25	12.50	25.00
—New number; purple label, small Capitol logo					
C1-46445 [P]	Yellow Submarine	1995	3.00	6.00	12.00
—Reissue has the British liner notes, which include a review of the White Album.					
C1-46446	Abbey Road	1988	6.25	12.50	25.00
—New number; purple label, small Capitol logo					
C1-46446	Abbey Road	1995	3.00	6.00	12.00
—Apple logo restored to back cover on reissue					
C1-46447	Let It Be	1995	3.00	6.00	12.00
—New number (the only 1995 reissue with a completely new number)					
C1-48062 [P]	Magical Mystery Tour	1988	6.25	12.50	25.00
—New number; purple label, small Capitol logo; no booklet					
C1-48062 [P]	Magical Mystery Tour	1992	3.00	6.00	12.00
—With Apple logo on back cover; reissue restores booklet to package					
C1-90435 [P]	The Beatles 1962-1966	1988	7.50	15.00	30.00
—New number; purple labels, small Capitol logo					
C1-90438 [B]	The Beatles 1967-1970	1988	7.50	15.00	30.00
—New number; purple labels, small Capitol logo					
C1-90441 [P]	Meet the Beatles!	1988	6.25	12.50	25.00
—New number; purple label, small Capitol logo					
C1-90442	Hey Jude	1988	6.25	12.50	25.00
—New number; purple label, small Capitol logo					
C1-90443 [S]	Something New	1988	6.25	12.50	25.00
—New number; purple label, small Capitol logo					
C1-90444 [P]	The Beatles' Second Album	1988	6.25	12.50	25.00
—New number; purple label, small Capitol logo					
C1-90445 [M]	Beatles VI	1988	6.25	12.50	25.00
—New number; purple label, small Capitol logo; plays in mono despite label designation					
C1-90446 [P]	Beatles '65	1988	6.25	12.50	25.00
—New number; purple label, small Capitol logo					
C1-90447 [P]	Yesterday and Today	1988	6.25	12.50	25.00
—New number; purple label, small Capitol logo; stereo content uncertain					
C1-90452 [S]	Revolver	1988	6.25	12.50	25.00
—New number; purple label, small Capitol logo					
C1-90453 [S]	Rubber Soul	1988	6.25	12.50	25.00
—New number; purple label, small Capitol logo					
C1-90454 [P]	Help!	1988	6.25	12.50	25.00
—New number; purple label, small Capitol logo					
C1-91135 [(2) B]	Past Masters Volume 1 and 2	1988	6.25	12.50	25.00
—Some early tracks are in mono, but "This Boy," "She's a Woman." "Yes It Is," and "The Inner Light" are in stereo.					
BBX1-91302 [(14)]	The Beatles Deluxe Box Set	1988	75.00	150.00	300.00
CICADELIC					
1960	Moviemania	1987	3.00	6.00	12.00
1961	Not a Second Time	1987	3.00	6.00	12.00
1962	Things We Said Today	1986	3.00	6.00	12.00
1963	All Our Loving	1986	3.00	6.00	12.00
1964	East Coast Invasion	1985	3.00	6.00	12.00
1965	Round the World	1986	3.00	6.00	12.00
1966	West Coast Invasion	1985	3.00	6.00	12.00
1967	From Britain with Beat!	1987	3.00	6.00	12.00
1968	Here, There and Everywhere	1988	3.00	6.00	12.00
CLARION					
601 [M]	The Amazing Beatles and Other Great English Group Sounds	1966	25.00	50.00	100.00
SD 601 [P]	The Amazing Beatles and Other Great English Group Sounds	1966	50.00	100.00	200.00
—All four Beatles tracks are rechanneled					
GREAT NORTHWEST					
GNW 4007	Beatle Talk	1978	2.50	5.00	10.00
GNW 4007	Beatle Talk	1978	12.50	25.00	50.00
—Columbia Record Club edition; "CRC" on spine					
HALL OF MUSIC					
HM-1-2200 [(2) M]	Live 1962, Hamburg, Germany	1981	12.50	25.00	50.00
—Only American LP with the original Eurpoean contents -- "I Saw Her Standing There," "Twist and Shout," "Ask Me Why" and "Reminiscing" replace the four songs listed with the Lingasong issue					
I-N-S RADIO NEWS					
DOC-1 [DJ]	Beatlemania Tour Coverage	1964	750.00	1125.	1500.
—Promo-only open-end interview with script in plain white jacket					
LINGASONG					
LS-2-7001 [(2) DJ]	Live at the Star Club in Hamburg, Germany, 1962	1977	75.00	150.00	300.00
—Promo only on blue vinyl					
LS-2-7001 [(2) DJ]	Live at the Star Club in Hamburg, Germany, 1962	1977	50.00	100.00	200.00
—Promo only on red vinyl					
LS-2-7001 [(2) DJ]	Live at the Star Club in Hamburg, Germany, 1962	1977	10.00	20.00	40.00
—Promo on black vinyl; "D.J. Copy Not for Sale" on labels					
LS-2-7001 [(2) R]	Live at the Star Club in Hamburg, Germany, 1962	1977	5.00	10.00	20.00
—American version contains "I'm Gonna Sit Right Down and Cry," "Where Have You Been All My Life," "Till There Was You," and "Sheila," not on imports					
LLOYDS					
ER-MC-LTD	The Great American Tour — 1965 Live Beatlemania Concert	1965	150.00	300.00	600.00
—Another interview album from the Ed Rudy people, with a live Beatles show in the background and the songs poorly overdubbed by the Liverpool Lads					
METRO					
M-563 [M]	This Is Where It Started	1966	25.00	50.00	100.00
—Reissue of MGM album with two of the "others" tracks deleted					
MS-563 [R]	This Is Where It Started	1966	37.50	75.00	150.00
—In stereo cover					
MS-563 [R]	This Is Where It Started	1966	50.00	100.00	200.00
—In mono cover with "Stereo" sticker					
MGM					
E-4215 [M]	The Beatles with Tony Sheridan and Their Guests	1964	50.00	100.00	200.00
—Without "And Guests" on cover					
E-4215 [M]	The Beatles with Tony Sheridan and Their Guests	1964	62.50	125.00	250.00
—With "And Guests" on cover					
SE-4215 [R]	The Beatles with Tony Sheridan and Their Guests	1964	150.00	300.00	600.00
—With "And Guests" on cover					
SE-4215 [R]	The Beatles with Tony Sheridan and Their Guests	1964	200.00	400.00	800.00
—Without "And Guests" on cover					
MOBILE FIDELITY					
BC-1 [(13)]	The Beatles Collection	1982	125.00	250.00	500.00
1-023	Abbey Road	1979	12.50	25.00	50.00
—Audiophile vinyl					
1-047 [P]	Magical Mystery Tour	1980	15.00	30.00	60.00
—Audiophile vinyl; yes, this contains the rechanneled stereo versions of "Penny Lane," "Baby You're a Rich Man" and "All You Need Is Love"					
2-072 [(2)]	The Beatles	1982	12.50	25.00	50.00
—Audiophile vinyl; not issued with photos or poster					
1-100 [S]	Sgt. Pepper's Lonely Hearts Club Band	1985	10.00	20.00	40.00
—Audiophile vinyl					
UHQR 1-100 [S]	Sgt. Pepper's Lonely Hearts Club Band	1982	75.00	150.00	300.00
—Ultra High Quality release with special cover; numbered edition of 5,000; numbers under 100 fetch even more					
1-101 [P]	Please Please Me	1986	10.00	20.00	40.00
—Audiophile vinyl; British version of album. "Love Me Do" and "P.S. I Love You" are rechanneled.					
1-102 [S]	With the Beatles	1986	37.50	75.00	150.00
—Audiophile vinyl; British version of album. Limited run because of a damaged stamper that was not replaced.					
1-103 [S]	A Hard Day's Night	1987	10.00	20.00	40.00
—Audiophile vinyl; British version of album					
1-104 [S]	Beatles for Sale	1986	10.00	20.00	40.00
—Audiophile vinyl; British version of album					
1-105 [S]	Help!	1985	10.00	20.00	40.00
—Audiophile vinyl; British version of album					
1-106 [S]	Rubber Soul	1985	10.00	20.00	40.00
—Audiophile vinyl; British version of album					
1-107 [S]	Revolver	1986	10.00	20.00	40.00
—Audiophile vinyl; British version of album					
1-108 [P]	Yellow Submarine	1987	15.00	30.00	60.00
—Audiophile vinyl					
1-109	Let It Be	1987	10.00	20.00	40.00
—Audiophile vinyl; gatefold cover					
1-109	Let It Be	1987	50.00	100.00	200.00
—Audiophile vinyl; regular cover					

Number	Title (A Side/B Side)	Yr	VG	VG+	NM
ORANGE					
ORC-12880 [DJ]	The Silver Beatles	1985	75.00	150.00	300.00
—Test pressing; white cover with title sticker					
ORC-12880 [DJ]	The Silver Beatles	1985	100.00	200.00	400.00
—Test pressing; full cover cover slick folded around a white cover. Both contain all 15 Decca audition tracks					
PBR INTERNATIONAL					
7005/6 [(2)]	The David Wigg Interviews (The Beatles Tapes)	1978	20.00	40.00	80.00
—Blue vinyl					
7005/6 [(2)]	The David Wigg Interviews (The Beatles Tapes)	1980	15.00	30.00	60.00
—Black vinyl					
PHOENIX					
PHX-352 [M]	Silver Beatles, Volume 1	1982	3.00	6.00	12.00
—Contains seven Decca audition tracks					
PHX-353 [M]	Silver Beatles, Volume 2	1982	3.00	6.00	12.00
—Contains seven Decca audition tracks (different seven than Phoenix 352)					
P20-623	20 Hits, Beatles	1983	5.00	10.00	20.00
—With 12 Decca audition tracks, four Beatles/Tony Sheridan tracks, and four Tony Sheridan solo tracks					
P20-629	20 Hits, Beatles	1983	5.00	10.00	20.00
—With 20 live Hamburg tracks					
PICKWICK					
PTP-2098 [(2) M]	The Historic First Live Recordings	1980	4.50	9.00	18.00
—Same contents as Lingasong LP, plus "Hully Gully"					
SPC-3661 [M]	The Beatles' First Live Recordings, Volume 1	1979	3.00	6.00	12.00
SPC-3662 [M]	The Beatles' First Live Recordings, Volume 2	1979	3.00	6.00	12.00
BAN-90051 [M]	Recorded Live in Hamburg, Vol. 1	1978	7.50	15.00	30.00
BAN-90061 [M]	Recorded Live in Hamburg, Vol. 2	1978	7.50	15.00	30.00
BAN-90071 [M]	Recorded Live in Hamburg, Vol. 3	1978	10.00	20.00	40.00
POLYDOR					
24-4504 [P]	The Beatles — Circa 1960 — In the Beginning Featuring Tony Sheridan	1970	6.25	12.50	25.00
—Originals have gatefold cover					
24-4504 [P]	The Beatles — Circa 1960 — In the Beginning Featuring Tony Sheridan	197?	10.00	20.00	40.00
—Some copies of the record contain only the title "The Beatles — In the Beginning"					
PD-4504 [P]	The Beatles — Circa 1960 — In the Beginning Featuring Tony Sheridan	1981	3.00	6.00	12.00
—Reissue without gatefold cover					
SKAO-93199 [P]	The Beatles — Circa 1960 — In the Beginning Featuring Tony Sheridan	1970	10.00	20.00	40.00
—Capitol Record Club edition					
825073-1 [P]	The Beatles — Circa 1960 — In the Beginning Featuring Tony Sheridan	1988	5.00	10.00	20.00
—Reissue with new number					
RADIO PULSEBEAT NEWS					
2	The American Tour with Ed Rudy	1964	25.00	50.00	100.00
—Yellow label; some copies came with a special edition of Teen Talk magazine (add 50%)					
2	The American Tour with Ed Rudy	1980	6.25	12.50	25.00
—Blue label; authorized reissue with Beatles' photo on cover					
3	1965 Talk Album — Ed Rudy with New U.S. Tour	1965	37.50	75.00	150.00
—"The Beatles" in black print under front cover photo (other versions appear to be bootlegs)					
RAVEN/PVC					
8911	Talk Downunder	1981	2.50	5.00	10.00
8911 [DJ]	Talk Downunder	1981	20.00	40.00	80.00
—Promo only in white cover with title sticker. Label reads "For Radio Play Only"					
SAVAGE					
BM-69 [M]	The Savage Young Beatles	1964	37.50	75.00	150.00
—Orange label; no legitimate copy says "Stereo" on cover					
BM-69 [M]	The Savage Young Beatles	1964	375.00	750.00	1500.
—Yellow label, glossy orange cover					
SILHOUETTE					
SM-10004 [PD]	Timeless	1981	5.00	10.00	20.00
—Picture disc with all interviews					
SM-10004 [PD]	Timeless	1981	6.25	12.50	25.00
—Picture disc with interviews plus remakes of "Imagine" and "Let It Be" (by non-Beatles)					
SM-10010 [PD]	Timeless II	1982	5.00	10.00	20.00
—Picture disc with mostly interviews					
SM-10013	The British Are Coming	1984	3.75	7.50	15.00
—Interview album with numbered sticker (very low numbers increase the value)					
SM-10013	The British Are Coming	1984	20.00	40.00	80.00
—Same as above, but on red vinyl					
SM-10013 [DJ]	The British Are Coming	1984	10.00	20.00	40.00
—White label promo; no numbered sticker					
SM-10015	Golden Beatles	1985	3.75	7.50	15.00
SM-10015	Golden Beatles	1985	20.00	40.00	80.00
—Gold vinyl					
PD-83010 [PD]	The British Are Coming	1985	7.50	15.00	30.00
—Picture disc					
STERLING					
8895-6481	I Apologize	1966	100.00	200.00	400.00
—One-sided LP with John Lennon's "apology" for supposed anti-Christian remarks; includes photo					
8895-6481	I Apologize	1966	75.00	150.00	300.00
—Same as above, but without photo					
UNITED ARTISTS					
SP-2359/60 [DJ]	United Artists Presents A Hard Day's Night	1964	1000.	1500.	2000.
—Open-end interview with script					
SP-2362/3 [DJ]	United Artists Presents A Hard Day's Night	1964	375.00	750.00	1500.
—Radio spots for movie					
UAL 3366 [M]	A Hard Day's Night	1964	50.00	100.00	200.00
—With "I Cry Instead" listing					
UAL 3366 [M]	A Hard Day's Night	1964	62.50	125.00	250.00
—With "I'll Cry Instead" listing					
UAL 3366 [M-DJ]	A Hard Day's Night	1964	750.00	1500.	3000.
—White label promo					
UAS 6366 [P]	A Hard Day's Night	1964	50.00	100.00	200.00
—With "I Cry Instead" listing					
UAS 6366 [P]	A Hard Day's Night	1964	62.50	125.00	250.00
—With "I'll Cry Instead" listing. Has incidental music by George Martin. All eight Beatles tracks are rechanneled; Martin's are in true stereo.					
UAS 6366 [P]	A Hard Day's Night	1964	6000.	9000.	12000.
—Pink vinyl; only one copy known, probably privately (and secretly) done by a pressing-plant employee					
UAS 6366 [P]	A Hard Day's Night	1968	12.50	25.00	50.00
—Pink and orange label					
UAS 6366 [P]	A Hard Day's Night	1970	12.50	25.00	50.00
—Black and orange label					
UAS 6366 [P]	A Hard Day's Night	1971	5.00	10.00	20.00
—Tan label					
UAS 6366 [P]	A Hard Day's Night	1975	5.00	10.00	20.00
—Tan label with "All Rights Reserved" in perimeter print					
UAS 6366 [P]	A Hard Day's Night	1977	5.00	10.00	20.00
—Sunrise label. Note: Any of the variations from 1968 on can have titles of songs incorrectly listed as "I Cry Instead" and "Tell Me Who," or only one can be wrong, or neither can be wrong. No difference in value at this time.					
ST-90828 [P]	A Hard Day's Night	1964	187.50	375.00	750.00
—Capitol Record Club edition					
T-90828 [M]	A Hard Day's Night	1964	750.00	1125.	1500.
—Capitol Record Club edition					
UA-Help-A/B [DJ]	United Artists Presents Help!	1965	500.00	1000.	1500.
—Radio spots for movie					
UA-Help-INT [DJ]	United Artists Presents Help!	1965	1000.	1500.	2000.
—Open-end interview with script (red label)					
UA-Help-Show [DJ]	United Artists Presents Help!	1965	1500.	2250.	3000.
—One-sided interview with script (blue label)					
UNITED DISTRIBUTORS					
UDL-2333 [M]	Dawn of the Silver Beatles	1981	15.00	30.00	60.00
—Hand-stamped numbers on back cover and label; contains 10 Decca audition tracks					
UDL-2333 [M]	Dawn of the Silver Beatles	1981	12.50	25.00	50.00
—With numbered registration card (deduct 20% if missing)					
UDL-2382 [M]	Lightning Strikes Twice	1981	15.00	30.00	60.00
—Side 1 has five Beatles' Decca audition tracks; Side 2 has live Elvis Presley performances from 1955					
VEE JAY					
DX-30 [(2) M]	The Beatles vs. The Four Seasons	1964	200.00	400.00	800.00
—Combines "Introducing the Beatles" with "Golden Hits of the Four Seasons" (Vee Jay 1065)					
DXS-30 [(2) S]	The Beatles vs. The Four Seasons	1964	1500.	2250.	3000.
—Combines "Introducing the Beatles" with "Golden Hits of the Four Seasons" (Vee Jay 1065)					
DX(S)-30	The Beatles vs. The Four Seasons Poster	1964	75.00	150.00	300.00
202 [M]	Hear the Beatles Tell All	1964	75.00	150.00	300.00
—Without "PRO" prefix on label					
PRO 202 [DJ]	Hear the Beatles Tell All.	1964	6000.	12000.	18000.
—White label promo with blue print					
PRO 202 [M]	Hear the Beatles Tell All.	1964	50.00	100.00	200.00
—With "PRO" prefix on label					
PRO 202 [PD]	Hear the Beatles Tell All.	1987	5.00	10.00	20.00
—Shaped picture disc with same recordings as the black vinyl versions					
PRO 202 [S]	Hear the Beatles Tell All.	1979	2.50	5.00	10.00
—Authorized reissue in stereo					
LP 1062 [M]	Introducing the Beatles.	1964	1500.	2750.	4000.
—"Ad back" cover; with "Love Me Do" and "P.S. I Love You"; oval Vee Jay logo with colorband only!					
LP 1062 [M]	Introducing the Beatles.	1964	400.00	800.00	1200.
—Blank back cover; with "Love Me Do" and "P.S. I Love You"; oval Vee Jay logo with colorband only!					
LP 1062 [M]	Introducing the Beatles.	1964	250.00	500.00	1000.
—Blank back cover; with "Please Please Me" and "Ask Me Why"; oval Vee Jay logo with colorband only!					
LP 1062 [M]	Introducing the Beatles.	1964	200.00	400.00	800.00
—Song titles cover; with "Love Me Do" and "P.S. I Love You"; oval Vee Jay logo with colorband only!					
LP 1062 [M]	Introducing the Beatles.	1964	75.00	150.00	300.00
—Song titles cover; with "Please Please Me" and "Ask Me Why"; oval Vee Jay logo with colorband					
LP 1062 [M]	Introducing the Beatles.	1964	62.50	125.00	250.00
—Song titles cover; with "Please Please Me" and "Ask Me Why"; brackets Vee Jay logo with colorband (most common authentic version)					
LP 1062 [M]	Introducing the Beatles.	1964	62.50	125.00	250.00
—Song titles cover; with "Please Please Me" and "Ask Me Why"; plain Vee Jay logo on solid black label					
LP 1062 [M]	Introducing the Beatles.	1964	75.00	150.00	300.00
—Song titles cover; with "Please Please Me" and "Ask Me Why"; oval Vee Jay logo on solid black label					
LP 1062 [M]	Introducing the Beatles.	1964	250.00	500.00	1000.
—Song titles cover; with "Please Please Me" and "Ask Me Why"; brackets Vee Jay logo on solid black label					
SR 1062 [B]	Introducing the Beatles.	1964	4000.	8000.	12000.
—"Ad back" cover; with "Love Me Do" and "P.S. I Love You" (both mono); oval Vee Jay logo with colorband only!					
SR 1062 [B]	Introducing the Beatles.	1964	625.00	1250.	2500.
—Blank back cover; with "Love Me Do" and "P.S. I Love You"; oval Vee Jay logo with colorband only!					
SR 1062 [B]	Introducing the Beatles.	1964	3000.	5500.	8000.
—Song titles cover; with "Love Me Do" and "P.S. I Love You"; oval Vee Jay logo with colorband only! Only two authentic copies are known, with hundreds of thousands of counterfeits					
SR 1062 [S]	Introducing the Beatles.	1964	400.00	800.00	1600.
—Song titles cover; with "Please Please Me" and "Ask Me Why"; oval Vee Jay logo with colorband					
SR 1062 [S]	Introducing the Beatles.	1964	375.00	750.00	1500.
—Song titles cover; with "Please Please Me" and "Ask Me Why"; brackets Vee Jay logo with colorband					
SR 1062 [S]	Introducing the Beatles.	1964	400.00	800.00	1600.
—Song titles cover; with "Please Please Me" and "Ask Me Why"; plain Vee Jay logo on solid black label					

Number	Title (A Side/B Side)	Yr	VG	VG+	NM
LP 1085 [M]	Jolly What! The Beatles and Frank Ifield on Stage	1964	62.50	125.00	250.00
	—Man in Beatle wig cover; originals have printing on spine and a dark blue/purple background (counterfeits have a black background and no spine print)				
LP 1085 [M]	The Beatles and Frank Ifield on Stage	1964	2000.	3500.	5000.
	—Portrait of Beatles cover; counterfeits are poorly reproduced and have no spine print				
SR 1085 [B]	Jolly What! The Beatles and Frank Ifield on Stage	1964	125.00	250.00	500.00
	—Man in Beatle wig cover; "Stereo" on both cover and label. "From Me to You" is mono.				
SR 1085 [B]	The Beatles and Frank Ifield on Stage	1964	4000.	8000.	12000.
	—Portrait of Beatles cover; "Stereo" on both cover and label				
LP 1092 [M]	Songs, Pictures and Stories of the Fabulous Beatles	1964	125.00	250.00	500.00
	—All copies have gatefold cover with 2/3 width on front; also, all copies have "Introducing the Beatles" records. Oval Vee Jay logo with colorband.				
LP 1092 [M]	Songs, Pictures and Stories of the Fabulous Beatles	1964	125.00	250.00	500.00
	—See above; brackets Vee Jay logo with colorband				
LP 1092 [M]	Songs, Pictures and Stories of the Fabulous Beatles	1964	125.00	250.00	500.00
	—See above; plain Vee Jay logo on solid black label				
LP 1092 [M]	Songs, Pictures and Stories of the Fabulous Beatles	1964	125.00	250.00	500.00
	—See above; oval Vee Jay logo on solid black label				
VJS 1092 [S]	Songs, Pictures and Stories of the Fabulous Beatles	1964	800.00	1600.	2400.
	—All copies have gatefold cover with 2/3 width on front; also, all copies have "Introducing the Beatles" records. Oval Vee Jay logo with colorband.				
VJS 1092 [S]	Songs, Pictures and Stories of the Fabulous Beatles	1964	800.00	1600.	2400.
	—See above; brackets Vee Jay logo with colorband				
VJS 1092 [S]	Songs, Pictures and Stories of the Fabulous Beatles	1964	800.00	1600.	2400.
	—See above; plain Vee Jay logo on solid black label. NOTE: Any non-gatefold copy or any copy called "Songs and Pictures of the Fabulous Beatles" is a counterfeit.				

BEST, PETER

Former drummer with THE BEATLES.

45s

CAMEO

Number	Title (A Side/B Side)	Yr	VG	VG+	NM
391	Boys/Kansas City	1965	20.00	40.00	80.00
391 [PS]	Boys/Kansas City	1965	25.00	50.00	100.00

HAPPENING

Number	Title (A Side/B Side)	Yr	VG	VG+	NM
405	If You Can't Get Her/Don't Play with Me	1964	45.00	90.00	180.00
1117/8	If You Can't Get Her/The Way I Feel About You	1966	37.50	75.00	150.00
	—Label credit: "Best of the Beatles (Peter Best)"				

MR. MAESTRO

Number	Title (A Side/B Side)	Yr	VG	VG+	NM
711	I Can't Do Without You Now/Keys to My Heart	1965	50.00	100.00	200.00
	—Label credit: "Best of the Beatles"; black vinyl				
711	I Can't Do Without You Now/Keys to My Heart	1965	37.50	75.00	150.00
	—Label credit: "Best of the Beatles"; blue vinyl				
712	Casting My Spell/I'm Blue	1965	37.50	75.00	150.00
	—Black vinyl				
712	Casting My Spell/I'm Blue	1965	50.00	100.00	200.00
	—Blue vinyl				

ORIGINAL BEATLES DRUMMER

Number	Title (A Side/B Side)	Yr	VG	VG+	NM
800	(I'll Try) Anyway/I Wanna Be There	1964	45.00	90.00	180.00

Albums

PHOENIX

Number	Title (A Side/B Side)	Yr	VG	VG+	NM
PHX-340	The Beatle That Time Forgot	1982	3.00	6.00	12.00

SAVAGE

Number	Title (A Side/B Side)	Yr	VG	VG+	NM
BM-71	Best of the Beatles	1966	50.00	100.00	200.00
	—Authentic copies have white circle around the word "Savage" and white circle around Pete Best's head on the album cover.				

HARRISON, GEORGE

12-Inch Singles

COLUMBIA

Number	Title (A Side/B Side)	Yr	VG	VG+	NM
CAS 2085 [DJ]	I Don't Want to Do It (same on both sides)	1985	5.00	10.00	20.00

DARK HORSE

Number	Title (A Side/B Side)	Yr	VG	VG+	NM
PRO-A-949 [DJ]	All Those Years Ago (same on both sides)	1981	6.25	12.50	25.00
PRO-A-1075 [DJ]	Wake Up My Love (same on both sides)	1982	6.25	12.50	25.00
PRO-A-2845 [DJ]	Got My Mind Set on You (same on both sides)	1987	6.25	12.50	25.00
PRO-A-2885 [DJ]	When We Was Fab (same on both sides)	1987	6.25	12.50	25.00
PRO-A-2889 [DJ]	Devil's Radio (Gossip) (same on both sides)	1987	7.50	15.00	30.00

45s

APPLE

Number	Title (A Side/B Side)	Yr	VG	VG+	NM
1828	What Is Life/Apple Scruffs	1971	3.75	7.50	15.00
	—With star on A-side label				
1828	What Is Life/Apple Scruffs	1971	2.00	4.00	8.00
	—Without star on A-side label				
1828 [PS]	What Is Life/Apple Scruffs	1971	10.00	20.00	40.00
1836	Bangla-Desh/Deep Blue	1971	6.25	12.50	25.00
	—Without star on A-side label				
1836	Bangla-Desh/Deep Blue	1971	2.00	4.00	8.00
	—With star on A-side label				
1836 [PS]	Bangla-Desh/Deep Blue	1971	5.00	10.00	20.00
1862	Give Me Love (Give Me Peace on Earth)/Miss O'Dell (2:30)	1973	2.00	4.00	8.00
	—With incorrect time for B-side listed				
1862	Give Me Love (Give Me Peace on Earth)/Miss O'Dell (2:20)	1973	2.00	4.00	8.00
	—B-side playing time corrected				
P-1862 [DJ]	Give Me Love (Give Me Peace on Earth) (mono/stereo)	1973	12.50	25.00	50.00
1877	Dark Horse/I Don't Care Anymore	1974	2.00	4.00	8.00
	—Light blue and white custom photo label				
1877	Dark Horse/I Don't Care Anymore	1974	2.50	5.00	10.00
	—White label; NOT a promo				
1877 [PS]	Dark Horse/I Don't Care Anymore	1974	20.00	40.00	80.00
P-1877 [DJ]	Dark Horse (full length mono/stereo)	1974	10.00	20.00	40.00
P-1877 [DJ]	Dark Horse (edited mono/stereo)	1974	15.00	30.00	60.00
1879	Ding Dong, Ding Dong/Hari's on Tour (Express)	1974	5.00	10.00	20.00
	—Black and white custom photo label				
1879	Ding Dong, Ding Dong/Hari's on Tour (Express)	1974	62.50	125.00	250.00
	—Blue and white custom photo label				
1879 [PS]	Ding Dong, Ding Dong/Hari's on Tour (Express)	1974	5.00	10.00	20.00
P-1879 [DJ]	Ding Dong, Ding Dong (remixed mono/edited stereo)	1974	10.00	20.00	40.00
1884	You/World of Stone	1975	—	3.00	6.00
1884 [PS]	You/World of Stone	1975	3.75	7.50	15.00
P-1884 [DJ]	You (mono/stereo)	1975	10.00	20.00	40.00
1885	This Guitar (Can't Keep from Crying)/Maya Love	1975	6.25	12.50	25.00
	—The last Apple 45 until 1995				
P-1885 [DJ]	This Guitar (Can't Keep from Crying) (mono/stereo)	1975	12.50	25.00	50.00
2995	My Sweet Lord/Isn't It a Pity	1970	10.00	20.00	40.00
	—With black star on label				
2995	My Sweet Lord/Isn't It a Pity	1970	2.00	4.00	8.00
	—With "Mfd. by Apple" on label				
2995	My Sweet Lord/Isn't It a Pity	1975	6.25	12.50	25.00
	—With "All Rights Reserved" disclaimer				
2995 [PS]	My Sweet Lord/Isn't It a Pity	1970	10.00	20.00	40.00

CAPITOL

Number	Title (A Side/B Side)	Yr	VG	VG+	NM
1828	What Is Life/Apple Scruffs	1976	7.50	15.00	30.00
	—Orange label				
1828	What Is Life/Apple Scruffs	1978	—	3.00	6.00
	—Purple late-1970s label				
1836	Bangla-Desh/Deep Blue	1976	7.50	15.00	30.00
	—Orange label				
1836	Bangla-Desh/Deep Blue	1978	—	3.00	6.00
	—Purple late-1970s label				
1836	Bangla-Desh/Deep Blue	1983	3.75	7.50	15.00
	—Black colorband label				
1862	Give Me Love (Give Me Peace on Earth)/Miss O'Dell	1978	2.00	4.00	8.00
	—Purple late-1970s label				
1862	Give Me Love (Give Me Peace on Earth)/Miss O'Dell	1978	3.75	7.50	15.00
	—Black colorband label				
1879	Ding Dong, Ding Dong/Hari's on Tour (Express)	1978	2.00	4.00	8.00
	—Purple late-1970s label				
2995	My Sweet Lord/Isn't It a Pity	1976	5.00	10.00	20.00
	—Orange label with "Capitol" at bottom				
2995	My Sweet Lord/Isn't It a Pity	1978	—	3.00	6.00
	—Purple label; label has reeded edge				
2995	My Sweet Lord/Isn't It a Pity	1983	—	3.00	6.00
	—Black label with colorband				
2995	My Sweet Lord/Isn't It a Pity	1988	—	2.50	5.00
	—Purple label; label has smooth edge				

COLUMBIA

Number	Title (A Side/B Side)	Yr	VG	VG+	NM
04887	I Don't Want to Do It/Queen of the Hop	1985	6.25	12.50	25.00
	—B-side by Dave Edmunds				

DARK HORSE

Number	Title (A Side/B Side)	Yr	VG	VG+	NM
8294	This Song/Learning How to Love You	1976	2.50	5.00	10.00
	—Tan label				
8294	This Song/Learning How to Love You	1976	2.00	4.00	8.00
	—White label, NOT a promo				
8294 [DJ]	This Song (mono/stereo)	1976	6.25	12.50	25.00
8294 [PS]	This Song/Learning How to Love You	1976	7.50	15.00	30.00
8294 [PS]	This Song (mono/stereo)	1976	10.00	20.00	40.00
	—Promotional only sleeve, different from stock sleeve				
8294 [PS]	This Song (mono/stereo)	1976	10.00	20.00	40.00
	—Flyer with "The Story Behind This Song"				
8313	Crackerbox Palace/Learning How to Love You	1977	—	2.50	5.00
8763	Blow Away/Soft-Hearted Hana	1979	—	2.50	5.00
	—With "RE-1" on label				
8763	Blow Away/Soft-Hearted Hana	1979	5.00	10.00	20.00
	—Without "RE-1" on label (no "Loka Productions S.A." on label)				
8763 [PS]	Blow Away/Soft-Hearted Hana.	1979	—	2.50	5.00
8844	Love Comes to Everyone/Soft Touch.	1979	2.50	5.00	10.00
8844 [PS]	Love Comes to Everyone/Soft Touch.	1979	250.00	500.00	750.00
27913	This Is Love/Breath Away from Heaven.	1988	—	2.50	5.00
27913 [PS]	This Is Love/Breath Away from Heaven.	1988	—	2.50	5.00
28131	When We Was Fab/Zig Zag.	1988	—	2.50	5.00
28131 [PS]	When We Was Fab/Zig Zag.	1988	—	2.50	5.00
28178	Got My Mind Set on You/Lay His Head.	1987	—	2.00	4.00
28178 [PS]	Got My Mind Set on You/Lay His Head.	1987	—	2.00	4.00
29744	I Really Love You/Circles.	1983	6.25	12.50	25.00
29864	Wake Up My Love/Greece.	1982	2.50	5.00	10.00
49725	All Those Years Ago/Writing's on the Wall.	1981	—	2.50	5.00
49725 [PS]	All Those Years Ago/Writing's on the Wall.	1981	—	2.50	5.00
49785	Teardrops/Save the World.	1981	2.50	5.00	10.00

WARNER BROS.

Number	Title (A Side/B Side)	Yr	VG	VG+	NM
22807	Cheer Down/That's What It Takes.	1989	3.75	7.50	15.00
22807 [DJ]	Cheer Down (same on both sides).	1989	50.00	100.00	200.00
22807 [PS]	Cheer Down/That's What It Takes.	1989	3.75	7.50	15.00

Number	Title (A Side/B Side)	Yr	VG	VG+	NM

Albums

APPLE

Number	Title (A Side/B Side)	Yr	VG	VG+	NM
STCH-639 [(3)]	All Things Must Pass	1970	10.00	20.00	40.00
—Apple labels on first two records and "Apple Jam" labels on third; includes poster and lyric innersleeves					
ST-3350	Wonderwall Music	1968	6.25	12.50	25.00
—With "Mfd. by Apple" on label					
ST-3350	Wonderwall Music	1968	37.50	75.00	150.00
—With Capitol logo on Side 2 bottom					
ST-3350	Wonderwall Music Bonus Photo	1968	—	2.50	5.00
SMAS-3410	Living in the Material World	1973	3.75	7.50	15.00
SMAS-3418	Dark Horse	1974	3.75	7.50	15.00
SW-3420	Extra Texture (Read All About It)	1975	3.75	7.50	15.00

CAPITOL

Number	Title (A Side/B Side)	Yr	VG	VG+	NM
STCH-639 [(3)]	All Things Must Pass	1976	7.50	15.00	30.00
—Orange labels with poster and lyric innersleeves					
STCH-639 [(3)]	All Things Must Pass	1978	6.25	12.50	25.00
—Purple labels with poster and lyric innersleeves					
STCH-639 [(3)]	All Things Must Pass	1983	25.00	50.00	100.00
—Black labels, print in colorband, with poster and lyric innersleeves					
ST-11578	The Best of George Harrison	1976	3.75	7.50	15.00
—Custom label, no bar code on back					
ST-11578	The Best of George Harrison	1976	45.00	90.00	180.00
—Orange label					
ST-11578	The Best of George Harrison	1978	2.50	5.00	10.00
—Purple label, large Capitol logo					
ST-11578	The Best of George Harrison	1983	6.25	12.50	25.00
—Black label, print in colorband					
ST-11578	The Best of George Harrison	1988	6.25	12.50	25.00
—Odd reissue with custom label; large stand-alone "S" in trail-off area; bar code on cover					
ST-11578	The Best of George Harrison	1989	20.00	40.00	80.00
—Purple label, small Capitol logo					
SN-16055	Dark Horse	1980	3.75	7.50	15.00
—Budget-line reissue; reverses front and back covers					
SN-16216	Living in the Material World	1980	5.00	10.00	20.00
—Budget-line reissue					
SN-16217	Extra Texture (Read All About It)	1980	6.25	12.50	25.00
—Budget-line reissue					

CAPITOL/APPLE

Number	Title (A Side/B Side)	Yr	VG	VG+	NM
STCH-639 [(3)]	All Things Must Pass	1988	20.00	40.00	80.00
—Odd pressing with Apple labels and Capitol cover (look for stand-alone "S" in trail-off wax); with large sticker on back cover					

DARK HORSE

Number	Title (A Side/B Side)	Yr	VG	VG+	NM
(no #) [DJ]	Dark Horse Radio Special	1974	100.00	200.00	400.00
—Promo-only; George Harrison introduces his new record label and artists					
PRO 649 [DJ]	A Personal Music Dialogue at Thirty Three and 1/3	1976	12.50	25.00	50.00
DH 3005	Thirty Three and 1/3	1976	2.50	5.00	10.00
—Deduct 30% for cut-outs					
DHK 3255	George Harrison	1979	2.50	5.00	10.00
—Deduct 30% for cut-outs					
DHK 3255	George Harrison	1979	10.00	20.00	40.00
—Columbia House edition (back cover says "Manufactured by Columbia House Under License"					
DHK 3492	Somewhere in England	1981	2.50	5.00	10.00
—Deduct 30% for cut-outs					
23724	Gone Troppo	1982	2.50	5.00	10.00
—Deduct 30% for cut-outs					

Number	Title (A Side/B Side)	Yr	VG	VG+	NM
23724 [DJ]	Gone Troppo	1982	6.25	12.50	25.00
—Promo on Quiex II vinyl					
25643	Cloud Nine	1987	2.50	5.00	10.00
W1-25643	Cloud Nine	1987	3.00	6.00	12.00
—Columbia House edition					
25726	Best of Dark Horse 1976-1989	1989	6.25	12.50	25.00
W1-25726	Best of Dark Horse 1976-1989	1989	3.75	7.50	15.00
—Columbia House edition					
R 174328	Cloud Nine	1987	3.75	7.50	15.00
—BMG Direct Marketing edition					
R 180307	Best of Dark Horse 1976-1989	1989	3.75	7.50	15.00
—BMG Direct Marketing edition					

ZAPPLE

Number	Title (A Side/B Side)	Yr	VG	VG+	NM
ST-3358	Electronic Sound	1969	10.00	20.00	40.00

HARRISON, GEORGE, AND FRIENDS

The "Friends" include BADFINGER; ERIC CLAPTON; BOB DYLAN; BILLY PRESTON; LEON RUSSELL; RAVI SHANKAR; RINGO STARR.

Albums

APPLE

Number	Title (A Side/B Side)	Yr	VG	VG+	NM
STCX-3385 [(3)]	The Concert for Bangla Desh	1971	10.00	20.00	40.00
—With 64-page booklet and custom innersleeves					
STCX-3385 [(3)]	The Concert for Bangla Desh	1975	12.50	25.00	50.00
—As above, but with "All Rights Reserved" on labels					

CAPITOL

Number	Title (A Side/B Side)	Yr	VG	VG+	NM
SABB-12248 [(2)]	The Concert for Bangla Desh	1982	75.00	150.00	300.00
—Scheduled reissue that was never officially released, though a few copies got out by mistake					

HARRISON, GEORGE/JEFF BECK/DAVE EDMUNDS

12-Inch Singles

COLUMBIA

Number	Title (A Side/B Side)	Yr	VG	VG+	NM
CAS 2034 [DJ]	I Don't Want to Do It/Sleepwalk/Queen of the Hop	1985	5.00	10.00	20.00
—Promo sampler from movie "Porky's Revenge"					

LENNON, JOHN

Includes records as "Plastic Ono Band," "John Ono Lennon," "John Lennon/Plastic Ono Band" and other records he made with Yoko Ono.

12-Inch Singles

CAPITOL

Number	Title (A Side/B Side)	Yr	VG	VG+	NM
SPRO-9585/6 [DJ]	Imagine/Come Together	1986	10.00	20.00	40.00
SPRO-9894 [DJ]	Happy Xmas (War Is Over) (same on both sides)	1986	50.00	100.00	200.00
—Limited edition for the Central Virginia Food Bank					
SPRO-9917 [DJ]	Rock and Roll People (same on both sides)	1986	15.00	30.00	60.00
SPRO-9929 [DJ]	Happy Xmas (War Is Over)/Listen, the Snow Is Falling	1986	12.50	25.00	50.00
—Custom silver label, plastic sleeve with sticker					
SPRO-79463 [DJ]	Stand By Me (same on both sides)	1988	10.00	20.00	40.00

GEFFEN

Number	Title (A Side/B Side)	Yr	VG	VG+	NM
PRO-A-919 [DJ]	(Just Like) Starting Over/Kiss Kiss Kiss	1980	20.00	40.00	80.00
—A-side is slightly longer (4:17) than any other release of this song					
PRO-A-1079 [DJ]	Happy Xmas (War Is Over)/Beautiful Boy (Darling Boy)	1982	7.50	15.00	30.00

POLYDOR

Number	Title (A Side/B Side)	Yr	VG	VG+	NM
PRO 250-1 [DJ]	Nobody Told Me/O' Sanity	1983	7.50	15.00	30.00

45s

APPLE

Number	Title (A Side/B Side)	Yr	VG	VG+	NM
1809	Give Peace a Chance/Remember Love	1969	—	2.50	5.00
—As "Plastic Ono Band"					
1809 [PS]	Give Peace a Chance/Remember Love	1969	3.75	7.50	15.00
—As "Plastic Ono Band"					
1813	Cold Turkey/Don't Worry Kyoko (Mummy's Only Looking for a Hand in the Snow)	1969	—	2.50	5.00
—As "Plastic Ono Band"; most copies skip on A-side on the third chorus because of a pressing defect					
1813	Cold Turkey/Don't Worry Kyoko (Mummy's Only Looking for a Hand in the Snow)	1969	2.50	5.00	10.00
—As "Plastic Ono Band"; some copies don't skip on A-side. They tend to have wider, bolder print than those that do.					
1813 [PS]	Cold Turkey/Don't Worry Kyoko (Mummy's Only Looking for a Hand in the Snow)	1969	10.00	20.00	40.00
—As "Plastic Ono Band"					
1818	Instant Karma! (We All Shine On)/Who Has Seen the Wind?	1970	—	2.00	4.00
—As "John Ono Lennon"; B-side by "Yoko Ono Lennon"					
1818 [DJ]	Instant Karma! (We All Shine On)	1970	50.00	100.00	200.00
—As "John Ono Lennon"; one-sided promo					
1818 [PS]	Instant Karma! (We All Shine On)/Who Has Seen the Wind?	1970	3.75	7.50	15.00
—As "John Ono Lennon"; B-side by "Yoko Ono Lennon"					
1827	Mother/Why	1970	2.00	4.00	8.00
—As "John Lennon/Plastic Ono Band"; B-side by "Yoko Ono/Plastic Ono Band"					
1827	Mother/Why	1970	3.00	6.00	12.00
—As "John Lennon/Plastic Ono Band"; star on A-side label					
1827	Mother/Why	1970	10.00	20.00	40.00
—As "John Lennon/Plastic Ono Band"; "MONO" on A-side label					
1827 [PS]	Mother/Why	1970	30.00	60.00	120.00
—As "John Lennon/Plastic Ono Band"; B-side by "Yoko Ono/Plastic Ono Band"					
1830	Power to the People/Touch Me	1971	2.00	4.00	8.00
—As "John Lennon/Plastic Ono Band"; B-side by "Yoko Ono/Plastic Ono Band"					
1830	Power to the People/Touch Me	1971	2.00	4.00	8.00
—As "John Lennon/Plastic Ono Band"; with star on A-side label					
1830 [PS]	Power to the People/Touch Me	1971	7.50	15.00	30.00
—As "John Lennon/Plastic Ono Band"; B-side by "Yoko Ono/Plastic Ono Band"					

Number	Title (A Side/B Side)	Yr	VG	VG+	NM
1840	Imagine/It's So Hard	1971	2.00	4.00	8.00
	—As "John Lennon Plastic Ono Band"; tan label				
1840	Imagine/It's So Hard	1975	3.00	6.00	12.00
	—As "John Lennon Plastic Ono Band"; green label with "All Rights Reserved"				
1842	Happy Xmas (War Is Over)/Listen, the Snow Is Falling	1971	3.75	7.50	15.00
	—As "John & Yoko/Plastic Ono Band with the Harlem Community Choir"; green vinyl, faces label				
1842	Happy Xmas (War Is Over)/Listen, the Snow Is Falling	1971	2.50	5.00	10.00
	—As "John & Yoko/Plastic Ono Band with the Harlem Community Choir"; green vinyl, Apple label				
1842 [PS]	Happy Xmas (War Is Over)/Listen, the Snow Is Falling	1971	5.00	10.00	20.00
	—As "John & Yoko/Plastic Ono Band with the Harlem Community Choir"				
1848	Woman Is the Nigger of the World/Sisters O Sisters	1972	2.00	4.00	8.00
	—As "John Lennon/Plastic Ono Band..."; B-side by "Yoko Ono/Plastic Ono Band..."				
1848 [PS]	Woman Is the Nigger of the World/Sisters O Sisters	1972	6.25	12.50	25.00
	—As "John Lennon/Plastic Ono Band..."; B-side by "Yoko Ono/Plastic Ono Band..."				
1868	Mind Games/Meat City	1973	—	3.00	6.00
1868 [PS]	Mind Games/Meat City	1973	3.75	7.50	15.00
P-1868 [DJ]	Mind Games (mono/stereo)	1973	12.50	25.00	50.00
1874	Whatever Gets You Thru the Night/Beef Jerky	1974	—	3.00	6.00
	—As "John Lennon and the Plastic Ono Nuclear Band"				
P-1874 [DJ]	Whatever Gets You Thru the Night (mono/stereo)	1974	12.50	25.00	50.00
	—As "John Lennon and the Plastic Ono Nuclear Band"				
1878	#9 Dream/What You Got	1974	2.00	4.00	8.00
P-1878 [DJ]	#9 Dream (edited mono/stereo)	1974	12.50	25.00	50.00
P-1878 [DJ]	What You Got (mono/stereo)	1974	25.00	50.00	100.00
1881	Stand By Me/Move Over Ms. L.	1975	2.00	4.00	8.00
P-1881 [DJ]	Stand By Me (mono/stereo)	1975	12.50	25.00	50.00
P-1883 [DJ]	Ain't That a Shame (mono/stereo)	1975	50.00	100.00	200.00
	—No stock copies issued				
P-1883 [DJ]	Slippin' and Slidin' (mono/stereo)	1975	50.00	100.00	200.00
	—No stock copies issued				
S45X-47663/4 [DJ]	Happy Xmas (War Is Over)/Listen, the Snow Is Falling	1971	187.50	375.00	750.00
	—As "John & Yoko/Plastic Ono Band with the Harlem Community Choir"; white label on styrene				

APPLE/AMERICOM

Number	Title (A Side/B Side)	Yr	VG	VG+	NM
1809P/M-435	Give Peace a Chance/Remember Love	1969	187.50	375.00	750.00
	—As "Plastic Ono Band"; four-inch flexi-disc sold from vending machines				

ATLANTIC

Number	Title (A Side/B Side)	Yr	VG	VG+	NM
PR-104/5 [DJ]	John Lennon on Ronnie Hawkins: The Short Rap/The Long Rap	1970	25.00	50.00	100.00

CAPITOL

Number	Title (A Side/B Side)	Yr	VG	VG+	NM
1840	Imagine/It's So Hard	1978	—	3.00	6.00
	—As "John Lennon Plastic Ono Band"; purple late 1970s label				
1840	Imagine/It's So Hard	1983	—	3.00	6.00
	—As "John Lennon Plastic Ono Band"; black colorband label				
1840	Imagine/It's So Hard	1988	—	2.50	5.00
	—As "John Lennon Plastic Ono Band"; purple late-1980s label (wider)				
1842	Happy Xmas (War Is Over)/Listen, the Snow Is Falling	1976	12.50	25.00	50.00
	—As "John & Yoko/Plastic Ono Band with the Harlem Community Choir"; orange label				
1842	Happy Xmas (War Is Over)/Listen, the Snow Is Falling	1978	—	3.00	6.00
	—As "John & Yoko/Plastic Ono Band with the Harlem Community Choir"; purple late-1970s label				

Number	Title (A Side/B Side)	Yr	VG	VG+	NM
1842	Happy Xmas (War Is Over)/Listen, the Snow Is Falling	1983	—	3.00	6.00
	—As "John & Yoko/Plastic Ono Band with the Harlem Community Choir"; black colorband label				
1842	Happy Xmas (War Is Over)/Listen, the Snow Is Falling	1988	5.00	10.00	20.00
	—As "John & Yoko/Plastic Ono Band with the Harlem Community Choir"; purple late-1980s label (wider)				
1868	Mind Games/Meat City	1978	—	3.00	6.00
	—Purple late-1970s label				
1868	Mind Games/Meat City	1983	3.00	6.00	12.00
	—Black colorband label				
1874	Whatever Gets You Thru the Night/Beef Jerky	1978	—	3.00	6.00
	—Purple late-1970s label				
1874	Whatever Gets You Thru the Night/Beef Jerky	1983	—	3.00	6.00
	—Black colorband label				
1874	Whatever Gets You Thru the Night/Beef Jerky	1988	—	3.00	6.00
	—Purple late-1980s label				
1878	#9 Dream/What You Got	1976	10.00	20.00	40.00
	—Orange label				
1878	#9 Dream/What You Got	1978	—	3.00	6.00
	—Purple late-1970s label				
1878	#9 Dream/What You Got	1983	2.50	5.00	10.00
	—Black colorband label				
S7-17644	Happy Xmas (War Is Over)/Listen, the Snow Is Falling	1993	—	2.00	4.00
	—John & Yoko/The Plastic Ono Band; green vinyl				
S7-17783	Give Peace a Chance/Remember Love	1994	25.00	50.00	100.00
	—CEMA Special Markets issue; meant for gold-plating in a special plaque. About 100 were not.				
B-44230	Jealous Guy/Give Peace a Chance	1988	—	2.50	5.00
B-44230 [PS]	Jealous Guy/Give Peace a Chance	1988	—	2.50	5.00
S7-57849	Imagine/It's So Hard	1992	12.50	25.00	50.00
	—CEMA Special Markets issue; meant for gold-plating in a special plaque. About 1,000 were not.				

COTILLION

Number	Title (A Side/B Side)	Yr	VG	VG+	NM
PR-104/5 [DJ]	John Lennon on Ronnie Hawkins: The Short Rap/The Long Rap	1970	20.00	40.00	80.00
	—White label with promo markings				
PR-104/5 [DJ]	John Lennon on Ronnie Hawkins: The Short Rap/The Long Rap	1970	22.50	45.00	90.00
	—No promo markings on white label				

GEFFEN

Number	Title (A Side/B Side)	Yr	VG	VG+	NM
29855	Happy Xmas (War Is Over)/Beautiful Boy (Darling Boy)	1982	—	2.50	5.00
29855 [PS]	Happy Xmas (War Is Over)/Beautiful Boy (Darling Boy)	1982	—	2.50	5.00
49604	(Just Like) Starting Over/Kiss Kiss Kiss	1980	—	2.00	4.00
	—B-side by Yoko Ono				
49604 [PS]	(Just Like) Starting Over/Kiss Kiss Kiss	1980	—	2.00	4.00
	—B-side by Yoko Ono				
49644	Woman/Beautiful Boys	1980	—	2.00	4.00
	—B-side by Yoko Ono				
49644 [PS]	Woman/Beautiful Boys	1980	—	2.00	4.00
	—B-side by Yoko Ono				
49695	Watching the Wheels/Yes, I'm Your Angel	1981	—	2.00	4.00
	—B-side by Yoko Ono				
49695 [PS]	Watching the Wheels/Yes, I'm Your Angel	1981	—	2.00	4.00
	—B-side by Yoko Ono				

KYA

Number	Title (A Side/B Side)	Yr	VG	VG+	NM
1260 [DJ]	The KYA 1969 Peace Talk	1969	50.00	100.00	200.00

NOISEVILLE

Number	Title (A Side/B Side)	Yr	VG	VG+	NM
43	John Lennon Talks About David Peel	199?	10.00	20.00	40.00
	—Red vinyl, signed by David Peel				
43	John Lennon Talks About David Peel	199?	2.50	5.00	10.00
	—Black vinyl				
43 [PS]	John Lennon Talks About David Peel	199?	2.50	5.00	10.00

POLYDOR

Number	Title (A Side/B Side)	Yr	VG	VG+	NM
817254-7	Nobody Told Me/O' Sanity	1983	2.50	5.00	10.00
	—With "Manufactured by Polydor Incorporated..." on label; B-side by Yoko Ono				
817254-7	Nobody Told Me/O' Sanity	1983	—	2.50	5.00
	—With "Manufactured and Marketed by Polygram..." on label; B-side by Yoko Ono				
817254-7 [PS]	Nobody Told Me/O' Sanity	1983	—	2.50	5.00
821107-7	I'm Stepping Out/Sleepless Night	1984	—	2.00	4.00
	—B-side by Yoko Ono				
821107-7 [PS]	I'm Stepping Out/Sleepless Night	1984	—	2.00	4.00
821204-7	Borrowed Time/Your Hands	1984	—	2.50	5.00
	—B-side by Yoko Ono				
821204-7 [PS]	Borrowed Time/Your Hands	1984	—	2.50	5.00
881378-7	Every Man Has a Woman Who Loves Him/It's Alright	1984	2.00	4.00	8.00
	—B-side by Sean Ono Lennon				
881378-7 [PS]	Every Man Has a Woman Who Loves Him/It's Alright	1984	2.00	4.00	8.00

QUAKER GRANOLA DIPPS

Number	Title (A Side/B Side)	Yr	VG	VG+	NM
(no #)	A Tribute to John Lennon	1986	3.75	7.50	15.00
	—Cardboard record included in specially marked boxes of Quaker Granola Dipps				

QUAYE/TRIDENT

Number	Title (A Side/B Side)	Yr	VG	VG+	NM
SK 3419 [DJ]	Rock 'N' Roll	1975	125.00	250.00	500.00
	—Radio spot to promote the album Rock 'N' Roll				

Albums

ADAM VIII

Number	Title (A Side/B Side)	Yr	VG	VG+	NM
A-8018	John Lennon Sings the Great Rock & Roll Hits (Roots)	1975	250.00	500.00	1000.
	—Counterfeits abound. On authentic copies, cover is posterboard (not slicks); labels are normal size (not overly large); printing on cover is sharp, not blurry; the word "Greatest" does NOT appear on the spine. Authentic copies usually have ad sleeve also.				

Number	Title (A Side/B Side)	Yr	VG	VG+	NM
APPLE					
SMAX-3361	Wedding Album	1969	37.50	75.00	150.00
—With photo strip, postcard, poster of wedding photos, poster of lithographs, "Bagism" bag, booklet, photo of slice of wedding cake. Missing inserts reduce the value.					
SW-3362	Live Peace in Toronto 1969	1970	3.75	7.50	15.00
—By "The Plastic Ono Band" ; without calendar					
SW-3362	Live Peace in Toronto 1969	1970	5.00	10.00	20.00
—By "The Plastic Ono Band"; with calendar					
SW-3372	John Lennon Plastic Ono Band	1970	5.00	10.00	20.00
SW-3379	Imagine	1971	5.00	10.00	20.00
—With either of two postcard inserts, lyric sleeve, poster					
SW-3379	Imagine.	1975	5.00	10.00	20.00
—"All Rights Reserved" label					
SVBB-3392 [(2)]	Some Time in New York City.	1972	7.50	15.00	30.00
—By John and Yoko; with photo card and petition					
SVBB-3392 [(2) DJ]	Some Time in New York City.	1972	250.00	500.00	1000.
—White label promo					
SW-3414	Mind Games.	1973	5.00	10.00	20.00
SW-3416	Walls and Bridges.	1974	5.00	10.00	20.00
—With fold-open segmented front cover					
SK-3419	Rock 'n' Roll.	1975	5.00	10.00	20.00
SW-3421	Shaved Fish.	1975	5.00	10.00	20.00
T-5001	Two Virgins — Unfinished Music No. 1.	1968	12.50	25.00	50.00
—With Yoko Ono; without brown bag					
T-5001	Two Virgins — Unfinished Music No. 1.	1968	37.50	75.00	150.00
—With Yoko Ono; price with brown bag					
T-5001	Two Virgins — Unfinished Music No. 1.	1968	37.50	75.00	150.00
—With Yoko Ono; with die-cut bag					
T-5001	Two Virgins — Unfinished Music No. 1.	1985	3.75	7.50	15.00
—With Yoko Ono; reissue, flat label					
CAPITOL					
SW-3372	John Lennon Plastic Ono Band.	1978	3.00	6.00	12.00
—Purple label, large Capitol logo					
SW-3372	John Lennon Plastic Ono Band.	1982	5.00	10.00	20.00
—Black label, print in colorband					
SW-3372	John Lennon Plastic Ono Band.	1988	7.50	15.00	30.00
—Purple label, small Capitol logo					
SW-3379	Imagine.	1978	2.50	5.00	10.00
—Purple label, large Capitol logo					
SW-3379	Imagine.	1986	7.50	15.00	30.00
—Black label, print in colorband					
SW-3379	Imagine.	1987	6.25	12.50	25.00
—Black label, print in colorband; "Digitally Re-Mastered" at top of front cover					
SW-3379	Imagine.	1988	7.50	15.00	30.00
—Purple label, small Capitol logo					
SVBB-3392 [(2)]	Some Time in New York City.	197?	6.25	12.50	25.00
—By John and Yoko; purple label, large Capitol logo					
SVBB-3392 [(2)]	Some Time in New York City.	197?	25.00	50.00	100.00
—Both discs in single-pocket gatefold (the other pocket is glued shut)					
SW-3414	Mind Games.	1978	10.00	20.00	40.00
—Purple label, large Capitol logo					
SW-3416	Walls and Bridges.	1978	3.75	7.50	15.00
—Purple label, large Capitol logo; standard front cover					
SW-3416	Walls and Bridges	1982	7.50	15.00	30.00
—Black label, print in colorband					
SW-3416	Walls and Bridges	1989	7.50	15.00	30.00
—Purple label, small Capitol logo					
SK-3419	Rock 'n' Roll	1978	10.00	20.00	40.00
—Purple label, large Capitol logo					
SW-3421	Shaved Fish.	1978	3.00	6.00	12.00
—Purple Capitol label with Apple logo on cover					
SW-3421	Shaved Fish.	1978	10.00	20.00	40.00
—Purple Capitol label with Capitol logo on cover					
SW-3421	Shaved Fish.	1983	5.00	10.00	20.00
—Black Capitol label with Apple logo on cover					
SW-3421	Shaved Fish.	1983	10.00	20.00	40.00
—Black Capitol label with Capitol logo on cover					
SW-3421	Shaved Fish.	1989	10.00	20.00	40.00
—Purple Capitol label (small logo) with Capitol logo on cover					
ST-12239	Live Peace in Toronto 1969.	1982	2.50	5.00	10.00
—By "The Plastic Ono Band"; reissue, purple Capitol label					
ST-12239	Live Peace in Toronto 1969.	1983	12.50	25.00	50.00
—By "The Plastic Ono Band"; reissue, black Capitol label					
SV-12451	Live in New York City.	1986	3.00	6.00	12.00
SJ-12533	Menlove Ave.	1986	3.75	7.50	15.00
SN-16068	Mind Games.	1980	3.00	6.00	12.00
—Budget-line reissue					
SN-16069	Rock 'n' Roll.	1980	3.00	6.00	12.00
—Budget-line reissue					
C1-90803 [(2)]	Imagine: Music from the Motion Picture	1988	5.00	10.00	20.00
C1-91425	Double Fantasy	1989	5.00	10.00	20.00
—Very briefly available reissue					
R 144136	Menlove Ave.	1986	12.50	25.00	50.00
—RCA Music Service edition					
R 144136	Menlove Ave.	198?	12.50	25.00	50.00
—BMG Direct Marketing edition					
R 144497	Live in New York City	1986	3.75	7.50	15.00
—RCA Music Service edition					
SV-512451	Live in New York City	1986	3.75	7.50	15.00
—Columbia House edition					
C1-591425	Double Fantasy	1989	15.00	30.00	60.00
—Columbia House edition of reissue					

Number	Title (A Side/B Side)	Yr	VG	VG+	NM
GEFFEN					
GHS 2001	Double Fantasy	1980	2.50	5.00	10.00
—Seven tracks by John, seven by Yoko; off-white label; titles on back cover out of order					
GHS 2001	Double Fantasy	1981	18.75	37.50	75.00
—Columbia House edition (all have corrected back cover) with "CH" on label					
GHS 2001	Double Fantasy	1981	3.00	6.00	12.00
—Off-white label, titles in order on the back cover					
GHS 2001	Double Fantasy	1981	3.00	6.00	12.00
—Columbia House edition (all have corrected back cover) without "CH" on label					
GHS 2001	Double Fantasy	1986	12.50	25.00	50.00
—Same as above, but with black Geffen label					
GHSP 2023	The John Lennon Collection	1982	5.00	10.00	20.00
GHSP 2023 [DJ]	The John Lennon Collection	1982	12.50	25.00	50.00
—Promo only on Quiex II audiophile vinyl					
R 104689	Double Fantasy	1981	10.00	20.00	40.00
—RCA Music Service edition					
MOBILE FIDELITY					
1-153	Imagine	1984	12.50	25.00	50.00
—Audiophile vinyl					
NAUTILUS					
NR-47	Double Fantasy	1982	20.00	40.00	80.00
—Half-speed master					
NR-47	Double Fantasy	1982	500.00	1000.	2000.
—Half-speed master; alternate experimental cover with yellow and red added to black and white front					
PARLOPHONE					
21954 [(2)]	Lennon Legend	1998	5.00	10.00	20.00
—"Made in U.S.A." on back cover					
POLYDOR					
817160-1	Milk and Honey	1983	2.50	5.00	10.00
—Six tracks by John, six by Yoko					
817160-1	Milk and Honey	1984	37.50	75.00	150.00
—Yellow or green vinyl; unauthorized "inside jobs"					
817238-1	Heart Play (Unfinished Dialogue)	1983	3.00	6.00	12.00
—Interviews with John Lennon and Yoko Ono					
SILHOUETTE					
SM-10012 [(2)]	Reflections and Poetry	1984	6.25	12.50	25.00
ZAPPLE					
ST-3357	Life with the Lions — Unfinished Music No. 2	1969	5.00	10.00	20.00
—With Yoko Ono					

MCCARTNEY, PAUL

Includes duets with Linda McCartney plus his work with Wings.

12-Inch Singles

Number	Title (A Side/B Side)	Yr	VG	VG+	NM
ATLANTIC					
PR 388 [DJ]	Every Night/Lucille	1981	62.50	125.00	250.00
CAPITOL					
SPRO-8574 [DJ]	Maybe I'm Amazed (mono/stereo)	1976	20.00	40.00	80.00
SPRO-9556 [DJ]	Spies Like Us (4:40)/Spies Like Us (3:46)	1985	7.50	15.00	30.00
SPRO-9763 [DJ]	Press (same on both sides)	1986	5.00	10.00	20.00
SPRO-9797 [DJ]	Angry (same on both sides)	1986	6.25	12.50	25.00
SPRO-9861 [DJ]	Stranglehold (same on both sides)	1986	6.25	12.50	25.00
SPRO-9928 [DJ]	Pretty Little Head (same on both sides)	1986	12.50	25.00	50.00
V-15212	Spies Like Us (Party Mix)/(Alternative Mix)//(DJ Version)/My Carnival	1985	5.00	10.00	20.00
—"MPL" correct on label					
V-15212	Spies Like Us (Party Mix)/(Alternative Mix)//(DJ Version)/My Carnival	1985	3.75	7.50	15.00
—"MLP" on label instead of "MPL"					
V-15235	Press (Video Mix)/It's Not True//Hanglide/Press (Dub Mix)	1986	3.00	6.00	12.00
V-15499	Ou Est Le Soleil//Ou Est Le Soleil (Tub Dub Mix)/(Instrumental)	1989	3.00	6.00	12.00
COLUMBIA					
AS 775 [DJ]	Coming Up/Coming Up (Live at Glasgow)	1980	15.00	30.00	60.00
—Red label					
AS 775 [DJ]	Coming Up/Coming Up (Live at Glasgow)	1980	12.50	25.00	50.00
—White label					
AS 1444 [DJ]	Ebony and Ivory//Ballroom Dancing/The Pound Is Sinking	1982	7.50	15.00	30.00
AS 1758 [DJ]	Say Say Say (same on both sides)	1983	3.00	6.00	12.00
—With Michael Jackson					
AS 1940 [DJ]	No More Lonely Nights (Ballad) (same on both sides)	1984	5.00	10.00	20.00
AS 1990 [DJ]	No More Lonely Nights (Special Dance Mix) (same on both sides)	1984	5.00	10.00	20.00
03019	Take It Away//I'll Give You a Ring/Dress Me Up as a Robber	1982	3.00	6.00	12.00
05077	No More Lonely Nights (Playout Version)//Silly Love Songs/No More Lonely Nights (Ballad)	1984	3.00	6.00	12.00
05077	No More Lonely Nights (Special Dance Mix)//Silly Love Songs/No More Lonely Nights (Ballad)	1984	7.50	15.00	30.00
10940	Goodnight Tonight (7:25)/Daytime Nighttime Suffering	1979	2.50	5.00	10.00
—Generic white cover, no picture cover or sticker					
10940	Goodnight Tonight (7:25)/Daytime Nighttime Suffering	1979	20.00	40.00	80.00
—Generic white cover with large blue and white sticker					
10940	Goodnight Tonight (7:25)/Daytime Nighttime Suffering	1979	3.75	7.50	15.00
—With picture cover					
10940 [DJ]	Goodnight Tonight (7:25)/Goodnight Tonight (4:18)	1979	6.25	12.50	25.00
8C8 39927-S1	No More Lonely Nights (2 versions)/Silly Love Songs	1984	5.00	10.00	20.00
—Picture disc					

45s

APPLE

Number	Title (A Side/B Side)	Yr	VG	VG+	NM
1829	Another Day/Oh Woman, Oh Why	1971	3.00	6.00	12.00
—With star on A-side label					
1829	Another Day/Oh Woman, Oh Why	1971	2.00	4.00	8.00
1837	Uncle Albert/Admiral Halsey//Too Many People	1971	3.75	7.50	15.00
—Paul and Linda McCartney; with "Pual" misspelling on producer credit					
1837	Uncle Albert/Admiral Halsey//Too Many People	1971	2.00	4.00	8.00
—Paul and Linda McCartney; with no misspelling					
1837	Uncle Albert/Admiral Halsey//Too Many People	1971	12.50	25.00	50.00
—Paul and Linda McCartney; with unsliced apple on B-side label					
1837	Uncle Albert/Admiral Halsey//Too Many People	1975	7.50	15.00	30.00
—Paul and Linda McCartney; with "All rights reserved" on label					
1847	Give Ireland Back to the Irish/Give Ireland Back to the Irish (Version)	1972	2.50	5.00	10.00
—Wings					
1847 [PS]	Give Ireland Back to the Irish/Give Ireland Back to the Irish (Version)	1972	7.50	15.00	30.00
—Wings; title sleeve with large center hole					
1851	Mary Had a Little Lamb/Little Woman Love	1972	2.50	5.00	10.00
—Wings					
1851 [DJ]	Mary Had a Little Lamb/Little Woman Love	1972	75.00	150.00	300.00
—White label promo, lists artist as Paul McCartney					
1851 [PS]	Mary Had a Little Lamb/Little Woman Love	1972	6.25	12.50	25.00
—Wings; without "Little Woman Love" on sleeve					
1851 [PS]	Mary Had a Little Lamb/Little Woman Love	1972	10.00	20.00	40.00
—Wings; with "Little Woman Love" on sleeve					
1857	Hi Hi Hi/C Moon	1972	2.50	5.00	10.00
—Wings; red label					
1861	My Love/The Mess	1973	2.00	4.00	8.00
—Paul McCartney and Wings; custom "Red Rose Speedway" label					
1861 [DJ]	My Love/The Mess	1973	50.00	100.00	200.00
—Paul McCartney and Wings; white label					
1863	Live and Let Die/I Lie Around	1973	2.00	4.00	8.00
—Wings					
1869	Helen Wheels/Country Dreamer	1973	2.00	4.00	8.00
—Paul McCartney and Wings					
1871	Jet/Mamunia	1974	2.50	5.00	10.00
—Paul McCartney and Wings					
1871	Jet/Mamunia	1974	25.00	50.00	100.00
—Paul McCartney and Wings; A-side incorrectly listed as playing for 2:49					
1871	Jet/Let Me Roll It	1974	2.00	4.00	8.00
—Paul McCartney and Wings					
P-1871 [DJ]	Jet (Edited Mono)/Jet (Stereo)	1974	12.50	25.00	50.00
—Paul McCartney and Wings					
1873	Band on the Run/Nineteen Hundred and Eighty-Five	1974	2.00	4.00	8.00
—Paul McCartney and Wings					
P-1873 [DJ]	Band on the Run (Edited Mono)/Band on the Run (Full-length Stereo)	1974	10.00	20.00	40.00
—Paul McCartney and Wings					
P-1873 [DJ]	Band on the Run (mono/stereo, both edits)	1974	25.00	50.00	100.00
—Paul McCartney and Wings					
1875	Junior's Farm/Sally G	1974	2.00	4.00	8.00
—Paul McCartney and Wings					
1875	Junior's Farm/Sally G	1975	20.00	40.00	80.00
—Paul McCartney and Wings; with "All Rights Reserved" on label					
P-1875 [DJ]	Junior's Farm (Edited Mono)/Junior's Farm (Full-length Stereo)	1974	12.50	25.00	50.00
—Paul McCartney and Wings					
P-1875 [DJ]	Sally G (mono/stereo)	1974	20.00	40.00	80.00
—Paul McCartney and Wings					
PRO-6193/4 [DJ]	Another Day/Oh Woman, Oh Why	1971	20.00	40.00	80.00
PRO-6786 [DJ]	Helen Wheels (mono/stereo)	1973	12.50	25.00	50.00
—Paul McCartney and Wings					
PRO-6787 [DJ]	Country Dreamer (mono/stereo)	1973	100.00	200.00	400.00
—Paul McCartney and Wings					

CAPITOL

Number	Title (A Side/B Side)	Yr	VG	VG+	NM
(no #) [DJ]	Figure of Eight (same on both sides)	1989	25.00	50.00	100.00
—Test pressings with blank label; most known copies come in a Capitol sleeve					
1829	Another Day/Oh Woman, Oh Why	1976	3.75	7.50	15.00
—Black label					
1837	Uncle Albert/Admiral Halsey//Too Many People	1976	3.75	7.50	15.00
—Black label					
1847	Give Ireland Back to the Irish/Give Ireland Back to the Irish	1976	5.00	10.00	20.00
—Wings; black label					
1851	Mary Had a Little Lamb/Little Woman Love	1976	3.00	6.00	12.00
—Wings; black label					
1857	Hi Hi Hi/C Moon	1976	3.75	7.50	15.00
—Wings; black label					
1861	My Love/The Mess	1976	5.00	10.00	20.00
—Paul McCartney and Wings; black label; "The Mess" plays too fast					
1861	My Love/The Mess	1976	5.00	10.00	20.00
—Paul McCartney and Wings; black label; "The Mess" plays normally					
1863	Live and Let Die/I Lie Around	1976	3.00	6.00	12.00
—Wings; black label					
1869	Helen Wheels/Country Dreamer	1976	3.75	7.50	15.00
—Paul McCartney and Wings; black label					
1871	Jet/Let Me Roll It	1976	3.75	7.50	15.00
—Paul McCartney and Wings; black label					
1873	Band on the Run/Nineteen Hundred and Eighty-Five	1976	3.75	7.50	15.00
—Paul McCartney and Wings; black label					
1875	Junior's Farm/Sally G	1976	3.75	7.50	15.00
—Paul McCartney and Wings; black label					
4091	Listen to What the Man Said/Love in Song	1975	—	2.50	5.00
4091 [PS]	Listen to What the Man Said/Love in Song	1975	3.00	6.00	12.00
—Wings					
4145	Letting Go/You Gave Me the Answer	1975	—	2.50	5.00
—Wings					
4175	Venus and Mars Rock Show/Magneto and Titanium Man	1975	—	2.50	5.00
—Wings					
4256	Silly Love Songs/Cook of the House	1976	2.00	4.00	8.00
—Wings; black label					
4256	Silly Love Songs/Cook of the House	1976	—	2.00	4.00
—Wings; "Speed of Sound" label (more common version)					
4293	Let 'Em In/Beware My Love	1976	—	3.00	6.00
—Wings; black label (more common version)					
4293	Let 'Em In/Beware My Love	1976	—	2.00	4.00
—Wings; "Speed of Sound" label					
4385	Maybe I'm Amazed/Soily	1976	—	2.00	4.00
—Wings; custom label (more common version)					
4385	Maybe I'm Amazed/Soily	1976	5.00	10.00	20.00
—Wings; black label					
4504	Girls' School/Mull of Kintyre	1977	—	2.50	5.00
—Wings; black label (more common version)					
4504	Girls' School/Mull of Kintyre	1978	30.00	60.00	120.00
—Wings; purple label, label has reeded edge					
4504 [PS]	Girls' School/Mull of Kintyre	1977	3.00	6.00	12.00
—Wings					
4559	With a Little Luck/Backwards Traveller-Cuff Link	1978	—	2.00	4.00
—Wings					
4594	I've Had Enough/Deliver Your Children	1978	—	2.00	4.00
—Wings					
4625	London Town/I'm Carrying	1978	—	2.00	4.00
—Wings					
B-5537	Spies Like Us/My Carnival	1985	—	—	3.00
B-5537 [PS]	Spies Like Us/My Carnival	1985	—	3.00	6.00
B-5597	Press/It's Not True	1986	—	2.50	5.00
B-5597 [PS]	Press/It's Not True	1986	—	2.50	5.00
B-5636	Stranglehold/Angry	1986	—	2.50	5.00
B-5636 [PS]	Stranglehold/Angry	1986	—	2.50	5.00
B-5672	Only Love Remains/Tough on a Tightrope	1987	—	2.50	5.00
B-5672 [PS]	Only Love Remains/Tough on a Tightrope	1987	—	2.50	5.00
S7-17318	Off the Ground/Cosmically Conscious	1993	—	3.00	6.00
—White vinyl standard issue					
S7-17318	Off the Ground/Cosmically Conscious	1993	—	3.00	6.00
—Black vinyl "error" issue					
S7-17319	Biker Like an Icon/Things We Said Today1993 —3.006.00—*Black vinyl "error" issue*				
S7-17319	Biker Like an Icon/Things We Said Today	1993	—	3.00	6.00
—White vinyl standard issue					
S7-17489	C'mon People/Down to the River19932.004.00 8.00—*All copies on white vinyl*				
S7-17643	Wonderful Christmastime/Rudolph, the Red-Nosed Reggae	1993	—	3.00	6.00
—Paul McCartney & Wings; red vinyl					
B-44367	My Brave Face/Flying to My Home	1989	2.50	5.00	10.00
—Version 1: Both title and artist in block print, time of A-side is "3:17"					
B-44367	My Brave Face/Flying to My Home	1989	2.00	4.00	8.00
—Version 2: Artist in custom print, title in block print, time of A-side is "3:17"					
B-44367	My Brave Face/Flying to My Home	1989	—	2.50	5.00
—Version 3: Same as Version 2, time of A-side is "3:16"					
B-44367 [PS]	My Brave Face/Flying to My Home	1989	—	2.50	5.00
S7-56946	Hope of Deliverance/Long Leather Coat	1993	—	3.00	6.00
58823	No Other Baby/Try Not to Cry	1999	—	2.00	4.00
7PRO-79700 [DJ]	This One (same on both sides)	1989	100.00	200.00	400.00
—Vinyl is promo only					

COLUMBIA

Number	Title (A Side/B Side)	Yr	VG	VG+	NM
02171	Silly Love Songs/Cook of the House	1981	6.25	12.50	25.00
—Wings; despite label information, this has an edited version of A-side					
03018	Take It Away/I'll Give You a Ring	1982	—	—	3.00
03018 [PS]	Take It Away/I'll Give You a Ring	1982	—	—	3.00
03235	Tug of War/Get It	1982	3.00	6.00	12.00
04127	Wonderful Christmastime/Rudolph the Red-Nosed Reggae	1983	7.50	15.00	30.00
—Scarce reissue with B-side in stereo					
04296	So Bad/Pipes of Peace	1983	—	2.50	5.00
04296 [PS]	So Bad/Pipes of Peace	1983	—	2.50	5.00
04581	No More Lonely Nights/No More Lonely Nights (playout version)	1984	—	2.00	4.00
04581	No More Lonely Nights/No More Lonely Nights (Special Dance Version)	1984	10.00	20.00	40.00
04581 [PS]	No More Lonely Nights/No More Lonely Nights (playout version)	1984	7.50	15.00	30.00
—Title print in gray, credit print in white					
04581 [PS]	No More Lonely Nights/No More Lonely Nights (playout version)	1984	—	2.50	5.00
—Title print in white, credit print in gray					
10939	Goodnight Tonight/Daytime Nighttime Suffering	1979	—	3.00	6.00
—Wings					
11020	Getting Closer/Spin It On	1979	—	3.00	6.00
—Wings					
11020 [PS]	Getting Closer/Spin It On	1979	7.50	15.00	30.00
—Title sleeve with large center hole					
11070	Arrow Through Me/Old Siam, Sir	1979	—	3.00	6.00
—Wings					

Number	Title (A Side/B Side)	Yr	VG	VG+	NM
11162	Wonderful Christmastime/Rudolph the Red-Nosed Reggae	1979	2.50	5.00	10.00
11162 [PS]	Wonderful Christmastime/Rudolph the Red-Nosed Reggae	1979	3.75	7.50	15.00
11263	Coming Up//Coming Up (Live at Glasgow)/Lunch Box-Odd Sox	1980	—	2.00	4.00
11263 [PS]	Coming Up//Coming Up (Live at Glasgow)/Lunch Box-Odd Sox	1980	—	2.50	5.00
11335	Waterfalls/Check My Machine	1980	—	3.00	6.00
11335 [PS]	Waterfalls/Check My Machine	1980	5.00	10.00	20.00
33405	Goodnight Tonight/Getting Closer	1980	2.50	5.00	10.00
—Wings; red label "Hall of Fame" series					
33407	My Love/Maybe I'm Amazed	1980	2.50	5.00	10.00
—Paul McCartney and Wings; red label "Hall of Fame" series					
33407	My Love/Maybe I'm Amazed	1985	7.50	15.00	30.00
—Paul McCartney and Wings; briefly available gray label reissue					
33408	Jet//Uncle Albert/Admiral Halsey	1980	2.50	5.00	10.00
—Paul McCartney and Wings; red label "Hall of Fame" series					
33408	Jet//Uncle Albert/Admiral Halsey	1985	7.50	15.00	30.00
—Paul McCartney and Wings; briefly available gray label reissue					
33409	Band on the Run/Helen Wheels	1980	2.50	5.00	10.00
—Paul McCartney and Wings; red label "Hall of Fame" series					
33409	Band on the Run/Helen Wheels	1985	7.50	15.00	30.00
—Paul McCartney and Wings; briefly available gray label reissue					

EMI

Number	Title (A Side/B Side)	Yr	VG	VG+	NM
3977	Walking in the Park with Eloise/Bridge on the River Suite	1974	15.00	30.00	60.00
3977 [PS]	Walking in the Park with Eloise/Bridge on the River Suite	1974	20.00	40.00	80.00
—As "The Country Hams"					

Albums

APPLE

Number	Title	Yr	VG	VG+	NM
SMAS-3363	McCartney	1975	25.00	50.00	100.00
—With "All Rights Reserved" on label					
SMAS-3363	McCartney	197?	5.00	10.00	20.00
—New prefix on label					
STAO-3363	McCartney	1970	6.25	12.50	25.00
—"McCartney" and "Paul McCartney" on separate lines on label; New York addess on back cover					
STAO-3363	McCartney	1970	7.50	15.00	30.00
—"McCartney" and "Paul McCartney" on separate lines on label; California addess on back cover					
STAO-3363	McCartney	1970	20.00	40.00	80.00
—Apple label with small Capitol logo on B-side					
STAO-3363	McCartney	1970	5.00	10.00	20.00
—Only "McCartney" on label; back cover does NOT say "An Abkco managed company"					
STAO-3363	McCartney	1970	6.25	12.50	25.00
—Only "McCartney" on label; back cover says "An Abkco managed company"					
MAS-3375 [M]	Ram	1971	1000.	2000.	4000.
—Credited to "Paul and Linda McCartney"; mono record in stereo cover for radio station use only					
SMAS-3375	Ram	1971	3.75	7.50	15.00
—Credited to "Paul and Linda McCartney"; unsliced apple on one label, sliced apple on other					
SMAS-3375	Ram	1971	7.50	15.00	30.00
—Credited to "Paul and Linda McCartney"; unsliced apple on both labels					
SMAS-3375	Ram	1971	12.50	25.00	50.00
—Credited to "Paul and Linda McCartney"; Apple label with small Capitol logo on B-side					
SMAS-3375	Ram	1975	25.00	50.00	100.00
—Credited to "Paul and Linda McCartney"; with "All Rights Reserved" on label					
SW-3386	Wild Life	1971	3.75	7.50	15.00
—Credited to "Wings"					
SMAL-3409	Red Rose Speedway	1973	5.00	10.00	20.00
—Credited to "Paul McCartney and Wings"; with bound-in booklet					
SO-3415	Band on the Run	1973	5.00	10.00	20.00
—Credited to "Paul McCartney and Wings"; with photo innersleeve and poster					
SPRO-6210 [DJ]	Brung to Ewe By	1971	100.00	200.00	400.00
—Promo-only radio spots for "Ram"; counterfeits have uneven spacing between tracks					

CAPITOL

Number	Title	Yr	VG	VG+	NM
SMAS-3363	McCartney	1976	6.25	12.50	25.00
—Black label, "Manufactured by McCartney Music Inc" at top					
SMAS-3363	McCartney	1976	5.00	10.00	20.00
—Black label, "Manufactured by MPL Communications Inc" at top					
SMAS-3375	Ram	1976	7.50	15.00	30.00
—Credited to "Paul and Linda McCartney"; black label, "Manufactured by McCartney Music Inc" at top					
SMAS-3375	Ram	197?	5.00	10.00	20.00
—Credited to "Paul and Linda McCartney"; black label, "Manufactured by MPL Communications Inc" at top					
SMAS-3375	Ram	197?	10.00	20.00	40.00
—Credited to "Paul and Linda McCartney"; black label, "Manufactured by Capitol RecordsÖ" on label					
SW-3386	Wild Life	1976	7.50	15.00	30.00
—Credited to "Wings"; black label, "Manufactured by McCartney Music Inc" at top					
SW-3386	Wild Life	197?	5.00	10.00	20.00
—Credited to "Wings"; black label, "Manufactured by MPL Communications Inc" at top					
SMAL-3409	Red Rose Speedway	1976	7.50	15.00	30.00
—Credited to "Paul McCartney and Wings"; black label, "Manufactured by McCartney Music Inc" at top					
SMAL-3409	Red Rose Speedway	197?	6.25	12.50	25.00
—Credited to "Paul McCartney and Wings"; black label, "Manufactured by MPL Communications Inc" at top					
SO-3415	Band on the Run	1975	5.00	10.00	20.00
—Credited to "Paul McCartney and Wings"; custom label with MPL logo					
SO-3415	Band on the Run	197?	12.50	25.00	50.00
—Credited to "Paul McCartney and Wings"; black label, "Manufactured by Capitol Records..."					
SO-3415	Band on the Run	197?	5.00	10.00	20.00
—Credited to "Paul McCartney and Wings"; black label, "Maunfactured by MPL Communications Inc." at top					
SMAS-11419	Venus and Mars	1975	3.75	7.50	15.00
—Credited to "Wings"; with two posters and two stickers					
SW-11525	Wings at the Speed of Sound	1976	2.50	5.00	10.00
—Credited to "Wings"; custom label					
SW-11525 [DJ]	Wings at the Speed of Sound	1976	75.00	150.00	300.00
—Credited to "Wings"; white label advance promo					
SWCO-11593 [(3)]	Wings Over America	1976	6.25	12.50	25.00
—Credited to "Wings"; custom labels with poster					
ST-11642	Thrillington	1977	25.00	50.00	100.00
—Credited to "Percy 'Thrills' Thrillington"; instrumental versions of songs from Ram LP					
SW-11777	London Town	1978	3.75	7.50	15.00
—Credited to "Wings"; custom label with poster					
SEAX-11901 [PD]	Band on the Run	1978	10.00	20.00	40.00
—Credited to "Paul McCartney and Wings"; picture disc					
SOO-11905	Wings Greatest	1978	3.75	7.50	15.00
—Credited to "Wings"; custom label with poster					
SOO-11905 [DJ]	Wings Greatest	1978	100.00	200.00	400.00
—Credited to "Wings"; white label advance promo/test pressing					
PJAS-12475	Press to Play	1986	3.00	6.00	12.00
CLW-48287 [(2)]	All the Best!	1987	5.00	10.00	20.00
C1-56500	Flaming Pie	1997	3.75	7.50	15.00
C1-91653	Flowers in the Dirt	1989	5.00	10.00	20.00
C1-94778 [(3)]	Tripping the Live Fantastic	1990	15.00	30.00	60.00
99176 [(2)]	Band on the Run	1999	10.00	20.00	40.00
—Limited-edition 180-gram reissue with original LP on one record and interviews and "The Making of.." on the second					
C1-595379	Tripping the Live Fantastic — Highlights!	1990	6.25	12.50	25.00
—Released on vinyl only through Columbia House; with U.S. address on back cover					
C1-595379	Tripping the Live Fantastic — Highlights!	1990	6.25	12.50	25.00
—Released on vinyl only through Columbia House; with Canada address on back cover, this was sold in the U.S. by Columbia House					

COLUMBIA

Number	Title	Yr	VG	VG+	NM
A2S 821 [(2) DJ]	The McCartney Interview	1980	10.00	20.00	40.00
—Promo-only set; one LP is the entire interview, the other is banded for airplay; white labels with black print; counterfeits have blank white labels					
FC 36057	Back to the Egg	1979	2.50	5.00	10.00
—Credited to "Wings"; custom label					
FC 36057 [DJ]	Back to the Egg	1979	10.00	20.00	40.00
—Credited to "Wings"; "Demonstration -- Not for Sale" on custom label					
PC 36057	Back to the Egg	1984	7.50	15.00	30.00
—Credited to "Wings"; "PC" cover with "FC" label					
PC 36057	Back to the Egg	1984	10.00	20.00	40.00
—Credited to "Wings"; "PC" cover with "PC" label					
JC 36478	McCartney	1979	3.75	7.50	15.00
PC 36478	McCartney	1984	3.75	7.50	15.00
—Budget-line reissue					
JC 36479	Ram	1980	3.75	7.50	15.00
—Credited to "Paul and Linda McCartney"					
PC 36479	Ram	1984	3.75	7.50	15.00
—Credited to "Paul and Linda McCartney"; budget-line reissue					
JC 36480	Wild Life	1980	3.75	7.50	15.00
—Credited to "Wings"					
PC 36480	Wild Life	1982	3.75	7.50	15.00
—Credited to "Wings"; budget-line reissue					
JC 36481	Red Rose Speedway	1980	3.75	7.50	15.00
—Credited to "Paul McCartney and Wings"; flat or glossy cover					
PC 36481	Red Rose Speedway.	198?	3.75	7.50	15.00
—Credited to "Paul McCartney and Wings"; not issued with booklet					
JC 36482	Band on the Run.	1980	3.75	7.50	15.00
—Credited to "Paul McCartney and Wings"; custom label					
JC 36482	Band on the Run	198?	25.00	50.00	100.00
—Credited to "Paul McCartney and Wings"; white "MPL" logo on lower left front cover					
PC 36482	Band on the Run.	198?	5.00	10.00	20.00
—Credited to "Paul McCartney and Wings"; "PC" cover with "JC" label					
PC 36482	Band on the Run.	198?	7.50	15.00	30.00
—Credited to "Paul McCartney and Wings"; "PC" cover with "PC" label					
FC 36511	McCartney II.	1980	2.50	5.00	10.00
—Add 80% if bonus single of "Coming Up (Live at Glasgow)" (AE7 1204) is with package					
FC 36511 [DJ]	McCartney II.	1980	7.50	15.00	30.00
—White label promo					
PC 36511	McCartney II.	1984	6.25	12.50	25.00
—"PC" cover with "FC" label					
PC 36511	McCartney II.	1984	25.00	50.00	100.00
—"PC" cover with "PC" label					
JC 36801	Venus and Mars.	1980	3.75	7.50	15.00
—Credited to "Wings"; with one poster and two stickers					
PC 36801	Venus and Mars.	1982	3.75	7.50	15.00
—Credited to "Wings"; budget-line reissue, not issued with inserts					
PC 36987	The McCartney Interview.	1980	3.00	6.00	12.00
—Stock release of interview originally intended for promotional use only					
FC 37409	Wings at the Speed of Sound.	1981	3.75	7.50	15.00
—Credited to "Wings"; custom label					
PC 37409	Wings at the Speed of Sound.	1982	3.75	7.50	15.00
—Credited to "Wings"; regular Columbia label, budget-line reissue					
PC 37462	Tug of War.	1984	7.50	15.00	30.00
—Custom label; "PC" cover with "TC" label					
PC 37462	Tug of War.	1984	25.00	50.00	100.00
—Regular Columbia label; "PC" cover with "PC" label					
TC 37462	Tug of War.	1982	2.50	5.00	10.00
C3X 37990 [(3)]	Wings Over America.	1982	12.50	25.00	50.00
—Credited to "Wings"; custom labels, no poster					
QC 39149	Pipes of Peace.	1983	3.00	6.00	12.00
SC 39613	Give My Regards to Broad Street.	1984	3.75	7.50	15.00

Number	Title (A Side/B Side)	Yr	VG	VG+	NM
HC 46382	Band on the Run	1981	12.50	25.00	50.00
—Credited to "Paul McCartney and Wings"; half-speed mastered edition					
MPL/PARLOPHONE					
96413	Unplugged (The Official Bootleg)	1991	18.75	37.50	75.00
—No U.S. pressings; "American" copies were U.K. imports with liner notes in Spanish!					
NATIONAL FEATURES CORP.					
2955/6	Band on the Run Radio Interview Special	1973	375.00	750.00	1500.
—Promo-only interview disc					

MCCARTNEY, PAUL, AND STEVIE WONDER

12-Inch Singles

Number	Title (A Side/B Side)	Yr	VG	VG+	NM
COLUMBIA					
02878	Ebony and Ivory//Rainclouds/Ebony and Ivory (Solo)	1982	3.00	6.00	12.00

45s

Number	Title (A Side/B Side)	Yr	VG	VG+	NM
COLUMBIA					
02860	Ebony and Ivory/Rainclouds	1982	—	2.00	4.00
02860 [PS]	Ebony and Ivory/Rainclouds	1982	—	2.00	4.00

ONO, YOKO

Also see JOHN LENNON.

12-Inch Singles

Number	Title (A Side/B Side)	Yr	VG	VG+	NM
GEFFEN					
PRO-A-934 [DJ]	Walking on Thin Ice (3:23)/Walking on Thin Ice (5:58)	1981	3.75	7.50	15.00
PRO-A-975 [DJ]	No, No, No (same on both sides)	1981	2.50	5.00	10.00
POLYDOR					
192 [DJ]	My Man/Let the Tears Dry	1982	—	3.00	6.00
810575-1	Never Say Goodbye/(B-side unknown)	1983	2.00	4.00	8.00
883455-1	Hell in Paradise (3 versions)	1985	—	3.00	6.00
883872-1 [DJ]	Walking on Thin Ice (Remix)/Cape Clear (2 versions)	1986	3.00	6.00	12.00

45s

Number	Title (A Side/B Side)	Yr	VG	VG+	NM
APPLE					
GM/OYB-1 [DJ]	Greenfield Morning/Open Your Box	1971	200.00	400.00	800.00
—Exactly six copies made for the personal use of Yoko Ono.					
1839	Mrs. Lennon/Midsummer New York	1971	—	3.50	7.00
—As "Yoko Ono/Plastic Ono Band"					
1853	Now or Never/Move On Fast	1972	—	3.50	7.00
1853 [PS]	Now or Never/Move On Fast	1972	2.00	4.00	8.00
1859	Death of Samantha/Yang Yang	1973	—	3.50	7.00
1867	Woman Power/Men, Men, Men	1973	—	3.50	7.00
CAPITOL					
S7-18550	Never Say Goodbye/We're All Water	1995	—	—	3.00
GEFFEN					
PRO-S-935 [DJ]	Walking on Thin Ice (3:23)/Walking on Thin Ice (5:58)	1981	2.50	5.00	10.00
49683	Walking on Thin Ice/It Happened	1981	—	2.00	4.00
49683 [PS]	Walking on Thin Ice/It Happened	1981	—	2.00	4.00
—Includes picture sleeve and lyric insert					
49802	No, No, No/Will You Touch Me	1981	—	2.00	4.00
49802 [PS]	No, No, No/Will You Touch Me	1981	—	2.00	4.00
49849	Goodbye Sadness/I Don't Know Why	1981	—	2.00	4.00
POLYDOR					
2224	My Man/Let the Tears Dry	1982	—	—	3.00
2224 [PS]	My Man/Let the Tears Dry	1982	—	—	3.00

Number	Title (A Side/B Side)	Yr	VG	VG+	NM
883455-7	Hell in Paradise/(Instrumental)	1985	—	—	3.00
883455-7 [PS]	Hell in Paradise/(Instrumental)	1985	—	—	3.00

Albums

Number	Title (A Side/B Side)	Yr	VG	VG+	NM
APPLE					
SW-3373	Yoko Ono Plastic Ono Band	1970	5.00	10.00	20.00
SVBB-3380 [(2)]	Fly	1971	6.50	12.50	25.00
SVBB-3399 [(2)]	Approximately Infinite Universe	1973	6.25	12.50	25.00
SW-3412	Feeling the Space	1973	5.00	10.00	20.00
CAPITOL					
(# unknown) [DJ]	Rising Mixes	1996	3.00	6.00	12.00
—Promo-only vinyl EP of six remixes from the CD "Rising"					
GEFFEN					
GHS 2004	Season of Glass	1981	3.00	6.00	12.00
POLYDOR					
PD1-6364	It's Alright (I See Rainbows)	1982	2.50	5.00	10.00
823289-1	It's Alright (I See Rainbows)	1984	2.00	4.00	8.00
—Reissue					
827530-1	Starpeace	1985	3.00	6.00	12.00

STARR, RINGO

Also see GEORGE HARRISON AND FRIENDS.

12-Inch Singles

Number	Title (A Side/B Side)	Yr	VG	VG+	NM
ATLANTIC					
DSKO 93 [DJ]	Drowning in the Sea of Love (5:08) (same on both sides)	1977	7.50	15.00	30.00

45s

Number	Title (A Side/B Side)	Yr	VG	VG+	NM
APPLE					
1826 [PS]	Beaucoups of Blues/Coochy-Coochy	1970	10.00	20.00	40.00
—Sleeve with wrong catalog number (actually 2969)					
1831	It Don't Come Easy/Early 1970	1971	2.00	4.00	8.00
1831	It Don't Come Easy/Early 1970	1971	3.00	6.00	12.00
—With star on A-side label					
1831	It Don't Come Easy/Early 1970	1975	7.50	15.00	30.00
—With "All rights reserved" on label					
1831 [PS]	It Don't Come Easy/Early 1970	1971	7.50	15.00	30.00
1849	Back Off Boogaloo/Blindman	1972	2.00	4.00	8.00
—Green-background label					
1849	Back Off Boogaloo/Blindman	1972	18.75	37.50	75.00
—Blue-background label					
1849 [DJ]	Back Off Boogaloo/Blindman	1972	37.50	75.00	150.00
—White label					
1849 [PS]	Back Off Boogaloo/Blindman	1972	3.75	7.50	15.00
—Black paper with flat finish					
1849 [PS]	Back Off Boogaloo/Blindman	1972	10.00	20.00	40.00
—Glossy black paper on both sides					
1849 [PS]	Back Off Boogaloo/Blindman	1972	10.00	20.00	40.00
—Glossy black on one side, gray on the other					
1865	Photograph/Down and Out	1973	—	3.00	6.00
—Custom star label					
1865 [PS]	Photograph/Down and Out	1973	5.00	10.00	20.00
P-1865 [DJ]	Photograph (mono/stereo)	1973	12.50	25.00	50.00
1870	You're Sixteen/Devil Woman	1973	—	3.00	6.00
—Custom star label					
1870	You're Sixteen/Devil Woman	1973	6.25	12.50	25.00
—Regular Apple label					
1870 [PS]	You're Sixteen/Devil Woman	1973	6.25	12.50	25.00
P-1870 [DJ]	You're Sixteen (mono/stereo)	1973	12.50	25.00	50.00
1872	Oh My My/Step Lightly	1974	—	3.00	6.00
—Custom star label					
1872	Oh My My/Step Lightly	1974	2.00	4.00	8.00
—Regular Apple label					
P-1872 [DJ]	Oh My My (Edited Mono)/Oh My My (Long Stereo)	1974	12.50	25.00	50.00
1876	Only You/Call Me	1974	—	3.00	6.00
—Custom nebula label					
1876	Only You/Call Me	1974	2.00	4.00	8.00
—Regular Apple label					
1876 [PS]	Only You/Call Me	1974	5.00	10.00	20.00
P-1876 [DJ]	Only You (mono/stereo)	1974	10.00	20.00	40.00
1880	No No Song/Snookeroo	1975	—	3.00	6.00
—Custom nebula label					
P-1880 [DJ]	No No Song/Snookeroo (both mono)	1975	10.00	20.00	40.00
P-1880 [DJ]	No No Song/Snookeroo (both stereo)	1975	10.00	20.00	40.00
1882	It's All Down to Goodnight Vienna/Oo-Wee	1975	—	3.00	6.00
—Custom nebula label					
1882 [PS]	It's All Down to Goodnight Vienna/Oo-Wee	1975	5.00	10.00	20.00
P-1882 [DJ]	It's All Down to Goodnight Vienna (mono/stereo)	1975	10.00	20.00	40.00
P-1882 [DJ]	Oo-Wee/Oo-Wee	1975	17.50	35.00	70.00
2969	Beaucoups of Blues/Coochy-Coochy	1970	6.25	12.50	25.00
—With small Capitol logo on bottom of B-side label and star on A-side label					
2969	Beaucoups of Blues/Coochy-Coochy	1970	10.00	20.00	40.00
—With "Mfd. by Apple" on label and star on A-side label					
2969	Beaucoups of Blues/Coochy-Coochy	1970	2.00	4.00	8.00
—With "Mfd. by Apple" on label and no star on A-side label					
2969 [PS]	Beaucoups of Blues/Coochy-Coochy	1970	12.50	25.00	50.00
—Sleeve with correct catalog number					
ATLANTIC					
3361	A Dose of Rock 'N' Roll/Cryin'	1976	2.50	5.00	10.00
3371	Hey Baby/Lady Gaye	1976	7.50	15.00	30.00
3412	Drowning in the Sea of Love/Just a Dream	1977	30.00	60.00	120.00
3429	Wings/Just a Dream	1977	7.50	15.00	30.00
BOARDWALK					
NB7-11-130	Wrack My Brain/Drumming Is My Madness	1981	—	2.50	5.00

Number	Title (A Side/B Side)	Yr	VG	VG+	NM
NB7-11-130 [PS]	Wrack My Brain/Drumming Is My Madness	1981	—	2.50	5.00
NB7-11-134	Private Property/Stop and Take the Time to Smell the Roses	1982	3.00	6.00	12.00

CAPITOL

Number	Title (A Side/B Side)	Yr	VG	VG+	NM
1831	It Don't Come Easy/Early 1970	1976	6.25	12.50	25.00
—Orange label					
1831	It Don't Come Easy/Early 1970	1978	—	3.00	6.00
—Purple late-1970s label					
1831	It Don't Come Easy/Early 1970	1983	—	3.00	6.00
—Black colorband label					
1831	It Don't Come Easy/Early 1970	1988	—	2.50	5.00
—Purple late-1980s label (wider)					
1849	Back Off Boogaloo/Blindman	1976	7.50	15.00	30.00
—Orange label					
1849	Back Off Boogaloo/Blindman	1978	2.00	4.00	8.00
—Purple late-1970s label					
1865	Photograph/Down and Out	1978	2.00	4.00	8.00
—Purple late-1970s label					
1865	Photograph/Down and Out	1983	2.00	4.00	8.00
—Black colorband label					
1865	Photograph/Down and Out	1988	—	3.00	6.00
—Purple late-1980s label (wider)					
1870	You're Sixteen/Devil Woman	1976	15.00	30.00	60.00
—Orange label					
1870	You're Sixteen/Devil Woman	1978	2.00	4.00	8.00
—Purple late-1970s label					
1870	You're Sixteen/Devil Woman	1983	2.00	4.00	8.00
—Black colorband label					
1870	You're Sixteen/Devil Woman	1988	—	2.50	5.00
—Purple late-1980s label (wider)					
1876	Only You/Call Me	1978	2.00	4.00	8.00
—Purple late-1970s label					
1876	Only You/Call Me	1983	25.00	50.00	100.00
—Black colorband label					
1880	No No Song/Snookeroo	1978	2.00	4.00	8.00
—Purple late-1970s label					
1880	No No Song/Snookeroo	1983	2.00	4.00	8.00
—Black colorband label					
1880	No No Song/Snookeroo	1988	7.50	15.00	30.00
—Purple late-1980s label (wider)					
1882	It's All Down to Goodnight Vienna/Oo-Wee	1978	2.00	4.00	8.00
—Purple late-1970s label					
2969	Beaucoups of Blues/Coochy-Coochy	1976	10.00	20.00	40.00
—Orange label					
B-44409	Act Naturally/Key's in the Mailbox	1989	3.75	7.50	15.00
—A-side with Buck Owens; B-side is Owens solo					

MERCURY

Number	Title (A Side/B Side)	Yr	VG	VG+	NM
MELP-195 [DJ]	La De Da/Everyday	1998	3.75	7.50	15.00
—Number only in the dead wax					
MELP-195 [PS]	La De Da/Everyday	1998	3.75	7.50	15.00

—The above record and sleeve were a giveaway from Beatlefest and J&R's Music World with advance purchase of the CD "Vertical Man" and later from Beatlefest with any Ringo Starr Mercury CD.

PORTRAIT

Number	Title (A Side/B Side)	Yr	VG	VG+	NM
70015	Lipstick Traces (On a Cigarette)/Old Time Relovin'	1978	3.75	7.50	15.00
70018	Heart on My Sleeve/Who Needs a Heart	1978	3.75	7.50	15.00

THE RIGHT STUFF

Number	Title (A Side/B Side)	Yr	VG	VG+	NM
S7-18178	In My Car/She's About a Mover	1994	2.00	4.00	8.00
—Gold/orange vinyl					
S7-18179	Wrack My Brain/Private Property	1994	2.00	4.00	8.00
—Red vinyl					

Albums

APPLE

Number	Title (A Side/B Side)	Yr	VG	VG+	NM
SW-3365	Sentimental Journey	1970	5.00	10.00	20.00
SMAS-3368	Beaucoups of Blues	1970	5.00	10.00	20.00
SWAL-3413	Ringo	1973	5.00	10.00	20.00
—Standard issue with booklet; Side 1, Song 2 identified on cover as "Hold On"					
SWAL-3413	Ringo	1973	100.00	200.00	400.00
—With a 5:26 version of "Six O'Clock." On later copies, the song is shortened to 4:05 though the label still says 5:26. All known copies have a promo punch-hole in top corner of jacket; on Side 2 record, "Six O'Clock" will be the widest track.					
SWAL-3413	Ringo	1974	6.25	12.50	25.00
—Later issue with booklet; Side 1, Song 2 identified on cover as "Have You Seen My Baby"					
SW-3417	Goodnight Vienna	1974	3.00	6.00	12.00
SW-3422	Blast from Your Past	1975	3.75	7.50	15.00

ATLANTIC

Number	Title (A Side/B Side)	Yr	VG	VG+	NM
SD 18193	Ringo's Rotogravure	1976	3.75	7.50	15.00
—Deduct 2/3 for cut-outs					
SD 18193 [DJ]	Ringo's Rotogravure	1976	7.50	15.00	30.00
—With "DJ Only" scrawled into trail-off area					
SD 19108	Ringo the 4th	1977	3.75	7.50	15.00
—Deduct 1/2 for cut-outs					
SD 19108 [DJ]	Ringo the 4th	1977	7.50	15.00	30.00
—With "DJ Only" scrawled into trail-off area					

BOARDWALK

Number	Title (A Side/B Side)	Yr	VG	VG+	NM
NB1-33246	Stop and Smell the Roses	1981	2.50	5.00	10.00
—Deduct 1/2 for cut-outs					

CAPITOL

Number	Title (A Side/B Side)	Yr	VG	VG+	NM
SW-3365	Sentimental Journey	197?	10.00	20.00	40.00
—Purple label, large Capitol logo					
SN-16114	Ringo	198?	3.75	7.50	15.00
—Green label budget-line reissue with all errors corrected					
SN-16218	Sentimental Journey	198?	6.25	12.50	25.00
—Green label budget-line reissue					
SN-16218	Goodnight Vienna	198?	6.25	12.50	25.00
—Green label budget-line reissue					
SN-16235	Beaucoups of Blues	198?	5.00	10.00	20.00
—Green label budget-line reissue					
SN-16236	Blast from Your Past	198?	3.75	7.50	15.00
—Green label budget-line reissue					

PORTRAIT

Number	Title (A Side/B Side)	Yr	VG	VG+	NM
JR 35378	Bad Boy	1978	3.75	7.50	15.00
—Deduct 1/3 for cut-outs					
JR 35378 [DJ]	Bad Boy	1978	25.00	50.00	100.00
—White label promo with "Advance Promotion" on label; in plain white cover					
JR 35378 [DJ]	Bad Boy	1978	7.50	15.00	30.00
—Regular white-label promo in standard jacket					

RHINO

Number	Title (A Side/B Side)	Yr	VG	VG+	NM
R1 70199	Starr Struck: Ringo's Best 1976-1983	1989	6.25	12.50	25.00

RYKODISC

Number	Title (A Side/B Side)	Yr	VG	VG+	NM
RALP 0190	Ringo Starr and His All-Starr Band	1990	7.50	15.00	30.00
—With limited, numbered obi (deduct $5 if missing)					

SUZY AND THE RED STRIPES

Actually Linda McCartney with Wings. Also see PAUL McCARTNEY.

12-Inch Singles

CAPITOL

Number	Title (A Side/B Side)	Yr	VG	VG+	NM
V-15244	Seaside Woman/B-Side to Seaside	1986	10.00	20.00	40.00

EPIC

Number	Title (A Side/B Side)	Yr	VG	VG+	NM
ASF 361 [DJ]	Seaside Woman (same on both sides)	1977	7.50	15.00	30.00
ASF [DJ]	Seaside Woman (same on both sides)	1977	7.50	15.00	30.00

45s

CAPITOL

Number	Title (A Side/B Side)	Yr	VG	VG+	NM
B-5608	Seaside Woman/B-Side to Seaside	1986	7.50	15.00	30.00

EPIC

Number	Title (A Side/B Side)	Yr	VG	VG+	NM
50403	Seaside Woman/B-Side to Seaside	1977	2.50	5.00	10.00
—Linda McCartney and Wings					
50403 [DJ]	Seaside Woman (mono/stereo)	1977	25.00	50.00	100.00
—"Advance Promotion" label, black vinyl					
50403 [DJ]	Seaside Woman (mono/stereo)	1977	6.25	12.50	25.00
—Red vinyl, orange label on one side, white on the other					
50403 [DJ]	Seaside Woman (mono/stereo)	1977	25.00	50.00	100.00
—Black vinyl, orange label on one side, white on the other					
[DJ]	Seaside Woman (mono/stereo)	1977	25.00	50.00	100.00
—"Advance Promotion" label, black vinyl					
[DJ]	Seaside Woman (mono/stereo)	1977	6.25	12.50	25.00
—Red vinyl, orange label on one side, white on the other					
[DJ]	Seaside Woman (mono/stereo)	1977	25.00	50.00	100.00
—Black vinyl, orange label on one side, white on the other					

TRAVELING WILBURYS

45s

WARNER BROS.

Number	Title (A Side/B Side)	Yr	VG	VG+	NM
19443	Wilbury Twist/New Blue Moon	1991	2.50	5.00	10.00
—Issued only in Europe					
19443 [PS]	Wilbury Twist/New Blue Moon	1991	2.50	5.00	10.00
19523	She's My Baby/New Blue Moon	1990	2.50	5.00	10.00
—"Wilbury" logo on label; issued only in Europe					
19523 [PS]	She's My Baby/New Blue Moon	1990	2.50	5.00	10.00
19773	Nobody's Child/Lumiere	1990	2.50	5.00	10.00
—B-side by Dave Stewart and the Spiritual Cowboys; "Wilbury" logo on label; issued only in Europe					
19773 [PS]	Nobody's Child/Lumiere	1989	2.50	5.00	10.00

WILBURY

Number	Title (A Side/B Side)	Yr	VG	VG+	NM
21867	Handle with Care/End of the Line	1990	3.75	7.50	15.00
—"Back to Back Hits" series					
27637	End of the Line/Congratulations	1989	3.75	7.50	15.00
27637 [DJ]	End of the Line (same on both sides)	1989	5.00	10.00	20.00
27637 [PS]	End of the Line/Congratulations	1989	5.00	10.00	20.00
27732	Handle with Care/Margarita	1988	2.00	4.00	8.00
27732 [DJ]	Handle with Care (same on both sides)	1988	3.75	7.50	15.00
27732 [PS]	Handle with Care/Margarita	1988	2.00	4.00	8.00

Albums

WILBURY

Number	Title (A Side/B Side)	Yr	VG	VG+	NM
25796	Traveling Wilburys (Volume One)	1988	5.00	10.00	20.00
26324	Traveling Wilburys, Vol. 3	1990	5.00	10.00	20.00

Label/Number	Artist	Title (A Side/B Side)	Year	NM

APPLE

45s

Label/Number	Artist	Title (A Side/B Side)	Year	NM
GM/OYB-1 [DJ]	Ono, Yoko	Greenfield Morning/Open Your Box	1971	800.00
	—Exactly six copies made for the personal use of Yoko Ono.			
1800	Foster, John, and Sons Black Dyke Mills Band	Thingumybob/Yellow Submarine	1968	100.00
	—With "Thingumybob" on uncut apple side			
1800	Foster, John, and Sons Black Dyke Mills Band	Thingumybob/Yellow Submarine	1968	100.00
	—With "Yellow Submarine" on uncut apple side			
1800	Foster, John, and Sons Black Dyke Mills Band	Thingumybob/Yellow Submarine	1968	120.00
	—With black star on uncut apple side			
1801	Hopkin, Mary	Those Were the Days/Turn, Turn, Turn	1968	10.00
1802	Lomax, Jackie	Sour Milk Sea/The Eagle Laughs at You	1968	20.00
	—With B-side author listed as "(George Harrison)"			
1802	Lomax, Jackie	Sour Milk Sea/The Eagle Laughs at You	1968	20.00
	—With B-side author listed as "(Jackie Lomax)"			
1803	Badfinger	Maybe Tomorrow/And Her Daddy's a Millionaire	1969	30.00
	—By "The Iveys"; with star on label			
1803	Badfinger	Maybe Tomorrow/And Her Daddy's a Millionaire	1969	20.00
	—By "The Iveys"; without star on label			
1804	Trash	Road to Nowhere/Illusions	1969	100.00
	—With star on A-side label			
1804	Trash	Road to Nowhere/Illusions	1969	50.00
	—Without star on A-side label			
1805	Taylor, James	Carolina in My Mind/Taking It In	1969	300.00
1805	Taylor, James	Carolina in My Mind/Something's Wrong	1970	10.00
	—With star on A-side label			
1805	Taylor, James	Carolina in My Mind/Something's Wrong	1970	8.00
	—Without star on A-side label			
1805 [DJ]	Taylor, James	Carolina on My Mind/Something's Wrong	1970	30.00
	—Promo with error in title on A-side			
1806	Hopkin, Mary	Goodbye/Sparrow	1969	8.00
1806 [PS]	Hopkin, Mary	Goodbye/Sparrow	1969	12.00
1807	Lomax, Jackie	New Day/Thumbin' a Ride	1969	75.00
	—With star on A-side label			
1807	Lomax, Jackie	New Day/Thumbin' a Ride	1969	60.00
	—Without star on A-side label			
1808	Preston, Billy	That's the Way God Planned It/What About You	1969	8.00
1808 [PS]	Preston, Billy	That's the Way God Planned It/What About You	1969	10.00
P-1808/PRO 6555 [DJ]	Preston, Billy	That's the Way God Planned It (Parts 1 & 2) (mono/stereo)	1969	60.00
1808	Preston, Billy	That's the Way God Planned It/What About You	1972	8.00
	—With "Mono" on both sides of record and reference to LP			
1809	Lennon, John	Give Peace a Chance/Remember Love	1969	5.00
	—As "Plastic Ono Band"			
1809 [PS]	Lennon, John	Give Peace a Chance/Remember Love	1969	15.00
	—As "Plastic Ono Band"			
1810	Radha Krishna Temple	Hare Krishna Mantra/Prayer to the Spiritual Masters	1969	8.00
1810 [PS]	Radha Krishna Temple	Hare Krishna Mantra/Prayer to the Spiritual Masters	1969	400.00
	—Only one copy is known to exist. The price is highly speculative.			
1811	Trash	Golden Slumbers-Carry That Weight/Trash Can	1969	15.00
	—A-side listed as "Golden Slumbers/Carry That Weight"			
1811	Trash	Golden Slumbers-Carry That Weight/Trash Can	1969	20.00
	—A-side listed as "Golden Slumbers and Carry That Weight"			
1811	Trash	Golden Slumbers-Carry That Weight/Trash Can	1969	20.00
	—A-side listed as "Golden Slumbers Carry That Weight"			
1812	Hot Chocolate	Give Peace a Chance/Living Without Tomorrow	1969	10.00
	—As "Hot Chocolate Band"			
1813	Lennon, John	Cold Turkey/Don't Worry Kyoko (Mummy's Only Looking for a Hand in the Snow)	1969	5.00
	—As "Plastic Ono Band"; most copies skip on A-side on the third chorus because of a pressing defect			
1813	Lennon, John	Cold Turkey/Don't Worry Kyoko (Mummy's Only Looking for a Hand in the Snow)	1969	10.00
	—As "Plastic Ono Band"; some copies don't skip on A-side. They tend to have wider, bolder print than those that do.			
1813 [PS]	Lennon, John	Cold Turkey/Don't Worry Kyoko (Mummy's Only Looking for a Hand in the Snow)	1969	40.00
	—As "Plastic Ono Band"			
1814	Preston, Billy	Everything's All Right/I Want to Thank You	1969	8.00
1815	Badfinger	Come and Get It/Rock of All Ages	1969	6.00
1815	Badfinger	Come and Get It/Rock of All Ages	1969	8.00
	—With Capitol logo on B-side bottom			
1816	Hopkin, Mary	Temma Harbour/Lantano Dagli Occhi	1970	8.00
1816 [PS]	Hopkin, Mary	Temma Harbour/Lantano Dagli Occhi	1970	12.00
1817	Preston, Billy	All That I've Got (I'm Gonna Give It to You)/As I Get Older	1970	8.00
1817 [PS]	Preston, Billy	All That I've Got (I'm Gonna Give It to You)/As I Get Older	1970	15.00
1818	Lennon, John	Instant Karma! (We All Shine On)/Who Has Seen the Wind?	1970	4.00
	—As "John Ono Lennon"; B-side by "Yoko Ono Lennon"			
1818 [DJ]	Lennon, John	Instant Karma! (We All Shine On)	1970	200.00
	—As "John Ono Lennon"; one-sided promo			
1818 [PS]	Lennon, John	Instant Karma! (We All Shine On)/Who Has Seen the Wind?	1970	15.00
	—As "John Ono Lennon"; B-side by "Yoko Ono Lennon"			
1819	Lomax, Jackie	How the Web Was Woven/I Fall Inside Your Eyes	1970	8.00
1819 [PS]	Lomax, Jackie	How the Web Was Woven/I Fall Inside Your Eyes	1970	10.00
1820	Troy, Doris	Ain't That Cute/Vaya Con Dios	1970	8.00
1821	Radha Krishna Temple	Govinda/Govinda Jai Jai	1970	8.00
1821	Radha Krishna Temple	Govinda/Govinda Jai Jai	1970	10.00
	—With Capitol logo on B-side label bottom			
1821 [PS]	Radha Krishna Temple	Govinda/Govinda Jai Jai	1970	10.00

Number	Artist	Title (A Side/B Side)	Year	NM
1822	Badfinger	No Matter What/Carry On Till Tomorrow	1970	6.00
1822	Badfinger	No Matter What/Carry On Till Tomorrow	1970	20.00
	—With star on A-side label			
1823	Hopkin, Mary	Que Sera, Sera (Whatever Will Be, Will Be)/Fields of St. Etienne	1970	8.00
1824	Troy, Doris	Jacob's Ladder/Get Back	1970	8.00
1825	Hopkin, Mary	Think About Your Children/Heritage	1970	8.00
1825	Hopkin, Mary	Think About Your Children/Heritage	1970	12.00
	—With star on A-side label			
1825 [PS]	Hopkin, Mary	Think About Your Children/Heritage	1970	12.00
1826	Preston, Billy	My Sweet Lord/Little Girl	1970	8.00
1826	Preston, Billy	My Sweet Lord/Little Girl	1970	12.00
	—With star on A-side label			
1826 [PS]	Starr, Ringo	Beaucoups of Blues/Coochy-Coochy	1970	40.00
	—Sleeve with wrong catalog number (actually 2969)			
1827	Lennon, John	Mother/Why	1970	8.00
	—As "John Lennon/Plastic Ono Band"; B-side by "Yoko Ono/Plastic Ono Band"			
1827	Lennon, John	Mother/Why	1970	12.00
	—As "John Lennon/Plastic Ono Band"; star on A-side label			
1827	Lennon, John	Mother/Why	1970	40.00
	—As "John Lennon/Plastic Ono Band"; "MONO" on A-side label			
1827 [PS]	Lennon, John	Mother/Why	1970	120.00
	—As "John Lennon/Plastic Ono Band"; B-side by "Yoko Ono/Plastic Ono Band"			
1828	Harrison, George	What Is Life/Apple Scruffs	1971	15.00
	—With star on A-side label			
1828	Harrison, George	What Is Life/Apple Scruffs	1971	8.00
	—Without star on A-side label			
1828 [PS]	Harrison, George	What Is Life/Apple Scruffs	1971	40.00
1829	McCartney, Paul	Another Day/Oh Woman, Oh Why	1971	12.00
	—With star on A-side label			
1829	McCartney, Paul	Another Day/Oh Woman, Oh Why	1971	8.00
1830	Lennon, John	Power to the People/Touch Me	1971	8.00
	—As "John Lennon/Plastic Ono Band"; B-side by "Yoko Ono/Plastic Ono Band"			
1830	Lennon, John	Power to the People/Touch Me	1971	8.00
	—As "John Lennon/Plastic Ono Band"; with star on A-side label			
1830 [PS]	Lennon, John	Power to the People/Touch Me	1971	30.00
	—As "John Lennon/Plastic Ono Band"; B-side by "Yoko Ono/Plastic Ono Band"			
1831	Starr, Ringo	It Don't Come Easy/Early 1970	1971	8.00
1831	Starr, Ringo	It Don't Come Easy/Early 1970	1971	12.00
	—With star on A-side label			
1831 [PS]	Starr, Ringo	It Don't Come Easy/Early 1970	1971	30.00
1831	Starr, Ringo	It Don't Come Easy/Early 1970	1975	30.00
	—With "All rights reserved" on label			
1832	Spector, Ronnie	Try Some, Buy Some/Tandoori Chicken	1971	7.00
1832	Spector, Ronnie	Try Some, Buy Some/Tandoori Chicken	1971	8.00
	—With star on A-side label			
1832 [PS]	Spector, Ronnie	Try Some, Buy Some/Tandoori Chicken	1971	10.00
1834	Lomax, Jackie	Sour Milk Sea/(I) Fall Inside Your Eyes	1971	8.00
1835	Elliott, Bill, and the Elastic Oz Band	God Save Us/Do the Oz	1971	8.00
1835 [PS]	Elliott, Bill, and the Elastic Oz Band	God Save Us/Do the Oz	1971	10.00
P-1835 [DJ]	Elliott, Bill, and the Elastic Oz Band	God Save Us/Do the Oz	1971	25.00
	—Has black star on A-side and unsliced apple on both sides			
1836	Harrison, George	Bangla-Desh/Deep Blue	1971	25.00
	—Without star on A-side label			
1836	Harrison, George	Bangla-Desh/Deep Blue	1971	8.00
	—With star on A-side label			
1836 [PS]	Harrison, George	Bangla-Desh/Deep Blue	1971	20.00
1837	McCartney, Paul	Uncle Albert/Admiral Halsey//Too Many People	1971	15.00
	—Paul and Linda McCartney; with "Pual" misspelling on producer credit			
1837	McCartney, Paul	Uncle Albert/Admiral Halsey//Too Many People	1971	8.00
	—Paul and Linda McCartney; with no misspelling			
1837	McCartney, Paul	Uncle Albert/Admiral Halsey//Too Many People	1971	50.00
	—Paul and Linda McCartney; with unsliced apple on B-side label			
1837	McCartney, Paul	Uncle Albert/Admiral Halsey//Too Many People	1975	30.00
	—Paul and Linda McCartney; with "All rights reserved" on label			
1838	Shankar, Ravi	Joi Bangla-Oh Bhaugowan/Raga Mishra-Jhinjhoti	1971	8.00
	—By Ravi Shankar & Ali Akbar with Alla Rakah			
1838 [PS]	Shankar, Ravi	Joi Bangla-Oh Bhaugowan/Raga Mishra-Jhinjhoti	1971	20.00
1839	Ono, Yoko	Mrs. Lennon/Midsummer New York	1971	7.00
	—As "Yoko Ono/Plastic Ono Band"			
1840	Lennon, John	Imagine/It's So Hard	1971	8.00
	—As "John Lennon Plastic Ono Band"; tan label			
1840	Lennon, John	Imagine/It's So Hard	1975	12.00
	—As "John Lennon Plastic Ono Band"; green label with "All Rights Reserved"			
1841	Badfinger	Day After Day/Money	1971	20.00
	—With star on A-side label			
1841	Badfinger	Day After Day/Money	1971	6.00
1841 [DJ]	Badfinger	Day After Day/Money	1971	120.00
	—White label			
1842	Lennon, John	Happy Xmas (War Is Over)/Listen, the Snow Is Falling	1971	15.00
	—As "John & Yoko/Plastic Ono Band with the Harlem Community Choir"; green vinyl, faces label			
1842	Lennon, John	Happy Xmas (War Is Over)/Listen, the Snow Is Falling	1971	10.00
	—As "John & Yoko/Plastic Ono Band with the Harlem Community Choir"; green vinyl, Apple label			
1842 [PS]	Lennon, John	Happy Xmas (War Is Over)/Listen, the Snow Is Falling	1971	20.00
	—As "John & Yoko/Plastic Ono Band with the Harlem Community Choir"			
1843	Hopkin, Mary	Water, Paper and Clay/Streets of London	1972	8.00
1843	Hopkin, Mary	Water, Paper and Clay/Streets of London	1972	12.00
	—With star on A-side label			
1844	Badfinger	Baby Blue/Flying	1972	6.00

Label/Number	Artist	Title (A Side/B Side)	Year	NM
1844 [DJ]	Badfinger	Baby Blue/Flying	1972	120.00
	—White label			
1844 [PS]	Badfinger	Baby Blue/Flying	1972	15.00
1845	Van Eaten, Lon and Derrek	Sweet Music/Song of Songs	1972	8.00
1845 [PS]	Van Eaten, Lon and Derrek	Sweet Music/Song of Songs	1972	10.00
1847	McCartney, Paul	Give Ireland Back to the Irish/Give Ireland Back to the Irish (Version)	1972	10.00
	—Wings			
1847 [PS]	McCartney, Paul	Give Ireland Back to the Irish/Give Ireland Back to the Irish (Version)	1972	30.00
	—Wings; title sleeve with large center hole			
1848	Lennon, John	Woman Is the Nigger of the World/Sisters O Sisters	1972	8.00
	—As "John Lennon/Plastic Ono Band..."; B-side by "Yoko Ono/Plastic Ono Band..."			
1848 [PS]	Lennon, John	Woman Is the Nigger of the World/Sisters O Sisters	1972	25.00
	—As "John Lennon/Plastic Ono Band..."; B-side by "Yoko Ono/Plastic Ono Band..."			
1849	Starr, Ringo	Back Off Boogaloo/Blindman	1972	8.00
	—Green-background label			
1849	Starr, Ringo	Back Off Boogaloo/Blindman	1972	75.00
	—Blue-background label			
1849 [DJ]	Starr, Ringo	Back Off Boogaloo/Blindman	1972	150.00
	—White label			
1849 [PS]	Starr, Ringo	Back Off Boogaloo/Blindman	1972	15.00
	—Black paper with flat finish			
1849 [PS]	Starr, Ringo	Back Off Boogaloo/Blindman	1972	40.00
	—Glossy black paper on both sides			
1849 [PS]	Starr, Ringo	Back Off Boogaloo/Blindman	1972	40.00
	—Glossy black on one side, gray on the other			
1850	Hodge, Chris	We're On Our Way/Supersoul	1972	8.00
1850 [PS]	Hodge, Chris	We're On Our Way/Supersoul	1972	10.00
1851	McCartney, Paul	Mary Had a Little Lamb/Little Woman Love	1972	10.00
	—Wings			
1851 [DJ]	McCartney, Paul	Mary Had a Little Lamb/Little Woman Love	1972	300.00
	—White label promo, lists artist as Paul McCartney			
1851 [PS]	McCartney, Paul	Mary Had a Little Lamb/Little Woman Love	1972	25.00
	—Wings; without "Little Woman Love" on sleeve			
1851 [PS]	McCartney, Paul	Mary Had a Little Lamb/Little Woman Love	1972	40.00
	—Wings; with "Little Woman Love" on sleeve			
1852	Sundown Playboys, The	Saturday Night Special/Valse De Soleil Coucher	1972	15.00
1853	Ono, Yoko	Now or Never/Move On Fast	1972	7.00
1853 [PS]	Ono, Yoko	Now or Never/Move On Fast	1972	8.00
1854	Elephants Memory	Liberation Special/Madness	1972	8.00
1854	Elephants Memory	Liberation Special/Power Boogie	1972	400.00
1854 [PS]	Elephants Memory	Liberation Special/Madness	1972	10.00
1855	Hopkin, Mary	Knock Knock Who's There/International	1972	8.00
1857	McCartney, Paul	Hi Hi Hi/C Moon	1972	10.00
	—Wings; red label			
1858	Hodge, Chris	Goodnight Sweet Lorraine/Contact Love	1973	8.00
1859	Ono, Yoko	Death of Samantha/Yang Yang	1973	7.00
1861	McCartney, Paul	My Love/The Mess	1973	8.00
	—Paul McCartney and Wings; custom "Red Rose Speedway" label			
1861 [DJ]	McCartney, Paul	My Love/The Mess	1973	200.00
	—Paul McCartney and Wings; white label			
1862	Harrison, George	Give Me Love (Give Me Peace on Earth)/Miss O'Dell (2:30)	1973	8.00
	—With incorrect time for B-side listed			
1862	Harrison, George	Give Me Love (Give Me Peace on Earth)/Miss O'Dell (2:20)	1973	8.00
	—B-side playing time corrected			
P-1862 [DJ]	Harrison, George	Give Me Love (Give Me Peace on Earth) (mono/stereo)	1973	50.00
1863	McCartney, Paul	Live and Let Die/I Lie Around	1973	8.00
	—Wings			
1864	Badfinger	Apple of My Eye/Blind Owl	1973	6.00
P-1864 [DJ]	Badfinger	Apple of My Eye (mono/stereo)	1973	25.00
1865	Starr, Ringo	Photograph/Down and Out	1973	6.00
	—Custom star label			
1865 [PS]	Starr, Ringo	Photograph/Down and Out	1973	20.00
P-1865 [DJ]	Starr, Ringo	Photograph (mono/stereo)	1973	50.00
1867	Ono, Yoko	Woman Power/Men, Men, Men	1973	7.00
1868	Lennon, John	Mind Games/Meat City	1973	6.00
1868 [PS]	Lennon, John	Mind Games/Meat City	1973	15.00
P-1868 [DJ]	Lennon, John	Mind Games (mono/stereo)	1973	50.00
1869	McCartney, Paul	Helen Wheels/Country Dreamer	1973	8.00
	—Paul McCartney and Wings			
1870	Starr, Ringo	You're Sixteen/Devil Woman	1973	6.00
	—Custom star label			
1870	Starr, Ringo	You're Sixteen/Devil Woman	1973	25.00
	—Regular Apple label			
1870 [PS]	Starr, Ringo	You're Sixteen/Devil Woman	1973	25.00
P-1870 [DJ]	Starr, Ringo	You're Sixteen (mono/stereo)	1973	50.00
1871	McCartney, Paul	Jet/Mamunia	1974	10.00
	—Paul McCartney and Wings			
1871	McCartney, Paul	Jet/Mamunia	1974	100.00
	—Paul McCartney and Wings; A-side incorrectly listed as playing for 2:49			
1871	McCartney, Paul	Jet/Let Me Roll It	1974	8.00
	—Paul McCartney and Wings			
P-1871 [DJ]	McCartney, Paul	Jet (Edited Mono)/Jet (Stereo)	1974	50.00
	—Paul McCartney and Wings			
1872	Starr, Ringo	Oh My My/Step Lightly	1974	6.00
	—Custom star label			
1872	Starr, Ringo	Oh My My/Step Lightly	1974	8.00
	—Regular Apple label			

Number	Artist	Title (A Side/B Side)	Year	NM

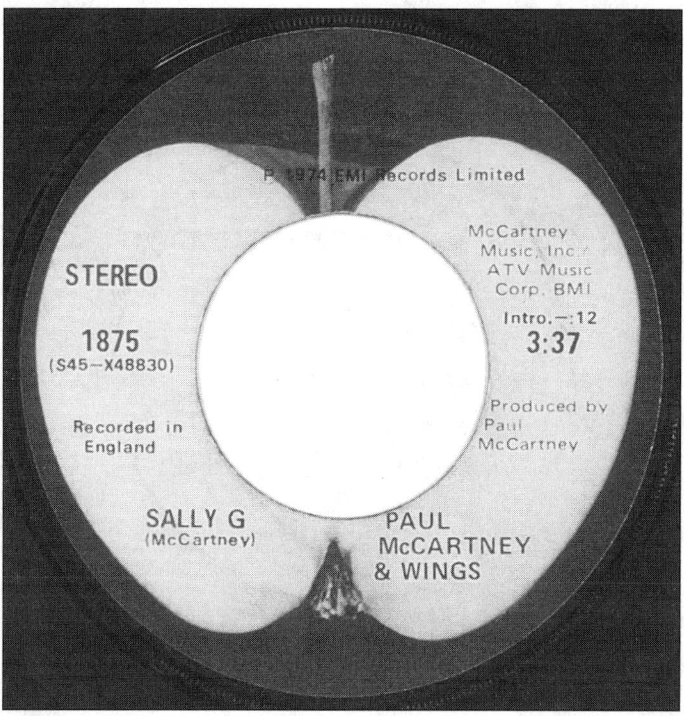

Number	Artist	Title (A Side/B Side)	Year	NM
P-1872 [DJ]	Starr, Ringo	Oh My My (Edited Mono)/Oh My My (Long Stereo)	1974	50.00
1873	McCartney, Paul *—Paul McCartney and Wings*	Band on the Run/Nineteen Hundred and Eighty-Five	1974	8.00
P-1873 [DJ]	McCartney, Paul *—Paul McCartney and Wings*	Band on the Run (Edited Mono)/Band on the Run (Full-length Stereo)	1974	40.00
P-1873 [DJ]	McCartney, Paul *—Paul McCartney and Wings*	Band on the Run (mono/stereo, both edits)	1974	100.00
1874	Lennon, John *—As "John Lennon and the Plastic Ono Nuclear Band"*	Whatever Gets You Thru the Night/Beef Jerky	1974	6.00
P-1874 [DJ]	Lennon, John *—As "John Lennon and the Plastic Ono Nuclear Band"*	Whatever Gets You Thru the Night (mono/stereo)	1974	50.00
1875	McCartney, Paul *—Paul McCartney and Wings*	Junior's Farm/Sally G	1974	8.00
P-1875 [DJ]	McCartney, Paul *—Paul McCartney and Wings*	Junior's Farm (Edited Mono)/Junior's Farm (Full-length Stereo)	1974	50.00
P-1875 [DJ]	McCartney, Paul *—Paul McCartney and Wings*	Sally G (mono/stereo)	1974	80.00
1875	McCartney, Paul *—Paul McCartney and Wings; with "All Rights Reserved" on label*	Junior's Farm/Sally G	1975	80.00
1876	Starr, Ringo *—Custom nebula label*	Only You/Call Me	1974	6.00
1876	Starr, Ringo *—Regular Apple label*	Only You/Call Me	1974	8.00
1876 [PS]	Starr, Ringo	Only You/Call Me	1974	20.00
P-1876 [DJ]	Starr, Ringo	Only You (mono/stereo)	1974	40.00
1877	Harrison, George *—Light blue and white custom photo label*	Dark Horse/I Don't Care Anymore	1974	8.00
1877	Harrison, George *—White label; NOT a promo*	Dark Horse/I Don't Care Anymore	1974	10.00
1877 [PS]	Harrison, George	Dark Horse/I Don't Care Anymore	1974	80.00
P-1877 [DJ]	Harrison, George	Dark Horse (full length mono/stereo)	1974	40.00
P-1877 [DJ]	Harrison, George	Dark Horse (edited mono/stereo)	1974	60.00
1878	Lennon, John	#9 Dream/What You Got	1974	8.00
P-1878 [DJ]	Lennon, John	#9 Dream (edited mono/stereo)	1974	50.00
P-1878 [DJ]	Lennon, John	What You Got (mono/stereo)	1974	100.00
1879	Harrison, George *—Black and white custom photo label*	Ding Dong, Ding Dong/Hari's on Tour (Express)	1974	20.00
1879	Harrison, George *—Blue and white custom photo label*	Ding Dong, Ding Dong/Hari's on Tour (Express)	1974	250.00
1879 [PS]	Harrison, George	Ding Dong, Ding Dong/Hari's on Tour (Express)	1974	20.00
P-1879 [DJ]	Harrison, George	Ding Dong, Ding Dong (remixed mono/edited stereo)	1974	40.00
1880	Starr, Ringo *—Custom nebula label*	No No Song/Snookeroo	1975	6.00
P-1880 [DJ]	Starr, Ringo	No No Song/Snookeroo (both mono)	1975	40.00
P-1880 [DJ]	Starr, Ringo	No No Song/Snookeroo (both stereo)	1975	40.00
1881	Lennon, John	Stand By Me/Move Over Ms. L.	1975	8.00
P-1881 [DJ]	Lennon, John	Stand By Me (mono/stereo)	1975	50.00
1882	Starr, Ringo *—Custom nebula label*	It's All Down to Goodnight Vienna/Oo-Wee	1975	6.00
1882 [PS]	Starr, Ringo	It's All Down to Goodnight Vienna/Oo-Wee	1975	20.00

Label/Number	Artist	Title (A Side/B Side)	Year	NM
P-1882 [DJ]	Starr, Ringo	It's All Down to Goodnight Vienna (mono/stereo)	1975	40.00
P-1882 [DJ]	Starr, Ringo	Oo-Wee/Oo-Wee	1975	70.00
P-1883 [DJ]	Lennon, John	Ain't That a Shame (mono/stereo)	1975	200.00
	—No stock copies issued			
P-1883 [DJ]	Lennon, John	Slippin' and Slidin' (mono/stereo)	1975	200.00
	—No stock copies issued			
1884	Harrison, George	You/World of Stone	1975	6.00
1884 [PS]	Harrison, George	You/World of Stone	1975	15.00
P-1884 [DJ]	Harrison, George	You (mono/stereo)	1975	40.00
1885	Harrison, George	This Guitar (Can't Keep from Crying)/Maya Love	1975	25.00
	—The last Apple 45 until 1995			
P-1885 [DJ]	Harrison, George	This Guitar (Can't Keep from Crying) (mono/stereo)	1975	50.00
Promo-1970 [DJ]	Beatles, The	Dialogue from the Beatles' Motion Picture "Let It Be"	1970	60.00
2056	Beatles, The	Hello Goodbye/I Am the Walrus	1971	30.00
	—With star on A-side label			
2056	Beatles, The	Hello Goodbye/I Am the Walrus	1971	10.00
	—Without star on A-side label			
2056	Beatles, The	Hello Goodbye/I Am the Walrus	1975	20.00
	—With "All Rights Reserved" disclaimer			
2138	Beatles, The	Lady Madonna/The Inner Light	1971	30.00
	—With star on A-side label			
2138	Beatles, The	Lady Madonna/The Inner Light	1971	10.00
	—Without star on A-side label			
2138	Beatles, The	Lady Madonna/The Inner Light	1975	20.00
	—With "All Rights Reserved" disclaimer			
2276	Beatles, The	Hey Jude/Revolution	1968	15.00
	—Original: With small Capitol logo on bottom of B-side label			
2276	Beatles, The	Hey Jude/Revolution	1968	10.00
	—With "Mfd. by Apple" on label			
2276	Beatles, The	Hey Jude/Revolution	1975	20.00
	—With "All Rights Reserved" disclaimer			
2490	Beatles, The	Get Back/Don't Let Me Down	1969	10.00
	—Original: With small Capitol logo on bottom of B-side label			
2490	Beatles, The	Get Back/Don't Let Me Down	1969	10.00
	—With "Mfd. by Apple" on label			
2490	Beatles, The	Get Back/Don't Let Me Down	1975	20.00
	—With "All Rights Reserved" disclaimer			
2531	Beatles, The	The Ballad of John and Yoko/Old Brown Shoe	1969	10.00
	—Original: With small Capitol logo on bottom of B-side label			
2531	Beatles, The	The Ballad of John and Yoko/Old Brown Shoe	1969	10.00
	—With "Mfd. by Apple" on label			
2531 [PS]	Beatles, The	The Ballad of John and Yoko/Old Brown Shoe	1969	100.00
2531	Beatles, The	The Ballad of John and Yoko/Old Brown Shoe	1975	20.00
	—With "All Rights Reserved" disclaimer			
2654	Beatles, The	Something/Come Together	1969	100.00
	—Original: With small Capitol logo on bottom of B-side label			
2654	Beatles, The	Something/Come Together	1969	10.00
	—With "Mfd. by Apple" on label			
2654	Beatles, The	Something/Come Together	1975	20.00
	—With "All Rights Reserved" disclaimer			
2764	Beatles, The	Let It Be/You Know My Name (Look Up My Number)	1970	12.00
	—Original: With small Capitol logo on bottom of B-side label			
2764	Beatles, The	Let It Be/You Know My Name (Look Up My Number)	1970	10.00
	—With "Mfd. by Apple" on label			
2764 [PS]	Beatles, The	Let It Be/You Know My Name (Look Up the Number)	1970	100.00
2764	Beatles, The	Let It Be/You Know My Name (Look Up My Number)	1975	20.00
	—With "All Rights Reserved" disclaimer			
2832	Beatles, The	The Long and Winding Road/For You Blue	1970	20.00
	—Original: With small Capitol logo on bottom of B-side label			
2832	Beatles, The	The Long and Winding Road/For You Blue	1970	10.00
	—With "Mfd. by Apple" on label			
2832 [PS]	Beatles, The	The Long and Winding Road/For You Blue	1970	100.00
2832	Beatles, The	The Long and Winding Road/For You Blue	1975	20.00
	—With "All Rights Reserved" disclaimer			
2969	Starr, Ringo	Beaucoups of Blues/Coochy-Coochy	1970	25.00
	—With small Capitol logo on bottom of B-side label and star on A-side label			
2969	Starr, Ringo	Beaucoups of Blues/Coochy-Coochy	1970	40.00
	—With "Mfd. by Apple" on label and star on A-side label			
2969	Starr, Ringo	Beaucoups of Blues/Coochy-Coochy	1970	8.00
	—With "Mfd. by Apple" on label and no star on A-side label			
2969 [PS]	Starr, Ringo	Beaucoups of Blues/Coochy-Coochy	1970	50.00
	—Sleeve with correct catalog number			
2995	Harrison, George	My Sweet Lord/Isn't It a Pity	1970	40.00
	—With black star on label			
2995	Harrison, George	My Sweet Lord/Isn't It a Pity	1970	8.00
	—With "Mfd. by Apple" on label			
2995 [PS]	Harrison, George	My Sweet Lord/Isn't It a Pity	1970	40.00
2995	Harrison, George	My Sweet Lord/Isn't It a Pity	1975	25.00
	—With "All Rights Reserved" disclaimer			
PRO-4671/2	Trash	Road to Nowhere (Edit)/Road to Nowhere	1969	80.00
PRO-5013/4 [DJ]	Radha Krishna Temple	Govinda/Govinda Jai Jai	1970	25.00
	—With an edit of the A-side			
SPRO-5067/8 [DJ]	Radha Krishna Temple	Govinda (Edit)/Govinda	1970	40.00
5112	Beatles, The	I Want to Hold Your Hand/I Saw Her Standing There	1971	30.00
	—With star on label			
5112	Beatles, The	I Want to Hold Your Hand/I Saw Her Standing There	1971	10.00
	—Without star on label			
5112	Beatles, The	I Want to Hold Your Hand/I Saw Her Standing There	1975	20.00
	—With "All Rights Reserved" disclaimer on label			

Number	Artist	Title (A Side/B Side)	Year	NM
5150	Beatles, The *—With star on A-side label*	Can't Buy Me Love/You Can't Do That	1971	30.00
5150	Beatles, The *—Without star on A-side label*	Can't Buy Me Love/You Can't Do That	1971	10.00
5150	Beatles, The *—With "All Rights Reserved" disclaimer on label*	Can't Buy Me Love/You Can't Do That	1975	15.00
5222	Beatles, The *—With star on A-side label*	A Hard Day's Night/I Should Have Known Better	1971	30.00
5222	Beatles, The *—Without star on A-side label*	A Hard Day's Night/I Should Have Known Better	1971	10.00
5222	Beatles, The *—With "All Rights Reserved" disclaimer*	A Hard Day's Night/I Should Have Known Better	1975	15.00
5234	Beatles, The *—With star on A-side label*	I'll Cry Instead/I'm Happy Just to Dance with You	1971	30.00
5234	Beatles, The *—Without star on A-side label*	I'll Cry Instead/I'm Happy Just to Dance with You	1971	10.00
5234	Beatles, The *—With "All Rights Reserved" disclaimer*	I'll Cry Instead/I'm Happy Just to Dance with You	1975	15.00
5235	Beatles, The *—With star on A-side label*	And I Love Her/If I Fell	1971	30.00
5235	Beatles, The *—Without star on A-side label*	And I Love Her/If I Fell	1971	10.00
5235	Beatles, The *—With "All Rights Reserved" disclaimer*	And I Love Her/If I Fell	1975	15.00
5255	Beatles, The *—With star on A-side label*	Matchbox/Slow Down	1971	30.00
5255	Beatles, The *—Without star on A-side label*	Matchbox/Slow Down	1971	10.00
5255	Beatles, The *—With "All Rights Reserved" disclaimer*	Matchbox/Slow Down	1975	15.00
5327	Beatles, The *—With star on A-side label*	I Feel Fine/She's a Woman	1971	30.00
5327	Beatles, The *—Without star on A-side label*	I Feel Fine/She's a Woman	1971	10.00
5327	Beatles, The *—With "All Rights Reserved" disclaimer*	I Feel Fine/She's a Woman	1975	15.00
5371	Beatles, The *—With star on A-side label*	Eight Days a Week/I Don't Want to Spoil the Party	1971	30.00
5371	Beatles, The *—Without star on A-side label*	Eight Days a Week/I Don't Want to Spoil the Party	1971	10.00
5371	Beatles, The *—With "All Rights Reserved" disclaimer*	Eight Days a Week/I Don't Want to Spoil the Party	1975	15.00
5407	Beatles, The *—With star on A-side label*	Ticket to Ride/Yes It Is	1971	30.00
5407	Beatles, The *—Without star on A-side label*	Ticket to Ride/Yes It Is	1971	10.00
5407	Beatles, The *—With "All Rights Reserved" disclaimer*	Ticket to Ride/Yes It Is	1975	15.00
5476	Beatles, The *—With star on A-side label*	Help!/I'm Down	1971	30.00
5476	Beatles, The *—Without star on A-side label*	Help!/I'm Down	1971	10.00
5476	Beatles, The *—With "All Rights Reserved" disclaimer*	Help!/I'm Down	1975	15.00
5498	Beatles, The *—With star on A-side label*	Yesterday/Act Naturally	1971	30.00
5498	Beatles, The *—Without star on A-side label*	Yesterday/Act Naturally	1971	10.00
5498	Beatles, The *—With "All Rights Reserved" disclaimer*	Yesterday/Act Naturally	1975	15.00
5555	Beatles, The *—With star on A-side label*	We Can Work It Out/Day Tripper	1971	30.00
5555	Beatles, The *—Without star on A-side label*	We Can Work It Out/Day Tripper	1971	10.00
5555	Beatles, The *—With "All Rights Reserved" disclaimer*	We Can Work It Out/Day Tripper	1975	15.00
5587	Beatles, The *—With star on A-side label*	Nowhere Man/What Goes On	1971	30.00
5587	Beatles, The *—Without star on A-side label*	Nowhere Man/What Goes On	1971	10.00
5587	Beatles, The *—With "All Rights Reserved" disclaimer*	Nowhere Man/What Goes On	1975	15.00
5651	Beatles, The *—With star on A-side label*	Paperback Writer/Rain	1971	30.00
5651	Beatles, The *—Without star on A-side label*	Paperback Writer/Rain	1971	10.00
5651	Beatles, The *—With "All Rights Reserved" disclaimer*	Paperback Writer/Rain	1975	15.00
5715	Beatles, The *—With star on A-side label*	Yellow Submarine/Eleanor Rigby	1971	30.00
5715	Beatles, The *—Without star on A-side label*	Yellow Submarine/Eleanor Rigby	1971	10.00
5715	Beatles, The *—With "All Rights Reserved" disclaimer*	Yellow Submarine/Eleanor Rigby	1975	15.00
5810	Beatles, The *—With star on A-side label*	Penny Lane/Strawberry Fields Forever	1971	30.00
5810	Beatles, The *—Without star on A-side label*	Penny Lane/Strawberry Fields Forever	1971	10.00
5810	Beatles, The *—With "All Rights Reserved" disclaimer*	Penny Lane/Strawberry Fields Forever	1975	15.00

Label/Number	Artist	Title (A Side/B Side)	Year	NM
5964	Beatles, The	All You Need Is Love/Baby, You're a Rich Man	1971	30.00
	—With star on A-side label			
5964	Beatles, The	All You Need Is Love/Baby, You're a Rich Man	1971	10.00
	—Without star on A-side label			
5964	Beatles, The	All You Need Is Love/Baby, You're a Rich Man	1975	15.00
	—With "All Rights Reserved" disclaimer			
PRO-6193/4 [DJ]	McCartney, Paul	Another Day/Oh Woman, Oh Why	1971	80.00
PRO-6240/1 [DJ]	Lomax, Jackie	Sour Milk Sea/(I) Fall Inside Your Eyes	1971	30.00
PRO-6498/9 [DJ]	Peel, David	F Is Not a Dirty Word/The Ballad of New York City	1972	120.00
PRO-6545/6 [DJ]	Peel, David	Hippie from New York City/The Ballad of New York City	1972	120.00
PRO-6786 [DJ]	McCartney, Paul	Helen Wheels (mono/stereo)	1973	50.00
	—Paul McCartney and Wings			
PRO-6787 [DJ]	McCartney, Paul	Country Dreamer (mono/stereo)	1973	400.00
	—Paul McCartney and Wings			
S45X-47663/4 [DJ]	Lennon, John	Happy Xmas (War Is Over)/Listen, the Snow Is Falling	1971	750.00
	—As "John & Yoko/Plastic Ono Band with the Harlem Community Choir"; white label on styrene			
58348	Beatles, The	Baby It's You/I'll Follow the Sun//Devil in Her Heart/Boys	1995	4.00
	—All 4 tracks from BBC sessions			
58348 [PS]	Beatles, The	Baby It's You/I'll Follow the Sun//Devil in Her Heart/Boys	1995	4.00
58497	Beatles, The	Free as a Bird/Christmas Time (Is Here Again)	1995	4.00
	—Small center hole; all with large hole were "dinked" somewhere other than when manufactured and have little, if any, value			
58497 [PS]	Beatles, The	Free as a Bird/Christmas Time (Is Here Again)	1995	4.00
58544	Beatles, The	Real Love/Baby's in Black (Live)	1996	3.00
	—Small center hole; all with large hole were "dinked" somewhere other than when manufactured and have little, if any, value			
58544 [PS]	Beatles, The	Real Love/Baby's in Black (Live)	1996	3.00

Albums

Label/Number	Artist	Title (A Side/B Side)	Year	NM
SBC-100 [M]	Beatles, The	The Beatles' Christmas Album	1970	400.00
	—Fan club issue of the seven Christmas messages; very good counterfeits exist			
SWBO-101 [(2)]	Beatles, The	The Beatles	1968	200.00
	—Numbered copy; includes four individual photos and large poster (included in value); because the white cover shows ring wear so readily, this is an EXTREMELY difficult album to find in near-mint condition			
SWBO-101 [(2)]	Beatles, The	The Beatles	1975	70.00
	—With "All Rights Reserved" on labels; title in black on cover; photos and poster of thinner stock than originals			
SWBO-101 [(2)]	Beatles, The	The Beatles	197?	60.00
	—Un-numbered copy; includes four individual photos and large poster (included in value)			
SW-153 [P]	Beatles, The	Yellow Submarine	1969	50.00
	—With Capitol logo on Side 2 bottom. "Only a Northern Song" is rechanneled.			
SW-153 [P]	Beatles, The	Yellow Submarine	1971	20.00
	—With "Mfd. by Apple" on label			
SW-153 [P]	Beatles, The	Yellow Submarine	1975	25.00
	—With "All Rights Reserved" on label			
SO-383	Beatles, The	Abbey Road	1969	75.00
	—With Capitol logo on Side 2 bottom; "Her Majesty" is NOT listed on either the jacket or the label			
SO-383	Beatles, The	Abbey Road	1969	40.00
	—With Capitol logo on Side 2 bottom; "Her Majesty" IS listed on both the jacket and the label			
SO-383	Beatles, The	Abbey Road	1969	20.00
	—With "Mfd. by Apple" on label; "Her Majesty" is NOT listed on the label			
SO-383	Beatles, The	Abbey Road	1969	20.00
	—With "Mfd. by Apple" on label; "Her Majesty" IS listed on the label			
SO-383	Beatles, The	Abbey Road	1975	25.00
	—With "All Rights Reserved" on label			
SO-385 [DJ]	Beatles, The	The Beatles Again	1970	8000.00
	—Prototypes with "The Beatles Again" on cover; not released to the general public			
SW-385	Beatles, The	Hey Jude	1970	40.00
	—Label calls the LP "The Beatles Again"; record is "SO-385" (this could be found in retail stores as late as 1973)			
SW-385	Beatles, The	Hey Jude	1970	25.00
	—Label calls the LP "The Beatles Again"; record is "SW-385"			
SW-385	Beatles, The	Hey Jude	1970	75.00
	—With Capitol logo on Side 2 bottom; label calls the LP "Hey Jude"			
SW-385	Beatles, The	Hey Jude	1970	20.00
	—With "Mfd. by Apple" on label; label calls the LP "Hey Jude"			
SW-385	Beatles, The	Hey Jude	1975	25.00
	—With "All Rights Reserved" on label; label calls the LP "Hey Jude"			
STCH-639 [(3)]	Harrison, George	All Things Must Pass	1970	40.00
	—Apple labels on first two records and "Apple Jam" labels on third; includes poster and lyric innersleeves			
ST-3350	Harrison, George	Wonderwall Music	1968	25.00
	—With "Mfd. by Apple" on label			
ST-3350	Harrison, George	Wonderwall Music	1968	150.00
	—With Capitol logo on Side 2 bottom			
ST-3350	Harrison, George	Wonderwall Music Bonus Photo	1968	5.00
SW-3351	Hopkin, Mary	Post Card	1969	25.00
SW-5-3351	Hopkin, Mary	Post Card	1969	30.00
	—Capitol Record Club edition			
SKAO 3352	Taylor, James	James Taylor	1969	25.00
	—With title in black print			
SKAO 3352	Taylor, James	James Taylor	1970	20.00
	—With title in orange print			
ST-3353	Modern Jazz Quartet, The	Under the Jasmine Tree	1969	25.00
ST-5-3353	Modern Jazz Quartet, The	Under the Jasmine Tree	1969	40.00
	—Capitol Record Club edition			
ST-3354	Lomax, Jackie	Is This What You Want?	1969	25.00
ST-3355	Badfinger	Maybe Tomorrow	1969	2000.00
	—As "The Iveys"; album not released in US; price is for an LP slick, which does exist			
ST-3359	Preston, Billy	That's the Way God Planned It	1969	50.00
	—Cover has close-up of Billy Preston			
ST-3359	Preston, Billy	That's the Way God Planned It	1972	20.00
	—Cover has multiple images of Billy Preston			
STAO-3360	Modern Jazz Quartet, The	Space	1970	25.00
STAO-5-3360	Modern Jazz Quartet, The	Space	1970	40.00
	—Capitol Record Club edition			

Number	Artist	Title (A Side/B Side)	Year	NM
SMAX-3361	Lennon, John	Wedding Album	1969	150.00
	—With photo strip, postcard, poster of wedding photos, poster of lithographs, "Bagism" bag, booklet, photo of slice of wedding cake. Missing inserts reduce the value.			
SW-3362	Lennon, John	Live Peace in Toronto 1969	1970	15.00
	—By "The Plastic Ono Band" ; without calendar			
SW-3362	Lennon, John	Live Peace in Toronto 1969	1970	20.00
	—By "The Plastic Ono Band"; with calendar			
STAO-3363	McCartney, Paul	McCartney	1970	25.00
	—"McCartney" and "Paul McCartney" on separate lines on label; New York addess on back cover			
STAO-3363	McCartney, Paul	McCartney	1970	30.00
	—"McCartney" and "Paul McCartney" on separate lines on label; California addess on back cover			
STAO-3363	McCartney, Paul	McCartney	1970	80.00
	—Apple label with small Capitol logo on B-side			
STAO-3363	McCartney, Paul	McCartney	1970	20.00
	—Only "McCartney" on label; back cover does NOT say "An Abkco managed company"			
STAO-3363	McCartney, Paul	McCartney	1970	25.00
	—Only "McCartney" on label; back cover says "An Abkco managed company"			
SMAS-3363	McCartney, Paul	McCartney	1975	100.00
	—With "All Rights Reserved" on label			
SMAS-3363	McCartney, Paul	McCartney	197?	20.00
	—New prefix on label			
ST 3364	Badfinger	Magic Christian Music	1970	30.00
	—With Capitol logo on Side 2 bottom			
ST 3364	Badfinger	Magic Christian Music	1970	20.00
SW-3365	Starr, Ringo	Sentimental Journey	1970	20.00
SKAO 3367	Badfinger	No Dice	1970	30.00
SMAS-3368	Starr, Ringo	Beaucoups of Blues	1970	20.00
SMAS-3369	Tavener, John	The Whale	1972	20.00
ST-3370	Preston, Billy	Encouraging Words	1970	20.00
ST-3371	Troy, Doris	Doris Troy	1970	25.00
SW-3372	Lennon, John	John Lennon Plastic Ono Band	1970	20.00
SW-3373	Ono, Yoko	Yoko Ono Plastic Ono Band	1970	20.00
MAS-3375 [M]	McCartney, Paul	Ram	1971	4000.00
	—Credited to "Paul and Linda McCartney"; mono record in stereo cover for radio station use only			
SMAS-3375	McCartney, Paul	Ram	1971	15.00
	—Credited to "Paul and Linda McCartney"; unsliced apple on one label, sliced apple on other			
SMAS-3375	McCartney, Paul	Ram	1971	30.00
	—Credited to "Paul and Linda McCartney"; unsliced apple on both labels			
SMAS-3375	McCartney, Paul	Ram	1971	50.00
	—Credited to "Paul and Linda McCartney"; Apple label with small Capitol logo on B-side			
SMAS-3375	McCartney, Paul	Ram	1975	100.00
	—Credited to "Paul and Linda McCartney"; with "All Rights Reserved" on label			
SKAO-3376	Radha Krishna Temple	The Radha Krishna Temple	1971	20.00
SW-3377	Soundtrack	Cometogether	1971	20.00
SW-3379	Lennon, John	Imagine	1971	20.00
	—With either of two postcard inserts, lyric sleeve, poster			
SW-3379	Lennon, John	Imagine	1975	20.00
	—"All Rights Reserved" label			
SVBB-3380 [(2)]	Ono, Yoko	Fly	1971	25.00
SMAS-3381	Hopkin, Mary	Earth Song/Ocean Song	1970	25.00
SWAO-3384	Shankar, Ravi	Raga	1971	25.00
STCX-3385 [(3)]	Harrison, George, and Friends	The Concert for Bangla Desh	1971	40.00
	—With 64-page booklet and custom innersleeves			
STCX-3385 [(3)]	Harrison, George, and Friends	The Concert for Bangla Desh	1975	50.00
	—As above, but with "All Rights Reserved" on labels			
SW-3386	McCartney, Paul	Wild Life	1971	15.00
	—Credited to "Wings"			
SW 3387	Badfinger	Straight Up	1971	60.00
SWAO-3388	Soundtrack	El Topo	1972	40.00
SMAS-3389	Elephants Memory	Elephants Memory	1972	25.00
SMAS-3390	Van Eaten, Lon and Derrek	Brother	1972	15.00
SW-3391	Peel, David	The Pope Smokes Dope	1972	75.00
SVBB-3392 [(2)]	Lennon, John	Some Time in New York City	1972	30.00
	—By John and Yoko; with photo card and petition			
SVBB-3392 [(2) DJ]	Lennon, John	Some Time in New York City	1972	1000.00
	—White label promo			
SW-3395	Hopkin, Mary	Those Were the Days	1972	40.00
SVBB-3396 [(2)]	Shankar, Ravi	Ravi Shankar In Concert	1973	40.00
SVBB-3399 [(2)]	Ono, Yoko	Approximately Infinite Universe	1973	25.00
SW 3400 [M]	Various Artists	Phil Spector's Christmas Album	1972	30.00
SKBO-3403 [P]	Beatles, The	The Beatles 1962-1966	1973	30.00
	—Custom red Apple labels. "Love Me Do" and "I Want to Hold Your Hand" are rechanneled; "She Loves You," "A Hard Day's Night," "I Feel Fine" and "Ticket to Ride" are mono; "From Me to You," "Can't Buy Me Love" and everything else is stereo.			
SKBO-3403 [P]	Beatles, The	The Beatles 1962-1966	1975	50.00
	—Custom red Apple labels with "All Rights Reserved" on labels			
SKBO-3404 [B]	Beatles, The	The Beatles 1967-1970	1973	30.00
	—Custom blue Apple labels. "Hello Goodbye" and "Penny Lane" are mono, all others stereo.			
SKBO-3404 [B]	Beatles, The	The Beatles 1967-1970	1975	50.00
	—Custom blue Apple labels with "All Rights Reserved" on labels			
SMAL-3409	McCartney, Paul	Red Rose Speedway	1973	20.00
	—Credited to "Paul McCartney and Wings"; with bound-in booklet			
SMAS-3410	Harrison, George	Living in the Material World	1973	15.00
SW 3411	Badfinger	Ass	1973	20.00
SW-3412	Ono, Yoko	Feeling the Space	1973	20.00
SWAL-3413	Starr, Ringo	Ringo	1973	20.00
	—Standard issue with booklet; Side 1, Song 2 identified on cover as "Hold On"			
SWAL-3413	Starr, Ringo	Ringo	1973	400.00
	—With a 5:26 version of "Six O'Clock." On later copies, the song is shortened to 4:05 though the label still says 5:26. All known copies have a promo punch-hole in top corner of jacket; on Side 2 record, "Six O'Clock" will be the widest track.			

Label/Number	Artist	Title (A Side/B Side)	Year	NM
SWAL-3413	Starr, Ringo	Ringo	1974	25.00
	—Later issue with booklet; Side 1, Song 2 identified on cover as "Have You Seen My Baby"			
SW-3414	Lennon, John	Mind Games	1973	20.00
SO-3415	McCartney, Paul	Band on the Run	1973	20.00
	—Credited to "Paul McCartney and Wings"; with photo innersleeve and poster			
SW-3416	Lennon, John	Walls and Bridges	1974	20.00
	—With fold-open segmented front cover			
SW-3417	Starr, Ringo	Goodnight Vienna	1974	12.00
SMAS-3418	Harrison, George	Dark Horse	1974	15.00
SK-3419	Lennon, John	Rock 'n' Roll	1975	20.00
SW-3420	Harrison, George	Extra Texture (Read All About It)	1975	15.00
SW-3421	Lennon, John	Shaved Fish	1975	20.00
SW-3422	Starr, Ringo	Blast from Your Past	1975	15.00
T-5001	Lennon, John	Two Virgins — Unfinished Music No. 1	1968	50.00
	—With Yoko Ono; without brown bag			
T-5001	Lennon, John	Two Virgins — Unfinished Music No. 1	1968	150.00
	—With Yoko Ono; price with brown bag			
T-5001	Lennon, John	Two Virgins — Unfinished Music No. 1	1968	150.00
	—With Yoko Ono; with die-cut bag			
T-5001	Lennon, John	Two Virgins — Unfinished Music No. 1	1985	15.00
	—With Yoko Ono; reissue, flat label			
SPRO-6210 [DJ]	McCartney, Paul	Brung to Ewe By	1971	400.00
	—Promo-only radio spots for "Ram"; counterfeits have uneven spacing between tracks			
SPRO 11206/7 [EP]	Beatles, The	Anthology 2 Sampler	1996	150.00
	—Promo-only collection sent to college radio stations			
C1-8-31796 [(2)]	Beatles, The	Live at the BBC	1994	50.00
AR-34001	Beatles, The	Let It Be	1970	25.00
	—Red Apple label; originals have "Bell Sound" stamped in trail-off area, counterfeits do not			
C1-8-34445 [(3)]	Beatles, The	Anthology 1	1995	40.00
	—All copies distributed in the U.S. were manufactured in the U.K. with no distinguishing marks (some LPs imported directly from the U.K. have "Made in England" stickers, which can be removed easily)			
C1-8-34448 [(3)]	Beatles, The	Anthology 2	1996	40.00
C1-8-34451 [(3)]	Beatles, The	Anthology 3	1996	30.00
C1-97036 [B]	Beatles, The	The Beatles 1962-1966	1993	25.00
	—Custom red Apple labels; red vinyl; all copies pressed in U.K; U.S. versions have a bar-code sticker over the international bar code on back cover. "Love Me Do," "Please Please Me," "From Me to You" and "She Loves You" are mono; all others are stereo.			
C1-97039	Beatles, The	The Beatles 1967-1970	1993	25.00
	—Custom blue Apple labels; blue vinyl; all copies pressed in U.K.; U.S. versions have a bar-code sticker over the international bar code on back cover			

APPLE FILMS

Label/Number	Artist	Title (A Side/B Side)	Year	NM
KAL 004 [DJ]	Beatles, The	The Yellow Submarine (A United Artists Release)	1969	2000.00
	—One-sided LP with radio spots for movie			

APPLE/AMERICOM

45s

Label/Number	Artist	Title (A Side/B Side)	Year	NM
2276/M-221	Beatles, The	Hey Jude/Revolution	1969	300.00
	—Four-inch flexi-disc sold from vending machines; "Hey Jude" is edited to 3:25			
1801P/M-238	Hopkin, Mary	Those Were the Days/Turn, Turn, Turn	1969	600.00
	—Four-inch flexi-disc sold from vending machines			
1803P/M-300	Badfinger	Maybe Tomorrow/And Her Daddy's a Millionaire	1969	600.00
	—By "The Iveys"; four-inch flexidisc sold from vending machines			
2490/M-335	Beatles, The	Get Back/Don't Let Me Down	1969	1000.00
	—Four-inch flexi-disc sold from vending machines			
2531/M-382	Beatles, The	The Ballad of John and Yoko/Old Brown Shoe	1969	800.00
	—Four-inch flexi-disc sold from vending machines			
1808P/M-433	Preston, Billy	That's the Way God Planned It (Edit)/What About You	1969	400.00
	—Four-inch flexi-disc sold from vending machines			
1809P/M-435	Lennon, John	Give Peace a Chance/Remember Love	1969	750.00
	—As "Plastic Ono Band"; four-inch flexi-disc sold from vending machines			
1809P/M-435	Ono, Yoko	Give Peace a Chance/Remember Love	1969	750.00
	—As "Plastic Ono Band"; four-inch flexi-disc sold from vending machines			
5715	Beatles, The	Yellow Submarine/Eleanor Rigby	1969	2000.00
	—Four-inch flexi-disc sold from vending machines			

APPLE/CAPITOL

Albums

Label/Number	Artist	Title (A Side/B Side)	Year	NM
(no #) [(10)]	Beatles, The	The Beatles Special Limited Edition	1974	1200.00
(no #) [(17)]	Beatles, The	The Beatles 10th Anniversary Box Set	1974	2000.00
ST 2047 [P]	Beatles, The	Meet the Beatles!	1968	40.00
	—With Capitol logo on Side 2 bottom			
ST 2047 [P]	Beatles, The	Meet the Beatles!	1971	20.00
	—With "Mfd. by Apple" on label			
ST 2047 [P]	Beatles, The	Meet the Beatles!	1975	25.00
	—With "All Rights Reserved" on label			
ST 2080 [P]	Beatles, The	The Beatles' Second Album	1968	40.00
	—With Capitol logo on Side 2 bottom			
ST 2080 [P]	Beatles, The	The Beatles' Second Album	1971	20.00
	—With "Mfd. by Apple" on label			
ST 2080 [P]	Beatles, The	The Beatles' Second Album	1975	25.00
	—With "All Rights Reserved" on label			
ST 2108 [S]	Beatles, The	Something New	1968	40.00
	—With Capitol logo on Side 2 bottom			
ST 2108 [S]	Beatles, The	Something New	1971	20.00
	—With "Mfd. by Apple" on label			
ST 2108 [S]	Beatles, The	Something New	1975	25.00
	—With "All Rights Reserved" on label			
STBO 2222 [(2) P]	Beatles, The	The Beatles' Story	1968	50.00
	—With Capitol logo on bottom of B-side of both records			

Number	Artist	Title (A Side/B Side)	Year	NM
STBO 2222 [(2) P]	Beatles, The *—With "Mfd. by Apple" on labels*	The Beatles' Story	1971	30.00
STBO 2222 [(2) P]	Beatles, The *—With "All Rights Reserved" on labels*	The Beatles' Story	1975	40.00
ST 2228 [P]	Beatles, The *—With Capitol logo on Side 2 bottom*	Beatles '65	1968	40.00
ST 2228 [P]	Beatles, The *—With "Mfd. by Apple" on label*	Beatles '65	1971	20.00
ST 2228 [P]	Beatles, The *—With "All Rights Reserved" on label*	Beatles '65	1975	25.00
ST 2309 [P]	Beatles, The *—With Capitol logo on Side 2 bottom*	The Early Beatles	1969	40.00
ST 2309 [P]	Beatles, The *—With "Mfd. by Apple" on label*	The Early Beatles	1971	20.00
ST 2309 [P]	Beatles, The *—With "All Rights Reserved" on label*	The Early Beatles	1975	25.00
ST 2358 [P]	Beatles, The *—With Capitol logo on Side 2 bottom*	Beatles VI	1969	40.00
ST 2358 [P]	Beatles, The *—With "Mfd. by Apple" on label*	Beatles VI	1971	20.00
ST 2358 [P]	Beatles, The *—With "All Rights Reserved" on label*	Beatles VI	1975	25.00
SMAS 2386 [P]	Beatles, The *—With Capitol logo on Side 2 bottom*	Help!	1969	40.00
SMAS 2386 [P]	Beatles, The *—With "Mfd. by Apple" on label*	Help!	1971	20.00
SMAS 2386 [P]	Beatles, The *—With "All Rights Reserved" on label*	Help!	1975	25.00
ST 2442 [S]	Beatles, The *—With Capitol logo on Side 2 bottom*	Rubber Soul	1969	40.00
ST 2442 [S]	Beatles, The *—With "Mfd. by Apple" on label*	Rubber Soul	1971	20.00
ST 2442 [S]	Beatles, The *—With "All Rights Reserved" on label*	Rubber Soul	1975	25.00
ST 2553 [P]	Beatles, The *—With Capitol logo on Side 2 bottom*	Yesterday and Today	1969	40.00
ST 2553 [P]	Beatles, The *—With "Mfd. by Apple" on label*	Yesterday and Today	1971	20.00
ST 2553 [S]	Beatles, The *—With "Mfd. by Apple" on label; all 11 tracks are in true stereo. Check for a triangle in the record's trail-off area.*	Yesterday and Today	1971	25.00
ST 2553 [P]	Beatles, The *—With "All Rights Reserved" on label*	Yesterday and Today	1975	25.00
ST 2576 [S]	Beatles, The *—With Capitol logo on Side 2 bottom*	Revolver	1969	40.00
ST 2576 [S]	Beatles, The *—With "Mfd. by Apple" on label*	Revolver	1971	20.00
ST 2576 [S]	Beatles, The *—With "All Rights Reserved" on label*	Revolver	1975	25.00
SMAS 2653 [S]	Beatles, The *—With Capitol logo on Side 2 bottom*	Sgt. Pepper's Lonely Hearts Club Band	1969	40.00
SMAS 2653 [S]	Beatles, The *—With "Mfd. by Apple" on label*	Sgt. Pepper's Lonely Hearts Club Band	1971	25.00
SMAS 2653 [S]	Beatles, The *—With "All Rights Reserved" on label*	Sgt. Pepper's Lonely Hearts Club Band	1975	25.00
SMAL 2835 [P]	Beatles, The *—With Capitol logo on Side 2 bottom; with 24-page booklet*	Magical Mystery Tour	1969	40.00
SMAL 2835 [P]	Beatles, The *—With "Mfd. by Apple" on label; with 24-page booklet*	Magical Mystery Tour	1971	20.00
SMAL 2835 [P]	Beatles, The *—With "All Rights Reserved" on label; with 24-page booklet*	Magical Mystery Tour	1975	25.00

CAPITOL/APPLE

Albums

Number	Artist	Title (A Side/B Side)	Year	NM
STCH-639 [(3)]	Harrison, George *—Odd pressing with Apple labels and Capitol cover (look for stand-alone "S" in trail-off wax); with large sticker on back cover*	All Things Must Pass	1988	80.00

ZAPPLE

Albums

Number	Artist	Title (A Side/B Side)	Year	NM
ST-3357	Lennon, John *—With Yoko Ono*	Life with the Lions — Unfinished Music No. 2	1969	20.00
ST-3358	Harrison, George	Electronic Sound	1969	40.00

Beatles Resources

Fan clubs, publications

For more information about the clubs listed here, most require that you send them a self-addressed stamped envelope. For more information about fan clubs in general, including clubs formed in honor of actors, non-recording artists, sports figures, etc., we recommed that you contact the excellent National Association of Fan Clubs at 818-763-3280, e-mail Linda Kay at lknafc@aol.com or visit http://members.aol.com/lknafc/nafc/index.htm. The information contained here comes more or less verbatim from the clubs or their publications and is not individually verified by *Goldmine*. *Goldmine* cannot accept responsibility for any claims made by the clubs. Costs noted with $ should be paid for in U.S. funds; $CA in Canadian funds; £ in British pounds sterling.

Beatlefan
PO Box 33515
Decatur GA 30033 USA
Fax: 404-321-3109
Charge line: 770-492-0444
E-mail: beatlefan@mindspring.com
Cost: $17 ($21 first class) USA; $25 ($31 printed matter airmail) U.K., Western Europe, Latin America; $27 ($33 printed matter airmail) overseas; credit card orders accepted
Special features: Exclusive interviews, photo-packed tour issues, retrospectives; sample issue $4 USA; $5.50 overseas; back issues also available; all major credit cards accepted.
Frequency: Six issues per year
Description: Been around 22 years; readership of 15,000+

Beatlefan/Extra!
PO Box 33515
Decatur GA 30033 USA
Fax: 404-321-3109
Charge line: 770-492-0444
E-mail: beatlefan@mindspring.com
Cost: $35 USA; $37.50 North America; $38 overseas; SASE for sample
Frequency: 18 issues per year
Special features: Fax subscriptions available for additional charge, inquire for rates; all major credit cards accepted.
Description: Our subscribers get the news while it's still news!

Beatlology Magazine
A magazine for collectors of Beatles Memorabilia
P.O. Box 90, 260 Adelaide Street East
Toronto, Ontario M5A 1N1 Canada
Phone: (416) 360-8902, 1-888-844-0826
Fax: (416) 360-0588, 1-888-831-5510
Web address: www.beatology.com
Cost: $24, $36CA, North America;
$30, $45CA international; or $6, $9CA single copy, incl. postage anywhere in the world.
Please note:The charges will appear in Canadian funds.
Frequency: Six times per year.
Special features: Mailed in a polybag for protection; secure online ordering.

Come Together — Southern California Beatles Fan Club

Attn: Carmen Salmon, president
PO Box 1793
Lakeside, CA 92040
Hotline: 619-687-3687
Best time to call: Anytime
Web address: http://cometogether.homepage.com/index.htm
E-mail: ctclub@aol.com
Cost: $10
Frequency: Quarterly
Special features: Club news, Beatles news, fan club directory
Description: We are a nonprofit organization in existence for seven years. Our members "come together" to share memories and news about the greatest musical band ever, The Beatles. We meet regularly throughout the year for social events. Our biggest event is our annual Beatlefair. This is an opportunity for Beatles fans to come together for a day of fun and music. Guests have included Pete Best, Tony Sheridan, Joey Molland, Gordon Waller, Lawrence Juber, and Denny Laine. Charities we have donated to in the past include The American Cancer Society, Joe Pop Memorial Fund, and the San Diego Youth Symphony. We collected more than 5,000 signatures to get The Beatles' star on the Hollywood Walk Of Fame and are also involved with the petition to keep John Lennon's killer from being released from prison.

Daytrippin'

Trina Yannicos, editor and publisher
Daytrippin'
1730 North Lynn St., Suite A-14
Arlington, VA 22209-2004
Phone: 703-312-4144
Fax: 703-312-4144
Web address: www.daytrippin.com
E-mail address: editor@daytrippin.com
Cost: $16
Frequency: Quarterly
Special features: The most Fab magazine for Beatles fans!
Description: From the fresh perspective of rock journalists, celebrate The Beatles with exclusive interviews and in-depth articles on the latest Beatle news, events and people, as well as columns by Martin Lewis and our own auction and memorabilia experts. Plus, book/CD/video reviews, calendar of events, artwork, convention info, contests and reader contributions.

Good Day Sunshine

Matt Hurwitz
PO Box 661008
Mar Vista CA 90066-9608 USA
Phone: 310-391-0778
Fax: 310-390-7475
Best time to call: 8 a.m. to 5 p.m. PT
Web address: www.gooddaysunshine.net
E-mail address: info@gooddaysunshine.net
Cost: $15 USA, $24 for first class; $18 Canada; $24 overseas
Frequency: Not on a set schedule; subscription includes five issues.
Description: The biggest, most detailed Beatles magazine in the world! Lots of behind-the-scenes facts and photos, plus information on Beatles record and memorabilia collecting from some of the country's experts.

Liverpool Beatlescene
Cavern Walks
Mathew Street
Liverpool L2 6RE England
Phone: 0151-207-0148
Fax: 0151-207-0148
Web address: http://come.to/Liverpoolbeatlescene
E-mail address: Jcathal@aol.com
Cost: £12 U.K.; £15 Europe; £17 worldwide
Frequency: Quarterly
Special features: Membership pack containing postcards, membership card, letter, other information, pen pal service, first-hand information on Liverpool Beatles convention, regular articles by Alistair Taylor.
Description: The only fan club in Liverpool since the early 1960s. Our aim is to bring together those who enjoy the music of the world's greatest musical phenomenon, The Beatles.

Octopus' Garden
Beth Shorten
21 Montclair Avenue
Verona NJ 07044 USA
Web address: http://members.home.net/hlnwheels
E-mail address: Beatles94@aol.com
Cost: $12 USA; $15 overseas
Frequency: Quarterly (March, June, Sept. Dec.)
Description: We are a quarterly fanzine registered with the National Association Of Fan Clubs. We've been around for 10 years and are dedicated to putting out a fanzine for all age groups. Our readers keep us alive with their input, short stories, news, opinions, games, etc... Whatever our readers want is what they get!

Tokyo Beatles Fan Club
Kenji Maeda & Otohei Shima
4-6-14-304 Toyotama-Kita Nerima-ku
Tokyo 176-0012 Japan
Fax: +81-48-773-6320 (24 hours)
Cost: $27
Frequency: Quarterly
Special features: Our magazine is written in English.
Description: We are the largest nonprofit Beatles fan club in Japan, established in 1991 to celebrate The Beatles' 25th anniversary of their visit to Japan.

Web sites

The following list of web sites was partially taken from recommendations given by Beatles fan clubs listed elsewhere in Beatles Resources.

Beatles

www.beatlefest.com/other.shtml
Description: A thorough page of links, arranged by category. U.S. fan pages are further divided by state of origin. Beatlefest is the host of annual fan conventions around the country.

www.beatlemix.com
Description: Coming soon, an online radio station devoted entirely to The Beatles.

www.beatlelinks.net
Description: This page, Beatlelinks.net, is a must-visit for any fan, beginner or longtime collector. The well-organized site lists links according to interest area, and it features a discussion group and free e-mail.

www.islandnet.com/~scliffor/beatles/fabhome.htm
Description: Steve Clifford's Beatles Web Page has all the information needed by casual fans or die-hard collectors. Read reviews of books, fanzines, and guidebooks; view U.K., U.S., and Canadian discographies; study Clifford's guide to starting a Beatles collection; visit the Virtual Beatles Museum; and much, much more.

beatles.about.com/musicperform/beatles/
Description: Another overall good site is The Beatles Fans Page on About.com.

News

www.best.com/~abbeyrd/
Description: This is the site to consult for breaking Beatles-

related news; it's set up by Steve Marinucci. The site also offers articles on collecting Beatles music and memorabilia as well as occasional interviews with figures such as Yoko Ono and Alistair Taylor. Recommended by every Beatles fan club listed here.

www.fabfour.addr.com
Description: The Beatles London News And Information Service page.

Albums and memorabilia

www.rarebeatles.com
Description: Mitch McGeary's Songs, Pictures And Stories Of The Beatles: This extremely helpful site lists current price guides for collectibles from the butcher cover to concert tickets to documents. Clear photos of the items are also provided. McGeary has posted other items of interest to Beatles fans, including rare photos of Paul McCartney and his family and images of John Lennon's "Listen To This Record" campaign. This is an excellent, thorough site.

www.dermon.com/Beatles/Beatles.htm
Description: This site, Dave Dermon III's Beatles Singles Pages, is for hard-core collectors only, but it is an invaluable resource. Dermon features photos of label variations used on U.S.Beatles and solo singles from 1963-1999. Dermon has expanded his site to cover non-U.S. singles, picture sleeves, and picture discs.

http://members.aol.com/agp78/index.html
Description: A site featuring Beatles 78s.

www.eskimo.com/~bpentium/butcher.html
Description: A site all about butcher covers.

www3.islandnet.com/~scliffor/beatles/museum/museum.htm
Description: A site created as a museum of the owner's personal collection.

Paul McCartney

www.photos.mccartney.net
Description: Photographer Jorie Gracen's exclusive Paul McCartney photos from the 1970s to the present, and Gracen frequently updates the "Macca News" section. Another outstanding aspect of the site is the thorough list of McCartney and Beatles-related links.

www.mplcommunications.com/mccartney/
Description: The official Paul McCartney page. Official fan club information is available here as well.

www.quipo.it/mccartney
Description: The site claims to be the largest Paul McCartney-related site on the web.

http://rgo.simplenet.com/macca/
Description: An unofficial Paul McCartney page.

www.macca-l.net/
Description: A Paul McCartney listserv.

John Lennon

www.bagism.com
Description: This extensive site offers a virtual library of letters and articles concerning John Lennon, a weekly poll, various related links, a discography and a timeline of Lennon's life. The fun quizzes also test your knowledge of Lennon and Beatles trivia.

www.instantkarma.com
Description: A John Lennon and Yoko Ono fan site, featuring a Q&A with Ono and news. It also has sections for Julian and Sean Lennon, including news and concert reviews.

George Harrison

www.bekkoame.ne.jp/~garp/hari/george.htm
Description: Hari's On The Web includes information on releases, film, TV and radio show appearances, as well as recording session information.

www.hariscruffs.com
Description: This site offers news, a biography, a day-by-day chronicle of Harrison's life, and a discography of his solo work. It also includes details of his participation in other groups such as Traveling Wilburys, interviews, promos, unreleased recordings, and his work with other artists.

Ringo Starr

www.ringotour.com/
Description: The official site of Ringo's tour dates, put together by David Fishof Presents.

http://web2.airmail.net/gschultz/
Description: The Ringo WWW Page includes an extensive biography, a timeline of events in his life, fan discussion rooms, and fan-written articles discussing Ringo's significance as a rock drummer.

Etc.

www.abbeyroad.co.uk/
Description: Abbey Road Studios' site on the Internet.

www.julianlennon.com/
Description: Julian Lennon's official site.

Laurence Juber played at Chicago Beatlefest in 1999 and 2000.

Gordon Waller of Peter And Gordon performed at Chicago Beatlefest in 1999.

From left: Astrid Kirchherr, Louise Harrison, and Martin Lewis at Chicago Beatlefest, 1999.

The Beatles cover band Liverpool has played Chicago Beatlefest for 21 years. On guitar and vocals is Jonathan Rupolo. Behind is puppeteer Bob Abdou with his John Lennon puppet.

Festivals

Beatlefest

Mark and Carol Lapidos
PO Box 436
Westwood, NJ 07675
Phone: 1-800-Beatles or 201-666-5450
For Tickets: 1-888-9Beatles
Fax: 201-666-8687
Web address: www.beatlefest.com
Description: A weekend jam-packed with Beatles-related activities, games, music, special guests and marketplace, located in various cities around the country.
2001 Beatlefests:
New York Metro: March 16-18, 2001 at the Crowne Plaza Meadowlands Hotel.
Chicago: August 17-19, 2001, Hyatt Regency O'Hare.

The Remnants from Chestnut Ridge, N.Y., played The Cavern during Beatles Week in Liverpool during 1999.

Liverpool Institute, Paul McCartney and George Harrison's high school, is now home to the Liverpool Institute For The Performing Arts, a school founded and partially funded by McCartney.

Festivals

Magical Mystery Tour
International Tours & Events
315 Derby Avenue, Orange, CT 06477
Phone: 800-777-5295, (203) 795-4737
Fax: (203) 891-8433
Web address: www.toursandevents.com
Description: A trip to Liverpool and London, among others, coinciding with International Beatle Week in Liverpool each August.
2001: The 18th annual Beatles vacation is Aug. 18-29, 2001; visiting Scotland, London and Liverpool Beatles landmarks.

Museums

Rock And Roll Hall Of Fame
Terry Stewart, executive director and CEO
1 Key Plaza
Cleveland OH 44114
Phone: 216-781-ROCK (7625)
Fax: 216-515-1284
Web address: www.rockhall.com
Admission: $14.95, adults 12-54; $11.50, seniors and children; free, members; group rates available, call 216-515-1228.
Hours open: 10 a.m.-5:30 p.m. seven days per week; open until 9 p.m. Wednesdays; closed Thanksgiving and Christmas Day.
Location: Shore of Lake Erie in downtown Cleveland's North Coast Harbor.

Special features: Interactive exhibits; exhibits that change periodically to showcase specific rock 'n' roll areas, styles, milestones and the many facets of the music's evolution.

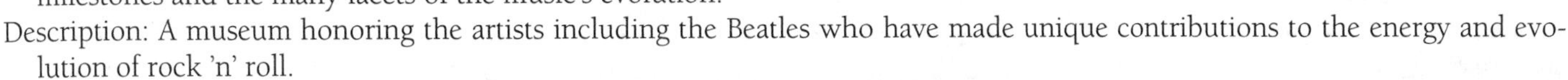

Description: A museum honoring the artists including the Beatles who have made unique contributions to the energy and evolution of rock 'n' roll.
2000 inductees: Eric Clapton; Earth, Wind & Fire; Lovin' Spoonful; The Moonglows; Bonnie Raitt; and James Taylor (performers). Nat "King" Cole and Billie Holiday (early influences). Hal Blaine, King Curtis, James Jamerson, Scotty Moore, and Earl Palmer (sidemen).
Special events in 2001: Call 216-515-8444

IMPROVE YOUR COLLECTING ABILITIES

The Complete Book of Doo-Wop
by Dr. Anthony J. Gribin & Dr. Matthew M. Schiff
This book transports you back to nostalgic times of hanging out with friends at the malt shop, dances at the hop, and first romances and makes you want to scan the radio in the hopes of hearing a song by Dion & the Belmonts, the Chiffons or Little Anthony & the Imperials. An extensive history of doo-wop from 1950 through the early 1970s is given, along with 150 photos, 64 sheet-music covers and prices for 1,000 top doo-wop records.

Softcover • 8-1/2 x 11 • 496 pages
150 b&w photos
Item# DWRB • $24.95

Goldmine Heavy Metal Record Price Guide
by Martin Popoff
When heavy metal hit the scene it roared and so did millions of fans. If you collect heavy metal records, the Goldmine Heavy Metal Record Price Guide will help you to find out what your heavy metal record collection is worth. This is the first book to provide you with pricing for more than 11,000 individual listings with proper discographies and descriptive notes. Featuring more than 300 photographs of record albums, releases from the 1960s to 1990s are covered.

Softcover • 8-1/2 x 11 • 368 pages
300+ b&w photos
Item# HVM1 • $23.95

Goldmine Price Guide to 45 RPM Records
2nd Edition
by Tim Neely
A new, larger format makes room for many new artists and 20,000 new listings - 50,000 records in all. All prices have been reviewed, providing the most accurate values in three grades of condition. Learn more about your favorite artists with the updated discographies from the '50s through the '90s. The handy checklist format helps you inventory your favorite records.

Softcover • 8-1/2 x 11 • 544 pages
100 b&w photos
Item# R452 • $22.95

Goldmine Roots of Rock Digest
Compiled by the Editors of Goldmine Magazine
From the pages of *Goldmine* magazine, come interviews and stories written by top-notch writers of the early pioneers of rock 'n' roll. Culled from 25 years of the magazine's history, the Digest also includes Top 25 lists (such as 25 Great Doo-wop Songs), Most Valuable Records lists, and helpful record collecting articles including Goldmine's record grading guide used by record dealers and collectors worldwide.

Softcover • 8-1/2 x 11 • 320 pages
50 b&w photos
Item# GM2000 • $19.95

Goldmine Record Album Price Guide
by Tim Neely
Now you can value record albums with confidence and celebrate 50 years of the LP, the 1940s through the 1990s. More than 40,000 albums, valued at $20.00 or more, are listed and priced in up to three grades of condition.
Softcover • 8-1/2 x 11
552 pages
100 b&w photos
Item# REA1 • $24.95

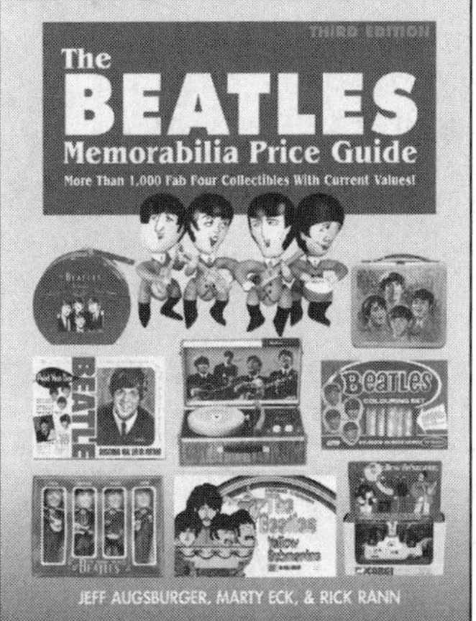

The Beatles Memorabilia Price Guide
Third Edition
by Jeff Augsburger, Marty Eck and Rick Rann
It all comes together in this extensively illustrated price guide with more than 1,500 Fab Four collectibles. Features previously undocumented items, 300 new listings, and 100 additional photos with more in full color.
Softcover • 8-1/2 x 11 • 240 pages
400 b&w photos
400 color photos
Item# AT5684 • $24.95

Shipping and Handling: $3.25 1st book; $2 ea. add'l. Foreign orders $20.95 1st item, $5.95 each add'l.
Sales tax: CA, IA, IL, PA, TN, VA, WA, WI residents please add appropriate sales tax.

To place a credit card order or for a FREE all-product catalog, call

800-258-0929 **Offer REBR**

M-F, 7 am - 8 pm • Sat, 8 am - 2 pm, CST
Krause Publications, Offer REBR
P.O. Box 5009, Iola, WI 54945-5009
www.krausebooks.com

Satisfaction Guarantee:
If for any reason you are not completely satisfied with your purchase, simply return it within 14 days and receive a full refund, less shipping.

Retailers call toll-free 888-457-2873 ext 880, M-F, 8 am - 5 pm